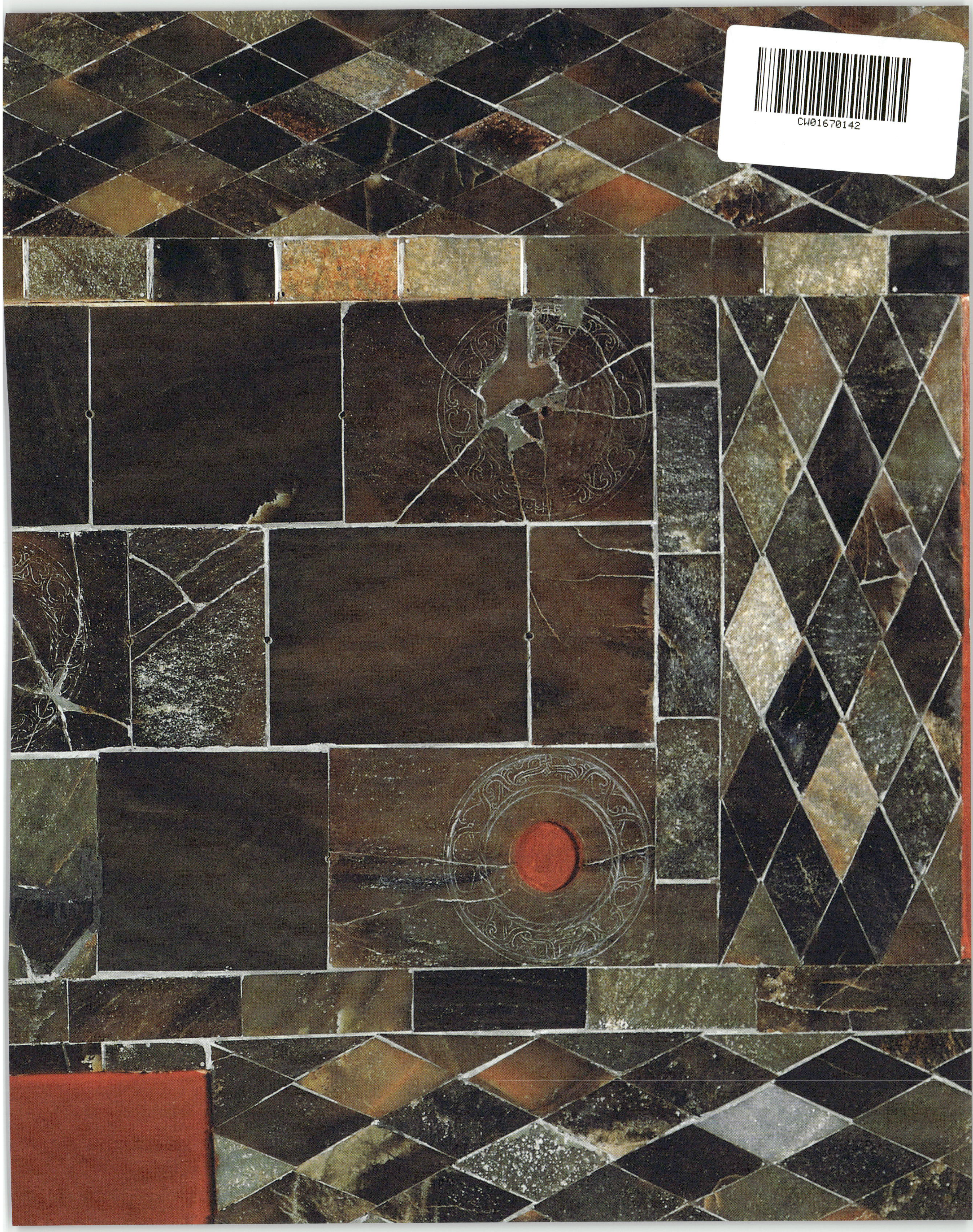

THE SEARCH FOR IMMORTALITY

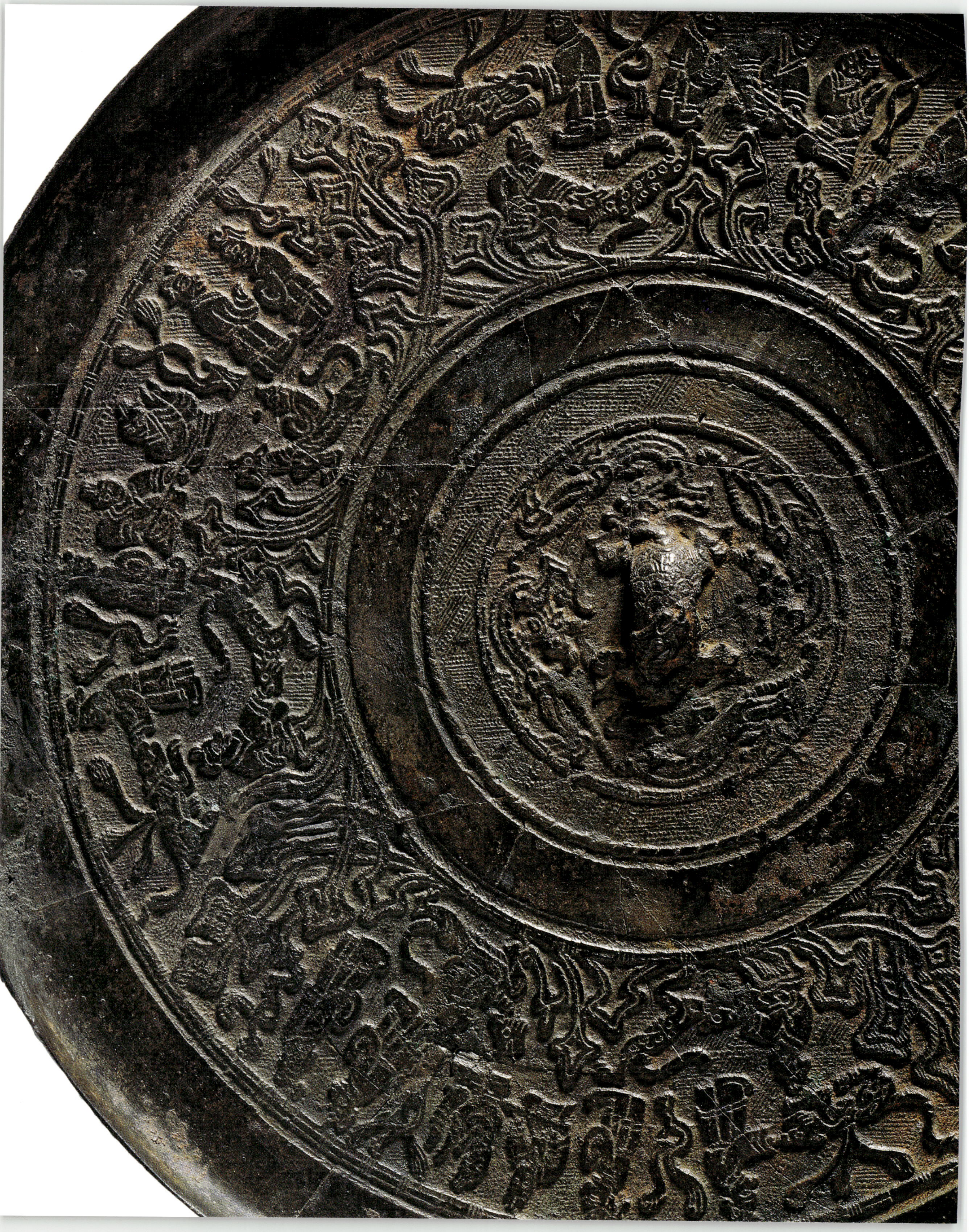

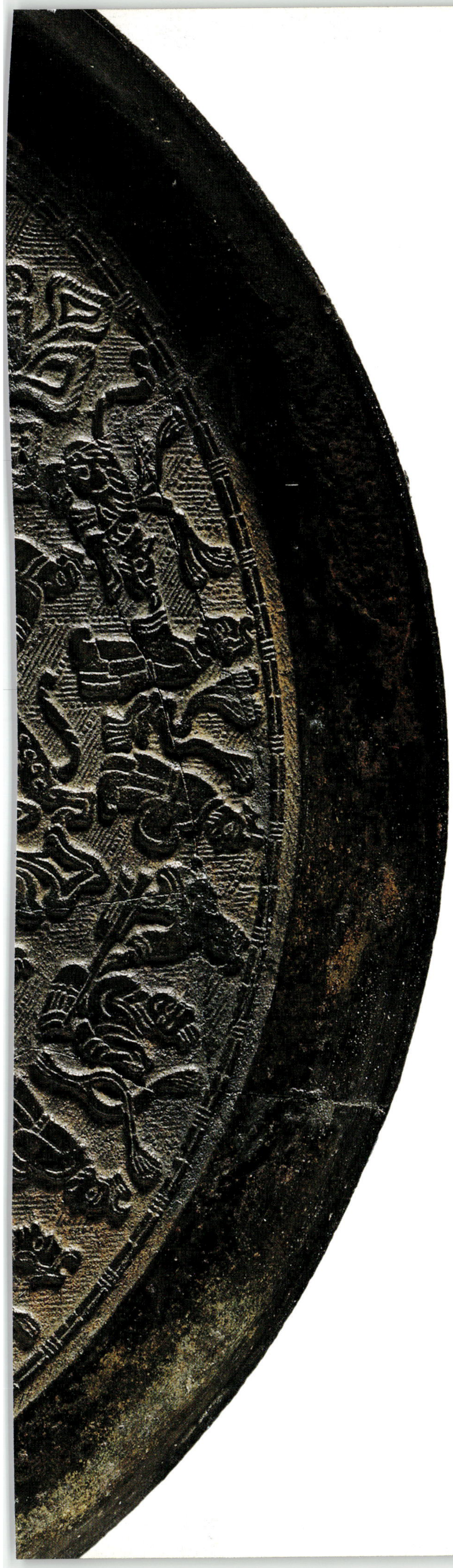

THE FITZWILLIAM MUSEUM
UNIVERSITY OF CAMBRIDGE

IN ASSOCIATION WITH

YALE UNIVERSITY PRESS
NEW HAVEN AND LONDON

THE SEARCH FOR IMMORTALITY

TOMB TREASURES OF HAN CHINA

EDITED BY JAMES C. S. LIN

Published to accompany the exhibition

THE SEARCH FOR IMMORTALITY:
TOMB TREASURES OF HAN CHINA

at the Fitzwilliam Museum, Cambridge
5 May–11 November 2012

Designed by Emily Lees
Printed in China

Library of Congress Cataloging-in-Publication Data
The search for immortality: tomb treasures of Han China / [edited by] James C. S. Lin.
p. cm.
Includes bibliographical references and index.
ISBN 978-0-300-18434-1 (cloth: alk. paper)
1. China – Antiquities. 2. China – History – Han dynasty, 202 BC–220 AD 3. Excavations (Archaeology) – China. 4. Tombs – China. 5. Grave goods – China. 6. Material culture – China. 7. Social archaeology – China. 8. Ethnoarchaeology – China. 9. Archaeology and history – China. I. Lin, James C. S.
DS748.13.S43 2012
931'.01 – dc23

2011047463

A catalogue record for this book is available from The British Library

FRONTISPIECE: Bronze mirror, second century BC, Western Han dynasty (detail of cat. 109).

EXHIBITION ORGANIZED BY

The Fitzwilliam Museum, University of Cambridge

UNIVERSITY OF CAMBRIDGE

IN PARTNERSHIP WITH

Art Exhibitions China (AEC)

Art Exhibitions China

WITH PARTICIPATION FROM

The Museum of the King of Nanyue (Guangzhou) and the Xuzhou Museum (Xuzhou)

EXHIBITION CURATED BY

James C. S. Lin, Fitzwilliam Museum

WITH INPUT BY

An Yao, Art Exhibitions China
Linna Li and Hong Quan, Museum of the King of Nanyue (Guangzhou)
Yinde Li, Xuzhou Museum (Xuzhou)

WITH THE ASSISTANCE OF

Wei Qian and Xue Feng, Art Exhibitions China
Wenjian Wang, Museum of the King of Nanyue (Guangzhou)
Lilin Wang, Xuzhou Museum (Xuzhou)

NOTE ON CHINESE EMPERORS' NAMES

The names of the Han emperors incorporate the title 'Emperor' (di), for example 'Wudi'. Some publications remove the suffix -di when adding the title 'Emperor' in English, thus yielding 'Emperor Wu'. Here the full version of the name is used even when the title is given, thus 'Emperor Wudi'.

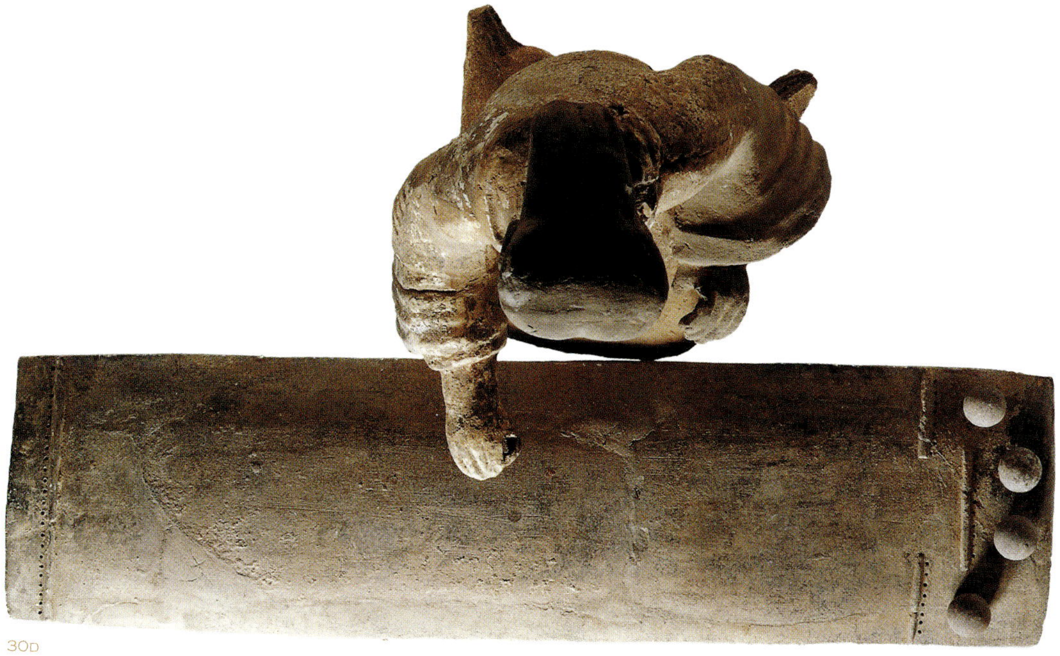

30D

Major support for the exhibition has been provided by:

The Monument Trust

CAMBRIDGE UNIVERSITY PRESS

With additional support from:

CAMBRIDGE ASSESSMENT

and a consortium of Cambridge businesses

CONTENTS

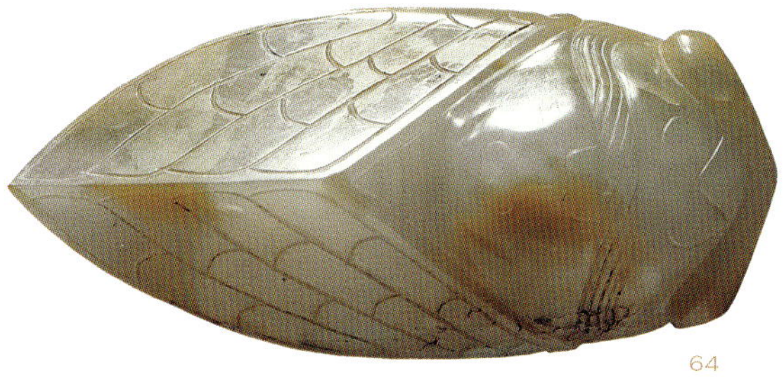

64

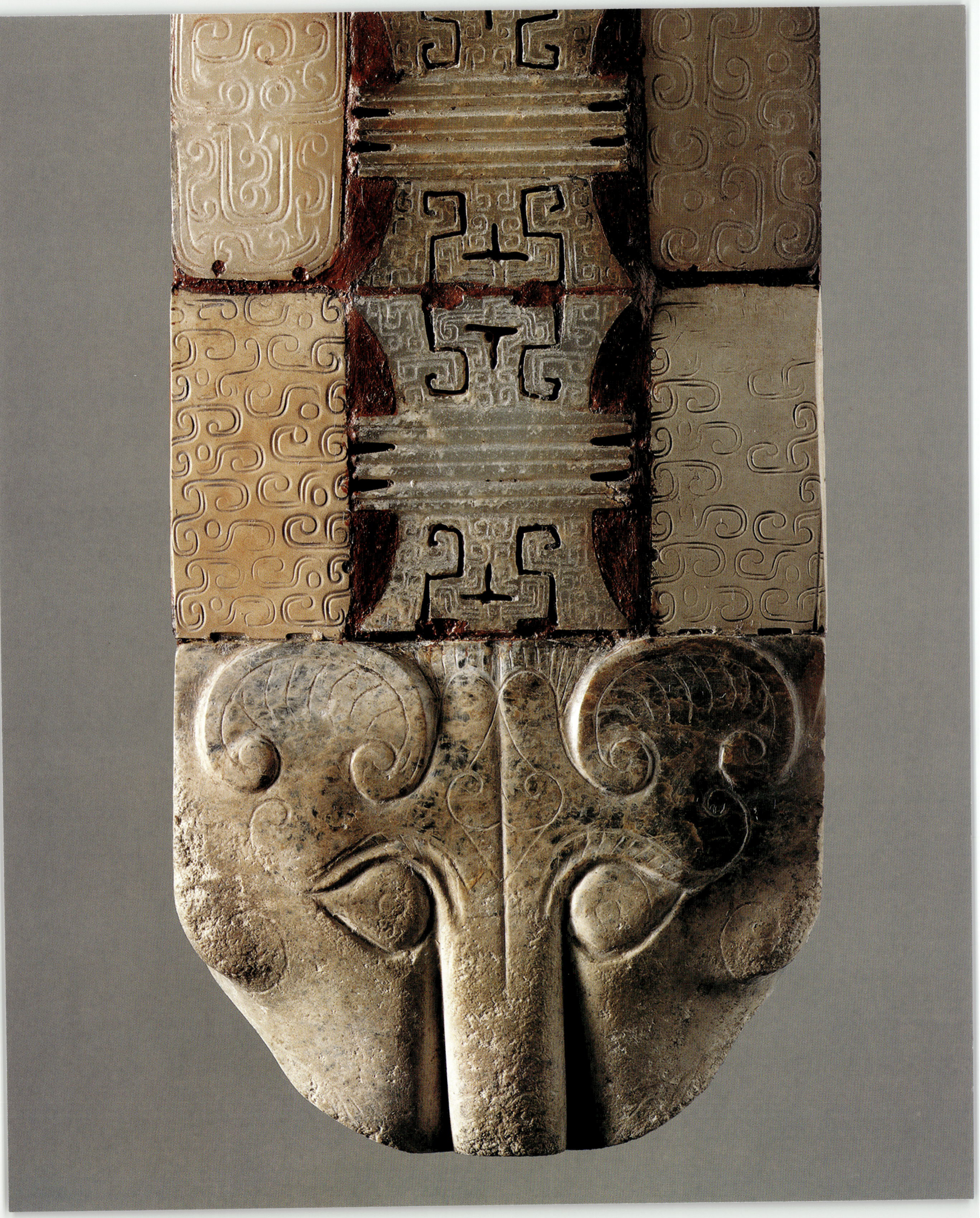

FOREWORD BY TIMOTHY POTTS

DIRECTOR OF THE FITZWILLIAM MUSEUM

The Search for Immortality: Tomb Treasures of Han China is the first exhibition in Britain, and one of few ever, to celebrate the artistic and cultural achievements of the Han dynasty (202 BC–AD 220). It comes to Cambridge with much symbolic appropriateness in the year the Olympic torch makes its parallel journey from Beijing to London. As a central part of the Cultural Olympiad it is our hope, and that of our colleagues in China, that the exhibition will greatly enhance understanding of this critical era in Chinese civilization, and indeed of ancient Chinese culture more generally.

This is the most ambitious exhibition mounted to date on the treasures discovered in the tombs of the Han royal family at Xuzhou and the first time this material has been brought together with the spectacular finds from the tomb of a contemporary King of Nanyue discovered in Guangzhou in 1983. Made of the most precious materials – jade, gold, silver, ivory, bronze and lacquer – by the most accomplished craftsmen of the day, the exquisite grave goods from these royal burials represent one of the pinnacles of ancient Chinese art. Many are unique in form and quality and have therefore been designated as 'grade one' treasures. In a gesture of great generosity, an unprecedented number of these exceptional objects has been allowed to travel to Cambridge, making the exhibition a landmark in British–Chinese relations. It is an additional advantage to British visitors that they were able in 2007–8 to see the *The First Emperor* exhibition at the British Museum, which provided the immediately preceding historical context to the Han achievement.

Cambridge's commitment to China as a subject of scholarly enquiry makes this event the culmination of a long and fruitful engagement. One of the first professorships of Chinese in Britain was established in Cambridge with the appointment of Sir Thomas Wade in 1888. Wade's gift of almost 4,000 books to the university formed the basis of a remarkable library that has since inspired generations of scholars to dedicate their lives to the study of China's peoples and civilizations. Joseph Needham (1900–1995), the greatest Western scholar of China, spent the major part of his professional life here writing many volumes of the landmark series *Science and Civilisation in China*, which is now continued by the Institute bearing his name. Many others have maintained this tradition: Denis Twitchett (1925–2006), founding editor of *The Cambridge History of China*, David McMullen, a leading authority on Tang China, Michael Loewe, co-editor of *The Cambridge History of Ancient China*, and Roel Sterckx, current holder of the Needham Professorship of Chinese History, Science and Civilization – the latter two also contributors to this catalogue.

No less important for Cambridge's reputation in China was the intellectual awakening that the Chinese poet Xu Zhimo experienced here in the 1920s, which inspired the poem 'A Farewell to Cambridge' that is still today learned by virtually every school child in China. Most recently, a life-size bronze sculpture of Confucius donated to Clare College in 2010 by the contemporary sculptor Wu Weishan has quickly become a destination point for the increasing number of Chinese visitors to the university. The reputation of Cambridge as a place to be inspired by learning and the world of the mind is clearly very much alive in China today, as manifested in the large numbers of Chinese students who attend the university, second only to those from Britain.

For the Fitzwilliam Museum, *The Search for Immortality* is the centrepiece of a broader collaboration with colleagues and institutions in China, which has already given rise to public festivals and displays of Chinese art and culture in Cambridge. More is planned: a reciprocal exhibition on

FACING PAGE: DETAIL OF CAT. 93

eighteenth-century Britain from the Fitzwilliam will be shown in China; opportunities for professional exchanges and curatorial training are being developed; and in July 2012 the distinguished writer and potter Edmund de Waal will be the Fitzwilliam Museum's inaugural artist-in-residence at the renowned pottery centre of Jingdezhen.

A profound debt of gratitude is owed to many institutions and colleagues in China who have made this exhibition possible: Jun Wang, Director, An Yao, Deputy Director, and Wei Qian, Head of Exhibitions of Art Exhibitions China; Yinde Li, Director of the Xuzhou Museum, Jiangsu; Linna Li and Lingyun Wu, past and current Directors of the Museum of the King of Nanyue, Guangzhou; Hong Quan, Director of the Museum of the Palace of Nanyue, Guangzhou; Lilin Wang, Head of Exhibitions, Xuzhou Museum; and Wenjian Wang, Head of Exhibitions, Museum of the King of Nanyue.

In Britain the exhibition has benefited greatly from the support and encouragement of the Rt Hon Jeremy Hunt MP, Secretary of State for Culture, Olympics, Media and Sport; the Rt Hon Ed Vaizey MP, Minister for Culture, Communications and Creative Industries; Keith Nichol, Head of Cultural Diplomacy, Department for Culture, Media and Sport; Hedley Swain, Director of Museums, Arts Council England, and Jane Weeks of the British Council.

In Cambridge the exhibition has found enthusiastic advocates in both the previous and current Vice-Chancellors, Professor Dame Alison Richard and Professor Sir Leszek Borysiewicz respectively, without whom the enterprise could not have been realised. For the Fitzwilliam Museum itself this exhibition has been the most complex and ambitious project it has undertaken and its success is due to the efforts of staff across all departments of the museum led by the originator and curator of the exhibition, James C. S. Lin, Senior Assistant Keeper, Applied Arts. Working with colleagues in China, Dr Lin has been responsible for selecting the objects and conceiving their display and interpretation as it is presented in the exhibition, tasks he has accomplished with great judgement and resourcefulness. Other critical contributions have been made by Helen Strudwick, Exhibitions Officer, Tao-Tao Chang, International Development Officer, Thyrza Smith, Registrar, Rachel Sinfield and Julia Tozer, Education, Ayshea Carter, Designer, Jo Dillon, Conservator, Nick Zolman, Technician, Anna Lloyd-Griffiths, Keepers' Assistant, Sue Rhodes and Emma White, Development, Cathy Giangrande and Dorian Jabri, fundraising consultants, Sean O'Neill, Lucy Theobold and Tracy Harding, Press and Marketing, and Sue Bond, communications consultant.

A number of scholars have been generous with their time and advice as the exhibition has evolved. I should note particularly Dr Michael Loewe, Professor Dame Jessica Rawson and Professor Roel Sterckx, as well as other China specialists at Cambridge University who agreed to serve on an advisory committee. We are especially grateful also to the Han specialists who have written for this catalogue, which will certainly be one of the most important and lasting legacies of this project.

FOREWORD BY JUN WANG

DIRECTOR OF ART EXHIBITIONS CHINA

The Han dynasty, more than two thousand years ago, was the East's most powerful empire. It was an era of economic strength and prosperity, and its social and political institutions, as well as Confucianism, its official ideology, have shaped Chinese history ever since. The Han was more than a historical period, but one that by amalgamating elements from cultures across China, gives its name to many of China's people.

This exhibition brings together nearly 400 excavated objects from the royal tombs of the Han kings of Chu and Nanyue. Highlights include two jade suits made of jade plaques held together with gold and silk threads respectively. By comparing the spectacular tombs of two rival power factions of the first time – the Han imperial family in the northern 'cradle' of Chinese history and the Kingdom of Nanyue in the south – this pioneering exhibition sheds light on the uniqueness and similarities of their burial customs. It is undoubtedly the largest and most important exhibition of ancient royal treasures from the Han period ever to travel outside China. It has been a great honour for Art Exhibitions China (AEC) to be involved in this exhibition with the Fitzwilliam Museum. I would also like to express my great appreciation of the hard work of my colleagues in the Museum of the King of Nanyue and the Xuzhou Museum.

Links between the University of Cambridge and China can be traced back more than 120 years to 1888, when Sir Thomas Wade was appointed Professor of Chinese – the first appointment of its kind in a British university. In 1921, Chinese poet Xu Zhimo was at Cambridge as a visiting scholar. His poem 'A Farewell to Cambridge' remains hugely popular to this day, its lines continuing to reverberate across the generations. In 1942, Cambridge biochemist Joseph Needham went to China for the first time. His stay awakened a life-long passion which resulted in the publication of the landmark work *Science and Civilisation in China*. For more than a century, the scholars of Cambridge University have sought through their research to build understanding of China in the West, becoming in every sense, the cultivators, the seed-planters of intellectual and cultural exchange between East and West. This exhibition, which takes place in Cambridge, continues that tradition and begins a new page in Cambridge–China relations.

This year is not only the year in which London hosts the Olympic Games. It also marks the fortieth anniversary of formal relations between Britain and the People's Republic of China. Art Exhibitions China is delighted to loan this exhibition to promote cultural exchange, celebrate the Olympic spirit and further the ties of friendship between Britain and China. I have no doubt that this exhibition will be one of the highlights of this year's Cultural Olympiad.

FOREWORD BY YINDE LI[1]

DIRECTOR OF THE XUZHOU MUSEUM

The 2012 Olympic Games in London are a celebration of sporting prowess, but they are also about the spirit of international understanding and co-operation. The exhibition *The Search for Immortality: Tomb Treasures of Han China*, organized by the Fitzwilliam Museum in Cambridge during the course of the Olympic and Paralympic Games, will raise widespread awareness of ancient Chinese civilization.

In the twenty-first century, technological advances in transport and telecommunications mean that we can command information on almost any subject at any time, and from any part of the world – nevertheless, ancient Chinese civilization remains a closed book to many people. Exchanges between China and the UK, in fact, started very early. During the second century AD, the fashion for wearing clothes made of Chinese silk had already spread to Roman Britain along the Silk Route. Chinese silk unearthed from Colchester Castle in Essex and dated to between the third and fifth centuries testifies to contacts between the two. Other museums in the UK, including the British Museum and the Victoria and Albert Museum, also preserve many Chinese antiquities, and in 2007, the British Museum held the exhibition *The First Emperor: China's Terracotta Army*. The collections and exhibitions have aroused interest in ancient Chinese civilization in the UK, as well as in Europe. The history of China is a long one. Every period has left its legacy – through archaeological finds, written records and collections. Each and every object tells its own unique story, and contributes to the richness of China's past and present. However, no period has left a more significant impact on the history of China and today's Chinese society than the Han dynasty. The language spoken and the characters written today, and the Han people, the largest ethnic group in China, are all a legacy, direct or indirect, of this formative period. As a result, *The Search for Immortality: Tomb Treasures of Han China* presents not only the society of the Han dynasty, but also in many ways opens a window to an understanding of modern China.

Liu Bang, the first emperor of the Han dynasty, rose to power from the position of a prefect at Sishui in Pei County. His strong attachment to his hometown is expressed in the 'Ode to the Great Wind' (*Dafengge*). Out of his love of his place of birth, Liu Bang conferred to his half-brother Liu Jiao the Kingdom of Chu, whose capital, Pengcheng, is the modern-day Xuzhou. Many gigantic tombs of the Kings of Chu were constructed by tunelling into hard rock. The longest tomb measures ninety metres. These underground palaces share many similarities with the pyramids in Egypt, and large numbers of treasures have been unearthed from them. As the mausoleums of the Han emperors have not yet been excavated, treasures from the tombs of the Chu kings represent the highest level of material culture and artistry of the Han dynasty known to date.

Numerous types of relic have been excavated from the tombs, all of which provide insights into every aspect of Han society. In politics, there are figurines of martial and civil servants. Kitchen and bathing utensils bear witness to everyday life. Food and merchandise reflect its economy. Objects related to court music and dance testify to its achievement and the importance of the arts. Jade burial suits and coffins used in funerals reveal the Han people's attitude towards death. Objects made of gold, silver and jade seem to have been particularly treasured by the court: some are delicate while others are massive in size. Many of these objects are being exhibited outside China and displayed as a group in the UK for the very first time. Furthermore, combining as it does cultural relics unearthed from both the tombs of Chu kings and the tomb of a Nanyue king, the exhibition will be the grandest display of Chinese Han tomb treasures to have been seen in the world so far.

For the Xuzhou Museum it has been a pleasure to collaborate with the Fitzwilliam Museum. I should like to express my heartfelt appreciation here. Since 2009, the Fitzwilliam has put its full energy into organizing *The Search for Immortality: Tomb Treasures of Han China*. Director Dr Timothy Potts has overseen the project. Dr James C. S. Lin, curator of the exhibition and an expert in the archaeology of the Han dynasty, has travelled to Xuzhou five times to make on-the-spot investigations. He has worked hard on the exhibition and as a result has made original contributions to knowledge of the subject. Ms Judy Z. Y. Xu and Ms Nicole T. C. Chiang have also worked intensively on preparations for the exhibition.

The organization of the exhibition is made possible by the generosity and great vision of the sponsors. I would like to express my sincere gratitude to them too.

I wish the exhibition every success.

NOTE

1 Translated by Nicole T. C. Chiang

FOREWORD BY LINNA LI

DIRECTOR OF THE MUSEUM OF THE KING OF NANYUE

With the passing of the Olympic torch from China to the UK, London will host the celebrated Games in 2012. In Cambridge, the Fitzwilliam Museum is mounting the exhibition *The Search for Immortality: Tomb Treasures of Han China*, which also promotes cultural exchanges and advances the friendship between the two countries. We are honoured to be involved in this project and have made every endeavour to provide our support.

Although the Han dynasty of China is at two thousand years' distance from today's world, its legacy is abundant and rich. More than 20,000 Han tombs have been discovered to date. As the mausoleums of the Han emperors have not been excavated, more than forty tombs of regional overlords and members of the imperial family represent the highest level of the burial culture of Han China. However, apart from a small number of tombs, most have been looted at some point in history. The Nanyue king's tomb of the Western Han dynasty is one of the few luckily found intact. A national museum has been built at the tomb site in Guangzhou to conserve and display its highly significant cultural artefacts.

The Nanyue king's tomb is the earliest stone tomb with painted decoration that has been discovered so far. The social status of the tomb occupant is also the highest among Nanyue kingdom burials. Large amounts of treasure and daily utensils, as well as the remains of fifteen sacrificial human victims, were found in the tomb. They are evidence of the desire at the time to permanently preserve the body, to help the soul ascend and to serve the dead as if they were alive. The burial goods also reflect the Nanyue kingdom's political structure, which follows the same bureaucracy of the Qin and Han periods. In addition, they testify to the economic growth and the multicultural aspect of the period. Through this tomb, many characteristics of Nanyue society are closely reflected. The tomb is one of the greatest treasures of the people of Guangzhou and one of the most important pieces of cultural heritage in China. The exhibits, which have been selected carefully by both the Museum of the King of Nanyue and the Fitzwilliam Museum, will display the essence of Nanyue culture, the rich history of Guangzhou and the depth of Chinese civilization.

Although China and the UK are thousands of miles apart, both have witnessed a long and splendid history and contributed to the progress of the civilization of mankind. Presenting the cultures of Han China to the world, the exhibition will surely win the hearts of both top athletes from around the globe and the general public, and add another fabulous feature to the London Olympic Games. I wish every success to the Games and to the exhibition *The Search for Immortality: Tomb Treasures of Han China*.

ACKNOWLEDGEMENTS BY JAMES C. S. LIN

CURATOR

This exhibition is the first time that such a large number of precious Han materials has been exhibited in Britain. The Han dynasty was the most important period in Chinese history. It developed into a highly sophisticated society that shaped all subsequent Chinese art and culture. The Han empire was arguably the most powerful empire in the world two thousand years ago. It was also a period in which China enjoyed extensive contact with central Asia and the wider world. Two millennia later, these materials again link China with the outside world through this exhibition.

Organizing a Han exhibition has been my dream since I studied Chinese art and archaeology at Oxford University in 1995. However, it has also been a most demanding task. During negotiations with our Chinese partners, I came to realize that this exhibition would represent the greatest Chinese treasure ever to be brought outside of China. This became an immense responsibility – for myself, and for my colleagues at the Fitzwilliam Museum. I would like to thank the Keeper of my department, Dr Vicky Avery, for her support, trust and understanding and for her help in smoothing the pressure of my workload. I am indebted to the contributors to this catalogue, who delivered their contributions on time to meet the publishing deadline. I would also like to acknowledge the help I received from my friends, Marcus Phipps and Peter Chare and from my colleagues, Timothy Potts, David Scrase, Tao-Tao Chang, Helen Strudwick and Sean O'Neill, who have kindly read through the text and entries and given me their comments and suggestions. I have known the Director of the Xuzhou Museum, Mr Yinde Li, for more than ten years; we have become firm friends. I would like to thank him in particular for his support, both academically and personally, and for helping to make this exhibition happen. Thanks also to Margaret Greeves for reminding me of the treasures at Guangzhou.

I have been fortunate to work with a team of three bright and hard-working assistants: Judy Xu, Nicole Chiang and Cheng Gang. Without their great contribution and efforts this catalogue and exhibition would not have been possible. Ayshea Carter has demonstrated her genius for design through her work on the galleries and the maps in this book. My student Cheng Gang has worked hard on the maps as well, and on the drawings for the catalogue. I would like to thank my colleagues, Helen Strudwick (Exhibitions Officer), Sue Rhodes and Emma White from the Development Office, Rachael Sinfield and Julia Tozer from the Education Department, Kate Carreno (Assistant Director), Tao-Tao Chang (International Development Officer), Sean O'Neill (Marketing and Press Manager), Tracy Harding, Lucy Theobald, Jo Dillon (Conservator) and the team of technicians, led by Nik Zolman, along with many others who have been involved with this project along the way. I would also like to thank Gillian Malpass and the talented Emily Lees at Yale University Press for their intense commitment to and patience in completing this catalogue. I am indebted to the British Academy for its generous sponsorship of my field trips to China.

An especial thanks goes to Dr Timothy Potts for his unwavering and tenacious stewardship of this project.

Finally, I owe a debt of gratitude to my parents and family in Taiwan. Without their support, I would not have been able to pursue my career in the United Kingdom, which has culminated in this exhibition.

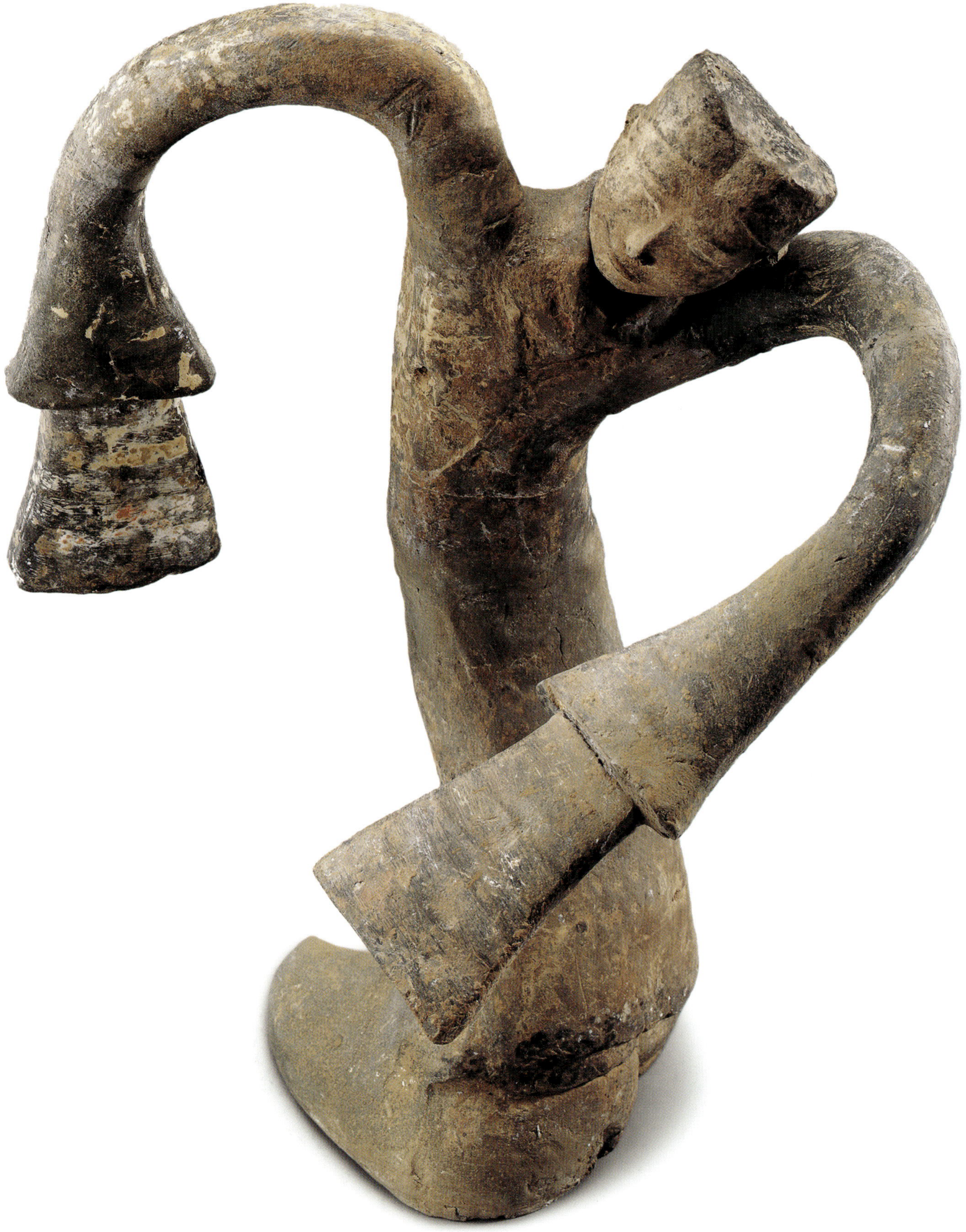

CONTRIBUTORS

CONTRIBUTORS OF ESSAYS

Yinde Li Director, Xuzhou Museum

James C. S. Lin Senior Assistant Keeper of Applied Arts, Fitzwilliam Museum, University of Cambridge

Michael Loewe Former Lecturer in Chinese Studies, University of Cambridge; currently Emeritus Fellow of Clare Hall, University of Cambridge

Timothy Potts Director of the Fitzwilliam Museum and Fellow of Clare College, University of Cambridge

Hong Quan Director of the Museum of the Palace of Nanyue

Jessica Rawson Former Warden of Merton College, University of Oxford; currently Professor, Oxford Centre for Asian Archaeology, Art and Culture

Roel Sterckx Joseph Needham Professor of Chinese History, Science and Civilization, Fellow of Clare College, University of Cambridge

CONTRIBUTORS OF CATALOGUE ENTRIES

Kuang-Jen Chang (KJC) Honorary Research Associate, Institute of Archaeology and Academic Secretary, International Centre for Chinese Heritage and Archaeology, Institute of Archaeology, University College London

Nicole T. C. Chiang (NC) Research Assistant, Fitzwilliam Museum, University of Cambridge; PhD candidate, School of Oriental and African Studies, University of London

Li-Kuei Chien (LKC) Postdoctoral Research and Teaching Fellow in Chinese Buddhism, University of Cambridge

James C. S. Lin (JCSL) Senior Assistant Keeper of Applied Arts, Fitzwilliam Museum, University of Cambridge

Lukas Nickel (LN) Reader in Chinese Art and Archaeology, School of Oriental and African Studies, University of London

Roel Sterckx (RS) Joseph Needham Professor of Chinese History, Science and Civilization, Fellow of Clare College, University of Cambridge

Sascha Priewe (SP) Curator of Chinese collections and Coordinating Curator of Korean collections, British Museum

Judy Z. Y. Xu (JX) Research Assistant, Fitzwilliam Museum, University of Cambridge

FACING PAGE: CAT. 30C

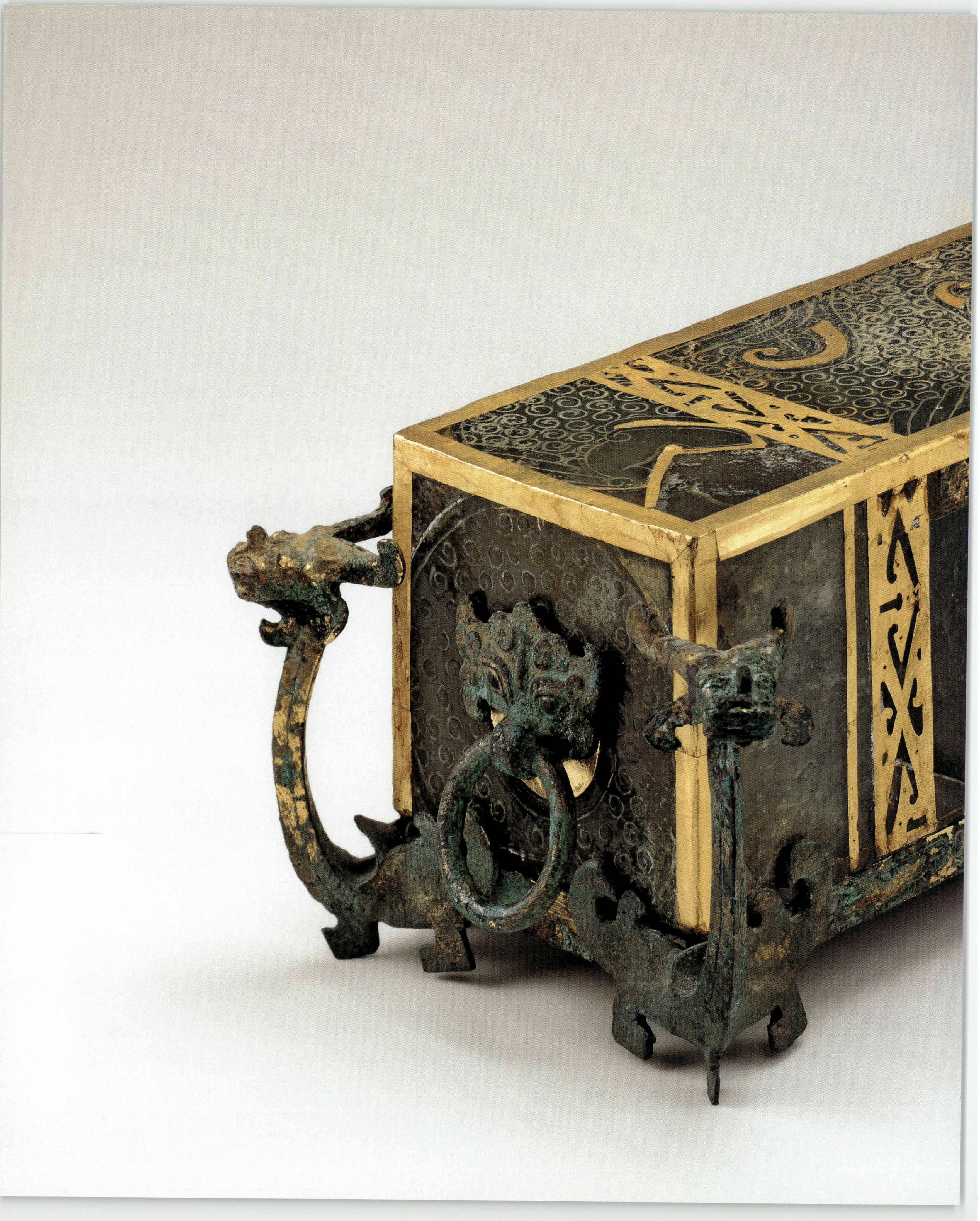

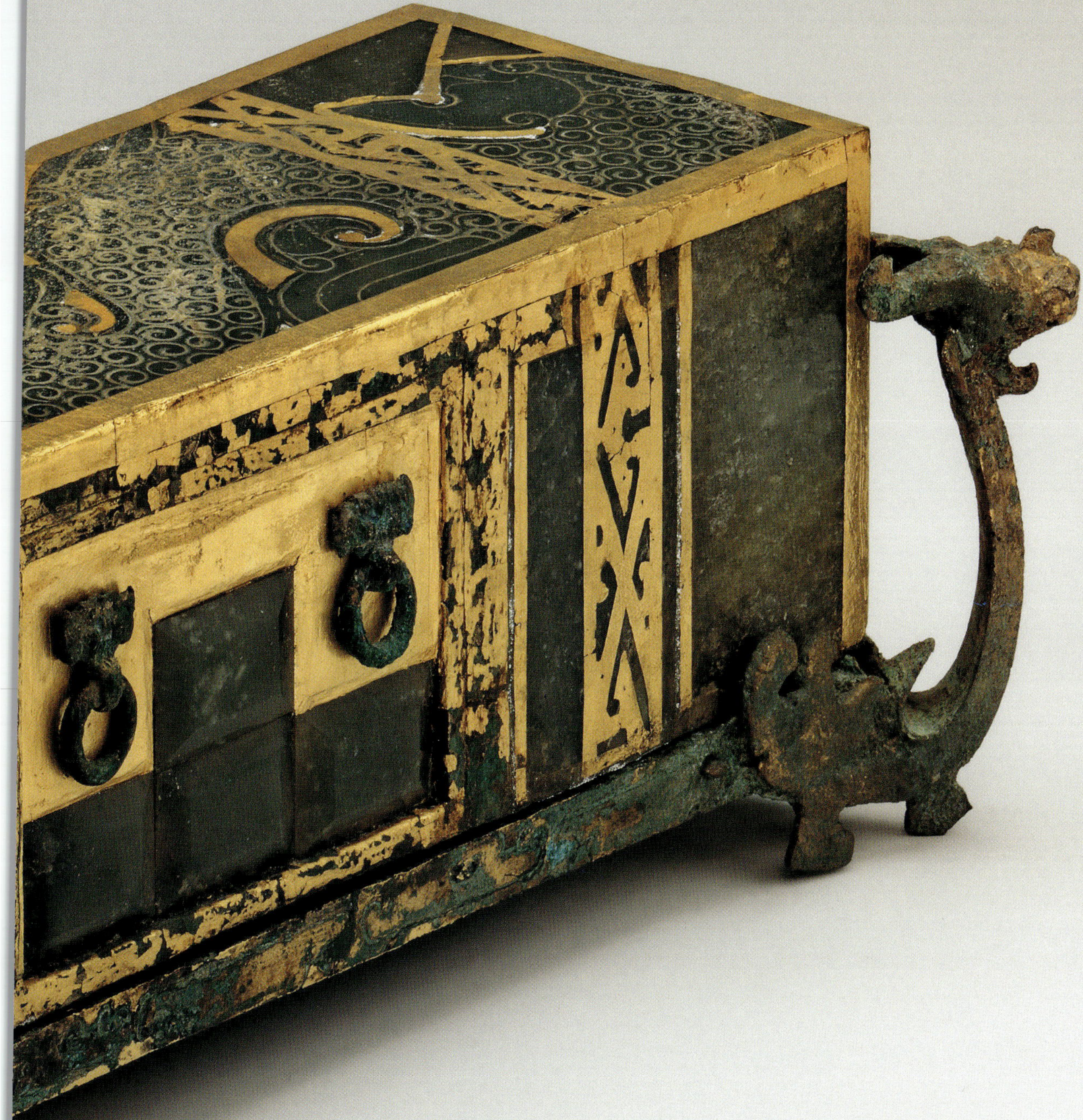

ESSAYS

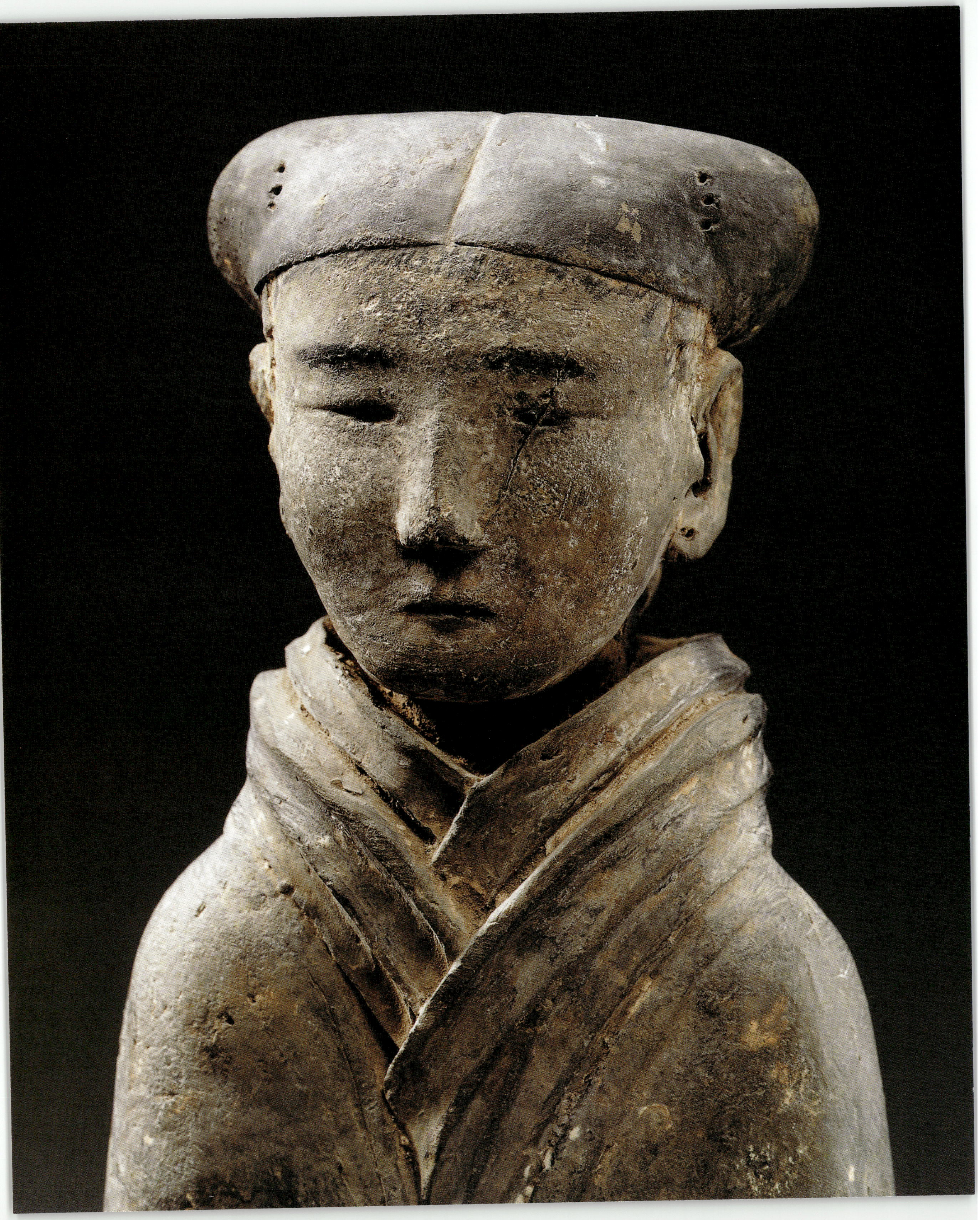

INTRODUCTION: THE HAN EMPIRE IN CONTEXT

TIMOTHY POTTS

As a political entity China was born of a great act of conquest: the military victory of Zheng, King of Qin, over six rival warring states in 221 BC. Uniting much of the territory we now know as China, Zheng was well justified in adopting the title 'First Emperor' (*Shi Huangdi*), by which he has been known ever since. After only ten years of rule, however, Shi Huangdi died and the infant empire he had forged fell apart, inaugurating another round of internecine warfare. Great as Shi Huangdi's military achievement had been – and spectacular as his tomb, guarded by the famous army of terracotta warriors, will one day prove to be – he was a flash in the pan.

Out of the battle for supremacy that followed it was Liu Bang, a rebel leader from the region of Pengcheng, modern Xuzhou, who emerged victorious in 206 BC, reunifying the empire and founding the Han dynasty (202 BC–AD 220). This time the centre held. Apart from a coup within the imperial family that lasted from AD 9 to 25, the Han dynasty ruled over a unified empire for over four hundred years, creating a paradigm of strong and successful leadership that all later dynasties would seek to emulate.

The foundational nature of this achievement is reflected in the fact that 'Han' has ever since been an epithet for the quintessentially Chinese: the Chinese language is *Hanyu*, the Chinese script is *Hanzi*, and the people who derive from the territories of the empire – now distributed much further afield and constituting over ninety percent of the population – are *Hanren*. Much of the central content and character of what has come to be considered the Chinese 'way of life' coalesced in the Western Han period (202 BC–AD 9): a system of imperial government through commanderies and counties; the adoption of 'Confucian' principles of respect and duty in court life and administration, giving rise to a civil service based on academic merit rather than birth; a mixed state–private economy, including long-distance trade; a qualified openness to foreign ideas, arts and beliefs; and a conception of the emperor as the unique object of beneficence from 'heaven' (*tian*), conveying thereby a semi-divine right to rule. This newly self-conscious, imperial culture was given tangible expression in the institutions, scholarship and monuments established in Han times.

It is in the Han period also that we find the first secure evidence for the practice of Buddhism in China, where it joined Daoist mysticism, Confucian ethics and statecraft and traditional folk religion as one more stream in a porous body of spiritual–philosophical–pragmatic thinking that defies Western conceptual categories. Literary criticism and historiography flourished as never before; scholars collated and analysed historical records, openly debating different approaches to government, human nature and the like. China's already millennium-long literary tradition was codified in the first imperial library (26 BC) and studied in the imperial university (founded 124 BC). Science, technology, the arts and crafts – more closely connected in China than anywhere – continued to flourish, reaching levels of technical and artistic excellence that match any in the ancient world. By any measure the Han period was a golden age for Chinese civilization and has been seen as such ever since.

EAST AND WEST

In Western historical terms the Han Empire aligns with the last two centuries of the Roman Republic and the first two centuries of the Roman Empire. As in China, this was a seminal period for European civilization, seeing the cre-

FACING PAGE: DETAIL OF CAT. 40A

ation of systems of government, law, economics and religious belief that have shaped Western life ever since.

In 202 BC, as the first Han ruler was ascending the imperial throne, at the other end of Eurasia the Romans were mustering their forces in north Africa for a final and decisive encounter with the most formidable enemy they had ever faced, the Carthaginian general Hannibal. Hannibal's defeat at the Battle of Zama was a turning point in the rise of Rome, which now forged ahead in its conquest of the Mediterranean. Over the following century, as the first Han emperors were consolidating their grip on power and their families were being buried with the grave goods we now see in Cambridge, the Greek kingdoms of Macedonia, Greece, Asia Minor (Turkey) and Syria were falling one by one to Rome's armies. By 100 BC more than half of the Mediterranean was firmly under Roman control and for the rest it was only a matter of time. By 30 BC the remainder of Asia Minor along with Syria, Palestine and Egypt had fallen too, completing Rome's circuit of the Mediterranean a generation before the birth of Christ.

Thus far the Romans had maintained a staunch adherence to republican government, despising in their rulers any hint of royal or imperial pretensions. But in their bloody battle for supremacy, the protagonists of the final push – Caesar, Antony and Octavian – ended up destroying the Republic in all but name and opening the way to Rome's own 'First Emperor', Augustus (as Octavian was hailed). From the year 27 BC it was two emperors who heard stories of exotic lands and distant empires at opposite ends of the world.

The Han emperors were well aware that they ruled an already ancient civilization and were heirs to a rich history stretching back far into antiquity. Modern archaeology has done much to document this pre-Han backdrop, allowing currents of continuity and change between periods and cultures to be charted. This shows that much of Han culture has a long ancestry, which it in turn adapted and bequeathed to later eras. Already in late Neolithic cultures (*c.*4000–2000 BC), jade was the favoured material for prestige objects in burials: skilfully carved blades, *cong*-cylinders, *bi*-discs and other enigmatic – presumably ritual – objects. Believed to have magical protective powers, these early jades were highly prized in later periods; some even turn up two thousand years later as part of the funerary vestments of Han kings. Pottery too had been expertly made and decorated for millennia, initiating a tradition of artistry in clay that flourished in the Han and has continued uninterrupted up to the present day. The development of early metalworking in copper and bronze begins somewhat later than in the Near East but by the Shang period (sixteenth–eleventh centuries BC) had reached unmatched heights of technical and artistic sophistication, especially in a variety of highly decorated ritual bronze vessels and in the striking life-size figurative sculptures from Sanxingdui in Sichuan Province.

China seems also to have been one of the few originators of an independent system of writing. The first such inscriptions appear around the twelfth century BC on 'oracle bones' (many in fact on turtle carapaces) using characters that are recognisably ancestral to the script used today – thus making Chinese the oldest continuously used writing system in the world. Despite the variety of spoken dialects, and an inevitable regionalism in material culture over such a great expanse, the Han hegemony served to reinforce an already considerable body of cultural practice that was distinctive of Chinese civilization as a whole.

THE HAN ROYAL TOMBS

By the Han period, poetry, literature and scholarly writing on a wide range of subjects had long histories and a 'core curriculum' of works was actively collated and studied by scholars, who could recount the deeds of earlier kings back a millennium and more. The Han emperors were therefore well aware of their place in history and likewise aspired to be seen as strong and successful rulers who left their mark on history.

Among the most important of all imperial acts was preparing for an afterlife as comfortable and glorious as that enjoyed on earth. Historical sources are almost entirely silent on the burials of earlier rulers, probably to avoid giving clues on the tombs' location to would-be robbers. However, archaeological discoveries of royal burials from the late Shang and Zhou dynasties (*c.*1200–221 BC) confirm that already in these earlier eras kings were sent on their journey to the afterlife in suitably resplendent fashion.[1]

The tombs of the eleven emperors of Western Han at the imperial capital of Chang'an, near modern Xi'an, have not been excavated. The emperors' brothers, sons and other close relatives, however, some of whom had been awarded the title of king and authority to rule a designated area, were laid to rest in the ancestral Han territories further east. A particularly dense cluster of these royal tombs surrounds the imperial family's home town of Pengcheng, modern Xuzhou (Maps 1, 5 and Table 3). These represent the burials of the Kings of Chu, one of the hereditary kingdoms granted to a branch of the imperial family by the Han emperors. A number of the Xuzhou tombs were excavated in the 1980s and 90s and, although they were found to have been opened by robbers in antiquity, some still contained most of their grave goods. The spectacular finds from three of these tombs, dating to the second century BC, form the core of the first half of the exhibition.

Least disturbed of the royal burials was the tomb at Shizishan, belonging to the second or third King of Chu, which contained a spectacular array of goldwork and jades, including the finest of all the jade suits known to date and a unique jade-inlaid coffin (cat. 87, 98). A two-storeyed tomb at Beidongshan belonging to one of the second through fifth Kings of Chu yielded a small army of terracotta warriors with remarkably preserved painted decoration and another rich group of distinctive jades (cat. 9, 86). The third tomb, at Guishan, usefully contained a royal silver seal (cat. 25) which allows the occupant to be identified as the sixth King of Chu, Liu Zhu (r. 128–116 BC).

In their provisioning for the afterlife these royal tombs provide a unique window onto the life of the Han royal courts. Unlike earlier dynasties, whose tombs consisted of large pits, most Han royal burials were cut horizontally into the living rock of the hillside. A shaft-like corridor led to a suite of rooms, presumably reflecting the layout of the deceased's palace, which was to be his residence in the afterlife. As such, the tomb would be provided with all the luxuries of court life: furniture, kitchen utensils, tools and weapons, ritual equipment, jewellery, foodstuffs, toilets and other appurtenances of royalty, including their unfortunate concubines, cooks and servants, who were sacrificed to serve their master's body–soul (*po*) in the hereafter.

Jade was believed to protect the body from decay and corrupting demons and therefore played a particularly important role in the funerary equipment of royal burials. Ornaments in this hard, pale green stone were applied lavishly to the body (some of them heirlooms from earlier centuries and millennia), while kings and their immediate family received the ultimate safeguard of an all-enveloping suit made of jade mosaic. For the first time outside China, two of these jade suits, including the finest one to survive, are included in the exhibition, along with a unique jade-inlaid coffin. Bronze musical bells, incense burners, lamps, braziers and mirrors suggest some of the rituals by which ancestors and other spirits were conjured into being. Other finely crafted objects from the royal workshops were made of lacquer, gold and silver, as well as silk and other perishables.

AN IMPERIAL PRETENDER: THE KING OF NANYUE

In 1983 one of the most spectacular discoveries of modern archaeology was made at Panyu, modern Guangzhou: the unlooted royal tomb of Zhao Mo, the second King of Nanyue (r. 137–122 BC), a vassal state on the southern periphery of the Han empire. The remarkable treasures recovered from this burial form the second section of the exhibition, seen here for the first time in juxtaposition with the material from Xuzhou.

Like those burials, Zhao Mo's tomb was dug into the hillside and consisted of a suite of rooms, first chambers stocked with the decorations and equipment of courtly entertainment and then three rooms containing the burials of the king, his concubines and servants. Many of the grave goods, including a spectacular array of jades, are of the same high quality as the Han royal burials at Xuzhou. Much was certainly made locally, but there are also bronzes and jades dating back a century or two to the Warring States period (481–221 BC), which must have come from the north.

In addition to their artistic and archaeological importance, the finds from Zhao Mo's tomb throw important

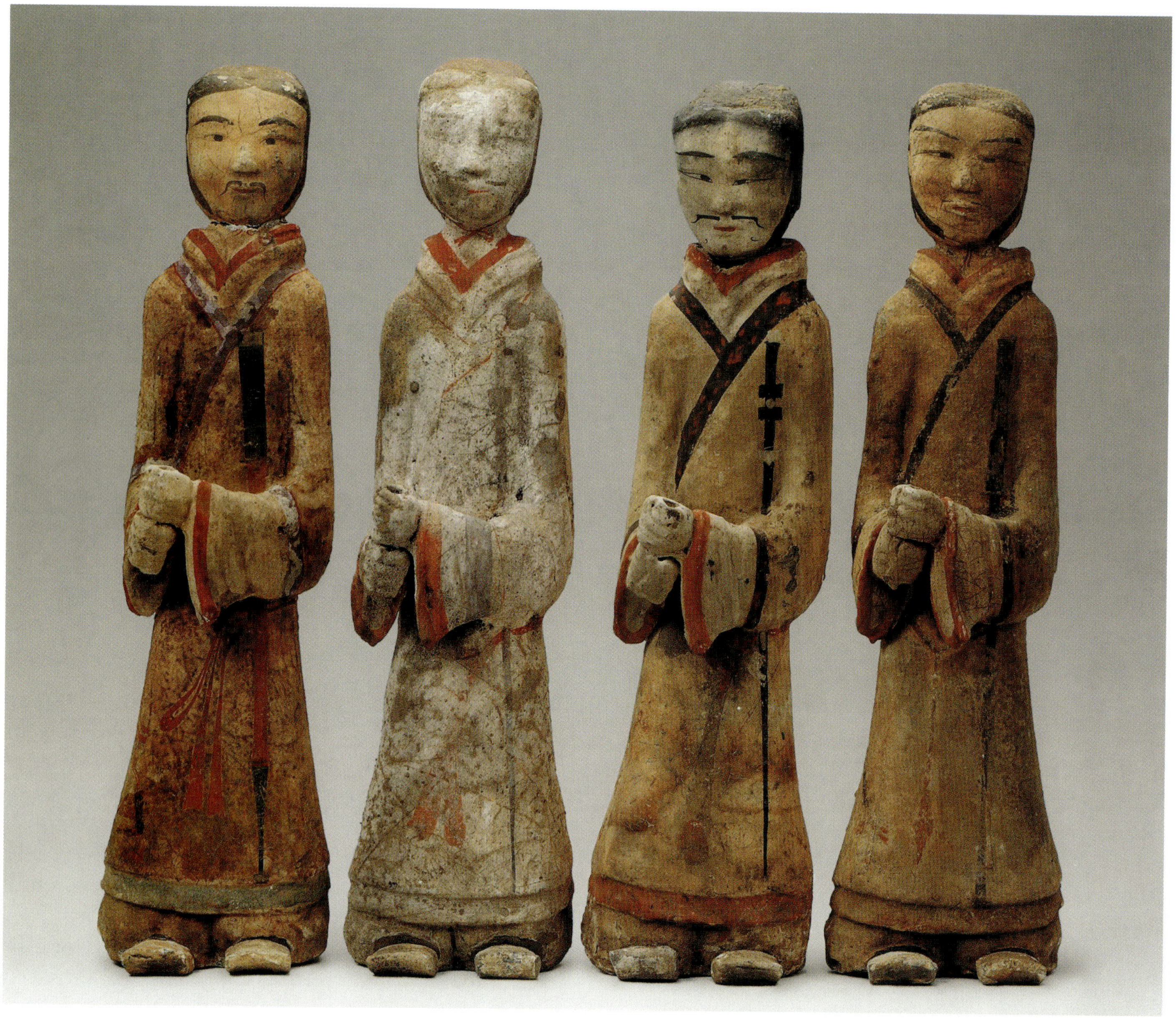

CAT.9B

light on the diplomatic vicissitudes of a kingdom just outside the Han realm and, more generally, on the degree of autonomy that the Han empire would tolerate – or not. Founded at the same time as the Han, the Nanyue dynasty may already have prospered from the lucrative maritime trade route (the so-called 'maritime Silk Route') that later ran from Guangzhou westward to India and the Middle East. By birth, language and culture the Kings of Nanyue were Chinese, and their aspiration for political status naturally led them to imitate the trappings of Han imperium. Nanyue's first ruler, Zhao Tuo (r. 203–137 BC), had twice taken the title 'emperor' and twice renounced it under threat from the Han emperor. His successor Zhao Mo, though weaker and more dependent on Han support, seems to have inherited his grandfather's imperial pretensions, as we see in the spectacular quality of his tomb's goldwork, bronzes and especially jades, which are every bit as fine as those from the Han royal burials. More than this, however, Zhao Mo emulated his grandfather in adopting the title 'emperor' on his gold seal (cat. 162). Not long after his death in 122 BC, pro- and anti-Han factions at the Nanyue court erupted in a coup that inspired the Han emperor Wudi to invade and absorb Nanyue entirely (111 BC). The treasonous *folie de grandeur* of Zhao Tuo and Zhao Mo perhaps made this an easier decision that it would otherwise have been.

EXOTICA FROM THE WEST

Among the most surprising objects found in the tombs at Xuzhou and Guangzhou are a few that show the influence of foreign types, styles and motifs: gold belt buckles in the 'animal style' favoured by nomadic tribes from the Xiongnu of present-day Mongolia (undoubtedly the source of influence here) right across the Eurasian steppelands to the Scythians of the Black Sea (cat. 82); a lobed silver vessel of Persian form (cat. 167); and floral scroll motifs in which some scholars see echoes of the Hellenistic and Roman cultures of the Mediterranean (pp. 26–8). Lacking any Chinese features, the silver vessel is likely to be an import from Parthian Persia. But more often these objects seem to have been made by Chinese artists who copied or adapted foreign imports for their exotic appeal, as here with the belt buckles and floral decorations. Was it only objects that travelled or did Western traders reach all the way to the courts of Chang'an and Panyu? Was the trade all by land or also by sea? The essays in this catalogue explore these and other aspects of the long-lived artistic interaction between East and West that began in the Han period.

The key period in the opening up of China to the West was the long reign of the greatest of all Han emperors, Wudi (r. 141–87 BC). From Dunhuang in the west to Korea in the east, and from Xiongnu in the north to Hainan Island in the south, Wudi's emissaries set up administrative posts and facilitated trade with China's neighbours. The Han's greatest rivals were the nomadic Xiongnu, with whom they alternately waged war and trade for over two hundred years. Further west, the fourth-century BC conquests of Alexander the Great had settled Greeks in Central Asia (Bactria, Sogdiana), where Tocharians and other Indo-European cultures already coexisted with Turkic, Mongolian and other peoples. In 139 BC, Wudi sent an envoy to seek alliance with the Yuezhi tribes of Uzbekistan against the Xiongnu, who were challenging the Han for control of the Tarim Basin. In this the envoy failed, but his return thirteen years later bearing stories of the riches to be found in these exotic lands led to the opening up of the Silk Route through Central Asia to the Mediterranean. Expeditions of a more military nature followed and by 100 BC Wudi's officials and other Han travellers were regularly reaching the Tarim Basin and oasis cities of the Fergana Valley – a precedent that has defined the limit of Han territorial ambition ever since.

In the Eastern Han period (AD 25–220) China's engagement with the outside world as far as Korea, Japan, Burma and the Kushan empire of western India / Pakistan continued to be conducted through a combination of trade, diplomacy and occasionally warfare. Mongolian and other Central Asian peoples from time to time challenged China for control of the Tarim Basin and the oasis towns of Central Asia but, despite these disruptions, for the most part the Silk Route continued to flourish as a conduit for garments, gems and other exotica between China and Rome. Known simply as *Seres*, '(the land of) silk', China was to the Romans little more than this – which itself was not always welcome: in the mid-first century Pliny and Seneca decried the unseemly fashion for wearing revealing silk garments among Roman women.

Han emperors received reports of many distant lands: the Parthians (*Anxi*) of Iran, the Seleucids and later rulers of Syro-Mesopotamia (*Tiaozhi*) and, at the far end of the world, the Roman Empire itself (*Daqin*). Han sources tell of an unsuccessful mission from western China to Daqin in AD 97, which turned back at the 'Great Sea' (Black Sea or Persian Gulf?). But in AD 166 a delegation from Emperor Antoninus Pius (*Andun*, who, by the time his envoys arrived, had been succeeded by Marcus Aurelius) is recorded in the *Book of Later Han* as reaching the Chinese court, the text emphasising that this was 'the very first time there was [direct] communication' between these great powers. This must surely have been one of the most symbolically charged encounters in history – despite the Han historian's disappointment at the delegation's meagre gifts of 'elephant tusks, rhinoceros horn, and turtleshell'.

The last century of the Eastern Han dynasty was plagued with power struggles between court eunuchs, dowager empresses, and high officials, this unrest further fomented by Daoist sects promising eternal bliss to the peasant poor. A series of weak and corrupt emperors in the final decades could do little to arrest the general deterioration in military, political and economic control which saw the Han dynasty collapse upon itself (AD 220). Things were not much better in Rome, where a young emperor of Syrian origin, Elagabalus, was increasingly reviled for his decadence, religious heresy and megalomania; his murder in AD 222 by his own praetorian guard went unlamented. The remainder of the third century proved to be one of crisis and instability at both ends of the world, with the rise of new religions – Christianity in the West and Buddhism in the East – adding to the currents of change. At both extremities of Eurasia, however, it was the legacy of the empires that had dominated the past four centuries that would continue to shape the outlines of civilization for centuries to come.

NOTE

1 Shang period: Lady Fu Hao, consort of King Wu Ding, *c.*1200 BC. Western Zhou period: marquisses of Jin State (*c.*1050–771 BC). Eastern Zhou period: King of Chu (*c.*550 BC), Marquis Yi of Zeng State (*c.*433 BC), and King Cuo of Zhongshan State (late fourth century BC).

FACING PAGE: DETAIL OF CAT. 61

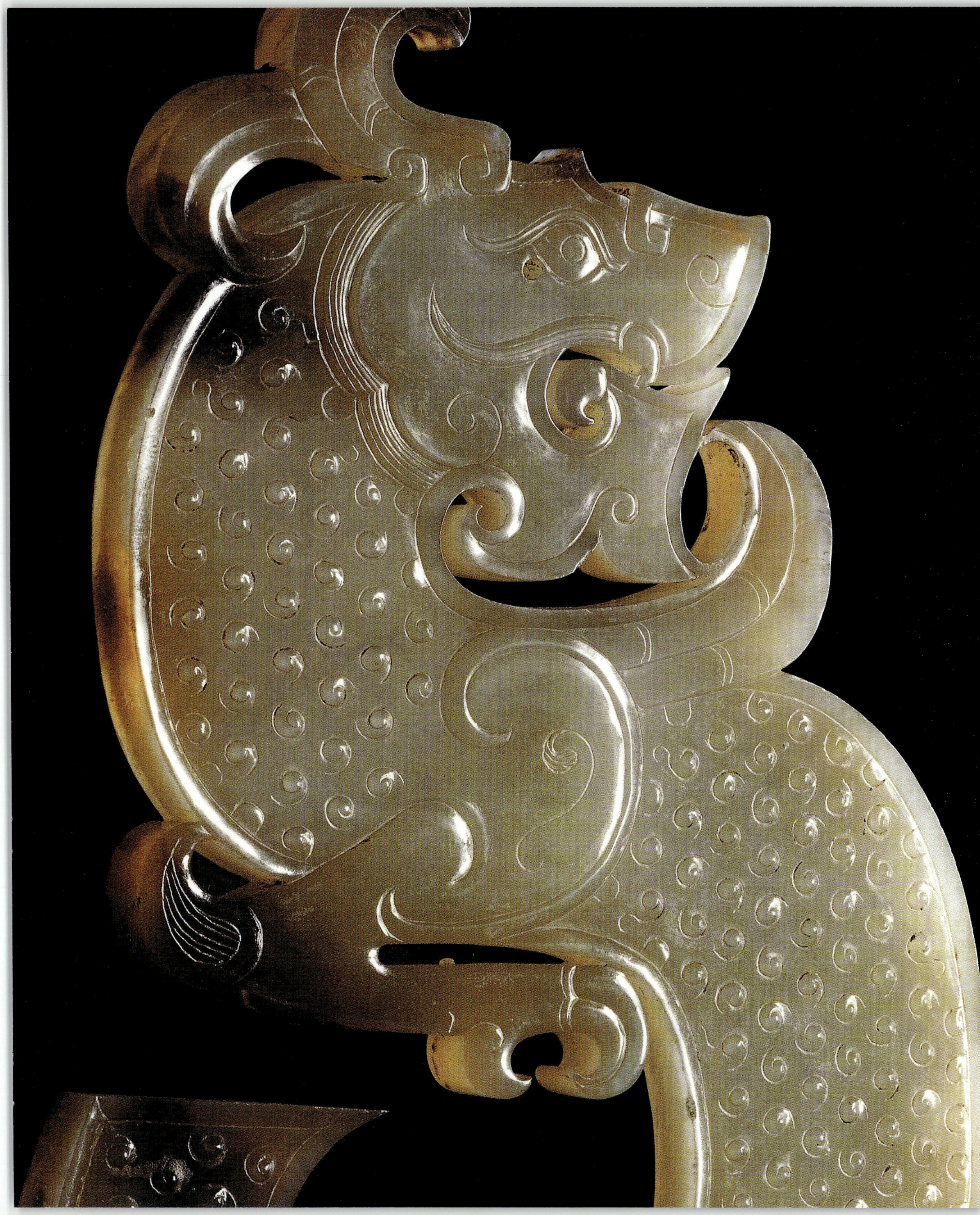

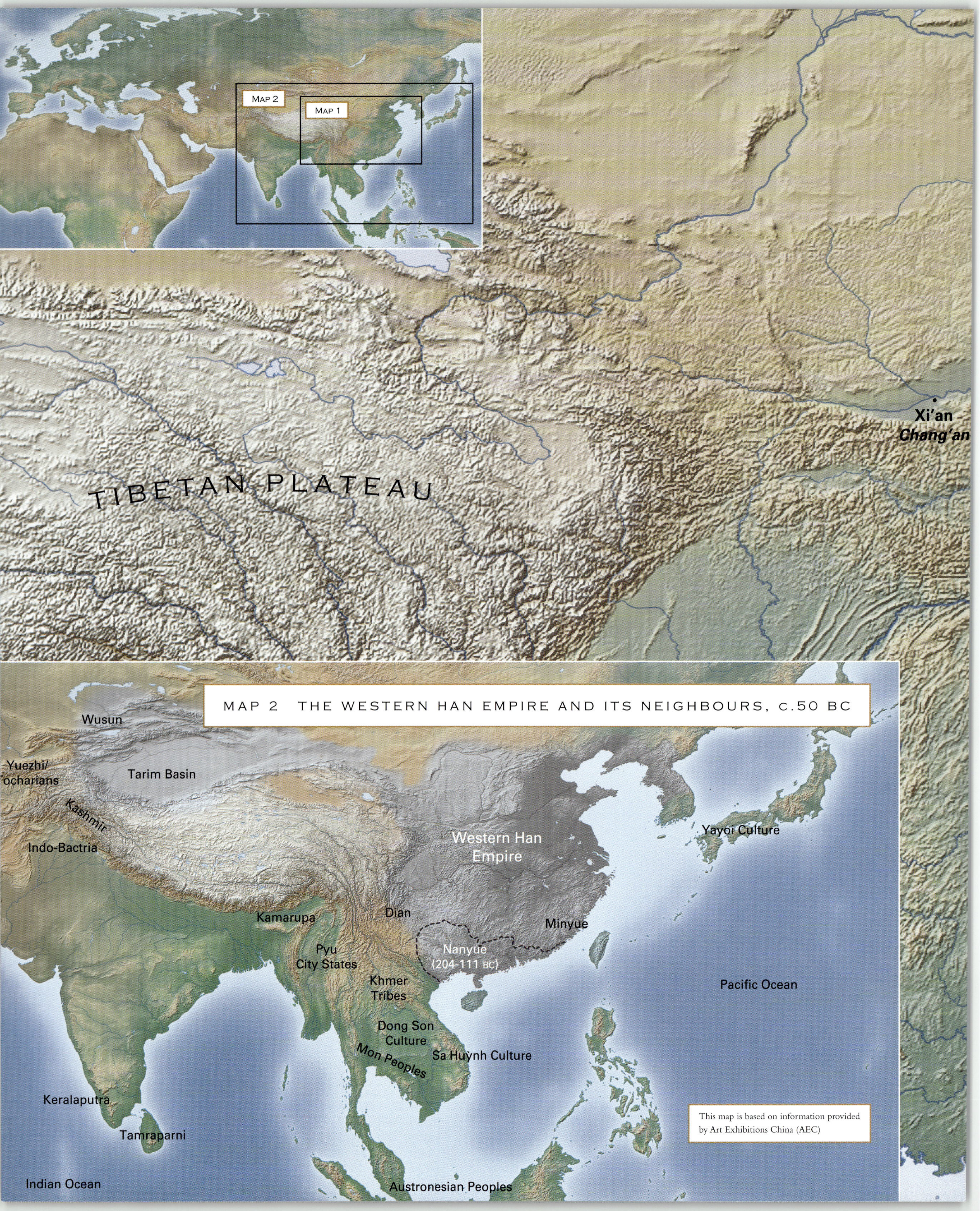

MAP 2 THE WESTERN HAN EMPIRE AND ITS NEIGHBOURS, C.50 BC

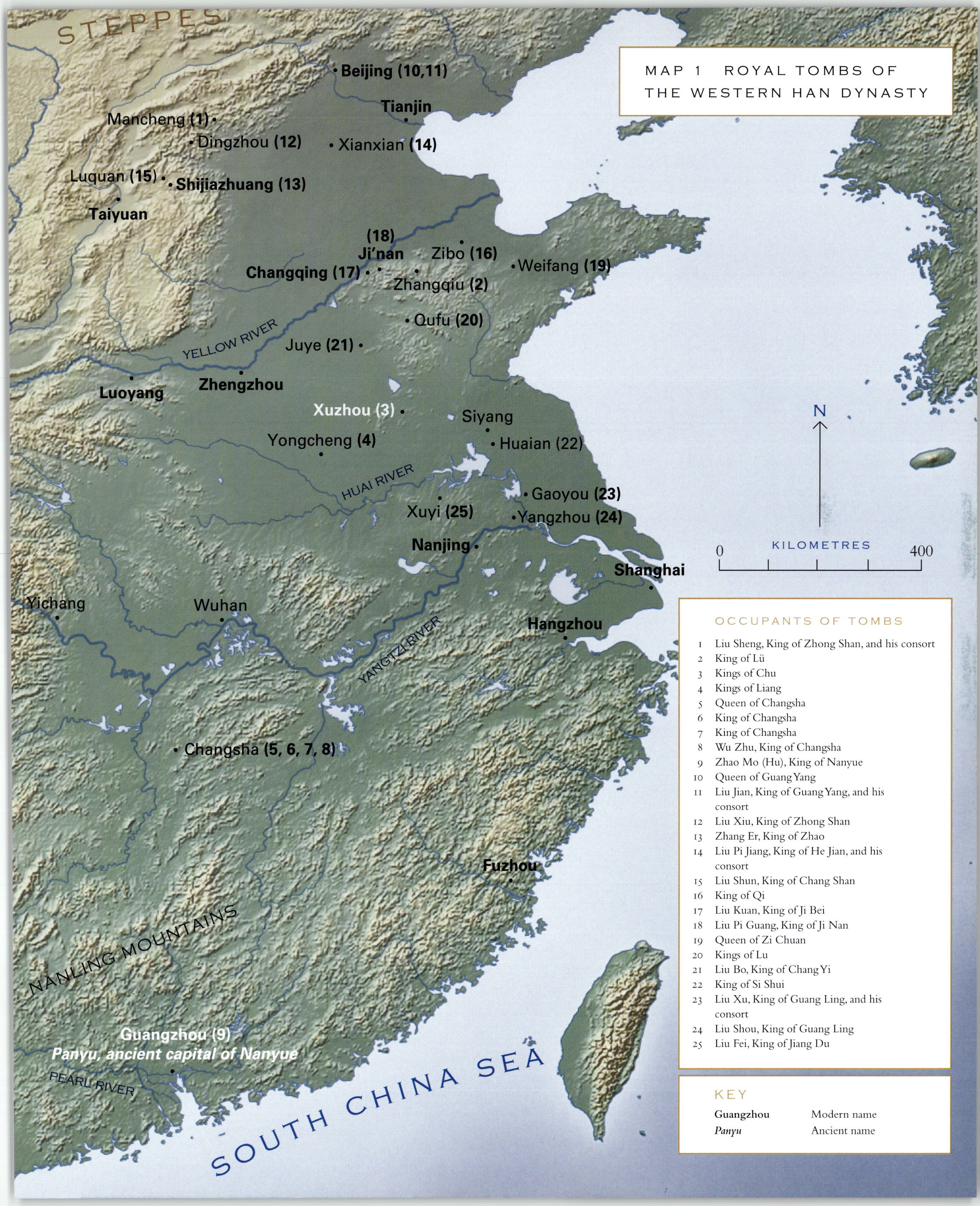

MAP 1 ROYAL TOMBS OF THE WESTERN HAN DYNASTY
STEPPES
Beijing (10,11)
Tianjin
Mancheng (1)
Dingzhou (12)
Xianxian (14)
Luquan (15)
Shijiazhuang (13)
Taiyuan
(18)
Ji'nan
Zibo (16)
Weifang (19)
Changqing (17)
Zhangqiu (2)
Qufu (20)
YELLOW RIVER
Juye (21)
Luoyang
Zhengzhou
Xuzhou (3)
Siyang
Yongcheng (4)
Huaian (22)
HUAI RIVER
Gaoyou (23)
Xuyi (25)
Yangzhou (24)
Nanjing
Shanghai
N
KILOMETRES
0
400
Yichang
Wuhan
Hangzhou
YANGTZI RIVER
Changsha (5, 6, 7, 8)
Fuzhou
NANLING MOUNTAINS
Guangzhou (9)
Panyu, ancient capital of Nanyue
PEARL RIVER
SOUTH CHINA SEA
OCCUPANTS OF TOMBS
1 Liu Sheng, King of Zhong Shan, and his consort
2 King of Lü
3 Kings of Chu
4 Kings of Liang
5 Queen of Changsha
6 King of Changsha
7 King of Changsha
8 Wu Zhu, King of Changsha
9 Zhao Mo (Hu), King of Nanyue
10 Queen of Guang Yang
11 Liu Jian, King of Guang Yang, and his consort
12 Liu Xiu, King of Zhong Shan
13 Zhang Er, King of Zhao
14 Liu Pi Jiang, King of He Jian, and his consort
15 Liu Shun, King of Chang Shan
16 King of Qi
17 Liu Kuan, King of Ji Bei
18 Liu Pi Guang, King of Ji Nan
19 Queen of Zi Chuan
20 Kings of Lu
21 Liu Bo, King of Chang Yi
22 King of Si Shui
23 Liu Xu, King of Guang Ling, and his consort
24 Liu Shou, King of Guang Ling
25 Liu Fei, King of Jiang Du
KEY
Guangzhou Modern name
Panyu Ancient name

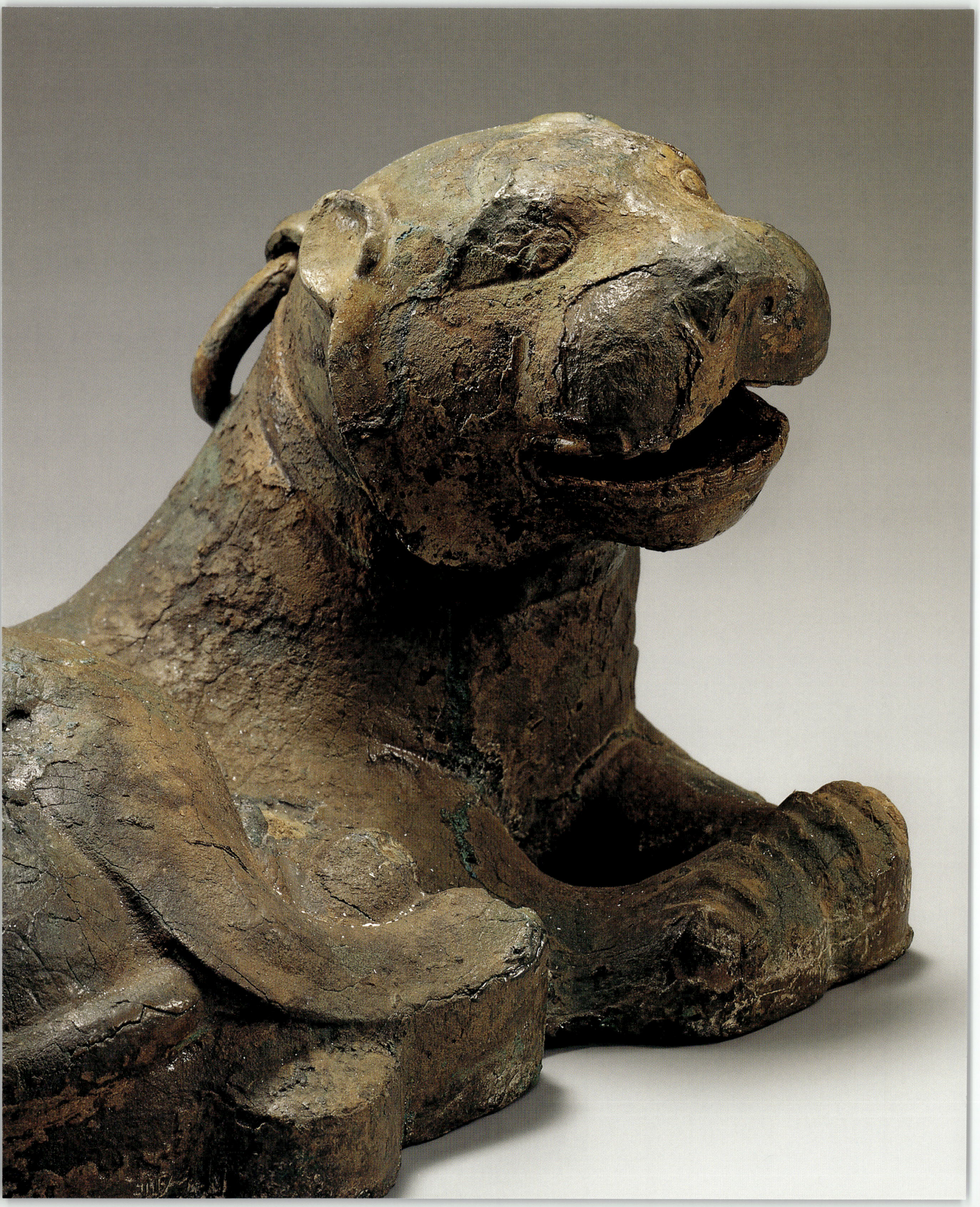

THE HAN EMPIRE IN CHINESE HISTORY AND CULTURE

MICHAEL LOEWE

Since perhaps 1600 BC kingdoms had ruled over limited areas in what we now call China for varying periods of time, but it was only in 221 BC that an empire was formed, ruling as a single authority without challenge from others. Shortlived as the hegemony of the Qin was (221–210 BC), it was followed by that of Western Han from 202 BC to AD 9 with its capital at Chang'an (present-day Xi'an), Xin (AD 9–25) and Eastern Han from AD 25–220, with its capital at Luoyang. As the first long-lasting empire, Han drew on the institutions, experience and practices of the previous kingdoms, now amalgamated under single control. Based in the north-west, Western Han ruled at first over lands that led into the lower parts of Gansu Province, the Liaodong peninsula and the fertile lands of Hunan and Sichuan. As yet the emperor did not rule in the deep south (Guangdong and Guangxi) or far west (Yunnan), but from around 100 BC his servicemen and officials were penetrating more widely and setting up their offices as far afield as Dunhuang, the Korean peninsula and Hainan Island.

Imperial government was designed to maintain law and order, defend the realm, suppress crime, collect revenue and to control the work of the population and the production of the land. The extent to which these aims were achieved varied widely between areas that had previously been governed intensively and those that had been unworked and were only recently brought under a government's attention; between those that were populated deeply or sparsely; between those where natural conditions favoured official supervision, and the woodlands and marshes that allowed inhabitants to live beyond an official's surveillance. It was thus only in particular areas that government could exercise a pervasive influence or maintain complete control. At times the authority of the emperor lay open to attempts by rebels to displace him and establish their own regime. Local outbreaks of dissidence were not infrequent, particularly during the latter years of the Eastern Han, when a strong-minded and popular local leader could at times set himself up in virtual independence, with the support of his own armed followers and control of large areas of land.

The position of emperor passed from father to son on a hereditary basis. Only a few of the eleven emperors of Western Han and the fourteen of Eastern Han can be judged to have been men of a compelling personality capable of leadership, decisiveness and initiative. In most cases they were below the age of twenty at the time of accession or indeed no more than infants, and as such they were subject to the immediate control of their mothers or grandmothers, as agreed with the latters' own relatives. The emperor's function was rarely that of an active head of an empire who gave direct orders to his subjects or played a leading role in determining matters of policy or administration. Nevertheless, it was of paramount importance to the government of the empire that emperors existed with an acknowledged title.

Initially the emperors of Qin, Western Han, Xin and Eastern Han had won their position thanks to their military success and it was due to their personal leadership and enduring strength of character that they could command obedience. But with the passage of time, maintenance of such authority came to require religious and intellectual support; it had to be demonstrated and believed that they had received a position that had been conferred upon them by a higher, superhuman authority whose will they represented on earth. In this way the emperor would constitute an unquestioned source of power that he devolved to his ministers or officials. With no emperor to command them,

FACING PAGE: DETAIL OF CAT. 36

TABLE 1 CHRONOLOGY OF THE EMPERORS OF THE WESTERN HAN DYNASTY

GENERATION	NAME	TITLE	RELATIONSHIP TO THE EMPEROR OR KING	REIGN
1	Liu Bang	Gaozu		202–195 BC
2	Liu Ying	Huidi	Son of Gaozu	195–188 BC
	Lü Zhi	Lühou	Wife of Gaozu	188–180 BC
3	Liu Gong	Shaodi	Son of Gaozu	184–180 BC
4	Liu Heng	Wendi	Son of Gaozu	180–157 BC
5	Liu Qi	Jingdi	Son of Wendi	157–141 BC
6	Liu Che	Wudi	Son of Jingdi	141–87 BC
7	Liu Fuling	Zhaodi	Son of Wudi	87–74 BC
8	Liu He	King of Changyi	Nephew of Zhaodi	74 BC
9	Liu Bingyi	Xuandi	Grandson of Wudi	74–49 BC
10	Liu Shi	Yuandi	Son of Xuandi	49–33 BC
11	Liu Ao	Chengdi	Son of Yuandi	33–7 BC
12	Liu Xin	Aidi	Grandson of Yuandi	7–1 BC
13	Liu Kan	Pingdi	Grandson of Yuandi	1 BC–AD 6

they would themselves have no authority to give orders; their call for obedience would ring true only if it came from their own superior, and if it was acknowledged that that superior person had himself received his charge to rule from a yet higher source. For these reasons Han emperors came at last to claim and see themselves as ruling thanks to the charge that they had received to do so, from a source that they came to identify as Heaven.

The appointment of officials, who came to number about 130,000, depended on merit or sponsorship, and in time on some rudimentary forms of testing and competition. Senior officials determined major policies and attended the emperor at court. With their juniors they staffed the government's offices and agencies at the capital city and in the provinces, promulgating imperial orders and implementing the laws. They counted, registered and controlled the population in units of as few as four or five members, calling up males to serve in the labour gangs or in the armed services. They judged criminal cases, set up schools and kept roads and waterways in good repair. They controlled the passage of individuals from one area to another. In outlying regions they introduced the ways of life of the civilized world, such as the use of clothing and forms of marriage. In all these duties they kept records, such as financial accounts that were carefully written on slats of wood, sometimes with duplicate copies.

In addition to the unknown number of persons who lived in the fastnesses of mountain or marshland and evaded the eyes of a prying official, by the beginning of the Christian era the registered population of the empire had come to number nearly sixty million individuals. Social distinctions rested on birth, merit, imperial orders or wealth. Some dozen male members of the imperial family of Liu who had been nominated kings transmitted their titles and the lands they governed to the keeping of their sons. Officials who showed promise rose from the low rank of humble clerk to that of minister of state in the central government. From time to time an imperial decree bestowed orders of social precedence on certain male members of the population according to a scale of twenty orders, each with its legal privileges and allotted land-holdings. The highest of these, the nobilities, provided a title and the right to raise tax and an income. A merchant's wealth could buy high social status. A comparatively small number of slaves worked either for private owners or at the behest of officials. Criminals sentenced to up to six years of hard labour, and sometimes mutilated, worked as was required in the provinces.

The great majority of the population lived off the land, sowing millet or hemp in their fields and rendering part of the produce as tax. To some extent the government controlled occupation of the land but much was available for purchase. For the rich, ingots of gold coins supplemented the bronze coins of a single denomination; private minting of coins was banned. Government monopolies for the mining, manufacture and sale of salt and iron wares operated on and off from *c.*120 BC, to the exclusion of private initiative. Merchants could make large fortunes by dealing in jades and pearls, lacquered wares and potteries, livestock, rare fruits and cooked meats. Conscript servicemen worked the mines and the iron foundries; skilled artisans produced polychrome silks, ornamental bronze vessels and pottery. These artisans fashioned the jades that filled the houses of the rich and might make their way outside the Han emperor's domains, sometimes reaching as far as the shores of the Mediterranean Sea.

No direct contact linked Han China with such lands. Tales of other peoples who were not subject to imperial rule, examples of rare products or commodities of exotic types reached the markets of Chang'an or Luoyang. A few travellers came back with accounts of the communities they had visited, their way of life, natural resources, living habits and organization. From perhaps 120 BC Han was extending its influence and expanding its interests into these unknown regions of the north-west. The Qin empire had unified a series of defence lines in the north as a protection from violent inroads, mainly by the Xiongnu (see pp. 23–4). Following a series of military campaigns against them, Han forces extended those lines of forts, staffed by conscript servicemen, to reach as far as Dunhuang in the north-west. They were to serve both as a measure of defence and as an armed causeway along which the Han caravans – numbering several hundred persons – could proceed safely with their bales of silk, bronze mirrors or potteries. Officials were posted to administer newly founded provincial units; contacts with local leaders could lead either to friendly relations or to conflict. Back in Chang'an, generals of the army welcomed the arrival of horses from the north to augment their forces; their wives enjoyed the luxury of furs and pelts; the newly arrived grape and its products enriched the emperor's banqueting table.

At the same time provincial governors were establishing offices in Korea, and the south-east, south and south-west of present-day China, with the intention of exploiting the land, controlling the population and raising tax. Some of these posts were isolated, such that appointment thereto could in effect be a type of banishment from the cultured and comfortable life known in the interior of the empire. Administration of these widely separated inhabitants was anything but complete or permanent and there were times when the Han government withdrew altogether from these outlying regions. Several centuries had to pass before the lands that led south to Hong Kong or present-day Yunnan formed integral parts of a united Chinese empire.

The first duty that fell upon a new emperor at his accession was to pay homage at the shrines dedicated to the memory of his ancestors, thereby confirming his own inheritance of their charge. Once adult, he performed the regular cults addressed to those superior powers from whom his authority derived. He would be buried in an imposing tomb furnished with valuables, such as jade jewellery, model farms or carriages, figures of attendants such as musicians, and consumables of food, drink and clothing. His tomb would include symbols intended to guide his soul to one of two paradises, either the east or the west, and it would be surmounted by a lofty tumulus for all to admire and revere.

Burial of those at lower levels of society followed this pattern, depending on the rank of the deceased person. Splendid tombs of some of the kings took the shape of stone-built mansions with their chambers and protective walls. For them and certain privileged persons a suit of jade – that treasured mineral that promised enduring life – encased the body, as it did that of the emperor. High-ranking officials were buried in brick-built tombs with richly decorated walls, lintels and vaults. At the lowest level a body was interred with no accompanying goods, save perhaps for a rough inscription of the man or woman's name. From perhaps AD 150, stone stelae carefully inscribed with an elaborate account of a high official's career stood beside his tomb.

Apart from the emperor's religious duties, others took care to render prayers and offerings to those mighty forces of nature, be they of hill or river, of wind or thunder, thought capable of fixing the destinies of mankind. Villagers spared products of their farms and ponds as offerings to appease those spirits and deflect their anger. Festivals to herald in the new year served as rites to bring it success, and could help to forge a sense of social identity. Faith in the ideals of the Buddha and the accompanying need for self-questioning and reverence came to China's countryside from India, perhaps about AD 150. The last decades of Eastern Han saw the emergence of self-proclaimed teachers who promised their adherents worldly bliss and perhaps spiritual happiness in return for an obedient life within a community. Such movements gave rise to a priesthood some of whose rites came to be addressed to Laozi, seen to be the author of the *Daodejing* (The Way and its Power).

Insecurity at times when the forces of nature could destroy a livelihood and a compelling need to maintain the continuity of a family were among the reasons why men and women adopted a number of means of enquiring how best to order their lives. Such guidance was to be found in messages that superhuman powers conveyed, perhaps by abnormal events such as an eclipse in the skies, the occurrence of an earthquake at a crucial time or the mere direction and force of the winds that blew on New Year's day. Specialist experts could make a living by manipulating a bundle of reeds to create a pattern of six lines, whose meaning could be found by consulting an old text to be called the *Yijing* (Book of Changes) and might serve to set the anxious mind of an enquirer at rest. Other methods were in use. Instruments displayed the cycles of the universe and the positions they had reached; books set out each day of the year with advice of what actions, such as marrying a wife or building a house, should be chosen as likely to be successful and those which should be avoided as leading to failure.

From about 100 BC, officials were paying attention to writings that were some centuries old with a view to inculcating moral standards. From perhaps 50 BC, there was a growing tendency to quote the sayings ascribed to Kongzi (Confucius; 551 to 479 BC) to sustain an argument; but as yet, despite some moves towards intellectual uniformity, there was no acknowledged system of 'Confucianism' that regulated public activities and individual conduct or stamped its ideas on literature. Particular moments of intense intellectual activity are recorded for the discussions on political principles in 81 BC and on the proper interpretation of certain old writings in 51 BC. The collection of books to form the imperial library, which was ordered in 26 BC, marked a new stage in China's literary history. The opening years of Emperor Zhangdi's reign in AD 76 witnessed an active interest in intellectual and literary matters.

A new form and style of writing history that was seen in a work completed *c.*100 BC formed a model for compiling dynastic histories thereafter. Men of letters were writing essays on matters such as the value of the past as against a need for innovation, or dialogues between advocates and opponents of imperial policies. Criticism of public life and its direction was being voiced in another literary form, that of the rhapsody; short poems drew on rigours of the time such as the hardships of the soldier; structured essays discussed the workings of nature and argued for or against well-known beliefs inherent in folklore. Elegant compositions disclosed personal points of view between friends. Occasionally we hear of the literary work of a woman.

Some writers were enquiring into the nature of the universe and its changes as manifested in the skies, on earth or among living creatures, and as affecting the destiny of empires. Scholars were laying down correct modes of behaviour that would maintain social distinctions and religious rituals in due order. Astronomers calculated the movements of the heavenly bodies and regulated the imperial calendar. Other thinkers drew attention to the part played by superhuman forces in human affairs, whether for good or ill. Working on silk paintings or stone reliefs, artists depicted scenes of the next world, figures and incidents from history and mythology or the luxuries of a banquet. Craftsmen produced their masterpieces in jade, bronze or lacquer. A new method of working the fields, introduced *c.* 100 BC, increased the yield of the land; builders supervised conscripted servicemen in the toil of pounding earth and clay to form the majestic walls of a city.

Such was the legacy of a mighty empire, ascribed with admiration and praise to Han for some two thousand years, and on several occasions between AD 338 and 1360 a short-lived regime chose to adopt Han as its title, by way of emulation. Before then a major difference of attitude affected views of the ideals of imperial government, as between the Western and Eastern Han; controversies and problems were no stranger to those who governed or lived in both the earlier and the later of these regimes. On several occasions, in 154 and 90 BC for example, survival of the dynasty was in question. Jealousies among the emperor's consorts and the claims of rivals to succeed him disrupted the peace of court and capital, at times with violence. Memorials to the throne protested against the improper selection of officials or their incompetence, corruption and oppression, particularly in the Eastern Han. Against those who advocated an intensive supervision of the working population and the products of the fields and mines, others argued for a laissez-faire policy that would reduce a government's interference to a minimum.

Occasionally an official suggested plans to restrict the size of land-holdings, but such attempts to soften the hardships of the poor met with scant success. Expansionist moves to promote contacts and trade with the peoples of Central Asia proved to be expensive; there were as many who proposed plans to do so as there were those who complained that they resulted in no more than the import of luxurious baubles. Advisors at court held widely divergent views both on the purposes and conduct of the religious cults of state and on the choice of ancient, revered writings that were fit for official adoption. There survives no positive disquisition on the nature of a life after death, but the design, embellishment and furnishing of tombs reveal differing approaches to this question. From time to time mother nature reminded men and women of their insignificance and weakness in the face of happenings that lay beyond their power, such as the floods that followed the changes of course of the Yellow River (AD 3 and 11), or the earthquake that shook Chang'an on the very same day as an eclipse (29 BC).

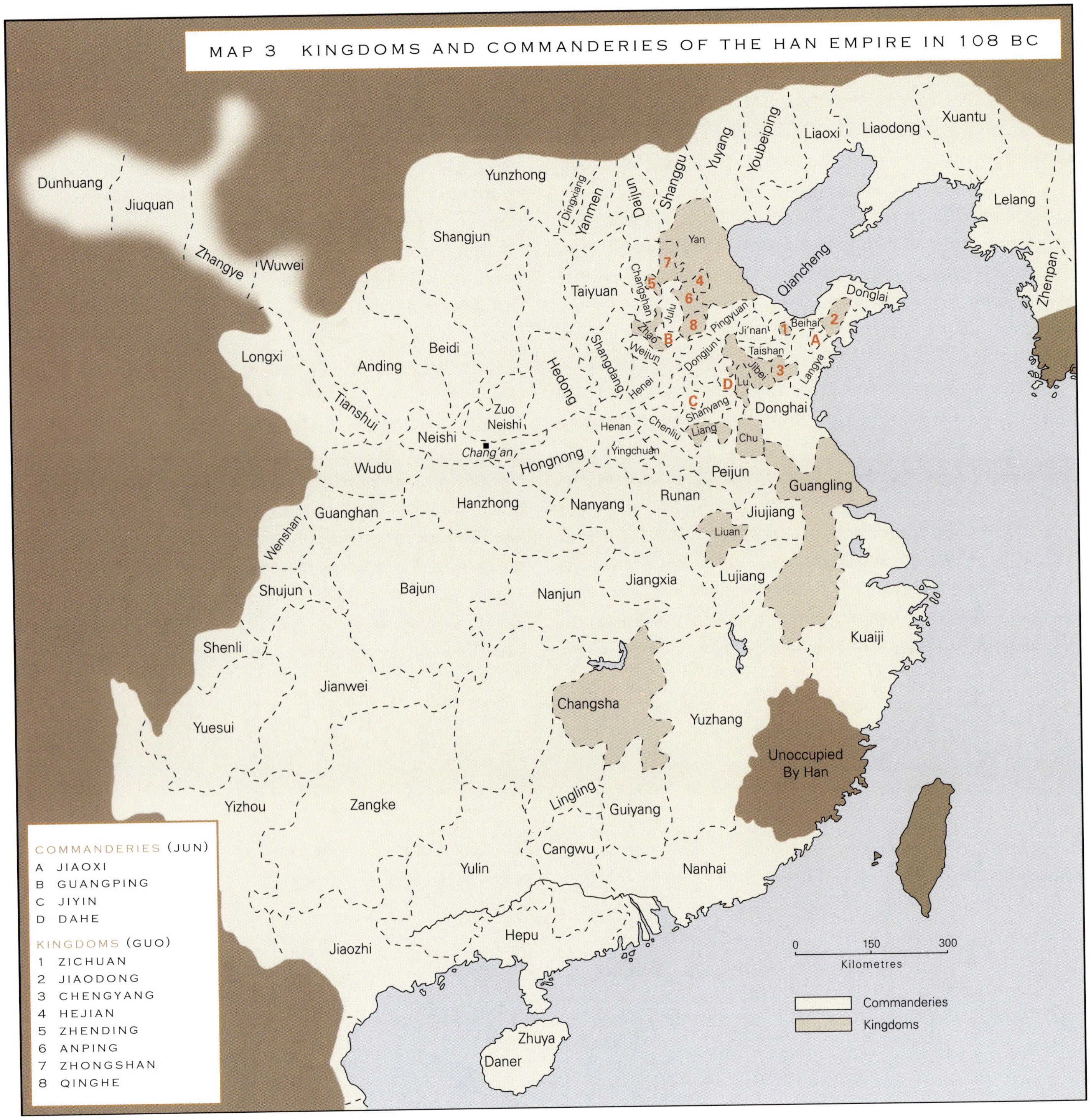

MAP 3 KINGDOMS AND COMMANDERIES OF THE HAN EMPIRE IN 108 BC

THE KINGDOMS OF CHU IN THE WARRING STATES AND HAN PERIODS

MICHAEL LOEWE

During the Warring States period (481–221 BC), Chu had been perhaps the largest, but not the strongest, of seven kingdoms that had occupied most of what we now call China. Its lands in present-day Anhui, Hubei and Hunan ran on either side of the Han and the Huai rivers, extending to the lower reaches of the Yangzi and as far as Sichuan in the west; they did not reach the eastern coast (Map 4). The region had given rise to a culture whose characteristics varied widely from those of the more northerly or easterly parts of China. It was marked by romantic rather than classical features; its artists drew on themes of mythology and painted their lacquers in brilliant scarlet and shining black; the designs of its bronzeware reflected an appeal to the mysterious. A historian of the first century AD noted something of the different lifestyle of a people whose agriculture was not advanced and who lived off fish. He also remarked on the prevalent belief in the powers of the spirits and the shamans, and the people's practice of irregular or even licentious religious rites. Such features are seen in the poetry of Chu, known as *Chu ci* (Songs of the South), although they were probably written at a slightly later date.

The lands of the pre-imperial Kingdom of Chu were incorporated into the short-lived empire of Qin (221–210 BC) and, following some years of civil warfare, into that of Han (founded 202 BC). The new empire included large areas made over to be governed by close relatives of the emperor, who were given the rank and title of king. It was in this way that the lands that had been the Kingdom of Chu were to be administered but they were now under the rule of kings who bore titles other than Chu, such as Huainan. At the same time a somewhat different area, situated in present-day Jiangsu and the south of Shandong (Map 3), was named Chu and made over as a kingdom to the emperor's younger brother.

There is thus a major distinction between the Kingdom of Chu of the Warring States and that of Han times. The earlier Kingdom of Chu, independent of all other authorities, had evolved its own series of offices and titles. In Han times, the kings controlled their lands and population, as constituent parts of the empire, in a form that was modelled on that of the emperor himself at the centre. Senior assistants or ministers of the kings bore titles, such as Chancellor, that corresponded with those of the central government. Their officials sought to keep the population in check and to promote production of the fields according to the rules that were ordered by the centre and followed throughout the provinces (or more properly 'commanderies') that its named governors administered. The kings themselves were duty-bound to attend the capital at regular intervals, there to confirm their allegiance to the emperor and to present their accounts. The Han Kingdom of Chu passed from father to son on a hereditary basis until 154 BC, when Chu joined six other kingdoms in staging a large-scale revolt against the emperor. At its suppression the King of Chu committed suicide and the kingdom was suspended. Refounded in 153 BC, it had been stripped of large territories that stretched from Feixian and Linyi in the north (present day Shandong) to Qingjiangshi in the south (Jiangsu). Roughly square in shape, the kingdom lay to the south-east of the Weishan lake, measuring no more than a hundred kilometres east to west and north to south, with Xuzhou to its west. The line of kings was broken in 69 BC but restored from 50 BC to AD 8, during Western Han.

Three of the Kings of Chu are known to have taken a part in dynastic matters in Western Han times. Liu Jiao (king from 201 to 179 BC) acted as an advisor to his elder brother, first of the emperors (known as Gaozu), and to his nephew the third emperor (Wendi). Liu Yingke (king from 179 to 175 BC) had held the post of Superintendent of the Imperial Clan and was one of the senior ministers who supported the accession of Liu Heng as emperor (Wendi). Liu Yanshou (king from 100 to 68 BC) was involved in an abortive plot to manipulate the imperial succession. Several tombs situated at Shizishan, Beidongshan and Guishan, close to Xuzhou, have been identified as those of some of the earlier of the Kings of Chu of Western Han times. The best materials from these imperial tombs are being exhibited at the Fitzwilliam Museum.

An even smaller Kingdom of Chu was created in Eastern Han for the person of Liu Ying who was a son of the first of the Eastern Han emperors and is best known for his patronage of Buddhism. This kingdom lasted from AD 41 to 71.

There is nothing to show that the small Kingdom of Chu was of any political importance or that it played any part in the economic operation of the empire in Western Han times. Nor is there reason to regard the Han Kingdom of Chu as a successor to the kingdom of Warring States times, with its characteristic, romantic culture. Lanling, birthplace of the writer and philosopher Xun Qing (*c.*313–235 BC), author of the *Xunzi* (Master Xun), is known to have been a centre of intellectual and scholarly activity at least from the time of Han Wudi (reigned 141–87 BC). It was situated in that part of the Western Han Kingdom of Chu that was detached in 153 BC and governed as the commandery of Donghai.

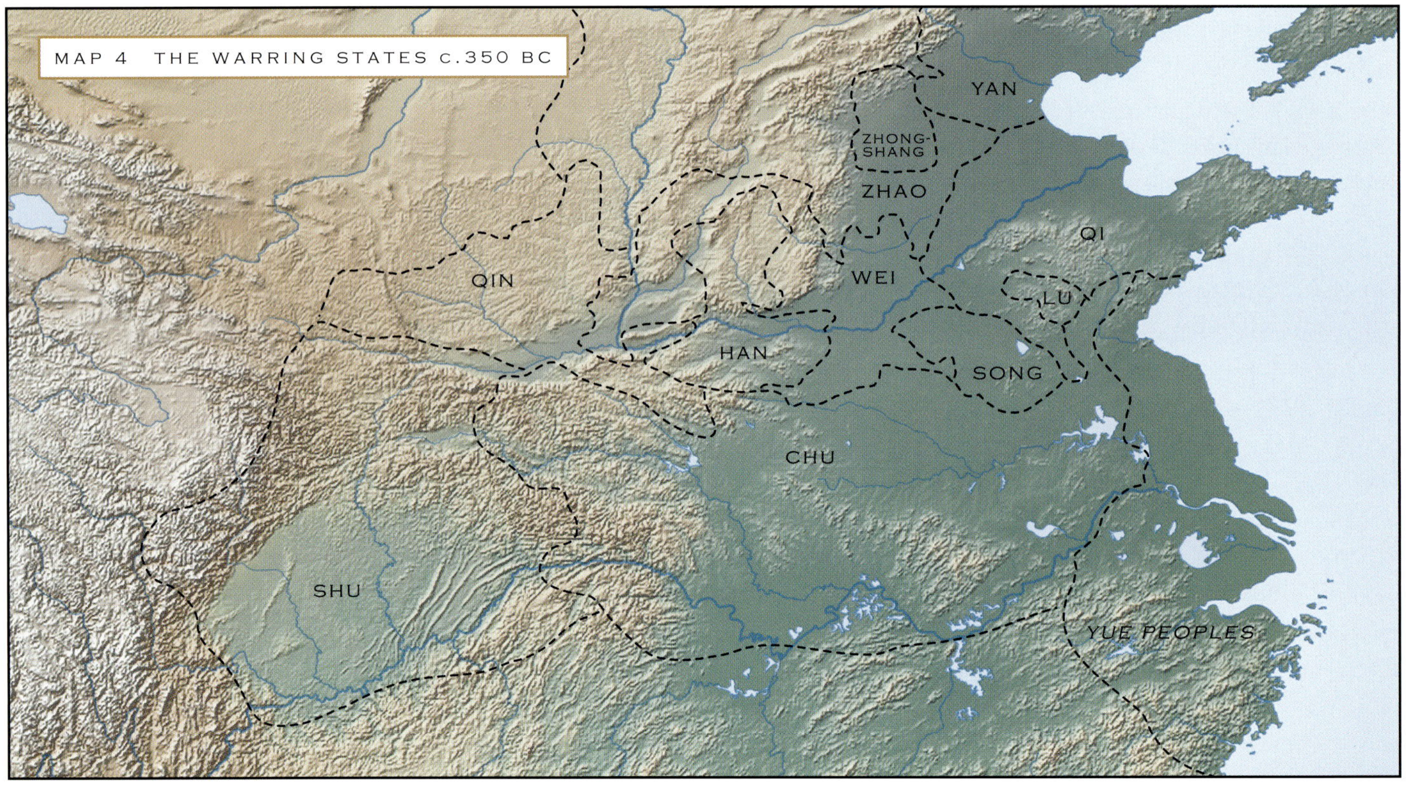

THE KINGDOM OF NANYUE

MICHAEL LOEWE

Nanyue of Han times, more properly Nan Yue, Yue of the South, or the region of Southern Yue, denotes the large area south of the Ling range of mountains that is administered now as the provinces of Guangdong and Guangxi. It was distinct from Min Yue of Han times, region of the Min Yue peoples, to the north-east in Fujian. The way of life of Nanyue was that of inhabitants of a mountainous and swampy land beset by a tropical climate, and little is known of the presence there of Chinese peoples from the north until the time of the Qin and Han empires. As late as the third century AD some of the inhabitants were still living naked, with no compunction, and they had yet to learn of the habit of paring off in orderly forms of marriage. A habitat of the elephant, Nanyue produced exotic fruit, and produce of the sea, including pearls, the latter serving both as an ornament and an aphrodisiac.

Han's relations with the south differed in one major respect from those with the north whose peoples, likewise unassimilated to the disciplines and habits of a settled way of life, would ride down into north China to wreak violence on the farmlands and could at times muster strength to fight Chinese forces in battle. The peoples of Nanyue posed no such threat and at the height of its powers the Qin empire established the commanderies of Nanhai, Xiang and Guilin to govern the lands; how effectively the governors were able to do so cannot be told, but it may be assumed that their rule was in no way as pervasive as that of their colleagues in the settled agricultural lands north of the Yangzi River.

Zhao Tuo, who came from present-day Hebei, had been one of the officials whom Qin had posted to this distant region. Aware (*c.*210 BC) that the Qin empire was breaking up he declared himself the King of Nanyue, with his centre probably at the city of Panyu (in present-day Guangzhou) and possibly exercised some authority north of the Ling range. His relations with the newly founded Han empire varied from friendly agreements to animosity, and he was at times tempted to attack one the nearest points of Han territory, in Changsha. From about 180 BC a compromise seems to have been reached; Han was not strong enough to take over Zhao Tuo's lands; Zhao Tuo perhaps realised the limits to his independence. With Han's acquiescence, he retained his kingdom and affirmed his position, while adopting part of the title and the forms of behaviour of a Han emperor, to whom he confirmed his loyalty. For its part the Han government was ready to assist his successor in the face of threats from Min Yue.

Zhao Mo, successor to the kingdom, died in 122 BC and was buried in a tomb that was modelled on the tombs of the Han kings. But by now the Han empire was able to embark on expansionist policies that took its officials, servicemen and merchants into the far reaches of the north and south, as far as Dunhuang, Korea and almost to Myanmar. When an official in Nanyue raised a revolt in protest against the king's proposal to make over to Han, Han sent forces to suppress it, both by land and sea; Panyu was set on fire in the course of the fighting. Incorporated now (111 BC) in the empire, the area was ruled as nine commanderies under governors appointed by the centre; two of these commanderies extended down the coast of Vietnam; two, which were withdrawn in 82 BC and 42 BC, were on Hainan Island.

A number of unsuccessful uprisings were directed against imperial authority in Eastern Han, beginning with that of the Tr'ung sisters in AD 40. Rather than send a large force to restore order at a time of a major revolt in AD 137, the Han government removed some of the potential dissidents and persuaded some of their leaders to join the imperial side. Following the Han dynasty, several leaders or regimes established themselves in different parts of the region, with increasingly stronger means of control. On one of the rare occasions in China's history of an attempt to set up a major imperial power that was based in the south, the 'dynasty' of Chen was established in 557, to last only until 589.

Sites of large cemeteries, as at Duimianshan and Luobowan, included several hundred graves, some dating from the seventh and sixth centuries BC, and some as late as Eastern Han. Possibly two tombs may be identified for certain as those of Han officials, one of a man of Western Han who may have been a governor of Jiuzhen commandery (on the coast of Northern Vietnam), and one, of a more junior official, in Kowloon. The most spectacular tomb to have been excavated is that of Zhao Mo, King of Nanyue (see pp. 59–62). The king was buried in a suit of jade pieces, a privilege reserved for the immediate relatives of the emperor, including the kings, and a few specially designated favourites. Whether the Han authorities gave permission to supply a jade suit for Zhao Mo, no blood relative of the imperial family, or whether it had been acquired by underhand means, may not be known.

Officials of Western Han had their duties, such as controlling the movement of wayfarers. They supervised two agencies for the production of salt, but a copper foundry in Beiliu (present-day Guangxi) was apparently independent of their control. Exotic products of the area such as rhinoceros horn, elephant tusks and rare fruit reached the court and city of Luoyang in Eastern Han times. A report tells of a long trade route that stretched from Guangxi or the coast of Vietnam, and continued partly by land, to reach the destination of Huangzhi, perhaps in India or perhaps the Persian Gulf, but as yet unidentified for certain.

THE HAN EMPIRE AND ITS NORTHERN NEIGHBOURS: THE FASCINATION OF THE EXOTIC

JESSICA RAWSON

Two magnificent gold belt plaques from the Shizishan tomb at Xuzhou (cat. 82) carry a vivid relief design of a wolf and a bear attacking a crouching, horned deer (fig. 1). The gold plaque's two animals in attack on a third and a deer whose horns are tipped with birds' heads link this piece to the world of northerners inhabiting the steppe, beyond the boundaries of Imperial China. Yet the plaques were almost certainly made in China. The high elites of the Han court owned not just such gold or gilded bronze plaques, but many other artefacts to be described here that demonstrate their fascination with their neighbours. This essay outlines the relationship of the Han court with these neighbours and describes some of the numerous artefacts, including many in the exhibition from the tombs of the Han Imperial princes and the King of Nanyue, that are evidence of this consuming interest.

INTERACTION WITH THE NORTHERN BORDERS

From the very earliest written records that survive, the oracle bones of the Shang (*c.*1250–1045 BC) and bronze inscriptions of the Shang and the Western Zhou (*c.*1045–771 BC), we learn that the people we today call the Chinese, the governing elites of the Yellow River basin, constantly engaged with their northern neighbours in warfare and trade.[1] They even integrated these outsiders in their societies as servants, horse managers and as trusted partners in official enterprises. Chinese military needs for chariots, horses to draw them, chariot drivers and their weaponry continued for many centuries to require repeatedly renewed contact with the borderlands where the horses were bred.[2]

For the early Han rulers, the impact of the horse-breeding nomads was intensified by the growth of the steppe-confederacy of the Xiongnu, a nomadic people who at different times dominated the northern steppes from Manchuria in the east to the far west, north of the great Tianshan mountain range. During the first part of the Han period, the Chinese were very much on the defensive, and suffered major defeats. They were forced to make pacts that gave the Xiongnu substantial gifts, or 'tribute'. From the reign of the Emperor Wudi (141–87 BC) the Chinese took a more aggressive position, inflicting defeats on the Xiongnu and driving them further north and west, as well as reducing the goods that they had to offer. In the last phase of Emperor Wudi's military policy, he sent an army westwards to seek allies against the Xiongnu. This move reinforced Han interest in the oasis cities around the Taklamakan desert along what is today called the Silk Route. The intention was to block Xiongnu access to the heartlands of China by obstructing these corridors of communication. And over a similar period, the emperor sent embassies to the courts in Bactria and other Central Asian states also seeking allies against the Xiongnu. The best known of these were led by Zhang Qian in 139 BC and 115 BC.[3]

The Chinese had themselves contributed to the continuous warfare by moving north under the leadership of the first emperor, during the late third century, to establish a boundary north of the Ordos region, which lies within the great northern bend of the Yellow River. This move had been one aspect of Chinese attempts to control the incursions of the border peoples and, at the same time, to acquire horses with which to match their northern foes. The more frequent warfare became, the greater the need the Chinese had for horses to mount their cavalry against

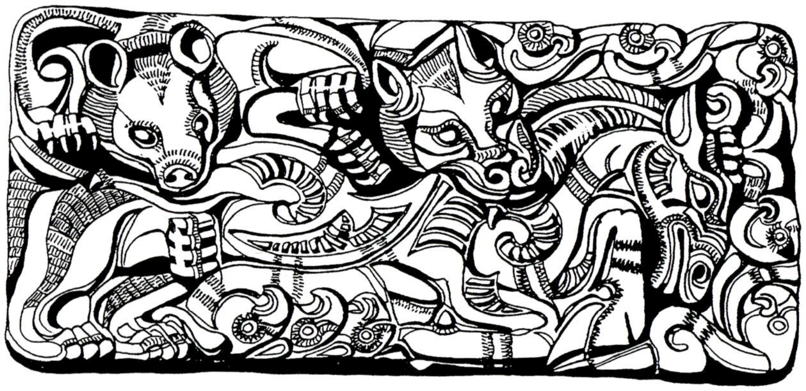

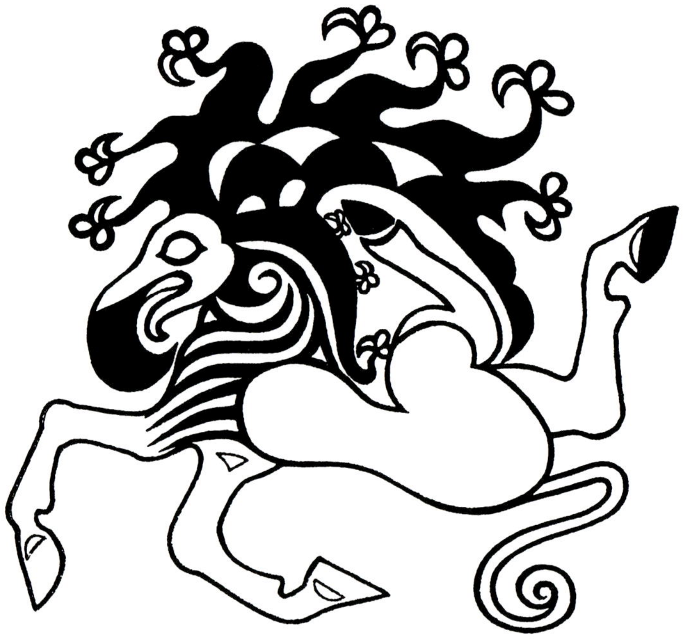

the nomads. Trade, as much as warfare, was an essential aspect of this relationship with the Xiongnu. During the early second century BC, while the Xiongnu had the upper hand in the relationship, treaties required the Chinese to send silk, gold and agricultural produce, such as cereals, to their neighbours. Evidence of both gifts and trade is seen in the metalwork, textiles and lacquers found in major Xiongnu tombs excavated at Noin Ula in Mongolia.[4]

People were another form of exchange between the Xiongnu and the Chinese. As guarantors of the treaties, marriages between Chinese women and Xiongnu *Chanyu*, or rulers, were a regular aspect of diplomacy. The Xiongnu leaders were entertained by the Han court and generals and other military figures on both sides defected to the other. Such continuous interchange between two major groups of peoples with very different cultures is the background against which we should view the gold belt plaques and many other exotic items in Han elite tombs. Here we will examine four topics to illustrate the impact of steppe or inner Asian cultures on the possessions of the Han princes and elites: belt and harness ornaments that imitate Xiongnu and other steppe work; major palace pieces that reflect the more distant cultures of Iran and Central Asia; the decoration of bronze, lacquer and ceramics with landscape motifs that originated in scroll patterns current in Western Asia; and the construction of tombs along horizontal corridors in small hills and mountains that recall, if distantly, rock-cut tombs in Central Asia and Iran.

IMITATIONS OF STEPPE ITEMS

The gold belt plaque (fig. 1) is only one of the most magnificent of the Han imitations of Xiongnu-type ornaments. Another gold belt plaque from Tongshan is exhibited (cat. 81). Much smaller pieces in gold, including four thin plaques decorated with rams' heads (cat. 77) and a more solid piece showing a bear with an open mouth (cat. 76), are likely to have been ornamented harnesses or similar artefacts. Large numbers of Xiongnu bronzes have been excavated in the Ordos area though quite a number may have been made by the Chinese expressly for the Xiongnu.[5] Such metalwork included many pieces displaying deer with long horns tipped with birds' heads, as seen on the gold belt plaque.[6] This very distinctive motif was, however, not confined to the Xiongnu but was used in fully three-dimensional, more elaborate forms in the Altai at the famous frozen tombs at Pazyryk. Here the same creature is found in tattoos on human bodies (fig. 2) and as a headdress for a horse.[7] In the latter example, the antlers tipped with birds' heads are free-standing.[8]

The tomb of the King of Nanyue also included a number of imitations of steppe metalwork. A rectangular plaque embellished with tortoises and a dragon is a hybrid of a

1 Drawing of a gold belt plaque from the tomb of the King of Chu at Shizishan, Xuzhou, Jiangsu Province (cat. 82). Western Han period, second century BC. Length 13.3 cm. Drawing by Mélanie Steiner.

2 Tattoo of a fantastic horned beast with small appendages on the horns similar to birds' heads. From kurgan No. 2 at Pazyryk, Altai Mountains, Siberia. Third–second century BC. After Rudenko 1972, fig. 131.

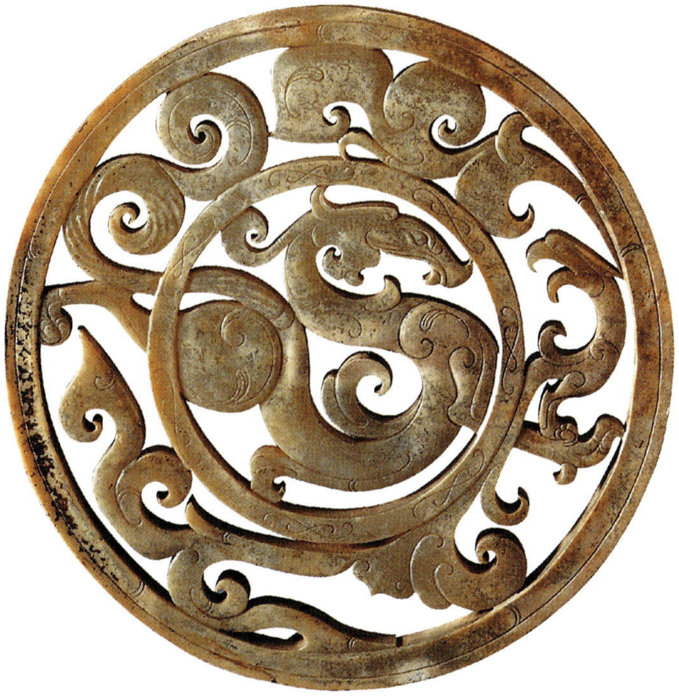

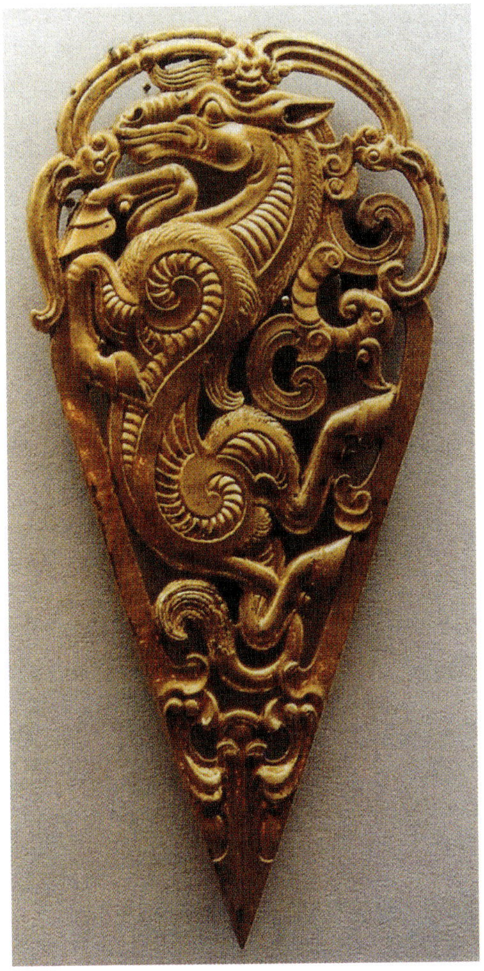

steppe artefact, a belt plaque and a Chinese motif (cat. 170). Even more unusual is a rectangular plaque inlaid with blue glass (cat. 145). Glass itself was rare in China, and its local manufacture was based upon foreign models. Blue, too, was a colour more closely associated with the steppe, or regions of present-day Iran or Afghanistan, than with the Han empire. The King of Nanyue, like the Chu king, owned many small items, including small gold plaques with rams' heads (cat. 159), of a variety similar to, but distinct from, those at Shizishan (cat. 77). The wider impact of such imitations of steppe artefacts is seen in a remarkable openwork jade disc with a phoenix and a dragon threatening each other (fig. 3). Such rendering of two creatures, otherwise associated with the four directions of the universe (north, south, west, east), in a combative pose is another hybrid combining Chinese and steppe taste.

The two areas of Xuzhou and Guangzhou celebrated in the exhibition are by no means the only regions from which Han period finds have come, illustrating the popularity of steppe-like ornaments with the Han elite. Tombs of other imperial princes, such as Liu Sheng, King of Zhongshan (d. *c.*113 BC), and those of the Kings of Liang at Yongcheng in Henan Province contained other examples of small gold or gilded fittings in steppe style. More dramatic is a gilded bronze horse bridle frontal part from a pit near a massive, unexcavated tomb at Luozhuang to the east of Ji'nan city in Shandong Province (fig. 4). The main subject is a horned deer with tiny birds' heads entwined in the schematic horns around the upper edge of the frontlet. A similar but narrower and less dramatic example is exhibited from the tomb of the King of Nanyue (cat. 127).[9] In all these cases, the hind legs of the main animal are twisted and lozenges of striped hatching, distantly derived from wood carving, enliven its body. Both such features are found on material at Pazyryk and on metalwork at Izzyk,

3 Jade openwork disc with a dragon and a phoenix. Excavated from the tomb of the King of Nanyue, Guangzhou, Guangdong Province. Second century BC. Diameter: 10.6 cm.

4 Gilt bronze horse frontal displaying a horned deer with small birds' heads in the horns along the edge and with a twisted body. From Luozhuang, Zhangqiu, Shandong Province. Western Han dynasty, second century BC. Length: 16.5 cm. After *Kaogu* 2004.8, pl. 2:1.

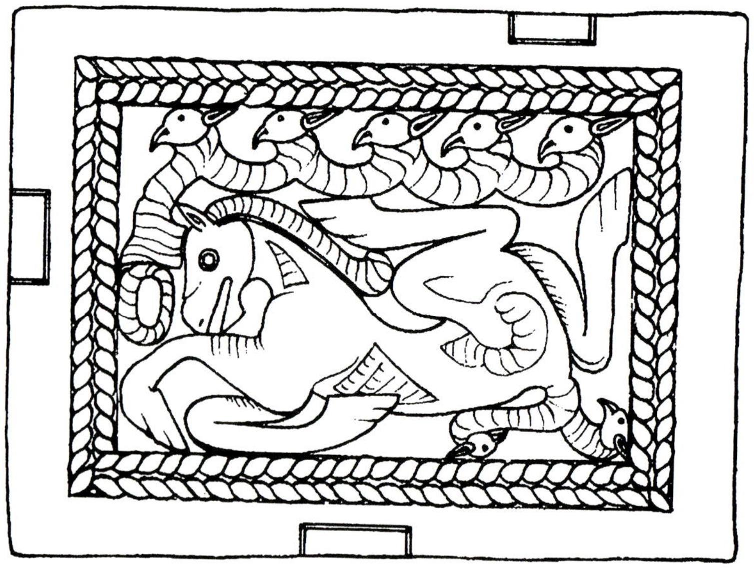

PALACE ITEMS IN CENTRAL ASIAN STYLE

While the plaques and harness fittings mimicked the fashions of the Xiongnu and other border groups, spectacular three-dimensional artefacts, here designated as palace items, were much more clearly adapted to Chinese taste. Among pieces from the tomb of the King of Nanyue that were clearly based upon models from Central Asia or Iran are a magnificent rhyton in jade (fig. 6) and a silver, lobed box (cat. 167). Rhytons, or horn-shaped cups, were especially popular with mounted warriors. An example made of horn has been found in modern-day Xinjiang Province.[13] In Mesopotamia

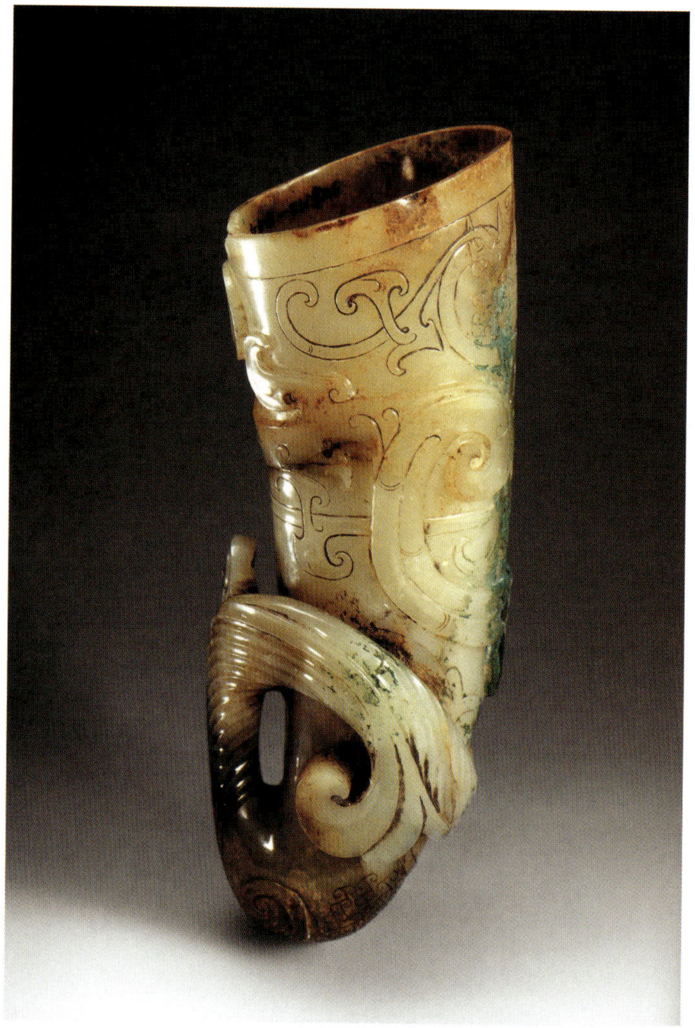

major burial sites in the Altai in Siberia and in Kazakhstan, as well as among the many bronzes from the Ordos region.[10] Despite the constant warfare and the disadvantageous treaties, it seems that the Han elite embraced Xiongnu and other steppe fashions enthusiastically, most especially for belt, weapon and harness ornaments. The imperial princes in particular, but also others, appear to have been eager to be recognized as equal to their mounted and threatening neighbours.

Most if not all of the pieces mentioned were probably made in China, both for the Xiongnu and for the Chinese.[11] We have evidence of workshops where such pieces might have been cast from the excavation of a tomb at Xi'an dating to the third century BC. Ceramic moulds and models for a variety of pieces, both traditionally Chinese and steppe in character, were found with the tomb occupant, who was probably a bronze caster. His repertoire included a ceramic model depicting a deer with horns tipped with birds' heads (fig. 5).[12] The occupant of this one tomb is not likely to be the sole example of a caster making bronzes in steppe form. Indeed, it would seem that many of the pieces found in the Ordos area are likely to have been cast by the Chinese and perhaps offered to the Xiongnu as part of the tribute they exacted.

5 Drawing of a pottery model showing a deer with small birds' heads at the tips of its horns. From the tomb of a bronze-caster, Xi'an, Shaanxi Province. Third century BC. Length: 9.4 cm. After Xi'an 2006, fig. 85.

6 Jade rhyton. Excavated from the tomb of the King of Nanyue, Guangzhou, Guangdon Province. Second century BC. Height: 18.4 cm.

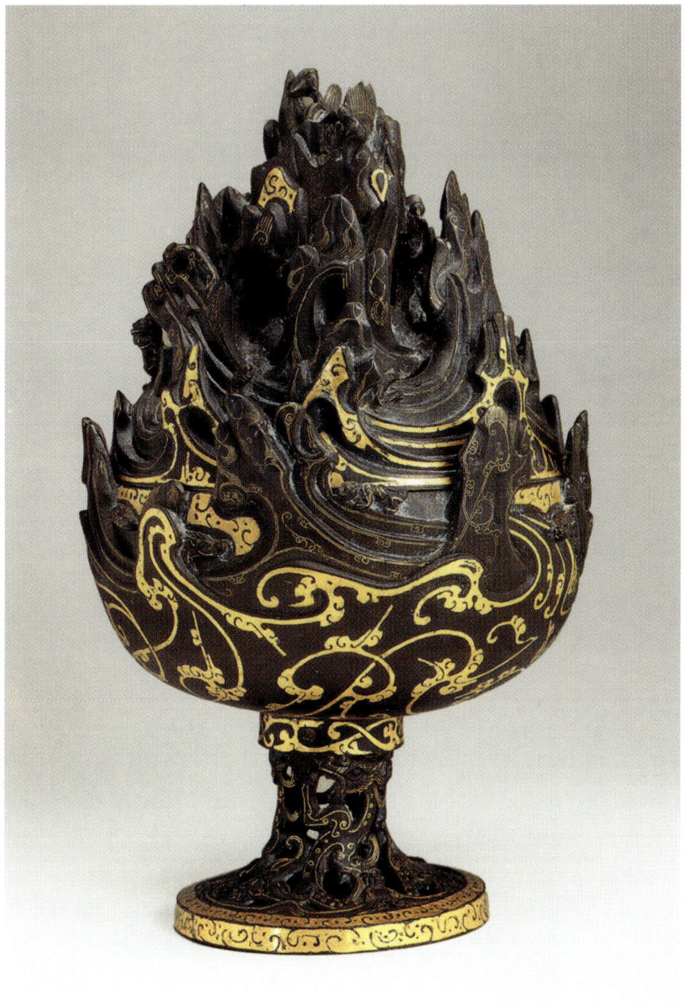

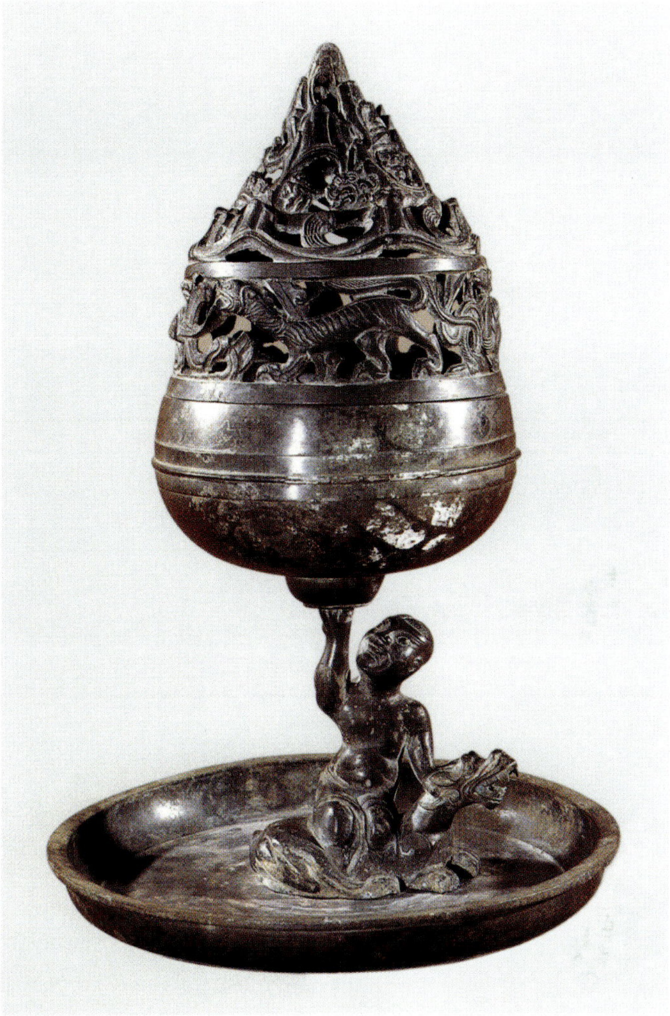

and Iran, elegant palace examples in ivory, gold and silver were popular with the kings and nobility.[14] For the Chinese, the shape was exotic but sufficiently intriguing for the foreign form to be copied in jade. Silver, on the other hand, was barely used in early China. The box, and a number like it found at other Han sites, are all based upon the lobed silver vessels developed in Achaemenid Iran and also used by their successors, the Parthians.[15] A recently excavated, turquoise glazed ewer from a Han tomb in Guangxi Province further points to trade with Iran, probably by sea and up the Persian Gulf, that may also have brought the prototypes for some of these silver boxes to the Pearl River delta.

Incense burners in the shape of peaked mountains were even more clearly hybrids, mixing features from Iran and the steppes with those from China. Two examples from the tombs of Liu Sheng, King of Zhongshan (fig. 7a), and his consort Dou Wan (fig. 7b), illustrate such combinations and can be compared with the exhibited example from a tomb at Dongdongshan at Xuzhou (cat. 43).[16] Overall, the peaked lid mounted on a cup and held on a stand was typical of incense burners popular in the Achaemenid Empire.[17] In China, the lid was turned into a mountain referring to Chinese legends.[18] Incense would have emerged from holes in the lid, creating an impression of mist among mountain

7 Incense burners. From the tombs of Liu Sheng, King of Zhongshan, and his consort Dou Wan, Mancheng, Hebei Province.
7a (left) Bronze inlaid with gold cloud scroll around the cup, held on a stem in the form of a dragon. Second century BC. Height: 26 cm. After Beijing 1998a, fig. 129.

7b (right) Bronze with the cup supported by a man riding on an imaginary creature. Second century BC. Height 32.3 cm. After Beijing 1998a, fig. 128.

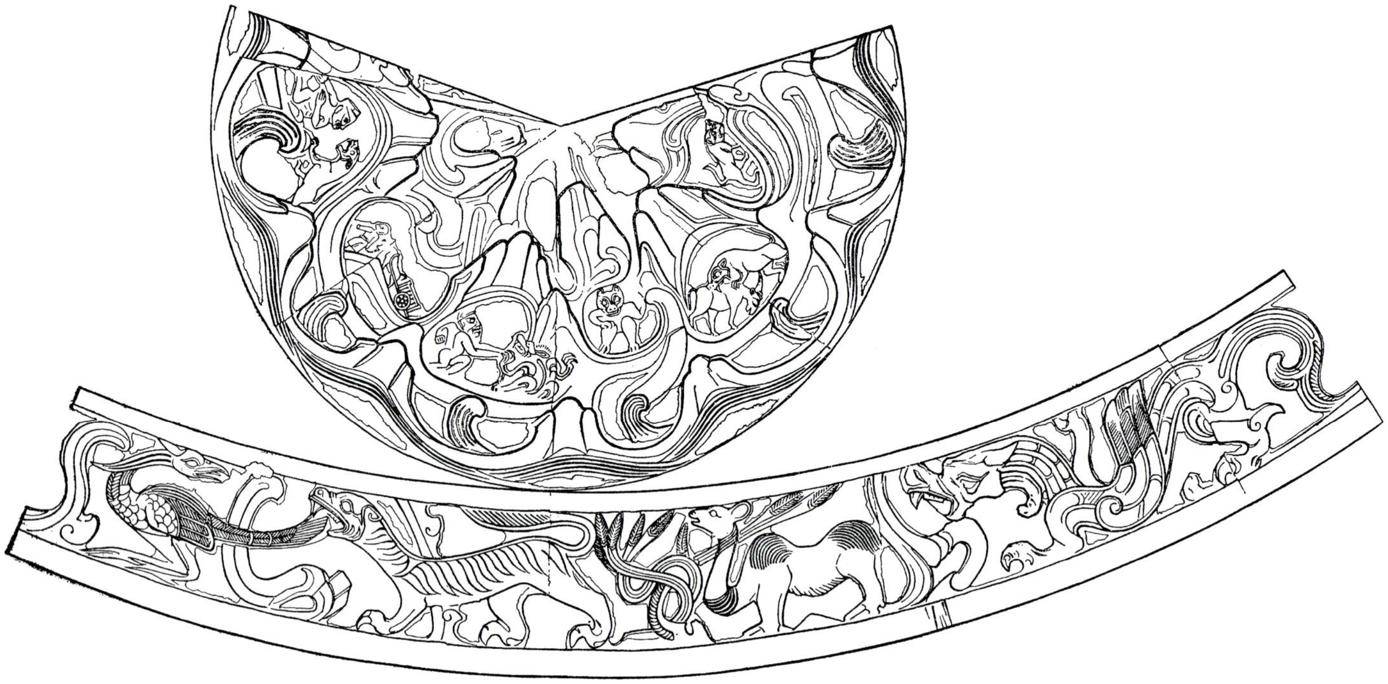

peaks. This hilly landscape seems to have signified the islands of Penglai for, as the two examples from the Zhongshan tombs illustrate, the mountains appear to be being lifted up above water, one by a dragon and the other by a man riding on an imaginary creature.[19] This appearance matches the legends about Penglai, thought to be a group of islands in the eastern sea inhabited by immortals, which, when approached by people in boats, would disappear beneath the waves.

Small, three-dimensional realistic creatures scale the mountain peaks on Liu Sheng's censer, while a bird, a tiger, a camel and a dragon march along the lower section of the incense burner belonging to Dou Wan (fig. 8). These four creatures symbolize the directions, with the camel here replacing the tortoise and snake, the more usual beasts to represent the north. The camel, indeed, belonged to the north and to the invading border peoples as one of their primary modes of transport. Even more closely linked to the steppe and the plaques discussed above are the small scenes of animals in combat or a man with a cart depicted in tiny scenes on the mountain above the directional creatures. These can be readily matched with plaques from the Ordos region that present almost identical subjects (fig. 9).

The diverse creatures that decorated both the incense burners and steppe-like plaques also feature prominently among other possessions of the imperial princes. And many of these were clearly inspired by Western Asian or steppe examples. One key piece is the crouching feline with a ring on its collar from Shizishan (cat. 35). As argued elsewhere, the prototypes include a gold weight from Nanjing (fig. 10) and ubiquitous bronze weights from Iran in the shape of crouching lions, with loops on their backs.[20] Two earlier examples reinforce the proposal that many realistic, three-dimensional, small animal sculptures owe their existence to stimulus from outside China. The first group includes the inlaid bronze creatures from the tomb of King Cuo at Zhongshan in the fourth century BC. Wings on a pair of beasts are Western in inspiration, as is the imagery of one animal devouring another, creating a magnificent inlaid bronze mount in the shape of a tiger with a deer in its jaws (fig. 11).[21] Later in date, two fittings in the form of upright lions standing on birds, from the tomb of Liu Sheng, seem

8 Drawing of the lid of Dou Wan's incense burner (fig. 7b). After Beijing 1980, vol. 1, fig. 171.

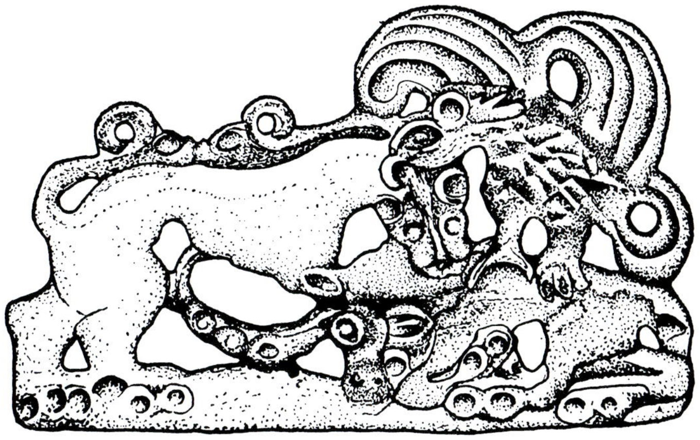

9a

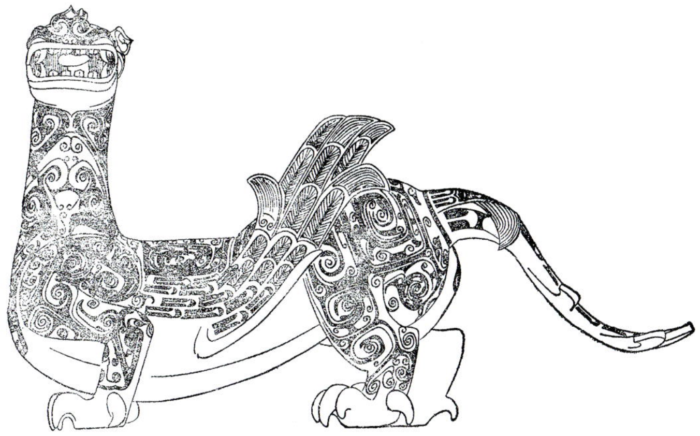

11a

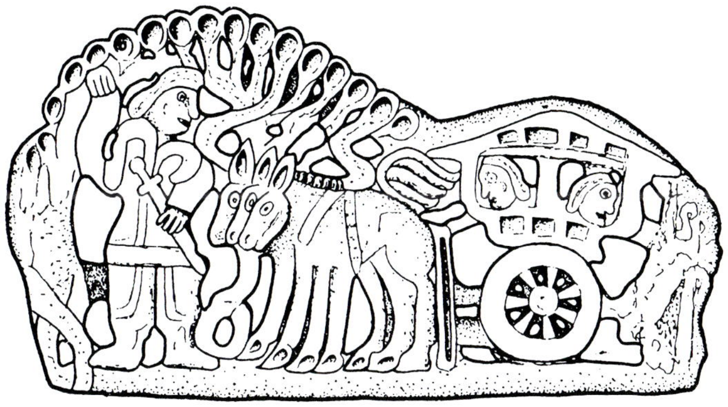

9b

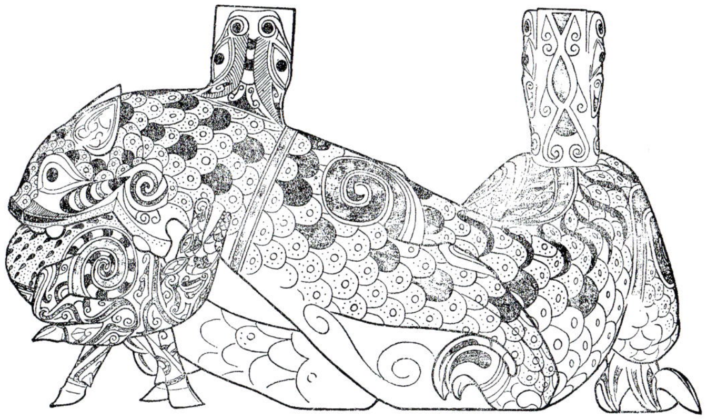

11b

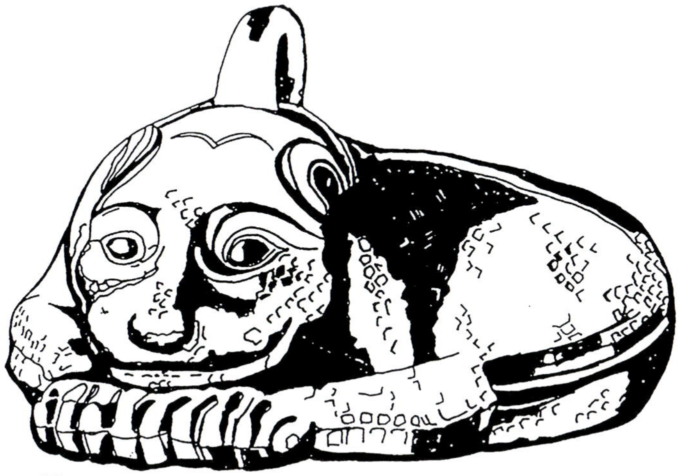

10

to have been based upon figures of the Egyptian god Tauert in a form known in Iran.[22] From such exotic examples, whose links with the steppe and Western Asia are relatively easy to detect, seem to have developed many small weights and fittings in the shape of realistic creatures, such as the felines in the tomb at Xuzhou or two entrancing leopards from the tomb of Liu Sheng. As with the incense burner, the stimulus to create these creatures seems to have come from outside the Chinese cultural centres, but once adopted, foreign traits were submerged and entirely new contexts and associations were developed for the creatures as ornaments and mat weights at the Han courts.[23]

9 Drawings of two openwork bronze belt plaques from the Ordos region showing a scene of animals in combat (9a) and a man with a cart (9b), both of which can be compared with the motifs on the lid of Dou Wan's incense burner, (fig. 7b). After Beijing 1986a, figs 63:3, 64:4.

10 Drawing of a gold weight in the shape of a crouching feline. Third–second century BC. Length: 17.8 cm. After Beijing 1992, no. 269.

11a Drawing of a winged beast in inlaid bronze. From the tomb of Cuo, King of Zhongshan at Pingshan, Hebei Province. Fourth century BC. Length: 40 cm. After Beijing 1995, fig. 51.

11b Drawing of a stand in the shape of a tiger devouring a deer in inlaid bronze. From the tomb of Cuo, King of Zhongshan, at Pingshan, Hebei Province. Fourth century BC. Length: 51 cm. After Beijing 1995, fig. 112.

THE CLOUD SCROLL AND INHABITED LANDSCAPES

In the previous two sections, we observed the ways in which the Chinese mimicked the metalwork of their northern neighbours or created their own hybrid versions of Central Asian and steppe items. We can explore an even more remarkable foreign borrowing in the cloud scrolls and inhabited landscapes of Han China that embellished the finest possessions of the elite. These highly flexible motifs stimulated a yet greater and longer-lasting response that was more creative, widespread and on a much larger and more significant scale than the examples just discussed.

A cloud scroll has an undulating stem with small frilly appendages seen, for example, on the cup of the incense burner from Liu Sheng's tomb (fig. 7a). Scrolls were deployed across numerous pieces of metalwork, lacquer and ceramics. And closely related undulating lines with crested peaks were the foundation for the scenes of animals in mountainous landscapes, as on an inlaid chariot pole from a tomb in Hebei Province (fig. 12). On this famous piece animals in combat and a hunting scene with a mounted archer shooting at a tiger to his rear (the Parthian shot) refer to subject matter preferred by the northern nomads, as do the small motifs on Dou Wan's incense burner (fig. 8). A predecessor of this elaborate piece is a much more compressed scroll with schematic leaves on a lacquer box from Gaotai in Jingzhou, Hubei Province (fig. 13).[24] The tightly rolled scroll or stem and the creatures among the foliage-like tufts along the tops suggest that the prototypes for such compositions come from much further west, from the foliage, flower and animal patterns developed in Greek and Hellenistic contexts and spread eastwards across Eurasia by the Scythians, the inhabitants of the Altai Mountains and the Xiongnu.[25]

A bow cover in Greek style, but found in a Scythian tomb, illustrates the two major forms of design that were popular in the Mediterranean area (figs 14a, b).[26] The uppermost motif consists of flowers set in the alternating sections of an undulating stem. On the next band below, schematic plants, palmettes, alternating with lotus blooms, sit upon S-shaped scrolls. These two versions were highly

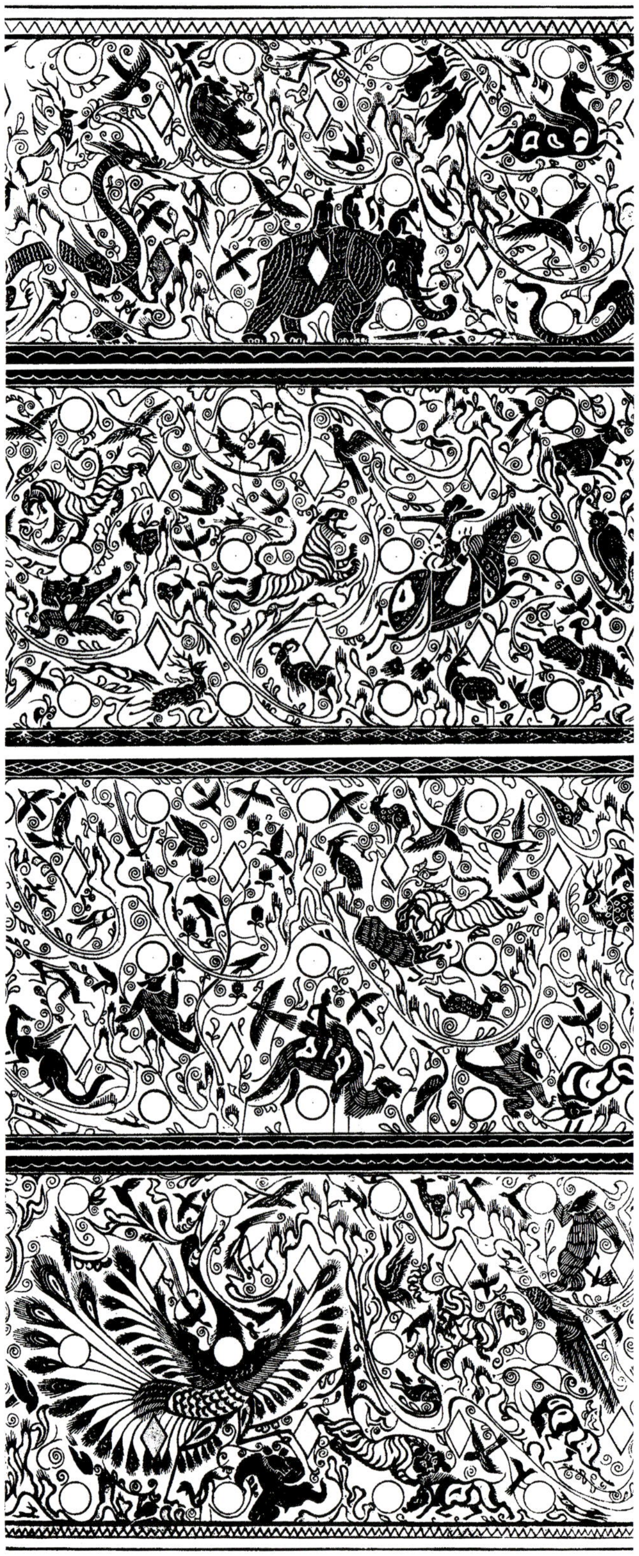

12 Drawing of the design on a tubular inlaid bronze fitting from a chariot parasol. From tomb M122 at Ding Xian, Hebei Province. First century BC. Height: 26.6 cm. After Beijing 1976, fig. 66.

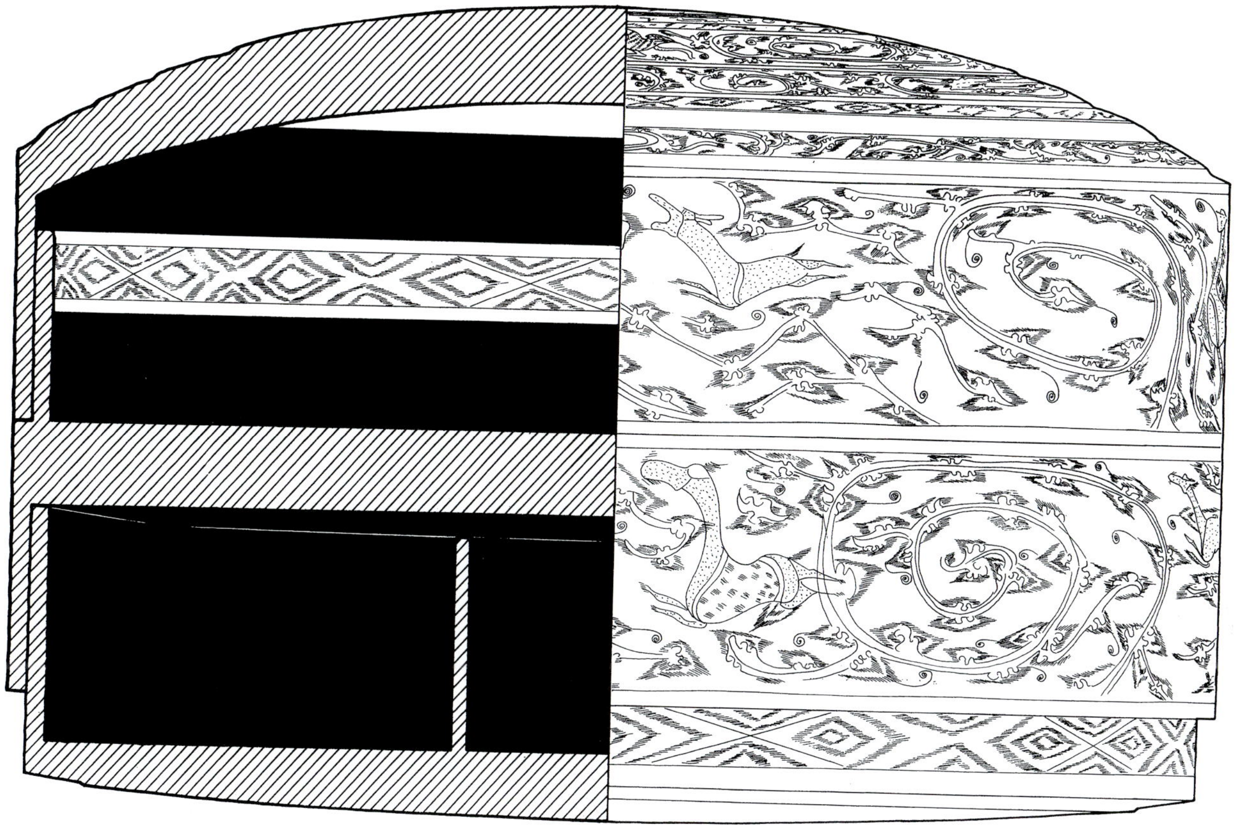

influential at different sites across Asia.[27] The undulating band is repeated on the two lower examples: a belt from Pazyryk and a textile from a Xiongnu tomb at Noin Ula (figs 14c, d). The S-shaped patterns, which could be arranged in widely varied configurations, were also deployed in Noin Ula and provided another form of pattern in China made up of S- and C-shapes, as on lacquer from Gaotai illustrated in figure 15. The various scrolls could be highly elaborated in lacquer painting[28] or simplified on ceramics, as on examples from the tomb of the King of Nanyue (fig. 16). A second phase of enthusiasm for the cloud scroll can be traced from the time of Wang Mang in the first century AD into the Eastern Han, when undulating scrolls with frilly appendages decorated mirrors and tomb bricks, for example. Renewed contact with the border peoples or with the cities along the Silk Route and the states of Central Asia may have been responsible for this new enthusiasm.[29]

This series of related designs was immensely influential throughout the Han period because the different parts (the S-shaped scrolls, the undulating stems, the schematic or realistic leaves, palmettes, flowers and creatures) could all be embellished or reinterpreted in several different ways. At Mangdangshan in Yongcheng, Henan Province, the site of the tombs of the Liang kings, a rare surviving wall painting displays a dragon that has been created out of the undulating foliage stem, with head and claws patently added to the original line (fig. 17). A famous coffin from a tomb at Mawangdui, Changsha in Hunan Province has dragons painted on it with a similar construction.[30] But much more common was the use of such scrolls to create a landscape (fig. 12). As the bottom of the panel from the Mangdangshan tomb illustrates, a stylized mountain is created up which a tiger prowls. This treatment was especially popular on textiles that have been found preserved

13 Drawing of a spiralling leaf scroll with leaping creatures on a lacquer box. From tomb M6 at Gaotai, Jingzhou, Hubei Province. Second–first century BC. After Beijing 2000, fig. 145.

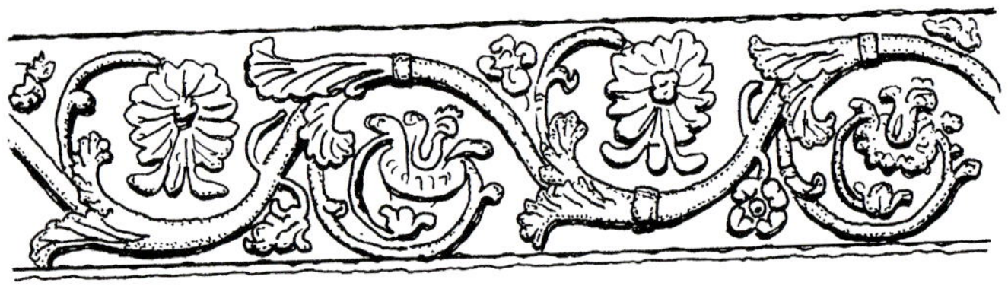

14a

14b

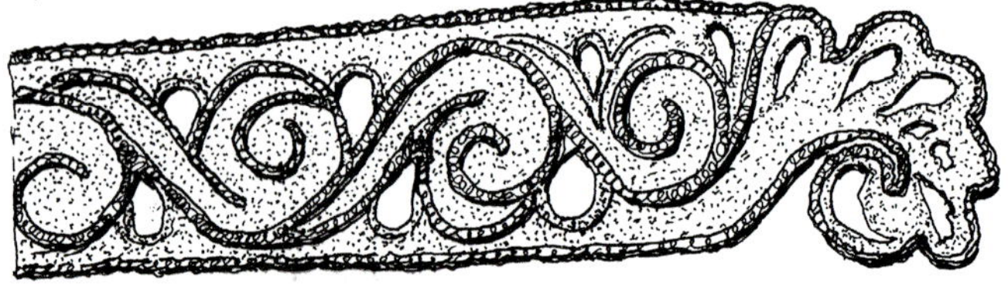

14c

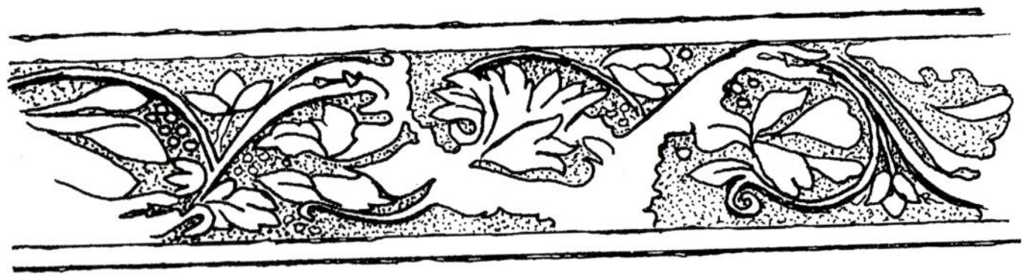

14d

15a

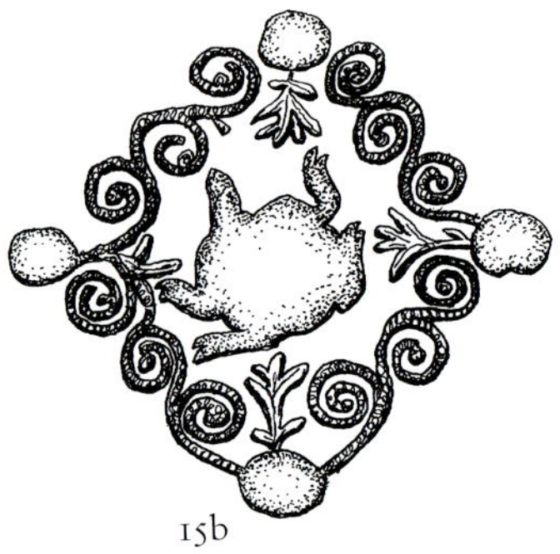

15b

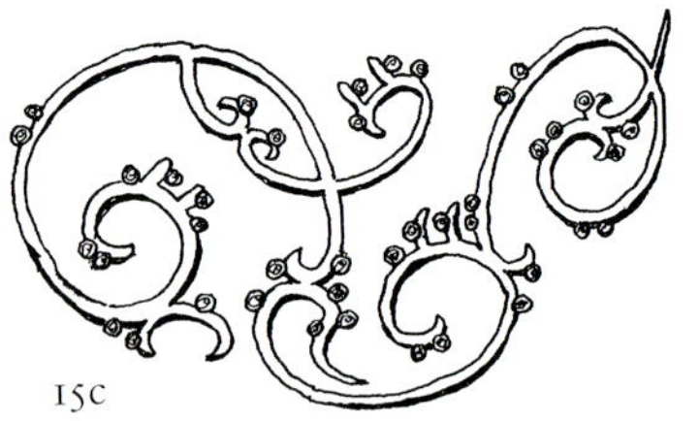

15c

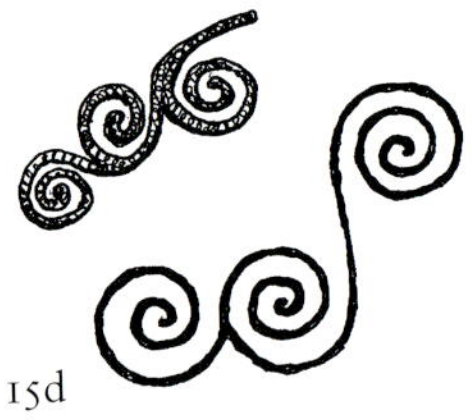

15d

in the dry conditions of Xinjiang Province, at Loulan and at Niya (fig. 18) and at Noin Ula in Mongolia.[31] With the exception of textiles and lacquers, later landscape images are presented in more concrete and realistic forms, with renderings of substantial hills and mountains. Images of hunting, riding and the nomadic peoples on the borders remained characteristic of these early landscapes. In Eastern Han tombs, mountainous landscapes were explicitly rendered as the territory of hostile border peoples, who were often shown crouching treacherously among the hills with their bows and arrows, awaiting the Han Chinese riding towards them.[32]

MOUNTAIN TOMBS

While mountains might be immediately associated with the fierce northern neighbours of the Han, they were also simultaneously recognized as the dwellings of the immortals. Legends surrounding the mountainous islands of Penglai as the place where immortals and herbs to make elixirs of immortality might be found have already been mentioned. Well before the Han came to power, the First Emperor of Qin sought in vain to engage with the immortals on Penglai. Both the First Emperor of Qin and Emperor

14a Drawing of an acanthus scroll with flowers from a gold bow cover (*gorytos*). Found in a kurgan at Chertomlyk, Pontic Steppe. Fourth century BC. After Riegl 1992, fig. 129.

14b Drawing of alternating lotus and palmette blooms on S-shaped paired scrolls from the same bow cover in fig. 14a. After Riegl 1992, fig. 129.

14c Drawing of a running scroll derived from Western Asian forms of palmette motifs. From a belt found in kurgan No. 2 at Pazyryk, Altai Mountains, Siberia. Third–second century BC. After Rudenko 1972, pl. 67F.

14d Drawing of a running scroll from a textile. From the Kondrat'ev kurgan at Noin Ula, Mongolia. Second–first century BC. After Rudenko 1969, fig. 75 (left). Drawing by John Rawson.

15a Drawing of S-shaped scrolls supporting large palmettes and less prominent lotus blooms on a Greek vase. Sixth–fifth century BC. After Jones 1982, pl. 20:12.

15b Drawing of embroidered motifs on a wall hanging. From kurgan No. 6 at Noin Ula, Mongolia. First century BC. After Rudenko 1969, fig. 60. Here a creature has been added. The spiky leaves are a local interpretation of the palmette.

15c Cloud scroll motif on a lacquer bowl. From tomb M28 at Gaotai, Jingzhou, Hubei Province. First century BC. After Beijing 2000, fig. 115.

15d A comparison of the S-scroll on the Greek vase (fig. 15a) with that of the Noin Ula textile (fig. 15b). On the Gaotai lacquer bowl (fig. 15c) the larger S-scroll has been divided but retains the S-shape and has an additional spiral at the right-hand end.

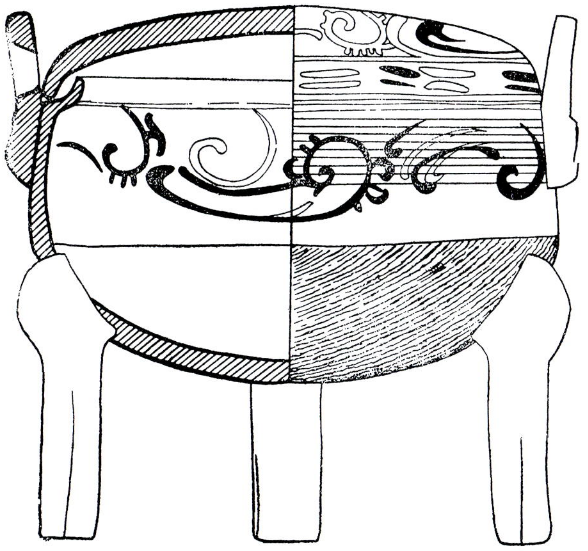

Wudi of the Han followed all possible routes in their search to avoid death: that is, to become immortal by meeting with and learning from immortals and also by drinking potions made from particular plants or minerals. Immortals and other strange beings appeared indeed among the cloud scrolls and imaginative landscapes painted on lacquer coffins or carved in stone tombs.[33] The Queen Mother of the West, a deity very popular and frequently depicted in Eastern Han, was thought to live high on the peaks of the Kunlun range in the extreme west.[34]

If the emperors and kings could not achieve immortality it seems possible that, as a form of additional insurance policy, they sought proximity to the immortals by arranging for their tombs to be cut into mountains. In the Wei River valley, the emperors were generally content with construct-

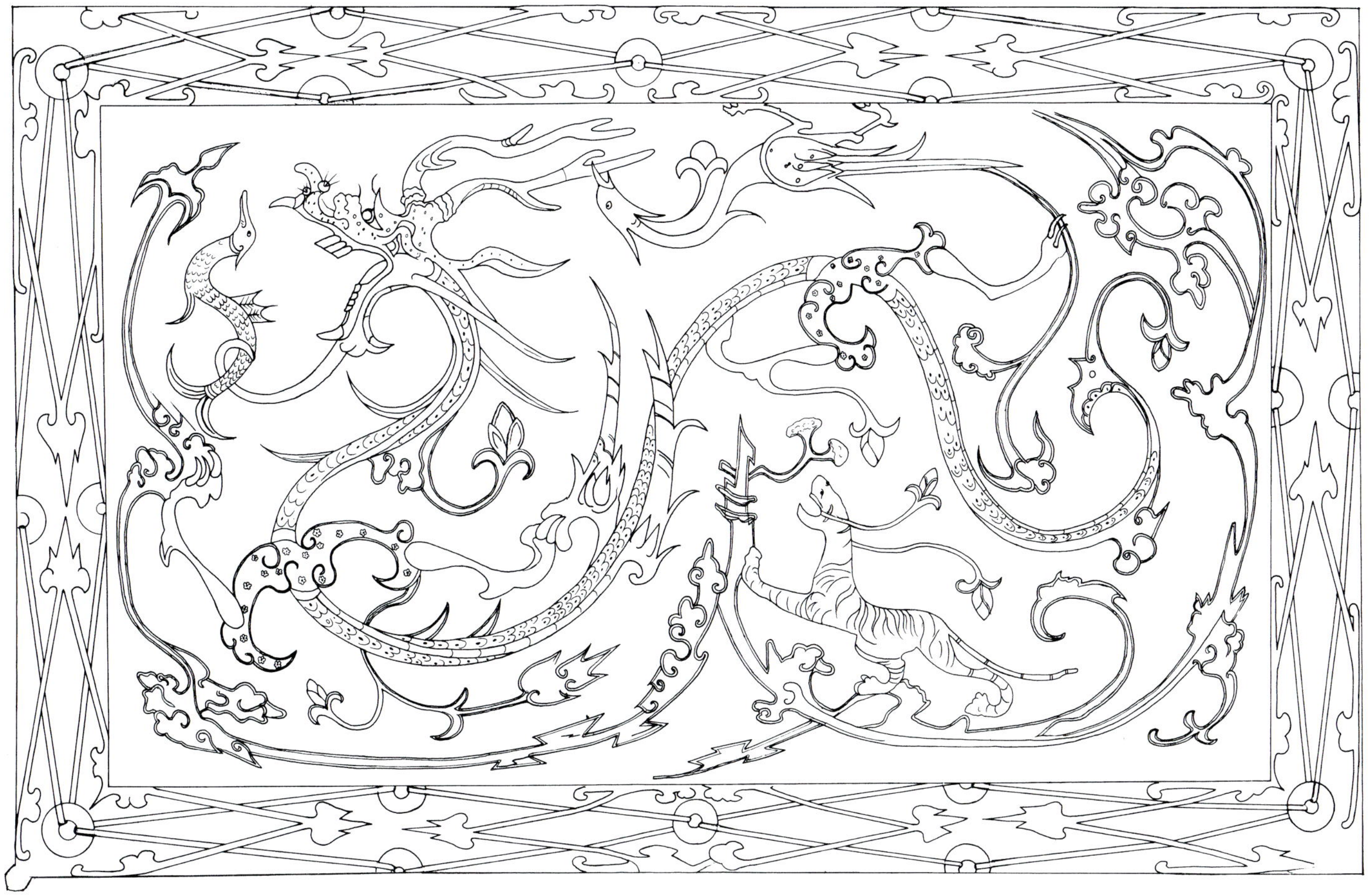

16 (above) Drawing of a ceramic *ding* vessel from the tomb of the King of Nanyue, decorated with scrolls similar to those of the Gaotai lacquer box (fig. 15c). Second century BC. Height: 20.2 cm. After Beijing 1991, vol. 1, fig. 160.

17 (below) Decorated wall painting. From a tomb at Shiyuan at Mangdangshan, Yongcheng, Henan Province, site of the tombs of the Kings of Liang. Second–first century BC. After Beijing 2001, fig. 49.

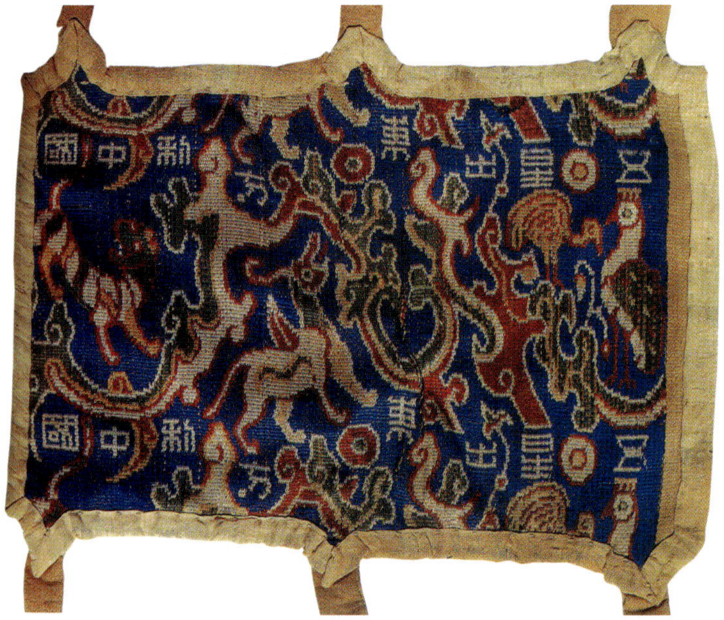

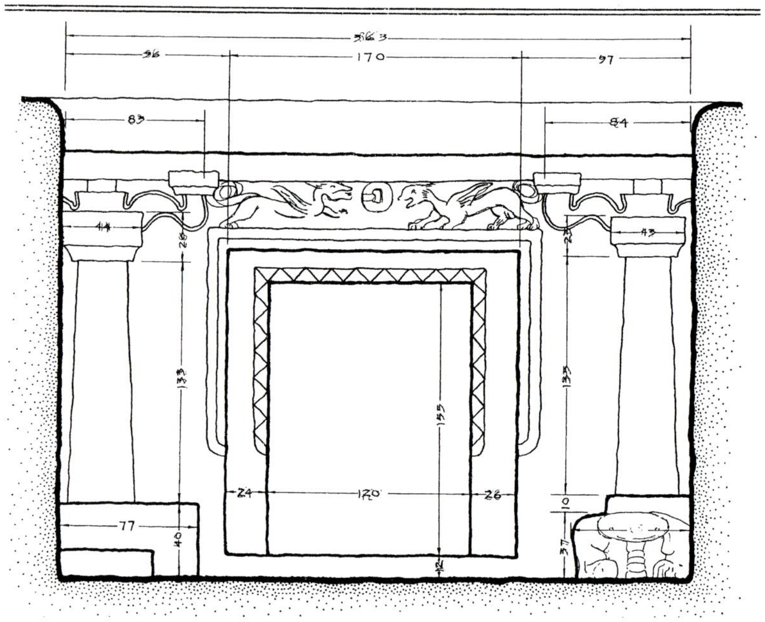

ing mounds as artificial mountains over their tombs. On the other hand, the Han princes who occupied their territories as Kings of Chu, of Liang, of Zhongshan and of Lu sought out limestone mountains in eastern China. Very complex tombs were hacked out with great labour in these hillsides. These multiple chamber tombs were a major departure from previous precedent. The choice of mountains and a structure with a number of rooms arranged along a corridor, as in the case of the many tombs at Xuzhou and the tomb of the King of Nanyue, were essentially innovations of the early Han. Tombs with separate rooms off the main shaft, known as catacomb tombs, had been introduced to the Wei River valley, perhaps by outsiders as early as the ninth century BC. In addition, systematic development of separate functional compartments, creating rooms within massive wooden coffins, was popular in the south in the earlier Chu state in Hubei Province. But the impetus that drove the creation of a completely new tomb type, often set in mountains, was an innovation of the third to second centuries BC.

Tombs cut into rock façades were, however, also features of Western Asia, where the most renowned were those of the Achaemenid rulers at Naqsh-e Rustam near Persepolis. The tombs of the great kings, including Darius, were much less complex than those at Xuzhou, comprising an entrance chamber and one or more coffin rooms off this entrance area.[35] It is possible that accounts of these or other similar rock-cut tombs were relayed by the various ambassadors to the West or by travellers, merchants and defectors to the Han court. Such accounts may have stimulated the choice of a new tomb type, which at the same time drew on several other traditions already well established in China.[36]

While these early Western Han tombs bear only a very distant relationship to tombs in the Achaemenid or Parthian Empires, there is much evidence in the Eastern Han period in the first and second centuries AD that Iranian or Central Asian models were known and copied.[37] Rock-cut tombs in Sichuan framed with two columns either side of a doorway at Pengshan recall Iranian tombs, as does decoration of creatures with wings above the doors (fig. 19). In eastern China, as well as in Sichuan, free-standing columns within stone-built or rock-cut tombs were popular.[38] Occasional examples in both regions in which columns were placed standing on animals, such as rams, certainly refer to a Western Asian practice (fig. 20).[39]

At a similar date, the Han adopted barrel vaults and domes within brick or stone tombs, both architectural

18 Brocade arm-band decorated with characters and creatures in a stylized landscape rendered by a cloud scroll. From tomb M8 at Niya, Minfeng, Xinjiang Province. Second century BC–first century AD. Length: 18.5 cm. After Shanghai 1998, no. 34.

19 Drawing of a façade of a tomb decorated with a pair of columns and winged beasts. Pengshan, Sichuan Province. Eastern Han period, second century AD.

forms much more common in the Western Asian Parthian Empire than in China. A particularly elaborate version was found at Mixian in Henan Province.[40] Ceiling ornaments of alternating lotus flowers with representations of wooden coffers are also details borrowed from further west. And at the same time, in central China and in the north-west, cloud scrolls were once more extremely popular, almost certainly growing out of a new stimulus from further west beyond the imperial borders.[41] These scrolls might again be simple abstract patterns, or they could be proxies for a landscape in which wild animals roamed.

Interaction with the Xiongnu and their neighbours had, therefore, a profound impact on Han Chinese cultural practices. The military dominance of the Xiongnu before the reign of Emperor Wudi may explain why the Chinese paid particular attention to steppe metalwork and invented new types of high-quality artefacts, new forms of decoration and new tomb types in response to their encounters. These exotic goods and practices were rapidly adopted and adapted, enriching Han palace life. Concurrently, Chinese goods and practices were penetrating far into Xiongnu territory. Once Emperor Wudi was on the throne, seeking out allies to help combat the Xiongnu, Chinese envoys had opportunities to see and even obtain exotic goods which may have formed the basis for yet newer fashions at the Han court. The diversity described here was a sign of the wealth and the drawing power of the empire of the Han.

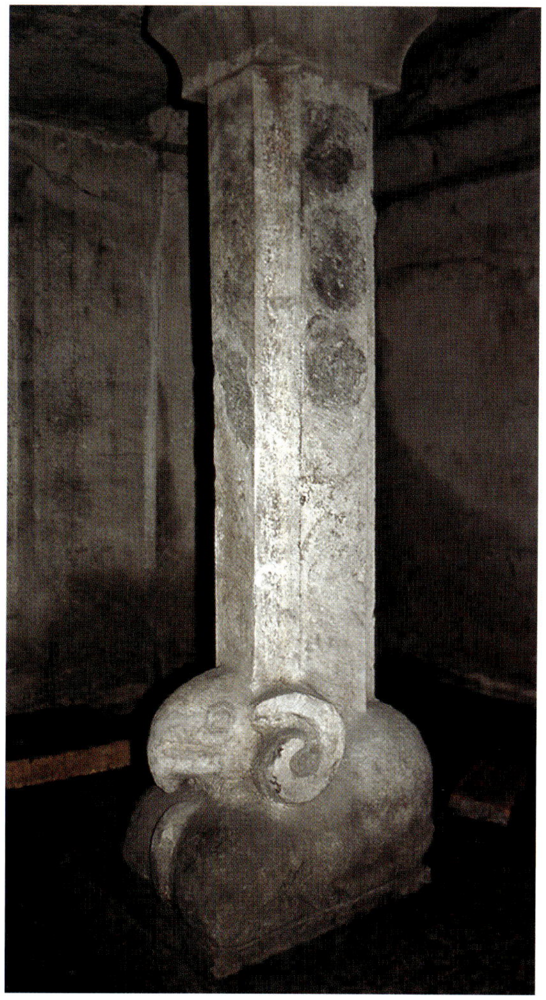

20 Stone column on the back of a ram. From a tomb at Baiji, Jiangsu Province. Eastern Han period, second century AD.

NOTES

1 Li 2006 describes the regular conflicts between the Western Zhou and their northern neighbours; see especially chapters 3 and 4.
2 Wu 2010a describes chariot and horse use from the Shang to the end of the Warring States.
3 For accounts of the interaction of the Han with the Xiongnu and areas in the extreme west, see di Cosmo 2002, pp. 161–252; Twitchett and Loewe 1986, pp. 377–421; Nylan and Loewe 2010, pp. 145–52; Psarras 2003.
4 The tombs are described in Rudenko 1969.
5 For such gold and bronze pieces see Beijing 1986a, pp. 72–96. Geographical divisions are proposed by Linduff 1997. These plaques and buckles from the Ordos region were formerly included in the general grouping of the 'animal-style' bronzes found in many parts of Eurasia. Examples so described are illustrated in many exhibition and collection catalogues.
6 Beijing 1986a, p. 90, figs 59–5, p. 65, fig. 64–1.
7 Rudenko 1972, p. 263, figs 130–1, pls 140E–142D.
8 Jacobson 1984 provides many examples of the motif.
9 For a discussion of the frontlet in the context of other steppe-type finds see *Zhongguo lishi wenwu* 2002.4, pp. 16–26.
10 The metalwork from Izzyk suggests that the hatching may have originated in a representation of ribs and muscles of the felines depicted; Chang and Guroff 2007, nos 47, 50, 51. At Pazyryk, the ribbing was reinterpreted as a hatching pattern in carved wood, Rudenko 1972, pl. 140A, which became yet more schematized on the gold and bronze plaques from the Ordos region and from China.
11 A limited number of the different types of plaque are considered in Boardman 2010, where many are attributed to Chinese craftsmen.
12 Xi'an 2006.
13 Shanghai 1998, no. 30.
14 Stierlin 2006, pp. 122–3; Miho Museum 2002, cat. 21, 29, 30, 116.
15 Özgen and Öztürk 1996 illustrates a number of Achaemenid silver bowls with lobes that provided the models for both the Parthian and Chinese versions; see also Miho Museum 2002, cat. 34, 101.
16 For the report on the two tombs, see Beijing 1980.
17 For illustrations of the examples shown in carvings at Persepolis, see Rawson 2006a. For examples in silver from Lydia, see Özgen and Öztürk 1996, nos 71, 72.
18 The transmission of the incense burner from the region of present-day Iran to China is discussed in Rawson 2006a.
19 A very full account of hill-shaped incense burners is given in Erickson 1992, although the meanings attributed to them are rather different from those suggested here.
20 For a discussion of the relationship of the Xuzhou feline with these earlier pieces used as weights, see Rawson 1998.
21 For the excavation report, see Beijing 1995. It is possible that the tiger and two other inlaid creatures were employed to support a screen, as were some gilded bronzes from the tomb of the King of Nanyue (cat.173).
22 Rawson 1998.
23 It is likely that the stimuli for making these exotic pieces was a consequence of the trade along the Silk Route and also of the embassies that the Chinese sent westwards; Watson 1961, pp. 264–89; compare Hulsewé 1979.
24 For other related lacquer designs, see Beijing 2000.
25 For earlier suggestions of the northern or even Mediterranean sources of the inhabited mountain ranges or scrolls, see Sullivan 1962; Jacobson 1985; Barbieri-Low 2001.
26 For a full photograph, see Reeder 1999, no. 105.
27 For further discussion on the creation of such motifs see Riegl 1992; Rawson 1984.2, pp. 19–43.
28 Some of the very finest examples appear on lacquer from Yaozhuang in Hanjiang, Jiangsu Province; *Wenwu* 1988.
29 See for example Eastern Han tombs in northern Shaanxi at Suide; see Xi'an 2000, pp. 108–9, where three different variants are illustrated.
30 Beijing 1973, vol. 1, fig. 25.
31 Sullivan 1962, pls 31–2.
32 See for example a lintel from a tomb door at Suide, Shaanxi Province; Stockholm 2010, no. 81. Other examples are shown in Sullivan 1962, pls 53, 54.
33 A famous example of strange figures among cloud scrolls appears on the black coffin from Mawangdui; Beijing 1973, fig. 17.
34 The introduction of the Queen Mother as a powerful deity can be discussed in terms of belief and in terms of the images adopted to represent her. For discussion of the growth of the religious belief, see Francasso 1988. For a discussion of the image type and its possible origins in Western Asia see Knauer 2006.
35 For the tombs, see Schmidt 1970. Achaemenid tombs in present-day Turkey are illustrated in von Gall 1966.
36 Wu 1995, pp. 126–36 describes the relationships between the early Han concepts of immortality, notions borrowed from further west and the interest in stone.
37 For intermediaries between Iran and China, see Pitschikjan 1992; Litvinskij and Pičkjan 2002.
38 For complex rock-cut tombs in Sichuan, see Beijing 2007.
39 For the report on the Baiji tomb, see *Kaogu* 1981.
40 The Mixian tombs are discussed and illustrated in Beijing 1993b. Compare tombs at Nanyang in Henan Province; Xi'an 2008.
41 Li 1998, fig. 3.24 provides a clear example of a Western running scroll rendered as a cloud scroll decorating a column and capital from Lishi in Shanxi Province.

ARCHAEOLOGICAL DISCOVERIES RELATING TO THE MARITIME TRADE OF THE KINGDOM OF NANYUE

HONG QUAN[1]

Following imperial envoy Zhang Qian's travels to Central Asia, the Han dynasty regularized and strengthened the traditional Silk Route linking China and the Mediterranean, now dominated by the Han capital Chang'an and Rome. This opened up an overland route through Asia and Europe, creating the means for cultural interchanges between the civilizations of China, India and the classical world. The overland Silk Route did much to facilitate cultural exchange between East and West, and was critical to the vibrant prosperity of the Han dynasty. And just as the Central Asia route linked Asia and Europe over land, so the South China Sea was the gateway to maritime trade during the Han period. Textual and archaeological evidence suggests that trade and even cultural exchange along China's south coast already existed in the third century BC during the Qin-Han period. The city of Guangzhou, located on the banks of the Pearl River and backing onto the Baiyun mountains, is ideally placed to control maritime traffic. Since the Qin-Han period, Guangzhou has served as China's largest commercial port, playing an important role in the economic and cultural interchange with coastal regions in the Pacific and Indian Oceans.

In 214 BC the First Emperor conquered Lingnan, establishing the commanderies of Guilin, Xiang and Nanhai. The First Emperor's military occupation of Lingnan was motivated by his long-term political ambitions, demonstrating his military might and expanding his empire. Establishing a hold over an extensive stretch of China's southern coastline and the prospect of additional wealth from overseas was doubtless a further reason for this conquest.

The main force behind the Qin army's advance on Nanyue came from the soldiers manning the turret-ships. Transporting troops and supplies would have required backup from a fleet of oceangoing ships. The site of a Qin dynasty shipyard, discovered in 1975 in the fourth section of Zhongshan Road, Guangzhou, provides material evidence of military action in the region. The slipway consists of two parallel planks of wood, at the base of which was placed a timber crosstie, in appearance not unlike a railway track. At the top of the slipway was a timber plançon on which the ship was placed. The distance between the two slipway planks could be adjusted according to the size of the ship being constructed. This facility enabled ships of differing sizes and specifications to be built. Research suggests that the Qin shipyard was capable of constructing flat-bottomed wooden ships with a load-bearing capacity of twenty-five to thirty metric tons. Although there is as yet no evidence proving that the ships constructed on this site were used for long voyages, it is likely that Qin shipbuilding skills provided the technological basis for the Kingdom of Nanyue's maritime economy. Quite a few model ships made of wood or pottery have been discovered in Guangzhou's Han burial sites. One of the objects found at the site of the King of Nanyue's tomb was a bronze barrel. Carved on the bilge were images of four warships, graphic representations of large, ocean-going vessels (fig. 21). These warships were not steered using rudders but relied on the wind and large sculling oars; and the compartments shown here are the earliest known graphics of watertight compartments.

Zhao Tuo, also known as Emperor Wudi of Nanyue, was a general serving in the army of the First Emperor of Qin who was posted south to the region of 'the hundred Yue tribes'. At the fall of the Qin dynasty, Zhao Tuo launched an attack on the three commanderies of Guilin, Xiang and Nanhai and established the Kingdom of Nanyue, with its

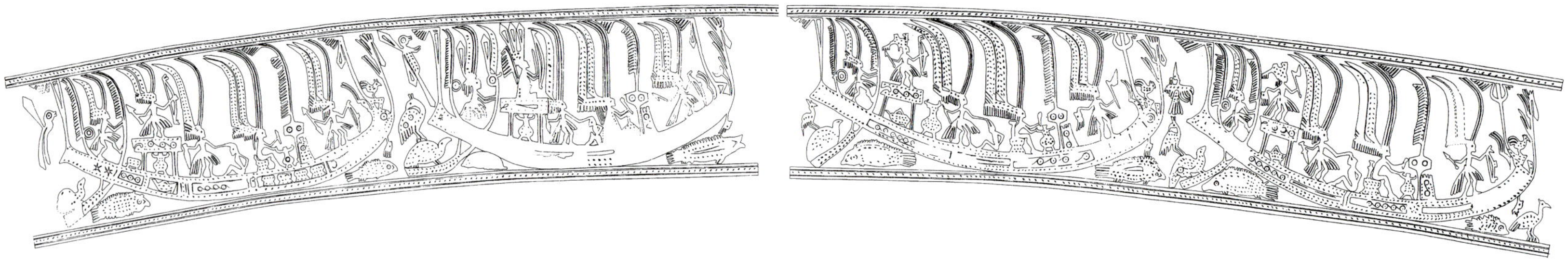

capital at Panyu (modern-day Guangzhou). Qin technology provided the material basis on which the Kingdom of Nanyue built its naval activities in the South China Sea and played a critical role in the development of the region's maritime trade. According to *Huozhi liezhuan* (Collective Biography of Great Merchants) in the *Shiji*, the city of Panyu was a trading hub for the world's rare treasures and one of the nineteen major cities of the empire.[2] The *Dilizhi* (The treatises on administrative geography) in *Hanshu* states that in Panyu, 'located close to the sea, there was an abundance of rhinoceros horn, ivory, tortoiseshell, gemstones, silver, copper, fruit and cloth – a wealth of choice for all those trading in China.'[3] From the descriptions of historians Sima Qian and Bangu, it is clear that by the early Han dynasty, Panyu was already a major seaport of the ancient world, a meeting point of East and West (see Maps 1, 2).

At the end of 2005, in the Huangpu district of Guangzhou, a site dating back to the period of the Nanyue kings was discovered at the Temple of the God of the Southern Sea. Fragments of pottery bearing geometric designs were among the items found. The site was on the banks of the Pearl River, facing towards the sea and is evidence of Nanyue's maritime activities. In the Pak Mong area in Hong Kong's Lantau Island and Wujiayuan site in the Ha Pak Nai area of Yuen Long District, New Territories, sites and objects dating to the Nanyue era have also been discovered. The coastal location of these sites indicates the extent to which Nanyue used the coastline to establish new settlements.

The archaeological evidence that most clearly demonstrates Nanyue's interactions with other cultures was discovered at the site of the royal palace and the tombs of the Nanyue kings. The pool in the palace grounds and its winding conduits are built from stone. Octagonal columns (fig. 22), balusters and lintels, all made of stone, indicate that the use of stone in construction and design was well advanced. Lying horizontally at the base of the stone pool were collapsed stone columns, the shafts of which were clearly composed of drum sections. This technique of constructing columns using drum sections is rarely found in China, but is more common in the architecture of ancient Egypt, Mesopotamia and Rome. Moreover, the wall of the pool is constructed entirely from sandstone using a 'crazy-paving' design. This technique of constructing a wall using irregular-shaped pieces of rock is again one that is common in Greek architecture. It is well known that the principal style of construction in traditional Chinese architecture is the timber frame and tamped earth structure, while in the West, ancient buildings were often constructed from stone. The use of wood or stone is one of the key differentiating

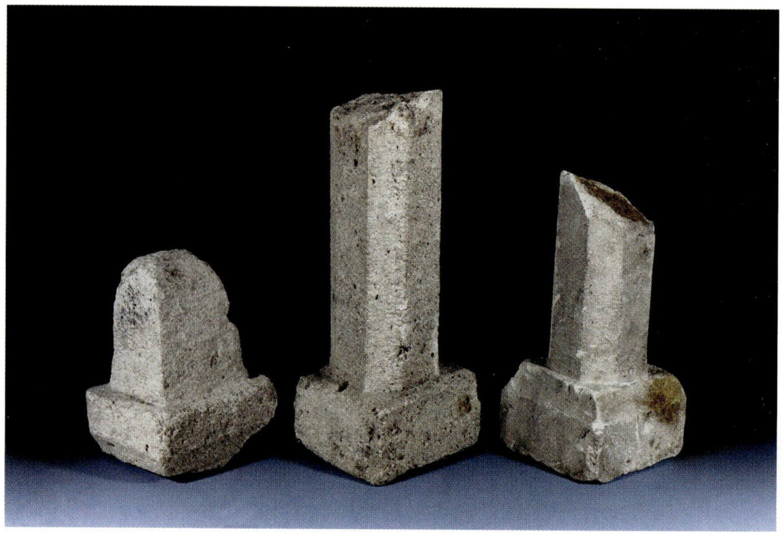

21 Drawings of a bronze container (*titong*) with boat images (cat. 122). Excavated from the tomb of the King of Nanyue, Guangzhou, Guangdong Province. Second century BC.

22 Octagon-shaped column. Found at the palace of the King of Nanyue, Guangzhou, Guangdong Province. Second century BC.

factors between the architecture of East Asia and the West. Yet both in terms of building materials and construction techniques, the palace of the Nanyue king has little in common with other Chinese buildings of the period. There are, however, striking similarities to contemporaneous buildings from Europe and Central Asia, suggesting that technologies were transmitted via maritime routes. Although there is no decisive evidence that the stone structure of the palace was transmitted directly from Egypt, Rome or Persia, we can reasonably infer that India served as a point of transfer.

The rectangular bricks, flat and semi-circular roof tiles and eave tiles of the main administrative building in the Palace complex are coated with a glass glaze. Tests show that they are not of the usual lead-barium composition normally found in tiles of Chinese manufacture but contain sodium and calcium, using potassium as a flux. This is the first time that early Han glazes containing sodium and potassium alkalis have been found in China. The glass-glazed tiles in Nanyue differ from those of the Shang and Zhou periods found in the rest of Guangdong, Jiangxi, Zhejiang and Fujian Provinces, suggesting that neither the technology nor the raw materials came from the Huanan region. Rather, their development was the result of absorbing and adapting technologies and formulae from outside China.

A silver box (cat. 167) was excavated from the tomb of Zhao Mo, styled Emperor Wendi. Also found were welded bulb-shaped gold ornaments with flower designs (cat. 158), glass beads, African ivory and frankincense, all of which are some of the earliest extant artefacts of imported goods found in Guangzhou and all of which point to Nanyue's extensive contact with other cultures.

The circular silver box and lid are decorated with a raised pattern of interlocking segments, similar to the cloves in a head of garlic, produced by hammering the silver in a mould. This style of decoration is different from that of other containers found in Han China, but can be found on gold and silverware from Western Asia and Persia. In Hamadan, Iran, silverware that was very similar in design to this box was discovered, bearing the mark of King Artaxerxes I of Persia. This technique of hammering silver was popular during the Persian Achaemenid Empire (533–330 BC). Following Alexander the Great's conquest of Western Asia and the establishment of the Seleucid Empire, the Parthians continued to develop the tradition of working gold and silver as the Achaemenians had, using moulds to achieve the raised design. Scholars have suggested that the Nanyue silver box was in fact imported from Parthia: before the East–West overland Silk Route was opened, it would have been very difficult to transport objects from Parthia to China overland. Transportation by sea was much more likely.

The body of the King of Nanyue is encased in a silk-edged jade suit. Over the torso of the jade suit was a short beaded outer garment decorated with glass beads, small glass discs, gold-plated copper and silver buttons. The bead workmanship on the gold flower-shaped buttons differs from traditional Chinese gold work of this period. Decorated beads dating back to the First Dynasty of Ur in the third millennium BC have been found in Sumer and were popular in ancient Egypt, Crete and Persia. Alexander's conquest of Asia introduced them to India. Apart from the tomb of the King of Nanyue, hollow decorated gold beads of this sort have also been found in Han tombs in Guangzhou, Hepu, Changsha and Yangzhou. All of these are either imported from overseas or are locally manufactured copies.

The frankincense discovered in the tomb of the King of Nanyue is not from China. Frankincense is mostly found in northern Ethiopia, Somalia and the southern part of the Arab Peninsula, whence it was imported to parts of Greece, Turkey and the Mediterranean. After the Punic Wars in the third century BC, when Rome gained control of Carthage and became the foremost power in the Mediterranean, Roman merchants often traded in the Red Sea area. It would not have been difficult for them to obtain both frankincense, which would have been native to the region, and African ivory, and then to trade these items with Han merchants. So the ivory and frankincense discovered in the tomb of the King of Nanyue could well have been obtained from Roman traders.

The ivory excavated in the King of Nanyue's tomb was badly damaged and the fragments cracked, but it was possible to retrieve the objects in their entirety. On average, the tusks measured about 120 centimetres in length. Experts have confirmed that this ivory differs from Asian ivory, and that in both shape and size it resembles the tusk of the African elephants of today. That African ivory has been discovered in the Lingnan region is again evidence of active overseas maritime trading.

Then there is the jade rhyton, carved from a single piece of stone (see fig. 6). It has an oval mouth, is hollow at the centre and its base curves upwards. Horn-shaped rhytons originated in the West and are similar to gold and silver rhytons found in Greece and elsewhere. The patterns and carvings on the Nanyue rhyton are all Chinese, but the shape is certainly not indigenous to China and is an example of how craftsmen in Nanyue created unique objects fusing a Western form with traditional Chinese materials and patterns. Just as the silver box made its way to China from Persia, so the jade rhyton stands as an example of Western elements that were absorbed and adapted by Nanyue's craftsmen in their work.

Many samples of fossilized/carbonized silk were excavated from the tomb of the King of Nanyue – over twenty types from all six major categories including tulle (*juan*), organza (*luo*), gauze, brocade, ribbon and figured silk. Also found was a bronze printing plate, currently the earliest extant fabric printing tool (cat. 134). The print block comprises two parts: a smaller plate acts as a positioner, the larger prints the actual pattern. The pattern on the plate is one of flames and is the same as the pattern depicted on many of the carbonized silk samples. From this we can infer that the printed silk fabrics found in the tomb were locally manufactured. In Han Tomb 1, discovered in the Lobowan area of Guangxi, a set of wooden weaving instruments was found, suggesting that Nanyue had its own textile industry and produced enough for export. It is recorded in the *Dilizhi* in *Hanshu* that when Han Wudi sent out fleets, in addition to trade in pearls, coloured glass beads, rhinoceros horn, ivory, tortoiseshell, gemstones, silver, copper, fruit, fabrics and other novelty objects, they took with them 'gold and assorted silk fabrics'.[4] The 'assorted silk fabrics' were native to China.

The best-known glass beads are in a necklace found in Egypt by a British archaeologist that dates back to 1400–1350 BC. The Phoenicians and the Persians also mastered bead manufacture. Many examples of faience beads have been found in the eastern Mediterranean and western Iran dating from the fifth to third centuries BC. In China, faience beads have been found dating from the end of the Spring and Autumn and early Warring States periods (early fifth–late third centuries BC). These early inlaid beads have only been found in the large tombs of the aristocracy, pointing to the fact that they were considered extremely rare. In the West, it is quite common to find a string of faience beads, but in China they are mostly found individually, or forming part of a necklace comprising other beads.

Two faience beads were found in the Nanyue tomb. The first was among Group A of the jades belonging to the 'Lady of the Right' (fig. 23); the second was found with the concubine in the Eastern side chamber. Short strings of beads were found in Nanyue, but were only worn by the senior aristocracy. During the Western Han, bead jewellery began to circulate more widely, with a noticeable increase during the Eastern Han. The beads found on the King of Nanyue's short outer garment were mostly quite small, and yellowish-white or grey in colour. Only a very few were green or pale blue. Their flat rounded shape is formed by stretching the glass under high temperatures. The design of these beads was probably influenced by beads from India and the Pacific.

After the First Emperor conquered Lingnan, China's south coast and estuaries came under centralized government control. Contact with neighbouring states and cul-

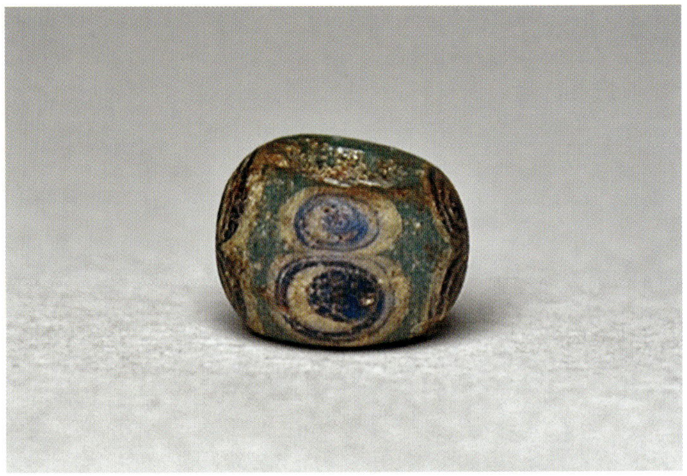

23 Glass bead that was part of a long pendant belonging to the Lady of the Right. Excavated from the tomb of the King of Nanyue, Guangzhou, Guangdong Province. Second century BC.

tures in the South China Sea increased considerably under the rule of Zhao Tuo, first King of Nanyue. From the non-indigenous artefacts found in the Nanyue tomb and from objects whose design bears evidence of outside influences, it is clear that ties between Nanyue and outside cultures existed on many levels. The so-called 'Maritime Silk Route' was certainly established by the Nanyue period.

In 111 BC, Han Emperor Wudi invaded and destroyed the Kingdom of Nanyue. He also further developed maritime trade in the South China Sea. The *Dilizhi* in *Hanshu* states that there were trading routes linking Southeast Asia and India. The Han fleet sailed from Rinan (modern Da Nang in Vietnam) through Xuwen before entering the sea at Hepu. It followed the coastline to the Indo-Chinese Peninsula, then sailed along the eastern coast of India to Conjevaram and Sri Lanka. All the countries along this route produced pearls, coloured glass beads and exotic gemstones, many of which were imported into China during the reign of Han Emperor Wudi. At the same time, China's gold and silks were exchanged as gifts and traded throughout the region. Panyu, located at the mouth of rivers flowing west, north and south, with the South China Sea to its south, was uniquely placed as Lingnan's hub. The shipbuilding skills that were developed and refined in Nanyue provided a sound foundation for maritime trade from the time of Han Emperor Wudi onwards. After the Eastern Han, written records of trade in the South China Sea and the arrival of Buddhist monks from India became richer still.

NOTES

1 Translated by Tao-Tao Chang
2 *Shiji*, p. 3268
3 *Hanshu*, p. 1670
4 *Hanshu*, p. 1670

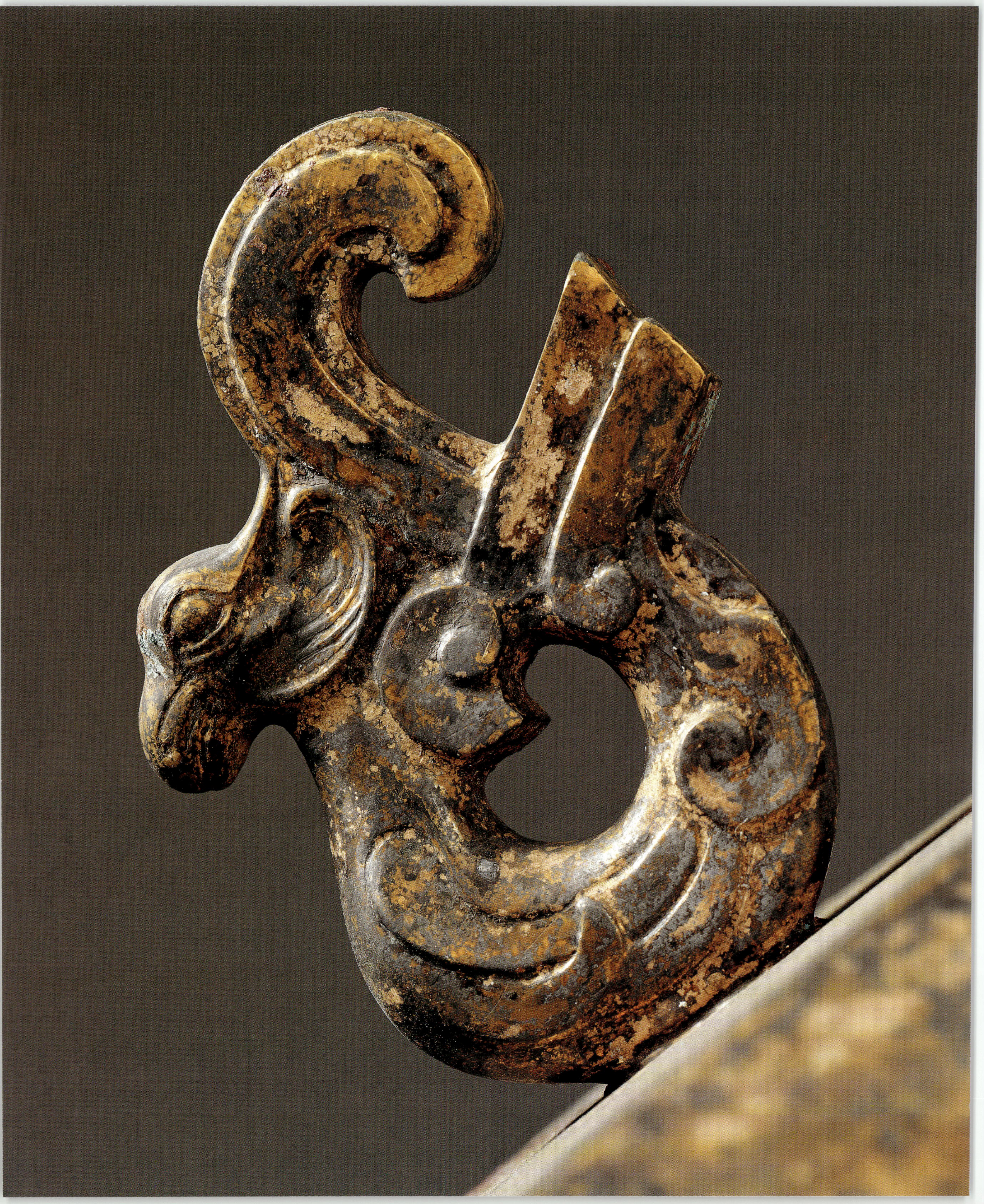

EXCAVATIONS AND STUDIES OF THE WESTERN HAN TOMBS OF THE CHU KINGS

YINDE LI[1]

Discoveries from Han dynasty archaeological sites in Xuzhou have been abundant, particularly in three areas: ancient city sites, workshops of artisans and tombs. Ancient city sites include Pengcheng and Shihucheng in Tongshan of the Qin and Han dynasties. Workshops include the remains of a bronze weapon casting workshop at Fushujie, a quarry at Yunlongshan, kiln sites at Cuipingshan and Liulou in Suining as well as sites of iron workshops at Liulou and Liguo in Tongshan.

More than a thousand Han tombs have been excavated. Among their number are grand-scale, horizontal, cave-like tombs carved into the mountains and vertical shaft tombs and stone sarcophagi of the Western Han dynasty; Huangchang-style[2] stone tombs; tombs with pictorial bricks; tombs made from a mixture of bricks and stones; and tombs made of bricks or earth, constructed during the Eastern Han period. The excavations give a clear picture of the sequence of developments and the transition of tomb types and are therefore useful in establishing relative dates. Since the mausoleums of the Han emperors have not yet been excavated, the tombs belonging to the Kings of Chu and the aristocracy are especially significant. In addition, these tombs contribute towards the understanding of regional cultures and the structure of Han society.

THE TOMBS OF CHU KINGS

Of all the archaeological discoveries in Xuzhou, the most significant are the tombs of the Western Han Chu kings in Xuzhou. They were discovered first by tomb robbers during the Wang Mang interregnum (AD 9–25). Historical texts, such as *Shuijingzhu* (Commentary on the Waterways Classic) by Li Daoyuan of the Northern Wei period and *Houhanshu* (Book of Later Han), record that the tomb of the first Chu king is located in the western suburb of the city. One chapter in *Shuijinzhu* also contains references to tombs of a Chu king and queen in Huanshan. The passageway in the Chu king's tomb in Nandongshan bears an inscription with the reign title *Zhida* (r. AD 1308–11), which implies that the tomb was looted between 1311 and 1368. The *Pengcheng zhi* gazetteer, compiled in 1473, refers to the Chu king's tomb at Dongdongshan as the 'grotto of immortals', which suggests that it had also been looted. Due to the fact that the tombs were empty, the gazetteers of Xuzhou during the Ming and Qing dynasties refer to the tombs according to their orientations as *dongshan* (empty caves) of the *dong* (east), *nan* (south), *xi* (west) and *bei* (north).

The Chu king's tomb (M1) at Woniushan was the first to be excavated scientifically, in the early 1980s. Since then, more than eighteen tombs of Western Han Chu kings and queens at nine different sites have been excavated, including three in Woniushan (1980, 2010) – tombs M2 and M3 after a robbery in 2010 – and Dongdongshan (1982, 1997) and two in each of the following sites: Guishan (1981–2), Beidongshan (1986), Huanshan, Tuolanshan (1989–90), Shizishan (1994–5), Yangguishan (2004), Chuwangshan (1997) and Nandongshan. The layout and burial objects of the tombs have become important evidence for the study of the Chu kings' tombs.

Unlike earlier Chinese mausoleums, which consist of deep pits and huge outer coffins, the tombs of Western Han

FACING PAGE: DETAIL OF CAT. 44

TABLE 2 CHRONOLOGY OF THE KINGS OF CHU IN THE HAN DYNASTY

GENERATION	NAME	TITLE	RELATIONSHIP TO THE EMPEROR OR KING	REIGN
	Han Xin			202–201 BC
1	Liu Jiao	King Yuan	Brother of Emperor Gaozu	201–179 BC
2	Liu Yingke	King Yi	Son of King Yuan	179–175 BC
3	Liu Wu		Son of King Yi	175–154 BC
4	Liu Li	King Wen	Son of King Yuan	154–150 BC
5	Liu Dao	King An	Son of King Wen	150–128 BC
6	Liu Zhu	King Xiang	Son of King An	128–116 BC
7	Liu Chun	King Jie	Son of King Xiang	116–100 BC
8	Liu Yanshou		Son of King Jie	100–68 BC
9	Liu Xiao	King Xiao	Son of Emperor Xuandi	50–25 BC
10	Liu Wen	King Huai	Son of King Xiao	25–23 BC
11	Liu Yan	King Si	Son of King Xiao	23–3 BC
12	Liu Yu		Son of King Si	3 BC–AD 8

Chu kings in Xuzhou are carved into mountains. Other states from the same period, including Liang, Lu and Zhongshan, also share this feature.

The capital of Chu contains segregated tomb sites. Early kings and queens are buried in separate chambers within the same site. At a later date, kings and queens might be buried in the same chamber. At Chuwangshan, Shizishan, Tuolanshan and Dongdongshan, unearthed architectural remains and building materials show that architectural structures were constructed within the tombs.

The tombs of Western Han Chu kings consist of enormous burial sites comprising a number of complicated underground building complexes. A tomb generally consists of an unsheltered passageway, corridors and chambers. Over time, the slope of the unsheltered passageway gradually reduces and becomes horizontal or even inclines towards the exterior of the tomb. The corridors become narrower and shorter. The number of chambers reduces from many to one, and their construction mirrors that of palaces above ground. Within the carved-out caves, wooden architectural structures and pottery tile roofs are constructed; some main chambers even have impressive columns carved out of stone (fig. 24). The walls in the early Chu king tombs are smooth. On top of the walls, layers of special fine clays were applied, followed by applications of lacquer and, sometimes, red pigments. In some, such as the one in Tuolanshan, the four walls of the main burial chamber have iron hooks for hanging curtains. Daily necessities, such as stoves, mortars, wells, bathrooms, toilets and fountains, are either carved out or built by layering stones.

BURIAL OBJECTS

The types of burial objects of feudal lords were consistent across the Western Han territory but, nevertheless, local traditions, customs and economic differences allowed the

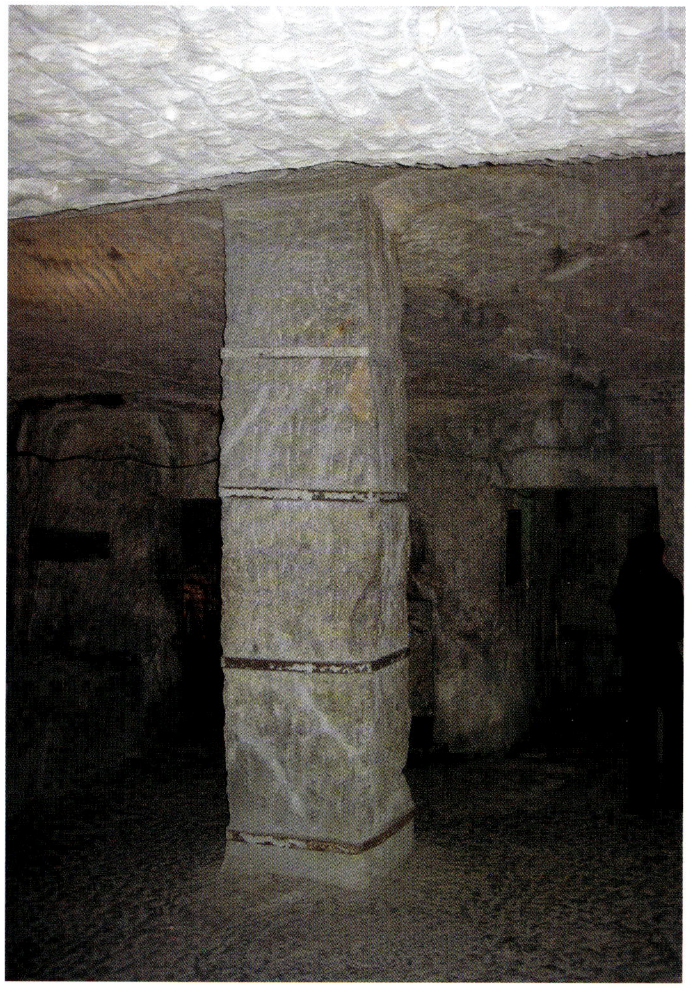

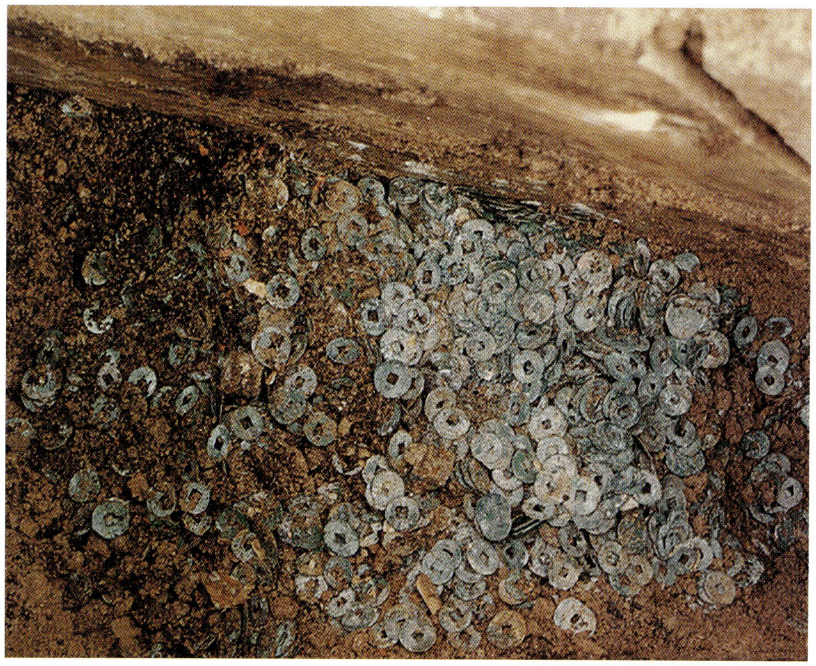

development of distinct characteristics in the burial goods of local kings. As a result, burial objects of the Chu kings and queens present unique features.

Coins

Since the reign of the Emperor Wendi (180–157 BC) of the Han dynasty, it was recorded in texts that large amounts of coin were buried along with the deceased as popular burial objects. Great quantities have been unearthed from the Kings of Chu in Shizishan and Beidongshan (fig. 25). Around 176,000 coins were found at Shizishan and around 52,640 relatively intact coins have been excavated from Beidongshan, not counting a further significant number of coins that had been damaged. As these tombs had been looted, the number of coins originally buried was most probably higher.

Seals

The tombs often contain a large numbers of seals, which bear the official titles of the deceased (cat. 24–9). More than two hundred such seals have been excavated from the king's tomb in Shizishan and thirteen bronze seals from the king's tomb in Beidongshan. Seals were very common burial objects, found in tombs of the high-ranking elite from the late Warring States period to the Han. These seals help archaeologists to identify the tomb owners and were probably intended as a method of identification in the underworld. If no seals had been found in the tomb of the King of Nanyue, we might have mistaken him for Zhao Hu, whose life was recorded in *Shiji*. Seals with the name or title of the owner were used in life, and the burial of these objects suggests that the owners wished to assert their status in the afterlife.

24 Carved stone columns. From Guishan, Xuzhou, Jiangsu Province. 128–117 BC.

25 Coins. Excavated from Beidongshan, Xuzhou, Jiangsu Province. Second century BC.

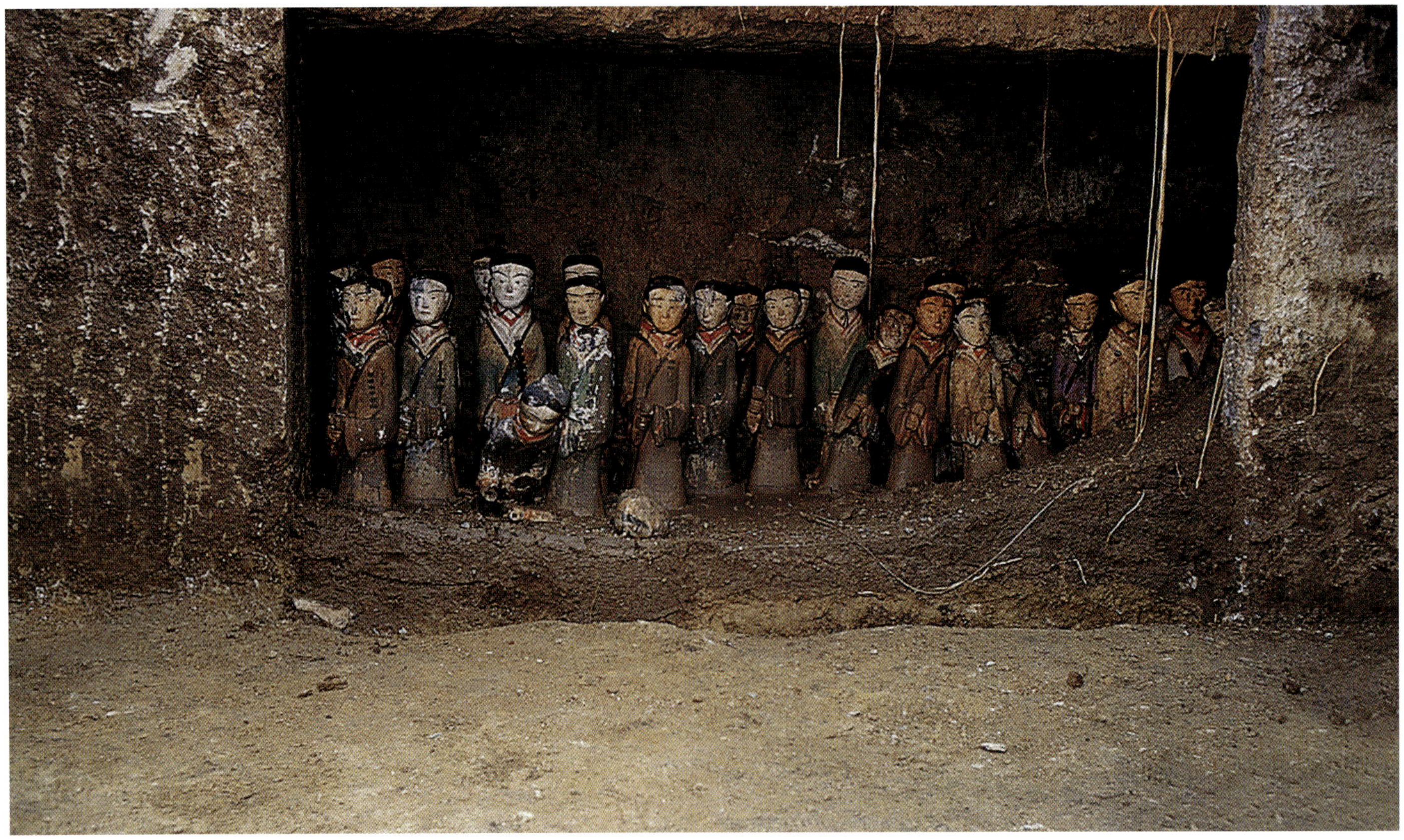

Earthenware figures

Earthenware figures are one of the most common burial goods found in the Western Han kings' tombs in Xuzhou. Excavated from burial pits and from within tomb chambers, they include soldiers, horses, servants, dancers and musicians. Nearly 3,000 figures of soldiers have been excavated from the pit of horses and soldiers at Shizishan and several hundred figures from the burial pits at Yangguishan, as well as from the burial pits and tomb chambers at Tuolanshan. 224 painted guardian figures were found at Beidongshan (fig. 26). A far greater number of earthenware figures was buried within the tombs of the Chu kings than in kings' tombs in other states of the Western Han period.

Jade suits

The Western Han kings commonly used jade suits in burials. They have been excavated from Chu kings' tombs at Shizishan, Beidongshan and Dongdongshan in Xuzhou. Considering that many royal tombs have been robbed, the number of jade suits must have exceeded that known today. Those of the Chu kings have a number of distinctive features. In particular, one sewn together with gold threads and excavated from Shizishan is the most delicate jade suit discovered to date (cat. 87). The pale jade is of the highest quality and is cut into the largest number and smallest size of plaques. The fish-scale-like plaques from Beidongshan (cat. 86) would have been tied together originally to form a jade suit. They were found scattered in the tomb passage. A passage from *Lüshi chunqiu* ('Mr Lü's Annals' by Lü Buwei, active third century BC) records that shrouds of this

26 Painted earthenware figures. Excavated from the niches of Beidongshan, Xuzhou, Jiangsu Province. Second century BC.

type were employed in rich burials during the Warring States period. In the Han dynasty, notes were added to his text by Gao You (*c.* AD 168–212), who explained that scale-like jade suits represented the covering of the body of the deceased to look like fish scales.

Jade coffins

Within the territory of the ancient state of Chu, a jade coffin (lacquer inlaid with jade) was discovered at Shizishan and consists of over 2,000 jade plaques cut into various forms and decorations, including disc patterns (cat. 98), which were attached to the surface of a lacquered coffin to form geometric designs. Jade nails were inserted into a central hole of the disc patterns, while gold nails were used to secure the four corners of the rhomboid jade plaques. The coffin's gold and jade glitter in the light, and to date this is a unique discovery in the history of Chinese archaeology.

A lacquer coffin inlaid with jade from the Chu king's tomb at Beidongshan consists of more jade discs than that from Shizishan and is also inlaid with gilt bronze discs. Coffins decorated with bronze discs are not common; the only other known example is from a Warring States period tomb located at Jiuliandun in Hubei Province, but the bronze discs do not feature any decoration, nor are they gilt. In addition, the bronze discs from Beidongshan bear patterns that generally appear on jades rather than bronzes.

THE TOMB OCCUPANTS

The dating of the twelve tombs of Chu kings from the nine sites that have been discovered so far covers the entire course of the Western Han dynasty. Their precise dates and the identities of their owners have been the focus of considerable discussion. Fortunately, a silver seal with a turtle-shaped knob and an inscription, which reads 'Liu Zhu', has been found at the M1 tomb at Guishan (cat. 25), clearly indicating that the owner of that tomb is the sixth King of Chu, Liu Zhu. This is the only tomb whose occupant can be definitively identified so far. Liu Zhu came to the throne in 128 BC and died in 116 BC, which would make him active in the early reign of Emperor Wudi. Being the sixth out of twelve Chu kings, his reign falls in the middle of the history of Chu. As a result, the layout and burial goods in his tomb serve as perfect markers against which other tombs of Chu kings can be compared for the dating and possible identification of their occupants.

The Chu king's tomb at Shizishan, with its grand scale, unique layout and abundant burial goods, has become a central point of discussion among archaeologists. It is commonly believed that it probably belongs to the third King of Chu, Liu Wu or the second King of Chu, Liu Yingke. However, neither of these two theories is backed up by concrete archaeological evidence. Liu Wu plotted an unsuccessful rebellion and then committed suicide: as a rebel, it is unlikely that he would have been allowed to take with him into the afterlife large numbers of earthenware soldiers, yet these were discovered in the tomb. Many scholars, therefore, tend to believe that the tomb belongs to the second King of Chu, Liu Yingke.

The identity of the tomb occupant at Chuwangshan is recorded in the historical texts mentioned above, which declare with confidence that the occupier is the first King of Chu. Until recently, scholars have quoted from these texts without questioning them. In 1997 the tomb was looted and archaeologists were therefore able for the first time to enter and investigate it. The tomb features domes constructed of stones. The bronzes and pottery and the style of inscriptions on stones found in the tomb clearly show that it dates from the mid- to late Western Han period. As a result, the owner of the tomb cannot be the first King of Chu, Liu Jiao, but must be a later king who was active in the latter half of the Western Han period.

From the tomb structures and burial goods that have been excavated so far, it can be concluded that the chronology of Chu kings' tombs, from earliest to latest, is as follows: Shizishan, Tuolanshan, Beidongshan, Woniushan, Guishan (tomb of Liu Zhu, the sixth Chu king), Nandongshan, Dongdongshan and Chuwangshan. In order to identify all twelve tombs further research and archaeological studies are required.

During the Eastern Han dynasty, Xuzhou was a fiefdom successively of the Chu and Pengcheng states, ruled over by one king of Chu and five kings of Pengcheng. In 1969, an Eastern Han period Pengcheng tomb (M1) of a noble was excavated at the site of the present day Xuzhou Museum. Relics, including a jade shroud sewn with silver thread, were unearthed. It has been inferred that the tomb might belong to a queen of the Pengcheng state. At the time of writing, excavations are ongoing at the main tomb (M2), and the project is due for completion in 2012.

Modern-day Suiningxian at Xuzhou was the fief of the Xiapi state. Its capital, which was also called Xiapi, is now known as the town of Gupi. To the west of Gupi is a pair of ancient artificial mounds that might be the tombs of a Xiapi king and his queen. The burial site of the Xiapi royal family is located in Liuluocun.

NOTE

1 Translated by Nicole T. C. Chiang

2 The term *ti cou* was first recorded in Lüshi Chunqiu ('Mr Lü's Annals', compiled under the auspices of Lü Buwei, probably in 240 BC). It was mentioned by Su Lin (fl. AD 196–227) in a commentary: 'It is called "yellow intestines (*huangchang*)" because the tomb structure employs the yellow core of cypress logs piled around the coffin. It is called "aligned together (*ti cou*)" because all of the logs are facing inward.' (Translation based on Thorp 1979, p. 145.)

THE HIERARCHICAL BURIAL SYSTEM OF HAN TOMBS AS SEEN IN XUZHOU

JAMES C. S. LIN

The excavations of tombs of the Chu kingdom at Xuzhou reveal an important aspect of Han burial practice. A hierarchical system from the highest levels of the elite down through to the lower levels can be observed in the tomb plans and their contents. The principal tombs at Xuzhou include those of the Kings of Chu from different generations who were buried at Beidongshan, Shizishan, Guishan, Dongdongshan, Nandongshan and Tuolanshan (Map 5). Each Chu king was buried in his individual hill or mountain with his spouse nearby. However, only one tomb, that in Guishan, has been positively linked to a particular king, Liu Zhu (r. 128–116 BC), on the basis of a seal found inside the tomb. The order of the other tomb occupants is still being debated.[1] Although most of them have been looted, the numbers of surviving jade plaques suggests that most of the tombs may have contained jade suits.

Below the hills are constellations of tombs of the kings' close relatives and high-ranking officials, such as those at Houloushan, Bojishan, Zifangshan, Jiulishan, Huoshan and Hanshan. The principal difference between the kings' tombs and the tombs of those of lower status are that the kings' tomb passages were dug horizontally into a hill and connected with several different functional chambers, while those of the relatives and officials were dug vertically into the ground and have a small horizontal chamber (fig. 27). Furthermore, the former were buried with real objects and with models and tomb figures, while the latter were generally equipped with models only. Seals bearing inscriptions containing the occupants' names from subordinate tombs, such as Huoshan (Liu He, *c.*179–141 BC), Bojishan (Liu Yi, early Western Han) and Hanshan (Liu Zai, early Western Han), indicate that these tombs belonged to members of the imperial Liu family, although their names were not recorded in any texts. In addition, a jade suit with silver thread from Huoshan and an incomplete jade suit from Hanshan, consisting of only five parts, highlight their unusual status and indicate that they must have enjoyed a close relationship with the King of Chu.

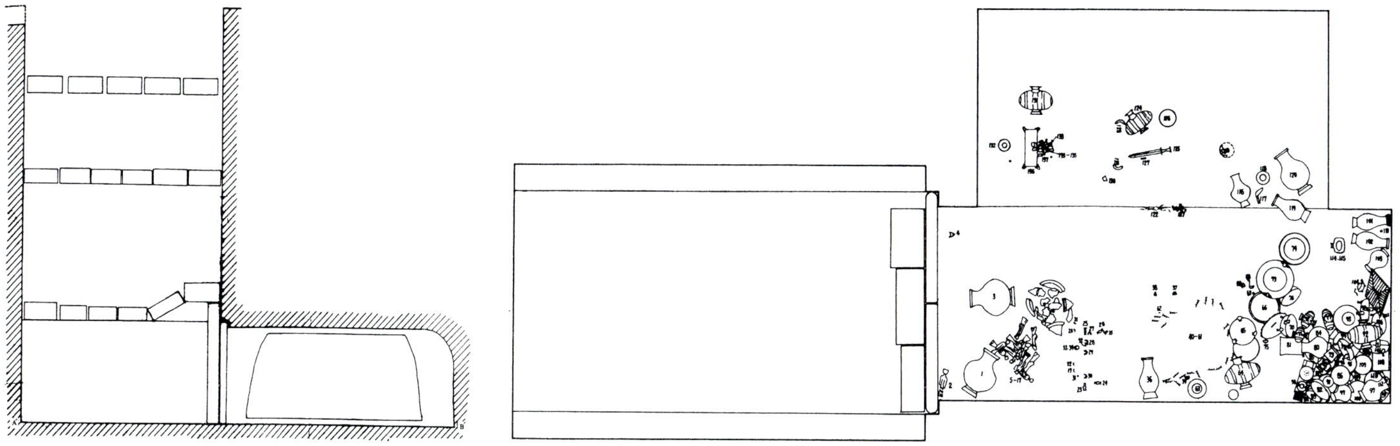

27 Catacomb tomb at Houloushan, Xuzhou, Jiangsu Province. After *Wenwu* 1993.4, figs 2, 3.

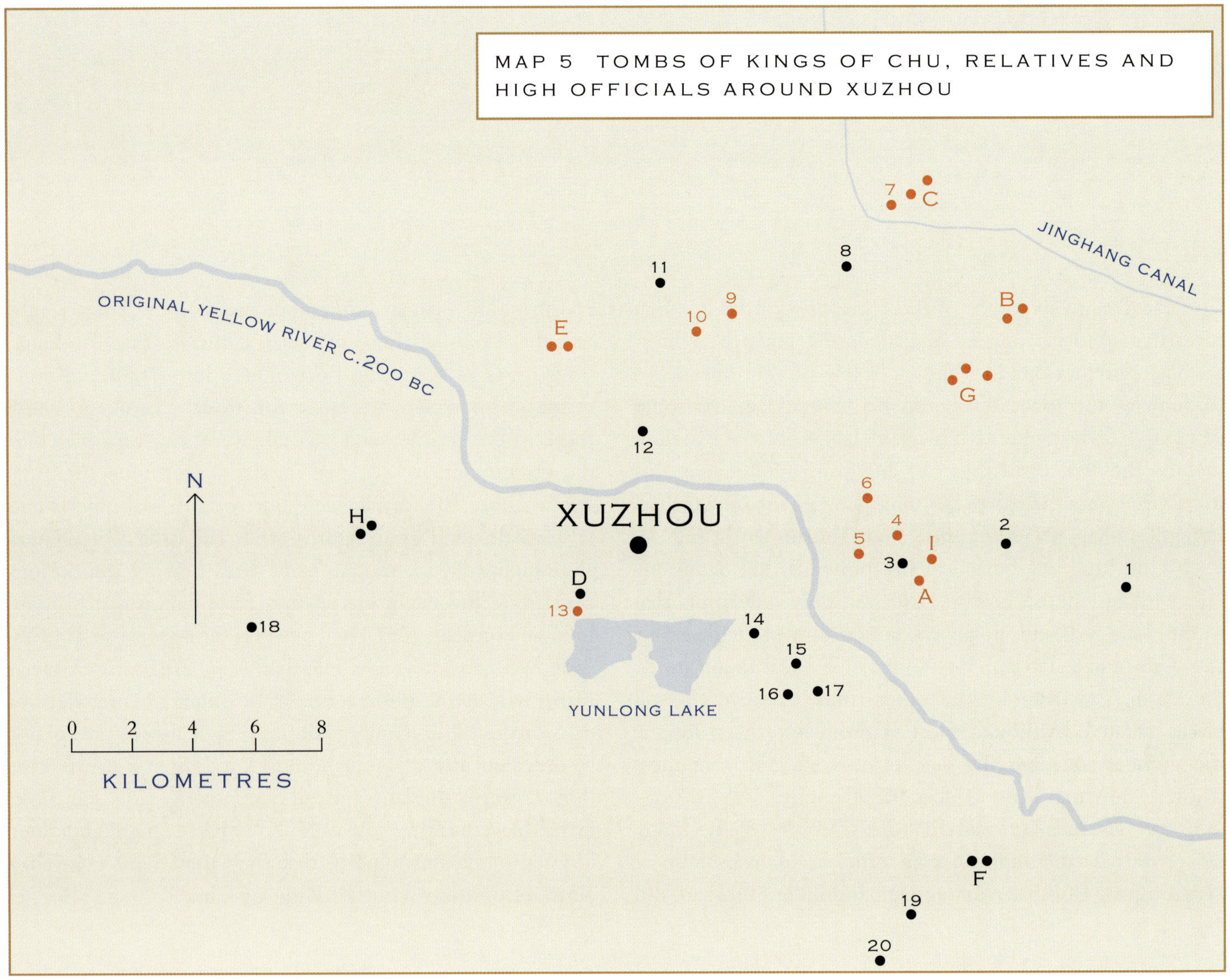

ROYAL TOMBS

A SHIZISHAN, KING OF CHU
B TUOLANSHAN, KING AND QUEEN OF CHU
C BEIDONGSHAN, KING OF CHU
D WONIUSHAN, KING OF CHU
E GUISHAN, KING AND QUEEN OF CHU
F NANDONGSHAN, KING AND QUEEN OF CHU
G DONGDONGSHAN, KING AND QUEENS OF CHU
H CHUWANGSHAN, KING OF CHU
I YANGGUISHAN, CONSORT OF SHIZISHAN

RELATIVES AND HIGH OFFICIALS

1 CUIPINGSHAN
2 HEITOUSHAN
3 XIUQIUSHAN
4 BAIYUNSHAN
5 ZIFANGSHAN
6 TAOJIASHAN
7 HOULOUSHAN
8 JIULISHAN
9 BOJISHAN
10 HUOSHAN
11 MISHAN
12 SUSHANTOU
13 HANSHAN
14 YUNLONGSHAN
15 YAOJIANSUO
16 FENGHUANGSHAN
17 KUISHAN
18 YIANSHAN
19 TUOLONGSHAN
20 YANSHAN

KEY

BEIDONGSHAN TOMBS REPRESENTED IN EXHIBITION
WONIUSHAN TOMBS NOT REPRESENTED IN EXHIBITION

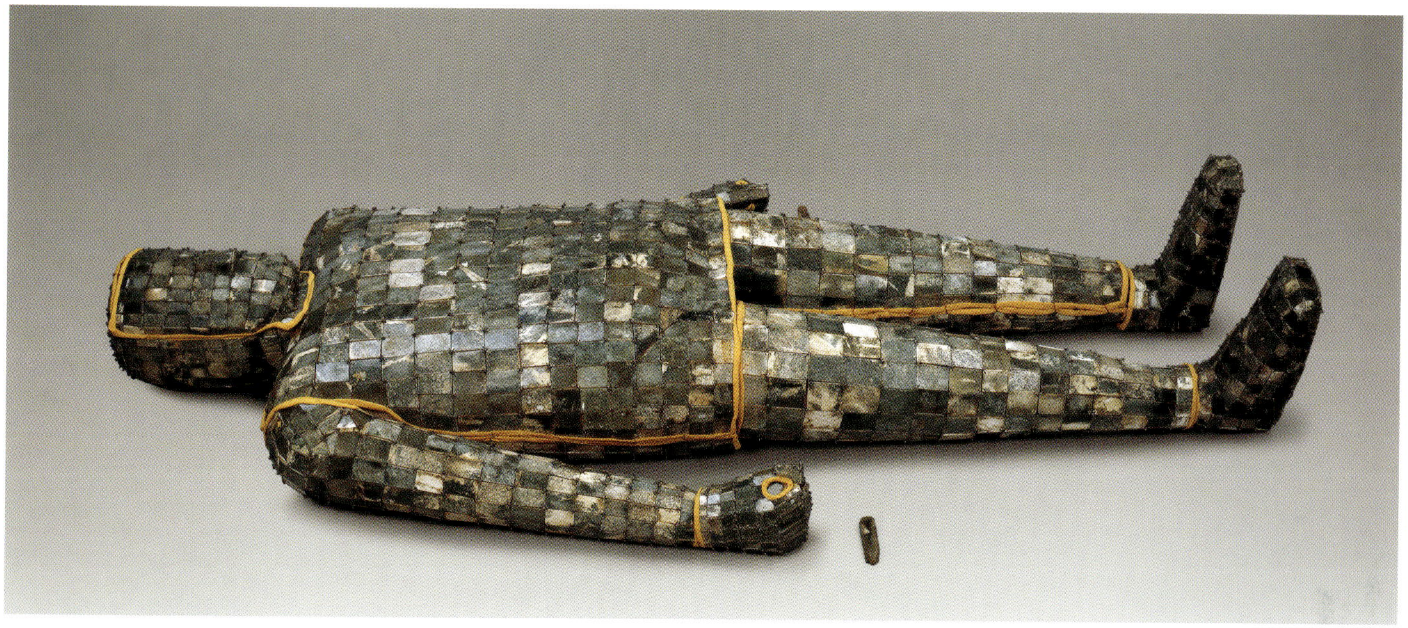

Liu He's jade suit is probably the earliest in date. His tomb was located at the top of Huoshan, north of Xuzhou city. It is a catacomb tomb with a long vertical tomb passage, east and west chambers, an attendant coffin and the main coffin chamber. The tomb occupant was identified from a seal inscription as Liu He. However, this name is not known from texts; it may be assumed that he is a member of the King of Chu's family. The *sizhu banliang* coins in the tomb indicate a date of between 179 and 141 BC.

The jade suit is composed of twelve parts, like most of those found so far (fig. 28). Most of the jade plaques are square, rectangular and trapezoid, with some irregular shapes used for the head, hands and feet. A jade pillow (cat. 95), seven jade orifice plugs, discs, bronze mirrors and an iron sword with a golden guard were found near the jade suit and a pair of *wo* (hand grips) in the shape of pigs was held in the hands. The eyes and mouth are represented by slits, like those found in Mancheng. The nose is composed of four long, narrow plaques. A jade disc with delicate decoration was placed on the top of the head. The soles of the feet are made of four jade plaques. The suit is bulky in appearance with a large abdomen.

Liu He's jade suit is unusual in that it is the only example found in a catacomb tomb in the Xuzhou area; most of the jade suits were found in the hill tombs carved out of rock.

The tomb of a King of Chu of the Western Han dynasty was excavated at the foot of Shizishan, Xuzhou from December 1994 to April 1995. It is a very complicated chamber tomb carved into a rocky mountain. The *banliang* coins date this tomb to the early Western Han. According to the *Houhanshu* and *Shuijingzhu*, the first King of Chu's tomb was located in Pengcheng, west of present-day Xuzhou; the sixth King of Chu's tomb has already been excavated at Guishan, Xuzhou. Therefore, there are two remaining possibilities that would fit the evidence of the coins; the tomb occupant is either the second king, Liu Yingke (r. 179–175 BC) or the third king, Liu Wu (r. 175–154 BC).[2] As some chambers in this giant tomb were incomplete, archaeologists have suggested that the tomb occupant may have been the King of Chu of the third generation, Liu Wu, who joined the rebellion with six other kingdoms in 154 BC and committed suicide soon after the failure of the rebellion. On this basis the tomb has been provisionally dated to 179–154 BC.[3]

28 Liu He's jade suit. Excavated from Huoshan, Xuzhou. Second century BC. Xuzhou Museum.

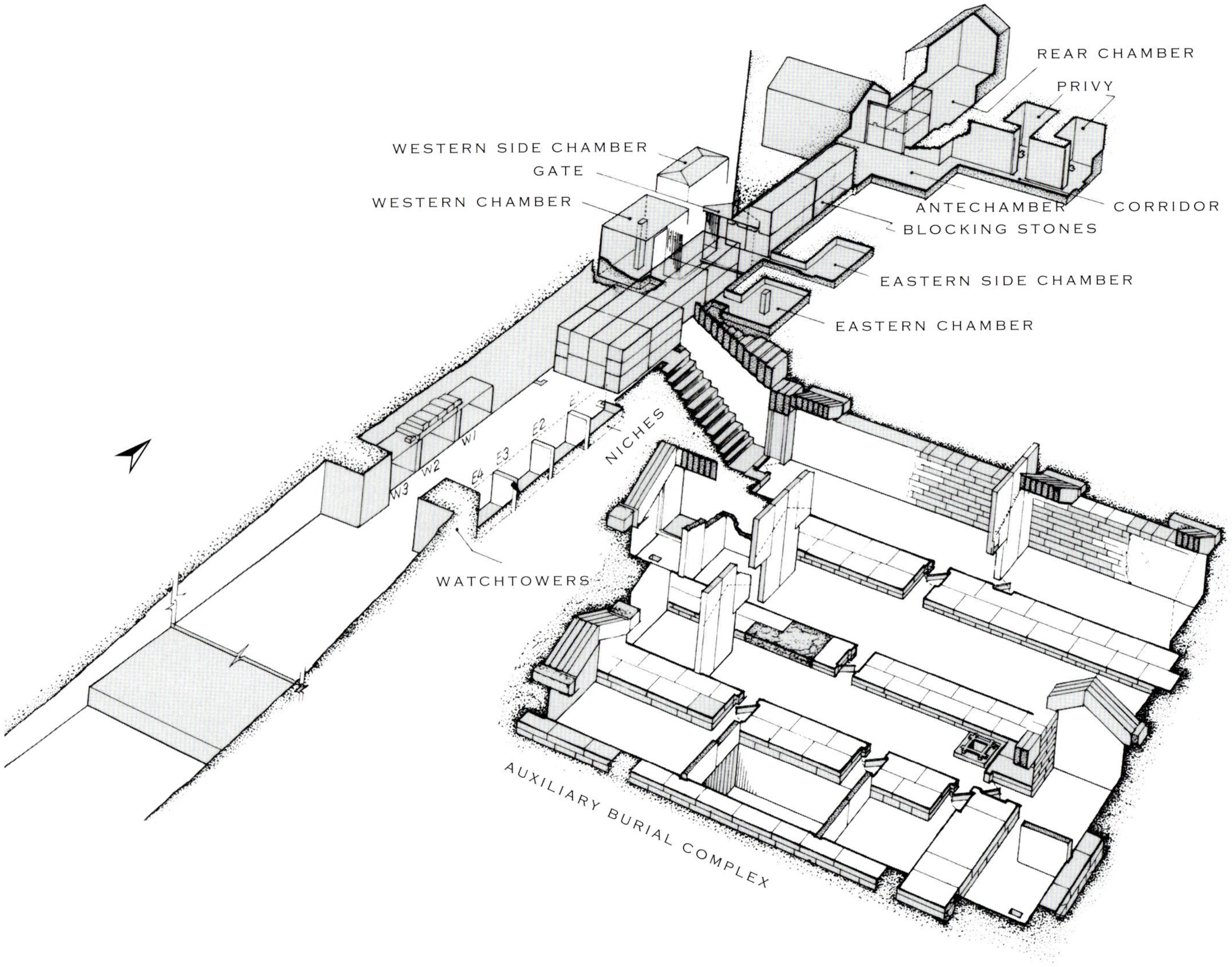

However, the discovery of a large group of terracotta soldiers in front of Shizishan and the delicate jade suit found inside the tomb appear to contradict this theory. This jade suit is the most delicate in terms of quality of jade and construction that has been found so far. It seems unlikely that the Han court would have given Liu Wu a grand burial if he had indeed been a rebel, as this could have risked the possibility of his continuing to pursue his rebellion in the afterlife.[4]

This jade suit is composed of 4,248 jade plaques, almost double the number of other jade suits, sewn together with 1,576 grams of gold thread (cat. 87). In addition to this jade suit, another 1,600 jade plaques for the coffin (cat. 98), 200 clay seals with inscriptions, gold ornaments and bronze weapons and another 200 jade objects were found in this tomb.[5]

Beidongshan is the most complicated of the Xuzhou tombs; it was dug into the side of the hill and was built partly of stone and partly of earth. It contains nineteen chambers and seven small niches. From the location of the surviving objects, the chambers can be identified as an arsenal, storerooms for pottery and lacquerware, a music and

29 Diagram of Beidongshan, Xuzhou, Jiangsu Province. Second century BC. After Yinde Li 1990, p. 57, fig. 1.

dance hall containing figures of dancers and musicians, a kitchen equipped with a stove and pots, a firewood store filled with charcoal, a *lingyin* (ice cellar), a food storeroom, three lavatories and a well (fig. 29).

Although the tomb contents have been plundered, more than a thousand funerary objects survived. A number of jade plaques resembling fish scales were recovered from the tomb (cat. 86), indicating that the tomb occupant was buried in a jade suit. The seal and coins help date the tomb to between 175 and 128 BC.

At least five sets of jade veils that were assembled to represent human facial features have been found in smaller-scale tombs in Xuzhou. The earliest archaeological evidence of jade veils can be traced back to the Western Zhou period in the western part of China. After 771 BC, the Zhou court was forced to move to Luoyi, near present-day Luoyang, and the custom of using jade facial plaques to cover the body became widespread in the area. It is sometimes suggested that the jade veils of Eastern Zhou were the precursors of veils that have been found in Han period tombs at Xuzhou. However, these veils are very different from their predecessors. In particular, these Han examples are more like masks than veils. We can consider them as a version of the jade protection developed in eastern China during the Han period, as they are different from Western Zhou jade veils from western China. They have primarily been found in lower-ranking tombs of the state of Chua in the Han period, or from poorer kingdoms. Evidence has come from medium sized catacomb tombs in Xuzhou. A veil from tomb M3 Zifangshan, dating to early Western Han (182–140 BC),[6] is composed of twenty-two jade plaques of various shapes – including square, rectangular, semi-circular, fan-shaped and ring-shaped with a nose-like piece – which together formed features like a human face. Most of these pieces were reworked from sword fittings (cat. 85). The tomb occupant has been identified as an aristocratic official.

A much simpler jade veil that is now in the Xuzhou museum was excavated from Yaojiansuo near Xuzhou. It is composed of fifteen broken jade pieces that form a very rough outline of a human face (fig. 30). According to the archaeologists, the tomb belonged to an official.

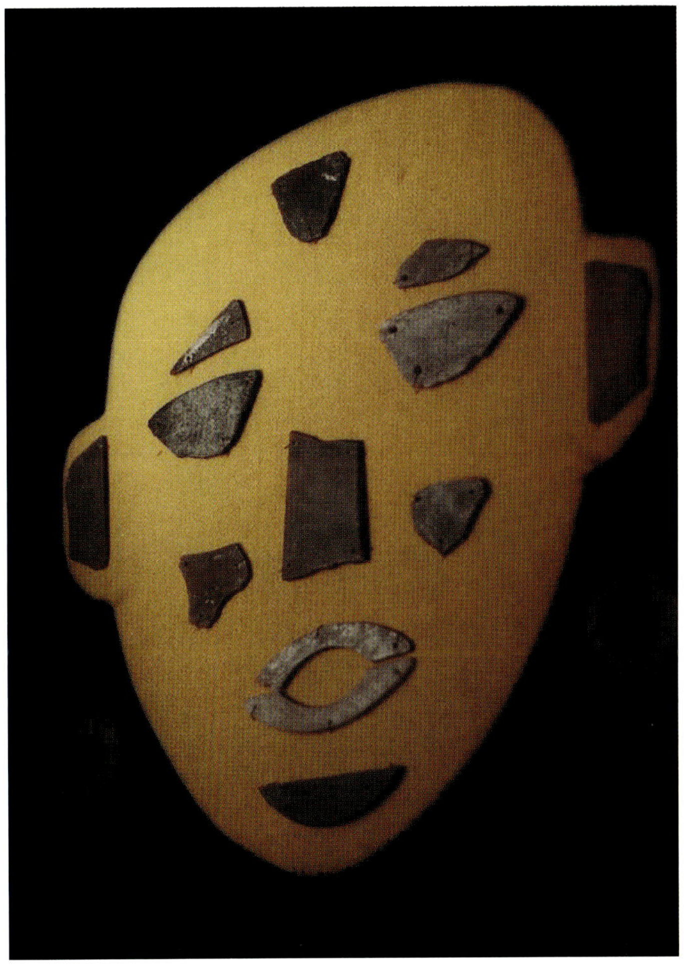

Another two jade veils dating to early Western Han from M1 Tuolongshan and M1 Houloushan, Xuzhou are quite similar to the jade suit in their physical construction. Both were found in vertical catacomb tombs. The face veil from Houloushan is composed of thirty-three jade plaques, including four earring-like ornaments. Most of the jade plaques are either rectangular or pentagonal and were used to cover the whole face; there are no eye, nose or mouth features. The closely fitting construction resembles the arrangement of plaques in the face cover of a jade suit (fig. 31).[7] In light of the tomb location – a satellite grave near the Chu king's mausoleum at Beidongshan – the occupant's status has been identified as either a relative of the King of Chu or a vassal of the Chu kingdom.

30 Jade plaques reworked from fifteen broken jade pieces. Excavated from a tomb at Yaojiansuo, Xuzhou, Jiangsu Province. Second century BC. James C. S. Lin, field research, Xuzhou Museum, 1998.

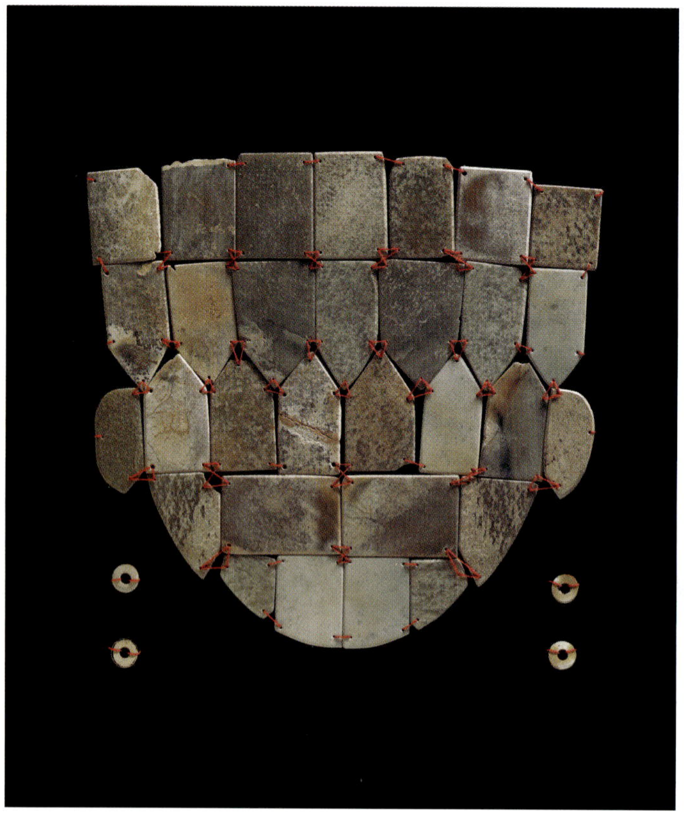

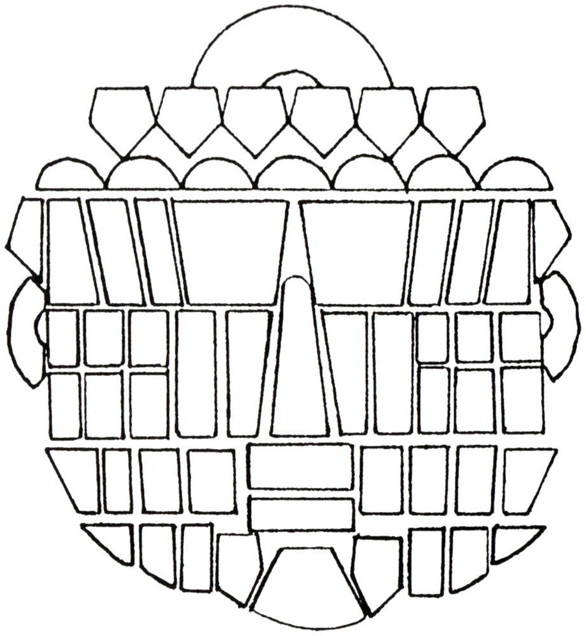

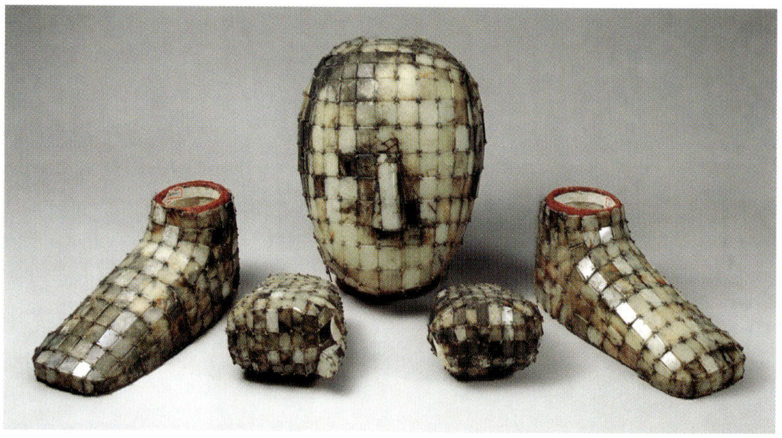

The tomb in Tuolongshan contained not only a jade veil, but also a jade helmet and two jade boots. The face veil and helmet are composed of some 150 jade plaques in a variety of shapes including pentagonal, semi-circular, triangular, fan-shaped, square and rectangular. Larger plaques were used to represent facial features such as the eyes, nose, mouth and chin. Although only a drawing of the veil has been published, it is obviously closely related to the jade suit (fig. 32) and is very similar to the incomplete jade suit from Liu Ci's tomb (fig. 33). A jade disc was placed on the top of the head, through which it was believed the souls of the dead could travel. The jade plaques are decorated with floating cloud patterns. Silk remains were found on the reverse of the jade plaques, suggesting that they were pasted onto a textile that was placed onto the head of the corpse. Holes were made in the sides of the plaques, but no metal traces were found, leading archaeologists to suggest that silk was used to thread together the face veil and helmet. These items may originally have been components of a complete jade suit.[8]

A similar example can be observed in tomb M1 at Hanshan, Xuzhou, a catacomb tomb surmounted by a large mound. The occupant was covered with some 600 jade plaques of various forms – square, rectangular, triangular, semi-circular and one irregular piece – sewn together with silk thread. Only the head, hands and feet were covered. The funeral objects help to date the tomb to the early

31 (above) Jade face covering. Excavated from tomb M1 at Houloushan, Xuzhou, Jiangsu Province in 1991. Height: 23cm; Width: 24.5 cm.

32 (below) Jade face covering from an incomplete jade suit. From Tuolongshan, Xuzhou, Jiangsu Province. Second century BC. After *Dongnan wenhua* 1996.1, p. 29, fig. 3.

33 Liu Ci's incomplete jade suit, which was composed of 1,140 jade plaques. From Linyi, Shandong Province. Second century BC. After Hong Kong 1996, p. 192, fig. 256.

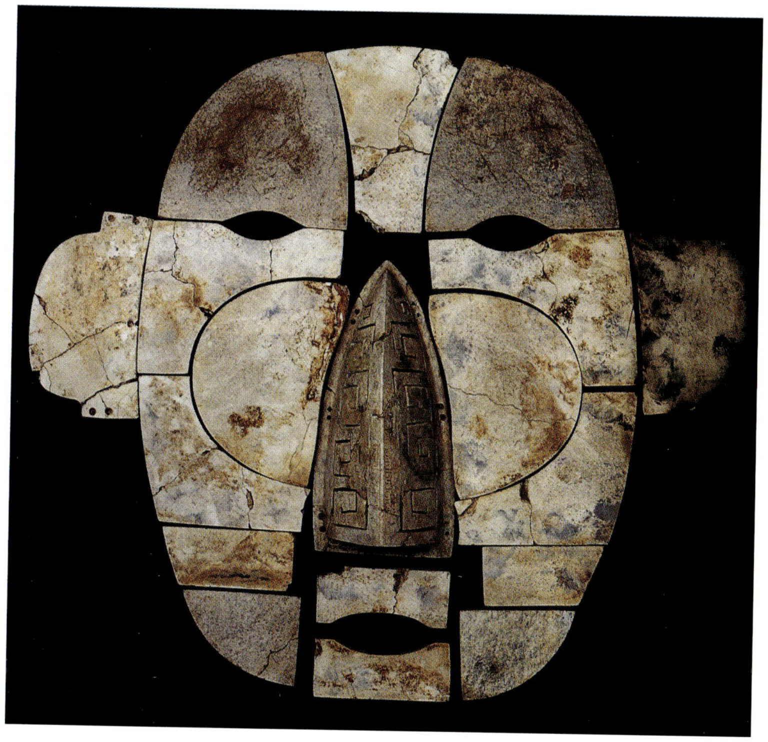

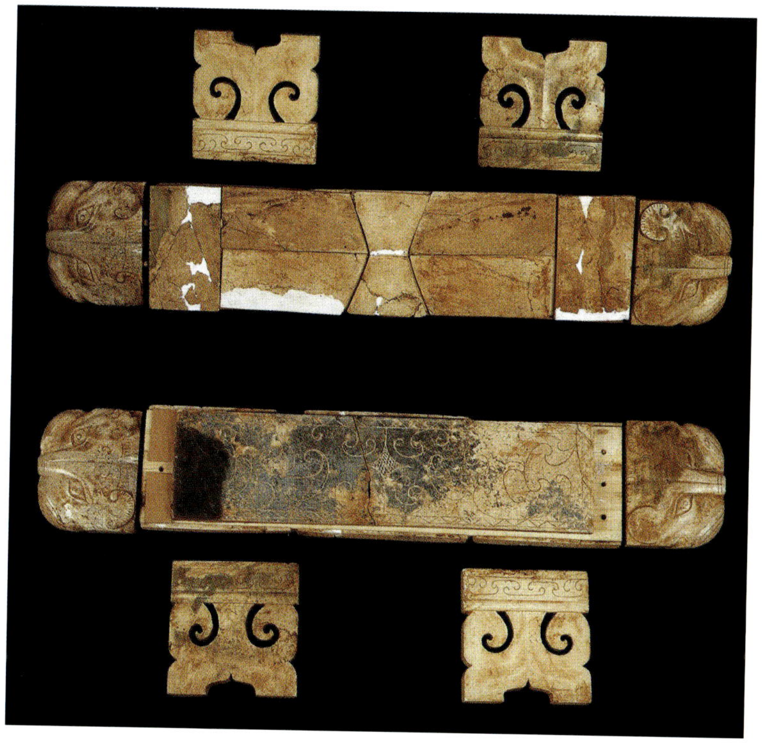

Western Han, and a jade seal bears the name of the tomb occupant, Liu Zai, who was obviously a member of the Liu family.[9]

The jade veils mentioned above are probably inferior alternatives to jade suits rather than early examples in a chronological development. As an alternative to a jade veil, parts of what were in effect jade suits might have been used. Liu Ci's incomplete jade suit found at Linyi, Shandong, is the best example.

Jade veils appeared in the Xuzhou area in a variety of forms during early Western Han. Those from Zifangshan and Yaojiansuo retained facial features and seem to be based on much earlier types, whereas the others from Tuolongshan, Houloushan and Hanshan are composed of geometric shapes and share characteristics with the jade suit. Obviously, the use of jade veils in the Xuzhou area depended on the status of the tomb occupants. Higher-ranking individuals were buried in more delicate and complicated veils, or even jade suits. Lower-ranking individuals were buried in veils that were much poorer in quality and much simpler in design.

One other example is comparable with the Xuzhou veils. Liu Kuan's jade veil is made of seventeen large jade plaques forming a human face (mask), including forehead, cheeks, nose, lips, ears and chin. There have been no other archaeological reports of such an unusual design (fig. 34). The tomb in which it was found is a large-scale vertical pit with a passage and chamber discovered at Shuangrushan, fifteen kilometres north-east of the Changqingxian, Shandong Province. The occupant was identified as the last king of the kingdom of Jibei, Liu Kuan (r. 97–87 BC).[10] In addition to the jade veil, a jade pillow (fig. 35) was placed under the neck, five jade discs were placed near the waist, on the stomach and beneath the back, and two jades in the shape of pigs were gripped in the hands. Nine orifice plugs were also found in this tomb, including a jade shroud for the penis, which enabled identification of the occupant's gender.[11] However, this noble was buried without a jade suit.

34 Jade mask, made for Liu Kuan (r. 97–87 BC). From Changqing, Shandong Province. After Gu 2005, vol. 4, pl. 230.

35 Jade pillow, made for Liu Kuan (r. 97–87 BC). From Changqing, Shandong Province. After Gu 2005, vol. 4, pl. 231.

TABLE 3 STRUCTURE, OCCUPANT AND THE STATUS OF OCCUPANT IN TOMBS OF THE XUZHOU AREA

SITE/TOMB	DATE	OCCUPANT	STATUS OF OCCUPANT	JADE SUIT/ VEIL	TOMB STRUCTURE
Shizishan	178–154 BC	Liu Yingke or Liu Wu	King of Chu	Gold-thread jade suit	Rock-cut chamber tomb
Tuolanshan M1	Early Western Han		King of Chu	Looted	Rock-cut chamber tomb
Tuolanshan M2	Early Western Han		Consort of King of Chu	Looted	Rock-cut chamber tomb
Beidongshan	175–128 BC	Liu Yingke, Liu Wu, Liu Li or Liu Dao	King of Chu	Jade plaques for suit	Rock-cut chamber tomb
Guishan M1	128–116 BC	Liu Zhu	King of Chu	Looted: Jade plaques	Rock-cut chamber tomb
Shiqiao M1	101 BC		King of Chu	Looted: Jade plaques	Rock-cut chamber tomb
Shiqiao M2	73–49 BC		Consort of King of Chu	Looted: Jade plaques	Rock-cut chamber tomb
Houloushan	Early Western Han		Unknown	Jade veil	Rock-cut pit tomb
Zifangshan M3	182–140 BC		Unknown	Jade veil	Rock-cut pit tomb
Tuolongshan			Unknown	Silk-thread incomplete jade suit	Rock-cut pit tomb
Huoshan	179–141 BC	Liu He	Relative of King of Chu	Silver-thread jade suit	Rock-cut pit tomb
Bojishan M3	Early Western Han	Liu Yi	Marquis of Wanqu	No veil or suit	Rock-cut pit tomb
Hanshan M1	Early Western Han	Liu Zai	Relative of King of Chu	Silk-thread incomplete jade suit	Rock-cut pit tomb
Cuipingshan M1	Early Western Han	Liu Zhi	Relative of King of Chu	Intact, no veil or suit	Rock-cut pit tomb
Heitoushan M1	Early Western Han	Liu Shen	Relative or official of King of Chu	Intact, no veil or suit	Rock-cut pit tomb

After Liu Bang unified China, he installed meritorious officials as kings and marquises. A few years later, kings who were not related to the emperor and those who were found guilty of rebellion were killed or replaced. From 201 to 195 BC, nine kings were replaced by Liu family members, either Liu Bang's brothers or his sons. As a result, Liu Bang's half brother, Liu Jiao, was installed as the first King of Chu in Xuzhou in 201 BC. Later, a secret meeting was organized by Liu Bang and other trusted courtiers, and a treaty was made, stating that 'if anyone not of the Liu family becomes a king, the empire must unite in attacking him'.[12] As a result, almost all of the catacomb tombs found in Xuzhou are related to the Liu family (Table 3).

The jade suits, which were designed for the afterlife and were mainly distributed among members of the imperial Liu family, clearly also manifested political allegiances. In the interests of political unity, use of a jade suit by non-Liu family members would be deemed illegal and would have implied improper access to political power. However, the outsider King of Nanyue in Guangzhou seems to be an unusual case. He may have had a jade suit made for himself without the Han emperor's permission as he was not a member of the imperial family. Indeed, the King of Nanyue was pretending to be a Han prince, as his suit, tomb structure and contents mimic those of the Han princes.

The imperial family members from the Xuzhou area may not be recorded in historical texts but their tomb structures and contents, particularly the use of the jade suit, incomplete jade suit or jade veil, distinguish their different statuses or kin distance from the Chu king. They also reflect the bureaucratic system during that time.

NOTES

1 *Wenwu* 1998.8, pp. 29–31; *Wenwu* 2001.10, pp. 71–84.

2 *Wenwu* 1998.8, p. 31.

3 *Kaogu* 1998.8, p. 10; *Kaogu yu wenwu* 2000.1, p. 24; Tang 1998, vol. III, pls. 437–47.

4 The Han imperial court worried that Grand Commandant Zhou Yafu might revolt in the afterlife when he prepared 500 sets of armour and shields for his funeral; see *Shiji*, p. 2079; Watson 1961, pp. 379–80.

5 *Wenwu* 1998.8, pp. 4–47; *Kaogu* 1998.8, pp. 1–20.

6 The date of this tomb was suggested by the archaeological examination of a bronze mirror and *bianliang* coins; *Wenwu ziliao congkan* 1981.4, pp. 59–69.

7 *Wenwu* 1993.4, pp. 29–49.

8 The excavation notes of Tuolongshan have not yet been published, but the information was recorded in *Dongnan wenhua* 1996.1, pp. 26–32.

9 *Wenwu* 1997.2, pp. 26–43.

10 No inscription was found in this tomb. However, judging from the large-scale tomb construction, location and the date from the *wuzhu* coins, Ren Xianghong suggests that the tomb occupant was the last King of Jibei; see Ren 1997, pp. 10–15.

11 See *Kaogu* 1997.3, pp. 1–9; *Gugong wenwu yuekan* (172) 1997.7, pp. 92–121; Tang 1998, vol. III, pl. 448.

12 Oath of White Horse (*baima mengshi*) was recorded in the Basic Annals of Empress Lü of *Shiji*, but the exact date was not recorded; Shiji 9.400. It is also in other chapters, such as that discussing the hereditary family of Marquis Jian, Zhou Bo; *Shiji* 27, p. 2077.

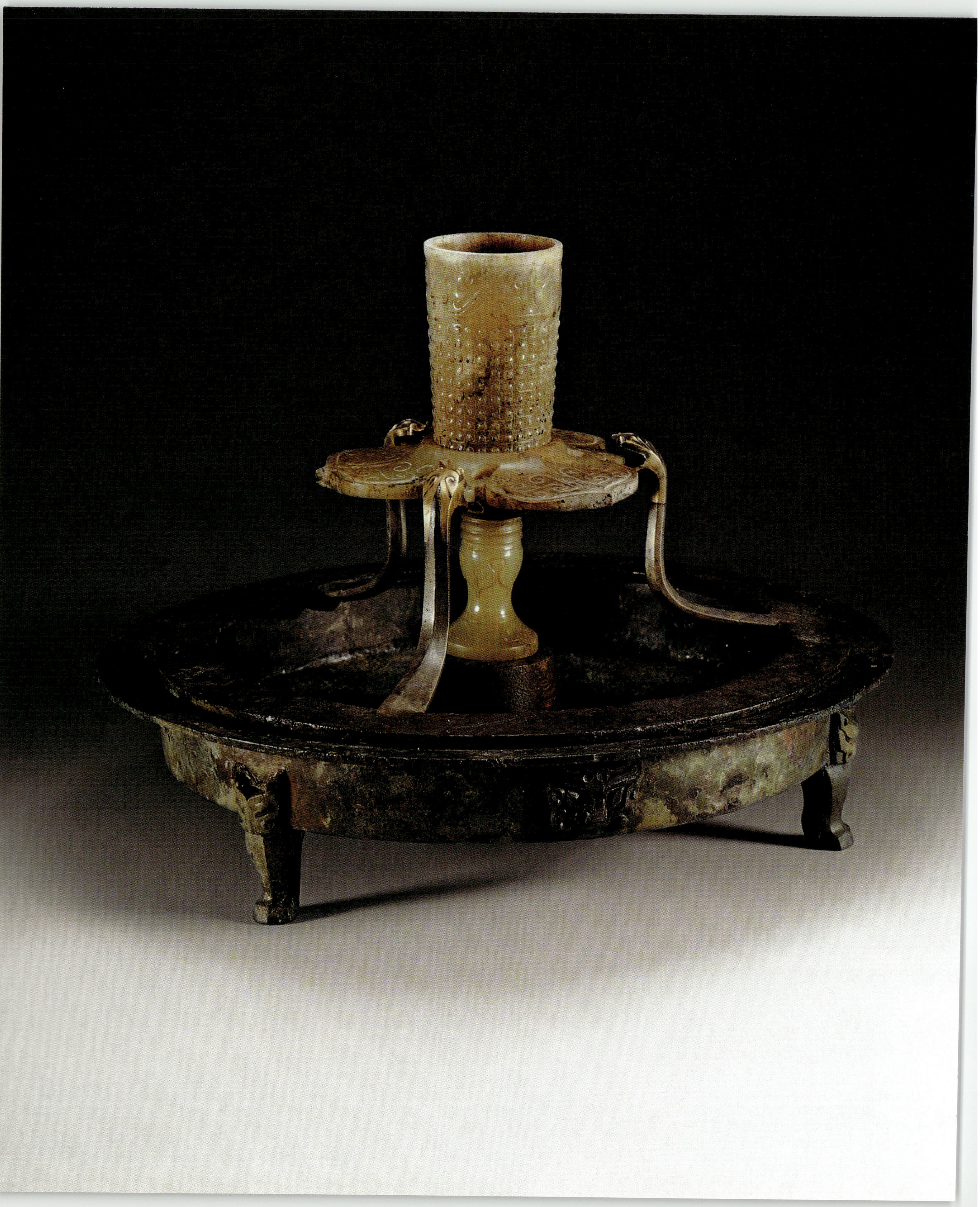

ARCHAEOLOGICAL DISCOVERIES OF THE NANYUE KINGDOM

LINNA LI[1]

In 1916, while foundations for residential houses were being built, an early Nanyue kingdom period wooden coffin was discovered at Guigang in the city of Guangzhou. The coffin, inscribed with numbers, became instantly famous. The tomb was mistakenly identified at the time as the resting place of the second King of Nanyue, Zhao Hu. Although unearthed accidentally and its occupant wrongly identified, the tomb was the first discovery of a series of Nanyue kingdom period burials in modern times. In 1975, at Yushan in Guangzhou, a large shipyard dating to the Qin and Han dynasties was discovered. On top of the shipyard were the remains of a grand passageway of a Nanyue palace. In 1980, when preparing land for residential flats at Xianggangshan in northern Guangzhou city, part of the tomb of the second King of Nanyue was found in a scientific excavation that was finished in 1983. From the unearthed architectural remains of these discoveries, as well as the sites of tombs and relevant historical records, it is possible to identify the precise site of the Nanyue kingdom's capital, which was known as the City of Panyu during the Han dynasty.

The locations of the Nanyue kings' tombs were kept secret. According to the *Shiji*, the combined reigns of the fourth and fifth Kings of Nanyue lasted only three years. Due to sibling rivalries and usurpations at court, it was impossible to build royal tombs during these final reigns. A Song dynasty record, *Hainan baiyong* ('A Hundred Songs of Hainan'), quoting a fifth-century text, *Guangzhou ji* ('Records of Guangzhou'), gives the further information that Sun Quan (AD 182–252), who heard about the numerous treasures buried with the first King of Nanyue, Zhao Tuo (r. 203–137 BC), sent thousands of people out to look for his tomb but failed to locate it. However, they did manage to find the tomb of Ying Qi, the third King of Nanyue, and obtained from it seals made of jade and gold, and bronze swords. Zhao Tuo died during the reign of the Han emperor Wudi (r. 141–87 BC), nearly three hundred years before the time of Sun Quan and a thousand years earlier than the completion of *Hainan baiyong*. If the historical text is to be trusted, the tomb of Ying Qi had already been emptied. Among the five Nanyue kings, only Zhao Tuo's tomb is yet to be discovered.

The Nanyue kingdom was a vassal state of the early Western Han dynasty. The earliest and relatively detailed accounts of its history can be found in the *Shiji* and *Hanshu*. According to these accounts, Zhao Tuo was originally from modern-day Hebei Province and was a general of the Qin dynasty. When peasants rebelled against authorities in the last years of the Qin, Zhao Tuo took over power in the Lingnan region and cut off communications with the Central Plain. In 203 BC he founded the Nanyue kingdom and built its capital in Panyu. The kingdom had five kings and lasted ninety-three years. In 111 BC the Han emperor Wudi annexed it.

THE TOMB OF THE SECOND KING OF NANYUE, ZHAO MO

The tomb has seven chambers, consisting of vertical shafts and chambers divided into a front area and a rear area, covering a total of about a hundred square metres (fig. 36). The chambers are constructed from more than 750 blocks of stones of various sizes. The tomb passage is located at the southern end. The front area of the tomb consists of

FACING PAGE: DETAIL OF CAT. 164

TABLE 4 CHRONOLOGY OF THE KINGS OF NANYUE

GENERATION	NAME	TITLE	RELATIONSHIP TO THE EMPEROR OR KING	REIGN
1	Zhao Tuo	Emperor Wudi		203–137 BC
2	Zhao Mo[2]	Emperor Wendi	Grandson of Emperor Wudi	137–122 BC
3	Zhao Yingqi	King Ming	Son of Emperor Wendi	122–113 BC
4	Zhao Xing		Son of King Ming	113 BC
5	Zhao Jiande		Eldest son of King Ming	113–111 BC

three chambers: an antechamber in the middle flanked by an eastern and western chamber. The rear area contains four chambers. The central space is occupied by the king's coffin chamber and is also flanked by eastern and western side chambers. The fourth chamber is located to the north of the king's coffin chamber. A wooden door bordered by two square columns forms the doorway that leads to the small rear storeroom. Both the antechamber and the king's coffin chamber have a double stone door. Underneath each, in the middle of the doorway, a self-locking device was installed (similar to cat. 11).

The various chambers of the underground palace of the King of Nanyue have their own distinctive functions; the antechamber probably represents a stable, as lacquered wooden models of a chariot and a sacrificial person were found here. The eastern chamber served as storage for utensils used in banqueting and entertainment. Many sets of musical instruments made of bronze, stone and lacquered wood, as well as numerous wine vessels, were neatly placed inside this chamber. In the western chamber, according to the archaeological excavation report, burial goods were stacked in three layers. The objects were likely placed on wooden shelves that have since perished. Most of the objects in this chamber contained traces of silk and fragments of bamboo or reed, indicating that the burial goods were originally packaged and stored in wrappings and containers made from these materials. The western chamber, therefore, seems to have served an imperial storage function.

The coffin of the occupant of the tomb was placed in the middle of the king's coffin chamber, with burial goods scattered around. Close to the eastern wall was a large lacquered wooden screen, which blocked the passageway leading to the eastern side chamber. As the eastern side chamber contained the burials of sacrificial concubines, the position of the screen was probably meant to provide them with privacy. When excavated, the wooden frame and panels of the screen were found to have rotted away. As a result, the bronze ornaments originally set on the screen had fallen onto the ground (cat. 173).

In the northern side of the chamber, close to the head of the king, burial goods were also discovered. An unusual-

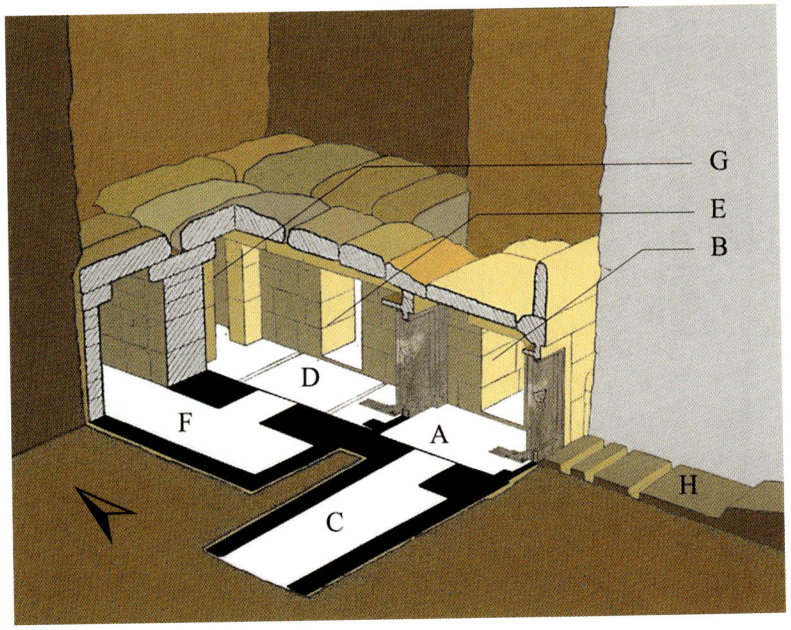

36 Plan of the tomb of the second King of Nanyue, Guangzhou, Guangdong Province. Second century BC.

looking jade cup with a bronze basin (cat. 164) was originally placed inside a lacquer container that had rotted away. Only traces of red and black lacquer were found on the surface of the jade cup.

To the west of the coffin under the western wall were a number of weapons, including four iron swords, seven iron spears (cat. 151), a pair of daggers, a bronze dagger-axe and an iron weapon that could not be identified. In addition were fifteen components of bronze crossbows and numerous lead pellets and arrowheads. These articles might have been placed on the coffin to offer protection and then fallen to the ground.

The placement of objects in the tomb is likely to have taken place as follows: first, coffins and burial goods were placed in the western and eastern side chambers; then more than a hundred bronze and iron cooking utensils were placed in the rear chamber; the lacquer wooden screen was installed; and, finally, the king's coffin was installed.

The burial goods inside the eastern chamber of the concubines mainly belonged to them, including sets of jade ornaments, seals and bronze and lacquered wooden utensils for daily use. There were also four seals bearing the inscription *Furen*, meaning 'lady' or 'wife'.

Seven human sacrifices were identified in the western side chamber, five lying directly on the ground to the south and two to the north. Judging from the small jade ornaments, belt plaques and bronze mirrors covering their faces, they were probably female. The most elderly woman in the chamber had the largest number of burial goods and a small jade seal without inscription. She might have been the head of the servants.

The rear chamber was used to store food, containers, washing implements and cooking utensils, such as *ding* (cat. 184–6), *mou* (cat. 190), cooking stoves (cat. 189), barrels, *jian* and *pen*, as well as earthenware pots and jars. Many objects were stacked on top of each other. In between the stacked objects were traces of wooden bars and boards, indicating that they had been placed on wooden shelves.

Among the more than one hundred objects inside the rear storeroom, most medium-sized and small-sized objects showed traces of wrappings made of silk or reeds. Silk textiles were mainly used to wrap bronze and iron objects. Reed wrappings were used for earthenware and food inside the containers. About thirty vessels of bronze and earthenware contained poultry, domestic animals and seafood. In addition, there were many clay seals with the seal impression *taiguan* (Grand Official), which indicates that the burial objects were inspected and sealed up by *taiguan* officials. Furthermore, on the floor by the doorway and in the south-eastern corner of the room a three- to five-centimetre thick layer of charcoal was found, which was stored as fuel for cooking.

THE PALACE OF THE NANYUE KINGDOM

The discovery of the ruins of the palace of the Nanyue kingdom in 1995 provided the first archaeological confirmation of the historical texts that place the capital of Nanyue within the city of Guangzhou. A large stone fountain, many stone columns (see fig. 22) and lintels, numerous stone fragments and eave tiles with inscriptions were found. In 1997, further excavations unearthed a stone moat leading to a crescent-shaped fountain, in which were two stone walls and two stone octagonal columns, suggesting that some architectural structures were probably built within

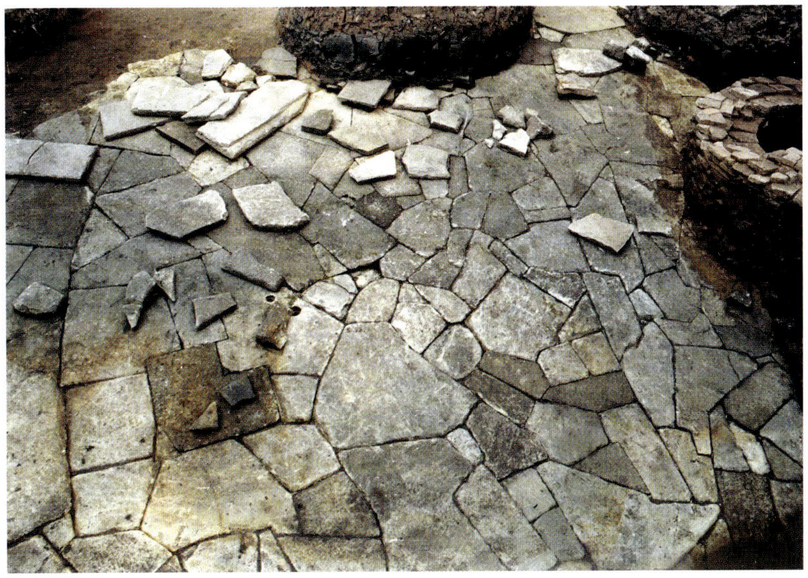

37 Stone pavement of a fountain. Excavated at the palace of the King of Nanyue, Guangzhou, Guangdong Province. Second century BC.

the fountains (fig. 37). According to the *Shiji*, the first emperor of China sent his court sorcerer, Xu Fu, accompanied by thousands of young boys and girls, on an expedition to the islands of immortals in the Eastern Sea to search for the elixir of immortality. As they failed to reach the islands, the emperor built a lake with three islands in the garden of his palace, and a pond with three islands thereafter became a standard element of imperial and royal gardens. In addition to the architectural components, at the bottom of the crescent-shaped fountain remains of tortoises and soft-shell turtles were also discovered. As symbols of longevity, these animals were commonly kept in royal and imperial gardens in China. The discoveries at the royal gardens of the Nanyue Palace have provided invaluable information for the study of early garden designs in the Lingnan region.

The archaeology of the Nanyue kingdom is distinctive in three respects. First, the finding of both the palace and the tomb of the King of Nanyue within the city of Guangzhou is unique in Han archaeology. From other states of the Han dynasty either tombs or palaces have been excavated, but never together. Second, archaeological evidence suggests that the Nanyue kingdom had established unusually strong connections with non-Chinese cultures. The stone architectural remains of the royal palace, together with the jade rhyton (see fig. 6), silver box (cat. 167) and glass beads, which were all unusual in China at the time, testify to trading and cultural exchanges with foreign lands, possibly at this time via sea routes rather than the Silk Route. Finally, many of the burial goods, such as the bronze stoves (cat. 189) and ginger grater (cat. 142), had been used before they were buried with the king. As utensils of daily use at the Nanyue court, the objects therefore not only testify to the burial customs of the Nanyue kingdom but also provide a vivid picture of the king's luxurious life some two thousand years ago.

NOTES

1 This essay is edited by Dr James C. S. Lin with reference to the original archaeological report (1991) and translated by Nicole T. C. Chiang.

2 Recorded as Zhao Hu in *Shiji* and *Hanshu*; see *Shiji* 1959, pp. 2970–1; *Hanshu* 1962, pp. 3853–4.

THE UNKNOWN EMPEROR AT GUANGZHOU

JAMES C. S. LIN

The relationship between the Nanyue kingdom and the Han court was ambiguous. After Liu Bang founded the Han dynasty, he sent an envoy, Lu Jia, to claim Zhao Tuo as a vassal of the Han court. In return, Zhao Tuo was given the title of king (*wang*). Although Zhao Tuo used this title in his dealings with the Han court, he remained virtually independent and styled himself Wudi (Emperor Wu) within his own kingdom.

In 183 BC, Empress Lü forbade the trade of iron tools to the Nanyue kingdom, which led Zhao Tuo to declare Nanyue's independence from the Han empire. Empress Lü sent an army to suppress Nanyue, but it was defeated and Zhao Tuo then openly used the title of emperor for four years. In 179 BC, soon after Emperor Wendi succeeded to the Han throne, Lu Jia was once again sent to claim Zhao Tuo as a vassal of the Han court, this time with more success: Zhao Tuo abandoned his title of emperor and gave allegiance as a king. The empire and vassal kingdom relationship between the Han court and the Nanyue kingdom continued until the latter ceased to exist.[1]

The spectacular tomb excavated in 1983 on the hill of Xianggang, west of Yuexiu Park in Guangzhou, was identified as the burial place of the second King of Nanyue, Zhao Mo, by the seals found among the funerary offerings. Zhao Mo was the grandson of Zhao Tuo and succeeded to the throne after his grandfather's sixty-seven year reign (r. 203–137 BC). Like his grandfather, he adopted the Han imperial title and referred to himself as Wendi (Emperor Wen, cat. 162).

Although there are very few written records about the Nanyue kingdom, it is clear that in many ways it was copying systems from the Han court. This can be seen from excavations that reveal the tomb structure, the bureaucratic system reflected in its inscriptions, the burial contents and the remains of a palace building.

The tomb of Zhao Mo was dug into the earth and then tunnelled into the rock of the hill to create six chambers for different functions. Utensils for daily use were found in the western chamber, which functioned as a storage room; musical instruments and banquet utensils were found in the eastern chamber, which functioned as living quarters; animal bones and the remains of seven human attendants were found in the western side chamber, which functioned as a kitchen (one of the attendants was identified as head chef from the seal found on her body); four concubines with luxurious burial jade pendants were found in the eastern side chamber; additional luxury personal objects, including pendants and seals were found in the main chamber, which functioned as the Nanyue king's bedroom; and cooking utensils and liquid containers were stacked behind the king's bedroom in a rear storage room. The tomb structure, its division into different chambers and the tomb contents bear a strong similarity to the tombs of members of the Han imperial Liu family.

Tomb contents included a pottery urn that bears the inscription *Changelegong qi* (utensil from the Eternal Happiness Palace, cat. 115), indicating that the Nanyue kingdom had a bureaucratic system copied from the Han court. This is confirmed by thirteen *feng ni* (clay seals) incised with *taiguan* (Grand Official) found in the rear storage room and five bronze *ding* incised with *Shaonei* (Privy Treasury, cat. 184) found in the rear chamber.

In addition, a set of eight bronze musical instruments, *goudiao*, incised with *wendi jiunian yuefu gongzao* (cast by the musicians of the Music Bureau in the ninth year of Emperor Wendi: 129 BC; cat. 116) reveals that Zhao Mo used his own calendar in his kingdom, but that it was copied from the Han system. However, no coins were found in his tomb or in the Guangzhou area in general, indicating that the Nanyue kingdom was still reliant on a primitive bartering system both within the kingdom and in trade with its neighbours.

The King of Nanyue collected many exotic objects and even practised Han imperial funeral rites, including the privileged use of a jade suit. His jade suit is composed of 2,291 jade plaques and can be divided into twelve parts like those of the imperial Liu family members (cat. 153), yet only the head, hands and feet were sewn together with silk thread. The jade plaques used for these parts were carefully cut and polished, while the other sections were prepared by pasting plaques onto linen, which was then used to cover the body. Almost all of the jade plaques used for the jacket and trouser sections are irregular in shape and of differing lengths. Most of them were reworked from discs and other jade objects. A disc was placed on top of the head. The nose is composed of triangular, trapezoidal and semi-circular plaques and is the only facial feature. No genital shroud or orifice plugs were found in his tomb.

Some scholars have raised doubts that the tomb owner was Zhao Mo as this name does not appear in any historical texts. Instead, the name of the second King of Nanyue is given as Zhao Hu (r. 137–122 BC), appearing eight times in Sima Qian's *Shiji* and seven times in Ban Gu's *Hanshu*. Since it seems unlikely that Sima Qian (141–86 BC) would have made such a mistake as he was almost contemporary with Zhao Hu, many believe the tomb occupant was another member from the same family.[2] Moreover, there was a considerable flow of communication between the Han court and the Nanyue kingdom, so a famous historian would likely have been clear about an important vassal leader's name. The scholar Haigui Wu has suggested that Zhao Mo may have been a king who reigned between Zhao Tuo and Zhao Hu.[3] However, this does not explain why his name was not mentioned in any texts. Sima Qian's records may not after all be comprehensive, as another omission has been identified. The tomb of Liu He, discovered in Xuzhou in 1996, can be dated to the early Western Han (*c.*179–141 BC), and Liu He was buried with a silver-thread jade suit. Like Zhao Mo, however, there is no reference to him in any textual records.

The tomb of the Nanyue king is the largest Han period tomb that has ever been found in the Guangzhou area. The scale is not as great as those of the imperial family members in Xuzhou but the contents reveal his unusual status, rivalling in material richness those of the Han imperial family. Nine seals made of gold and jade were found between his chest and stomach, on top of his jade suit. Traces of cinnabar lacquer indicate that these seals were kept inside a lacquer box. They include a gold seal with a dragon-shaped ornamental knob that is incised with *Wendi xing xi* (the imperial seal of Emperor Wendi; cat. 162), a jade seal incised with *taizi* (Crown Prince), a gold seal with *taizi* (cat. 163), a jade seal with Zhao Mo (cat. 160) and a jade seal with *di yin* (Seal of the Emperor; cat. 161). In addition there are three plain jade seals and one plain turquoise seal.

Apart from these seals, a long pendant set composed of thirty-two jade rings, pendants, figurines and gold, black, amber and glass beads was also found on the body, from the chest down to the stomach (fig. 38). Jade pendants were laid in the grave as part of the personal possessions of the deceased. They were also a mark of the deceased's status, with more intricate jade pendants reserved for people of higher status. For example, among the eleven sets of pendants excavated from the Nanyue king's tomb, the most elaborate belonged to the king himself, and among those found on his four concubines, the one on the body of 'Lady of the Right' is the finest (cat. 174).

Seals and pendants were common burial objects in tombs of the high-ranking elite from the late Warring States period to the Han. These objects, particularly seals, help archaeologists to identify the tomb owners' names and status and were probably intended as a method of identification in the world of the afterlife.[4] If no seals had been found in the tomb of the King of Nanyue, we might have mistaken him for Zhao Hu.

Unlike the imperial Liu princes who were buried with pottery terracotta warriors, no such figures were found in the tomb of the King of Nanyue or within this region. According to the *Shiji*, the neighbouring Minyue kingdom attacked the Nanyue kingdom during Zhao Hu's reign in

137 BC. Zhao Hu asked for help from the Han court but the invasion was halted before the Han army arrived when the King of Minyue was killed by his brother, who then surrendered to the Han court.[5] However, a tiger-shaped object known as a *jie* found in the Nanyue king's tomb provides evidence that the kingdom was an independent military power. *Jie* were used to convey orders and messages for military and diplomatic purposes. This example was modelled in the shape of a tiger inlaid with gold stripes on the body (cat. 143). The inscription can be read as 'The king orders the troops to muster'. Half of it was kept in the court and the other half with the military leader. The two halves of the *jie* had to be brought together in order to mobilize the troops. The fact that the Nanyue kingdom attacked the Changsha kingdom in revenge against Empress Lü is further evidence of its considerable military strength.[6]

As an independent kingdom at the edge of the powerful Han empire, the semi-sinicized Nanyue had to play a game of skilful diplomacy with the Han court in order to survive. It also built connections with foreign neighbours, evidenced by a Persian-style silver box believed to have been imported from Central Asia but which has a base that was added and incised with an inscription on the lid after it arrived in Nanyue (cat. 167). In addition, thirty-two gold ornaments decorated with flowers, of non-Chinese design, along with many glass beads, glass shells, gilded bronze bulbs and silver ornaments, were found on the three belts attached to the lower part of the Nanyue king's jade suit (cat. 158). A set of eight gold foil plaques was also found; they are decorated with two symmetrical sheep's heads in profile facing in opposite directions and a smaller sheep's head at the top depicted full face. All the plaques were embossed and pierced with tiny holes at the edges. They were sewn onto a veil used to cover the face of the Nanyue king; this design was clearly another Central Asian import (cat. 159). Almost identical examples have been excavated from Mancheng from the tomb of the first king of the kingdom of Zhongshan. Contact with Iran or Central Asia can also be shown by a jade rhyton based on the shape of a drinking vessel typical of those western lands, but made from a material that is distinctively Chinese (see fig. 6), and by the inclusion of a jade rhinoceros as part of a long pendant that belonged

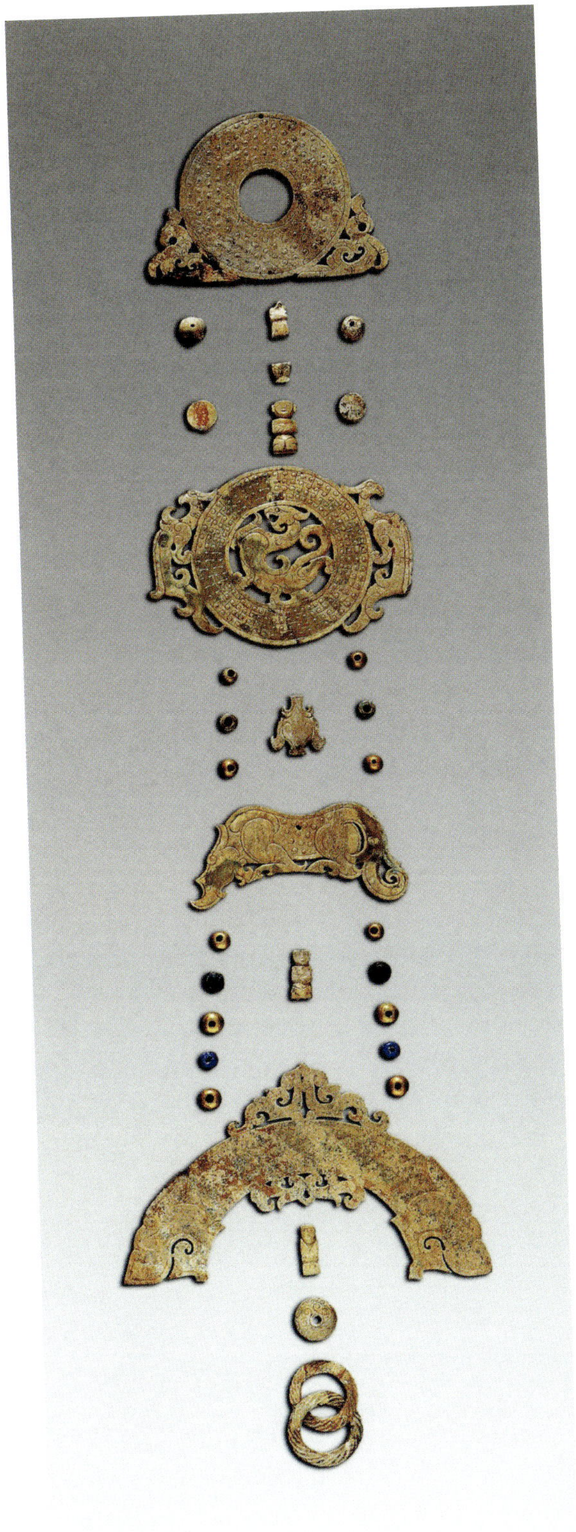

38 Jade pendant. Excavated from the tomb of the King of Nanyue, Guangzhou, Guangdong Province. Second century BC. Length: 60 cm.

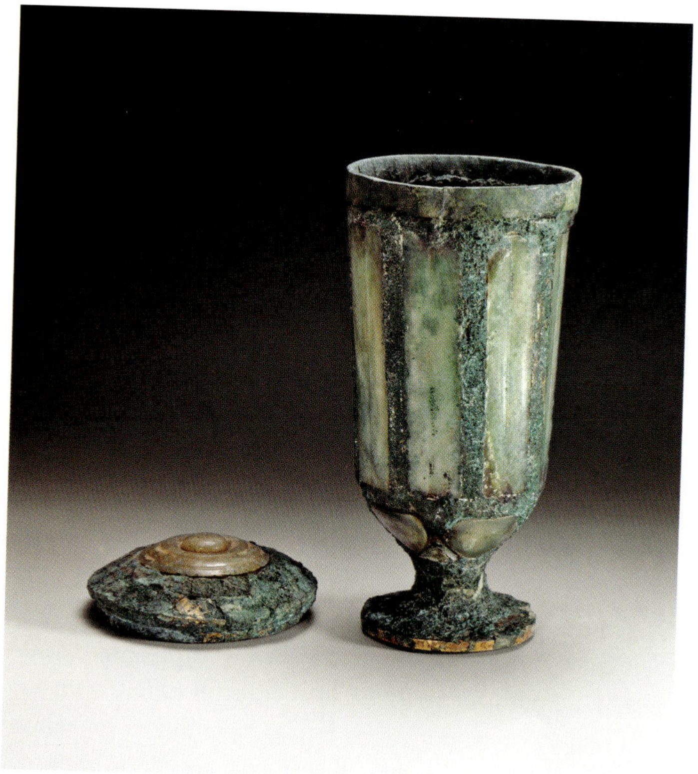

to the King of Nanyue (fig. 38). So far, we have no clue as to how these exotic objects, or the prototypes on which they were based, arrived in the southern Nanyue kingdom. It is possible that they came via the maritime silk route, as suggested by Hong Quan, director of the Museum of the Palace of Nanyue.

As well as exotic objects, antiques were also collected by the King of Nanyue. A large fifth-century BC bronze wine container (cat. 118) was found in the kitchen. Several objects, including mirrors that date several centuries earlier and from various regions, were collected and buried in his tomb (cat. 176, 177). In addition, traditional Chinese musical instruments, including a set of *yongzhong* consisting of five bells and a set of *niuzhong* composed of fourteen bells, were also found. These types of instruments were played during ritual banquets before the unification of China and had almost disappeared from the Han imperial princes' tombs by this time. Local Yue instruments, such as *goudiao* and percussion instruments that produced a rustling sound when shaken while dancing (cat. 150, 193), were also deposited in his tomb.

The rich burial objects from this tomb help us to understand the tastes and lifestyle of the Nanyue kingdom. Eating, drinking and music clearly played an important role in the Nanyue king's life. Bronze vessels from regions such as Chu and Han were collected and buried alongside local vessels from Yue (cat. 184–6). In addition, the Nanyue imperial kitchen had specific and idiosyncratic cooking utensils for roasting, baking and frying. Unusual low stoves with wide, flat rims were also found in the rear storeroom; each was supported on four owl-shaped legs and the four corners were tilted upwards to hold tongs or skewers for roasting meats (cat. 189). A large quantity of skeletons of domestic animals and seafood was found in four of the tomb chambers. These foods had been prepared as offerings to the tomb owner, his guests and four concubines. Moreover, a chef and some attendants were buried with the king to ensure his comfortable afterlife.

Like the majority of Han princes, the King of Nanyue was also obsessed with collecting jades. Apart from a jade suit, two jade discs were placed near his head, four between the chest and abdomen and another eight between the arms and the body. Exquisite jades with exaggerated designs, such as the one that has been adopted as the Museum of the King of Nanyue logo (see fig. 3), were placed over the king's right eye and a jade ornament based on the design of a bronze door-knocker was found on his forehead (cat. 171). Forty-three jade sword fittings were wrapped in red silk within a lacquered box and kept in the storage chamber. Only a small number of them show signs of having been used; the rest were from his personal collection. In addition, a jade box with a lid (cat. 165), a jade rhyton (see fig. 6) and a bronze drinking vessel inlaid with jade (fig. 39) were found in the space between the inner and outer coffins.

The search for immortality was a common preoccupation of emperors and princes soon after the unification of China. The first emperor of Qin was described as sending his court physician, Xu Fu, accompanied by thousands of young boys and girls, to search a distant island for the elixir of immortality. Emperor Wudi of the Han dynasty built a device for collecting dewdrops in the Jian Zhang Palace, as

39 Bronze drinking vessel inlaid with jade. Excavated from the tomb of the King of Nanyue, Guangzhou, Guangdong Province. Second century BC. Height: 16 cm.

he believed that drinking dew and jade powder from a jade cup conferred longevity.[7] A narrow-stemmed tubular jade cup with a bronze basin stand was found placed squarely in front of the outer coffin of the King of Nanyue (cat. 164). To its left was a lacquer cup with gilded bronze handles and to its right a deep bronze basin. All three were placed in a line in front of the outer coffin and were probably used in a sacrificial or burial ceremony. The tall jade cup is held upright by being placed through the hole in a quatrefoil jade disc, which itself is supported by three gold-headed silver feline dragons that soar upwards from the broad rim of a bronze basin. It is believed to be a device to collect dew so that it could be used to prepare a life-extending elixir.[8] In addition, a mortar, pestle and multi-coloured stones were found in the storage room (cat. 132). The drinking of elixirs to prolong life or even achieve immortality was widespread during this period and the multi-coloured stones are thought to represent drugs taken by the King of Nanyue to grant immortality.

If the tomb of the King of Nanyue had not been found by accident during construction work in 1983, this emperor would probably still remain unknown. Although written records about Zhao Hu are more limited than those referring to his grandfather, the rich materials excavated from his tomb highlight his achievements as ruler of an independent kingdom against a powerful Han empire. He successfully adopted both Han Chinese and local Yue cultures, and built links with the outside world.

NOTES

1 *Shiji*, pp. 2969–70
2 Wu 2000, pp. 72–7
3 Wu 2000, pp. 76–7
4 Rawson 1999, p. 11.
5 *Shiji*, p. 2970
6 *Shiji*, pp. 2969–70; *Hanshu*, p. 100
7 See *Shiji*, 'Wudi ji', p. 459.
8 Another two, almost identical examples of stemmed tubular jade cups were excavated in Guangxi and from the Epang Palace site at Chezhangcun in Xi'an city, Shaanxi, dating to the Qin dynasty, third century BC. See *Wenwu* 1978. 9, pp. 25–35; Hebei 1991–3, vol. 4, pl. 19; also see Beijing 1993a, pl. 64. This evidence shows that there is a standard type for this particular vessel.

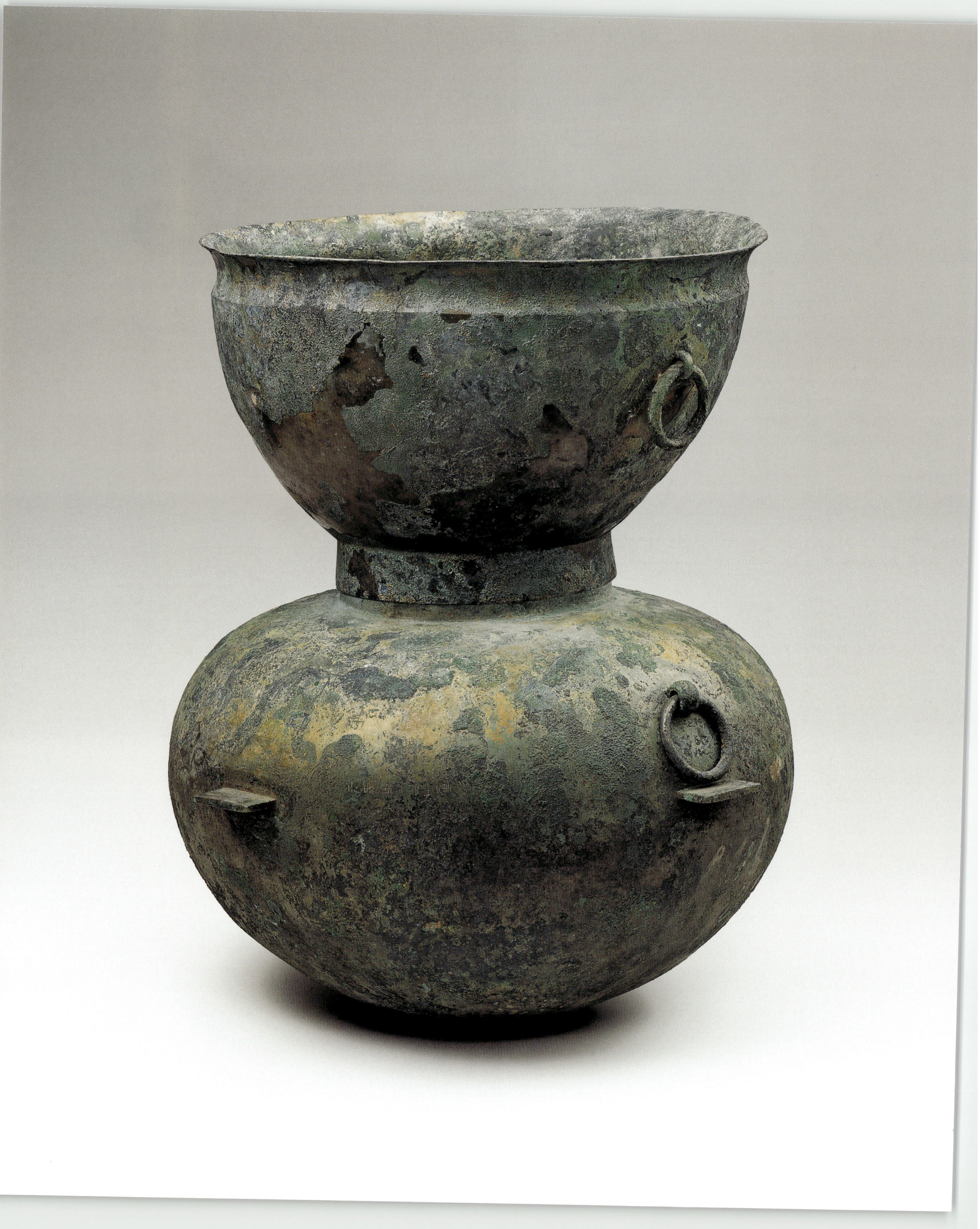

FEEDING IN THE AFTERLIFE

ROEL STERCKX

The interior spaces of Han tombs indicate a desire to perpetuate and replicate the welfare of the deceased in the afterlife. The idea that the living should comfort the dead and cater for their sensual pleasures beyond this life is manifest in several ways. First, multi-chambered elite tombs were architectural spaces constructed with a layout that mimicked the residences of the living. These structures could include entrance halls, bathrooms, a privy, food storage compartments and dining rooms, and each of the spaces could be equipped with appropriate grave furnishings and mortuary goods. Once a tomb was sealed, the intent was that its contents were never to be seen again by the living. Meticulous planning therefore preceded the closing of a tomb and, just as lavishing goods on the living in the form of feasts and luxury goods had sparked debate among philosophers and intellectuals ever since the Warring States period, so funerary expenditure forms a topic of perpetual discussion in texts of the period. Second, a central mechanism to help sustain the welfare of the departed was the presentation of food offerings. Ancestor worship in the form of sacrifices, a process also referred to as 'feeding' the dead,[1] constituted the single most important cultic practice. The presentation of offerings was a ritual procedure aimed at appeasing ancestral spirits and the spirit world at large. Successful communication with ancestral spirits or, to paraphrase a line from a poem in the *Shijing*, 'getting the spirits drunk',[2] required maintaining a sensory bond with those unseen forces through the careful selection of both sacrificial offerings and the techniques used to prepare and present them.

The belief that the dead needed to be fed inside the tomb and the expectation that they, in turn, would continue to offer sacrifice in the hereafter, emerges before the Han. The plan of the late fifth-century BC tomb, Changtaiguan Tomb 1, Xinyang, Henan, already allows for a kitchen compartment and storage room with food samples, cooking utensils and figurines of cooks and a servant.[3] A register of grave goods recovered from Tomb 2 at Baoshan, Jingmen, Hubei (burial dated *c*.316 BC) refers to the compartment east of the burial chamber containing the coffin as a 'food chamber' (*si/shishi*). This space may have served as a post-mortem dining room for the tomb occupant or, possibly, as a sacrificial hall where the departed would continue to receive offerings or feed their respective ancestors with sacrifices. The inventory itself spares no details regarding the provisions the tomb occupant could expect to enjoy: 'one basket of spiced dried meat, one basket of sliced dried meat, one jar of wren mincemeat, one jar of honey, two jars of scallions, one jar of chives, one jar of water chestnuts, one jar of honeyed plums, one jar of honeyed meat mince, one container of sliced meat mince, one container of dried fish mincemeat.'[4]

As the locus for ancestral rituals gradually shifted from the lineage temple to the actual gravesite over the course of the Eastern Zhou, by Han times tombs increasingly included spaces designated as post-mortem sacrificial chambers.[5] The rock-cut tomb of Liu Sheng, King of Zhongshan (d. 112 BC) at Mancheng (present-day Hebei) contained a large rectangular room arranged as a hall for sacrificial banquets. It included two empty seats, possibly designed for the souls of the king and his consort, and sacrificial vessels and figurines were lined up to imitate the scene of a sacrificial offering.[6] Similarly, in the northern compartment of Mawangdui Tomb 1, Changsha, Hunan (closed 168 BC), a seating mat was laid out for the occupant, Lady Dai, in front of a tray with lacquer tableware. An entire meal was

FACING PAGE: DETAIL OF CAT. 52

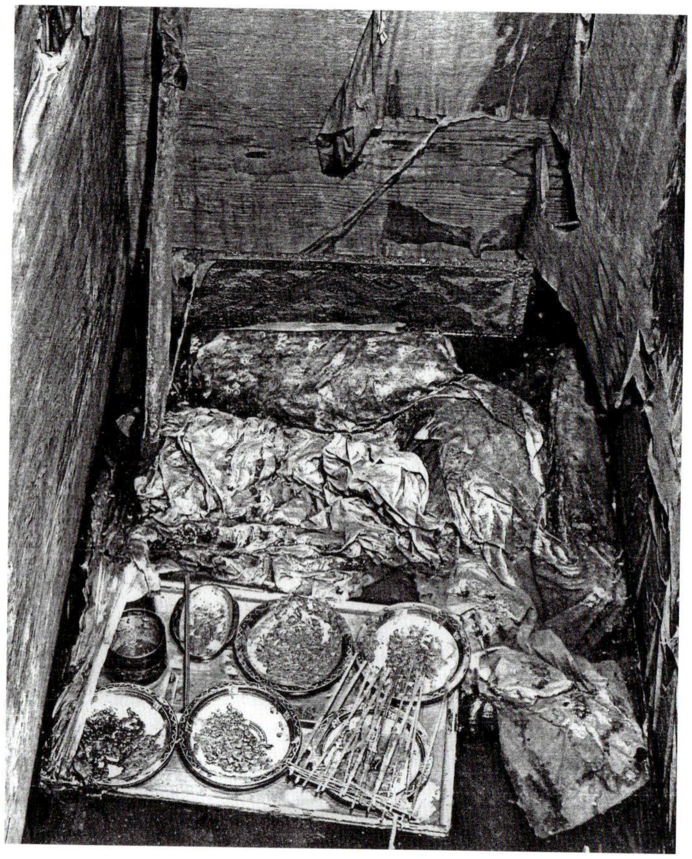

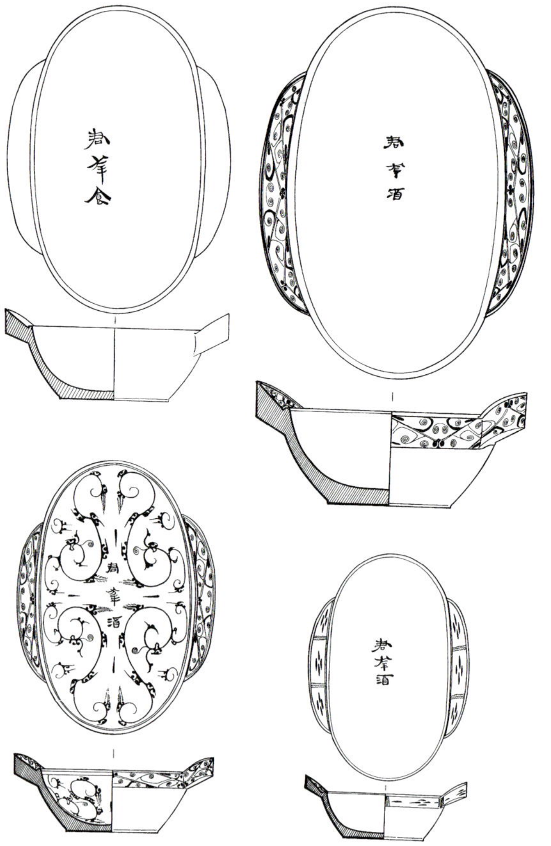

served on the tray, complete with cups, goblets, bamboo skewers and a pair of bamboo chopsticks (fig. 40). Inscriptions on the plates and cup reading 'food for the enjoyment of the master/mistress' and 'ale for the enjoyment of the master/mistress' (fig. 41) indicate that they were meant to hold ingredients for the gastronomic delight of the tomb occupant. The tomb further contained an extensive sample of food containers, cooking utensils, food vessels and over three hundred inventory slips identifying foodstuffs and food vessels.[7]

Catering personnel too could follow the departed to the afterlife. The Han prince buried at Shizishan north-west of Xuzhou, Jiangsu, was interred together with his cook. Seals of catering officials with the titles 'Inspector of Food Officers' (*shiguanjian*; cat. 28) and 'Food Official from Chu' (*Chu shiguan*) were recovered from the tomb.[8] At Yangling, near Xi'an, seals of catering officers were recovered from the mausoleum of Han emperor Jingdi (r. 157–141 BC), which also contained an underground granary.[9]

In addition to lacquered tableware, food containers and actual or figurine replicas of kitchen and catering staff and a host of other funerary goods could accompany the dead. These included ceramic vessels and earthenware replicas (*mingqi*) of kitchen stoves, water-wells, storehouses, granaries and animals. The Yangling pits revealed a hitherto unmatched assembly of pottery farmyard animals and livestock including chickens, roosters, dogs, pigs, goats, sheep, horses and oxen. The figurines were lined up in rows and flocks by species.[10] Remnants of food and samples of desiccated millet contained in pottery granaries suggest that these supplies were entombed with a wish to supply food and wealth in the afterlife.[11] Noticeable among Han grave furnishings are the wide range of miniature pottery stoves and replicas of entire cooking ranges and kitchen sheds. Some of these

40 Food and lacquerware. Found in the northern compartment of tomb M1, Mawangdui, Changsha, identified as a reception hall. After Beijing 1973, vol. 2, pl.11.

41 Inscriptions on cups reading: 'May you enjoy the food!' and 'May you enjoy the wine!' (cat. 57). From tomb M1, Mawangdui, Changsha. After Beijing 1973, vol. 2, pl. 191.

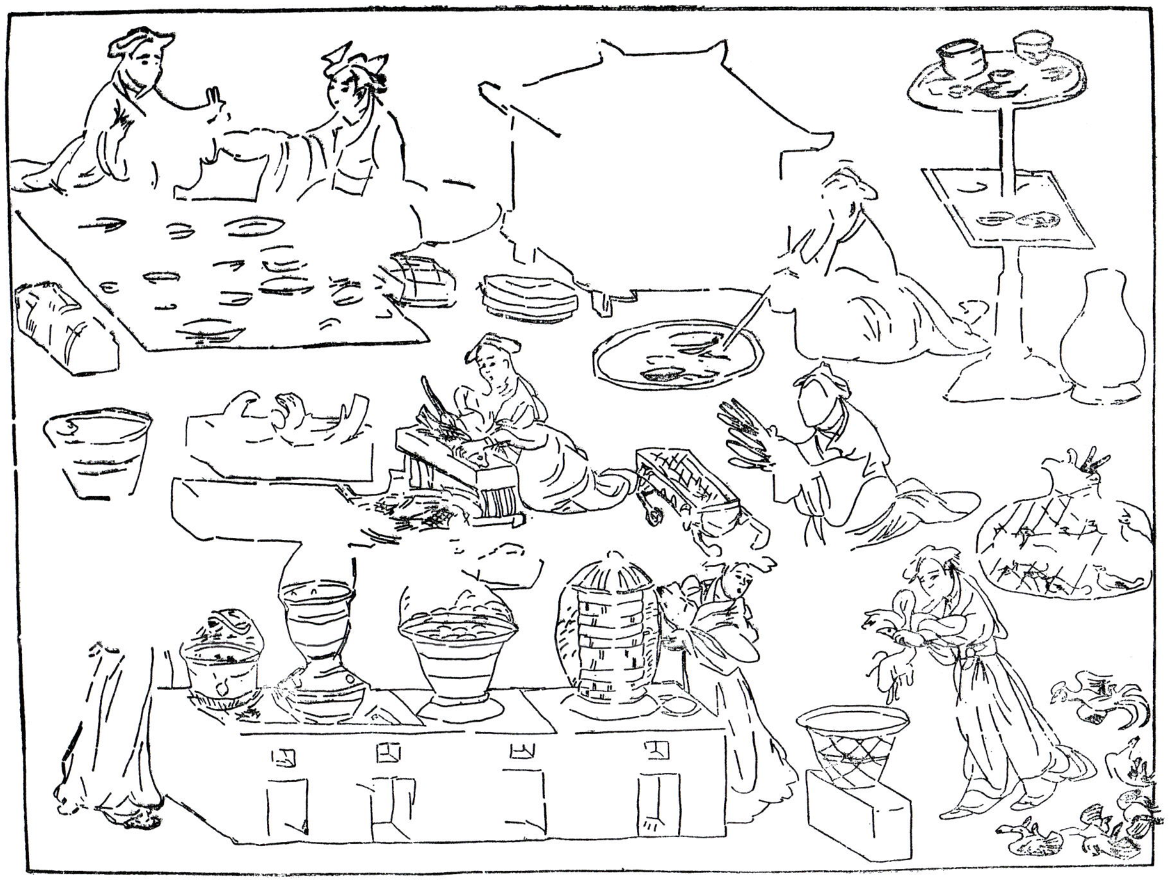

models contain kitchen furniture, cupboards, screen walls and chimneys.[12] It appears that miniature replicas of buildings and objects that would ensure continued economic and material welfare in the afterlife (farmyards, granaries, privies, stoves, etc.) occupied a significant place in Han funerary culture.

Not unimportant in this context is that many tombs also include texts written on silk or bamboo among their grave goods. Scholars have put forward several hypotheses regarding the function of texts buried in tombs and, in some cases, their physical location within. In many cases, however, one can only speculate why certain texts have ended up in certain tombs. Yet judging by their content we must assume that some of these texts were buried with the intention that they would help secure good health and wellbeing for the deceased in the afterlife. Given that the boundaries between food as nutrition and food as medicine were often blurred, securing good health through, for instance, a balanced diet, may have been one of the reasons that prompted the inclusion of medical treatises and self-cultivation literature at Mawangdui Tomb 3. One recently uncovered tomb of a noble man of Yuanling (*c.*187–162 BC) buried at Huxishan, Wuling, Hunan contained recipes for the preparation of food.[13]

Finally, another way in which elites could perpetuate conviviality and hospitality beyond this life was by decorating their tombs with murals depicting cooks, kitchens and banquets.[14] Tomb 2 at Dahuting, Mixian county, Henan (late Eastern Han, *c.*AD 160–90) contained a painted banquet scene in its central chamber, and a detailed kitchen scene is preserved on a wall in Tomb 1 at the same cemetery complex (fig. 42), possibly containing the earliest visual representation

42 Detailed kitchen scene. Preserved on a wall in tomb No. 1 at Dahuting, Mixian county, Henan Province. Late Eastern Han, *c.*AD 160–90. After Beijing 1993b, fig. 143.

of the fermentation of bean curd (*doufu*). Scholars have suggested that the emphasis in murals on banquets and festive occasions involving the hosting of guests reflects the relatively high rank of the tomb occupants.[15]

Yet tomb architecture, funerary goods and decorative scenes in the form of murals were not the only mechanisms to ensure that the deceased would continue to be catered for in the afterlife. The most important act of religious worship to sustain a bond between the living and the departed was the presentation of sacrificial food offerings. Food offerings and sacrificial rituals forged a sensory bond with ancestral spirits, yet the nature of the relationship between the living and the dead was not uncontroversial: in fact, it was marked by an ambivalent tension. On the one hand, to bury someone (*Zang*) meant, to paraphrase the 'Book of Rites' (*Liji*), to 'hide' (*cang*) the corpse away and conceal the dead for ever from the eyes of the living.[16] Thus the deceased had to be appeased and placated in luxury tombs and receive offerings to ensure they would not return and avenge themselves. On the other hand, by presenting the dead with food offerings a sensory bond and obligation to the living was created, and this relationship needed to be mediated by ritual specialists. In short, in order to placate the spirits and ultimately keep them at bay, worshippers were obliged to seek a spirit response though the medium of the sanctified food offering. Laying out offerings for the spirits, however, did not invariably mean that the spirits would actually consume them and respond fortuitously. Success in feeding the spirits depended on several factors, including the correct timing of the procedure in the ritual calendar, the proper selection and preparation of offerings, the order in which sacrificial dishes and platters were presented and the site where they would be displayed.

According to third- and second-century BC liturgies associated with the southern state of Chu, some may have held the belief that, prior to burial, the souls of the recently departed could be recalled and persuaded to rejoin the body when reminded of the gustatory pleasures they enjoyed while alive. The canonized version of this soul-summoning ritual describes how, between the point of death and prior to burial, a priest would mount the roof of the deceased's house to recall the ethereal *hun* soul. Reminding the departed of the feasts enjoyed during life was clearly thought to be an effective means to help secure their return, as the 'Great Summons' (*Dazhao*) intones:

> Oh soul, come back! Indulge your appetite!
> Fresh turtle, succulent chicken, dressed with the sauce of Chu;
> Pickled pork, dog cooked in bitter herbs, and ginger-flavoured mince,
> And sour Wu salad of artemisia, not too wet or tasteless.
> Oh soul, come back! Indulge in your own choice!
> Roast crane next is served, steamed duck and boiled quails,
> Fried bream, stewed magpies, and green goose, broiled.
> Oh soul, come back! Choice things are spread before you.
> Four kinds of wine have been subtly blended, not rasping to the throat.
> Clear, fragrant, ice-cool liquor, not for base men to drink;
> And white yeast has been mixed with must of Wu to make the clear Chu wine.
> O soul, come back and do not be afraid![17]

After death and prior to burial, the oral cavity of the corpse was stuffed with jade or shells according to rank. According to the *Liji* the mouth of the Son of Heaven was stuffed with nine shells, that of a feudal lord with seven, that of a grandee with five and that of an officer with three pieces.[18] The ritual canon also specifies the number of food baskets and types of food the dead were entitled to depending on their rank and status.[19] What might look like simply plugging up the oral cavity may have had a significance related to the act of feeding the corpse, since the ritual code refers to it as a process in which one *fan* 'feeds' the oral cavity. Prescriptions to plug the oral cavity with uncooked grains, shells or a jade pearl possibly expressed the desire to continue feeding one's superior or soon-to-be ancestor beyond the extent of this life. 'Since a person has eaten as a living being,' one Han text notes, 'now that he is dead, one does not wish to leave his mouth empty, and therefore it is filled.'[20] However, beneath this at first sight well-intended attempt to ensure continuity with the departed also lurks a wish to placate the corpse before burial and avoid the wrath of potentially unhappy ancestors. Reports suggest that the custom of feeding the corpse may have survived in modern times, although its link to classical funerary ritual is not certain. Modern anthropology has documented that in the early 1980s Taiwan mourners still put food in the mouths of the deceased or used chopsticks to present items of food that are touched to their lips.[21]

But what offerings were deemed most efficient in feeding the spirit world? One Han author remarks that when spirits appreciate offerings they do so because essentially spirits 'eat vapour' (*shiqi*).[22] Some texts suggest that, in terms of the efficiency and reach of sacrificial offerings, there existed a direct relationship between flavour and memory. In other words, living ritual participants and their immediate ancestors may appreciate the flavour conveyed by a particular food offering, but more distant ancestors and more intangible spirits prefer ethereal ingredients above individual physical foodstuffs. The most powerful offerings therefore are those that belong to the realm of fragrance or *qi*. For instance, offerings containing blood – tasteless, bland, uncooked and pure – are highly valued because blood was thought to be a good conduit of *qi*.[23] Fragrance, smell or scent appears to take precedence over flavour. The more elevated the recipient of a sacrifice, the more vapour is to be conveyed through the offerings. The dichotomy between flavour and vapour sets apart human participants from the spirits, as one passage in the *Guanzi* makes clear:

> On the *gengzi* day [the 217th day in a sacrificial cycle] the phase of metal takes control. The Son of Heaven issues orders and commands the priest in charge of sacrifices to select suitable animals and birds from their sacrificial pens and suitable offerings of early ripening grains to present in ancestral temples and the five household sacrifices. Ghosts and spirits will absorb the *qi* contained in them, whereas gentlemen [the human participants in the ritual] will enjoy their taste [*wei*].[24]

It is not easy to link sacrificial models prescribed in texts to concrete practice, let alone to attempt the matching of archaeological evidence to references in texts (a methodological approach that is not without controversy in itself). For instance, it remains hard to establish whether certain foodstuffs were exclusively destined for spirit consumption or whether, as ritual texts intimate, most offerings were to be shared by humans in sacrificial banquets at the end of the procedure. We know that a rich variety of stews was consumed in Han times by most social strata, from noblemen to commoners. They could include meat, fish, vegetables and cereals or, according to manuscripts uncovered at Mawangdui, ingredients as rich as ox, sheep, deer, pig, carp, sturgeon, wild duck and pheasant. Some sources speak of stews that include turtle, dog, rabbit and quail. Yet against this diversity of ingredients and worldly flavours, ritual literature insists that the bland and unseasoned stew (*geng*) is the most highly valued dish in sacrifice and that, ultimately, flavourless offerings and water should take precedence over well-seasoned sacrifices and ale. Offerings that are insipid and bland are said to transcend the powers of ordinary foodstuffs.[25] Interestingly, the diet prescribed to descendants during the mourning period seems to mirror the same paradigms. The height of the mourning period is punctuated by a short period of total abstention that was gradually alleviated by the intake of gruel, solid foods, fruits and vegetables and, ultimately, meat and ale. Mourners progressively returned to a full diet, via a vegetarian stage, as they gradually distanced themselves from the departed in the tomb and re-entered the world of the living and its habitual cuisine.[26]

Leaving the contents of offerings aside, facilitating the transfer of sacrificial offerings to the spirits required human agency. One ritual functionary who was central to help ensure that the dead partook of their offerings was known as the 'corpse' or 'representative of the dead' (*shi*). This was a living descendant of the deceased who acted as a proxy of the ancestral spirits. The impersonator physically mimics the ancestral spirits and gives form to invisible spirits during a sacrifice. He tastes and drinks from the offerings, moves and speaks on behalf of the dead and toasts the living clan members during the banquet that follows the sacrifice.[27] Once the impersonator has symbolically tasted the offerings, the leftovers are consumed by the ritual participants in a cascading order according to status. The consumption of tangible sacrificial leftovers was a mechanism to establish sensory contact with an invisible spirit world through the medium of the impersonator.[28]

While the dead may have been comfortable in their tombs, for the living a great deal of apprehension continued to surround the performance of sacrificial rituals, despite the meticulous preparations that preceded them. Indeed, the obligation to establish contact with the spirits in an effort to placate them went hand in hand with fears and uncertainties about the efficacy of the goods on offer and the type of response they would provoke from the spirits. Feeding the spirits was a process marked by doubts and insecurity among the ritual participants. Once the offerings were set forth, repeated announcements had to be made, each performed with reverence and care as if the spirits were spatially present. Yet a spirit response was no immediate guarantee, as the following passage illustrates:

> Within the great ancestral temple reverence prevailed. The ruler personally led the victim forward while the grandees assisted and followed, carrying the offerings of silk. While the ruler personally took charge of the preliminary sacrificial preparations, his wife presented the dish in which [the offering] would be presented. The ruler personally cut up the victim, while his wife presented the sacrificial ale. The ministers and grandees followed the ruler and ordered their wives to follow the ruler's wife. How grave and solemn was their reverence! How absorbing their serenity! How intense was their desire that [the spirits] would accept the offerings! The arrival of the victim was announced [to the spirits] in the courtyard; upon presentation of the blood and the flesh with the hair on it, an announcement was made [to the spirits] in the chamber; when the sacrificial stew was ready, it was announced [to the spirits] in the hall. Announcements were made thrice, each time in a different place; indicating how they were seeking for the spirits but had not yet found them. Then the sacrifice was set forth in the hall, and was repeated outside the gate of the temple; and thus arose the saying, 'Are they in there? Are they over here?'[29]

Before being able to feed the spirits, these invisible and intangible forces had to be located near the site of worship. And to ensure that spirits would make themselves visible near a tomb, shrine or ancestral hall, the worshippers were under a continuous obligation to provide ritual maintenance. For all the ritual paraphernalia and tomb furnishings that could be lavished on the dead, the presentation of sacrifice demanded more than material requirements. The offering of sacrifice to the departed also required empathy and mental concentration from the ritual participants. Sacrifices were most likely to reach those for whom they were intended when the living descendants could mentally recall the place where the ancestors used to sit, remember how they smiled or spoke, what intentions and ideas they had, what they found pleasurable and what they relished.[30] Feeding the spirits therefore was about more than simply placating the dead. Sacrificial ritual reinforced hierarchies among the living descendants and strategies for commemoration among ritual participants. Without feasting the spirits – to conclude with one Han text – there could be no feasting among the living: 'It is permissible to sacrifice first and hold a banquet afterwards. Yet banqueting first and sacrificing afterwards is not permissible.'[31]

NOTES

1 Wang 1998, p. 66.143
2 *Mao shi zhengyi*, p. 13B.4a–16a
3 Beijing 1986b, 18–20, pls 46, 71, 112.
4 Hubei 1991, p. 37 (slip 251); Lai 2002, pp. 49–50. For the inventory see Cook 2006, pp. 214–15 (slip 255).
5 Wu 1988, pp. 78–115. For a critique of the argument, see Lewis 2006, pp. 119–30.
6 Wu 2010b, pp. 28–9, 67–8, 86–7.
7 Pirazzolli-t'Serstevens 1991, pp. 209–19.
8 Beijing 2005, pp. 52, 70.
9 *Kaogu yu wenwu* 2008.3, pp. 27–8.
10 Chongqing 2001, pp. 10–12, 24–5, 51–9, 154.
11 For a typology of pottery granaries and storehouses see Guo 2010, pp. 86–104.
12 Guo 2010, pp. 110–14.
13 *Wenwu* 2003.1, pp. 36–55.
14 Wang 1995, pp. 125–63.
15 Pirazzolli-t'Serstevens 2010, p. 84, fig. 2.8, pp. 107–9, pp. 168–9 (colour pl. 10).
16 *Liji jijie*, 9.227 (Tan gong).
17 *Chuci jin zhu* 1997, p. 247; tr. Hawkes 1985, pp. 234–5.
18 *Liji jijie*, 42.1110 (*Za ji xia*).
19 *Liji jijie*, 44.1183 (*Sang da ji*).
20 *Baihutong shu zheng*, 11.548 (*Beng hong*).
21 Thompson 1988, p. 83.
22 *Shuowen jiezi*, 8B.26a.
23 *Liji jijie*, 26.711, 26.717.
24 *Guanzi jiaozhu*, 14.876 (*Wu xing*).
25 Sterckx 2011, pp. 16–17, 84–95.
26 Sterckx 2011, pp. 32–4.
27 *Yili zhushu*, 42.8a–14a (*Shi yu li*); *Liji jijie*, 19.542 (*Zengzi wen*).
28 *Liji jijie*, 47.1242 (*Ji tong*).
29 *Liji jijie*, 24.663–665 (*Li qi*)
30 *Liji jijie*, 46.1208–9, 46.1210 (*Ji yi*).
31 *Huainanzi honglie jijie*, 16.551 (*Shui shan*).

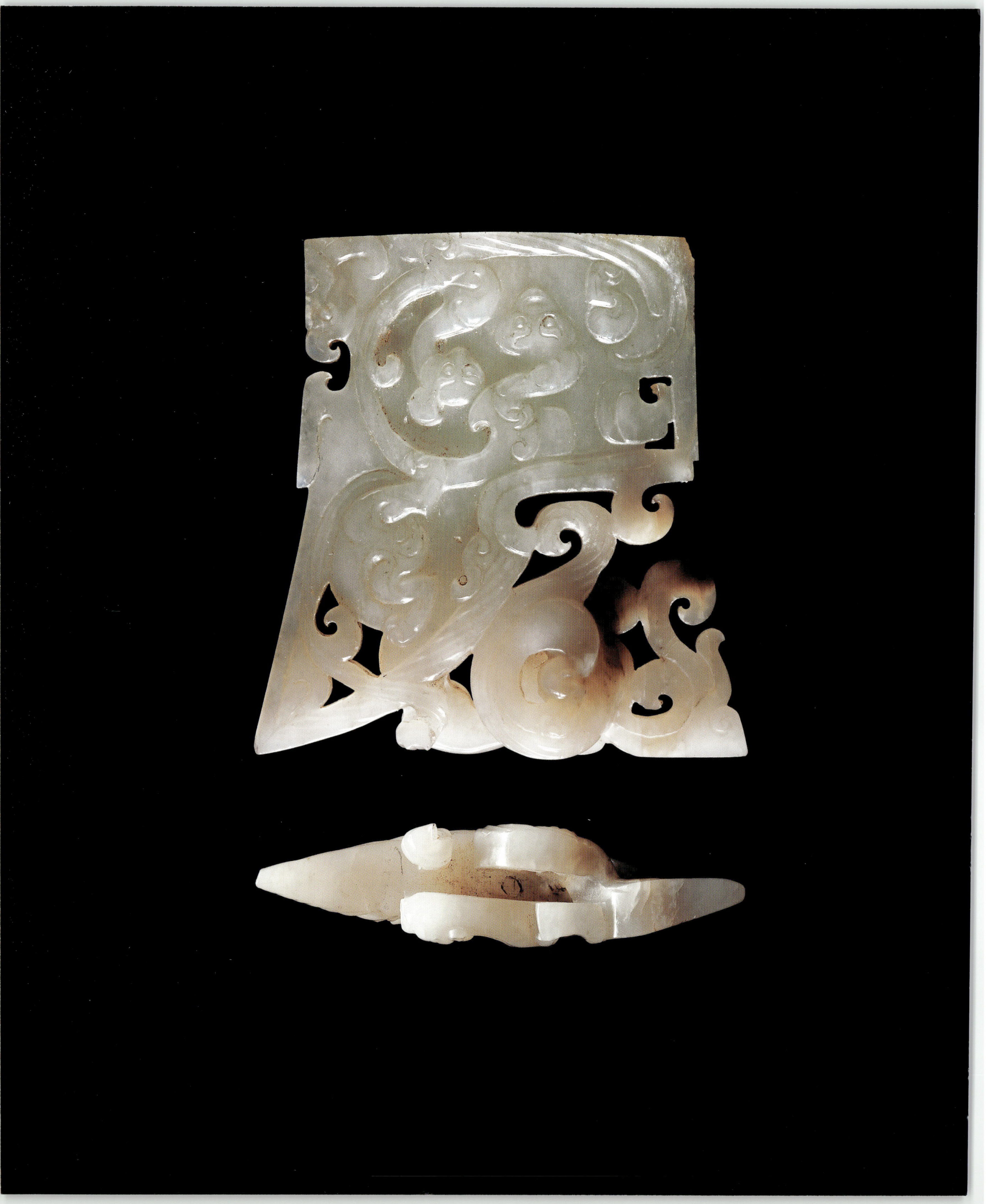

PROTECTION IN THE AFTERLIFE

JAMES C. S. LIN

The structure and arrangement of the contents within tombs of the Han period present two aspects for consideration: first, the tomb was designed both as a dwelling and as a universe for the afterlife; and second, it was a place in which the maximum possible protection for the deceased and his afterlife within the tomb was required.

The intact tombs of the Kings of Zhongshan in Mancheng, Hebei and Nanyue in Guangzhou and surviving weapons from imperial tombs in Xuzhou clearly indicate that the tomb was thought to require protection from intruders and any other form of disturbance. The tomb of Liu Sheng, for example, was dug into a rocky mountainside and its entrance has two walls of pounded earth and a cast-iron door. For the King of Nanyue a stone gate with a self-locking device in the floor was installed. Large stone blocks were used to block the tomb passages of tombs at Shizishan and Beidongshan, Xuzhou (fig. 43). In addition, bronze self-locking devices were commonly found in most of the imperial tombs during the Han period (cat. 11).

More than 200 tomb guardians with miniature weapons were installed in niches along the passage in Beidongshan, protecting the tomb from any intruders (see fig. 26). As one approached the rear chamber the number and variety of weapons increased. For example, three bronze swords, a dagger, knife, crossbow, arrowheads, four iron swords, two halberds, a spear, bow and armour were found in Liu Sheng's rear chamber. The entrance to the rear chamber was blocked with a thick stone slab that was fitted with a self-locking device. Two iron swords and one knife accompanied Liu Sheng, who was buried inside a jade suit. On the western side of the King of Nanyue's coffin, four iron swords, seven iron spears, a pair of iron halberds, a bronze dagger and one unidentifiable iron weapon were found. Fifteen bronze crossbows, arrowheads and lead pellets were also found nearby. Ten iron swords, half of them decorated with jade fittings, were found next to the jade suit. Fourteen jade discs – thought to have protective power – were placed inside the jade suit and another five underneath it. In addition, 139 discs made of pottery were piled up in the space near the feet (cat. 157; fig. 44). These pottery discs are likely to be substitutes for jade versions, as a pottery disc was buried with a servant in the western side chamber. However, the most unusual burial items from these imperial members' tombs are weapons made of jade (cat. 19), found in the tombs at Shizishan, Xuzhou, at Yongcheng, Henan and at Qufu, Shandong.

Large quantities of weapons were commonly found in Han tombs, emphasizing the tomb occupant's desire for protection in the afterlife. These well-designed defence systems call to mind the description of the First Qin Emperor's mausoleum at Lishan by Sima Qian: 'Replicas of palaces, scenic towers, and the hundred officials, as well as rare utensils and wonderful objects, were brought to fill up the tomb. Craftsmen were ordered to set up crossbows and arrows, rigged so they would immediately shoot down anyone attempting to break in'.[1]

Bronze crossbows and arrowheads have often been found in the passages, stables, ceremonial chambers and rear chambers of tombs. These types of weapons seem to have been popular devices for countering spectral attacks.[2] Therefore, it appears that the tomb was guarded as much against spirits as mortal robbers.

The *Jie* ('Spellbinding') section of daybooks from the Shuihudi bamboo slips (the burial has been dated to 217 BC) instructs people on how to protect themselves from

FACING PAGE: DETAIL OF CAT. 20C

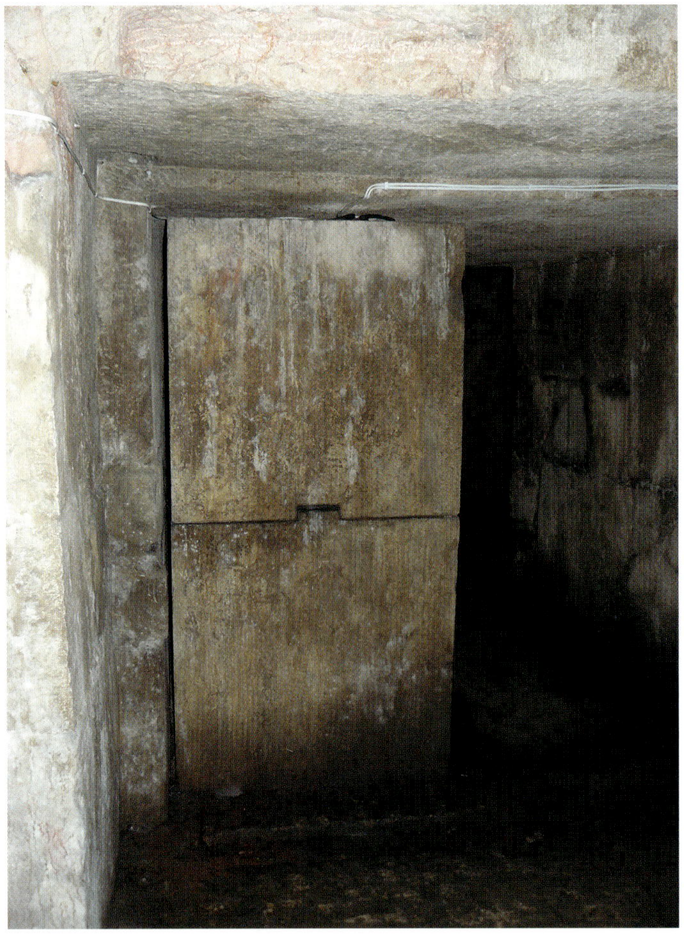

demons. Similar records were also seen in the *Wushier bing fang* ('Recipes for fifty-two ailments') from Mawangdui.[3] The slips reveal that during these centuries peoples in the south, and probably elsewhere, believed that demonic intrusion was a significant cause of illness to the living. Therefore, magical, exorcistic recipes were used for compounding drugs and therapeutic treatments taken to cure the disease.[4]

It is very likely that, instead of believing that decomposition was a natural process, the Han people may have thought that the body decomposed due to attack by evil spirits. A ritual was recorded in the *Zhouli*, in which the *Fangxiangshi* shaman enters the tomb wearing an animal skin and mask and uses a spear to attack the demon *fangliang*.[5] This rite was performed before the burial of the dead and was intended to protect the corpse from attack by demons. It was imperative to purify the grave and make it safely habitable for the dead. This custom was clearly explained by an Eastern Han text, *Fengsu tongyi* ('Comprehensive Meaning of Customs' by Ying Shao, *c.*140–206 BC) as follows:

> On the tomb a thuja is planted and at the head of the path a stone tiger. The *Chou li* (says), 'On the day of burial the *fang-hsiang* enters the pit to drive out the *Wang-hsiang*'. The *Wang-hsiang* likes to eat the liver and brain of the deceased. People cannot constantly have the *fang-hsiang* stand by the side of the tomb to bar it. But the *Wang-hsiang* fears the tiger and the thuja. Thus the tiger and thuja are placed before the tomb.[6]

From the daybooks we know that these demons could be expelled or even killed. Many of the preparations of the tomb may have been intended to prevent demons from attacking the deceased's body, causing it to decompose. Weapons such as bows, arrows, swords, armour, white stone and peachwood were also commonly recorded in bamboo slips.[7]

Apart from the actual weapons and security devices found in high-ranking tombs, images of demon quellers and guardian animals were also found on the coffins of lower-ranking tombs.[8] A famous example was found in Lady Dai's tomb at Changsha, Hunan, dating to the early second century BC. Two of her coffins were decorated with strange horned creatures that were depicted devouring snakes, presumably to protect the tomb occupant (fig. 45). The inner coffin carried images of dragons, tigers and other auspicious beings. We know from texts that the interest in deities and fear of spirits and demons during the Han period was founded on beliefs already well entrenched in the southern Chu area during the Warring States period. The use of images in tombs to protect the dead also developed from this time.

The most prominent example is the decoration on coffins from the fifth century BC tomb of Marquis Yi of Zeng (fig. 46). The inner coffin was painted with doors and windows. Each of the painted creatures on the inner coffin holds a *ge* halberd in its claws, with the points of the *ge* directed away from the openings. They were obviously intended to

43 Large stone slabs blocking a tomb passage at Beidongshan, Xuzhou, Jiangsu Province.

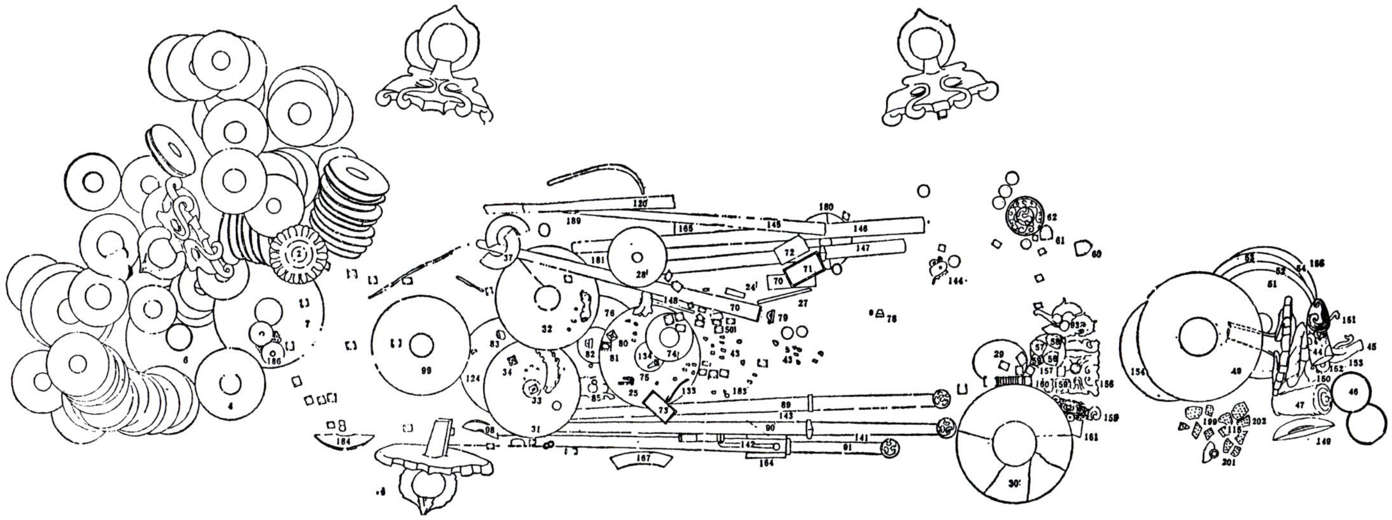

be in charge of the doors and should be regarded as guardians.[9] Apart from the images on the inner coffin, more than 4,500 bronze weapons were also found in this tomb.[10]

The founder of the Han dynasty, Liu Bang, came from the present-day Xuzhou area, which is located in eastern China, but ruled by the Chu state during the late Warring States period. While the Han adopted artefacts and practices from many parts of the empire they ruled, the objects and burial practices of Qi and Lu in the east and Chu in the south played particularly significant roles.[11] These included the method that they used to protect the body, the fear of demons mentioned and an interest in jades.

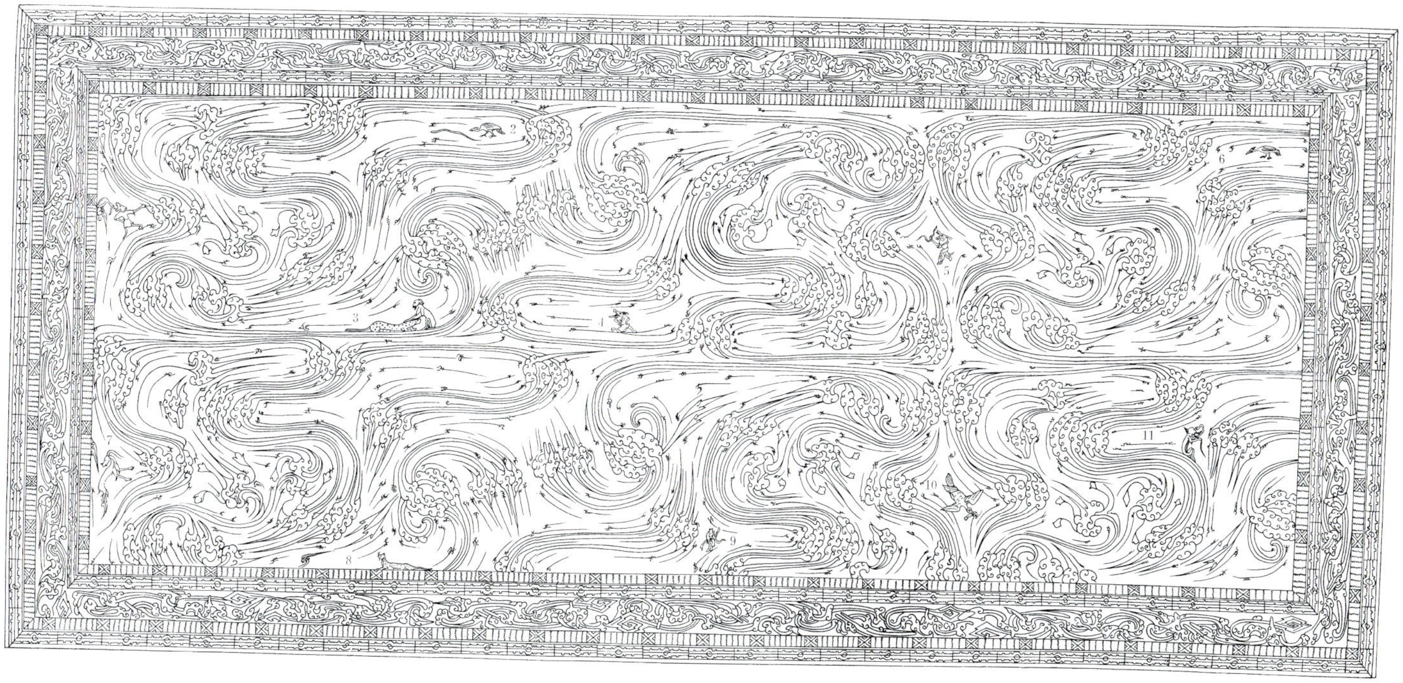

44 (above) Line drawing showing the position of 139 pottery discs piled up in the space near the feet of the King of Nanyue in his tomb, Guangzhou, Guangdong Province. After Beijing 1991, vol. 1, fig. 99.

45 (below) Coffin decorated with horned creatures devouring snakes, presumably to protect the tomb occupant. From Mawangdui, Changsha. After Beijing 1973, vol. 1, pp. 19–20, pls 18, 19.

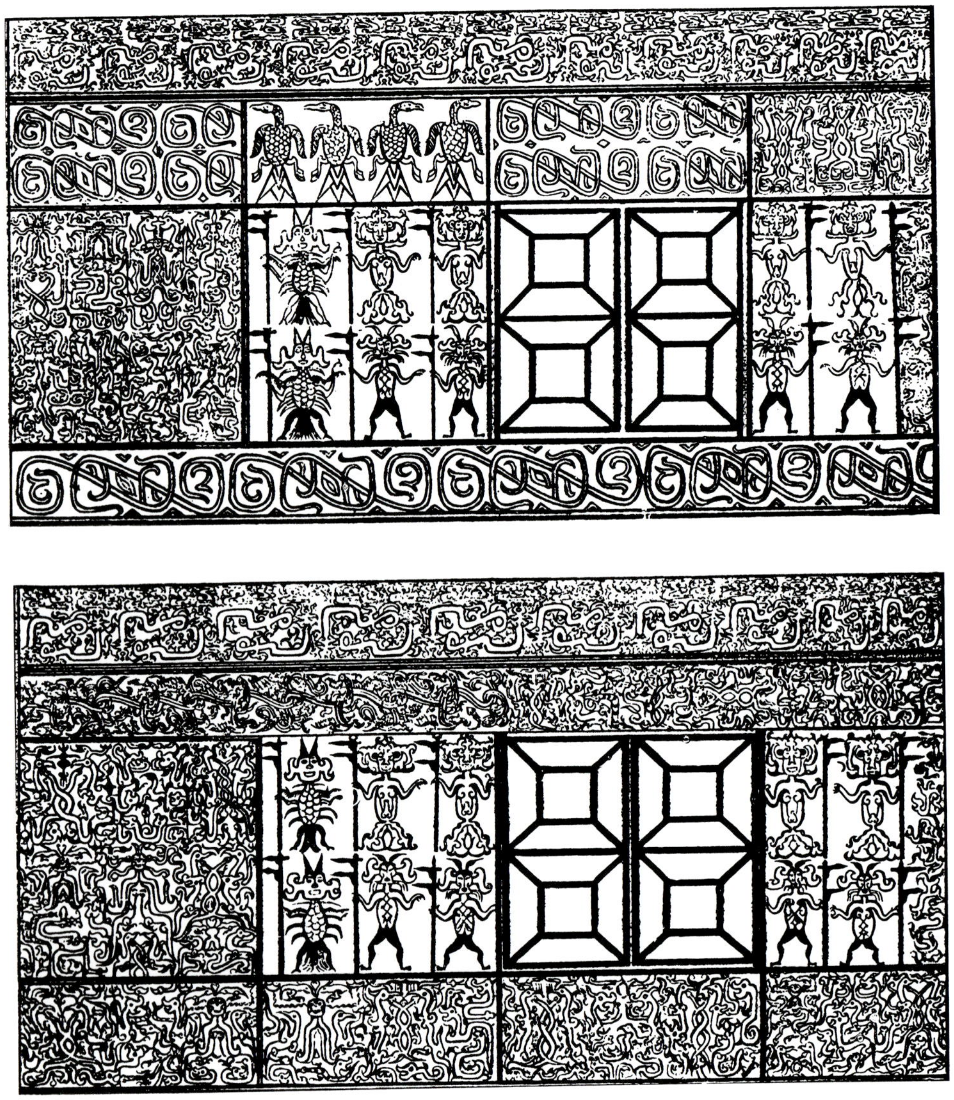

Stone and jade played an important role in Han imperial burial practices because they are permanent and unchanging. In addition, from some contemporary texts and bamboo slips we know that the ancient Chinese people regarded stones and jade as offering a defence against demons and spirits.

In the imperial family members' tombs that have been excavated, jade and other stones were used almost obsessively near the bodies of the Liu princes to protect them from demons. Stone was used for the chambers, furniture and some figures of auspicious animals, while jade was employed for suits, discs, pendants, seals, weapons, vessels and also inlaid on coffins. These jades were found close to the body of imperial family members, where jade plugs (cat. 91) also were inserted into the nine orifices before the body was covered with jade discs (cat. 88, 89) and then encased by a jade suit (cat. 87), which was placed inside a lacquered wood coffin that was sometimes inlaid with jade discs or plaques (cat. 98). In this way, the whole body was completely covered with several layers of jades.

46 Decoration on the two long sides of the inner coffin of the Marquis Yi of Zeng (d. 433 BC). Excavated from Leigudun, Suixian, Hubei Province. After Thote 1991, p. 37, fig. 17.

In the Han period, Liu An's (*c.*180–122 BC) *Huainan wanbishu* ('The Ten Thousand Infallible Arts of the Prince of Huainan') mentions that burying stones at the four corners of the house would prevent it from being disturbed by ghosts.[12] The bamboo slips (*rishu*) excavated from Shuihudi mention that peachwood and white stones could ward off evil.[13] The magical power of white stones and their use as a defence is confirmed by an early fourth-century Daoist work, *Baopuzi* ('Master Embracing Simplicity', *c.*320):

> If you encounter an official in the mountains, but only hear his voice without seeing any shape as it keeps shouting to you, throw a white stone at it, and it will stop.[14]

In the *Shuowen jiezi* ('Explaining Simple and Analysing Compound Characters'), Xu Shen describes jade as the 'finest among stones' (*shi zhi mei zhe*),[15] implying that it should be regarded as possessed of the same or even stronger magical power than other stones.

Jade suits with wide, densely fitting plaques provide the most extraordinary evidence of the fears and concerns of the Han rulers. Fitting tightly around the body, like armour, these suits were made from the most enduring and protective of materials and would thus – it was assumed – be difficult even for a demon to penetrate.

The stone armour and helmets found near the First Qin Emperor Shihuangdi's mausoleum were probably prepared specifically for the terracotta army and other guards in the afterlife, as they were too heavy to wear in life. Like the stone armour used by the terracotta army, the jade suits worn by the Liu princes were analogous to real armour and would be expected to have powers in the afterlife.

It is clear therefore that the Han imperial family and other high officials hoped to use the jade suits as defence against outside forces that threatened their bodies with decay. If the body could be protected from attacks by demons it might be preserved eternally.[16] A story in *Houhanshu* records that the bodies of Empress Lü and others from the imperial tombs that were encased in jade suits were well preserved and still looked lifelike after 200 years when the Vermilion Eyebrows Soldiers dug out the tombs.[17] A similar belief that the body would be well preserved by several discs is recorded in *Baopuzi* and in *Sanguozhi* ('Records of Three Kingdoms').

> During the reign of Emperor Jing of Wu (r. AD 259–264) the soldiers guarding Jiangling dug out tombs in order to obtain slabs to build the city wall. They discovered a large tomb with double doors and a stone door-leaf inside; all were hinged. The surrounding perimeter had passages for chariots and was wide enough for horse riding. In addition, bronze was used to cast ten figures which were five feet tall, clothed and with tall hats and swords . . . It seemed to be a prince's or nobleman's tomb. When the coffin was opened a body was found inside. His sideburns were white and bright and his face and body were lifelike. Inside the coffin was a piece of mica more than one foot thick. In addition, 30 white jade discs were laid on the body. When the soldiers removed the body, a piece of jade more than one foot long and shaped like a wax gourd fell from his clasped arms. Both the ears and nostrils were filled with pieces of gold that were as big as dates. This was to try to preserve the body from decay by using the power of objects.[18]

The records about the use of jade discs, jade suits and orifice plugs in texts are confirmed by archaeological finds from the imperial family members' tombs. Most of the imperial Liu members were found buried in jade suits and covered with jade discs. In addition, varying numbers of jade plugs were found around the body. One theory proposes that the purpose of inserting jade plugs into the orifices of the body was to prevent the 'escape' of vital essence from the body.[19] However, an alternative view of the function of such orifice plugs might be to prevent evil spirits or ghosts taking up residence in the body and wreaking havoc therein.[20]

The use of jades to cover the body of the deceased might have served more than one purpose. A record of about AD 195 in an Eastern Han text, *Fengsu tongyi* ('Comprehensive Meaning of Customs', by Ying Shao, *c.*AD 140–204), mentions 'The vital energy of the *hun* of a dead person floats away; therefore a mask is made in order to retain it.'[21]

It is possible that the use of jade orifice plugs and the jade suit in top-ranking tombs might also be expected to prevent the intangible *hun* from leaving the body *po*.[22] The concept of *po* is derived from Daoism: a person's spirit is believed to combine aspects of both *yin* and *yang*; the *po* is the corporeal soul that returns to earth at death, and the *hun* is the ethereal, volatile soul. In the later Daoist rites a liturgical or magical ceremony was designed to keep the *hun* and *po* souls together in an incorrupt body after death, defeating the malevolent influences of the earth (*di sha*) and their spirits (*shashen*).[23] Once the *hun* and *po* souls were retained in the body, then the immortal souls of the dead were ready to rise up into the heavens or begin their wanderings over the earth[24] – or, as we have seen from the tombs themselves, reside in the tomb.

NOTES

1 Watson 1993, p. 63.
2 Harper 1985, pp. 492–3.
3 Most of the contents of daybooks from the Shuihudi, such as that entitled *Ren zi* and *Yu xu yu* ('Promptuary of Yu') were also found in the section *Taichanshu* ('Book of the production of the foetus') and *Yang sheng fang* ('Recipes for nurturing life') from the Western Han Mawangdui texts. As Donald Harper has pointed out, 'The manuscripts from Shui-hu-ti and Ma-wang-tui are clearly writings which circulated among the literate elite of the period, and they may be treated as exemplars of books used in life.' See Harper 1985, p. 470. He suggests that these procedures were in general use at that time. Therefore, these manuscripts were not a special category of tomb literature but were in themselves aids in life, which therefore made them appropriate items to be included among the burial goods.
4 Harper 1999, pp. 244–5.
5 *Zhouli*, *Xiaguan sima* ('Summer offices domain of the overseer of military affairs'); Taipei 1972, p. 324.
6 *Fengsu tongyi*, p. 88. Tr Harper 1985, p. 482. The terms *Wang-liang*, *Wang-hsiang* and *Fang-liang* are related to each other as binomial demon names. For more discussion see Harper 1985, p. 481.
7 Liu 1994, pp. 225–68.
8 An unusual example features an image believed to be *Fangxiangshi* and was incised on the jade stand used to support a jade pillow belonging to the King of Chu at Shizishan.
9 Thote 1991, pp. 37–8.
10 Beijing 1989; Keightley 1987, p. 19.
11 Rawson has suggested that the Han tombs with many rooms, each dedicated to a specific and different function, derived from Chu practice; while the Han imperial members' interest in jades may be related to the practice in eastern China; Rawson 1999, pp. 30–52.
12 *Huainan wanbishu*.
13 Liu 1994, p. 257.
14 *Baopuzi* 17.278; Ware 1966, p. 288.
15 *Shuowen jiezi*, p. 10.
16 Wu Hung's contention is that, in Liu Sheng's case, the jade suit's function was to transform the flesh into a 'jade body', and at Mawangdui the aim was to protect the body, not to transform it. He further explained that the incomplete jade suit from Liu Ci's tomb was '*metonymic*, a representation in which parts stand for the whole. The Mancheng set, on the other hand, is *metaphoric*'. However, he does not take into account the different statuses and the regional burial characteristics among these three tombs. Indeed, the intention of protecting the body is quite clear in these Han tombs, but the methods they used and the objects with which they were buried varied according to the status of their owners. The jade suit is analogous to iron armour, indicating a fear of external enemies, spirits that caused bodily decay. Thus Wu Hung's suggestion that the jade suit turned the body into a jade-like substance is likely to need further discussion. See Wu 1997, pp. 162–4.
17 *Houhanshu*, pp. 483–4.
18 *Baopuzi*, p. 332; *Sanguozhi*, p. 1162.
19 Xia Nai was the first scholar to suggest that the nine orifice plugs were designed to prevent the escape of vital essences; Xia Nai 1983, p. 31. The notion of vital essence, *qi*, was combined with that of *yin* and *yang* (the positive and negative forces) and accounted for all phenomena in the universe. It was widely disscussed in the Han texts. Graham 1989, IV; Harper 1999, pp. 813–84.
20 Yates 1994, p. 73.
21 Wu 1980, p. 428; tr. Brashier 1997, p. 13.
22 During the 1970s and 1980s, sinologists such as Yü Ying-shih and Michael Loewe followed the commentators of both Confucian and Daoist works in believing that the two aspects of the soul, that is the *hun* and *po*, returned to heaven and earth respectively at death; Yü 1987, pp. 376–8; Loewe 1979, pp. 9–10. In 1987, Anna Seidel distinguished between the literati theories of *hun / po* dualism and the concept of *hun* and *po* of the dead from the Han funerary texts, such as celestial ordinances on pottery jars excavated from tombs. She pointed out that 'the souls do not separate at death but *hun* and *po* together descend into the mountain netherworld'; Seidel 1987, pp. 21–57, particularly p. 30. Her position has taken root and has been cited by other scholars such as Lothar von Falkenhausen and K. E. Brashier; Falkenhausen 1994, p. 6. Brashier further suggests that in terms of ancestral worship, the *hun*, *po* and the body were grouped together and venerated at the individual's grave, while a separate entity, the *shen*, was often worshipped at the lineage shrine; Brashier 1997, pp. 1–35, particularly p. 11. From this new approach we can develop the argument that the dead lived in their tombs and did not leave them to ascend permanently to Heaven.
23 The rites went by several names: sometimes called *yang xing tai yin fa* (nourishing the form) or *tai yin lain xing* (re-moulding the form by the aid of the Yin force at its fullness); sometimes they were called *wu lian sheng shi zhi fa* (keeping life in the corpse by the five transformations). See Needham 1974, vol. 5, part 2, sec. 33, pp. 302–3.
24 Needham 1974, vol. 5, part 2, sec. 33, p. 302.

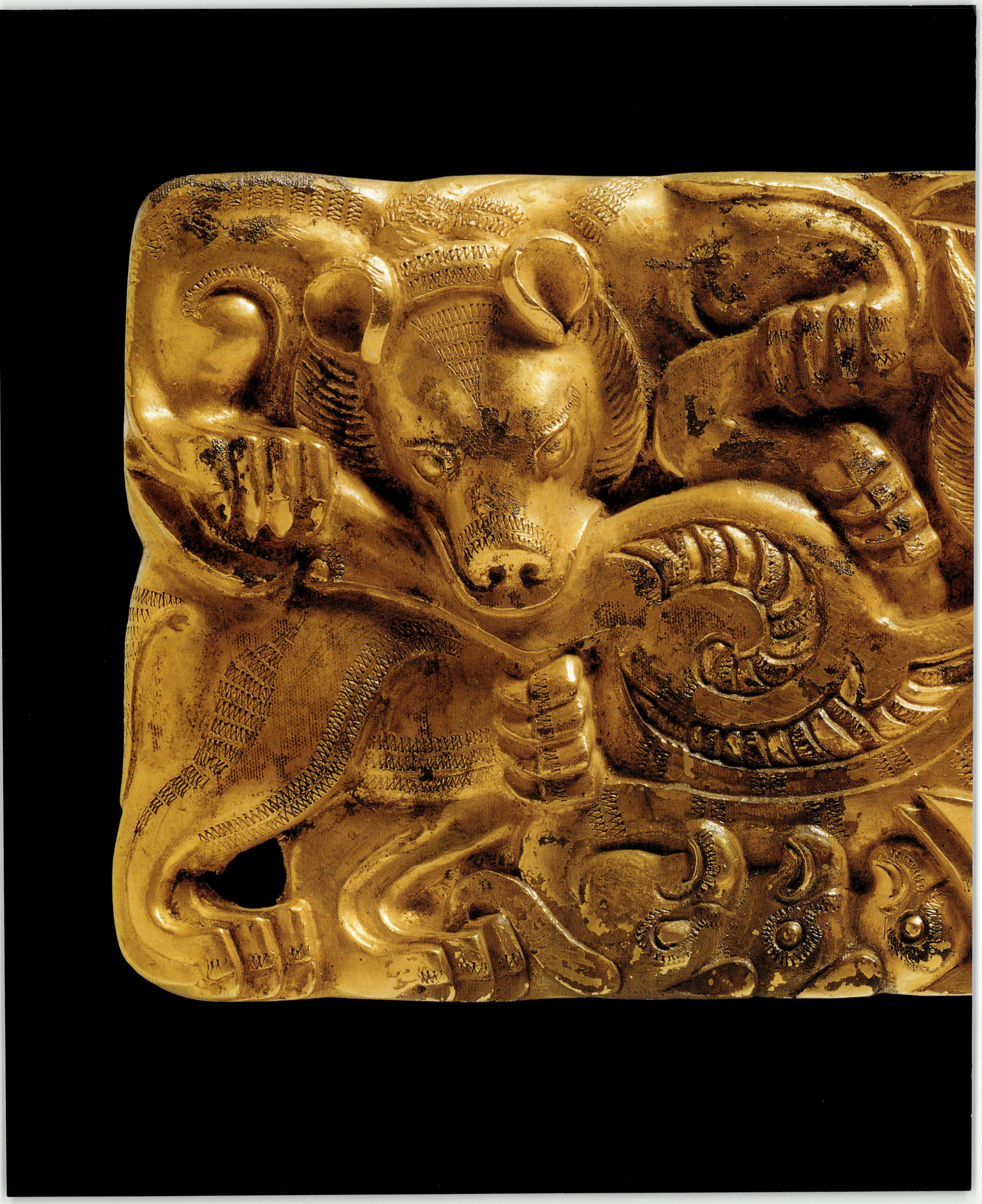

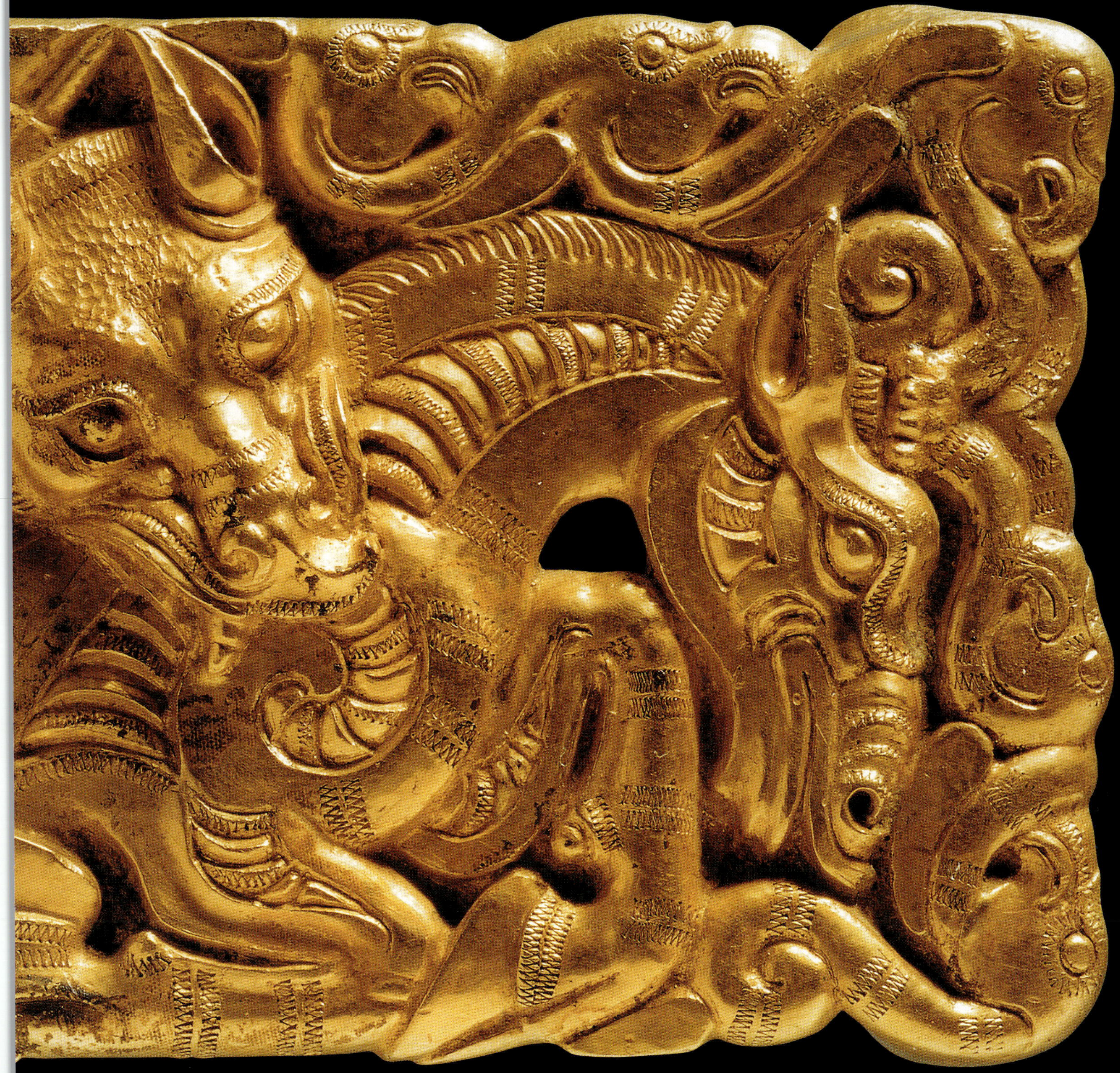

HAN TOMBS OF XUZHOU

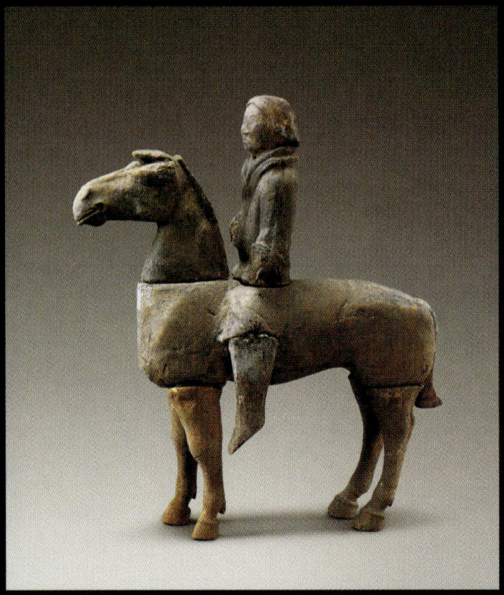
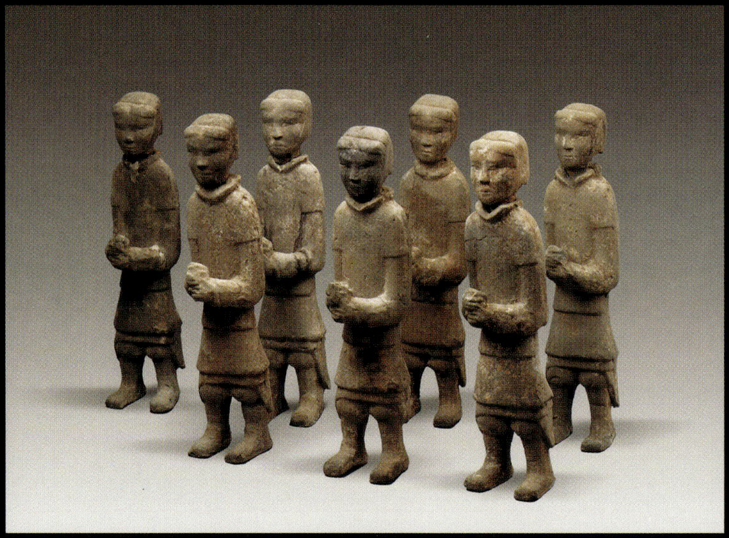
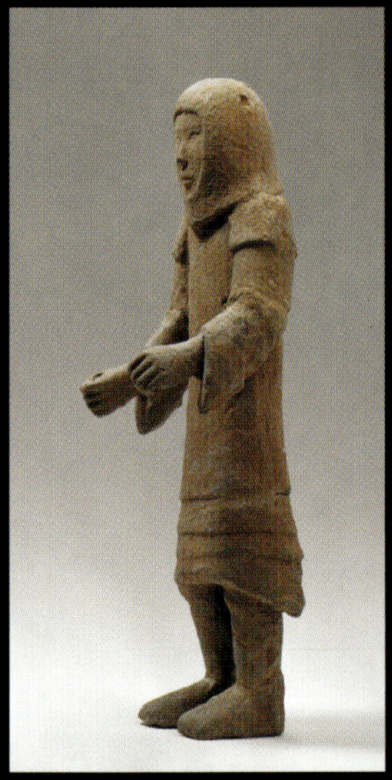

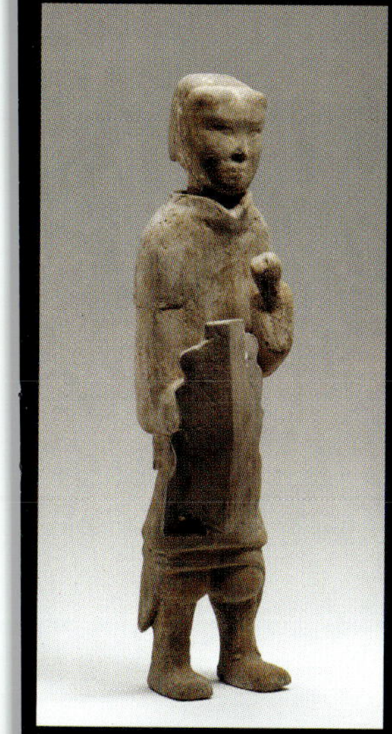 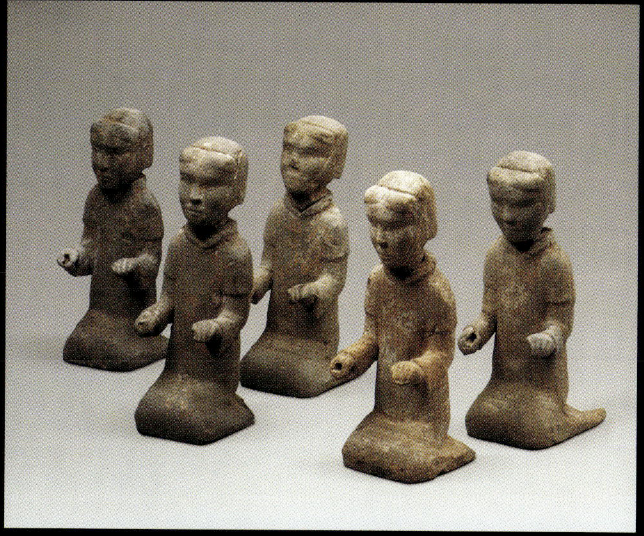 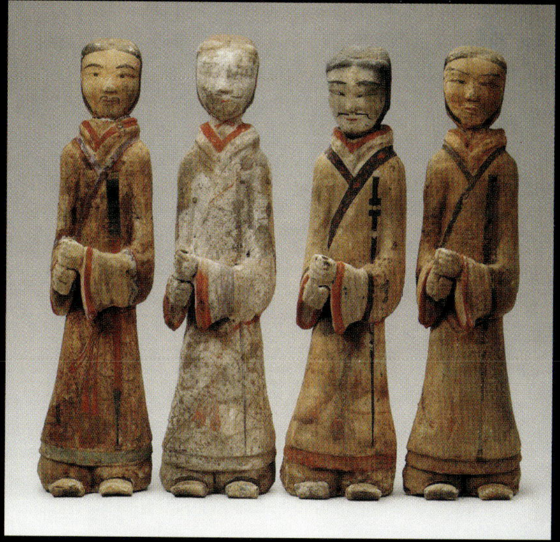

GUARDIANS FOR THE AFTERLIFE

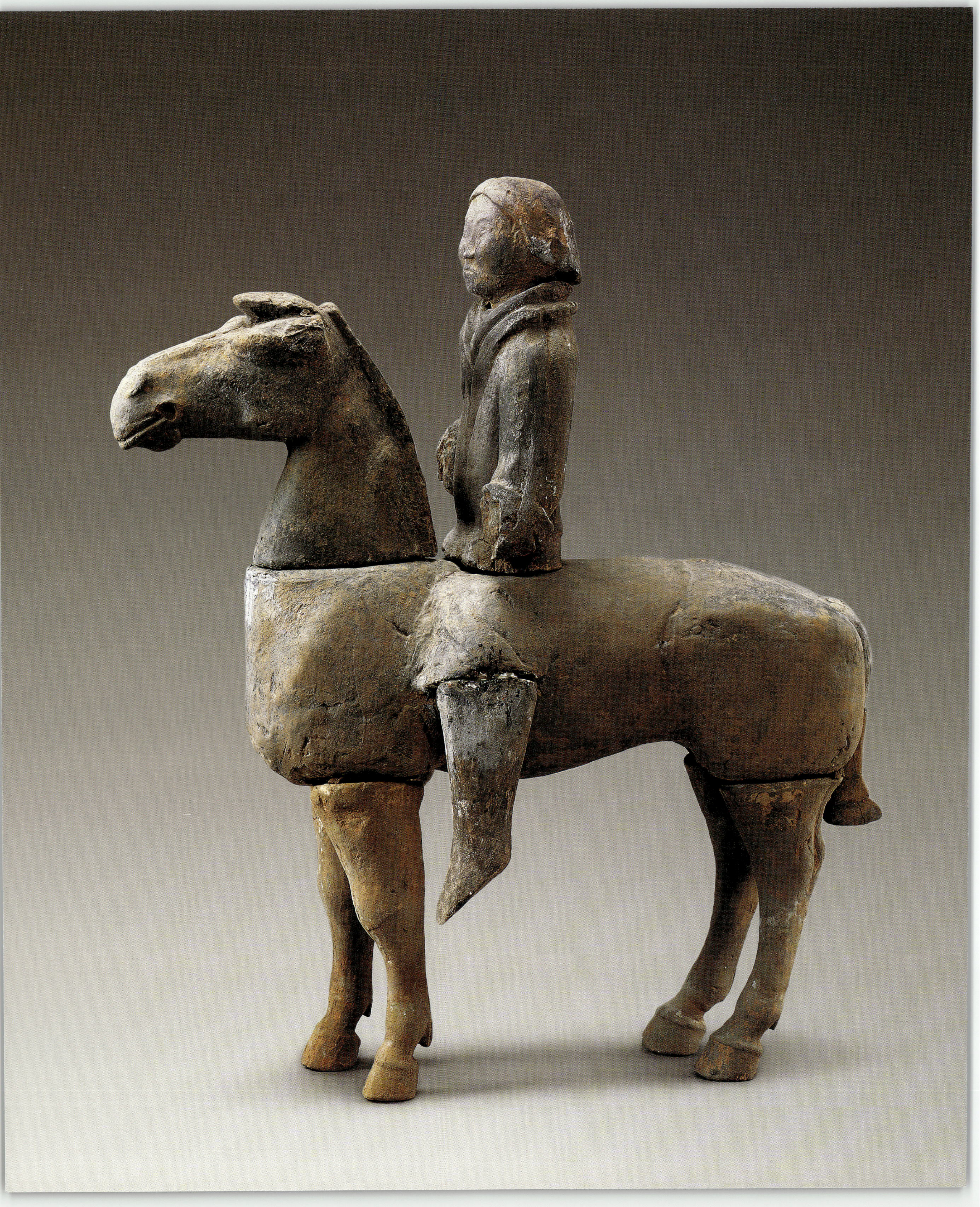

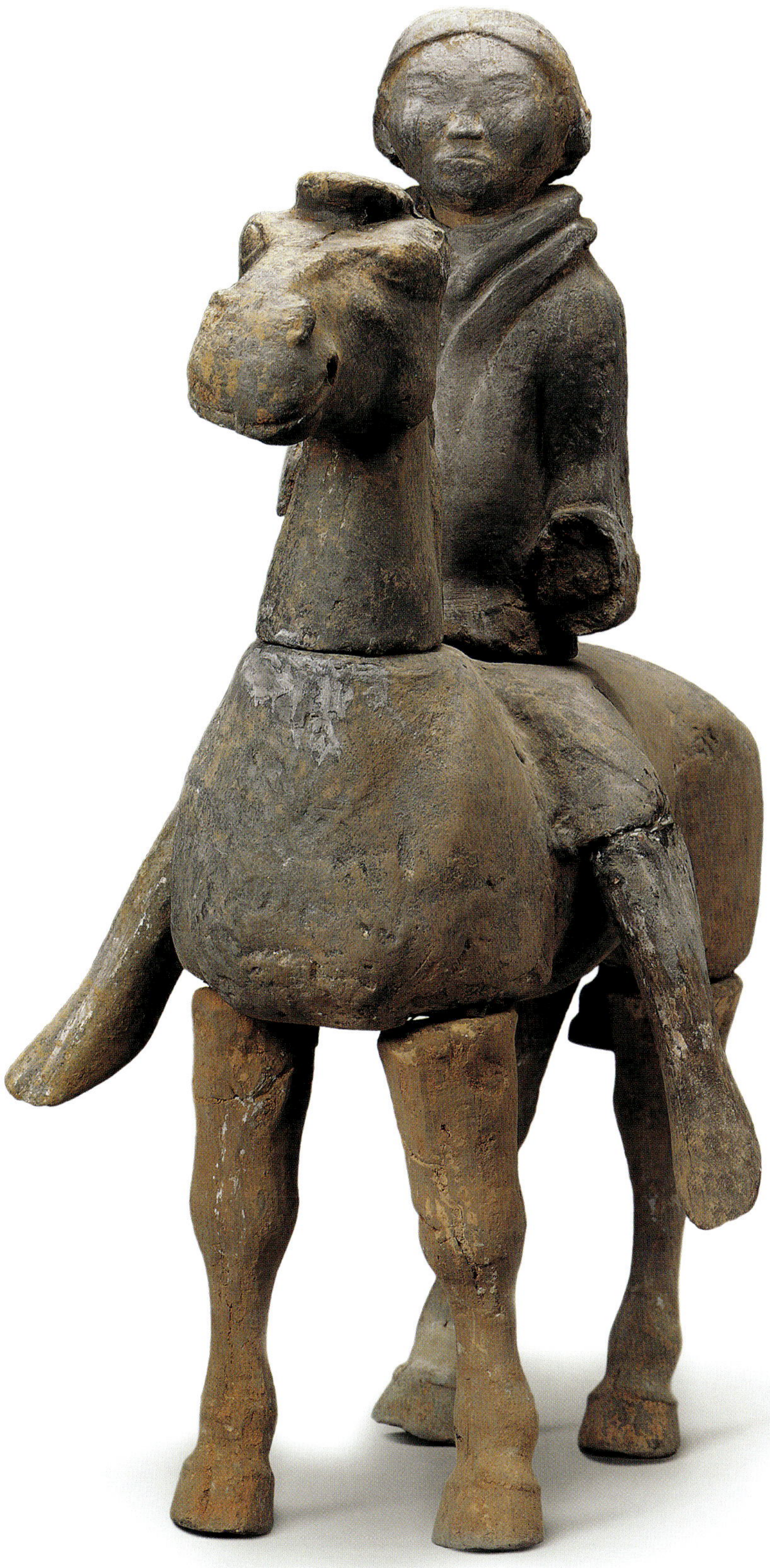

1

1

Earthenware cavalryman on horseback with inscription of 'feiji'

Second century BC, Western Han dynasty
Height: 59 cm
Excavated at Shizishan in 1984
Xuzhou Museum, Jiangsu Province

This sculpture of a cavalryman riding on a horse was one of the most extraordinary finds from the earthenware army at Shizishan. The horse was moulded in three parts: the head, body and four legs. The cavalryman wears two high-collared robes that fasten on the right. The lower section of the figure was made as part of the horse's body and his legs were inserted after being produced separately. An inscription of two Chinese characters, *feiji*, meaning speedy horse, was found on the horse's abdomen. JX

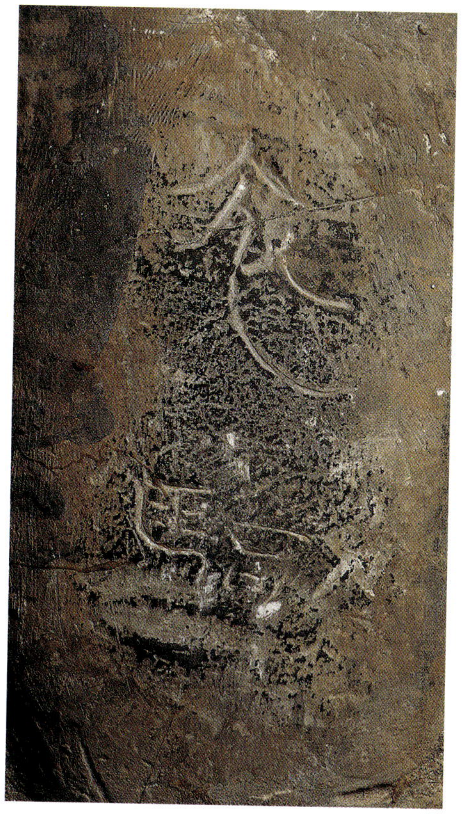

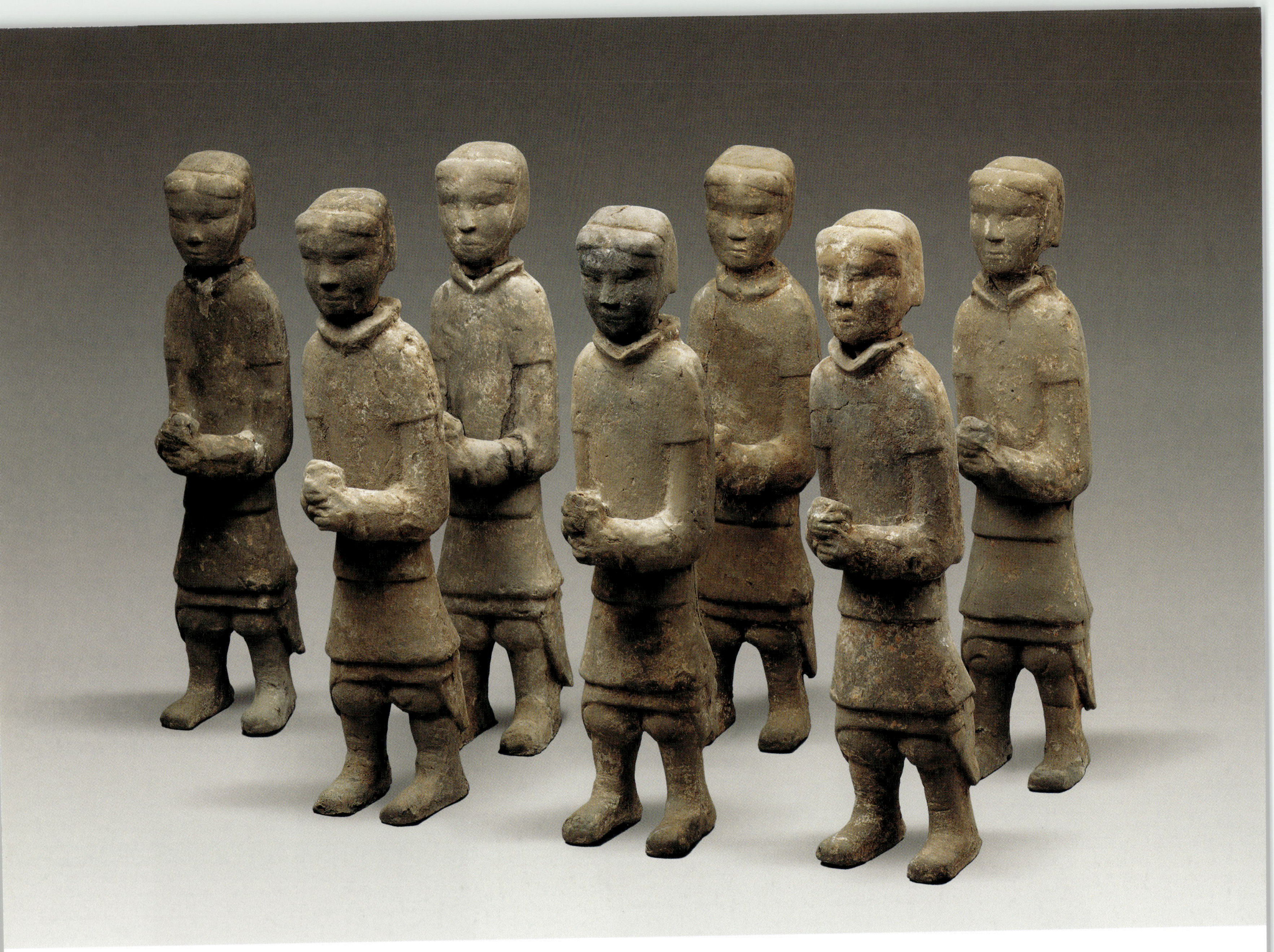

2

2

Earthenware standing figures formerly holding weapons

Second century BC, Western Han dynasty
Height: 42.5 cm
Excavated at Shizishan in 1984
Xuzhou Museum, Jiangsu Province

The standing figures are wearing helmets and knee-length inner robes with triangular points at the bottom on both sides. Beneath the robes, they wear loose trousers and round-toed boots. Their hands are clasped in front of the chest with a round hole through the fists to hold a long weapon. These infantry figures were by far the most common figures discovered at Shizishan. Both heads and bodies were made in two sections, front and back, which were later joined together. There are still some traces of the original colour on the uniform. JX

3

Earthenware standing soldiers formerly holding weapons

Second century BC, Western Han dynasty
Height: 48.5 cm
Excavated at Yangguishan in 2005
Xuzhou Museum, Jiangsu Province

These standing soldiers have serious and solemn expressions on their faces. Their hair is divided in the middle and tied up in a bun at the back of the head. Their attire is typical for men of the Han dynasty including a loose-sleeved robe

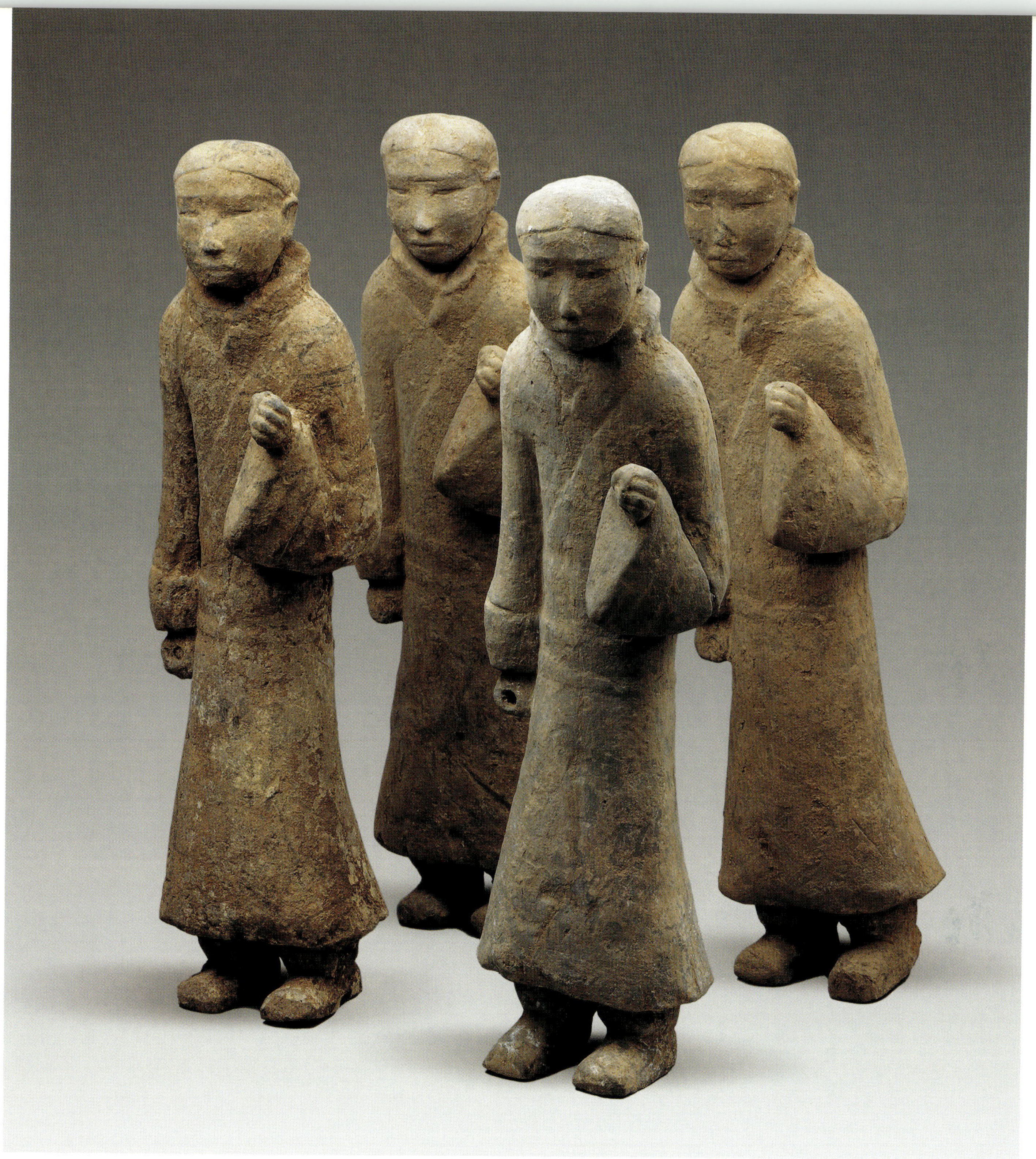

3

with its left lapel crossing over the right and a belt tied around the waist. The soldiers also wear trousers beneath the robe and boots.

The right arm of the soldiers is relaxed while the left arm is raised to chest height. They clench both fists, which are hollow. It is likely that the soldiers originally held something, possibly weapons, in their hands. While the earthenware figures have survived, the weapons, probably made of wood, have rotted away.

The soldiers were originally painted, but most of the colours had already gone when the figures were unearthed from Yangguishan in 2005.[1] NC

1 Beijing 2005, p. 101.

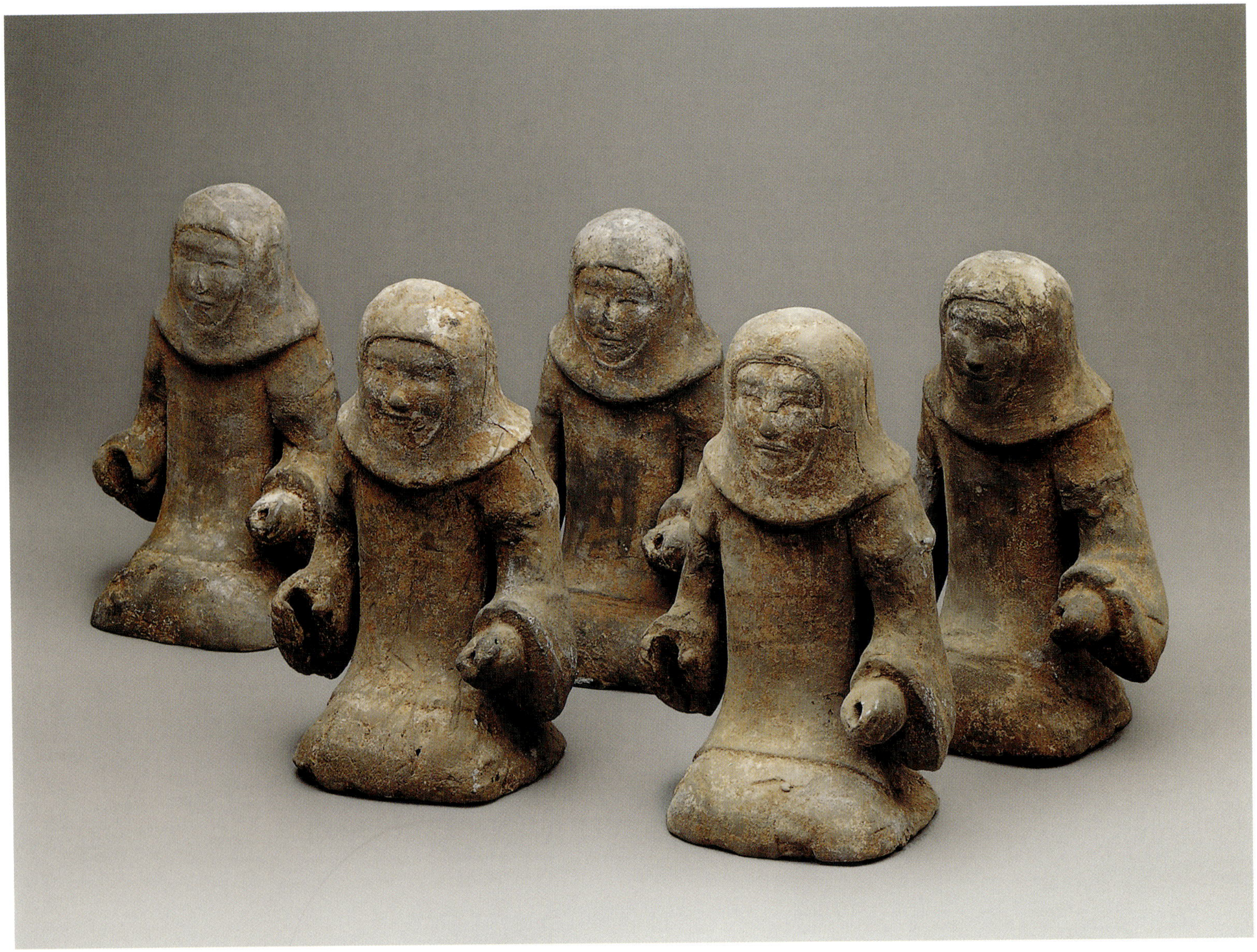

4

4

Earthenware kneeling figures in armour

Second century BC, Western Han dynasty
Height: 25.5 cm
Excavated at Shizishan in 1984
Xuzhou Museum, Jiangsu Province

These kneeling figures wear a helmet, similar to an iron helmet excavated from the same site, which covers the neck and shoulders. They have round faces and clearly defined eyebrows, eyes, noses and mouths. Underneath the short-sleeved armour is a long wide-sleeved robe. The figures are believed to be soldiers on chariots. The forearms are outstretched, with both hands cupped as if to hold something. The hole in the right hand is bigger, probably for a long pole weapon. The soldiers were assembled by joining the front and back sections together. The kneeling armoured figures were found with kneeling charioteers (cat. 5) in the same formation, arranged in twenty-two rows; 212 figures in total. The discovery of both types of figures indicates that chariots still played an important role in battle in the early Han dynasty. JX

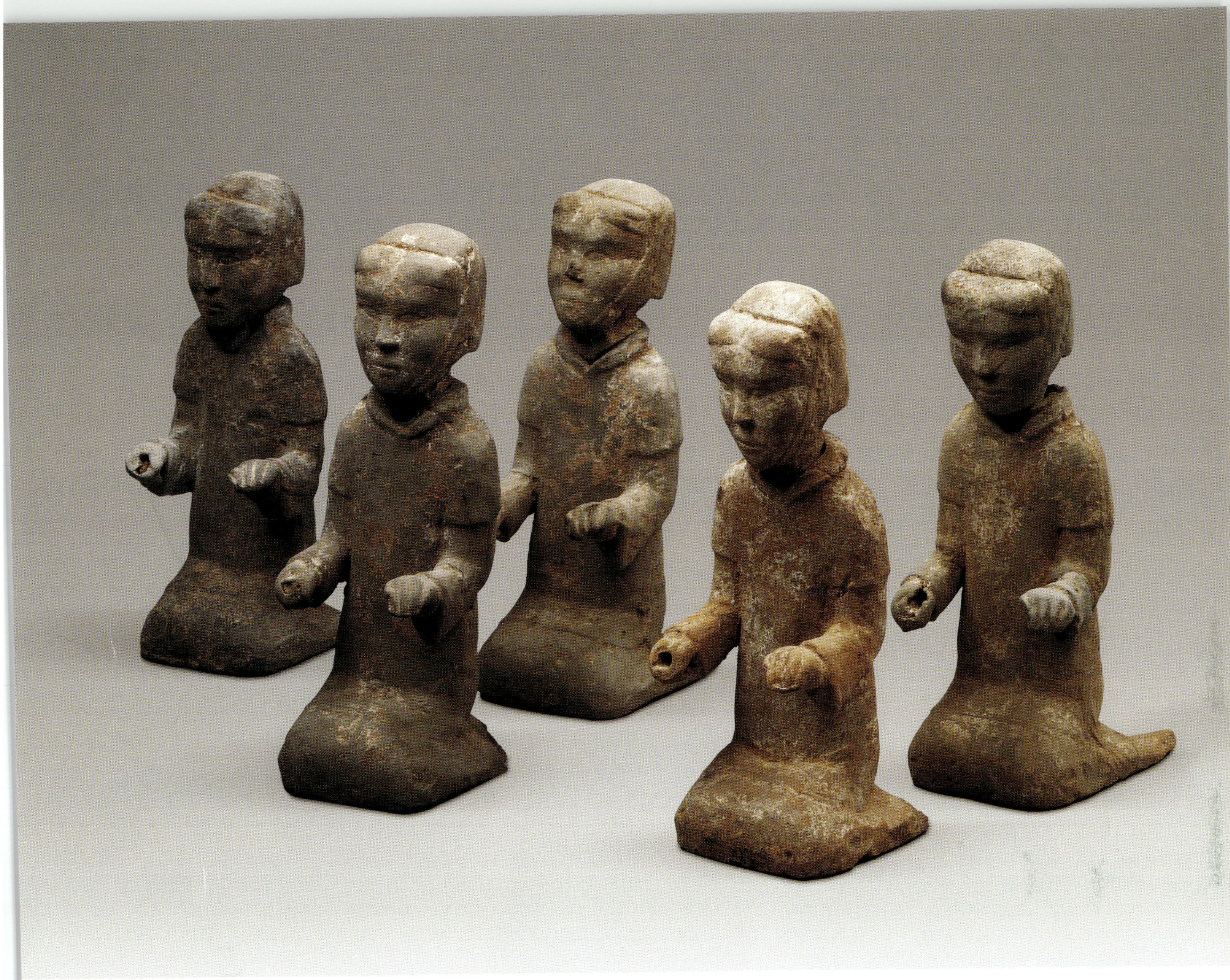

5

5

Earthenware kneeling charioteers

Second century BC, Western Han dynasty
Height: around 28 cm
Excavated at Shizishan in 1984
Xuzhou Museum, Jiangsu Province

Each kneeling figure is wearing a helmet, with the hair divided in the centre and parted into two locks, and a long robe under V-necked short-sleeved armour. The forearms are outstretched, left hand cupped with palm facing downwards and the right fist hollowed, as if to rein a chariot. Similar figures have been found in the chariot and horses pit No. 2 at the mausoleum of the First Emperor of Qin. The head and body were produced separately. The neck was made in a cone shape and later inserted into the torso. It was originally colourfully painted but the pigments have faded completely with time. JX

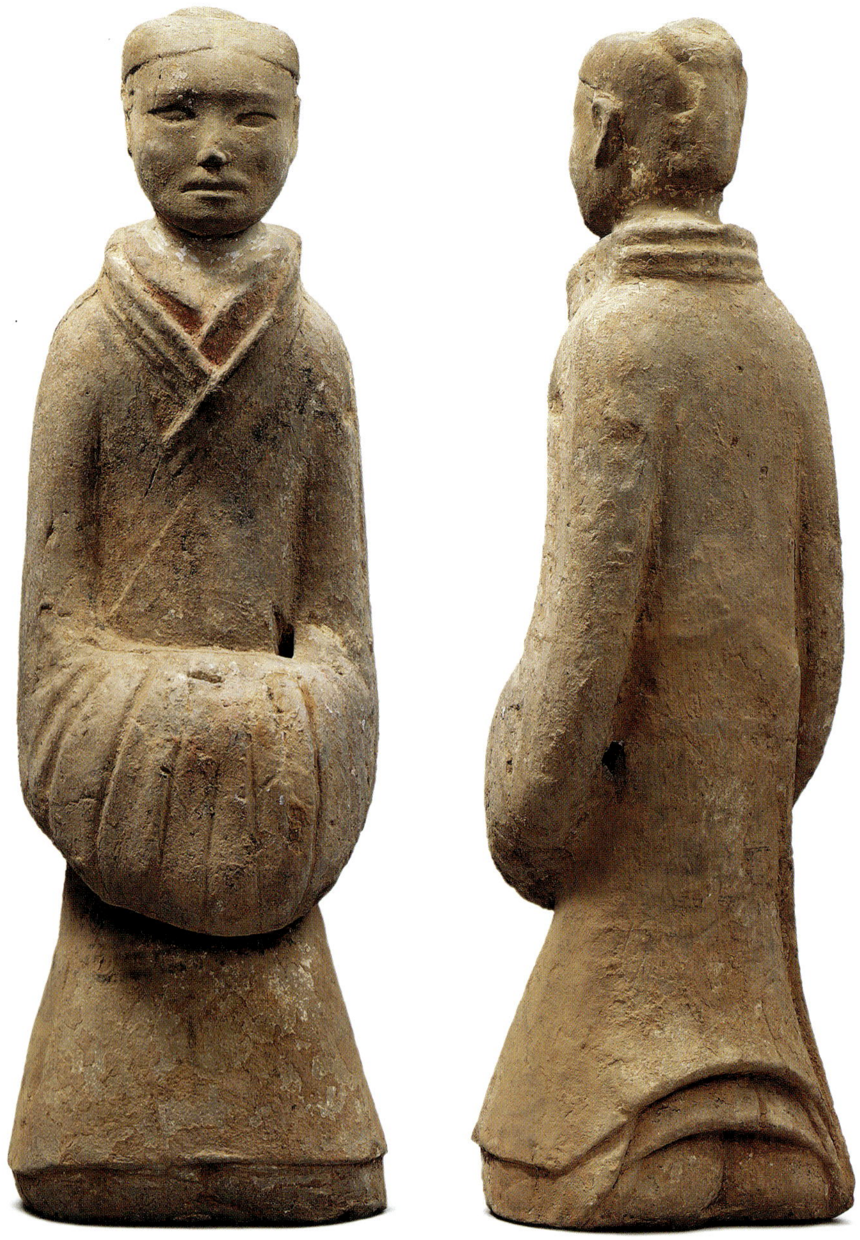

6

6

Earthenware official

Second century BC, Western Han dynasty
Height: around 54 cm
Excavated at Yangguishan in 2005
Xuzhou Museum, Jiangsu Province

This figure wears two long, high-collared and wide-sleeved robes fastened on the right. Hands are held together inside the sleeves. There is a rectangular slit in the hands, presumably to hold a *hu* (tablet denoting rank), and a similar slit under the left arm, probably for a sword.
This figure, almost identical to a standing official found in Shizishan, is believed to be a civil servant. Traces of a wooden chariot were found alongside the figure. JX

7

Earthenware figure wearing helmet

Second century BC, Western Han dynasty
Height: 50 cm
Found at Tuolanshan
Xuzhou Museum, Jiangsu Province
NOT EXHIBITED

The figure of a soldier wears a helmet that covers his entire head, neck and shoulders, revealing only his face. He wears a long robe with wide sleeves. On top of the robe is what might be a piece of armour with short sleeves to protect the body and the upper arms. His fingers are curled up yet his fists are hollowed, which suggests that originally he might have carried weapons in his hands. Many figures of kneeling chariot drivers unearthed from Shizishan wear similar helmets (cat. 4). However, not many standing figures with helmets are known. The figure was found in one of the sacrificial pits of the king's tomb at Tuolanshan by chance. Excavation of this pit is not yet complete. NC

8

Earthenware figure with shield

Second century BC
Height: 42.5 cm
Excavated at Dingwanhe, Wanzhai, Xuzhou in 1985
Xuzhou Museum, Jiangsu Province
NOT EXHIBITED

The figure holds a ladder-shaped shield with foliated borders in his right hand. The shield has a slight convex curvature, which allows the soldier to place his hand in the concave side. In his left hand would have been a weapon such as a sword or a spear, which has not survived. The figure was originally painted but the pigments have faded.

Many figures of shield-bearers have been discovered in Han tombs. Apart

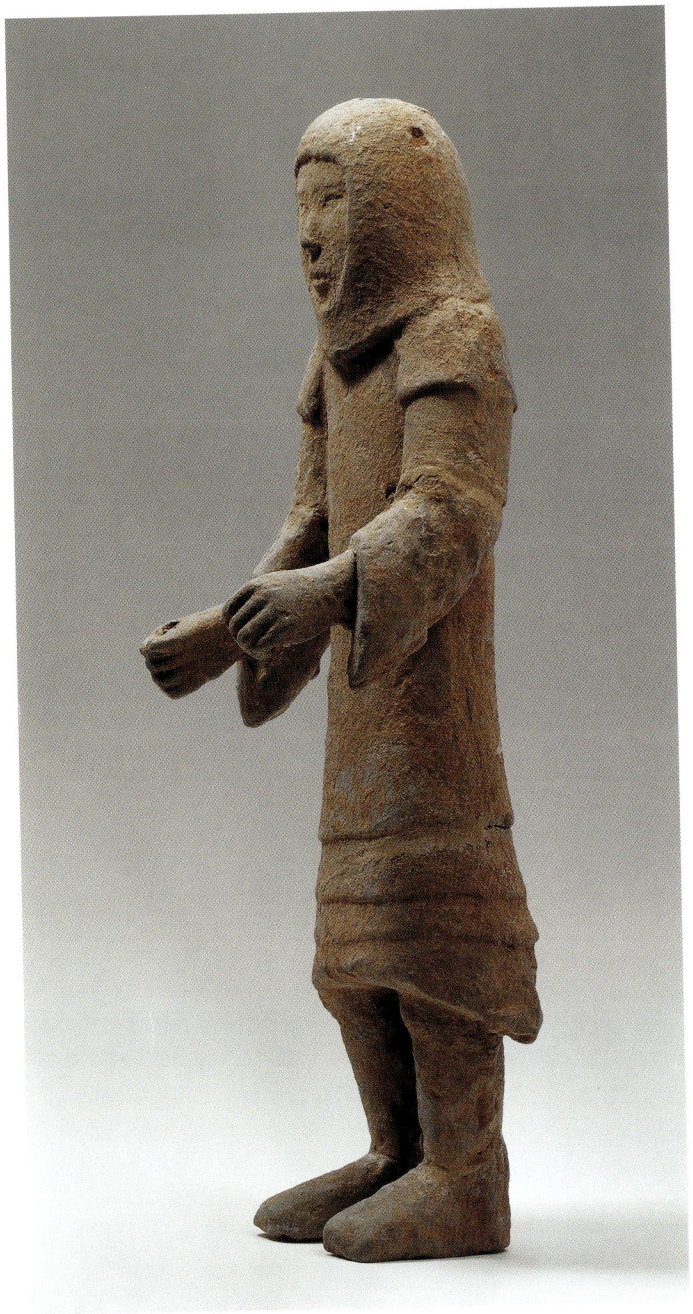

7

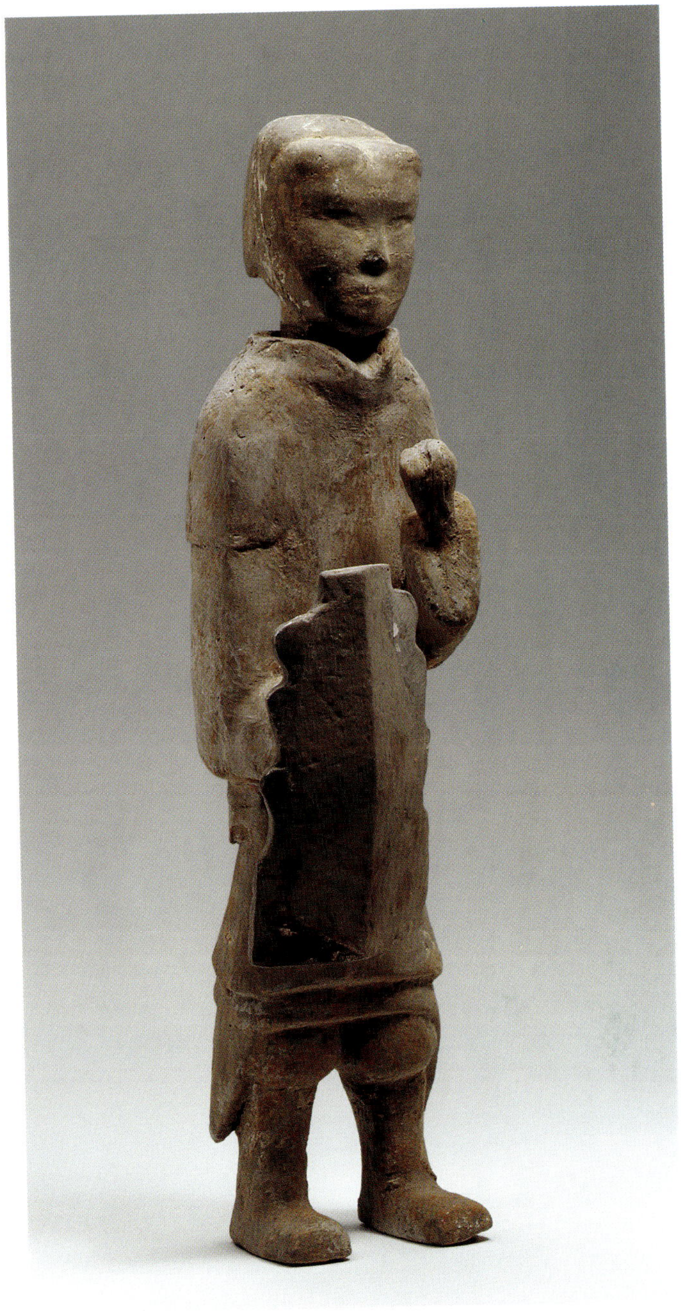

8

from ceramic ones, wooden statuettes with shields have also been excavated.[1] They provide clues to the types of defensive armour used at the time. Apart from relatively small rectangular and ladder-shaped shields, such as this one, circular ones and much larger shields, which have a greater convex surface and are sometimes decorated with what appears to be a tree design, are also known from texts and illustrations.[2]

In addition to earthenware figures, images of shield-bearers can also be found on Han monuments. In some cases, the soldiers carry the shield in their left hand while using a weapon with their right. It has been suggested that fighters might seek relief by changing weapons from one hand to the other when fatigued.[3] NC

1 A Western Han period wooden figure with a shield was unearthed from Lianyungang, Jiangsu Province in 1980; Cao and Sun 1996, pp. 108–10.
2 Laufer 1914, pp. 201–4.
3 Laufer 1914, p. 201.

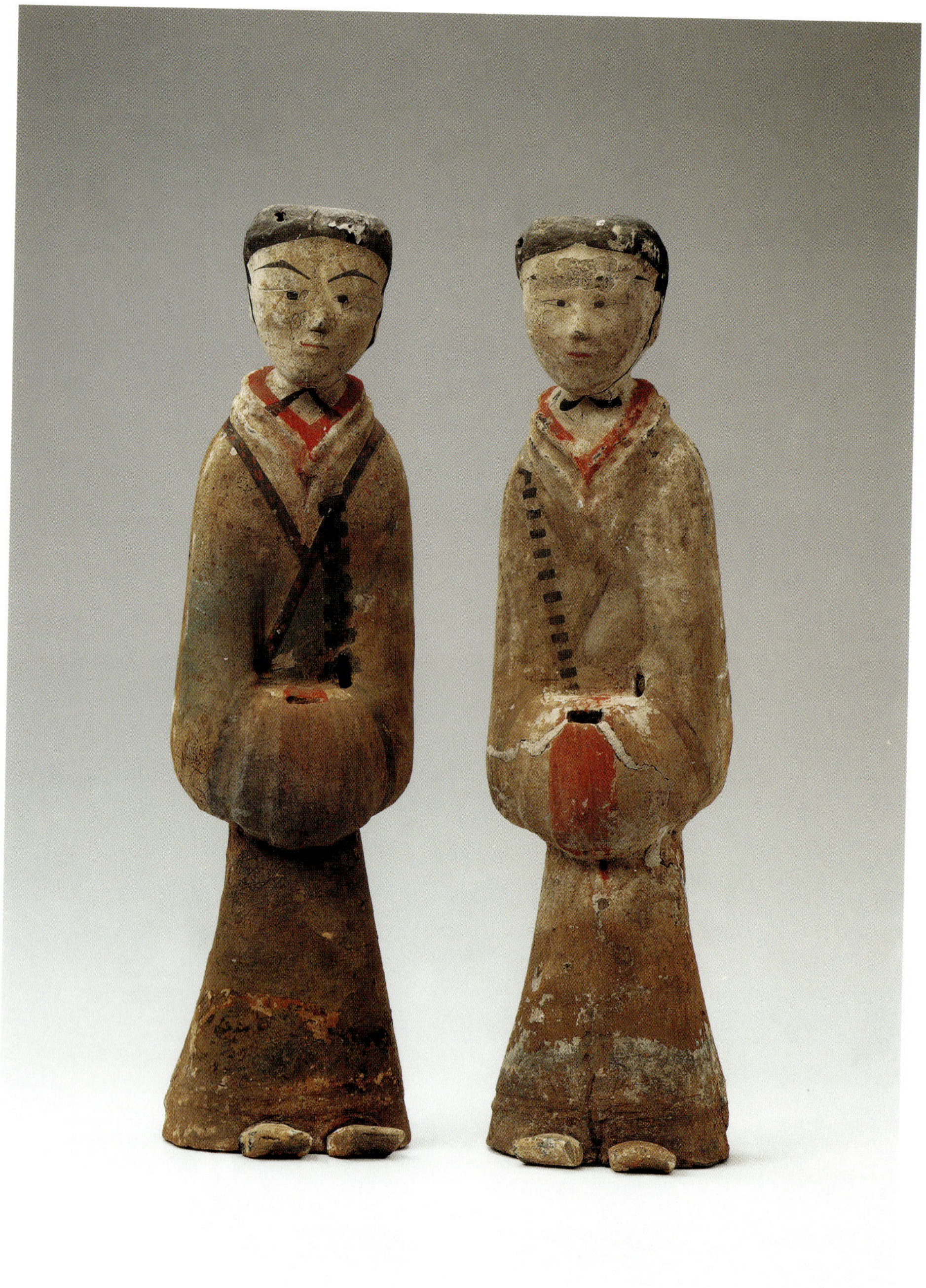

9A

9

Painted earthenware figures from Beidongshan

Second century BC, Western Han dynasty
Excavated at the tomb of the King of Chu at Beidongshan in 1986
Xuzhou Museum, Jiangsu Province

The 224 painted earthenware figures from the wall niches of Beidongshan tomb, mainly representing officials and guards, is the largest group of its kind ever discovered intact from a Han tomb. The mould-made figures are painted in red, white, black, green, bluish-purple and pale yellow colours.

A Painted earthenware figures formerly holding *hu* (tablet denoting rank)

Height: 54 cm, 55 cm

These figures are portrayed standing, each wearing a cap fastened under the chin with a strap. A hairpin originally would have been on the right of the forehead where there is now a hole. There is a space between the hands for holding a *hu*. A wooden sword was originally worn at the waist on the left. Both the *hu* and the sword have long since decomposed. The sword sheath was painted and decorated with jade ornaments and the designs vary from figure to figure. Nine officials of this type were found in Niche 1E. According to costume rituals recorded in historical texts, those wearing a cap with a hairpin and holding a *hu* tablet are believed to be high-ranking officials.

B Painted earthenware figures formerly holding weapons

Height: 48 cm, 51 cm

These figures wear the same costume as the painted officials: a V-neck robe fastened on the right, a belt, a sword or knife with a ring handle on the left chest and a pair of shoes with upward-curving toes. The differences are that these figures have various kinds of moustaches and their fists are joined at the waist on the right presumably to hold a long weapon such as a halberd. Traces of painted wood remain inside the hands. A hook is sometimes added to the belt and a silk ribbon is tied in a knot at the waist. Attached to the ribbon is a rectangular container containing a seal carved with the characters *Langzhong*.[1] The post of *Langzhong* was already in existence in the Spring and Autumn period (770–476 BC). During the early Western Han, a *Langzhong* served not

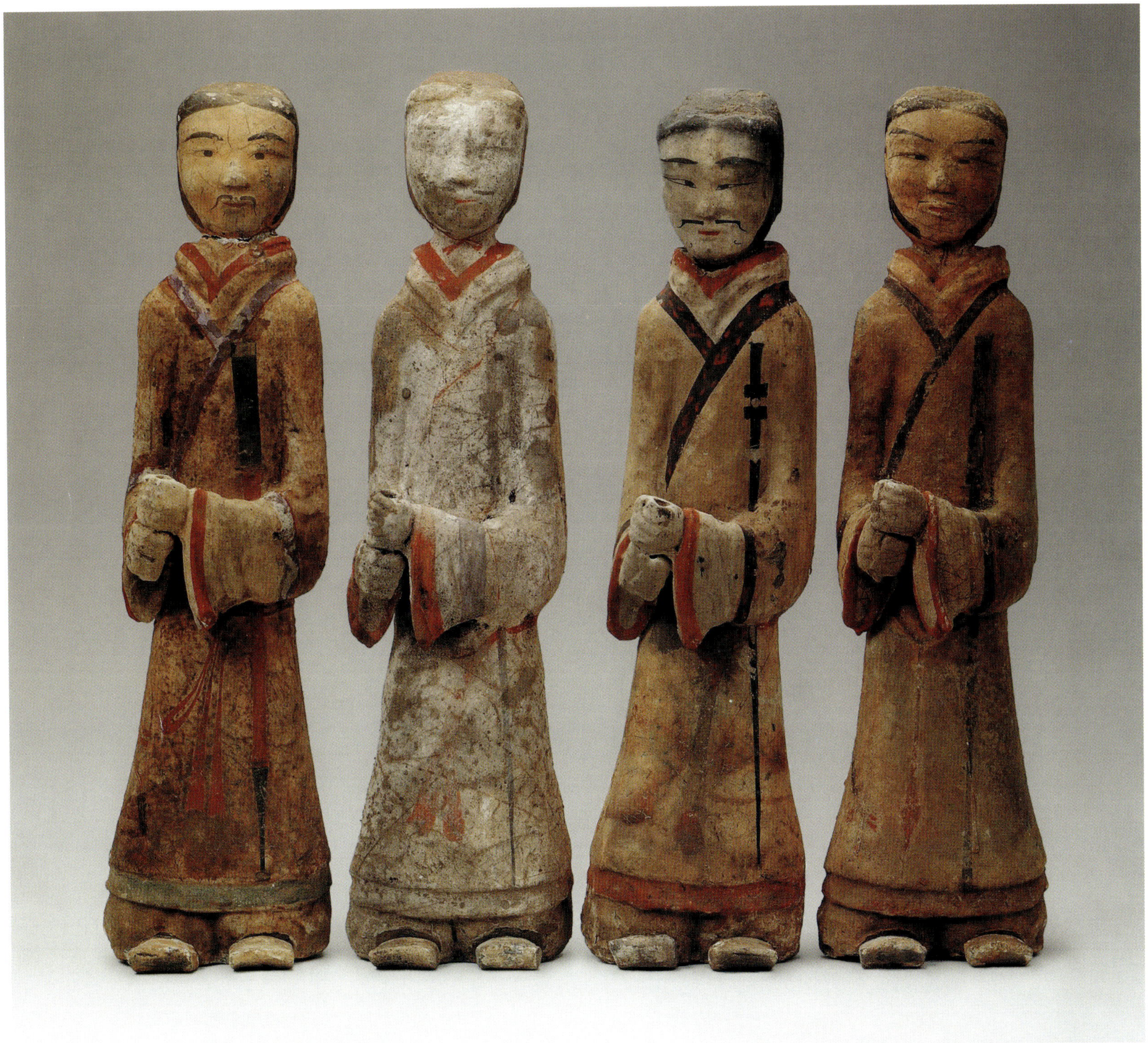

9B

only the emperor, but also vassals, since the system of the court in nobles' fiefdoms followed that of the capital.

The post could be either of civil or military ranking, serving in a palace and being close to the emperor or king.

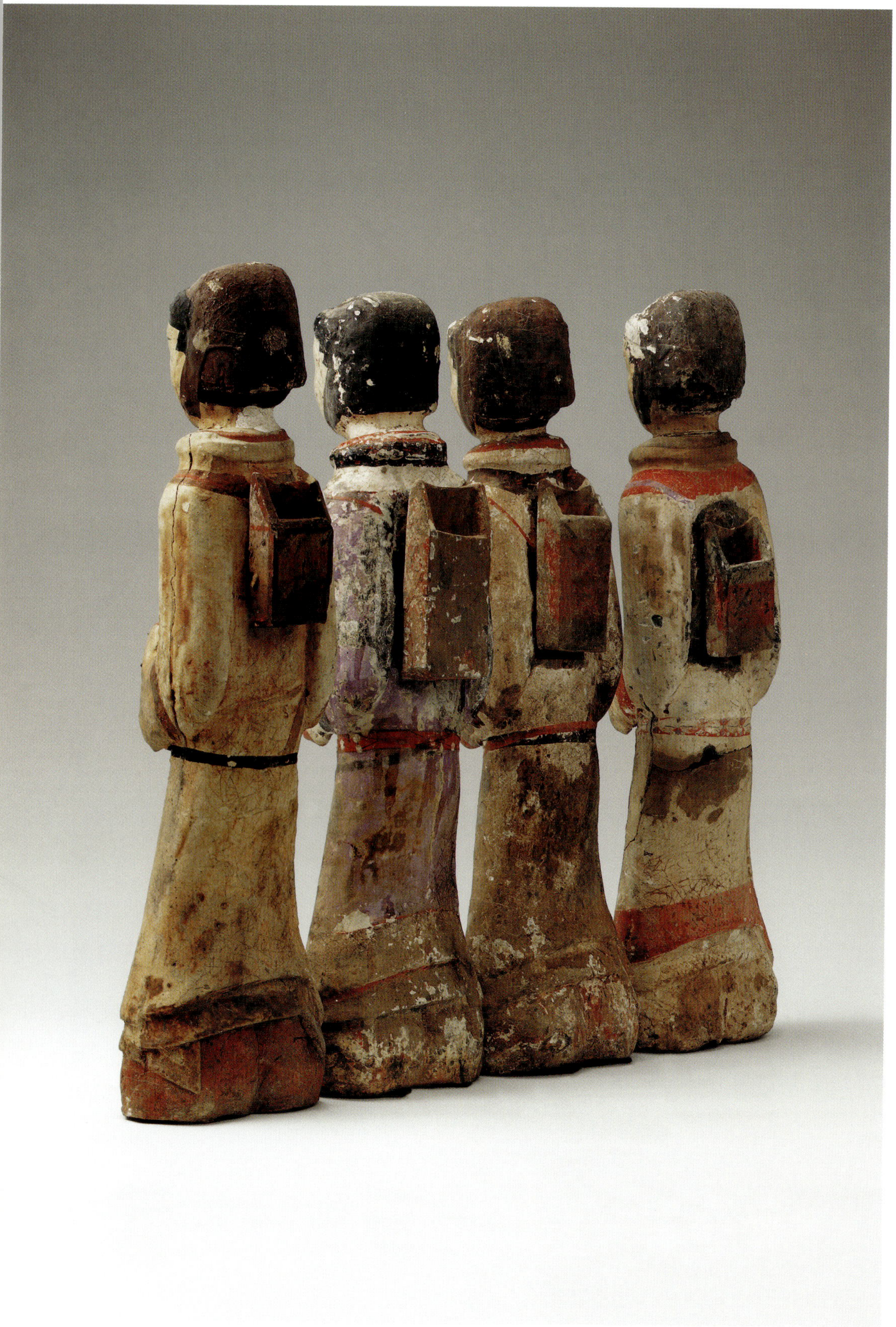

C Painted earthenware figures carrying quivers

Height: 49.5 cm, 50.5 cm

This type of figure wears a purple hat, a long robe fastened on the right, loose trousers and shoes with upturned toes. Each figure has a quiver on its back decorated in dark red with cloud and geometric designs. These figures have their arms bent and hands clasped as if holding bows and arrows. All three groups of painted figures carry swords as both a fashionable ornament and a weapon to hand confirming a text in the *Jinshu* ('Book of Jin'), which states that in the Han dynasty everyone in the court from the emperor to the hundreds of officials carried a sword. JX

1 On some figures, the seal was carved with *Zhonglang*, another post of officials serving the emperor or the king. It was ranked slightly higher than *Langzhong*.

10

Earthenware horses

Second century BC, Western Han dynasty
Height: 64 cm
Excavated at Yangguishan in 2005
Xuzhou Museum, Jiangsu Province

The four horses found in Yangguishan are identical to the ones unearthed from the pit of earthenware armies at Shizishan. They have broad bodies and thighs, wide-open eyes, erect ears and slightly closed mouths with a horizontal hole through the corners, presumably for fixing a gag bit. The horses were made of grey clay and moulded in separate parts: the ears; the head and the body, produced in two vertical sections; the four legs and the tail. After the horses were assembled and refined, they were fired and painted. JX

9C

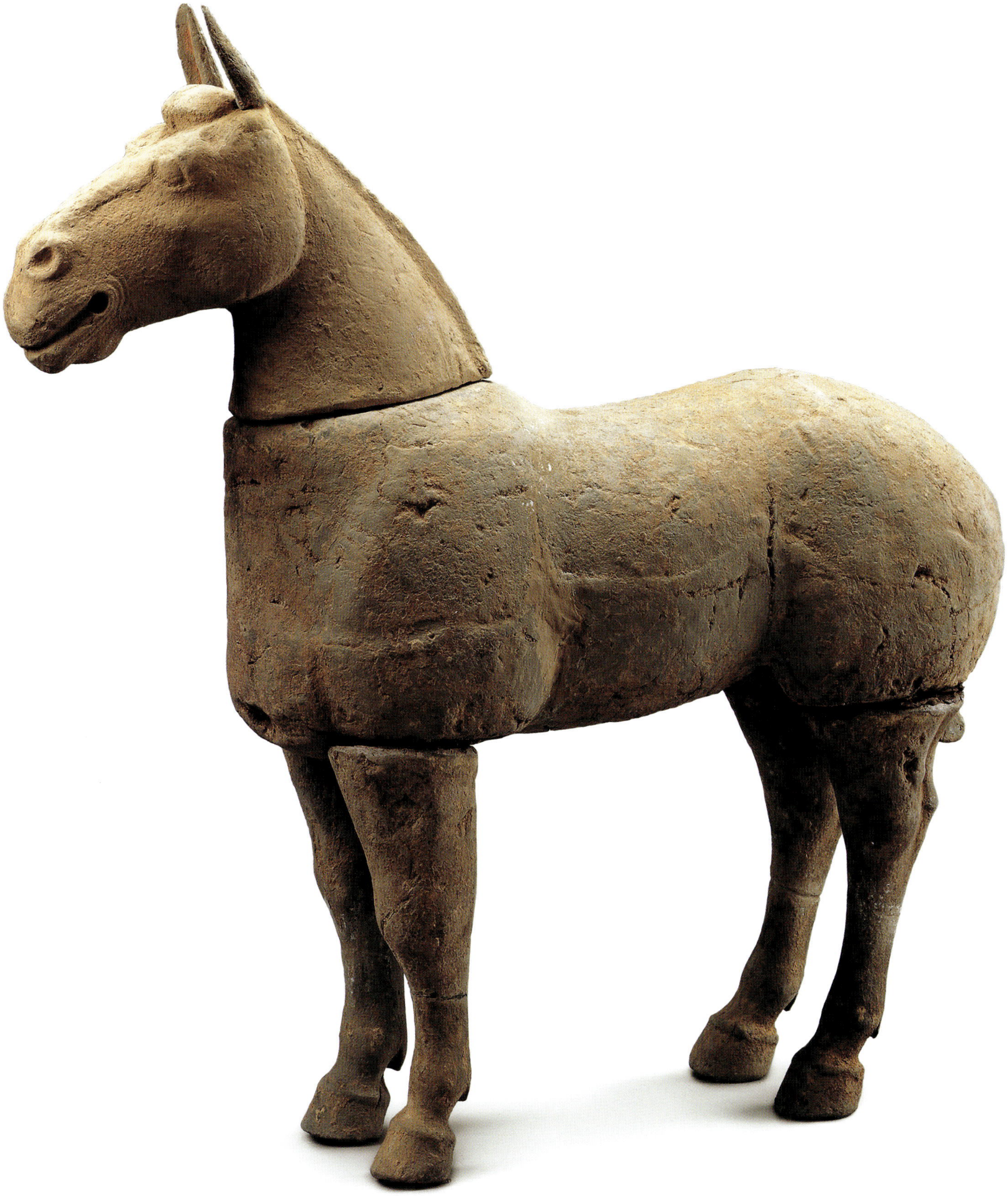

10

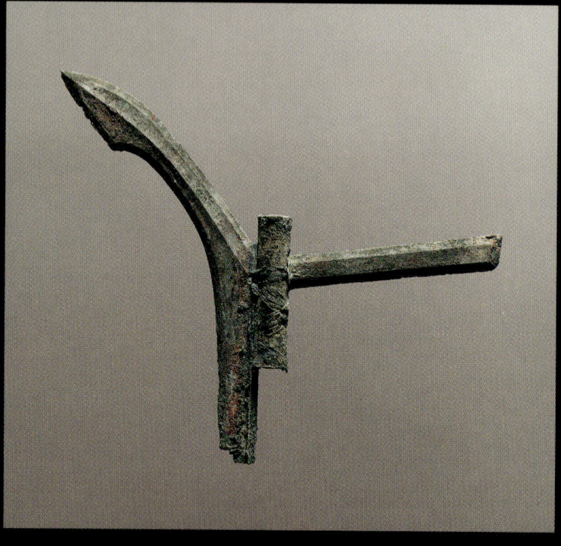
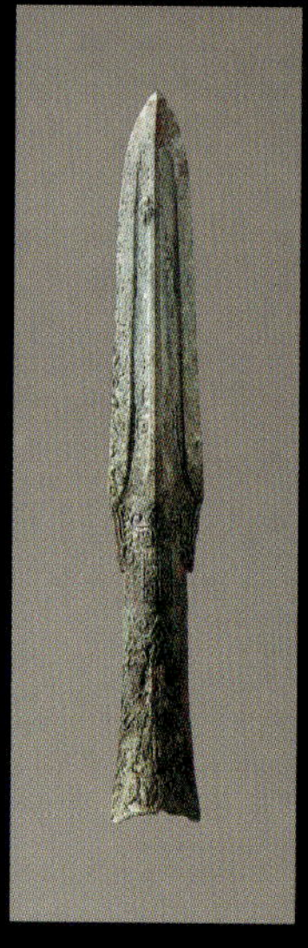
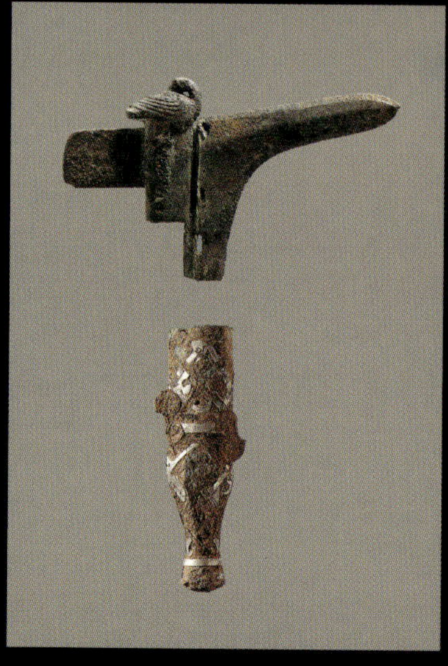
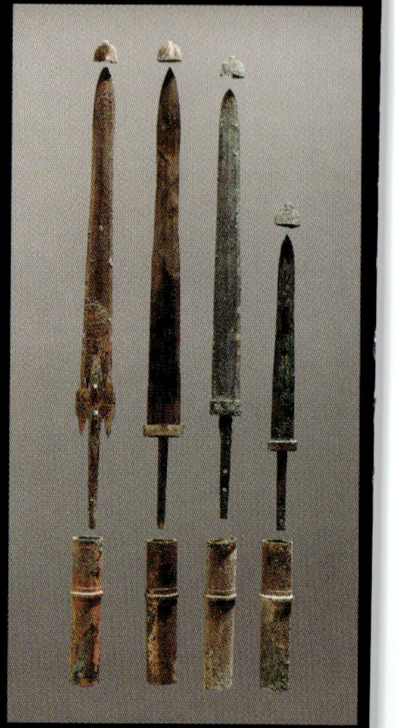

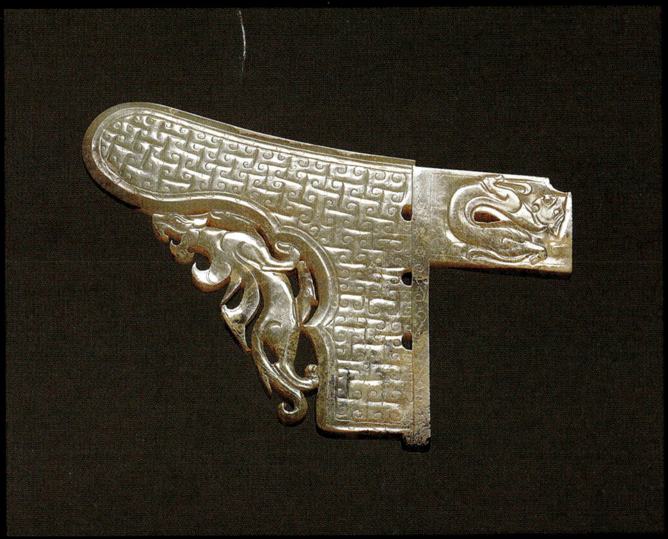
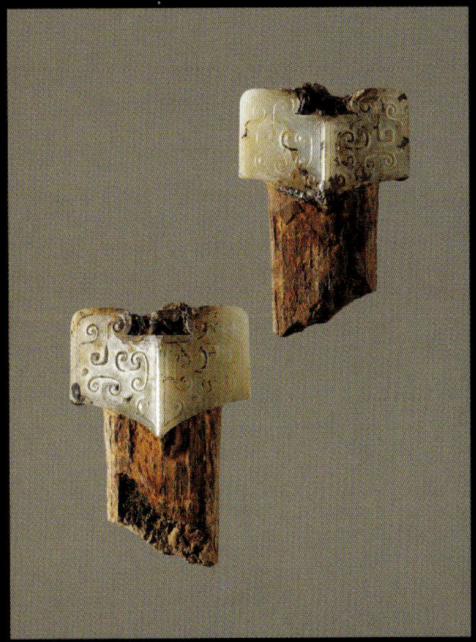
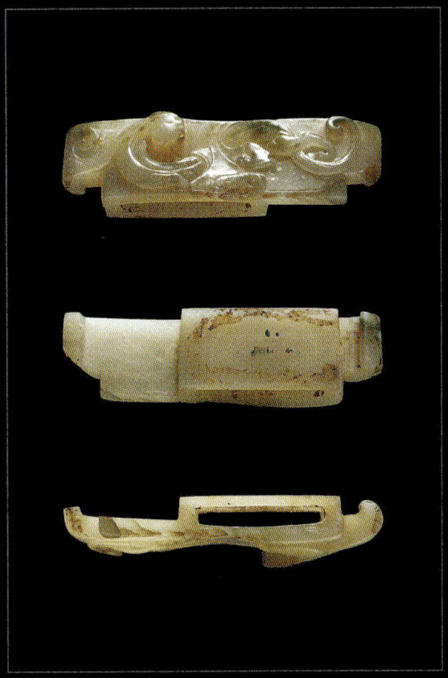

DEFENCE

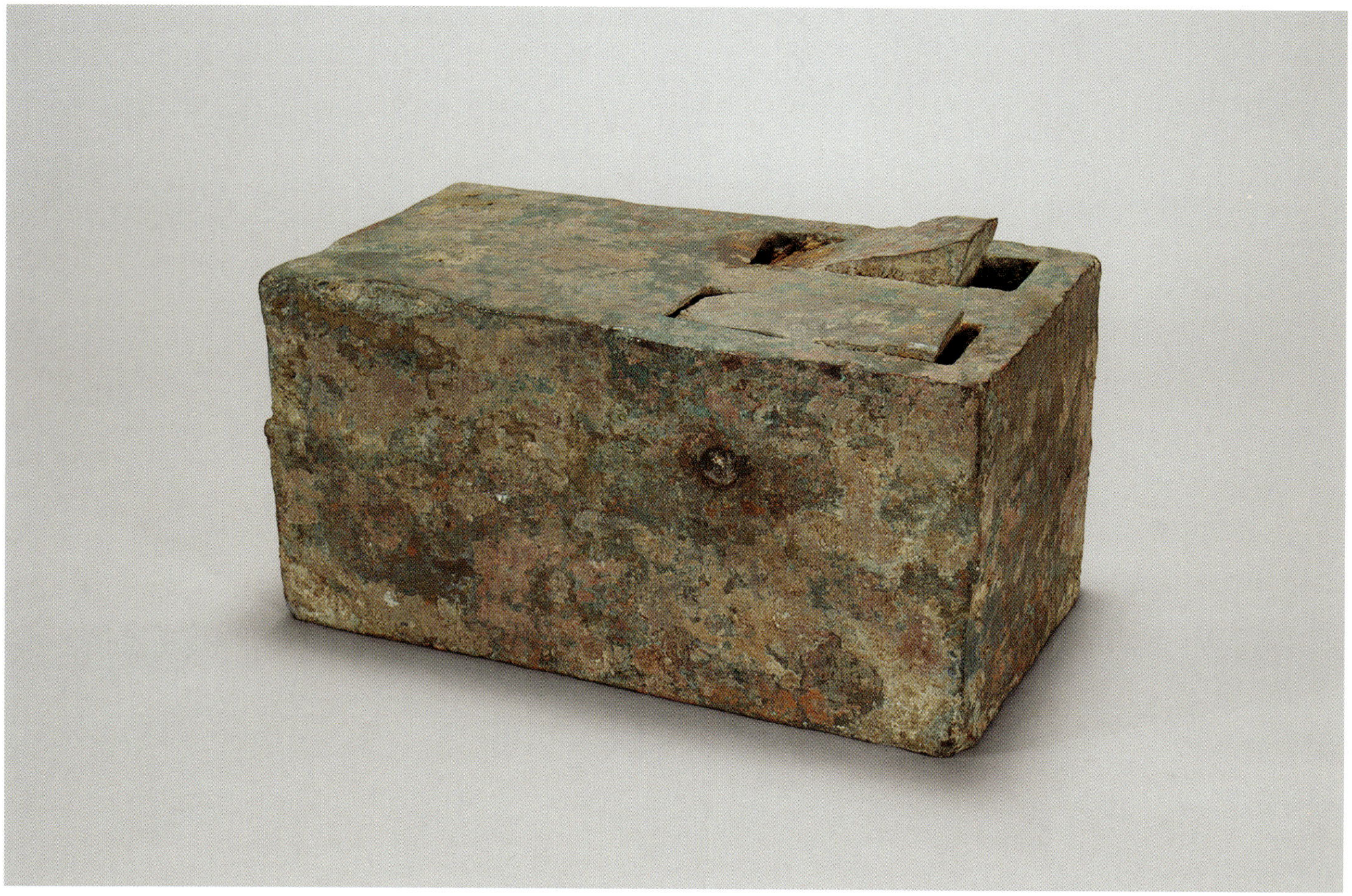

11

11

Self-locking device

Second century BC, Western Han dynasty
Length: 17.8 cm; Width: 9.6 cm; Thickness: 8.9 cm
Excavated at the tomb of the King of Chu at Beidongshan in 1986
Xuzhou Museum, Jiangsu Province

This self-locking device is made of bronze and has two teeth connected to an iron core inside a rectangular outer casing. The double tooth lock was discovered in the middle of the doorway at the end of the sloping tomb passage at Beidongshan. Traces of wood found on either side of the doorway indicate that originally two wooden doors were installed, for which the self-locking device was recessed into the ground. Once the door was closed, the teeth raised into position behind the door, locking it in place. Three locks in all were unearthed from this tomb. The other two are single tooth examples.

Looting of tombs in China dates back several thousand years. *Lüshi chunqiu* ('The Spring and Autumn [Annals] of Mr. Lü') record that tomb looting was considered a major crime as early as the pre-Qin period (eighth–third century BC) and anyone who looted a tomb would be severely punished. However, the practice continued in spite of these laws and the severity of the punishment. Many scholars linked the emergence of tomb looting to the tradition of 'treating the dead as the living'[1] and burying elaborate funerary goods.[2] In order to prevent robberies, stone blocks were often used in various places in Han tomb complexes. The Beidongshan tomb, for example, used nine huge, dovetailed stone blocks, mostly over two metres long, one metre high and weighing between 3 and 7.8 tons, to seal the outer passage; nine smaller blocks and eight big boulders for the inner passage; and another four big stones outside the front chamber (fig. 143). In addition to the stone blocks, self-locking devices were used in early Han tombs to maximize security.[3] Despite all these defensive measures, very few Han tombs survived undisturbed. Most of the tombs of the Kings of Chu in Xuzhou, including Beidongshan, were

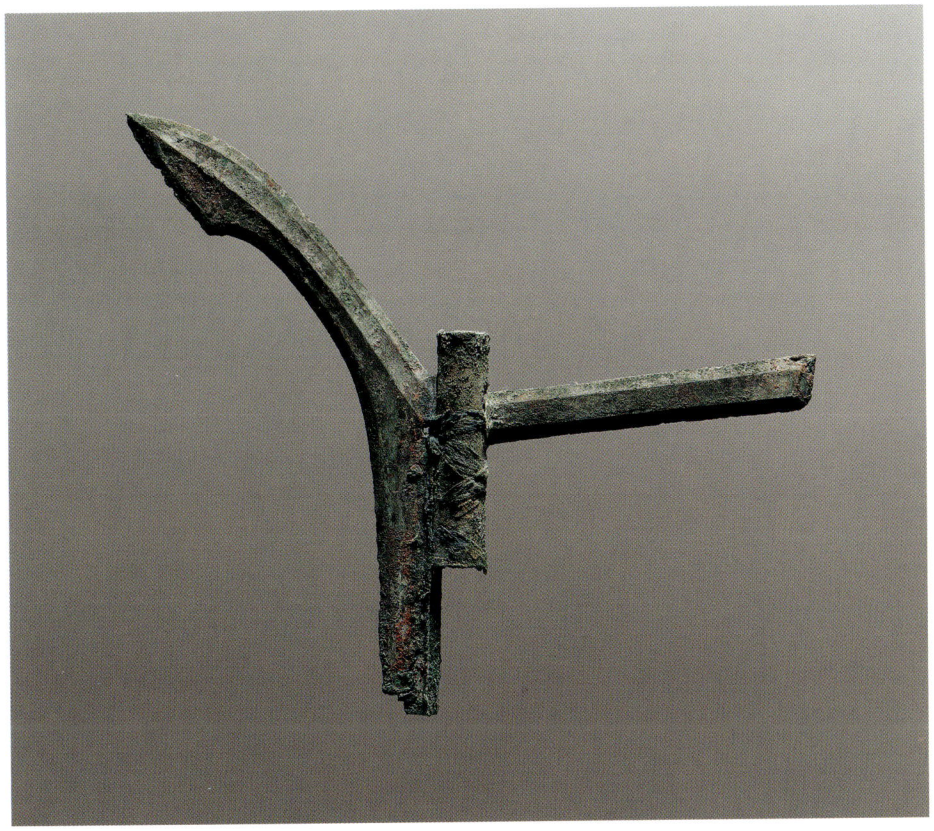 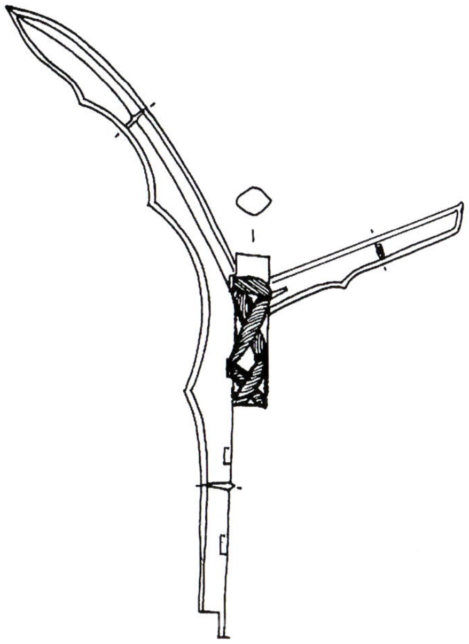

12

severely plundered several times over the past two thousand years. The King of Nanyue's tomb in Guangzhou is one of very few that have survived intact. JX

1 *Shisanjing zhushu*, p. 1593.
2 See Wang 2007b for a detailed discussion on the emergence of tomb looting in ancient China.
3 Li 2005, p. 19.

12

Bronze halberds (*ji*)

Second century BC, Western Han dynasty
Length 33.5 cm, 53 cm
Excavated at the tomb of the King of Chu at Shizishan in 1994–5
Xuzhou Museum, Jiangsu Province

Found in the first chamber in the west of the tomb along with ferrules, these two halberds are among five finds of the same form. The weapon was made of bronze, combining a dagger-axe and a spear. The single blade curves upward towards a sharp point at an oblique angle to the vertical shaft. The lower edge of the blade is in one or three broad concave curves,[1] merging with the vertical part, which has four holes for fastening the head to the shaft. Between the tang of the head and the blade is a gilded hollow column of oval cross-section where the wooden shaft was inserted. The column was tied to the dagger with silk strings. All three parts were cast in one piece.

Archaeological evidence suggests that halberds were used in China for at least 3,000 years. The earliest prototype halberd was discovered in an early Shang dynasty tomb at Taixi in Hebei Province, where the tomb occupant was found with a bronze spear with a dagger-axe perpendicularly attached to its shaft on the left side of the body.[2] Since the late Warring States period (476–221 BC), iron began to replace bronze in weapon production. The shape of halberds changed accordingly to a '卜' shape: that is, the tang of the dagger disappeared and the horizontal and vertical blades became longer and narrower, making sharper points. In the Western Han dynasty, a halberd was listed as one of the necessary 'five weapons' for every patrol officer – the basic official position at the time – for maintaining local law and order.[3] JX

1 The lower edge of the blade of the bigger halberd is in three concave curves.
2 As it was the only find of Shang dynasty date and the way of assembling the two weapons together was rather simple, Yang Hong thought that it could be a trial piece for weapon improvement during that time, but was not used in battle; Yang 1985, p. 157.
3 Yang 1985, p. 175. The other four were crossbow, shield, sword and armour.

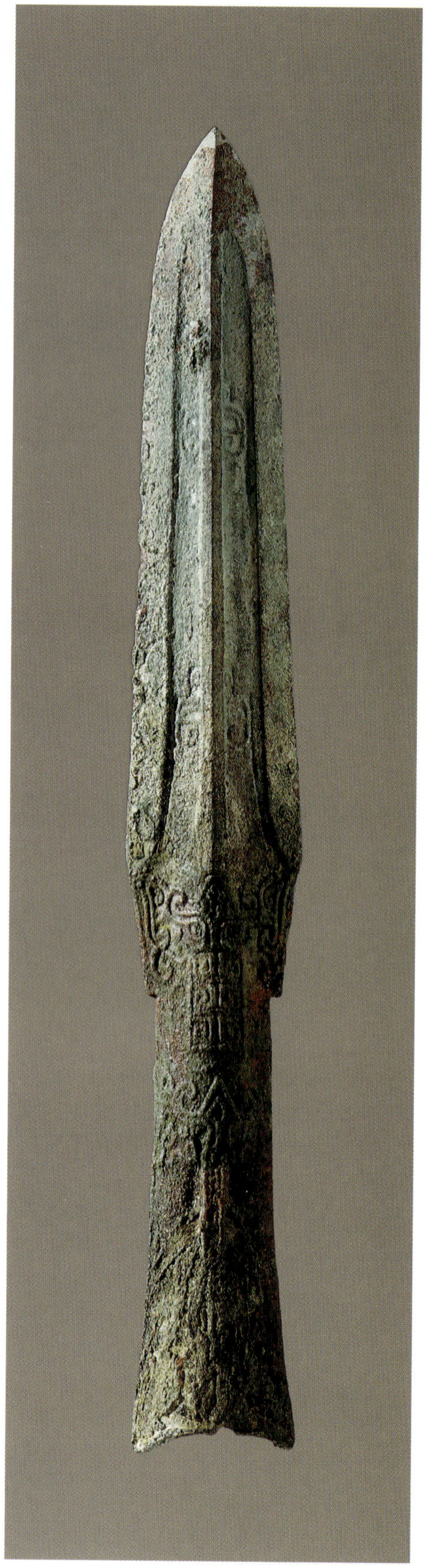

13

13

Bronze spearhead

Second century BC, Western Han dynasty
Length: 20.8 cm
Excavated at the tomb of the King of Chu at Shizishan in 1994–5
Xuzhou Museum, Jiangsu Province

Decorated with a mask relief pattern, this bronze spearhead is among the five finds excavated from the W1 chamber, which appeared to be a storehouse for weapons and vessels. The blade has a raised median crest with a rhomboid cross-section. The lower portion of the spearhead is an oval-shaped socket into which would have been fixed a long wooden pole. There is a loop on one side of the cylinder possibly for attaching a tassel. The original spear was 216 cm long including the wooden shaft and the silver ferrule. Spears are one of the most common weapons used in China from the Neolithic period and are still in use today in contemporary martial arts. JX

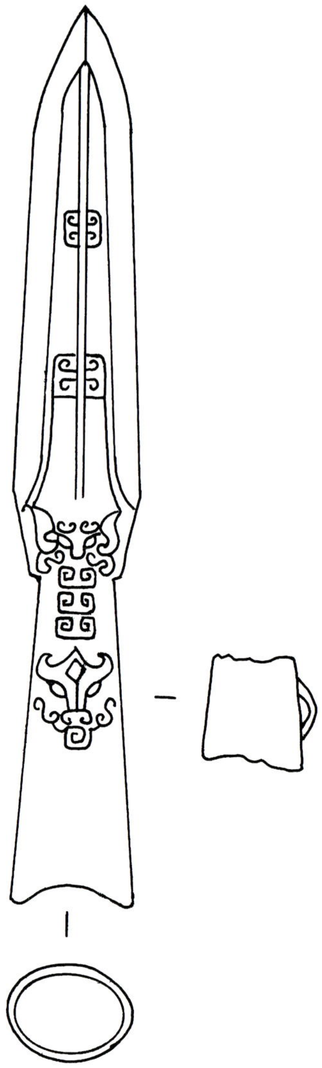

14

Bronze dagger-axe (*ge*)

Second century BC, Western Han dynasty
Width of the *ge* head: 19 cm; Length of *zun* (bronze ferrule): 13.6 cm
Excavated at the tomb of Marquis Wanqu at Bojishan in 1994
Xuzhou Museum, Jiangsu Province

This highly elaborate and decorated dagger-axe was found in the west corner of the tomb of Marquis Wanqu and is dated to the early Western Han period. It is in a good state of preservation, with light patination. The head is made of bronze with a long, straight double-edged blade and a sharp point.[1] The lower edge curves downwards, merging with the vertical elongation of the edge called a *hu*. This piece has three holes on the *hu* to help fasten the head to the shaft. A crouching bird looking back was cast at the top of the *yue*, a tubular part attached to the tang (*na*) of the dagger. The perpendicular wooden pole had completely decomposed.

Evolved from prehistoric tools, the *ge* was the primary weapon of the early Chinese armies from the Shang dynasty (*c.*sixteenth–eleventh century BC) to the Spring and Autumn period (*c.*770–476 BC).[2] This early pole weapon was very effective in battle, usually used with a thrusting and swinging motion. *Ge* with longer shafts were carried on war

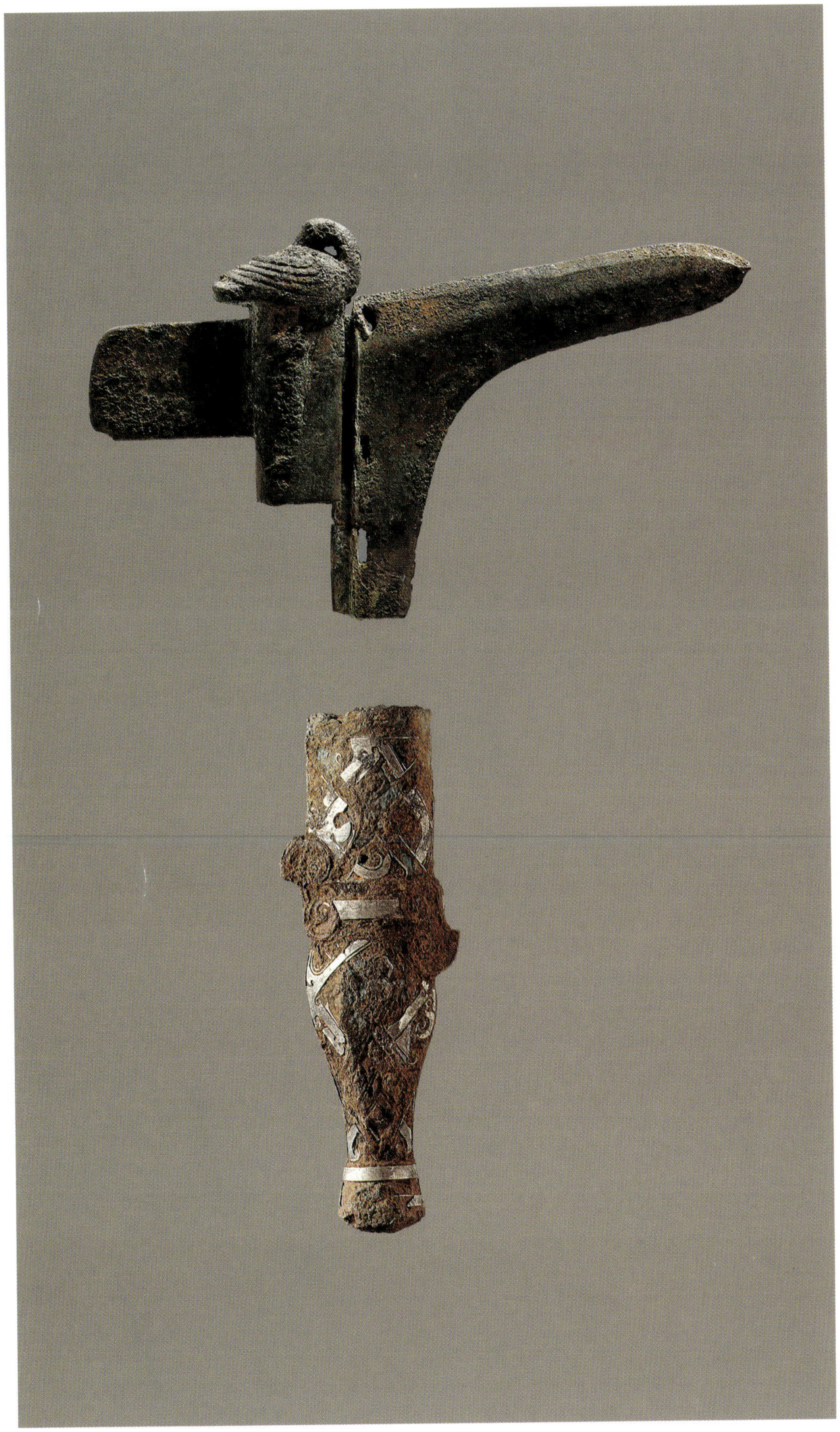

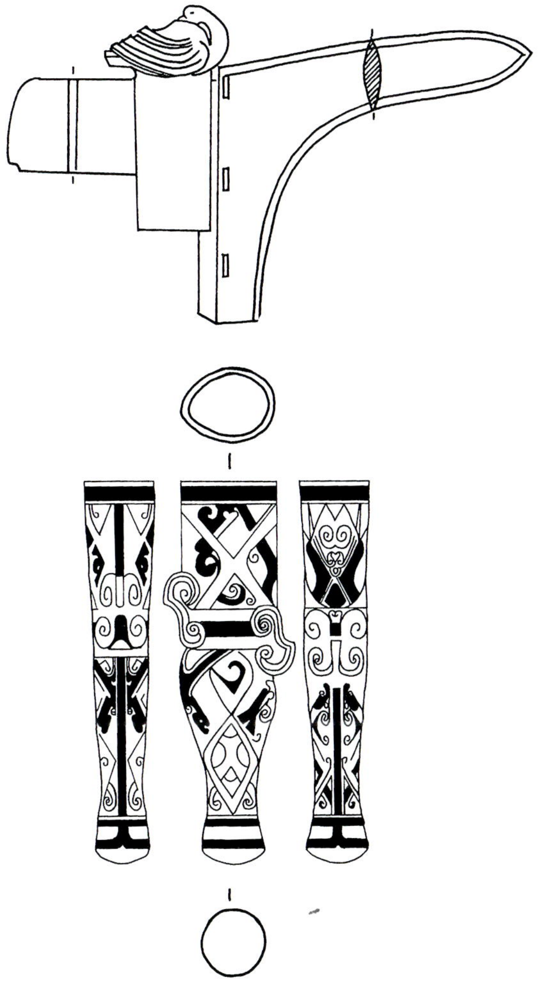

chariots to push the enemy to the ground. The use of bronze *ge* declined in combat during the Warring States period because of the introduction of more versatile halberds. In the meantime iron began to be used widely in weapon production, replacing bronze. Bronze *ge*, especially with unusual designs and fine decoration like this piece, continued to be used as ritual or ceremonial objects.
JX

1 A dagger-axe head can also be made of jade for ritual or ceremonial purpose, such as the piece excavated from the tomb of the King of Chu at Shizishan (cat. 19).
2 The earliest bronze dagger-axe was discovered in Fu Hao's tomb in Yinxu, Henan Province, the ruined site of the last capital of China's Shang dynasty.

14

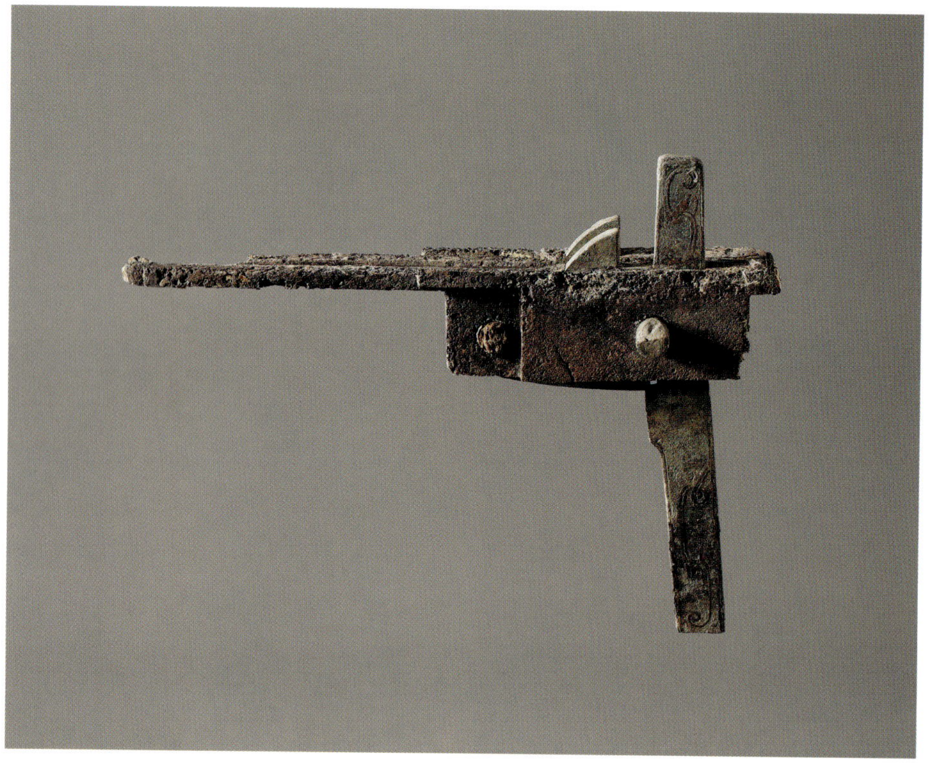

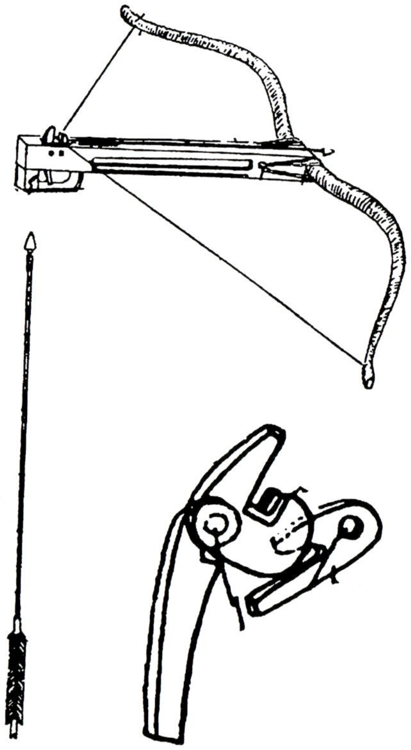

15

15

Bronze crossbow mechanism

Second century BC, Western Han dynasty
Width 19.3 cm; Height 14.7 cm
Excavated at the tomb of Marquis Wanqu at Bojishan in 1994
Xuzhou Museum, Jiangsu Province

This piece was the trigger mechanism of a Han dynasty crossbow found next to the bronze dagger-axe (cat. 14) in the west corner of the Marquis Wanqu's tomb. The whole assembly consists of the tumbler (which included two elements cast in one piece, the teeth *ya* to hold the bow string and the aiming element, *wangshan*), the sear (or *gouxin*) and the trigger (*xuandao*) in its bronze casing, called *guo*. Some traces of the original wood from the stock were found within the casing. The working parts of the trigger system were connected to the outer casing with two axles, a wooden one in the front and a metal one in the rear. The surfaces of the tumbler, the trigger and the casing were inlaid with gold and silver cloud patterns. No other decoration or inscription is discernable on this piece. According to the archaeological excavation report, this trigger mechanism was a working weapon, that is, not a ritual item for burial. The trigger and sear were stuck together by corrosion.

The earliest crossbow to appear in an archaeological context is from the sixth century BC grave burial at Qufu, Shangdong.[1] Since the Qin and Han dynasties, the crossbow had been widely used as the military projectile weapon of choice.[2] Apart from being used for infantry engagements, crossbows were also weapons used by cavalry and by warriors on war chariots.[3] JX

1 See Selby 2001 for a detailed examination of this bronze crossbow trigger.

2 Over 260 crossbows of at least three different types were found in the First Emperor's tomb. Techniques of making crossbows were well developed at that time.

3 As is shown in the example from the First Emperor's tomb; Yates 2007, pp. 37–45, fig. 23.

16

Four bronze lances (*pi*)

Second century BC, Western Han dynasty
Length 33–51.6 cm
Excavated at the tomb of the King of Chu at Shizishan in 1994–5
Xuzhou Museum, Jiangsu Province

Twenty-four lances in all have been excavated from the tomb of the King of Chu at Shizishan and they can be grouped into four types, in two basic shapes with different patterns. These four lances were buried as a complete set, consisting of a sheath, a body, a shaft and a ferrule. Double-edged, flat and sharp-

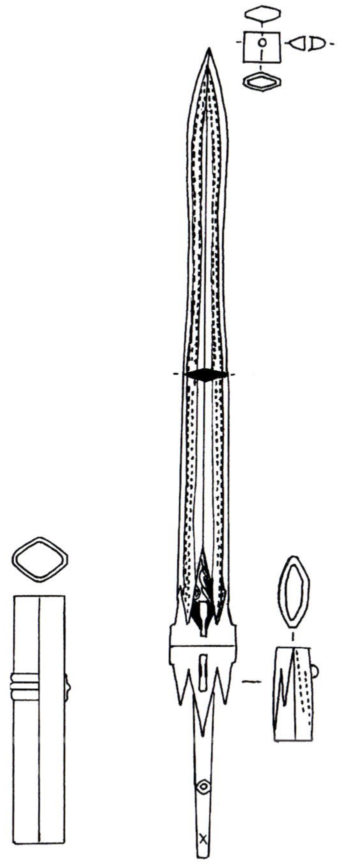

pointed, the blades of the *pi* are very similar in shape to those of swords. The wooden shafts had decomposed, as had the sheaths. Only the bronze caps at the top and metal decorations on the mouth of some sheaths were left. The lances' surfaces are covered with patina and accretions of earth. Two lines of dotted decoration along the edges of the blade are discernible on one of the four lances. This piece also has a jagged-shaped sheath mouth. The other three are plain in design. With its wooden shaft, a lance could be over two metres long. According to historical texts, this pole weapon appeared between the Shang (*c.*sixteenth–eleventh century BC) and Zhou dynasties (*c.*eleventh century–771 BC) and became popular from the Spring and Autumn period (*c.*770–476 BC) to the Western Han (202 BC–AD 9) dynasty.

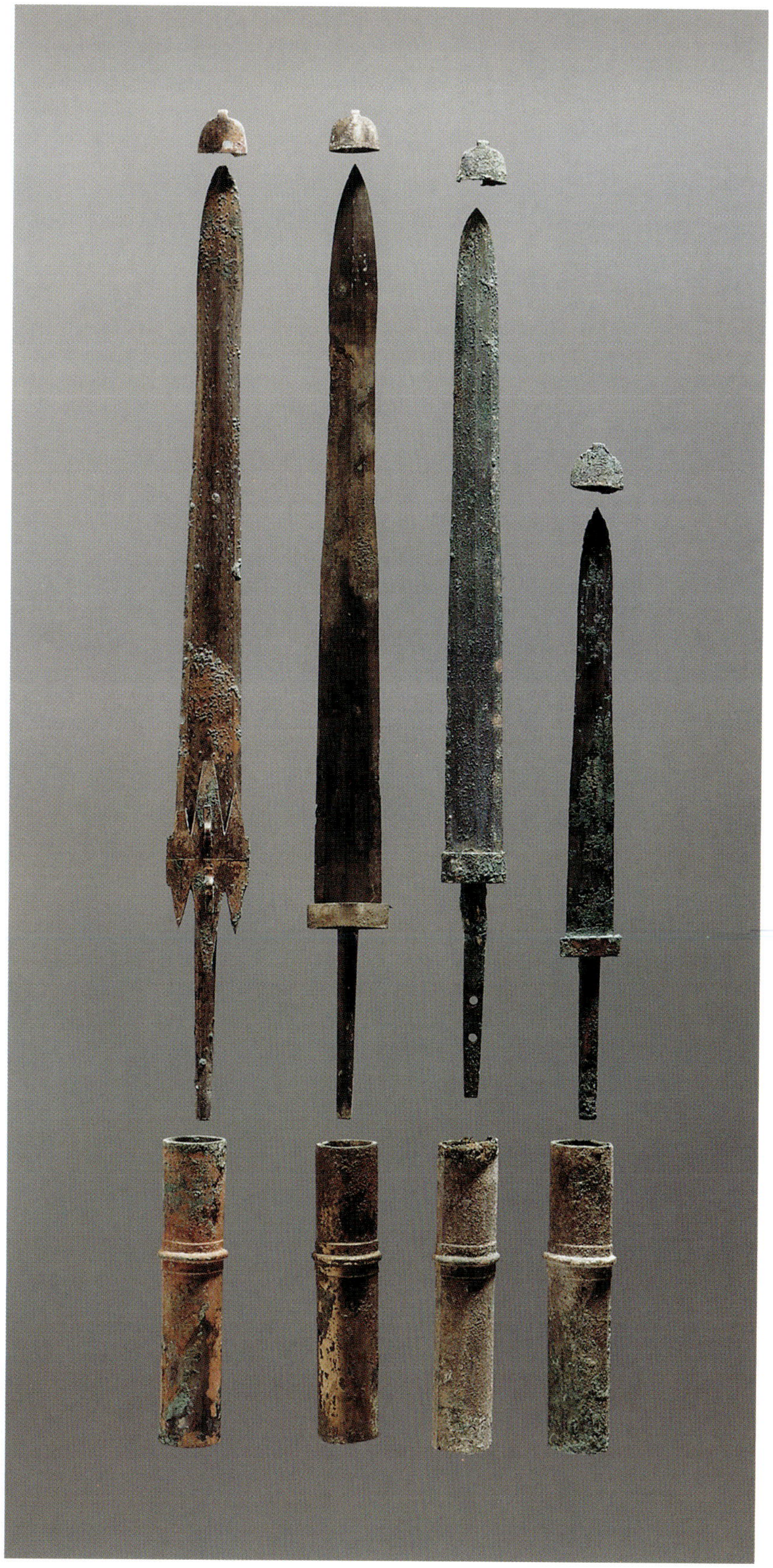

16

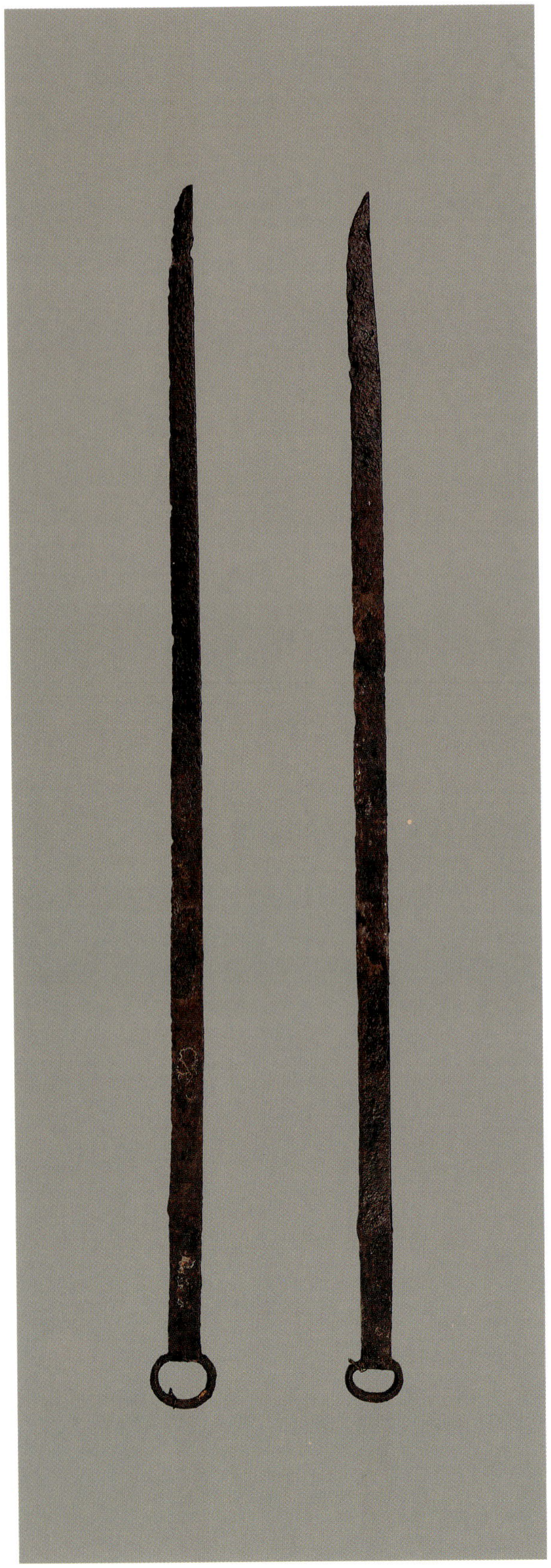

17

Lances discovered from the First Emperor's tomb are normally inscribed with the names of the workshop and maker as part of the process of quality control.[1] However, no inscriptions are found on any of the lances excavated at this tomb. JX

1 Yates 2007, p. 50.

17

Two iron knives with ring handles

Second century BC, Western Han dynasty
Length: 97 cm, 98 cm
Excavated at the tomb of the King of Chu at Shizishan in 1994–5
Xuzhou Museum, Jiangsu Province

These two wrought-iron knives have long, flat blades, which are joined to a ring handle. Both pieces are badly corroded. This type of knife was designed for military use, especially in close combat. Since the late Qin and early Western Han period, cavalry started to play a crucial role in warfare. Developed from swords to maximize strength when used in a cleaver motion, such long knives were generally used by soldiers on horseback.

Another type of long knife, used by the court as a ceremonial object, is frequently found in Han aristocrat tombs. They generally have fine decorations. For example, the long knife excavated at the tomb of King Mu at Zhongshan in Ding County in Hebei Province has a beautifully inlaid gold cloud pattern.[1] During the Eastern Han period, knives became part of official attire. The *Houhanshu* has a specific section on costume providing standard rules for the wearing of knives.[2] JX

1 See Excavation Report of Han Tomb No. 43 in Ding County, Hebei Province in *Wenwu* 1973.11, pp. 8–20.
2 *Houhanshu*, p. 3672, as quoted in Yang 1985, p. 125.

18

Two iron swords and a sheath

Second century BC, Western Han dynasty
Sword length: 87 cm, 103.5 cm; Sheath length: 33.7 cm; Width: 5 cm
Excavated at the tomb of the King of Chu at Shizishan in 1994–5
Xuzhou Museum, Jiangsu Province

Twenty-five iron swords in two bundles were found at the north corner of the W1 chamber of the tomb, along with other bronze and iron weapons. Because the tomb was flooded in antiquity, most organic materials such as wood and textiles had decomposed and iron objects were severely corroded. Iron swords of the Han dynasty represented by these two examples were made with elongated blades, almost twice as long as the bronze swords discovered in the same room. Traces of cords around the hilts are clearly discernible. The shorter piece has an oval-shaped jade guard between the blade and hilt.

The swords from Shizishan were all originally buried with oblate sheaths made of woven silk yarn, but only a few have survived. This piece is preserved in relatively good condition. The details of weaving provide rare material evidence of the craftsmanship of sword sheath making in the early Western Han period.

Swords were one of the basic weapons for infantry. During the Zhou dynasty (eleventh–third century BC), when chariots played the main role in combat, swords were auxiliary to long weapons such as dagger-axes and spears. The introduction of iron in weapon production during the Warring States period improved the toughness of the sword, enabling it to be made longer and sharper. JX

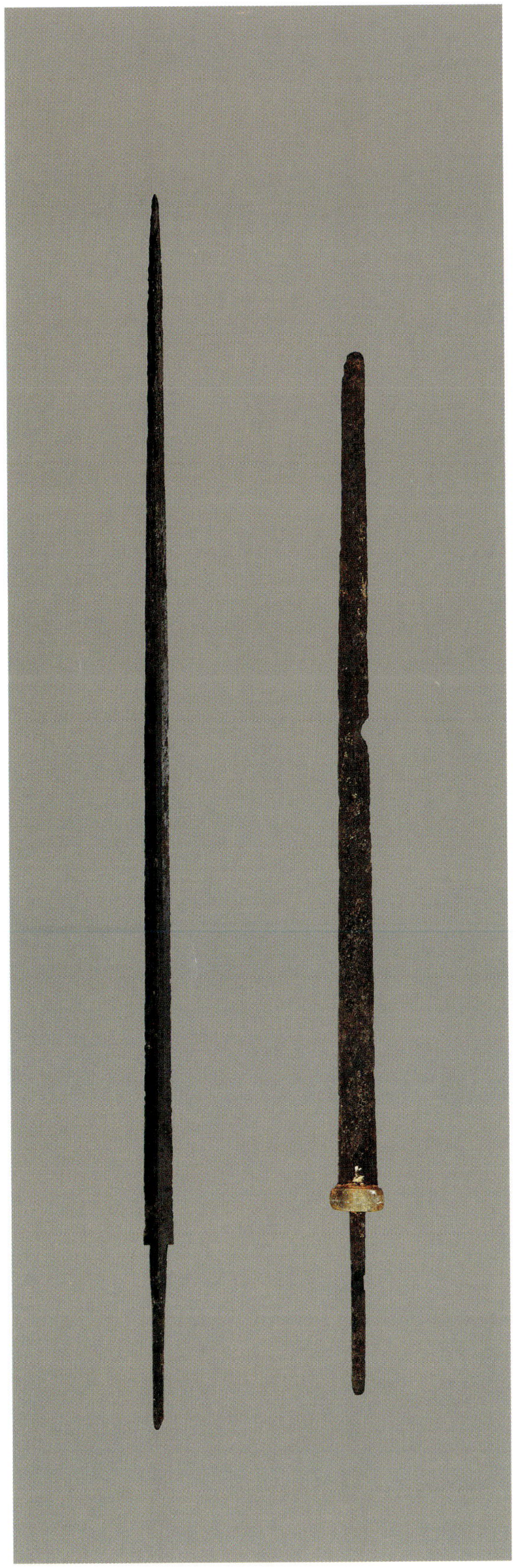

18

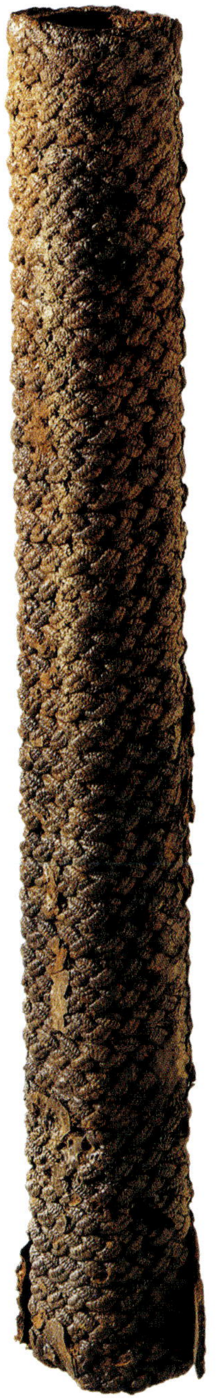

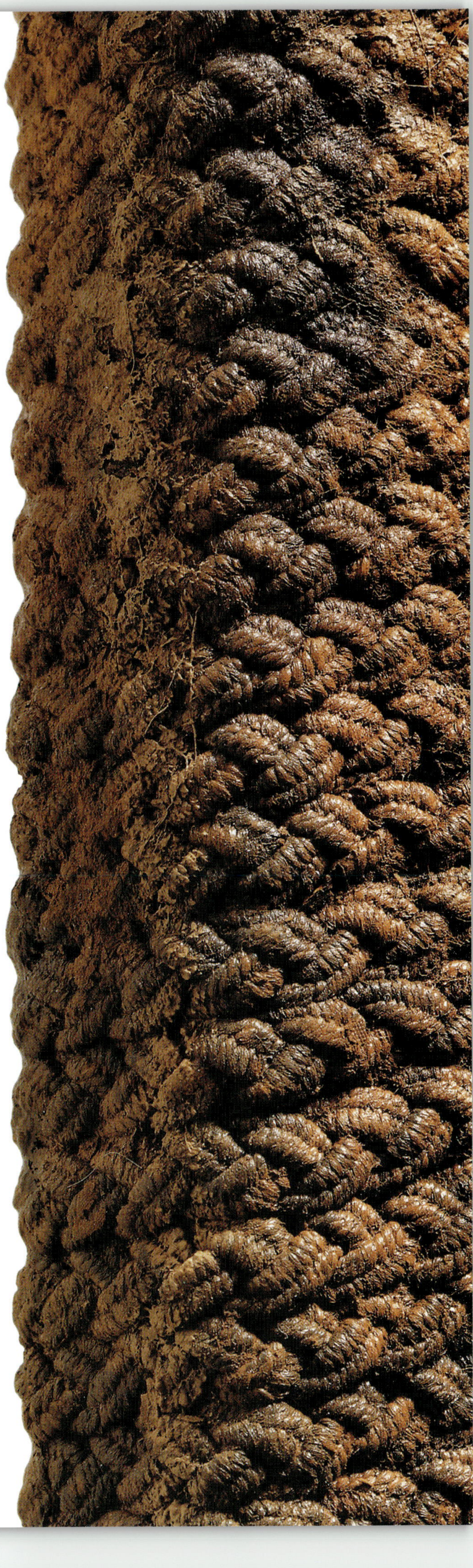

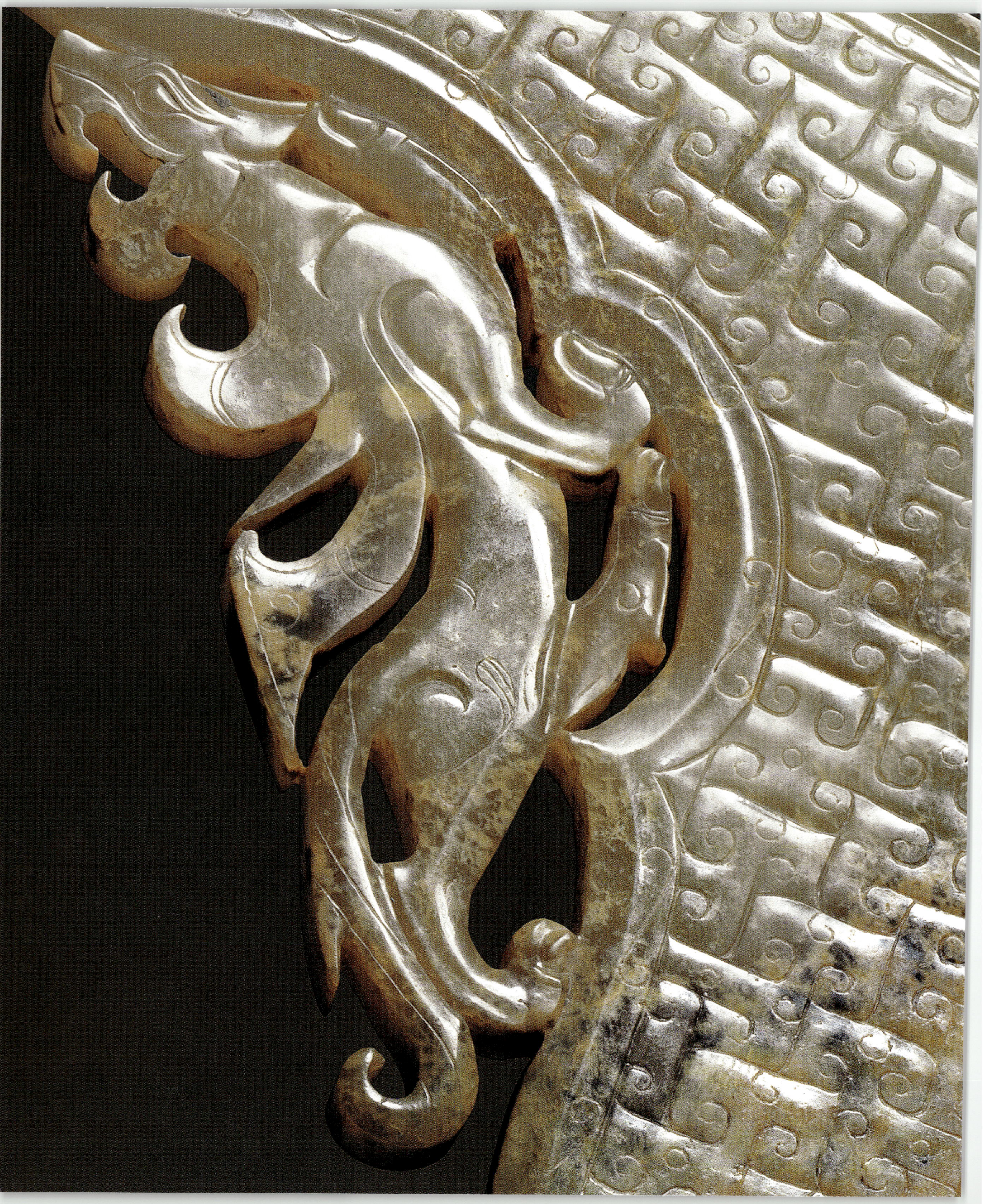

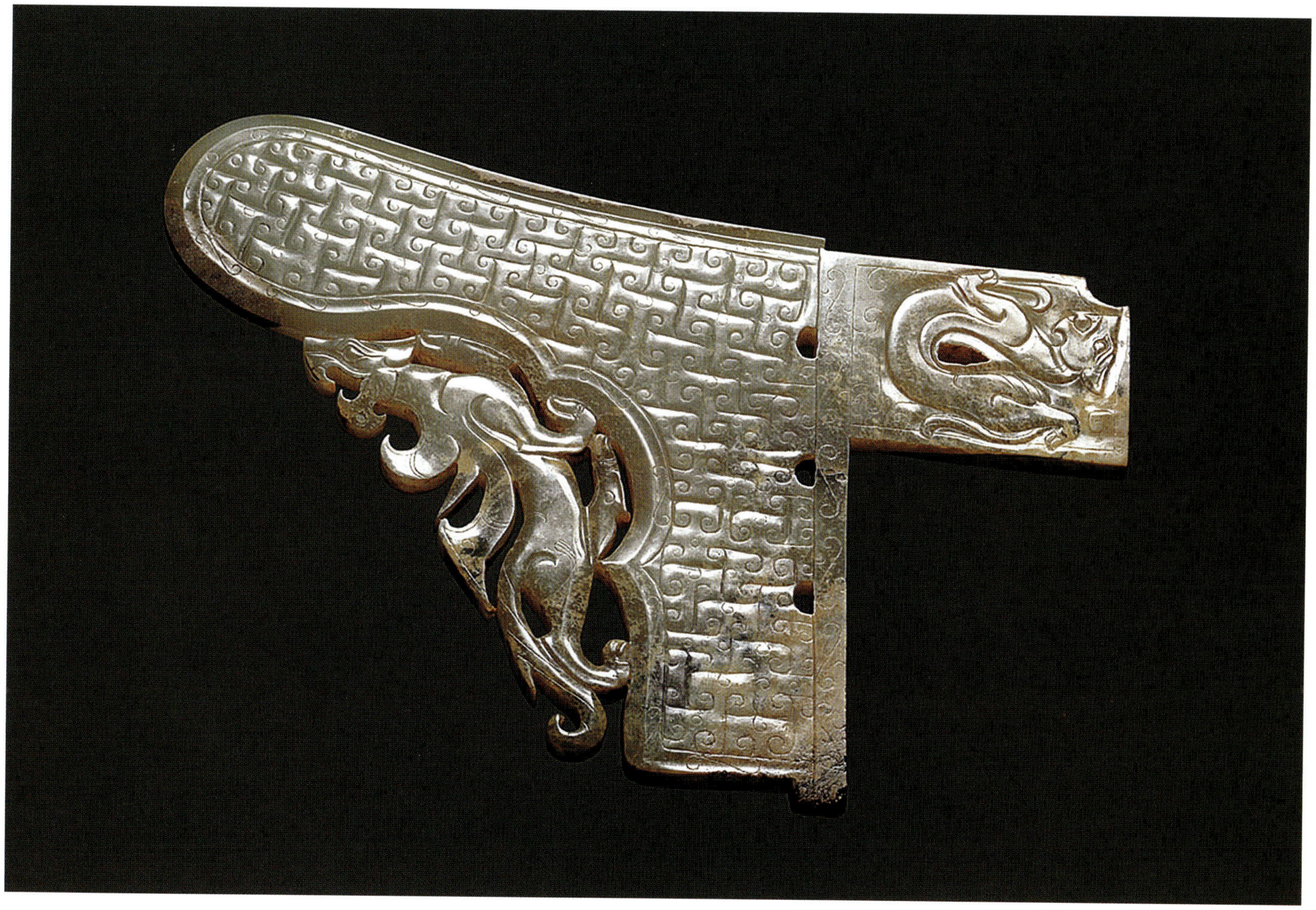

19

19

Jade dagger-axe (*ge*)

Second century BC, Western Han dynasty
Width: 17.2 cm; Height: 11.2 cm
Excavated at Shizishan in 1994–5
Xuzhou Museum, Jiangsu Province

A translucent jade dagger-axe is carved in the shape of a bronze weapon (*ge*). The jade has been identified as originating from Khotan. The surface of this dagger-axe is decorated with interlinked scrolls in low relief. A feline dragon was incised on the tang, and another dragon with wide-open jaws was carved below the arc in openwork style.

The use of jade, rather than bronze or iron, for the dagger-axe suggests that it was not designed as a weapon for use by the living. Jade weapons buried in tombs may have had a similar function to their bronze or iron counterparts but would also have been expected to provide protection against evil forces of the spirit world.[1]

Two other jade dagger-axes were found in the tombs of the King of Liang at Yongcheng, Henan Province, and of the King of Lu at Qufu, Shandong Province;[2] both locations are geographically close to Xuzhou. This piece from Shizishan, Xuzhou, however, is the best in terms of the quality of jade material used, the skill of carving and its overall design. JCSL

1 Lin 2007, pp. 188–9.
2 Hebei 1991–3, vol. 4, pls. 162, 190.

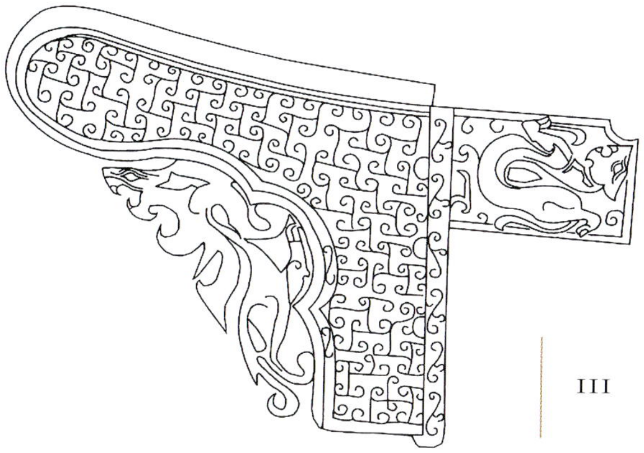

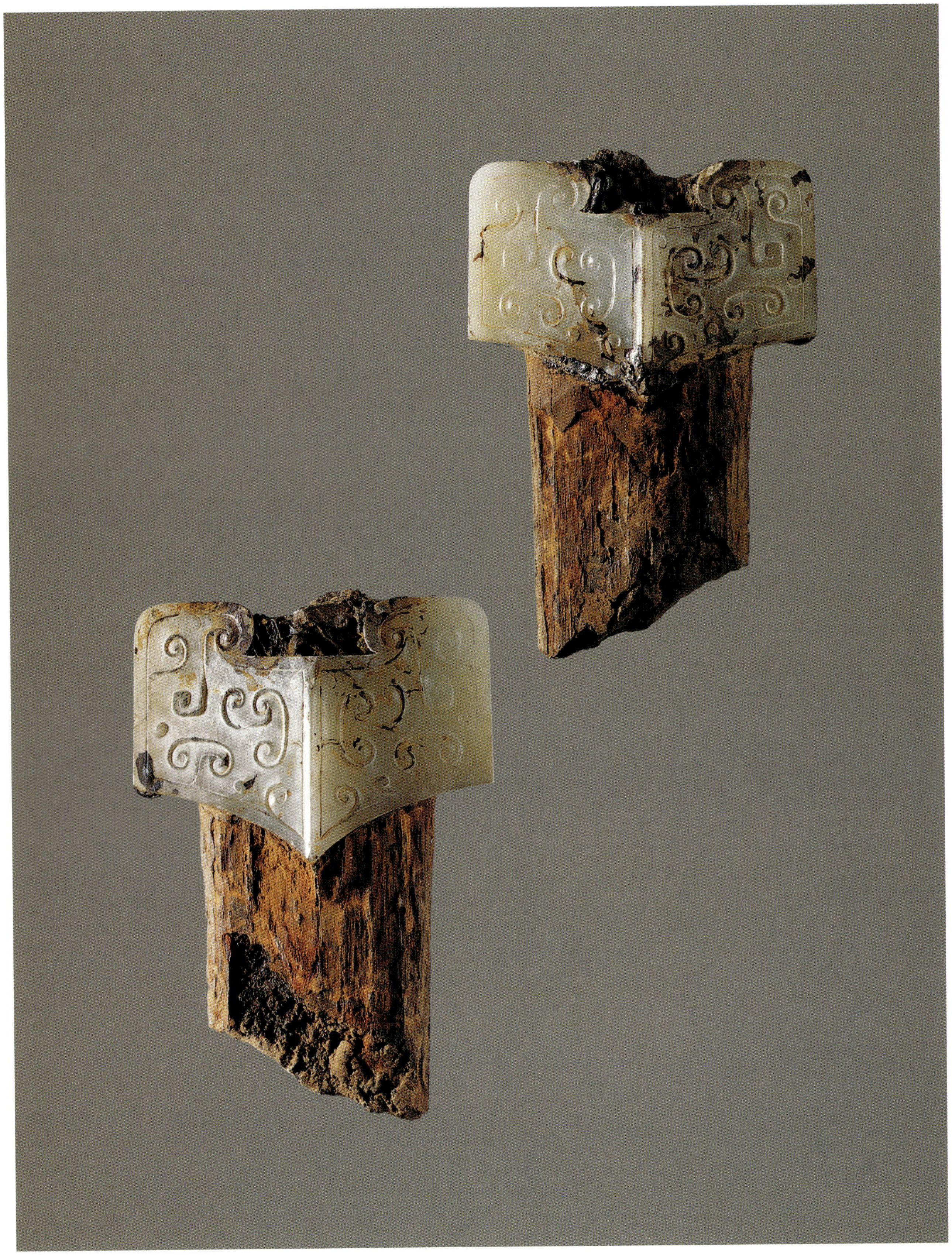

20A

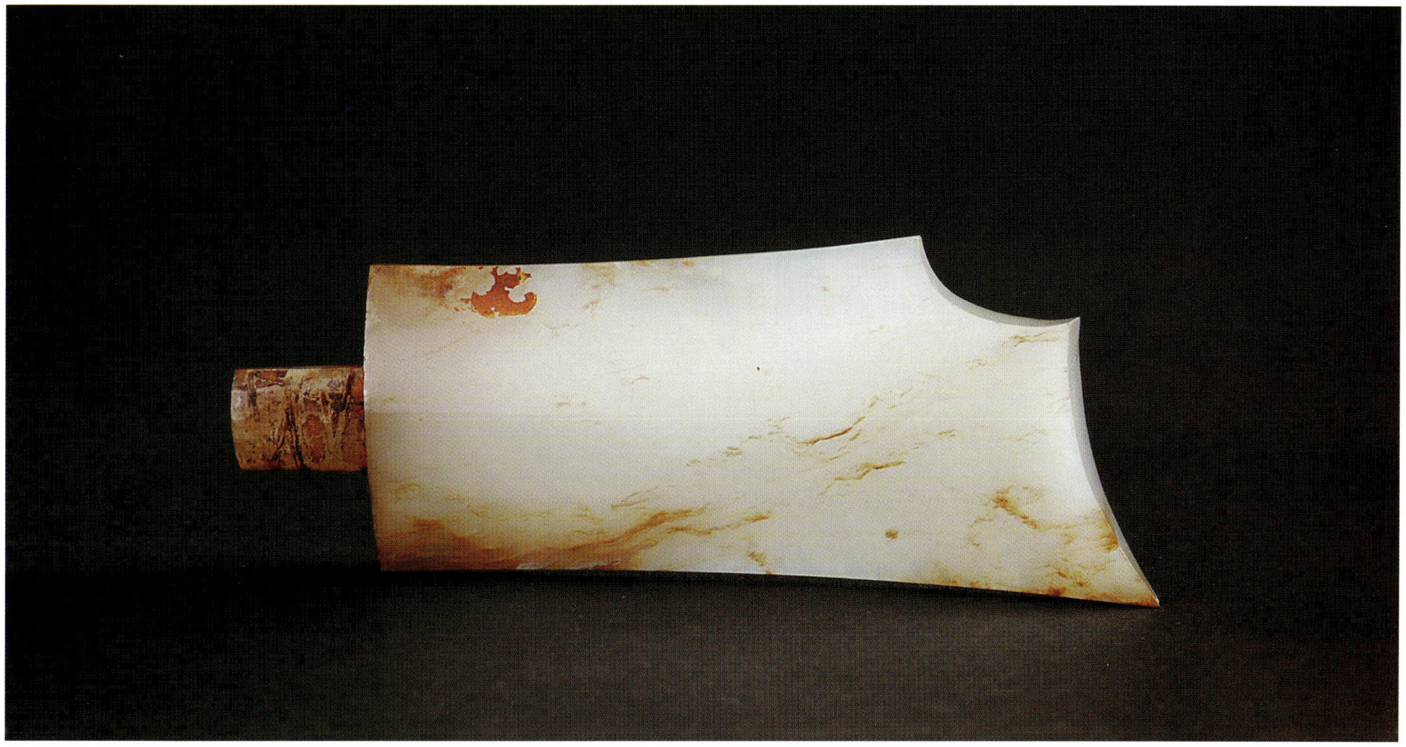

20B

20

Jade sword fittings

Second century BC, Western Han dynasty
Guard length: 5.6 cm; Width 4 cm;
Pommel length: 9.8 cm; Width 4 cm;
Scabbard chape length: 6 cm; Width 4.6–5.9 cm;
Scabbard chape width: 7.5 cm; Height: 4 cm;
Scabbard slide length: 9.5 cm; Width; 2.4 cm
Excavated at Shizishan in 1994–5 and
Beidongshan in 1986
Xuzhou Museum, Jiangsu Province

Sword fittings usually included a sword pommel, a sword guard, a scabbard slide and a scabbard chape (fig. 47). The artisans in Xuzhou varied their designs, particularly for the pommel and the scabbard chape, which are very different from those found in other Han kingdoms. The pommel from Shizishan is carved into a rectangular shape but has two large chips on the edge which makes it look unfinished or damaged (cat. 20B). The scabbard chape from Beidongshan was carved both in high relief and with openwork which gives the impression that it was ornamental rather than functional (cat. 20C). The scabbard chape from Shizishan is completely abstract to the point that no one can identify what it represents (cat. 20D). The sword guard (cat. 20A) and scabbard slide (cat. 20E) are more consistent in design due to constraints imposed by their positions on the sword.

These jade sword fittings were not only for decorative purposes and to represent the social status of the owner, but also might have been used to reinforce the power of the weapon through the 'magical' properties of jade. JCSL

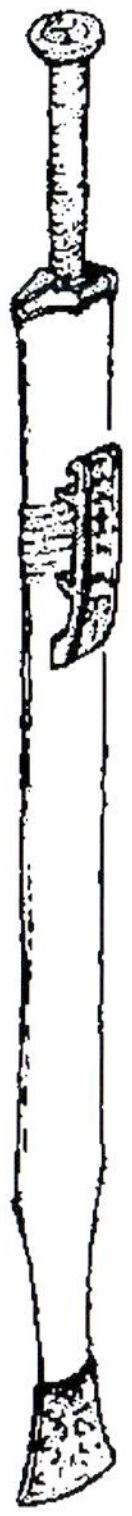

47 A sword with all its fittings

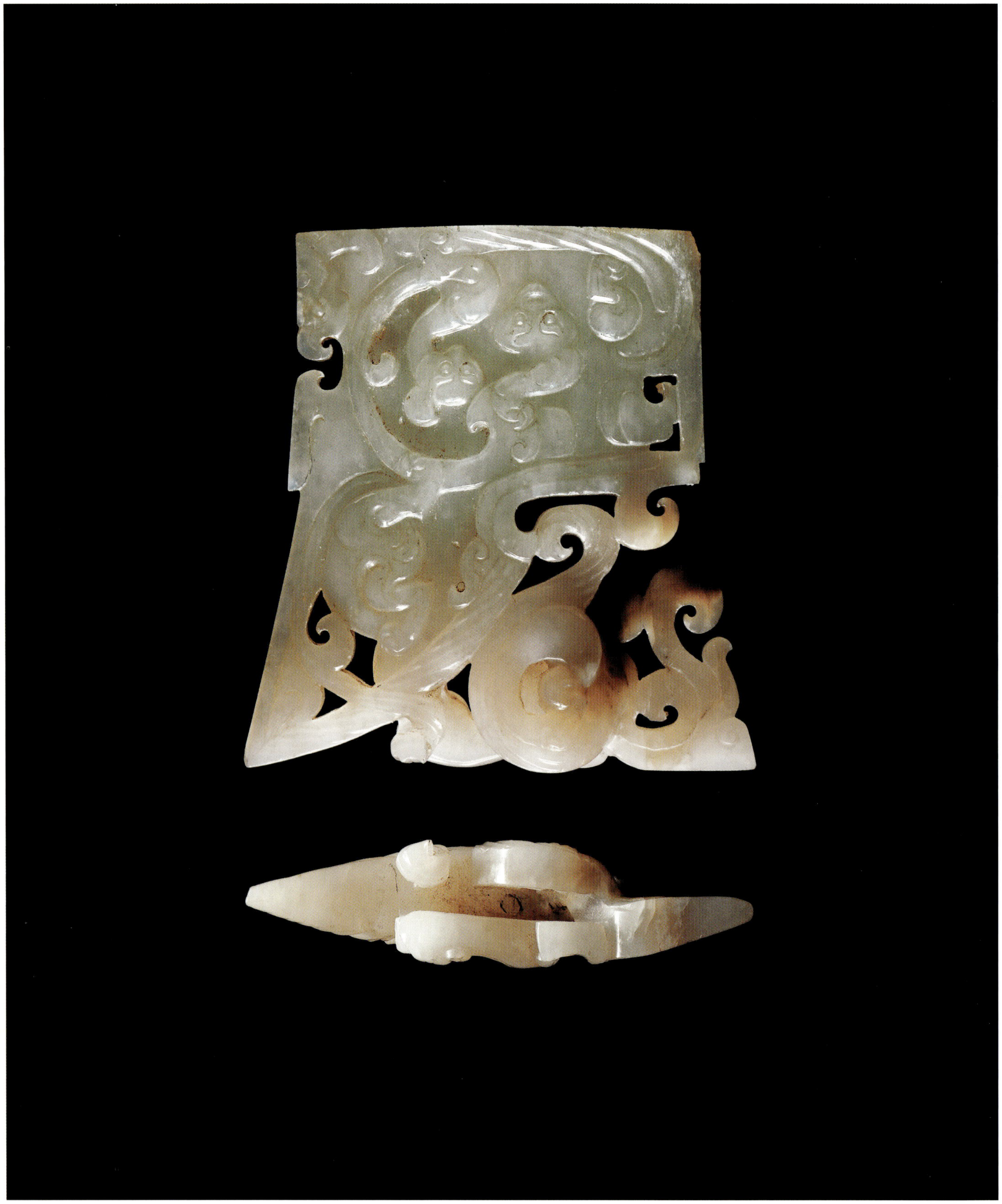

20c

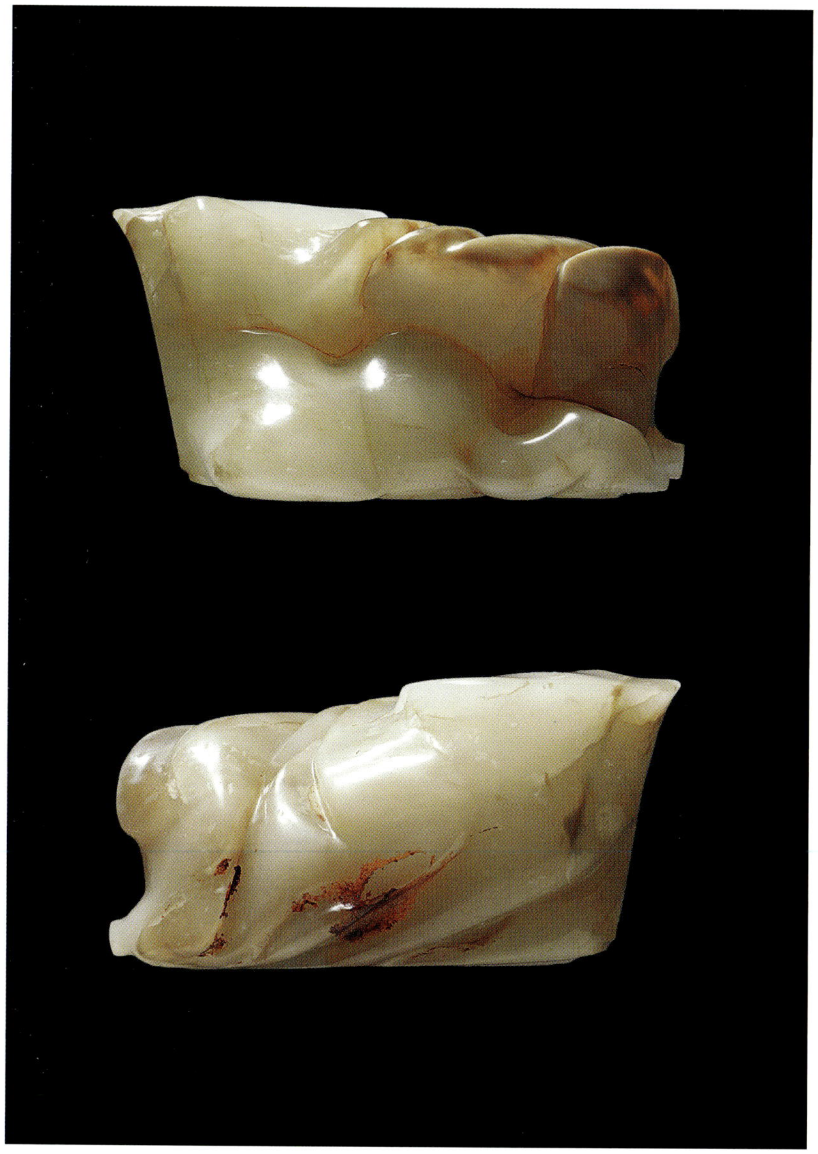

20D

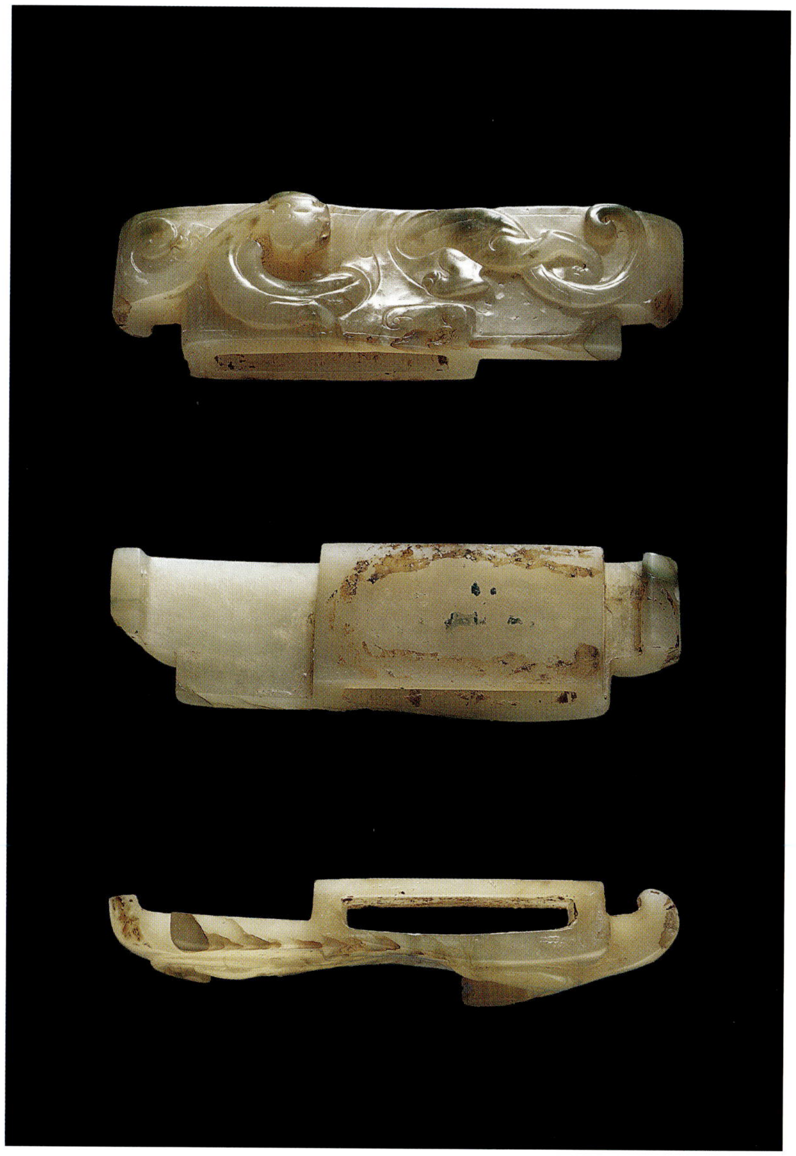

20E

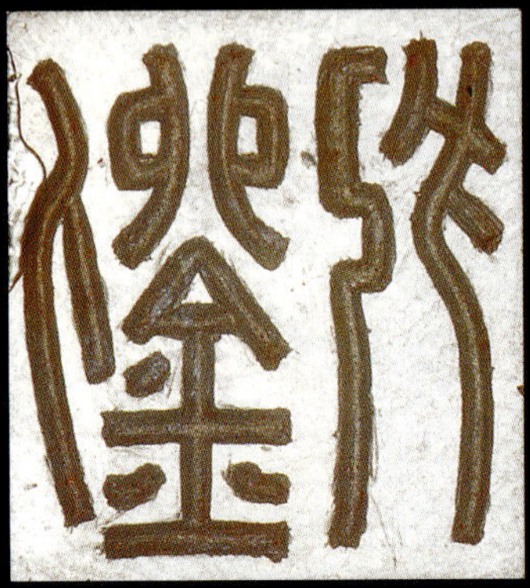

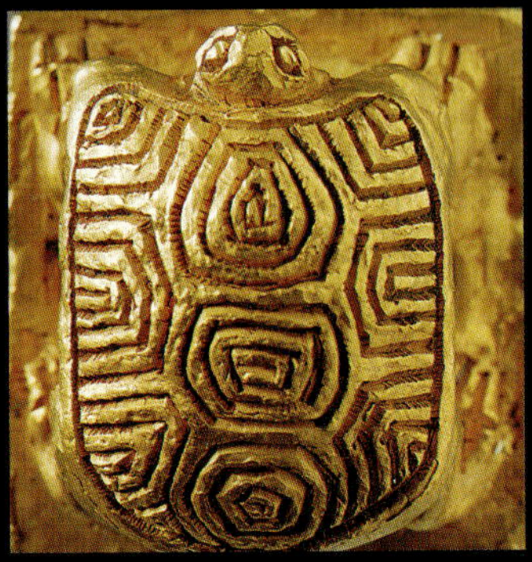

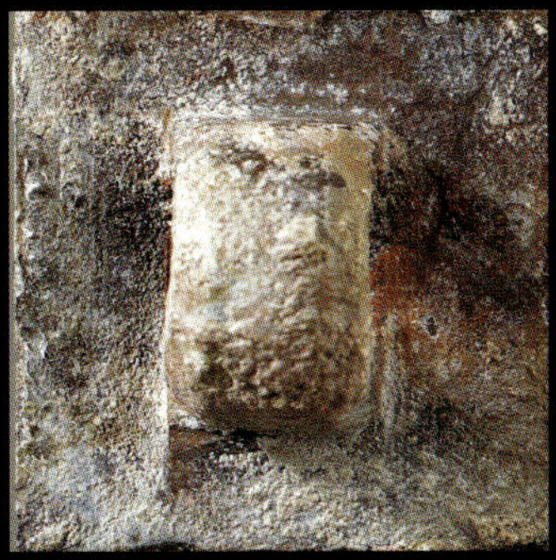

SOCIAL STATUS

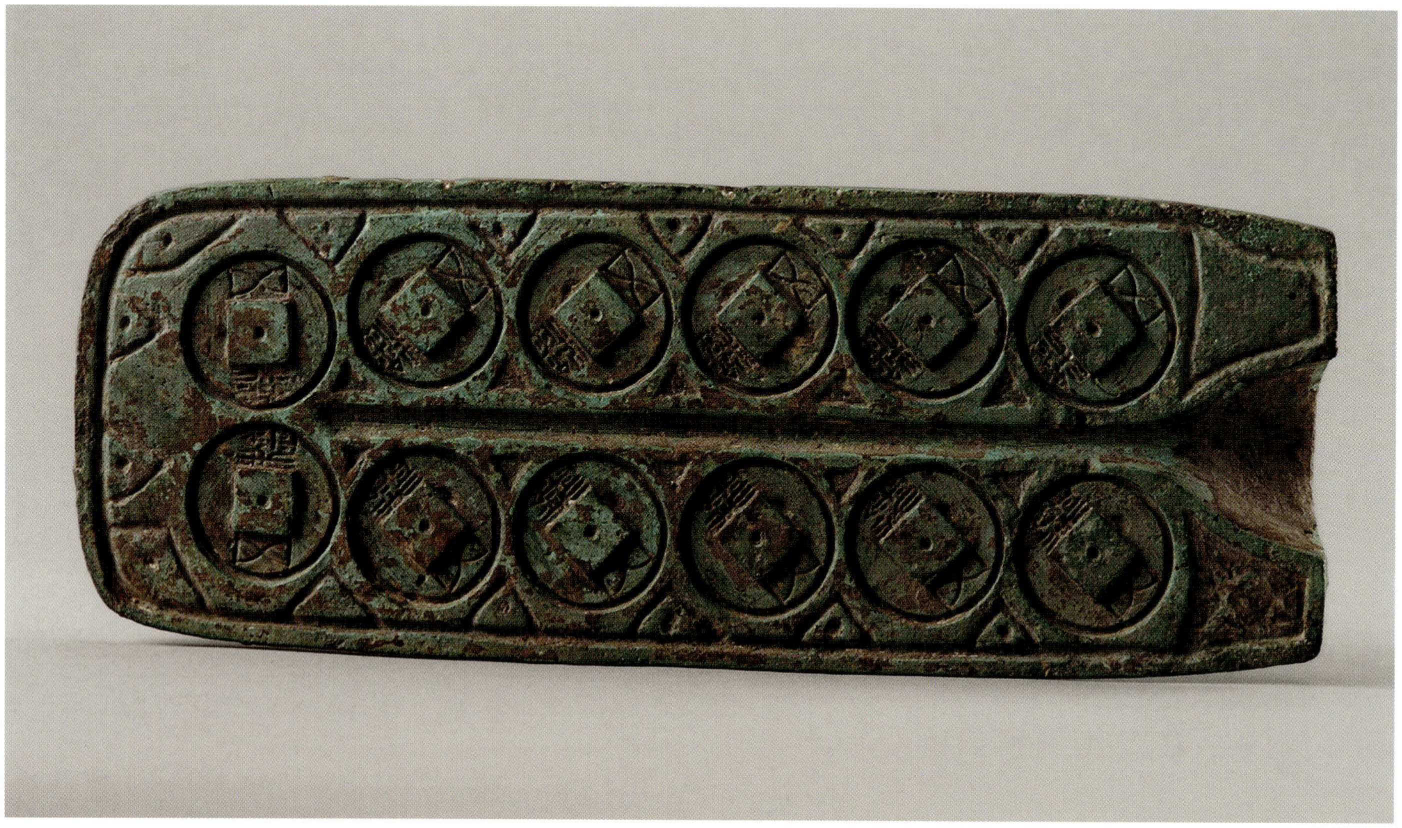

21

21

Mould for *wuzhu* coins

Western Han dynasty (202 BC–AD 24)
Length: 17.4 cm; Width: 7.5 cm; Thickness: 0.6 cm
Discovered at Yunlongshan in 1955
Xuzhou Museum, Jiangsu Province

This coin mould was discovered on the east slope of the Yunlongshan hill in Xuzhou during an archaeological survey in 1955. The mould was found with 530 *wuzhu* coins, under which there was one shard of a broken earthenware jar with an inscribed *wuzhu* coin pattern.[1] This site has not been excavated, but judging from the types of objects found on site, archaeologists excluded the possibility of it being a coin-manufacturing workshop.

The mould is made from bronze. Twelve coins in two rows can be cast simultaneously. *Wuzhu* coinage, which weighed five *zhu*[2] (hence its name), was issued in 118 BC as a result of Emperor Wu's efforts to regain the monopoly on coin production. The official *wuzhu* coins were called *Sanguan Wuzhu*, meaning *wuzhu* coins made under supervision of three officers.[3] Coins during that time were of consistently good quality and were edged with a hard lip to prevent forgers from clipping fragments off to cast new ones.[4] *Wuzhu* was one of the most influential circulating coinages in Chinese history as its use continued until the Tang dynasty (AD 618–906). JX

1 *Wenwu cankao ziliao* 1955.12, pp. 127–8.
2 *Zhu* was a weight unit. 24 *zhu*, equivalent of about 16 grams, equalled one *liang*.
3 Sun 1991, pp. 82–3.
4 Lewis 2007, p. 65.

22

Coins (*bazhu*, *sizhu*, *yujia banliang*, *wuzhu*, *daquan wushi*, *huoquan*, *dabu huangqian*)

Second century BC, Western Han dynasty
Diameter: 1.9–3.0 cm
Excavated at tombs of the Kings of Chu at Beidongshan in 1986, Shizishan in 1994–5 and Woniushan in 1980
Xuzhou Museum, Jiangsu Province

These selected examples are from a huge quantity of coins unearthed at the tombs of the Kings of Chu in the Xuzhou area. Most of them were found at the Beidongshan site, of which about 52,640 were well preserved (fig. 48),[1] and at the Shizishan site, where more than 176,000 *banliang* coins were found. Some of those coins were probably funeral money, not

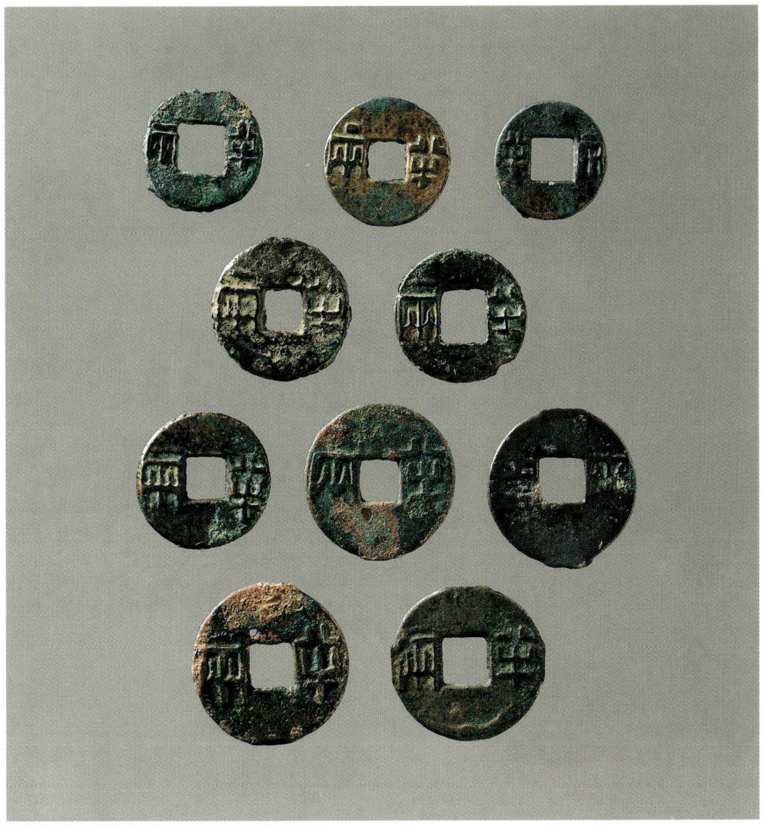

22

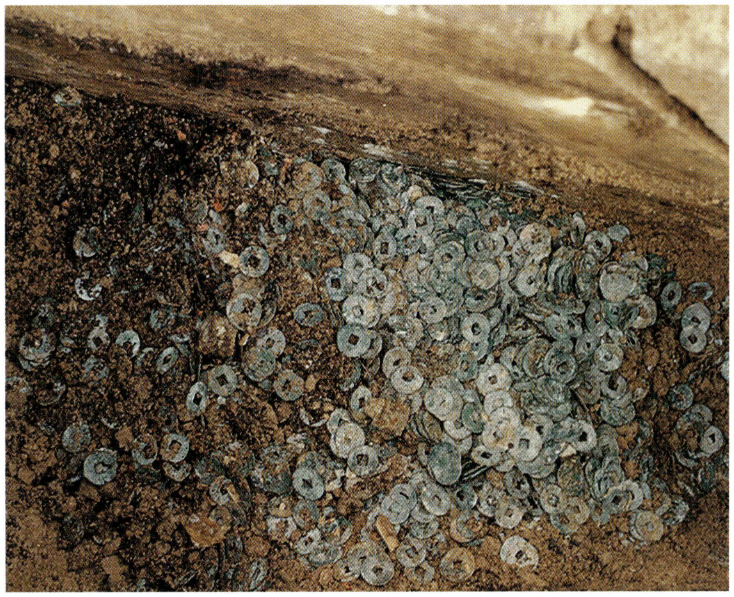

Fig. 48

coinage for circulation, as they were never recorded in use.

This selection of coins includes *bazhu*, *sizhu*, *yujia banliang*, *wuzhu*, *daquan wushi*, *huoquan*, and *dabu huangqian*, covering the coinage issued from the Warring States period (476–221 BC) through to the Wang Mang interregnum (AD 8–23). The first three are all categorized as *banliang* coinage but represent different periods of time.

The Qin state (778–207 BC) first issued the *banliang* coin, which was round with a square hole in the middle, in 336 BC. As the new Qin empire standardized the coinage throughout its conquered territory, the dominance of the *banliang* was not only essential for the effective running of the state administration, but also politically symbolic of unification.[2]

The subsequent Han dynasty adopted the Qin coinage along with many other practices but essentially managed to make gradual alterations to ensure the long-term survival of the empire.[3] *Banliang* coins were used from the beginning of the Han dynasty until Emperor Wudi's reign (141–87 BC) when the new *wuzhu* coins were issued, signalling a start of the central court's monopoly of coin production. Although *banliang* means half a *liang*, or twelve *zhu*,[4] the actual weight of different types of *banliang* coins varies enormously.

During the Wang Mang interregnum, there were four large-scale coinage reforms.[5] The emperor tried to revive ancient forms of coinage. Both *dabu huangqian* and *huoquan* were spade money (an ancient form of money modelled on farming tools) that used to be popular in the pre-Qin era. The four coinage reforms created very complicated and confusing monetary systems. Under the Eastern Han, when the Liu clan reclaimed the throne, the *wuzhu* coinage was re-established. Although the coins issued during Wang Mang's reign represented an untidy economy, they were beautifully made. The craftsmanship of the coins and the calligraphy of the inscriptions are considered to be fine examples of the art of the period and are still highly sought after by collectors today. JX

1 The total number of coins buried in this tomb is thought to be over 100,000, including the stolen and broken ones. Most of them are *banliang* coins.

2 Wang 2007a, p. 80.

3 See Lewis 2007, pp. 60–70 for a discussion on how Han inherited and altered Qin's practices.

4 *Zhu* was a weight unit. The *liang* consisted of 24 *zhu*, equivalent to about 16 grams.

5 See Sun 1991, pp. 85–6 for a discussion of the four coinage reforms.

48 Coins. Excavated from Beidongshan, Xuzhou, Jiangsu Province. Second century BC.

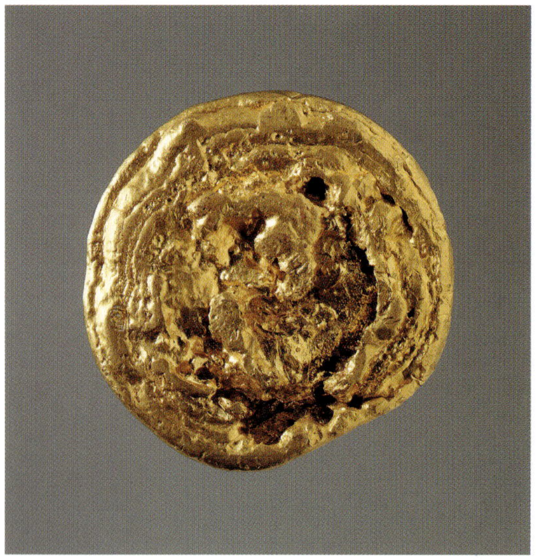

23

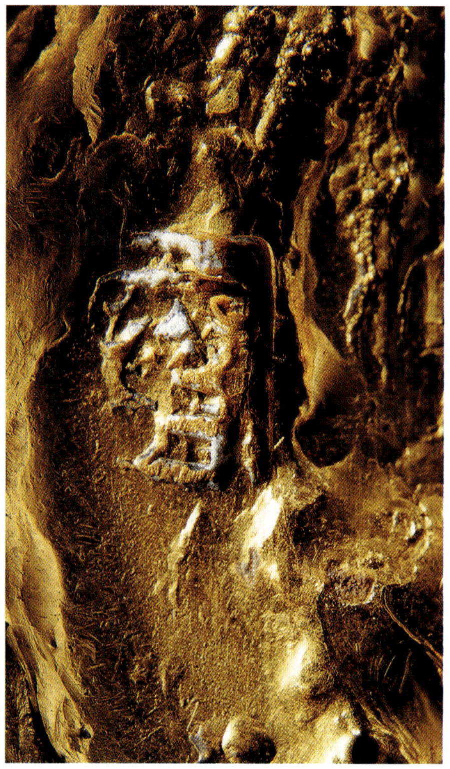

23

Gold disc

Second century BC, Western Han dynasty
Diameter: 6.2–6.5 cm; Thickness: 0.6–0.7 cm
Excavated at tomb No. 1 at Bojishan in 1990
Xuzhou Museum, Jiangsu Province

This gold disc, weighing 247.5 grams, has an irregular circular shape and an inscription engraved in *li* (seal) script on its front. A stamped impression can be seen close to the edge of the back but the characters are too obscure to read. The policy of defining two grades of money, gold in the upper grade and coins in the lower grade, derived from Qin dynasty practice and it was adopted by the Han. There were two different types of gold money based on shape in the Han dynasty: horsehoof shaped and a flat, round disc. This piece belongs to the latter group.

Burying gold money to symbolize wealth was a common burial practice during this period. Gold discs, or ceramic discs imitating gold ones, have been found in many Han tombs.[1] Archaeological evidence shows that the size and weight of gold discs in the Han dynasty vary. For example, the diameters of big pieces range from 5 to 6.6 centimetres and small ones measure 3 centimetres on average.[2] Some gold discs bear the inscription *lingzhi yijin* (toe of a Chinese dragon), which was an official name given by Emperor Wudi to round gold discs in 95 BC because of its auspicious implication. *Yijin*, or one *jin*, referred to the standard unit of gold and was equivalent in value to 10,000 *qian* (coins). Gold and gold discs were often used to reckon the quantity of money in historical records, indicating that gold was a form of circulating money.[3] JX

1 Examples include Guishan tomb No. 1, two gold discs and 600 pottery ones; the King of Chu's tomb at Beidongshan, two pottery discs; both the Kings of Chu's tombs at Guishan and at Tuolanshan, a number of pottery discs; Liusheng and his consort's tombs in Hebei, forty and twenty-nine gold discs respectively, as well as a few pottery and stone pieces.
2 Sun 1991, p. 83.
3 Sun 1991, p. 84.

24

Jade seal

Second century BC, Western Han dynasty
Length: 1.5 cm; Width: 1.4 cm; Height: 0.7 cm
Excavated at Fenghuangshan, Tianqi in 2001
Xuzhou Museum, Jiangsu Province

This small translucent jade seal was excavated from a medium-sized catacomb tomb at Fenghuangshan, Tianqi, Xuzhou. It has a perforation so that it can be worn and is carved with inscriptions on both sides. One side is inscribed with the characters of the owner's name, Liu Fan, a member of the imperial Liu family. The other is inscribed with the characters *Chen Fan* (Your Servant Fan),

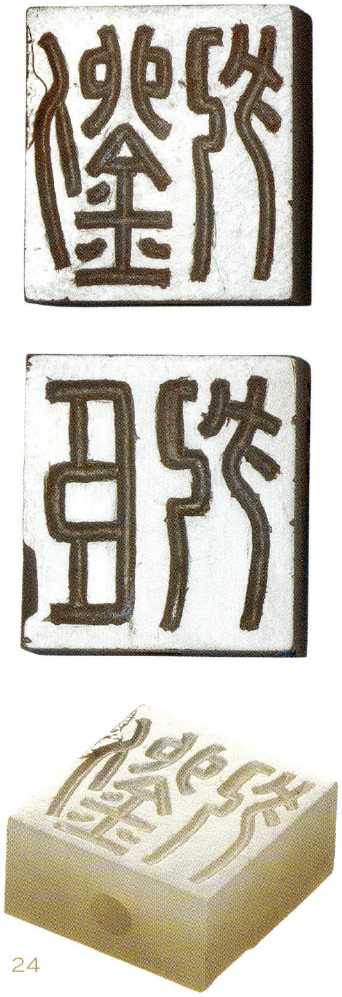

24

which identifies him as a state official of the Chu kingdom. The inscriptions on both sides of the seal, together with seals found in imperial family tombs in the Xuzhou region, seem to confirm that, after the *baima mengshi* (the Oath of White Horse), a secret meeting between Liu Bang and trusted supporters, a treaty was made which included terms agreeing that 'if anyone not of the Liu family becomes a king, the empire must unite in attacking him.'[1] State officials in the Xuzhou area all appear to be under the control of members of the Liu imperial family. JCSL

1 The history of the *baima mengshi* was recorded in the 'Basic Annals of Empress Lu' in *Shiji*, although the exact date was not recorded; *Shiji* 9.400. It is also referred to in other chapters, such as the hereditary family of Marquis Jian, Zhou Bo; *Shiji* 27.2077.

25

Silver seal

Second century BC, Western Han dynasty
Height: 1.7 cm; Knob Height: 1 cm; Length: 2.1 cm
Retrieved in 1985, originally from Guishan
Xuzhou Museum, Jiangsu Province

This silver seal has a square base with a turtle knob. The inscription, carved in negative relief, is the name of the sixth King of Chu, Liu Zhu (r. 128–116 BC). Seals were symbolic of social status and were usually buried with their owners as tokens for the afterlife. The higher the individual's status, the more seals were buried with him or her.

In the intact tomb of the King of Nanyue, nine seals made of gold, jade and turquoise, most carved with his name and title, were found in three lacquer boxes on top of his body. At Mancheng, in the intact tomb of Liu Sheng, the King of Zhongshan, four jade seals, two uncarved, were found. Nearby, in his queen's tomb, nineteen bronze seals, two with the name of the tomb owner, were buried in the main chamber.

As most of the imperial tombs in Xuzhou were looted, few seals have survived. This silver seal was the only one found to support the tomb owner's status that also matches the records in Sima Qian's *Shiji*. JCSL

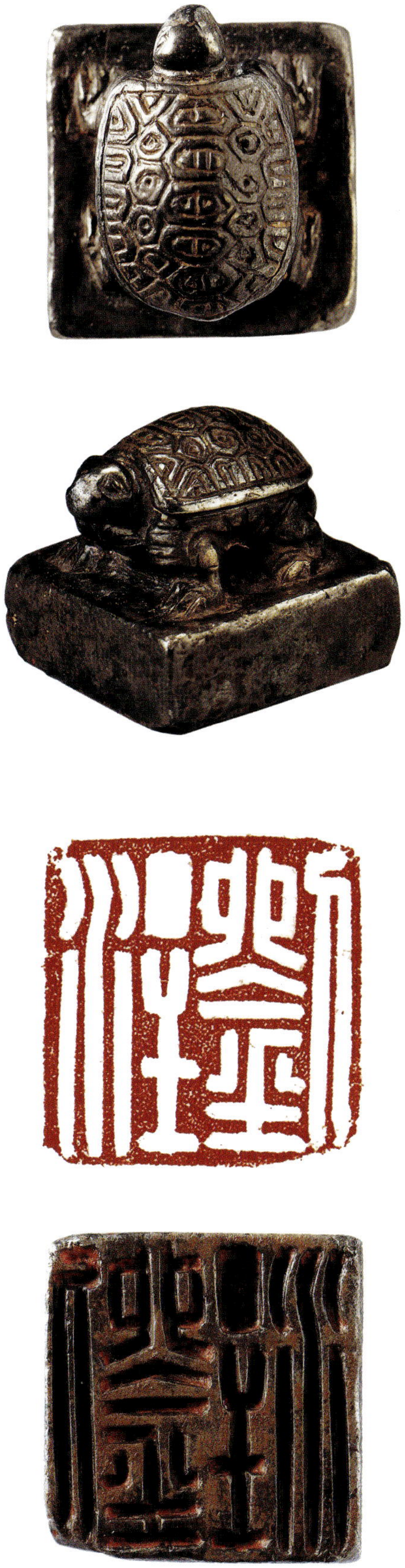

25

26

Gold seal belonging to the Marquis of Wanqu

Second century BC, Western Han dynasty
Height: 2.1 cm; Length: 2.3 cm
Excavated at tomb M3 at Bojishan in 1994
Xuzhou Museum, Jiangsu Province

This gold seal was found near the waist of the deceased Marquis. It was cast with an ornamental turtle knob, with the

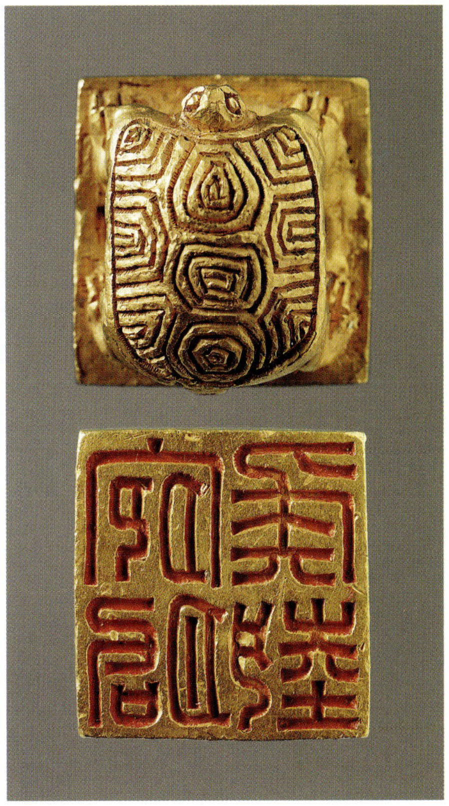

26

details of the turtle incised afterwards. The base is square with a negative relief inscription, *Wanqu Hou Yi* (Marquis Wanqu of Yi). Liu Yi was the sixth son of the first King of Chu, Liu Jiao, and was enfeoffed with Wanqu in modern Heze county, Shandong Province. He took part in the revolt against the central government in 154 BC. After the revolt, the Wanqu March was dissolved.

A Song dynasty text, *Hanjiuyi buyi* ('Addendum to the Ancient Rituals of the Han dynasty'), recorded that, during the Han dynasty, the carving of the seal knob indicated social status: the emperor used a jade seal with a tiger knob; the Empress used a gold seal with a tiger knob; kings of vassal states used gold seals with a camel knob; marquises, prime ministers, Grand Commandant and great generals used gold seals with a turtle knob.[1] The discovery of this seal with the Marquis's title matches the records in Sima Qian's *Shiji*. Most seals in the Han dynasty were either carved with an official title or a personal name. This gold seal is the only example that combined both title and personal name. It has been suggested by some scholars that it was probably produced for burial purposes. JCSL

1 *Hanjiuyi buyi* 1930, p. 4.

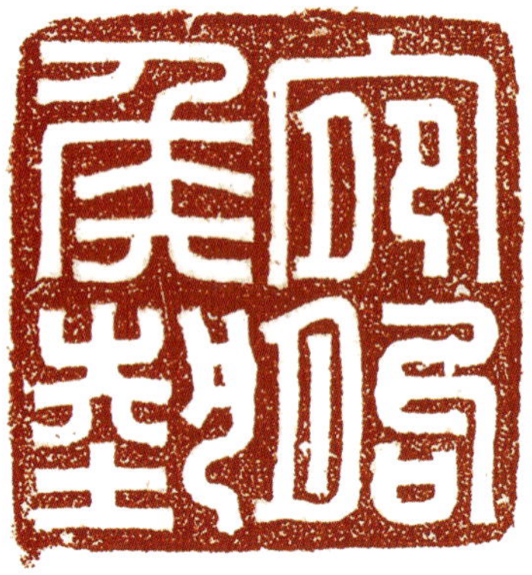

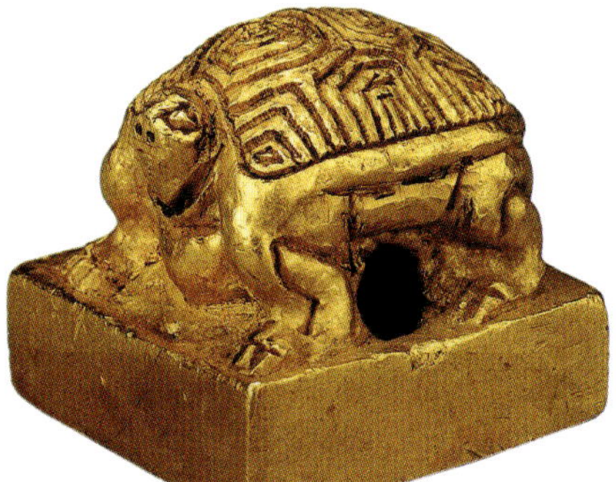

27

Bronze seal belonging to a minister

Second century BC, Western Han dynasty
Height: 1.7 cm; Length: 2.2 cm; Width: 2.1 cm
Excavated at Shizishan in 1994–5
Xuzhou Museum, Jiangsu Province

This bronze seal is cast with a bridge-shaped ornamental knob. The inscription is carved in negative relief with the characters *Chu Sima Yin*. *Sima* was the title of a senior Chu military official. Approximately 200 bronze seals were found in Shizishan bearing inscriptions indicating the titles of court officials, military officials and county officials who served the Chu kingdom. JCSL

28

Bronze seal belonging to the Inspector of Food Officer

Second century BC, Western Han dynasty
Length: 2.3 cm; Width: 2.3 cm; Height: 1.5 cm
Excavated at Shizishan in 1994–5
Xuzhou Museum, Jiangsu Province

This seal was found at the waist of an attendant who was buried in the tomb passage at Shizishan. The inscription *shiguanjian yin* reveals the title of its owner as Inspector of Food Officer. Two categories of *shiguan* were described in the *Hanshu* texts: one was responsible for providing sacrificial materials for the

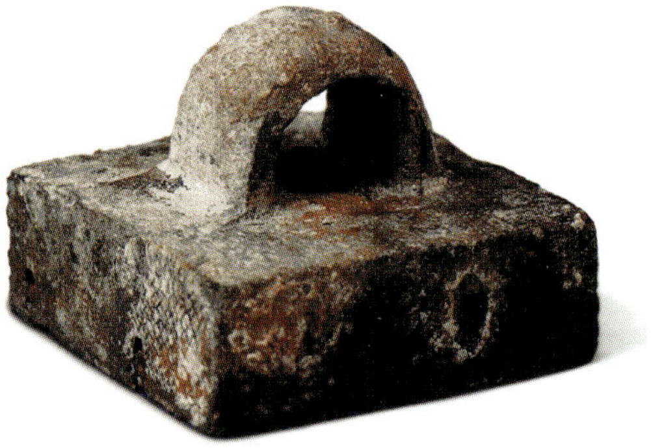

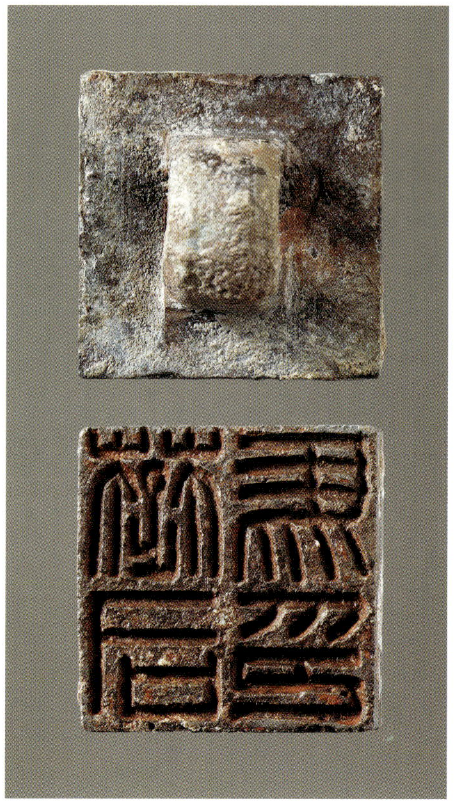

27

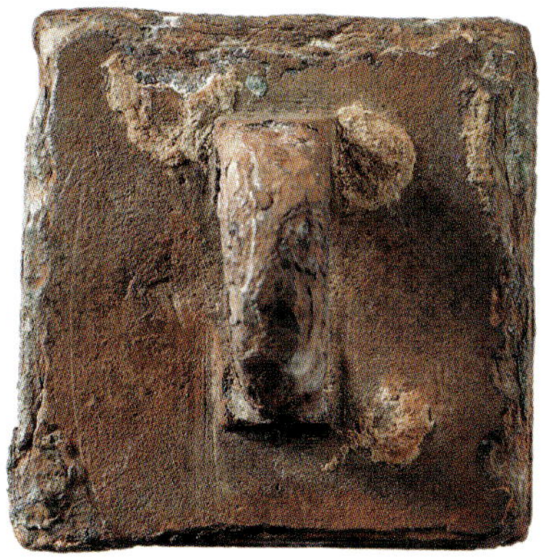

28

imperial tombs, the other food for the court. The owner of this seal belonged to the latter category. Preparing food for the afterlife was an important activity during the Han dynasty. Human sacrifice was rare during this time and had mostly been replaced in burials by earthenware figures. However, there were a few examples of attendants being buried with their masters, including the King of Nanyue's chef. It is possible that these chefs were considered so irreplaceable that their masters wished them to continue their service in the afterlife.

During the Han dynasty, chefs must have enjoyed considerable status at court as they were buried with honours and luxury objects along with their masters. This Inspector of Food Officer of the Chu kingdom was buried with a pillow inlaid with jade plaques (cat. 93), in addition to other personal belongings. Another example, dating to the early Western Han, can be found at the M1 tomb at Zaoyuancun, northern Xi'an. One attendant was identified as a leading chef for the imperial court and was buried with seven jade discs and bronze and iron weapons, and more than 200 broken jade fragments wrapped with silk were placed in each hand.[1] JCSL

1 Liu 2009, p. 5.

29

Two clay seals

Second century BC, Western Han dynasty
Lieutenant of Chu (Chu zhongwei) Length: 2.8 cm; Width: 2.7 cm; Thickness: 1.1 cm
Interior Minister (Chu neishi): Length: 3 cm; Width: 2.4 cm; Thickness: 1.1 cm
Excavated at Shizishan in 1994–5
Xuzhou Museum, Jiangsu Province

More than eighty clay seals were found in the inner tomb passage, the first and second western chambers, and the first eastern chamber at Shizishan. Inscriptions on the seals' lutes can be classified into three major categories: Chu court officials, Chu army officials and Chu county officials. These clay seals accompanied burial items included in the tomb. The inscriptions on the clay seals identify the origins of these burial goods as being presented for the Chu king's funeral by members of the imperial court, army or county governments.

The inscription on the seal on the bottom, *Chu zhongwei*, identifies the Lieutenant of Chu, the highest-ranking military officer charged with equipping the Chu army. The seal on the top belongs to *Chu neishi*, which identifies the Interior Minister, the highest-ranking Chu civil official charged with administering the peoples of the Chu kingdom. JCSL

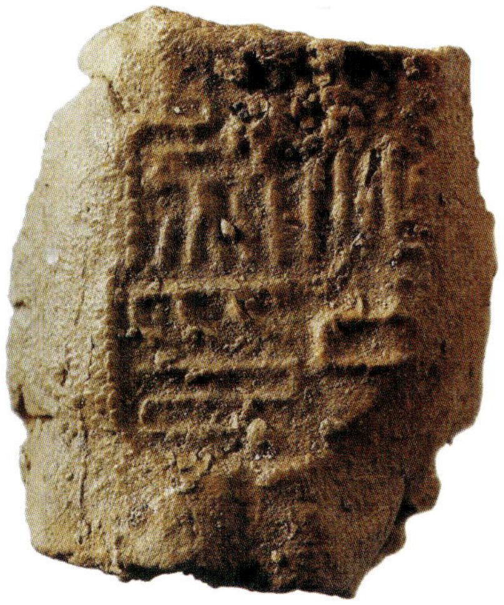

29

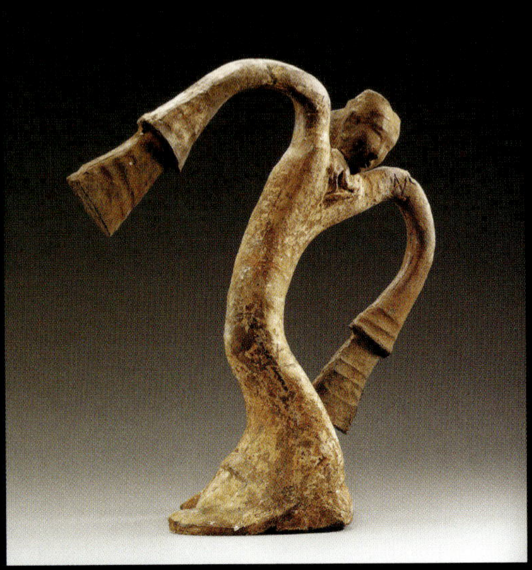
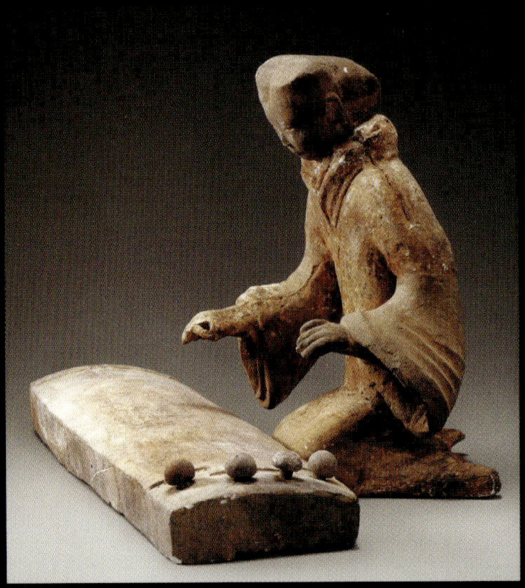
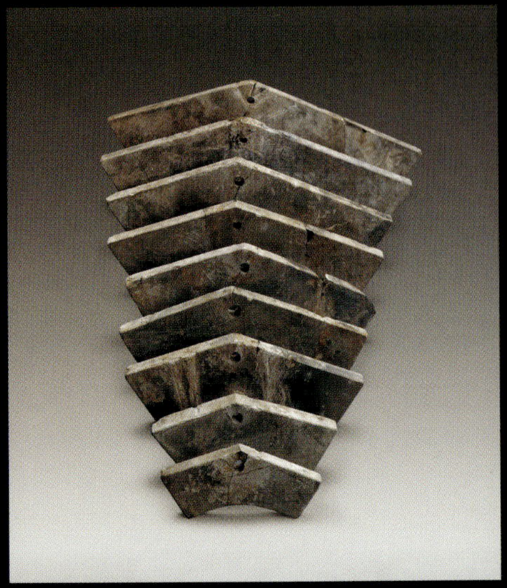

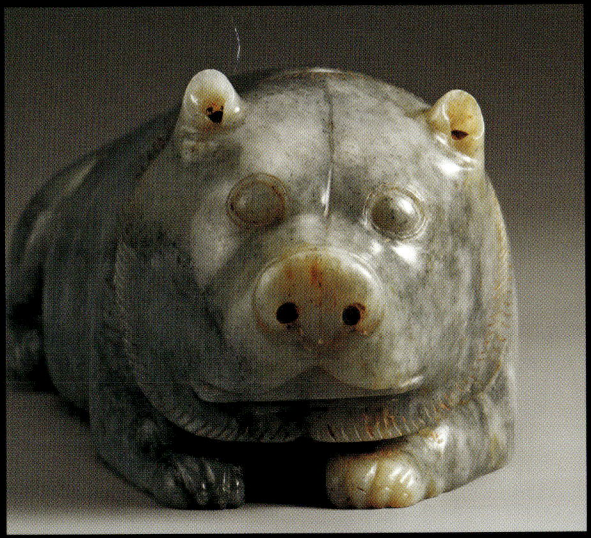
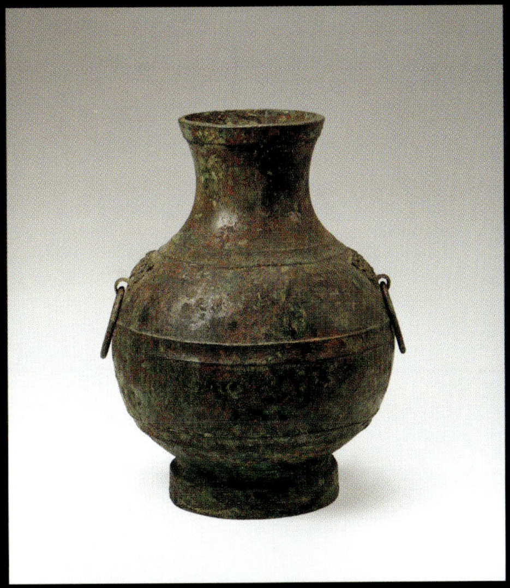
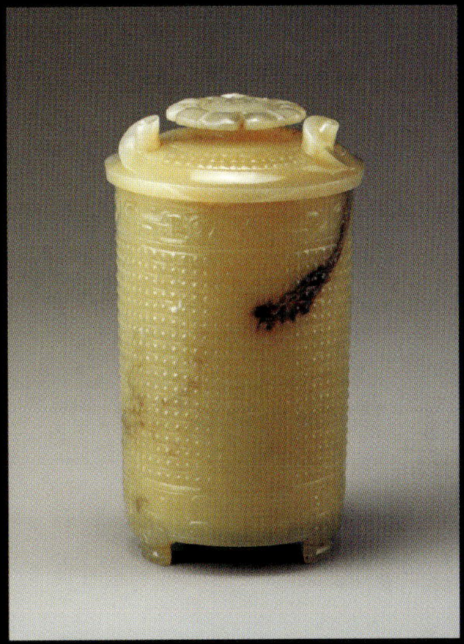

ENTERTAINMENT FOR THE AFTERLIFE

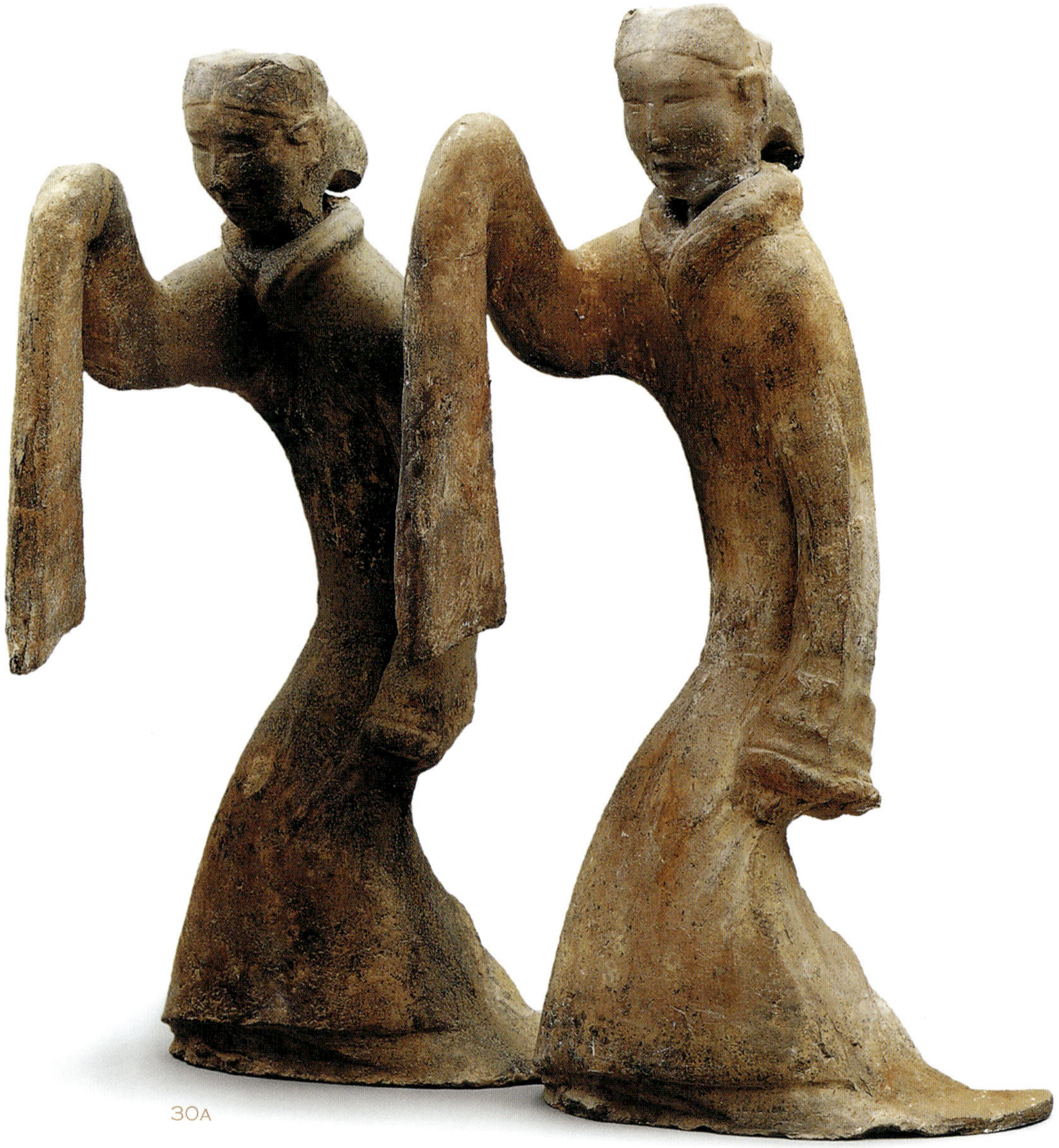

30A

30

Earthenware dancing figures and musicians

Second century BC, Western Han dynasty
Height: 47–9 cm
Excavated at the tomb of the King of Chu at Tuolanshan in 1989–90
Xuzhou Museum, Jiangsu Province

These exquisite dancers and musician figures found at Tuolanshan provide a fascinating insight into the rich, colourful life of the Han. This group consists of four dancers in different postures and musicians. The performance seems to be a popular Chu dance of the period that featured long waving sleeves and swaying movements. The realistic depiction of the *se* (an ancient Chinese musical instrument) provides important information for the study of Han musical instruments. Similar earthenware dancers and musicians were also found in the entertainment hall in the auxiliary complex of the tomb at Beidongshan.

A These two dancers are portrayed standing with their bodies slightly bending forward and right arms raised. The hair is divided in a centred parting and tied up in a bun at the back of the head. The head and body were made in separate moulds and later joined together. The original paint has almost completely disappeared.

B This lively dancing figure has both arms raised on either side and the body is posed in a graceful S-shape bending to the left. The flowing arms and sleeves

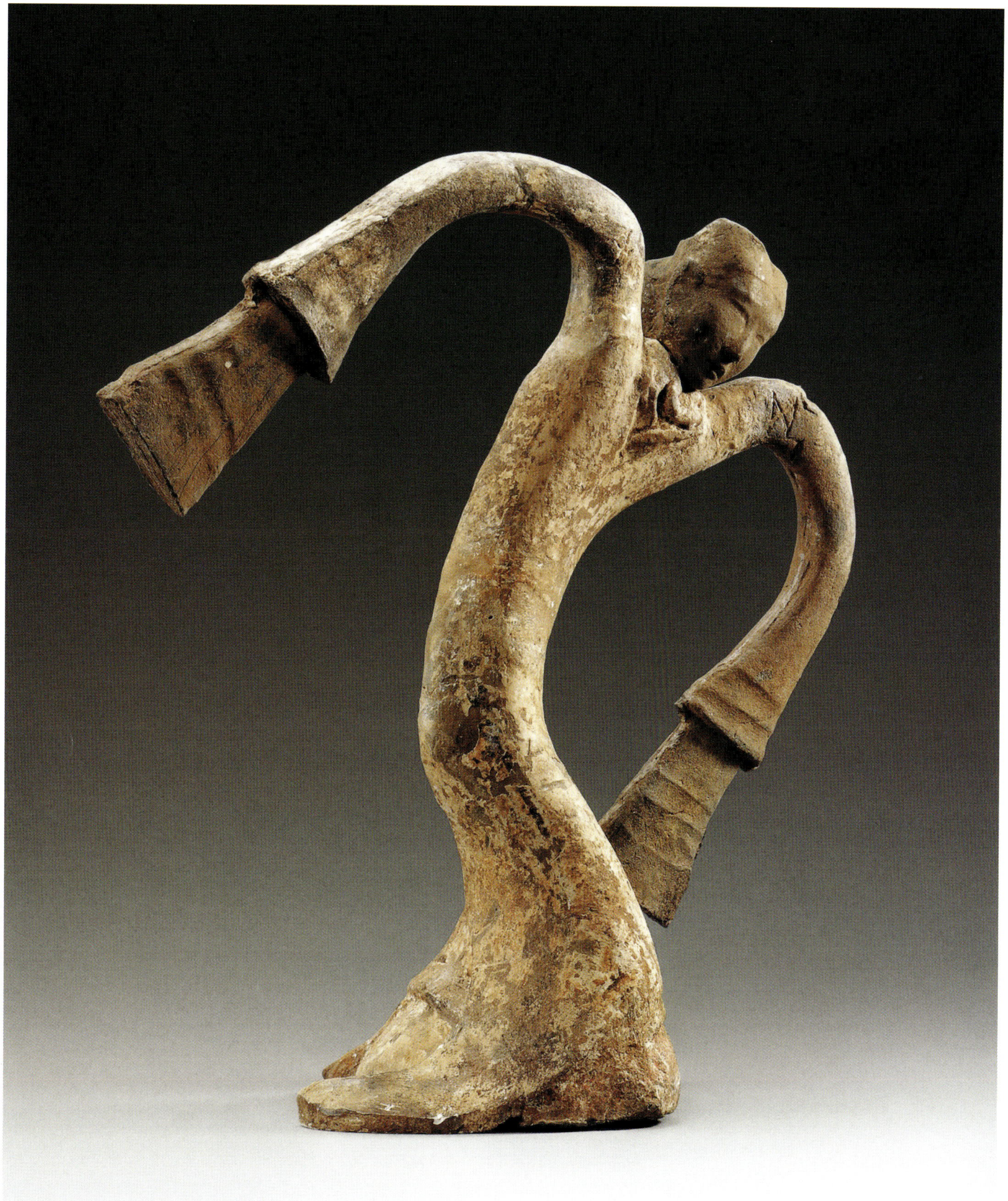

30B

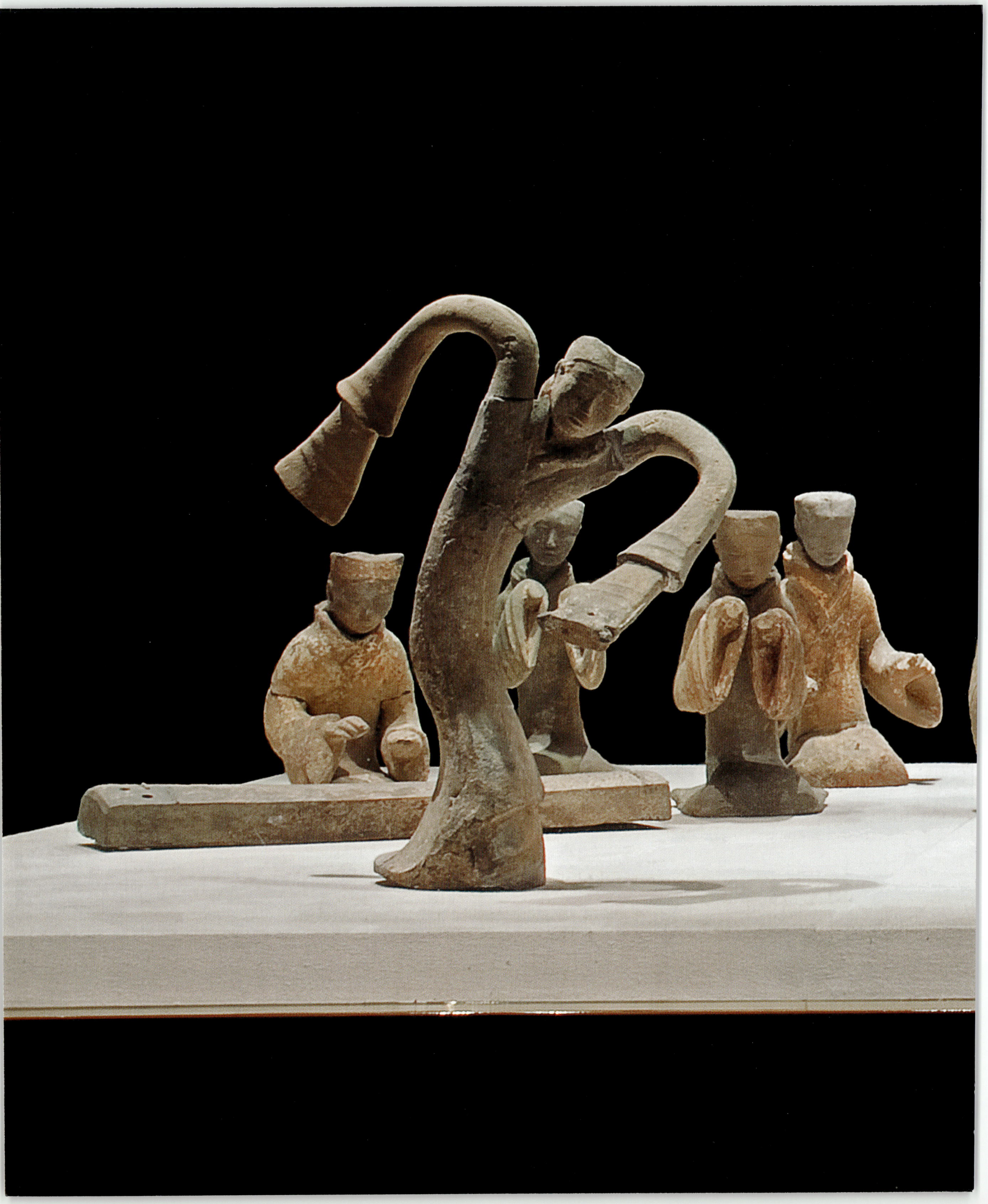

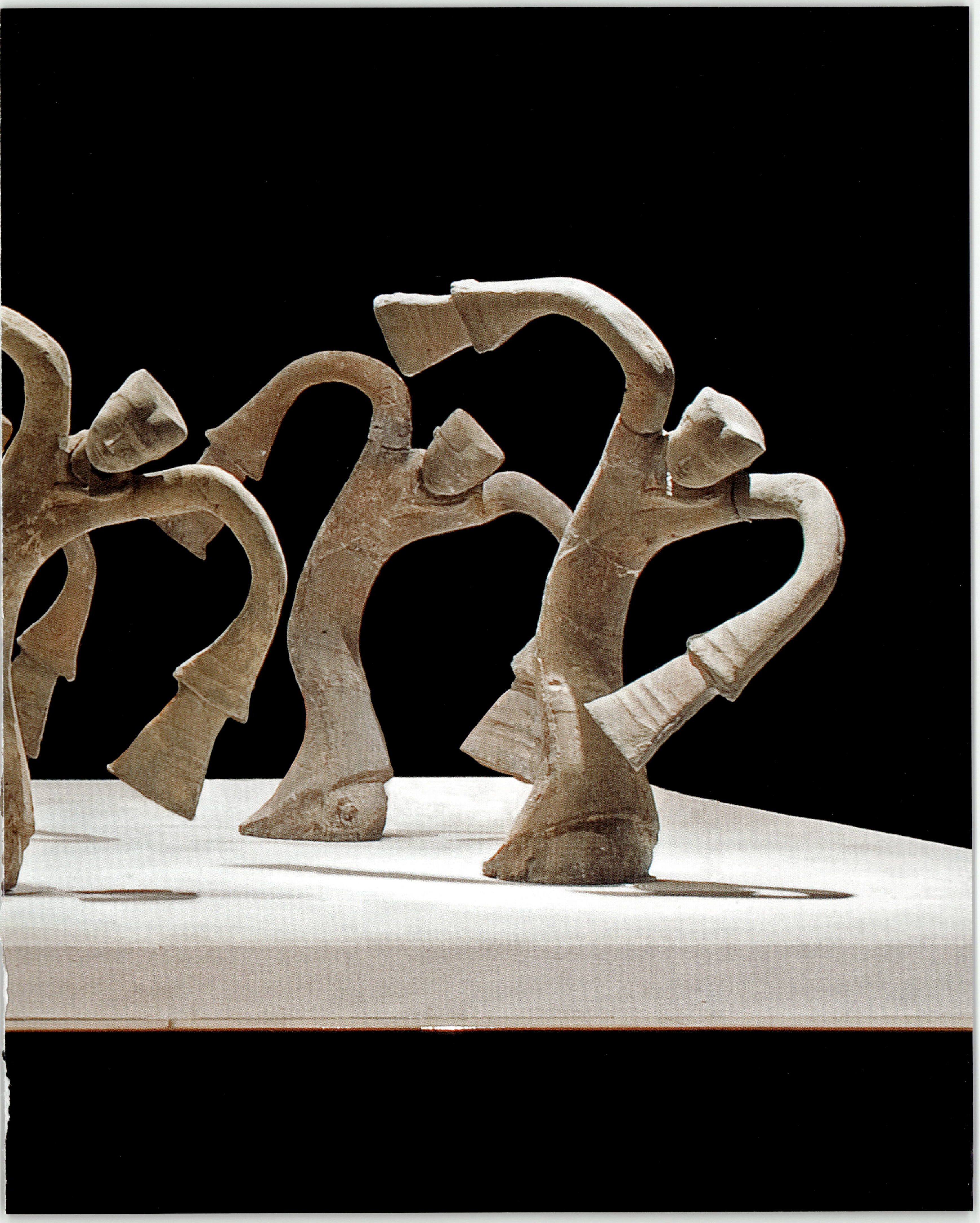

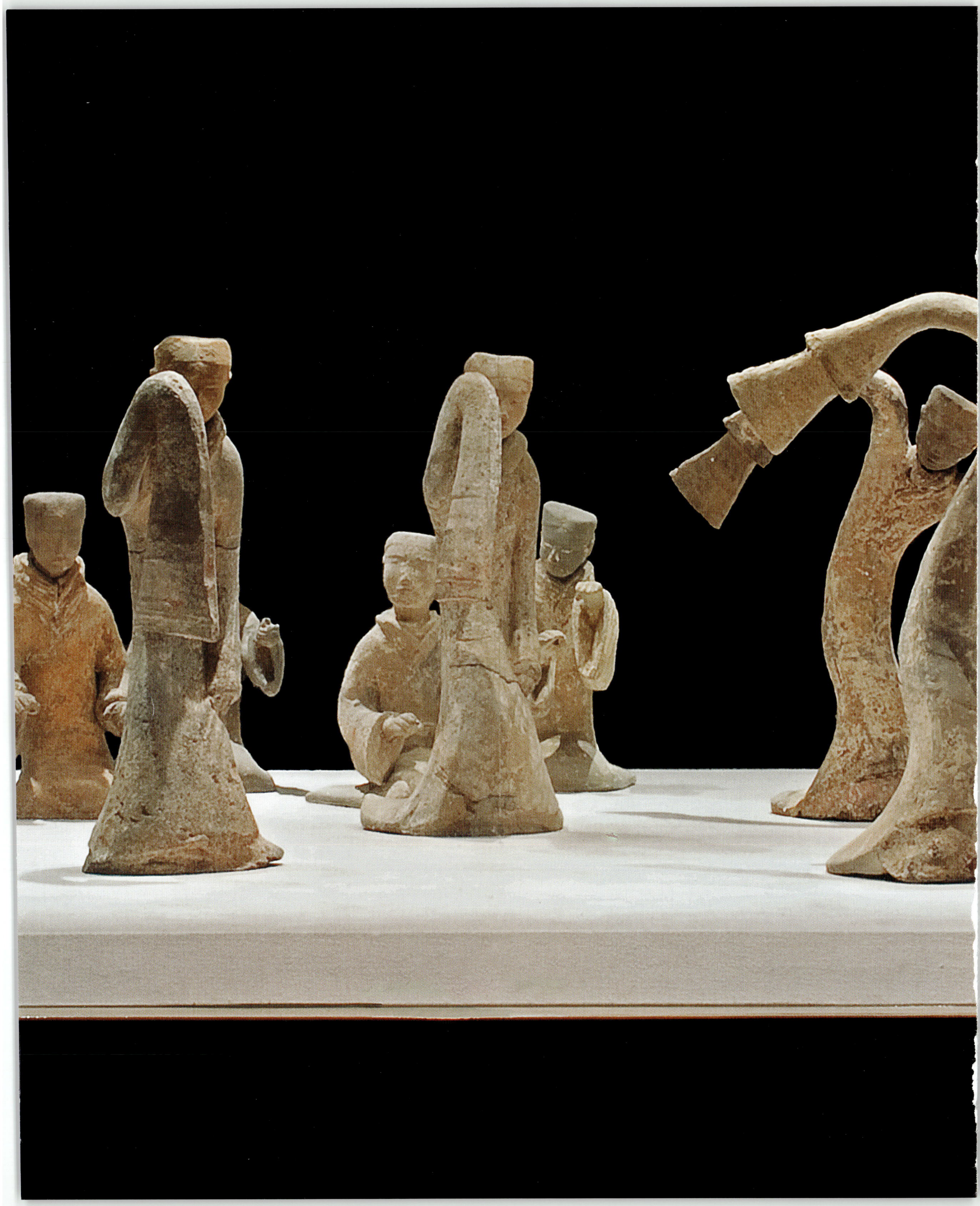

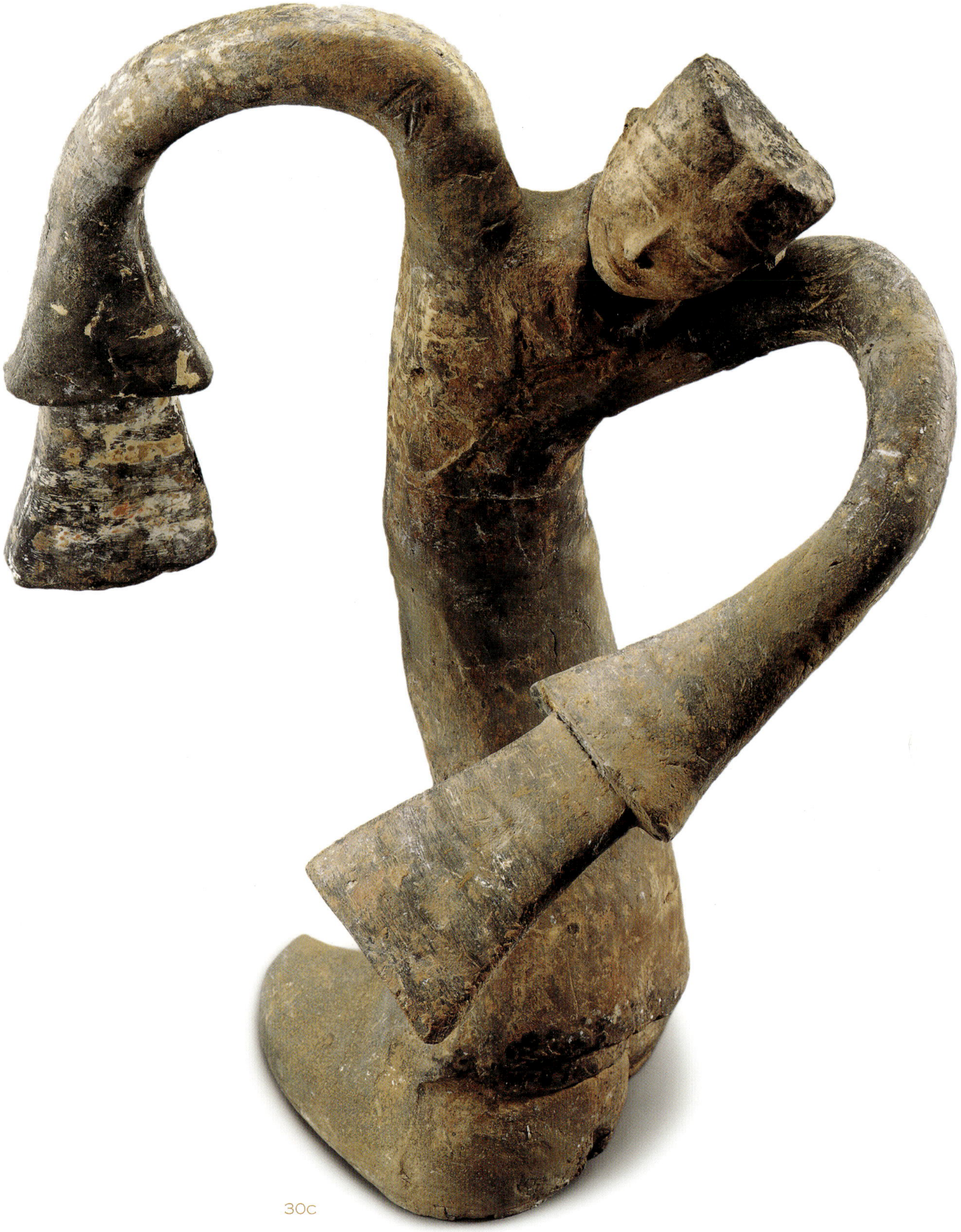

30c

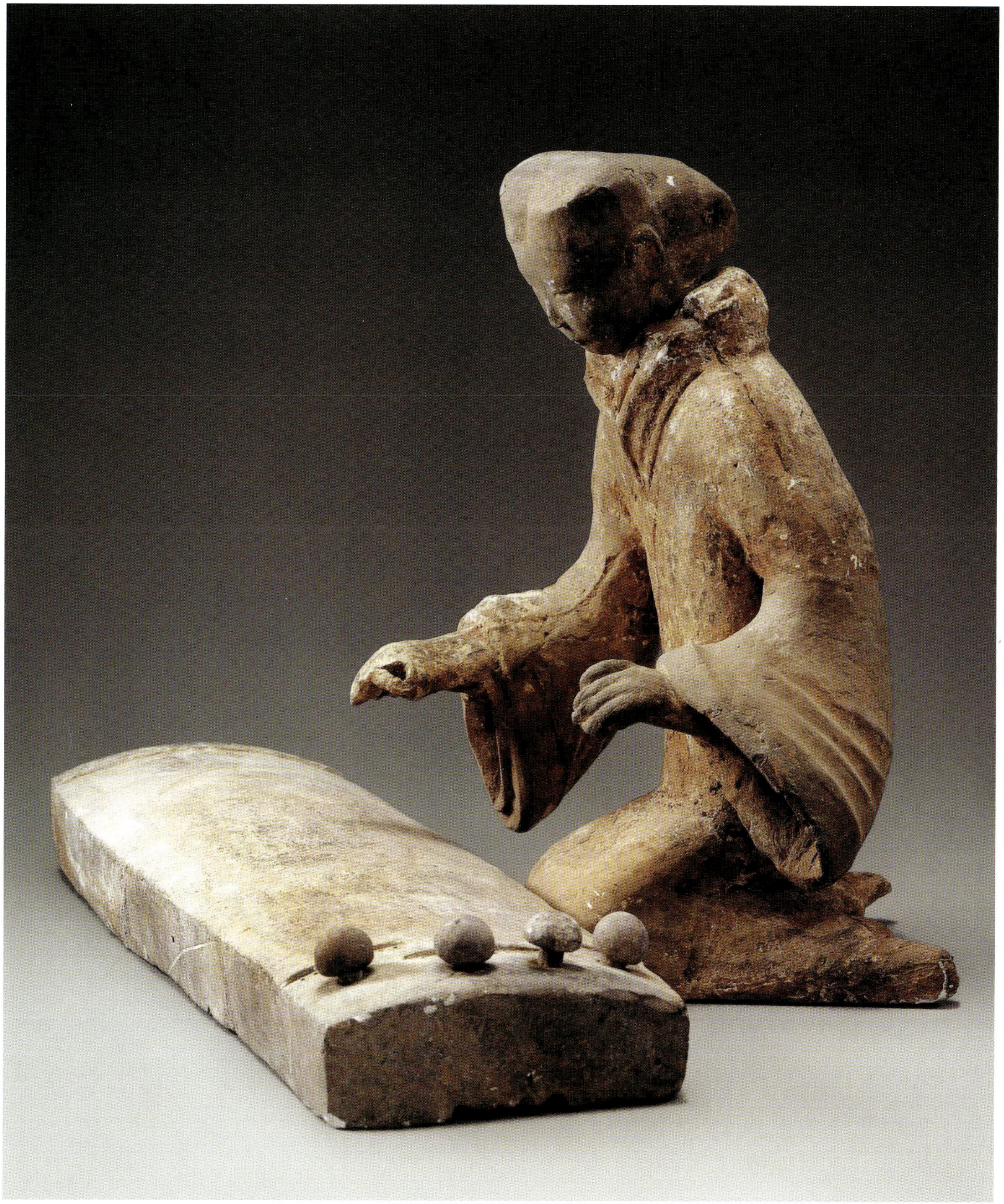

30D

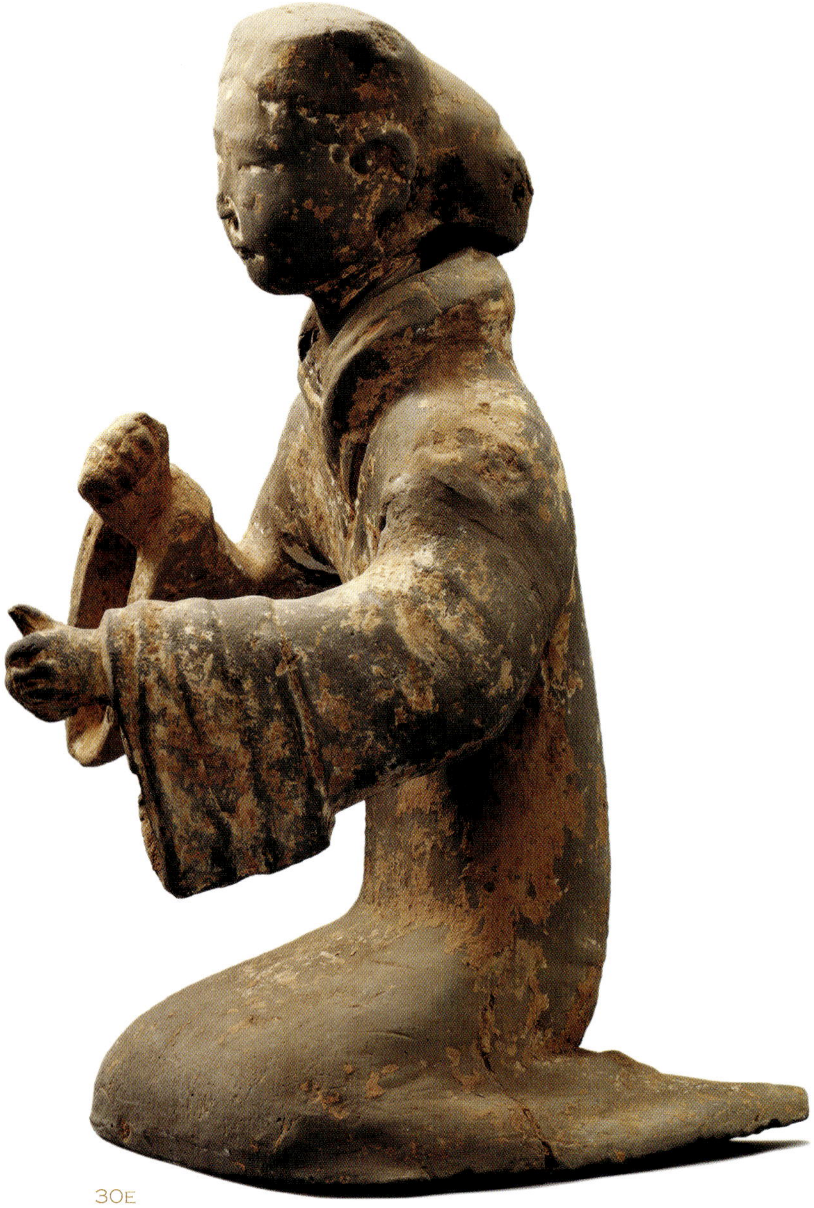

30E

were moulded separately. Both arms have been carved with the character *wu* (five) on the front and back.

C This figure is portrayed in a more dramatic dance movement, with the right arm raised on one side and the left arm swinging to the front; the body is twisted in an S-shape and the head slants left towards the left arm.

D The *se* player sits on her knees with her body leaning slightly forward. Both arms are outstretched as if playing the instrument. An earthenware *se* was discovered with the figure. A *se* is a twenty-five-stringed plucked instrument, rather like a zither.

E The chime player has both arms outstretched, but the right arm is raised slightly higher. Originally there might have been a wooden hammer in her hand with which to strike a chime of bells. The chime bells were normally made of stone or earthenware and were hung on a wooden rack during the Han dynasty.

F The musician figure is kneeling, with both arms raised as if to hold a flute to her mouth. The hands were missing when excavated. A panpipe and *sheng*, a reed-pipe wind instrument, were unearthed alongside the musician. JX

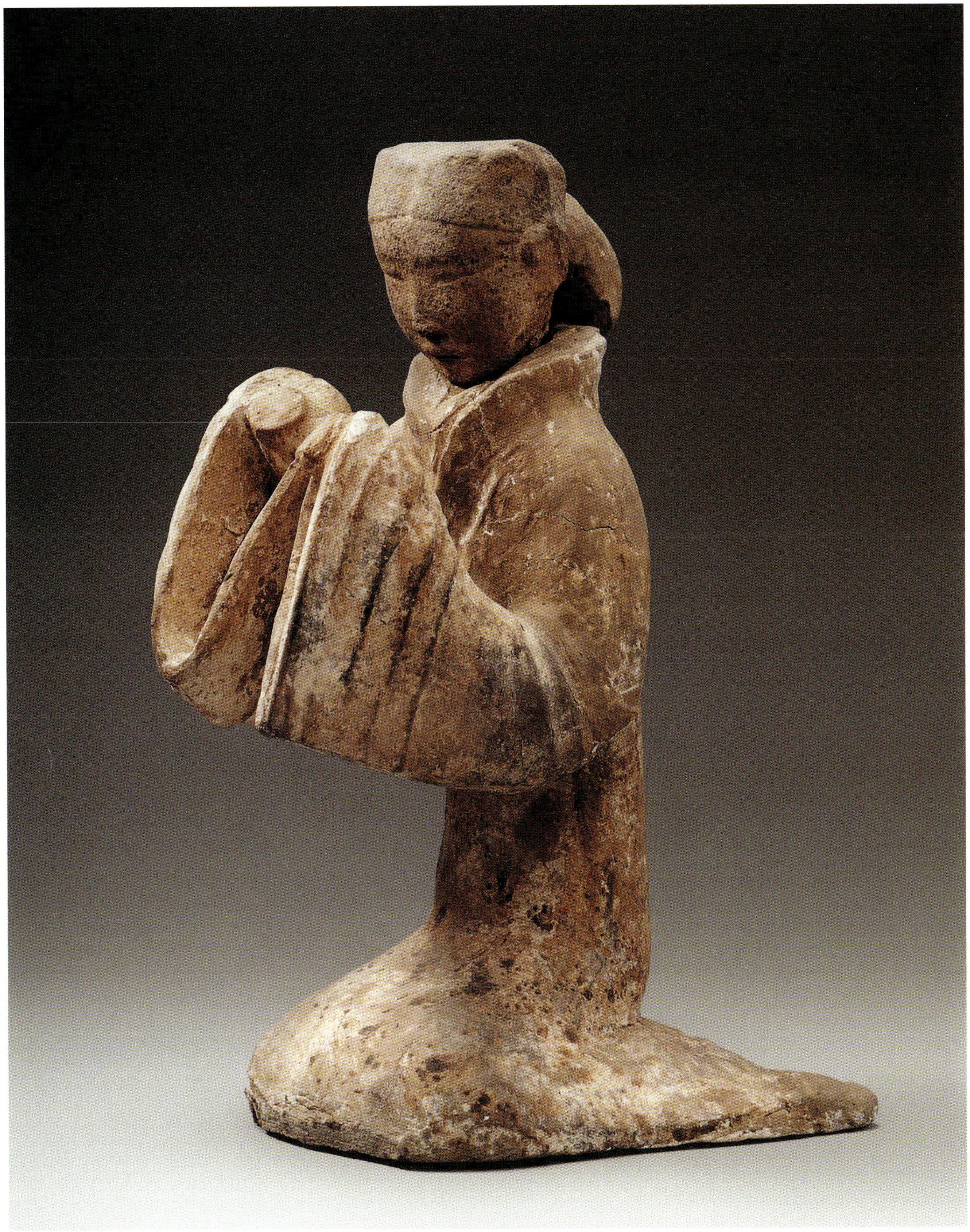

30F

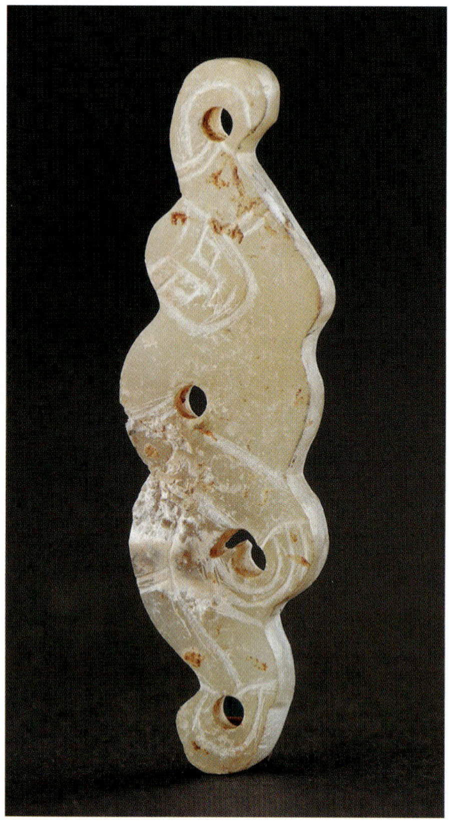

31

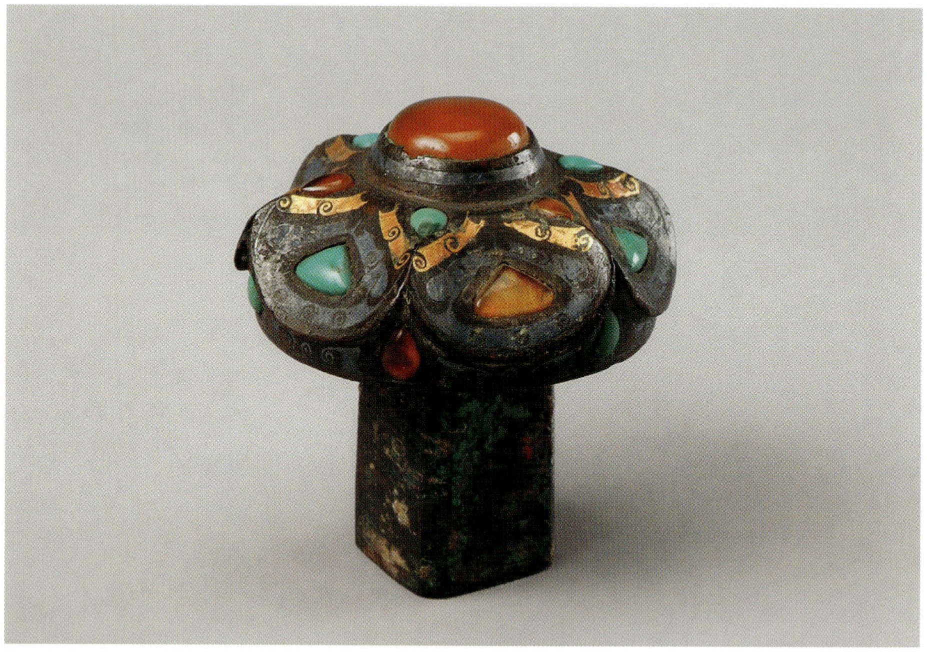

32

31

Jade plaque representing a dancer

Second century BC, Western Han dynasty
Height: 4.5 cm; Width: 1.5 cm
Excavated at the Sushantou Han tomb in 2003
Xuzhou Museum, Jiangsu Province
NOT EXHIBITED

Judging from the white colour and the translucent quality of the jade, the material is likely to have come from Khotan (modern Hetian, Xinjiang). After the overland Silk Route was established, commerce between China and Central Asia brought luxurious products to the cultures through which it passed. Jade from Khotan was one of the most important and sought-after commodities of trade with Han China.

This plaque is carved in the shape of a long-sleeved dancer, a common theme for jade carvings in the Han dynasty. The dancer is delineated in simple lines, almost abstract in style, with flowing, cursive contours. The dancer raises one of her arms up above her head, while the other is positioned down beside the waist. Her body has been left unadorned. Simple lines delineate the face, sleeves and lower garment. Close examination of the incised lines reveals that they have been scratched in roughly, suggesting that the piece may have been unfinished. The holes in the jade may have been made to fix this plaque onto the object it was designed to adorn. LKC

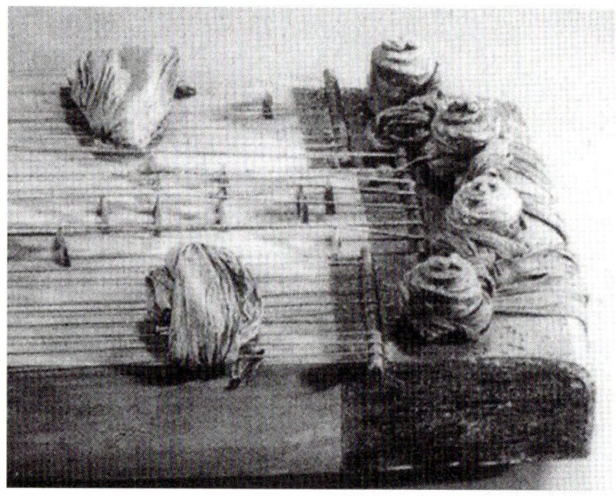

49 Musical instrument *se* found in tomb No. 1 at Mawangdui, Changsha, Hunan Provincial Museum. Second century BC.

32

Bronze peg for a stringed instrument (*se*)

First century BC, Western Han dynasty
Height: 4.2 cm; Diameter: 4.1 cm
Excavated at tomb No. 2 at Dongdongshan in 1982
Xuzhou Museum, Jiangsu Province

This bronze peg was used to fasten the strings of the musical instrument known as a *se* (fig. 49). Viewed from the top, it takes the form of a flower with six petals, with precious stones adorning the surface in two layers. The inner layer is decorated with scrolls in gold, while the outer layer is decorated with similar scrolls in blue pigment. The peg is inlaid with turquoise and other precious stones. LKC

33

Stone chimes

Second century BC, Western Han dynasty
Length: 69 cm, 61.5 cm, 51 cm, 45.5 cm, 44 cm, 40.5 cm, 36 cm, 30.5 cm, 21.5 cm;
Width: 17 cm, 15.5 cm, 13 cm, 12 cm, 11.8 cm, 11 cm, 10 cm, 9.5 cm, 7.5 cm
Excavated at the tomb of the King of Chu at Shizishan in 1994–5
Xuzhou Museum, Jiangsu Province

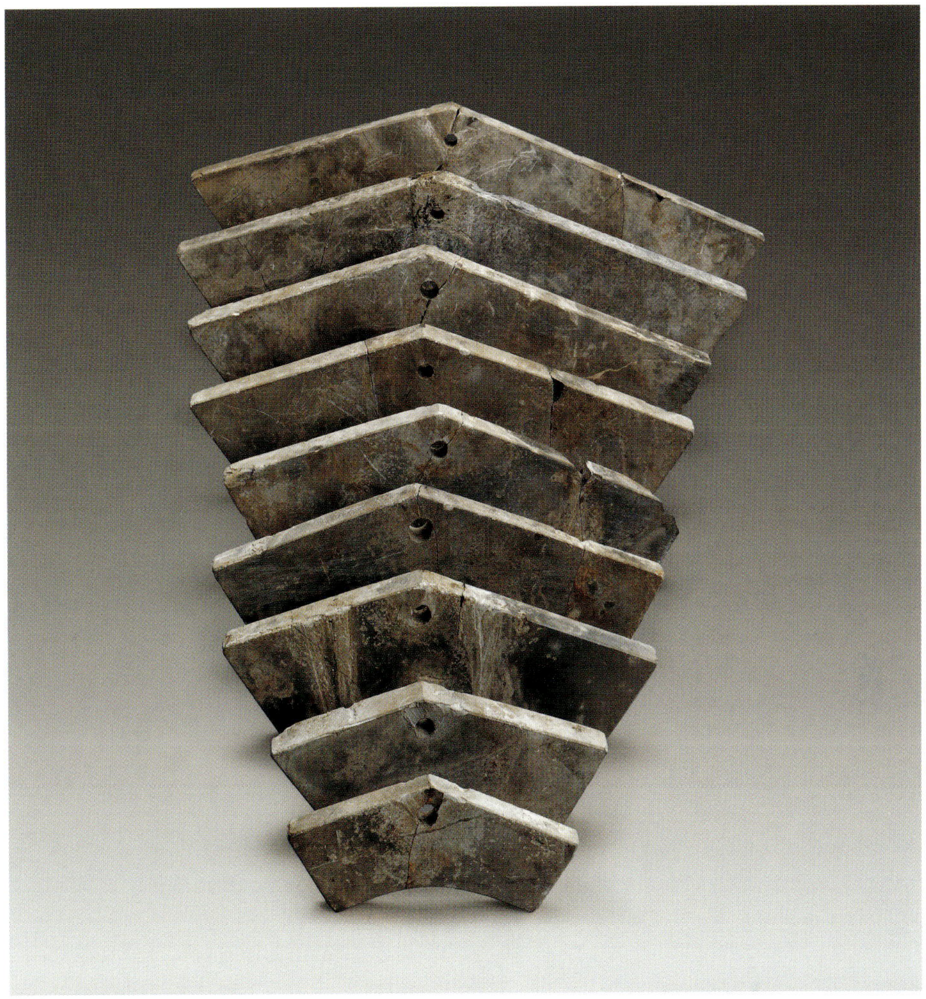

Chimes were used as musical instruments in a wide range of contexts, from solemn ritual ceremonies to aristocratic banquets. The use of stone chimes can be traced back to the Neolithic age, but the use of sets first appeared in the late Shang dynasty (seventeenth–eleventh century BC). At this early stage, the shapes of individual pieces in a set had to be adjusted in order to obtain the correct pitch for each chime. Beginning in the Western Zhou dynasty (eleventh–eighth century BC), the development of more sophisticated production techniques allowed the manufacture of standardized sets in a uniform pattern. At the same time, the number of the chimes in each

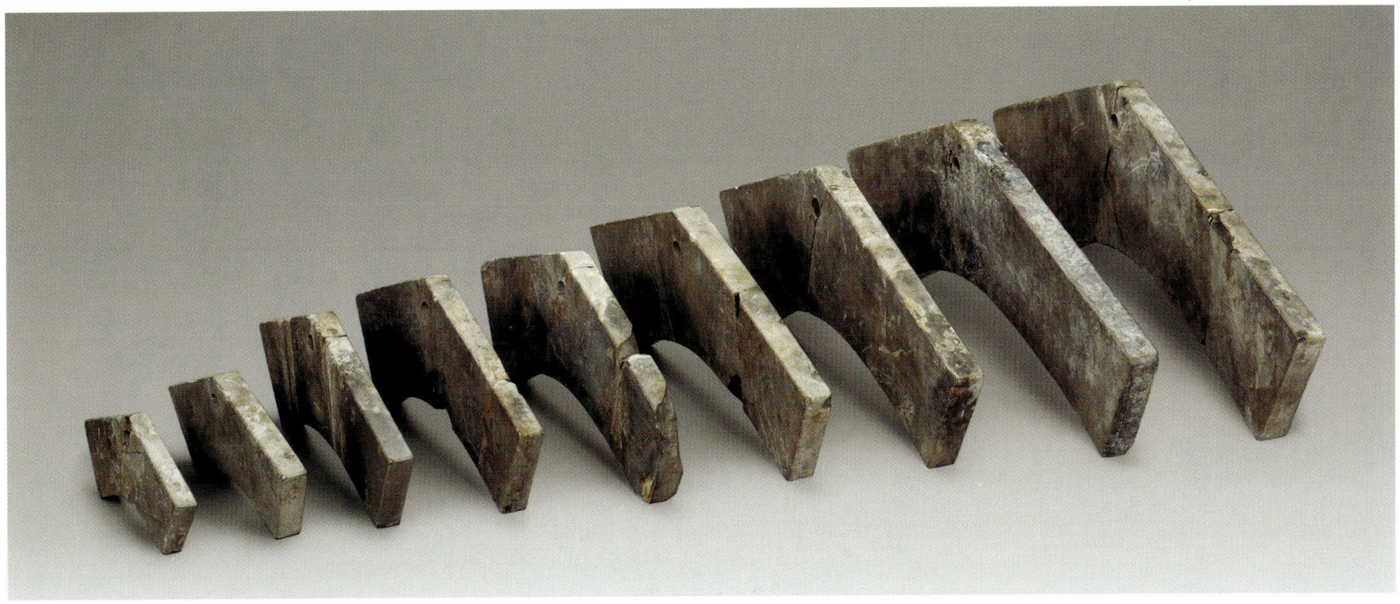

33

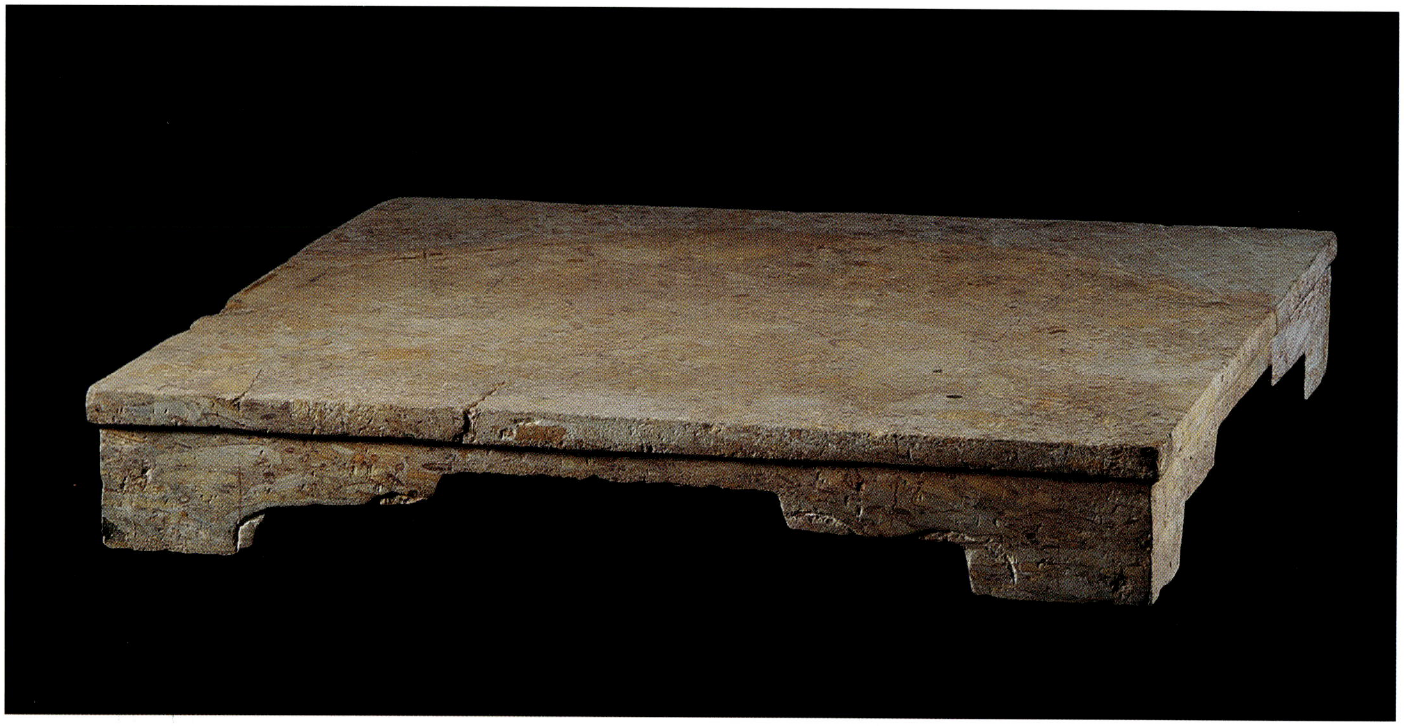

34

set continued to increase. In the Spring and Autumn period (eighth–fifth century BC), stone chimes reached a peak both in quality of manufacture and in ritual importance. Ritual regulations stipulated rules for the use of chimes in accordance with the gradations of social rank.

The chimes in this set vary in size to provide nine different pitches. They were suspended from a rack by strings passing through the holes drilled in the top of each piece. The holes show signs of wear, indicating that this set had been in use before it was buried with its owner in his underground palace. LKC

34

Stone *ping* seat

First–second century AD, Eastern Han dynasty
Length: 72 cm; Width: 72 cm; Thickness: 11 cm
Found at the Yi'an Eastern Han tomb at Tongshan, Xuzhou in 1999
Xuzhou Museum, Jiangsu Province

A *ping* is a piece of furniture that has been recorded in various early Chinese texts and has been found in many Han tombs.[1] Commonly made of stone or board, a *ping* had a square, flat surface supported by four feet (fig. 50). It was used as a seat for one person. Another piece of furniture, similar in shape, a *ta*, was larger than a *ping*. Both *ping* and *ta* were usually covered with a straw or bamboo mat. Weights were placed at the four corners of the mat to prevent it from curling up.

Apart from being used as a seat, a *ping* can also be used as a board for a game called *Liubo*, popular between the Warring States and the Han periods (cat. 121). A scene of two players playing *Liubo* on a *ping* can be found on some painted tomb stones such as those discovered at Xinjin in Sichuan and at Weishan in Shangdong.[2]

This stone *ping* was unearthed at the Yi'an tomb of the Eastern Han period in Tongshan county, Xuzhou. This site has not been excavated, but it was largely exposed after local villagers took tomb stones away for construction materials. The *ping* seat was the only object left in the front chamber when archaeologists conducted a survey of this site. JX

1 Apart from this Yi'an piece, other examples include those from Liu Qian's tomb of the Western Han period in Beichencun, Xingtai, Hebei and Liu Xiu's tomb of the Western Han period in Bajiaolang, Dingxian, Hebei.
2 Sun 1991, pp. 394–6.

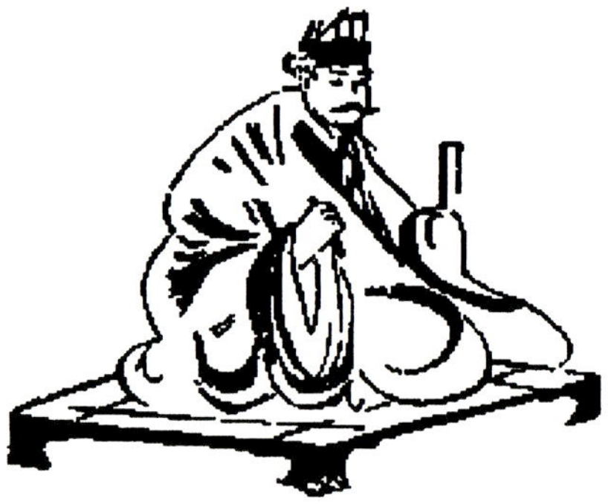

50 Tomb painting of a man sitting on a *ping* seat. From tomb No. 1 at Wangdu, Hebei Province. After Sun 1991, fig. 55–1

35

Stone weight in the form of a lion

Second century BC, Western Han dynasty
Length: 23.5 cm; Width: 13 cm; Height: 14.5 cm
Excavated at Shizishan in 1994–5
Xuzhou Museum, Jiangsu Province

This greyish-green marble weight in the form of a lion was found at the first western chamber in Shizishan. It is seated on a platform and wears a collar made of cowrie shells, suggesting it had been tamed. Initially, this figure was recorded in the archaeological report as a leopard simply because most of the animal sculptures and images found in Han tombs have been leopards. However, it lacks the most basic characteristic of a leopard – spots. Judging from the muzzle and the mane of this creature, it more likely represents a lion. This type of weight usually appeared in a set of four to secure the four corners of a mat placed on top of a *ping* or seating platform (cat. 34). The design of this sculpture, including the platform, a loop on the neck and the seashell collar, all suggest Central Asian influences. Taming fierce animals for hunting was popular among imperial family members during the Han period, a practice that might show Indian or Central Asian influence.
JCSL

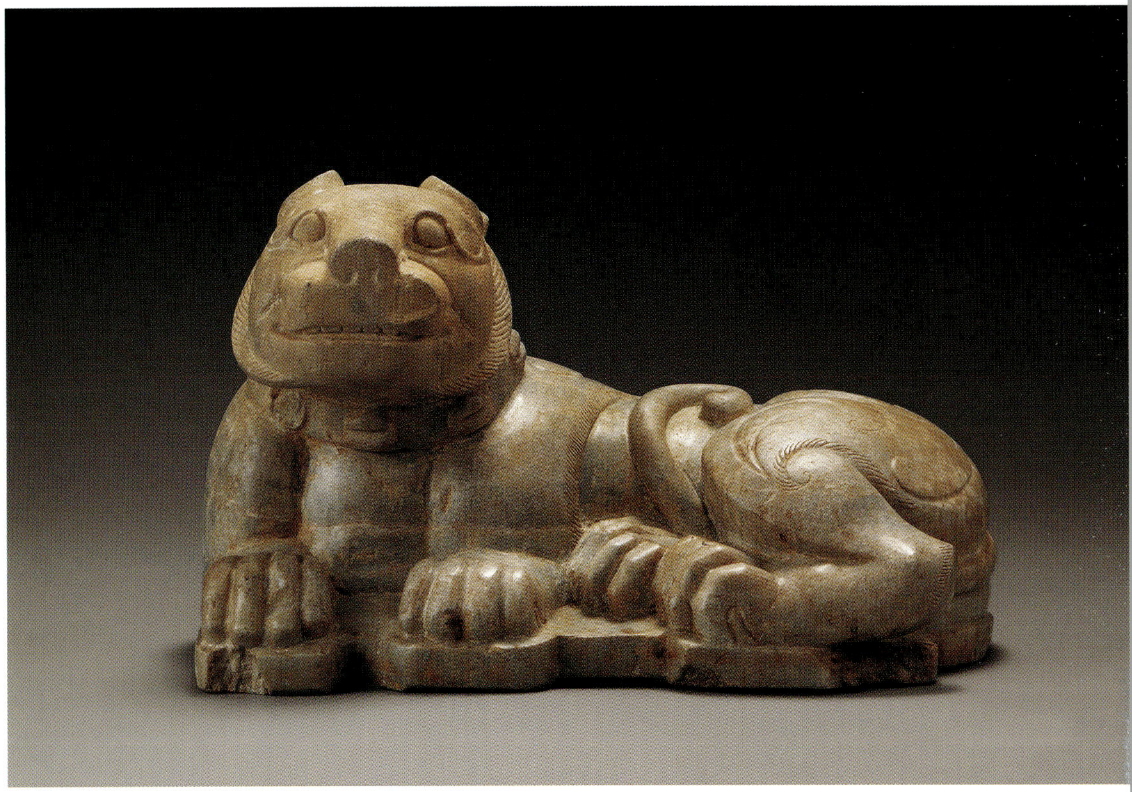

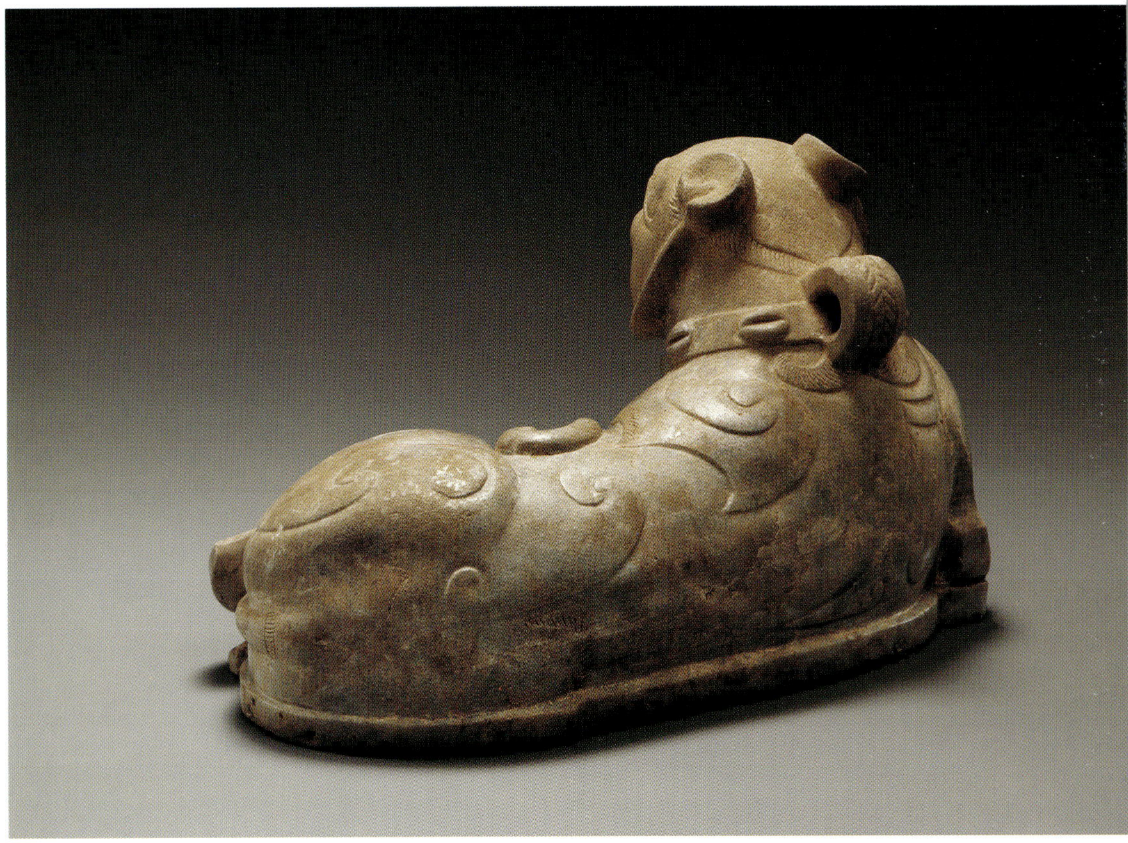

35

36

Bronze weight in the form of a lion

Second century BC, Western Han dynasty
Length: 19.7 cm; Height: 11.1 cm
Excavated at Shizishan in 1994–5
Xuzhou Museum, Jiangsu Province
NOT EXHIBITED

Two bronze weights of this type were found in the second western chamber at Shizishan. This one is formed of a bronze cast that is filled with lead. The design of

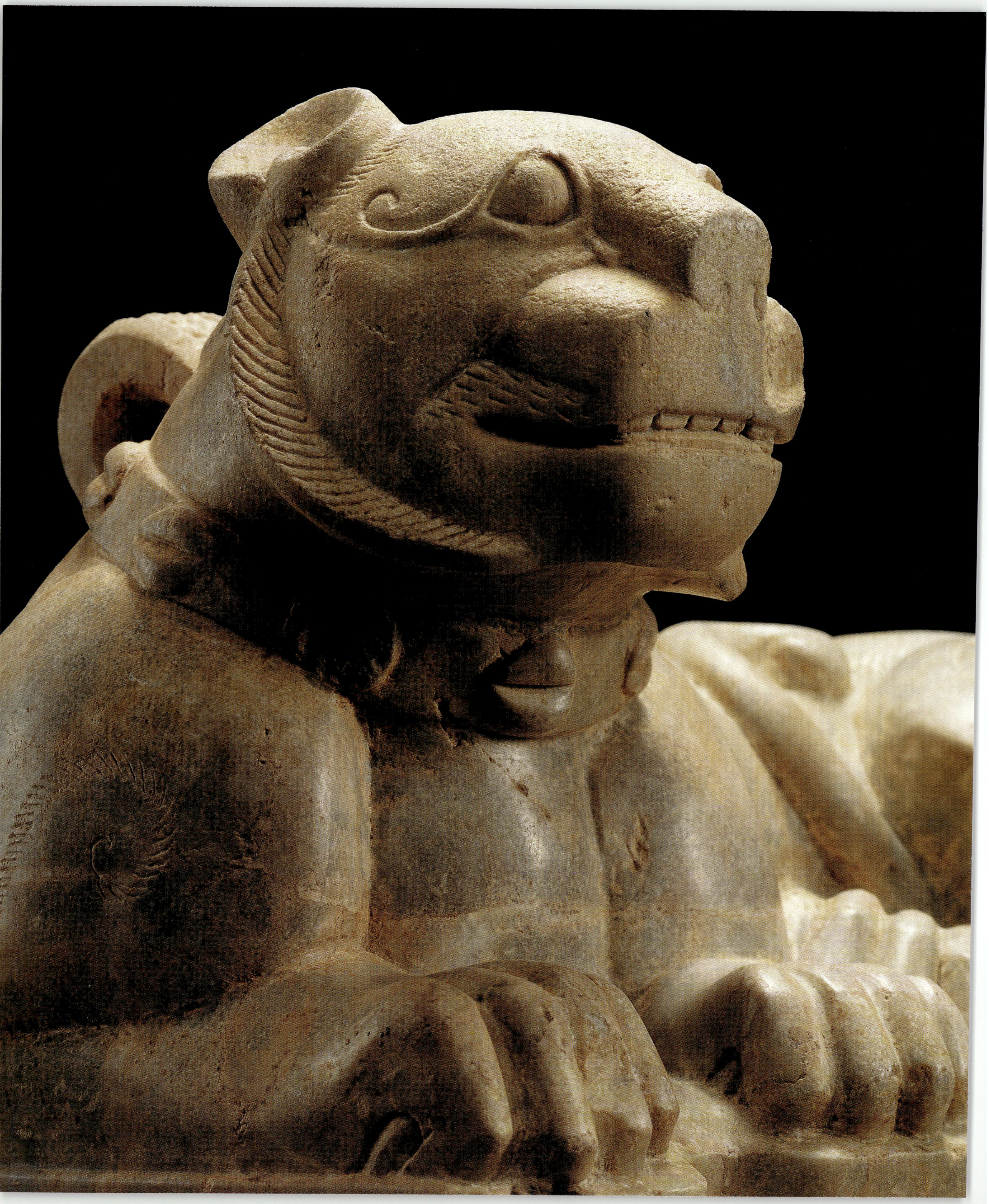

this weight is very similar to the marble one from the same tomb (cat. 35). It depicts a crouching lion with its tail curled up onto its back and with wide-open jaws. Incised onto the body are characters that indicate the weights of bronze used to cast the mould and the weights of lead used for the body of the lion. Commonly used materials for weights included bronze, jade and stone, although occasionally amber and iron were also used. Weights made during the Han period were cast or carved into animal forms such as deer, lambs, bears, turtles and snakes, but lions and leopards were the most popular. The size of these weights indicates the status of the owner.
JCSL

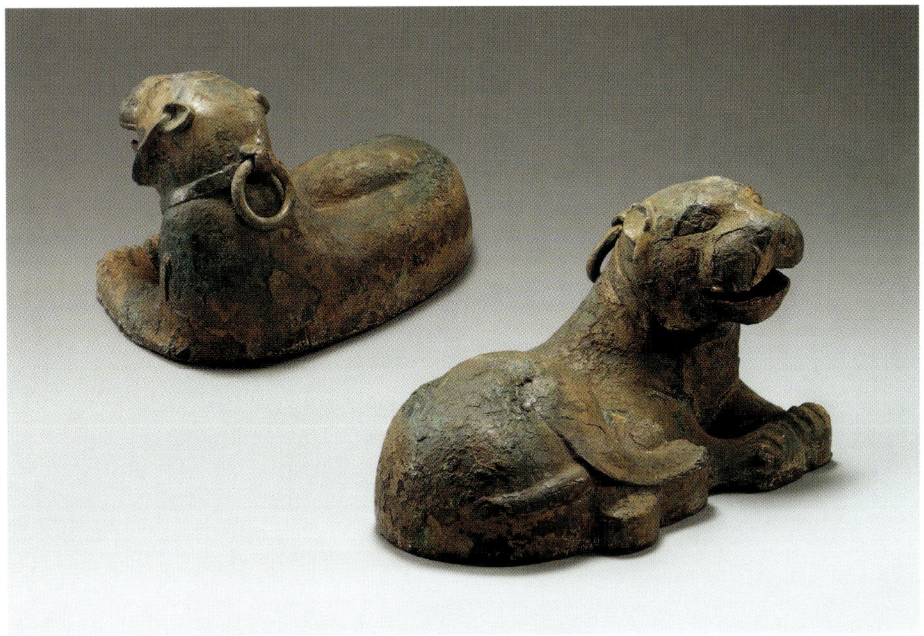

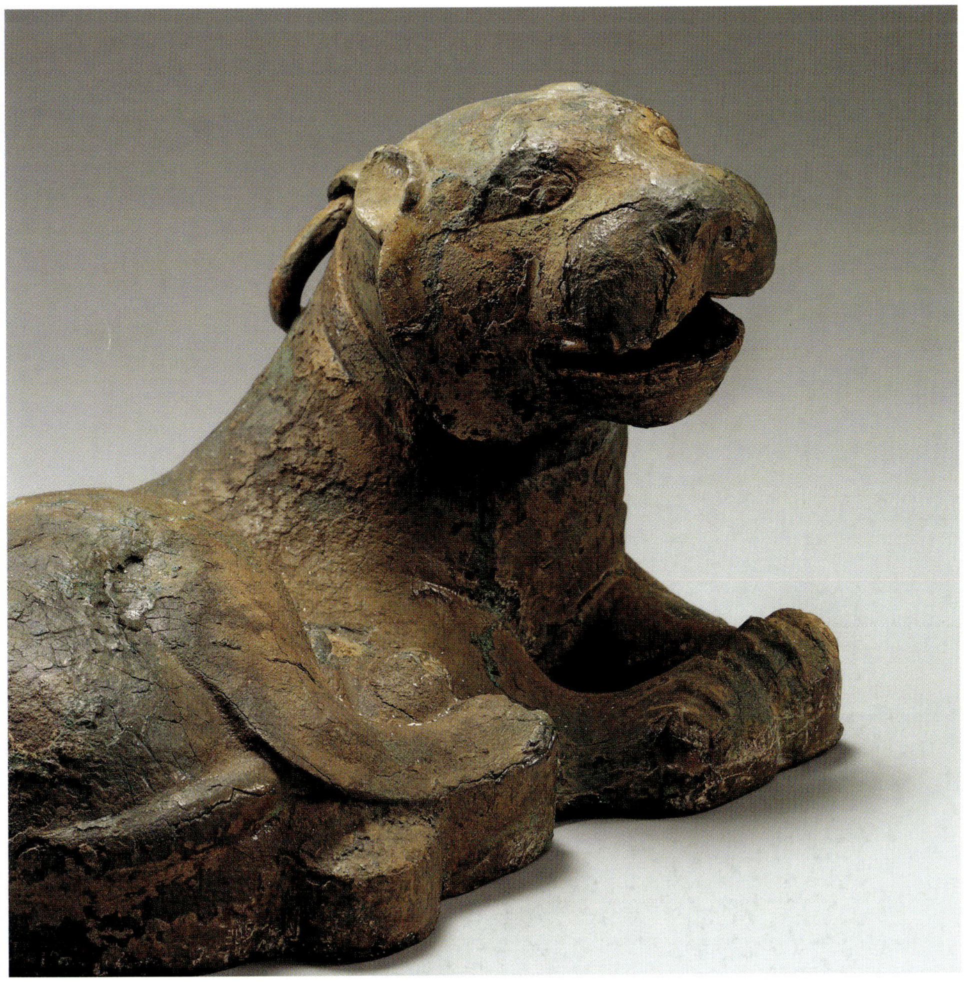

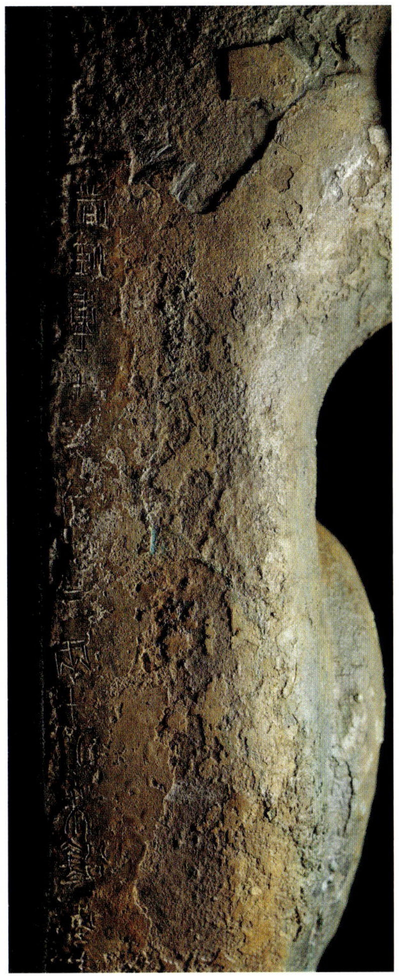

36

FACING PAGE: DETAIL OF CAT. 35

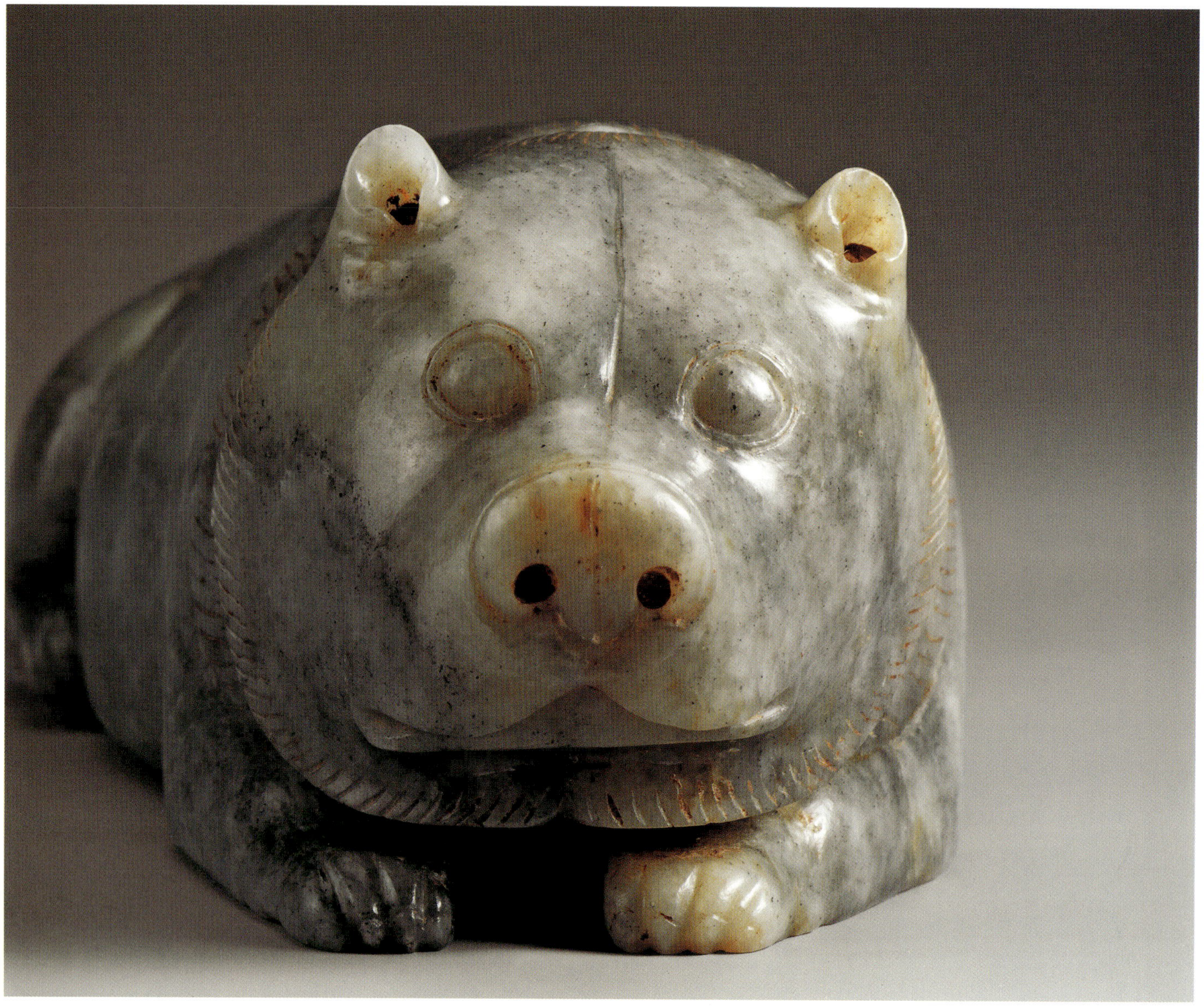

37

37

Jade weight in the form of a bear

Second century BC, Western Han dynasty
Length: 20.3 cm; Width: 8.3 cm; Height: 6.6 cm
Excavated at Beidongshan in 1986
Xuzhou Museum, Jiangsu Province

This weight in the form of a bear was carved from a piece of greyish-green jade stone. It depicts a crouching bear resting on its front paws with a collar around its neck, suggesting it was a tamed animal. The details of the bear, including the tail and ruff, are incised with fine lines. Judging from the stone and bronze lion weights found in Shizishan (cat. 35, 36), a stone tiger weight from the tomb at Jushan in Pizhou (cat. 39) and this jade bear from the tomb at Beidongshan, the keeping of exotic wild animals in captivity was popular among the Kings of Chu. JCSL

38

Gilt bronze weight in the shape of a performer

First–second century AD, Eastern Han dynasty
Height: 7.5 cm; Width: 6.0 cm; Thickness: 4.0 cm
Found at Chefushan Han tomb at Pizhou, Xuzhou, 1992
Pizhou Museum, Jiangsu Province

This palm-sized statue of an old man sitting on his knees is made from bronze,

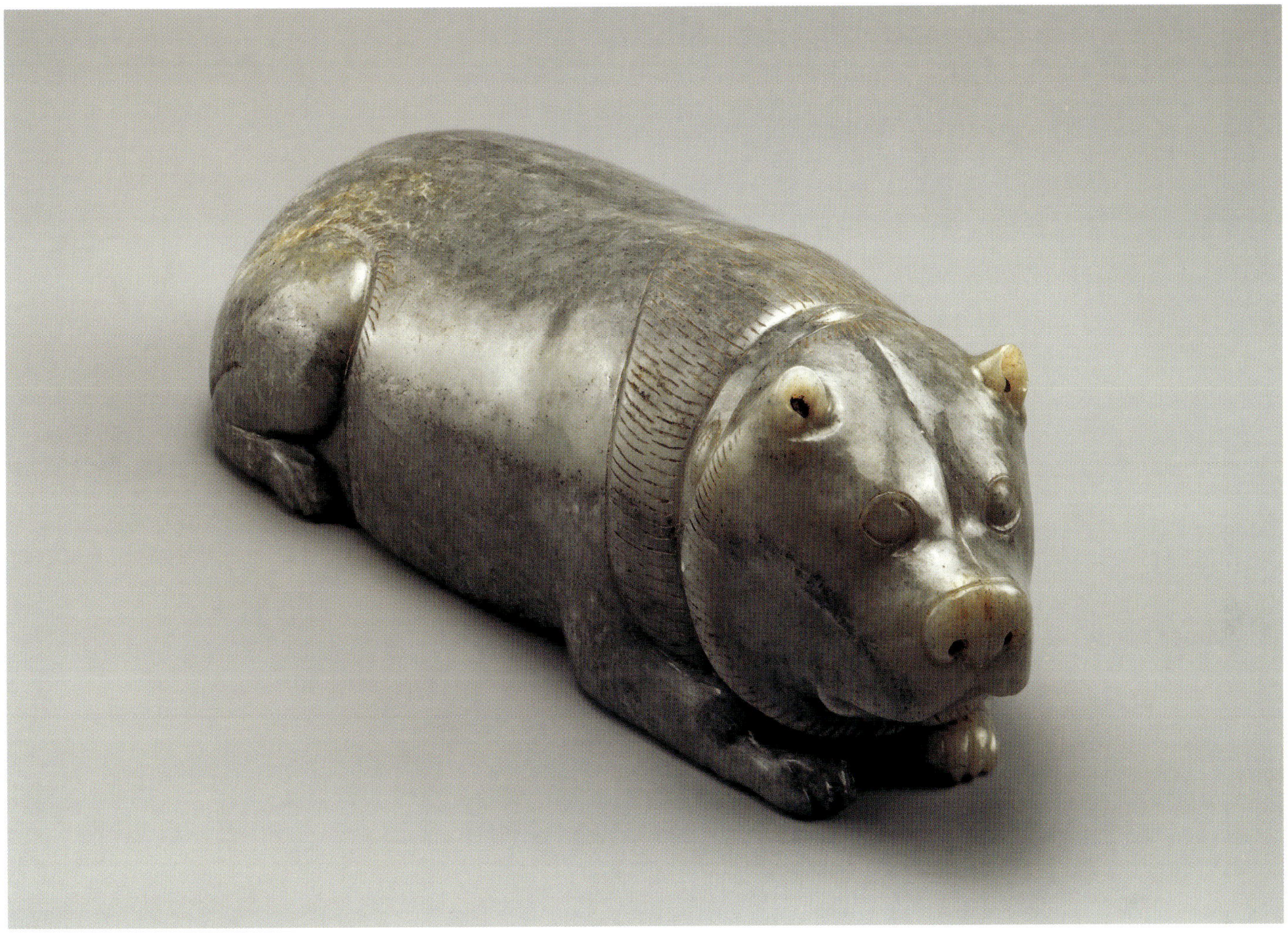

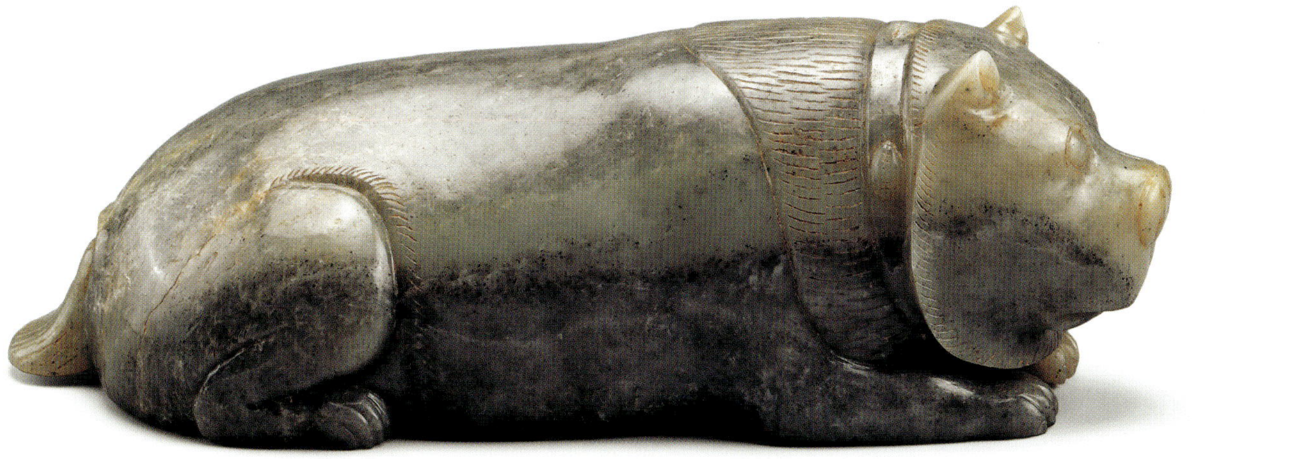

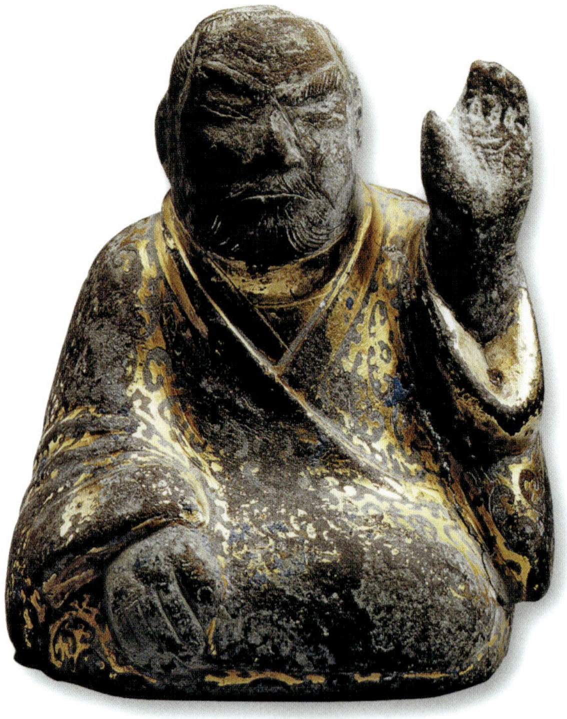

38

and the figure wears a gilt-painted robe with wide sleeves. His left hand is raised up above his ear and his right hand rests on his knee. A lively dramatic facial expression depicted with lifted eyebrows, wide-open eyes and a firmly closed mouth with drooping corners, seems to demand the viewer's attention.

When it was excavated from an Eastern Han tomb (first–second century AD) in Pizhou county, this statue was originally considered to be a bronze figure of Buddha, as Buddhism was gaining in popularity at that time after being first introduced to China along the Silk Route at the end of the Western Han dynasty (*c.*first century AD). However, a recent re-examination of this object has questioned this interpretation.[1] Judging from the body posture, the nearly domed top shape and the size,[2] scholars from Xuzhou argued that the statue was actually a mat weight, depicting a performer who was employed to tell jokes and provide entertainment in the royal court or for aristocrats.

The socket at the bottom of the statue has traces of lead, which was commonly added to increase the weight for mat weights at the time. It provided additional evidence as to its original use.

Mat weights in archaeological finds are usually found in a set of four, and most have animal designs. This human figure is a rare example of its kind. Another similar figure is the bronze statue of a young *Paiyou* performer discovered at the Han tomb in Mancheng, Hebei Province.[3] JX

1 Zhao and Liu 2009.

2 The dimensions of this statue fall into the range of a weight for mats or curtains, which on average measures about 3.5–7.5 cm high, 6–9 cm long in base diameter and weighs about 6–800 g. See Zhao and Liu 2009.

3 Archaeological report of the Han tomb at Mancheng; Beijing 1980, p. 275.

39

Stone weight in the form of a tiger

Second century BC, Western Han dynasty
Length: 10 cm; Width: 7.5 cm; Height: 4.5 cm
Found at Jushan Han tomb at Pizhou, Xuzhou in 1989
Xuzhou Museum, Jiangsu Province

This stone mat weight, which is in the shape of a tiger with a curling tail, is one of a set of four weights discovered at a small Han shaft tomb located in Pizhou. Unfortunately, archaeologists did not excavate the tomb systematically. Not much is known of its original context when it was unearthed.

In addition to their practical functions, mat weights in the shapes of predatory animals might also have served to ward off evil spirits.[1] Such designs were popular during the Han dynasty. Apart from these four mat weights in the shape of tigers, bronze and stone lion weights have been unearthed from Shizishan (cat. 35 and 36) and jade bear weights have

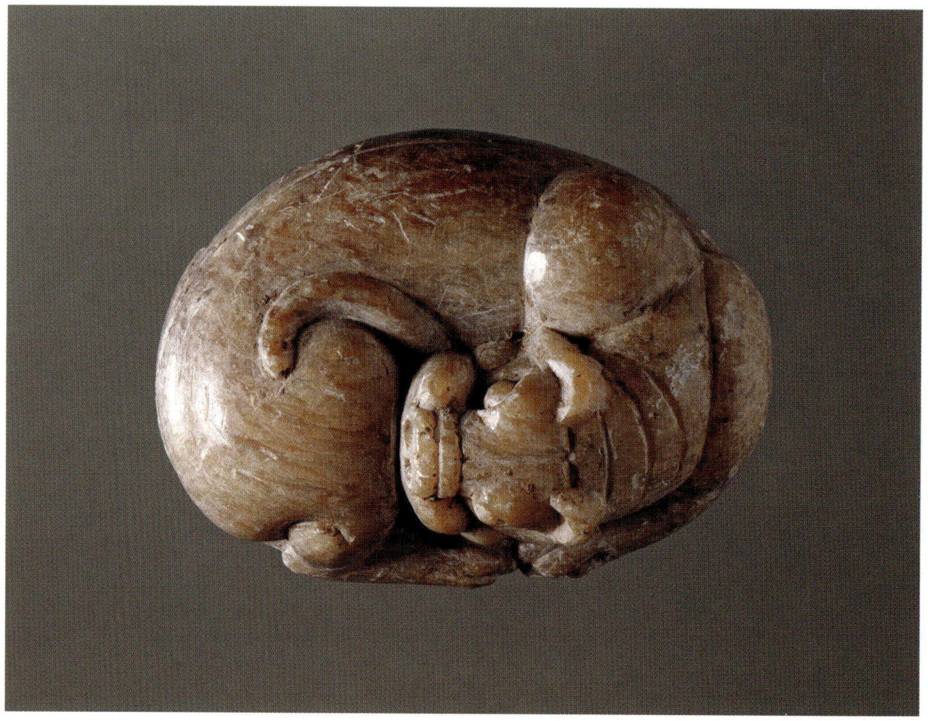

39

been excavated at Beidongshan (cat. 37). These animals are portrayed with collars around their necks, which suggests that they were domesticated. It has been known that noblemen in Western Han trained ferocious animals for hunting purposes.[2] NC

1 Beijing 2005, p. 264.
2 Beijing 2005, p. 257.

40

Female earthenware figures

Second century BC, Western Han dynasty
Height: 52 cm
Excavated at the tomb of the King of Chu at Beidongshan in 1986
Xuzhou Museum, Jiangsu Province
40B AND 40C NOT EXHIBITED

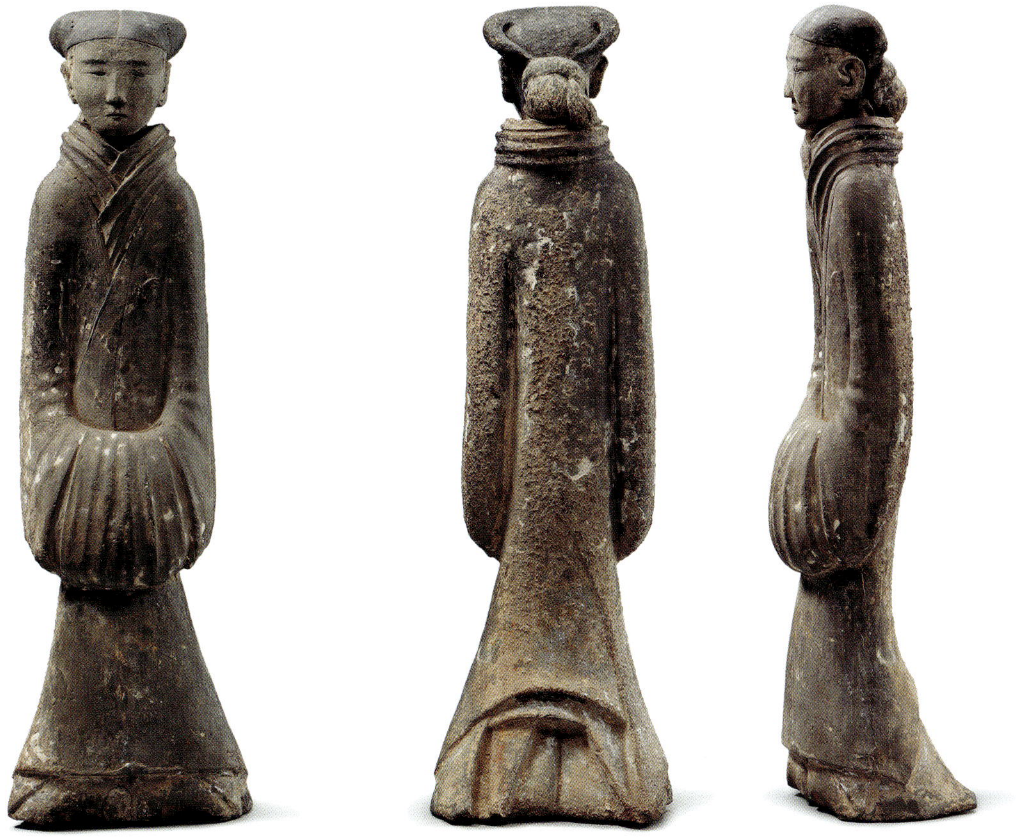

40A

The standing female attendants have their hair dressed in a 'bird-tail' bun style or in the form of a pony-tail with the hair less tightly bound (cat. 40A). There are three holes on each side of the forehead, presumably for hairpins. The ears are pierced for earrings. The faces are painted white and the hair black. They have fine eyebrows, narrow eyes, straight noses and tiny mouths. They are clothed in long robes. Judging from the costume, these figures are believed to be high-ranking attendants or female officials close to the King of Chu.

The figures of kneeling females can be divided into two types. Type 1 (cat. 40B) wears a silk-like robe richly decorated and painted with exquisite designs (fig. 51). The collars and hems have intricate borders adorned with pearls and tassels. The feet are folded inwards below her hips. The gorgeous apparel indicates that the figure might represent a noble lady or favourite concubine of the king. Type 2 (cat. 40C) has the same hairstyle and the hands are clasped. The feet are invisible under the robe, which is fastened on the right and decorated with red and black leaf patterns. This female figure seems to be a high-ranking attendant, a close servant of the King of Chu. JX

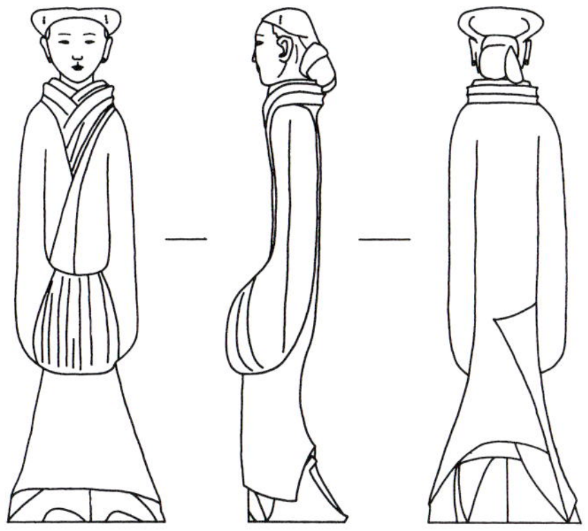

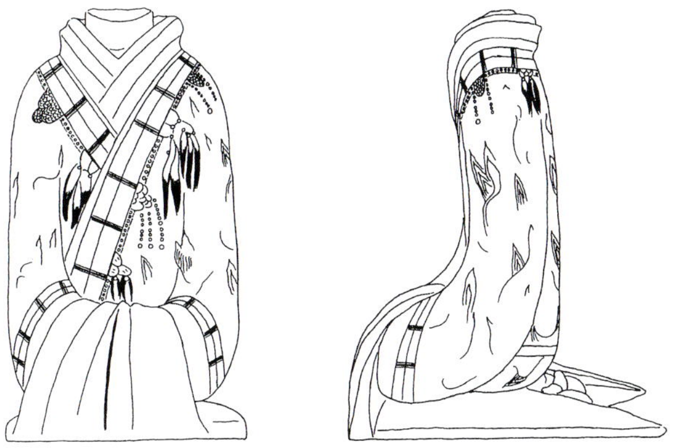

51 Details of the design of Type 1 figure apparel.

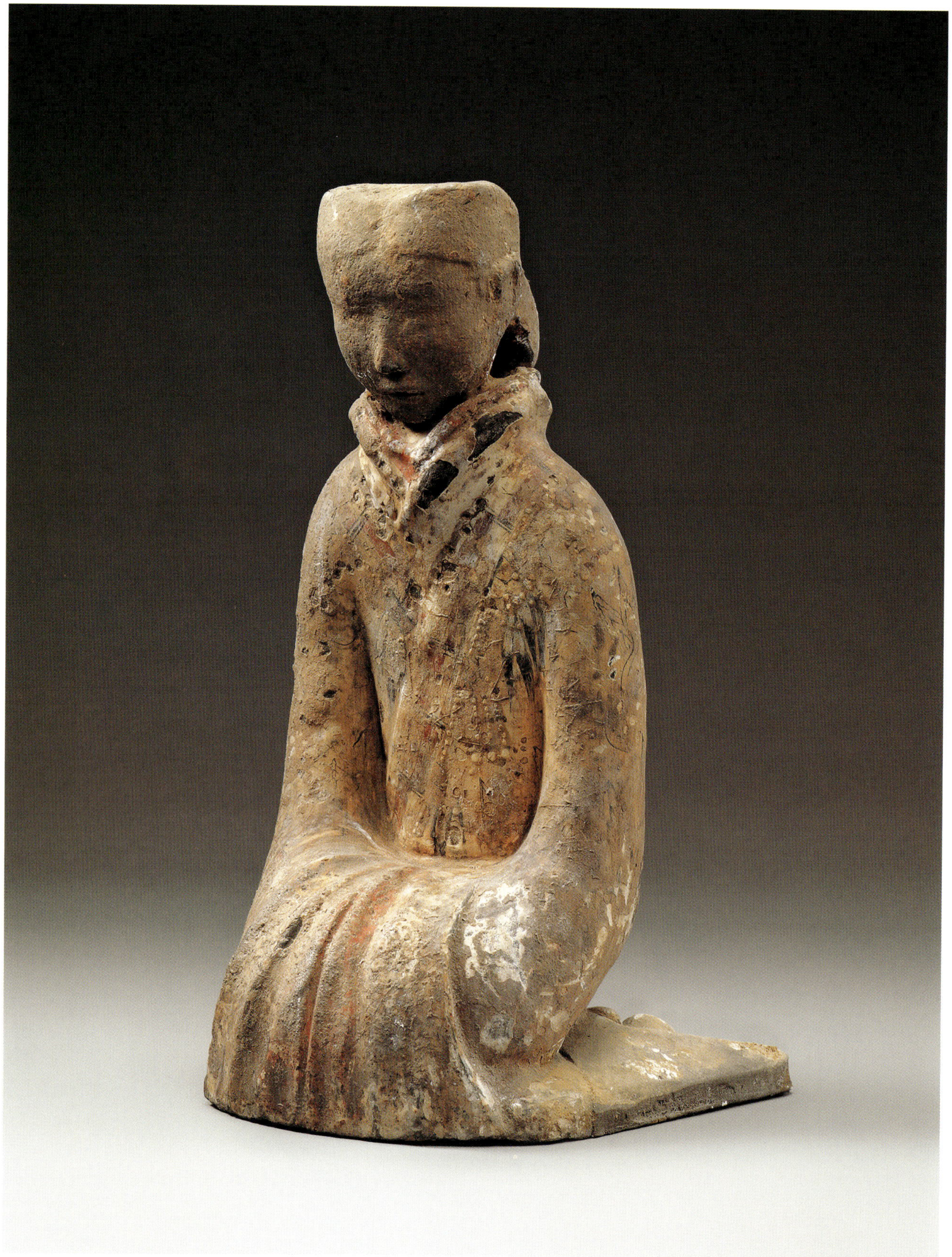

40B

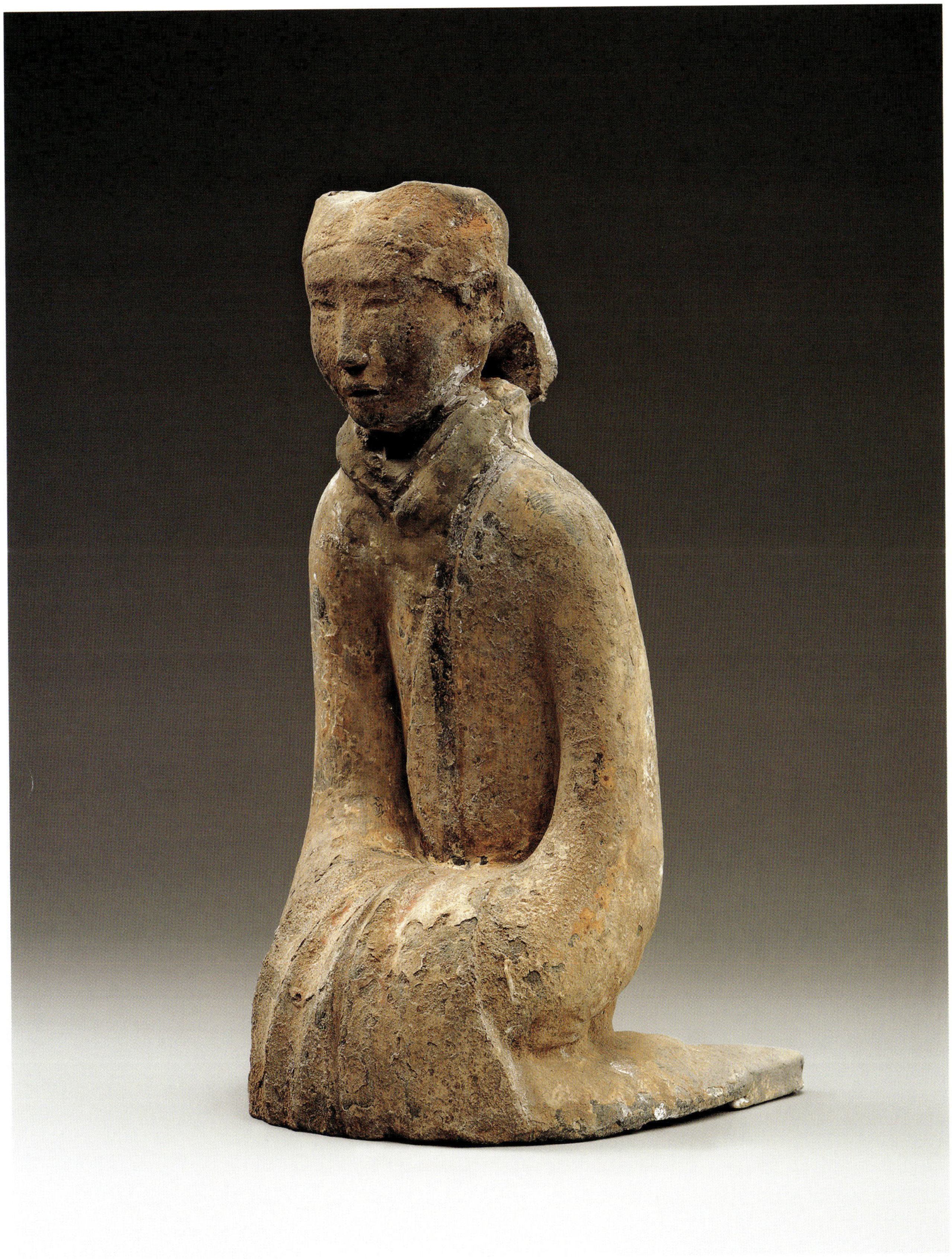

40c

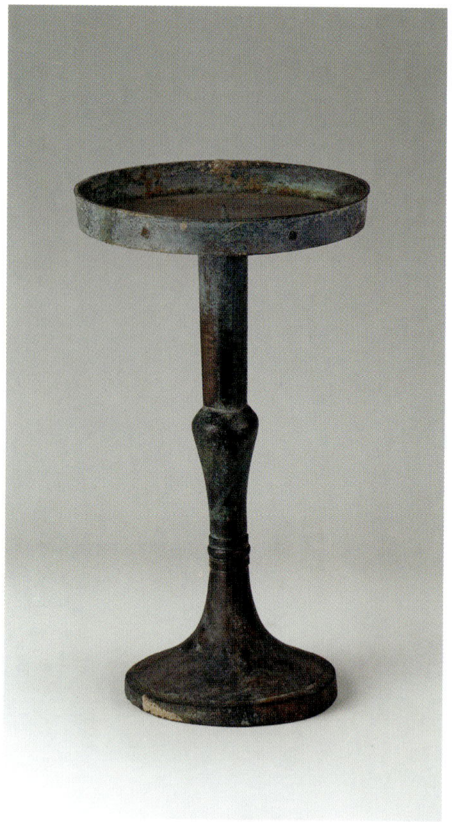

41

41

High stem bronze lamp (*deng*)

First century BC, Western Han dynasty
Height: 30.5 cm; Diameter of plate: 18.5 cm;
Diameter of base: 13.5 cm
Excavated at tomb M2 at Dongdongshan in 1982
Xuzhou Museum, Jiangsu Province
NOT EXHIBITED

This lamp was found at the M2 site at Dongdongshan, a severely plundered and disturbed tomb. Most of the burial objects had been moved out of the tomb by local villagers before the excavation began in 1982. It is therefore impossible to identify the exact original location of the lamp at the time of burial. This is one of three identical lamps found at the same site. Made from bronze, the lamp is composed of a round shallow plate, a long stem projecting in the middle with three raised bands in the lower section and a flaring foot. In the centre of the plate stands a fixed awl-shaped nail one centimetre long, which was used to support a lamp wick. Twelve copper sheets were cast onto the inner surface of the plate.

This type of lamp is believed to be evolved from the *dou*, an ancient form of food vessel usually made from bronze. A bronze lamp from the King of Nanyue's tomb, similar in shape but slightly larger and with three lamp wick support nails, is shown in this exhibition (cat. 188). The chemical analysis of the remaining substance in the lamp found in tomb No. 1 at Mancheng shows that animal fat was used as a fuel source for lamps during the Han dynasty.[1]

Of some forty bronze objects found in this tomb, ten were inscribed with characters *Mingguang gong* (Palace of Bright Radience), a royal palace in the capital city of Chang'an built during Emperor Wudi's reign that was in use for 109 years. How these palace utensils of the central court came to the Chu kingdom is still a matter for speculation.
JX

1 Archaeological report of the Han tomb at Mancheng; Beijing 1980.

42

Bronze cup-shaped lamp

Third century BC–first century AD, Han dynasty
Height: 17.8 cm; Diameter: 8 cm
Museum Acquisition
Xuzhou Museum, Jiangsu Province

This unusually designed bronze lamp consists of five parts. There is a cylindrical body to which two round shallow plates attached at the top. One of these is foldable, and the other is movable around the central body. There are two further plates attached to the base of the cylinder. The top plates work in a similar way to the *dou*-shaped lamps (cat. 41). The bottom plate with a hole

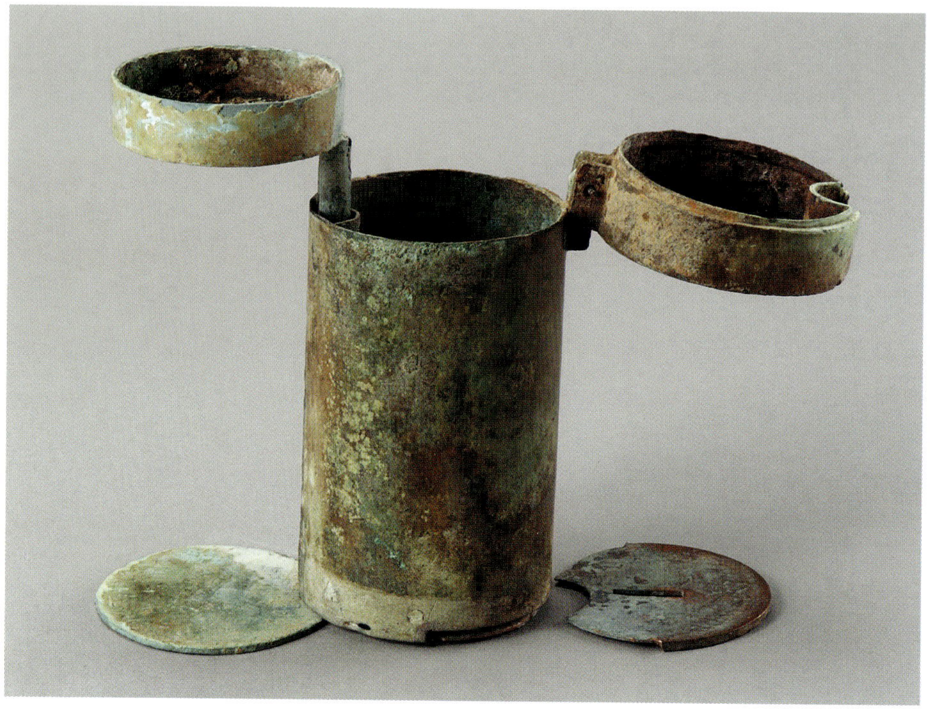

42

on the edge can be taken out and inserted into the body. When folded completely, the lamp looks like a cup and is easily portable.

It is believed this lamp was designed for travel, but how exactly it was used still remains in question. One speculation is that the supplementary base plates were designed for storing fuel. There are traces remaining of a black substance found on the plates. Chemical analysis has yet to be conducted to determine what this is. A lamp similar in shape was found at the Shangyuanjia cun site in Gansu,[1] but it is a three-in-one lamp, which can be assembled into a *dou*-shaped lamp, a walking lamp and a *zhi*- (cup) shaped lamp separately. JX

1 Zhu and Li 2004, pp. 212.

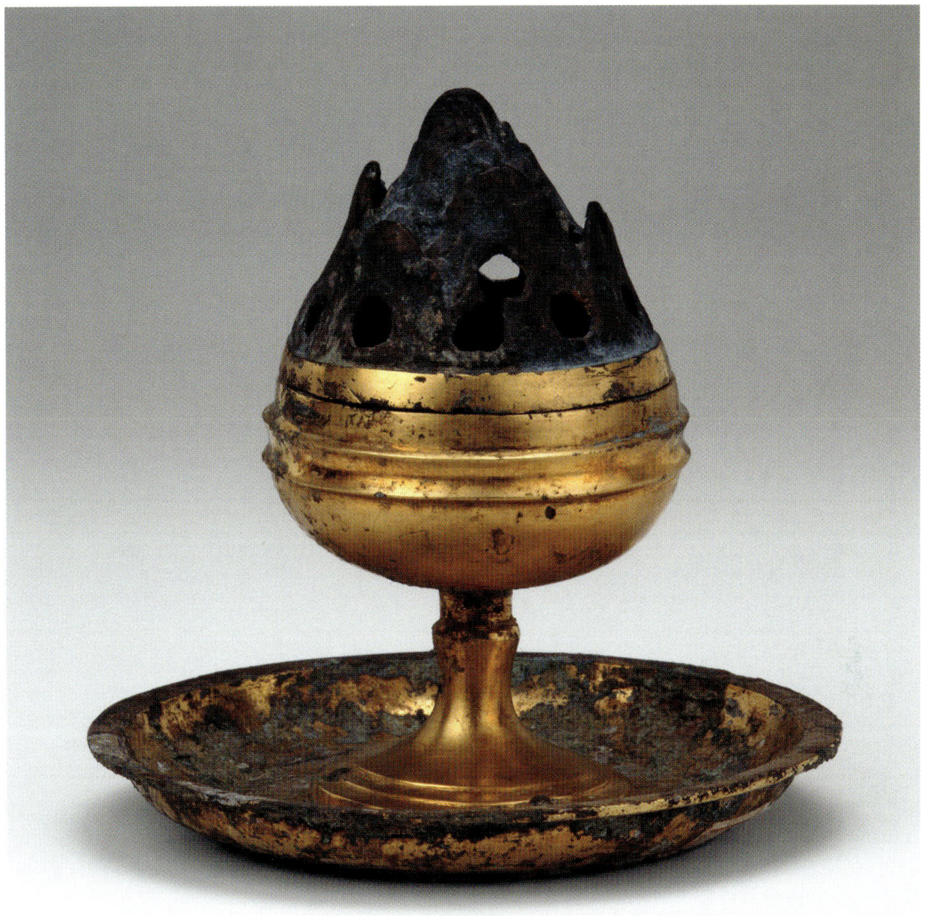

43

43

Bronze incense burner in the shape of Bo Mountain (*Boshan*)

First century BC, Western Han dynasty
Height: 12.4 cm; Diameter: 12 cm
Excavated at tomb M2 at Dongdongshan in 1982
Xuzhou Museum, Jiangsu Province

Incense burners were widely used in the Han dynasty and were cast in various forms (other examples can be seen in cat. 125, 146, 179). This bronze burner is designed in the shape of *Boshan*, one of the three imaginary celestial mountains in Daoist myth. The *Boshan* burner was very popular in the Han dynasty, coinciding with the practice of seeking immortality. When used, the smoke issuing from the burner would resemble the mist and clouds that surrounded mountain peaks.

A *Boshan* incense burner consists of a conical top bearing irregular mountain-like projections, a bowl to hold incense, a stem and sometimes a plate serving as a base. The Song dynasty scholar Lü Dalin explained in his 'Illustrated Enquiries into Antiquity' (*Kaogutu*, 1092 AD) the symbolism and functions of the shape of the conical top and plate: 'The incense burner symbolizes *Boshan* in the sea. The plate underneath is filled with water, moisturizing and perfuming the air. The water in the plate resembles the sea surrounding the mountain.'[1] LKC

1 *Kaogutu* 10:15b.

44

Gilt bronze container (*fang*)

Second century BC, Western Han dynasty
Height: 58.8 cm
Excavated at Shizishan in 1994–5
Xuzhou Museum, Jiangsu Province

This container was excavated from the first chamber to the west in the tomb at Shizishan.[1] Lying on its side, it was found next to the entrance area to the chamber. An almost identical *fang* was found close by, suggesting that these were intended as a pair, which is often the case in Han burials. The vessel, square in cross-section, sits on a tall, splayed foot. On two faces

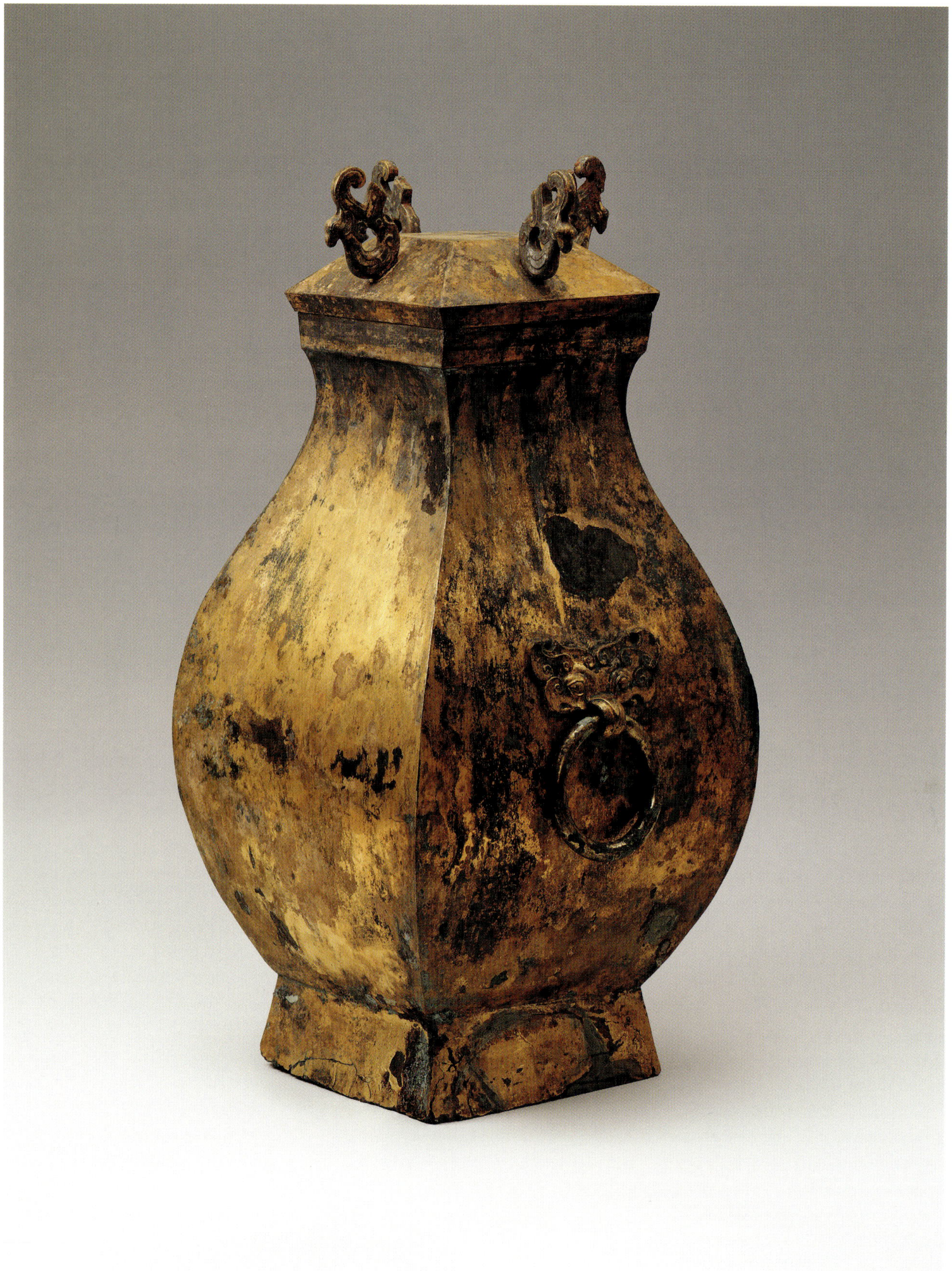

44

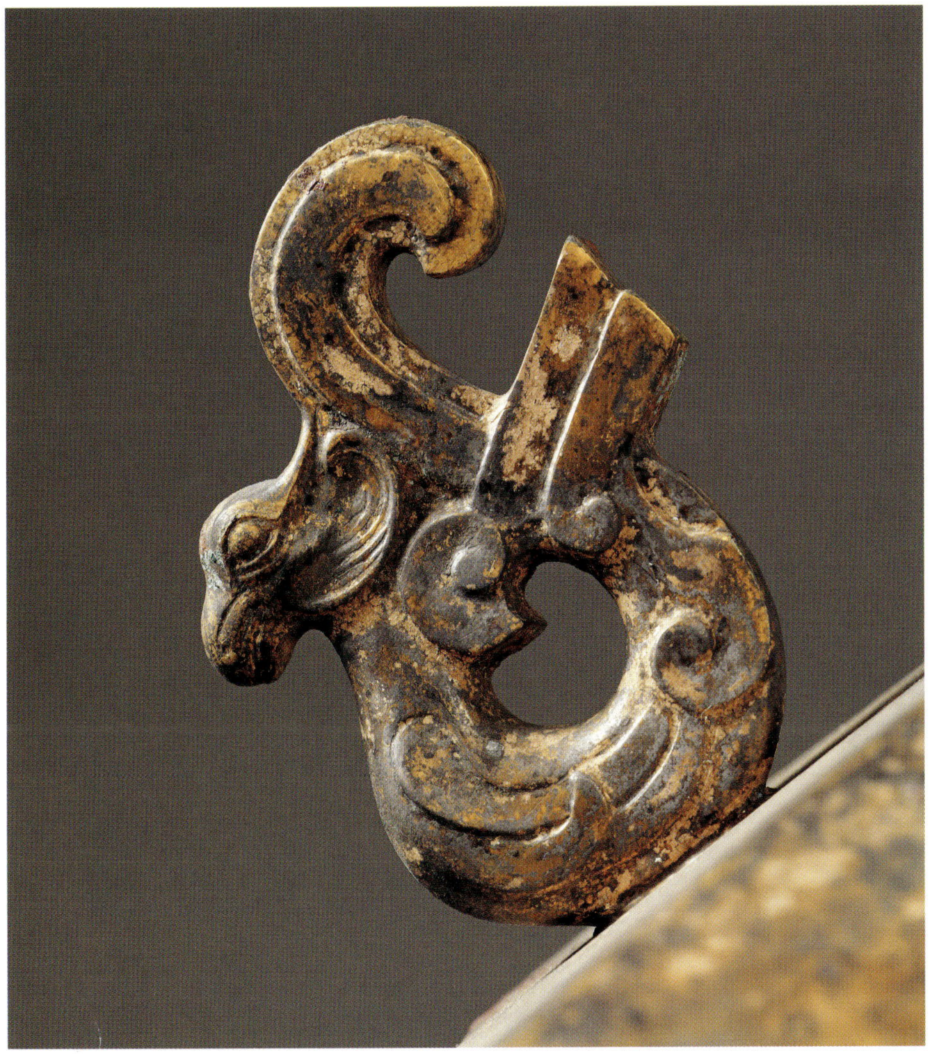

of the body is an animal face with a ring in its snout. The lid could be taken off and made to stand using the four bird appendages as feet to serve as an additional vessel. Apart from the animal faces and birds, the vessel is otherwise undecorated but entirely covered with mercury-amalgam gilding, which has come off in places, allowing the bronze beneath to patinate.

Fang are vessels for alcohol, as revealed by the inscriptions on bamboo slips from tomb No. 1 at Mawangdui, which refers to a lidded *fang* containing alcohol made from rice.[2] Four lacquered wooden *fang* excavated from this tomb still had alcohol dregs in them.[3] *Fang* first appeared in the Spring and Autumn period and became more popular in Warring States and Western Han times. We know from an inscription on a *fang* from tomb No. 1 at Mancheng that this type of vessel was actually referred to as such during the Han period.[4] In addition to bronze and lacquer, *fang* were also produced in ceramics, as seen in the example from Shizishan that was found in the main tomb chamber.[5] SP[6]

1 *Wenwu* 1998.8, p. 15.
2 Beijing 1973, vol. 1, p. 144.
3 Beijing 1973, vol. 1, pp. 79–80.
4 Beijing 1980, vol. 1, p. 49.
5 *Wenwu* 1998.8, p. 20.
6 Sascha Priewe would like to acknowledge Carol Michaelson for her helpful comments on his entries in this catalogue.

45

Lacquer-covered earthenware *fang*

Second century BC, early Western Han dynasty
Height: 34 cm
Excavated at Baiyunshan in the 1970s
Xuzhou Museum, Jiangsu Province
NOT EXHIBITED

This lacquer-covered earthenware wine container (*fang*), is an accurate copy of a bronze vessel of the Warring States period. It is square in cross-section with a pear-shaped body sitting on a tall, splayed foot. The surface is painted with black lacquer and decorated in red with a frieze of pendent triangles below the neck. A bronze version, incised with a Han inscription, formerly in the Arthur M. Sackler Collection, is now in a private collection (fig. 52). This earthenware *fang*

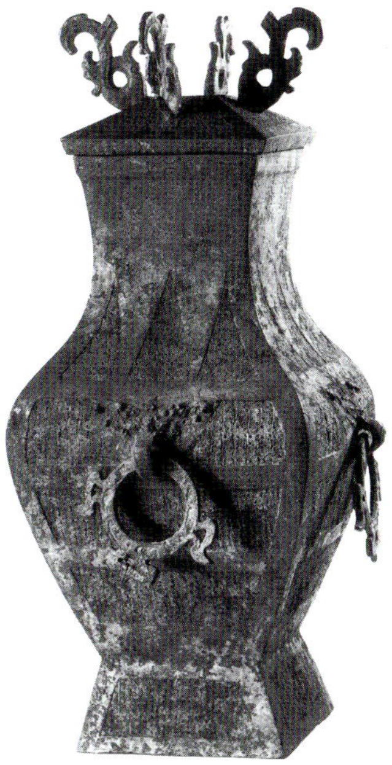

52 A bronze *fang*. Incised inscription dated to 1 BC, Western Han period. Formely Arthur M. Sackler Collection, New York, now private collection.

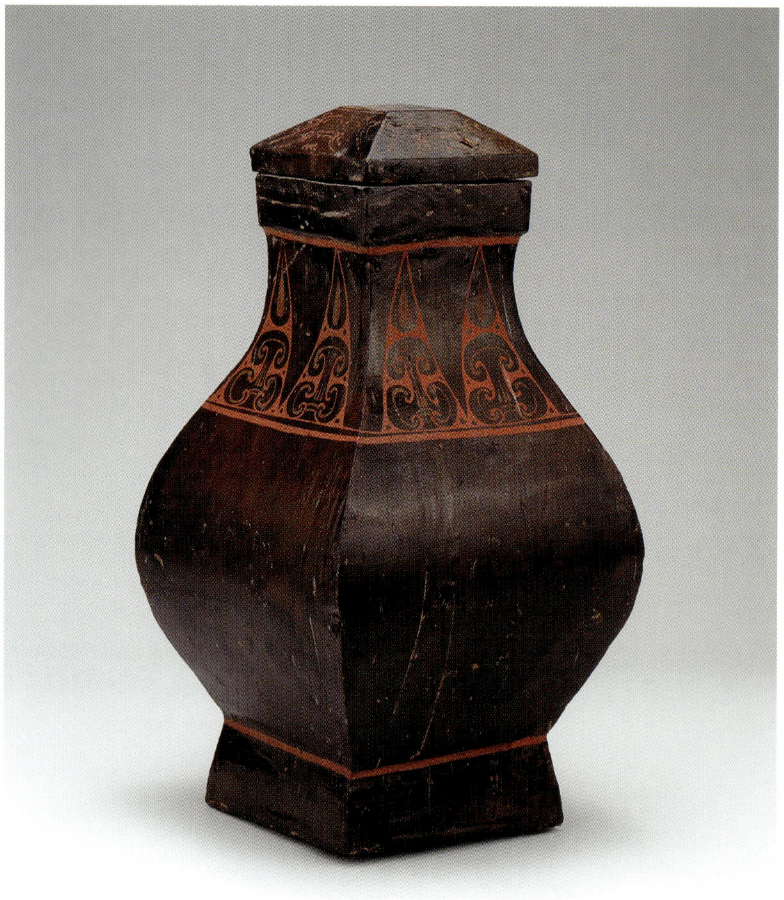

45

was excavated from the tomb of a low-ranking individual whose status has been identified as that of the official in charge of jade carving at the imperial workshop (cat. 99). JCSL

46

Bronze wine container (*pi*)

Third century BC–first century BC,
Western Han dynasty
Height: 30.5 cm; Width: 33 cm
Museum Acquisition
Xuzhou Museum, Jiangsu Province

Bronze wine vessels of this shape are found from the Spring and Autumn period (770–476 BC). Ceramic and lacquer containers of this shape have also been discovered. Vessels of this type have a square base, a flattened, oval-shaped body with ring-shaped handles and a round neck. The lid has a loop for the attachment of a cord that could be used to tether the lid to the neck while still allowing for it to be removed easily. The ring-shaped handles are held in place by an attachment in the form of a mythical beast. The pattern on the vessel has not yet been determined. LKC

47

Bronze container (*zhong*)

First century BC, Western Han dynasty
Height: 44.5 cm; Diameter: 33.5 cm
Excavated at tomb No. 2 at Dongdongshan
in 1982
Xuzhou Museum, Jiangsu Province

This vessel is one of two similar *zhong* from tomb No. 2 at Dongdongshan. While one bears the inscription *Mingguan gong* (Palace of Bright Radiance), the

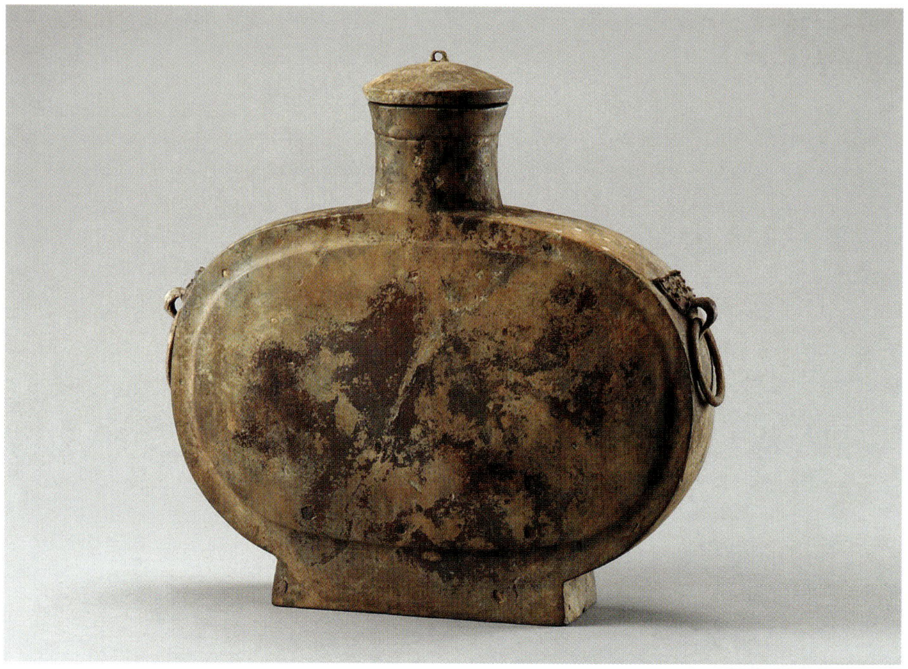

46

present example has a slightly longer inscription of six characters on the foot ring reading *Mingguang gong Zhao Ji zhong*, which could be translated as '*Zhong* of concubine Zhao; Palace of Bright Radiance'. Zhao Ji, possibly the first owner of the vessel, is also named on another, a gilt bronze *pan* from the same tomb (cat. 100). The *Mingguang gong* was constructed in the Han capital at Chang'an, present-day Xi'an in Shaanxi Province, in 101 BC. Whether Zhao Ji can be identified as the tomb occupant remains to be seen, but it is possible that this vessel ended up in Xuzhou as a gift. Interestingly, the inscription refers to this vessel as a *zhong* as opposed to a *hu*. Both terms seem to have been used interchangeably for such types of vessel during the Han period.

This vessel is very similar to the one from Shizishan (cat. 48). Four concentric bands adorn the body. Animal masks are placed between the second and third band. The foot ring is slightly more recessed and the mouth is less flared than those of the Shizishan example. While in overall good condition when discovered, the neck of the vessel was partly missing and the foot ring was also partly damaged, but both have since been restored.[1] SP

1 *Wenwu* 1984.11, p. 27, fig. 20.

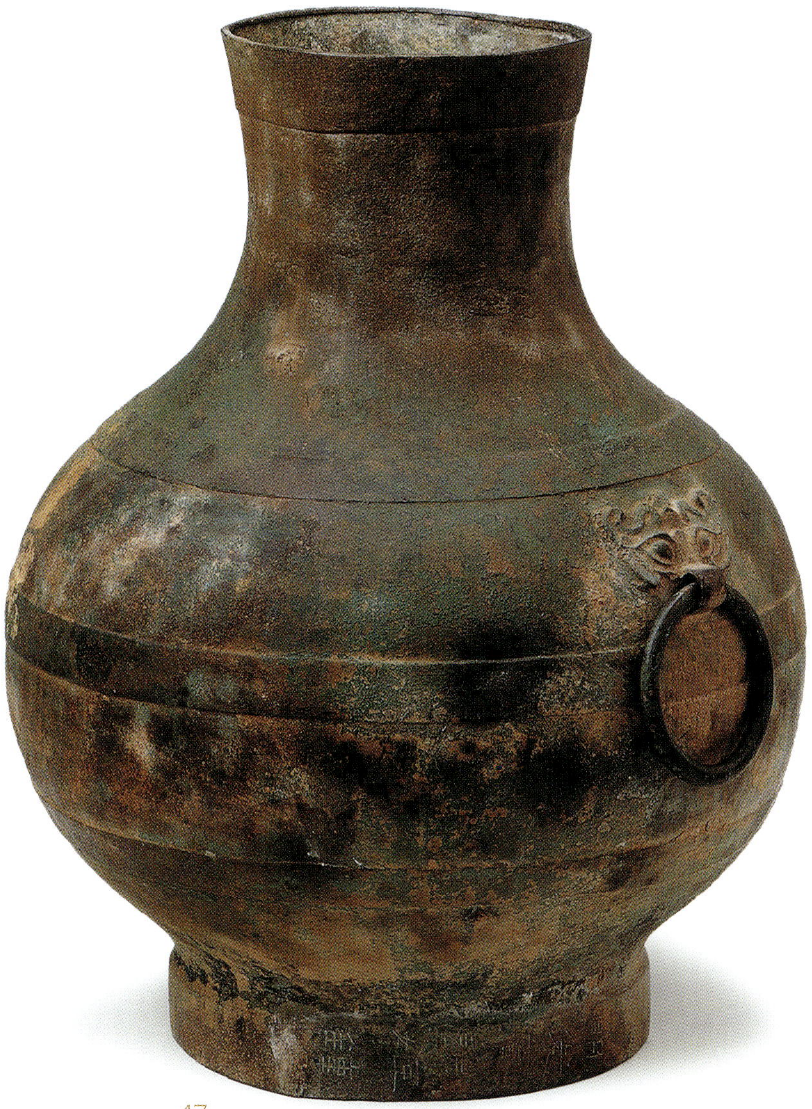

47

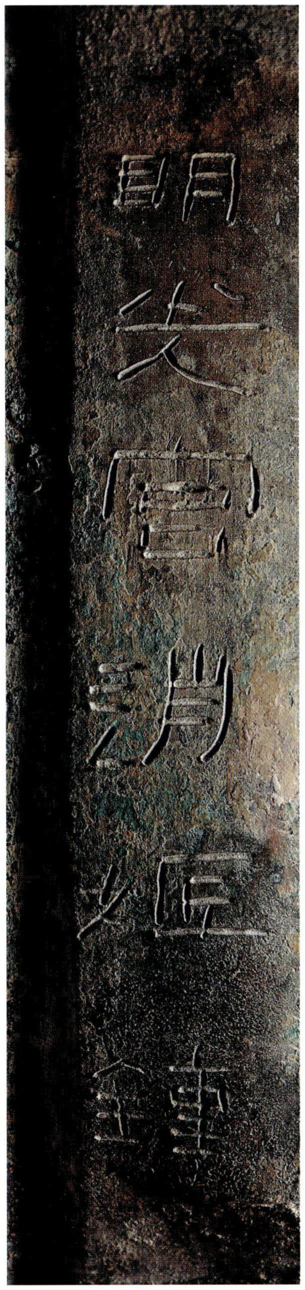

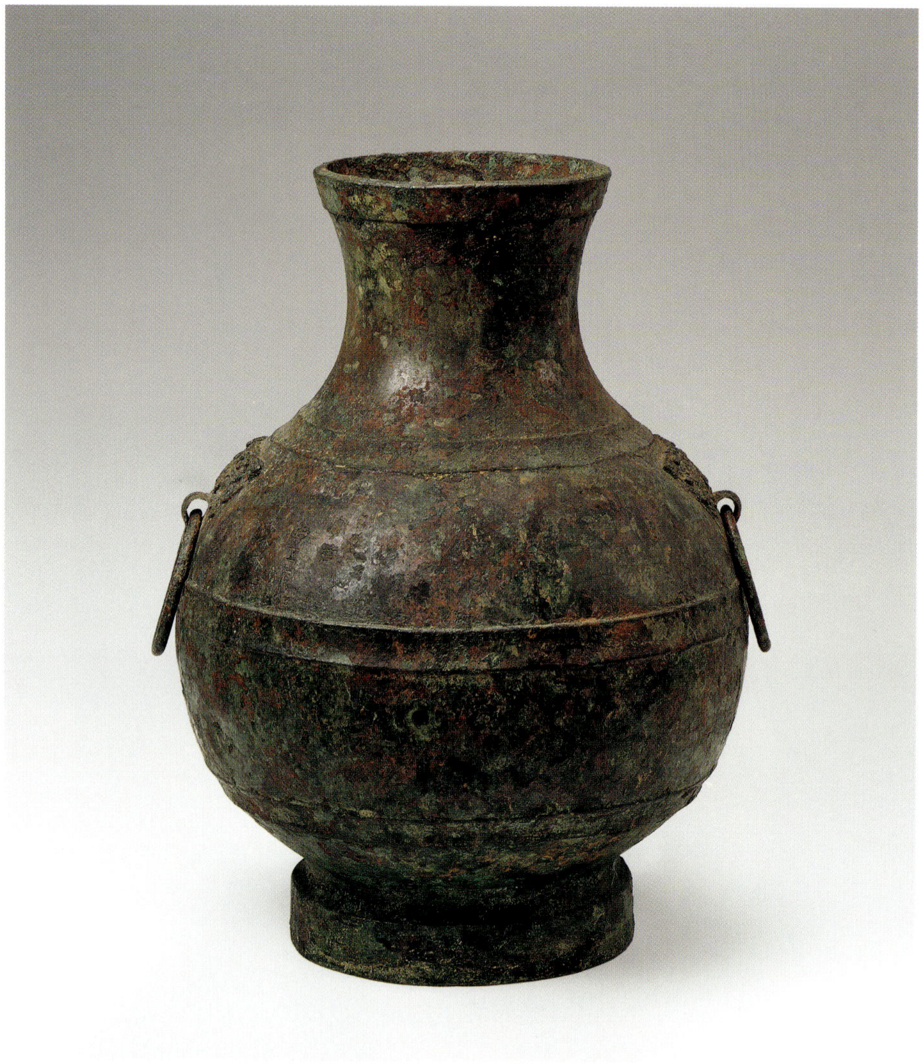

48

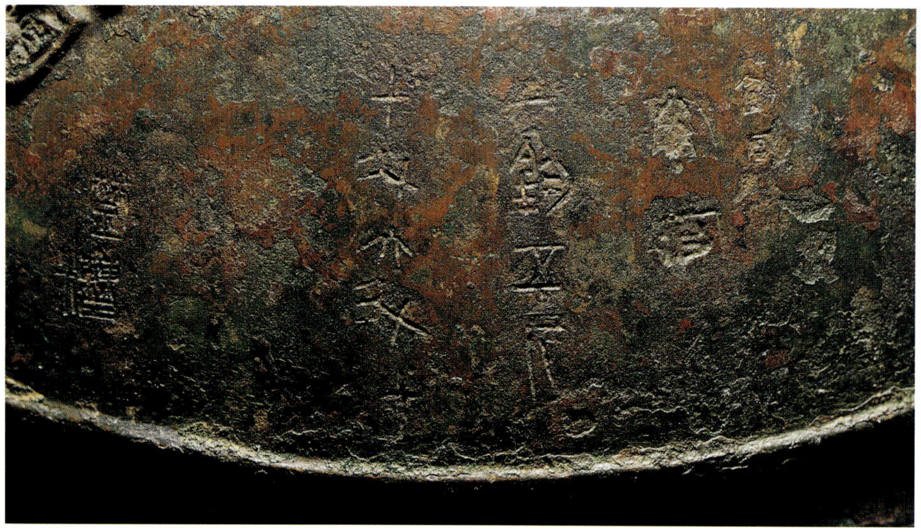

48

Bronze container (*zhong*)

Second century BC, Western Han dynasty
Height: 47.4 cm; Diameter: 35 cm
Excavated at Shizishan in 1994–5
Xuzhou Museum, Jiangsu Province
NOT EXHIBITED

This *zhong* container was excavated from the tomb at Shizishan. Its precise location within the tomb cannot be ascertained from published sources. Five such vessels seem to have been excavated from this tomb. Four come from the first side chamber to the west. Two were standing right next to a *yi* (cat. 53), while another was lying on its side at the entrance area next to a *fang* (cat. 44). The fourth example was also lying on its side but along the western wall with its mouth facing south. It was lying among many weapons and it is possible that weapons may have once been placed in this container, which later were spilled onto the floor when the chamber was flooded. The fifth *zhong*, said to be similar to the others, was found in the second side chamber to the west.[1] The present example carries an inscription giving its capacity on the shoulders at the height of the handles. It also mentions a Chu Zao, which probably refers to the owner of the piece.

This vessel has a pear-shaped body resting on a stepped foot ring. Four concentric bands are the only adornment. One is found just below the mouth, the second just below the neck and above the shoulder, the third sits just above where the vessel has the widest circumference and the fourth sits a bit lower down. Two animal masks grasping ring handles are just below the second band. SP

1 *Wenwu* 1998.8, p. 8, figs 7, 17.

49

Bronze ladle

Second century BC, Western Han dynasty
Length: 34 cm
Excavated at Shizishan in 1994–5
Xuzhou Museum, Jiangsu Province

This ladle comes from the first side chamber to the east in the tomb at Shizishan, which was identified as a kitchen.[1] It contained items of ceramic, bronze and iron, but also clay sealings and bird and animal bones. This ladle was found together with three others of similar design inside an earthenware cauldron (*fu*). It bears a twelve-character inscription on the handle giving its weight. A pair of similar ladles was found in a bronze tripod *ding* in the chamber across the hall. The ladle has a deep almost rectangular bowl with rounded edges. The part of the handle closest to the bowl is angular but becomes rounder, ending in a raised band. Beyond the band the head of a creature with flattened ears, possibly a dragon, grasps a loop in its snout from which the ladle can be suspended. Similar ladles but in larger quantities were found in the royal tomb of Nanyue in Guangzhou.[2]

Much of the other kitchen equipment also bore inscriptions as to their content: for example, one was inscribed as containing a sauce made from water chestnuts. Some inscriptions also refer to the *Shiguan*, the office of the food provisioner with responsibilities to furnish the queen, heir apparent and the princely establishment with food.[3] This office apparently not only existed at the Han court in Chang'an, but also at the court of Chu at Xuzhou. SP

1 *Wenwu* 1998.8, pp. 4, 8.
2 Beijing 1991, vol. 1, p. 81, fig. 54:1.
3 Hucker 1985, p. 426.

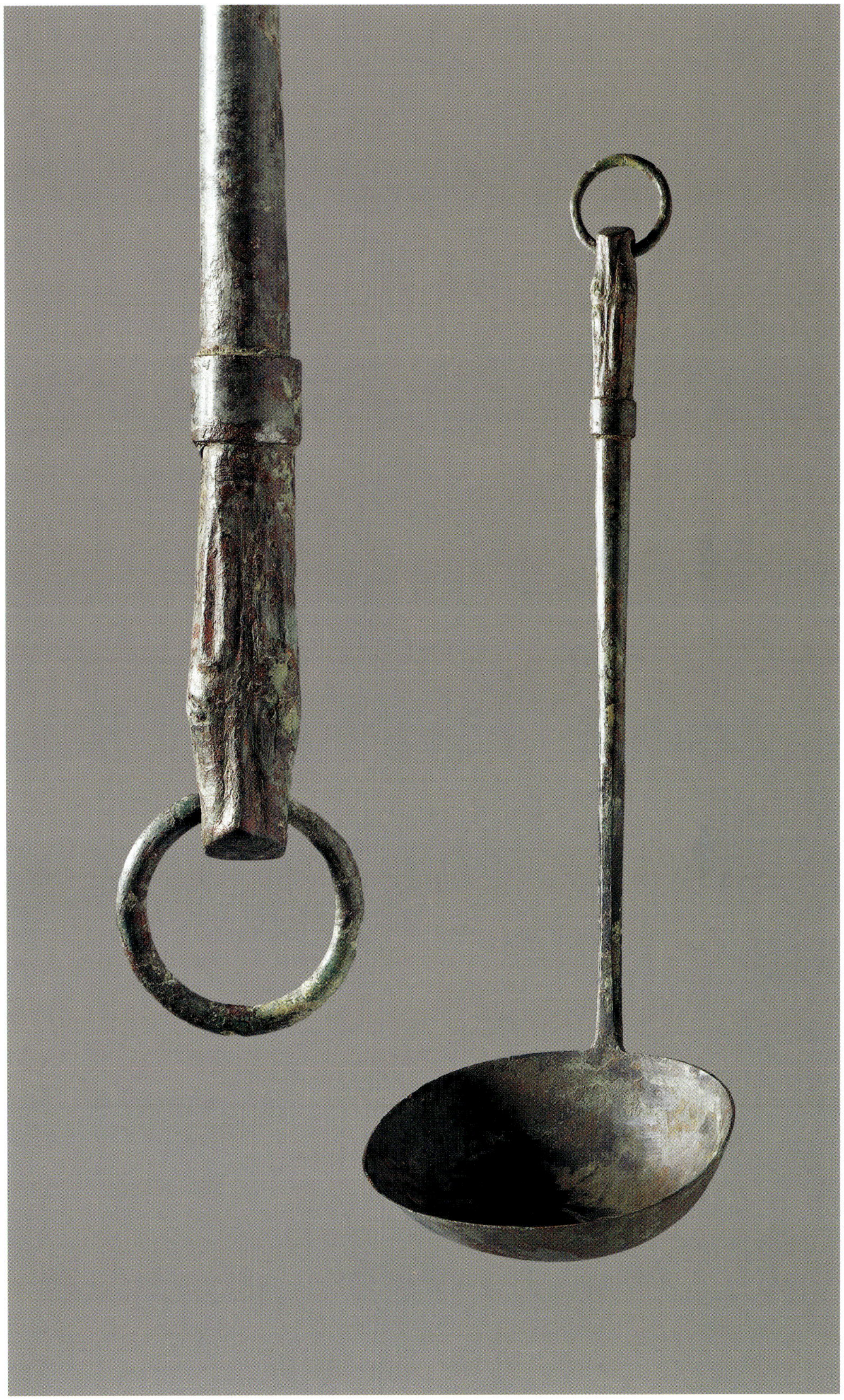

49

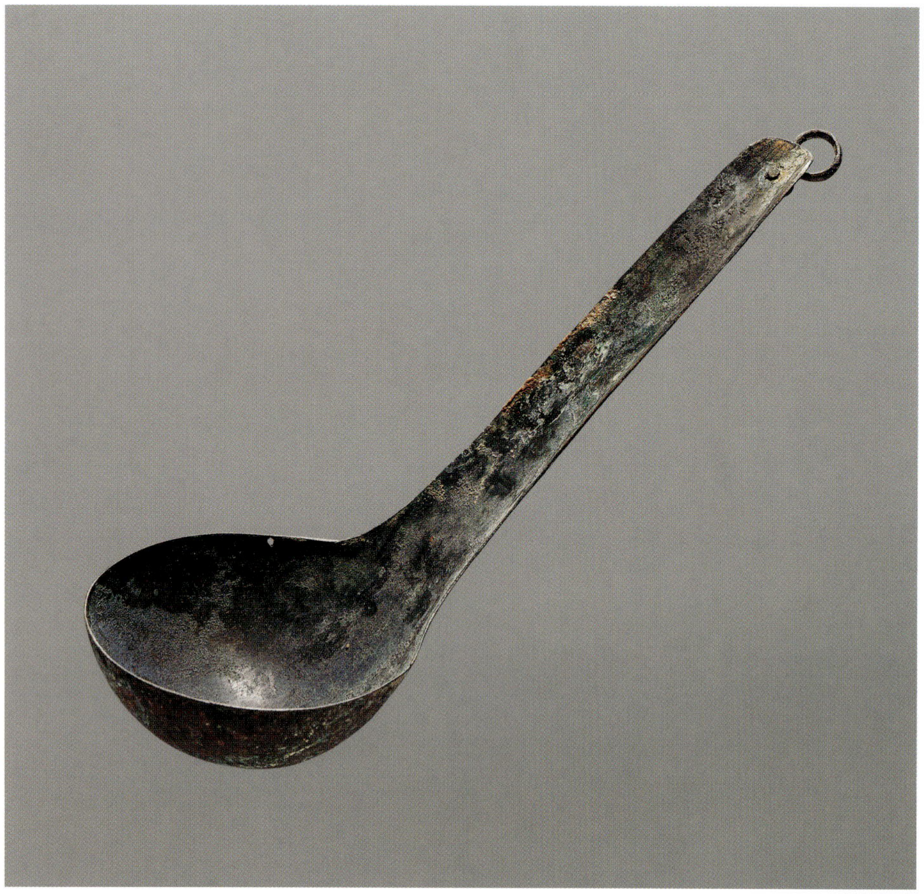

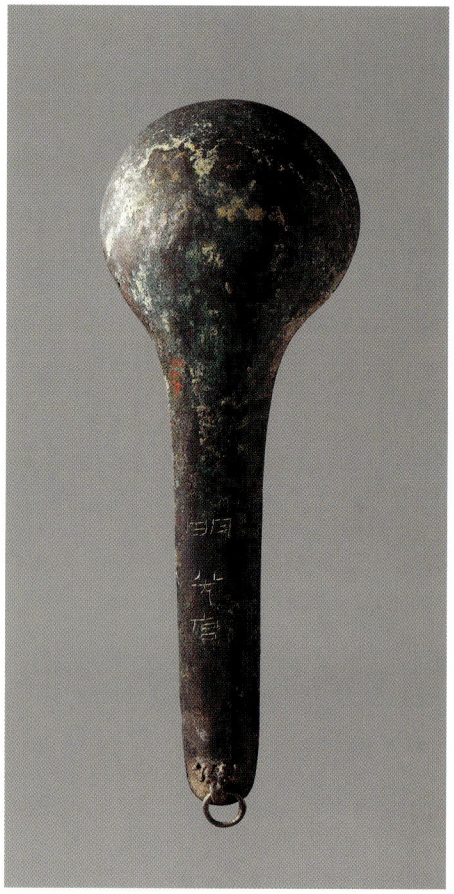

50

50

Bronze spoon

Early first century BC, Western Han dynasty
Length: 26 cm
Excavated at tomb No. 2 at Dongdongshan in 1982
Xuzhou Museum, Jiangsu Province

One of two more or less identical spoons, this was excavated from tomb No. 2 at Dongdongshan.[1] Unfortunately, the majority of the grave goods, including this spoon, were removed before their position in the tomb could be properly recorded. The spoon has an arched, straight handle ending in a deep, round bowl. At the tip of the handle a rivet holds an animal mask grasping a loop its snout from which the spoon could be suspended. Like its counterpart from the same tomb, it bears an inscription on the underside of the handle reading *Mingguan gong*, Palace of Bright Radiance. In addition to the two spoons, eight bronze vessels carry the name of this palace, which was constructed in the Han capital at Chang'an, present-day Xi'an in Shaanxi Province, in 101 BC, providing an earliest possible date for the construction of tomb No. 2 at Dongdongshan.[2] The spoons were originally produced for this palace in the capital, but how they ended up in the possession of the tomb occupant in Xuzhou remains a mystery.
SP

1 *Wenwu* 1984.11, p. 26.
2 *Wenwu* 1984.11, pp. 38–9.

51

Bronze stove (*kaolu*)

Second century BC, Western Han dynasty
Height: 16 cm; Diameter: 45.4 cm
Excavated at Shizishan in 1994–5
Xuzhou Museum, Jiangsu Province
NOT EXHIBITED

This stove was probably found in the second chamber to the west in the tomb at Shizishan. The flat vessel with slightly S-shaped sides is sitting on three cabriole legs. Four animal masks holding loops are affixed onto the body of the oven between the legs. The loop of one of these faces still has one smaller loop linked to it, suggesting chains of loops may have once connected the masks, making the stove easier to transport.

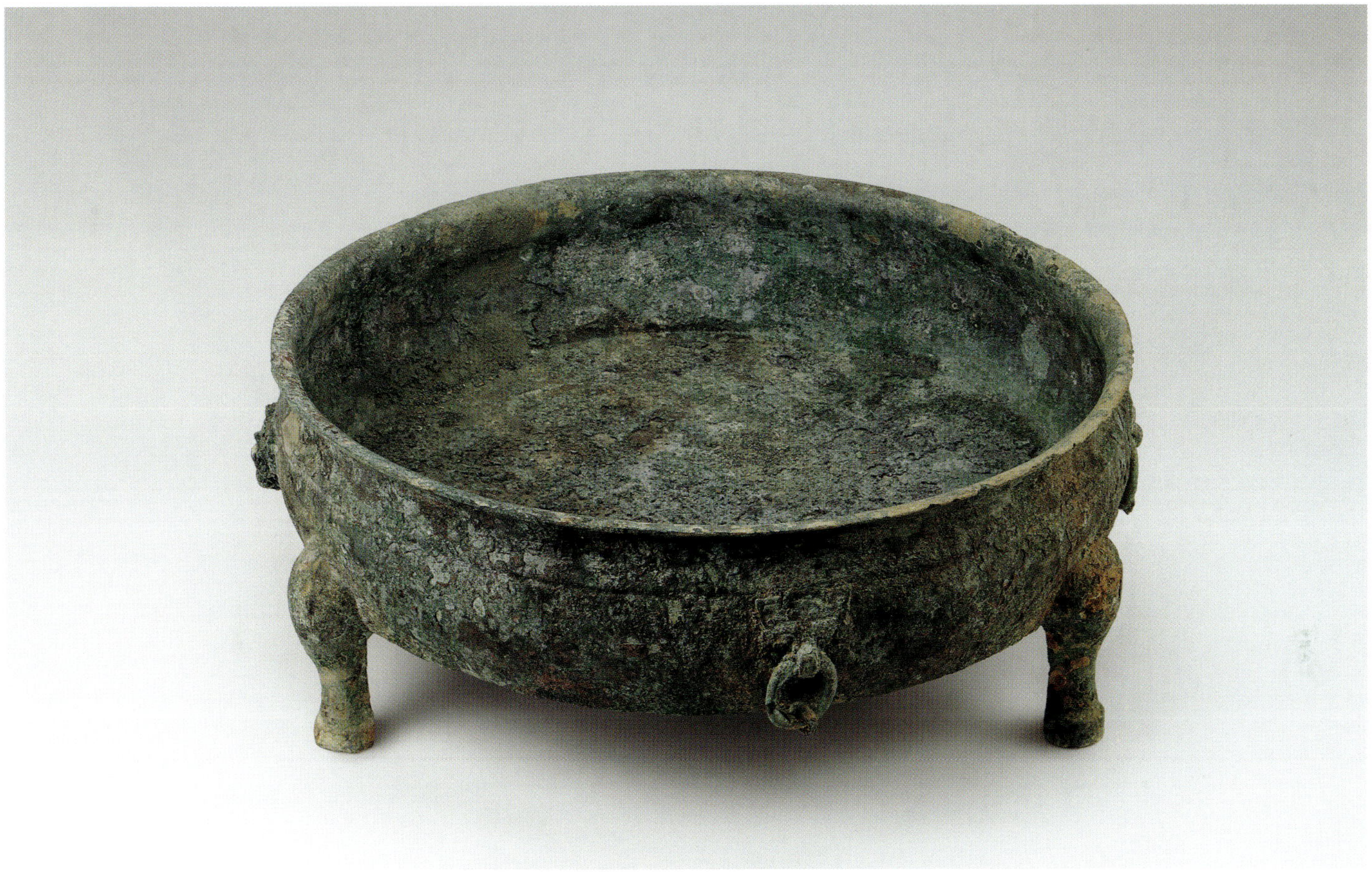

51

Such stoves were used to roast or broil meat, held over the stove by an iron or bronze fork-like implement. Such stoves were also rectangular or square in shape, such as the example from the royal tomb of Nanyue (cat. 189). A stove of this type in use is depicted on a mural in a Western Han period tomb in Luoyang, Henan.[1] It shows a kneeling man leaning towards a square or rectangular stove, holding a stick with a large chunk of meat on it over the fire. The Nanyue examples illustrate that the meat could also be held over the fire by a support, which was inserted into openings on the side of the stove.[2] SP

1 *Kaogu* 1964.2, pl. 2.
2 Prüch 1998, cat. 88.

52

Bronze steamer and cauldron

Second century BC, Western Han dynasty
Height: 44.5 cm; Maximum diameter: 38 cm
Excavated at Yangguishan in 2005
Xuzhou Museum, Jiangsu Province

This set of bronze vessels comes from one of the many pits surrounding an as yet unopened tomb, probably that of the consort of the king who was buried at Shizishan close to where Yangguishan is located. The set consists of a steamer *zeng* whose foot ring perfectly fits the cauldron *fu* below. The cauldron would have been filled with water and placed on a tripod over fire. The steam that built up would escape through the perforations in the steamer, allowing the food to cook. Alternatively, the cauldron and steamer could be placed on a stove resting on the four projections that are cast on where the circumference is widest. Two loop handles on each allow both steamer and cauldron to be lifted. Models of stoves holding steamers and cauldrons illustrating such use have been found in Han period tombs, such as in a Western Han period burial excavated in Luoyang, Henan (fig. 53).[1]

This combination of vessels became popular from the mid- to late Western Han period (first century BC). Previously, a legged cauldron that sat directly on the fire without a tripod or stove had been used. Bronze steamer sets are seen less frequently in the Eastern Han period and later and it is probable that vessels made of iron replaced them.[2] The majority of

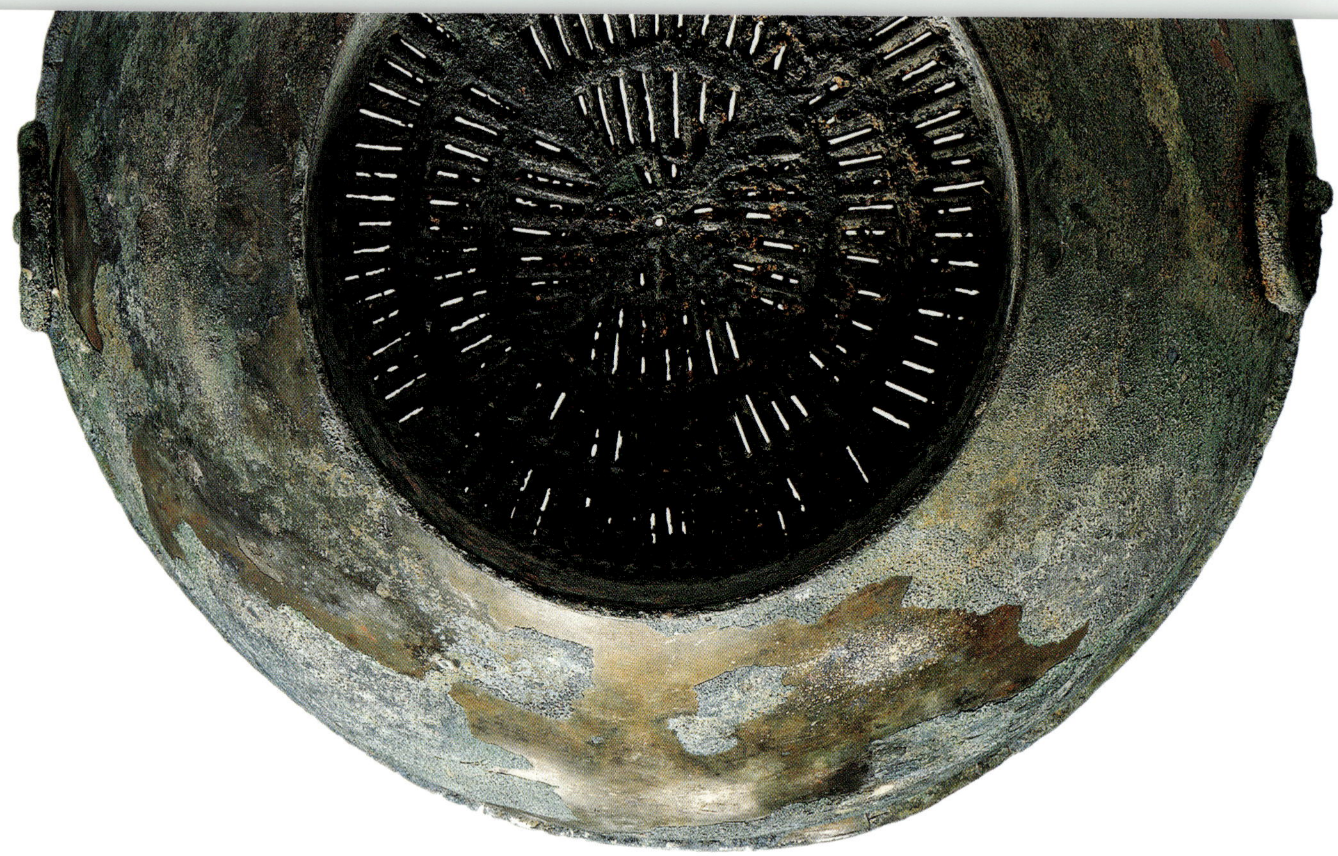

sets of steamer and cauldron were made from pottery. Steaming was an essential part of Han period cuisine and *zeng* and *fu*, as a set, were used to prepare grains.[3] SP

1 *Kaogu* 1964.2, p. 119, fig. 8:8.
2 Beijing 2005, p. 198.
3 Yü 1977, p. 79.

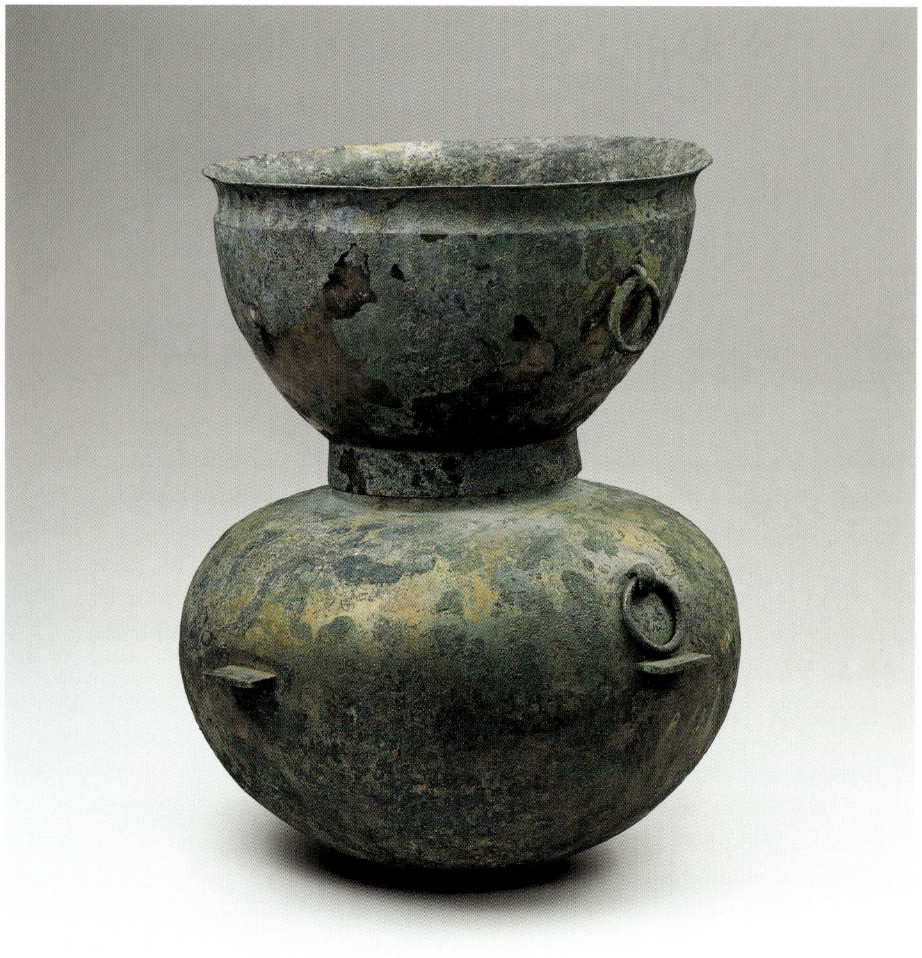

52

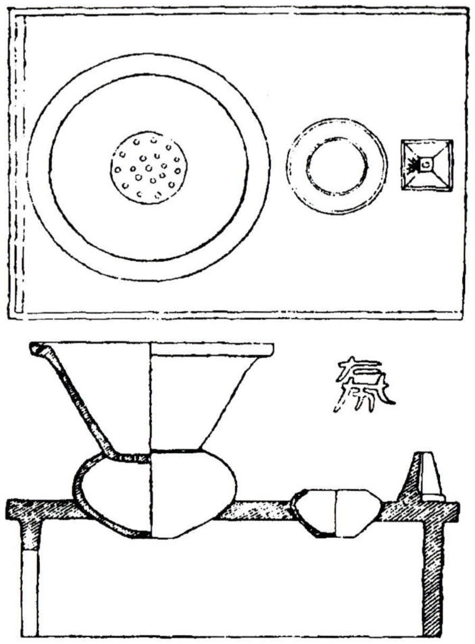

53 Drawing of the steamer and cauldron in use.

53

Bronze pouring vessel (*yi*)

Second century BC, Western Han dynasty
Length: 33.7 cm; Width: 26.7 cm; Height: 10.7 cm
Excavated at Shizishan in 1994–5
Xuzhou Museum, Jiangsu Province
NOT EXHIBITED

This vessel was found in the first chamber to the west in the tomb at Shizishan. The chamber contained large numbers of bronze and iron weapons, as well as lacquer and jade items, and the excavators suggested it may have been a storage room.[1] It also housed a number of containers and vessels for liquids, including the present piece, and food vessels. Lying on its right side, the vessel was sandwiched between a container *zhong* to the north and two tripod *ding*, one to the south and one to the southwest.

The underside of the *yi*'s spout bears the sixteen-character inscription *Shiguan 13 1 dou 10 sheng 6 jin 20 liang*, detailing the vessel's weight and volume. The term *Shiguan* refers to the office at the court of Chu at Xuzhou of those responsible for providing food for the empress, the heir apparent and the princely establishment.[2] The inscription confirms the use of the group of vessels in this chamber. The *yi* was probably used like a ewer, held by a servant, to pour water over hands for washing with a basin placed below. *Yi* and basins are often found together and it is tempting to suggest that the bronze basin that was also found in this chamber was once used for this purpose along with this *yi*. With a flat base instead of a more rounded one, the present example is based on pieces from the late Warring States. The loop on the surface opposite the spout could be used to suspend the *yi*. SP

1 *Wenwu* 1998.8, p. 6.
2 Hucker 1985, p. 426.

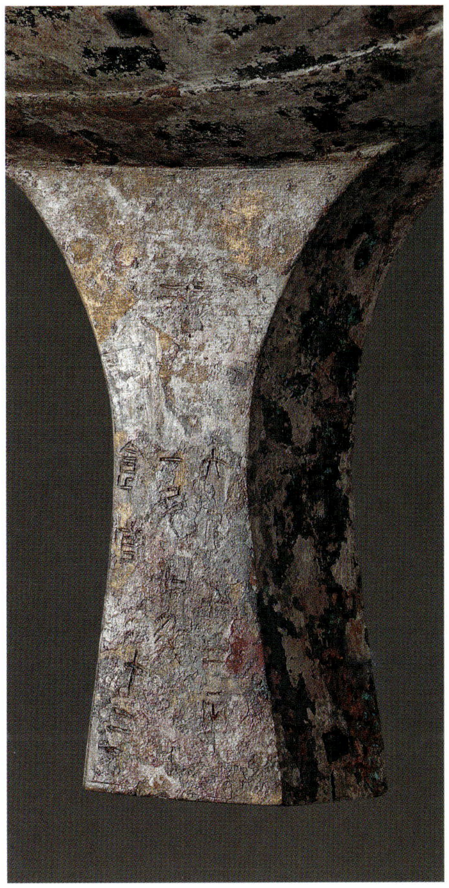

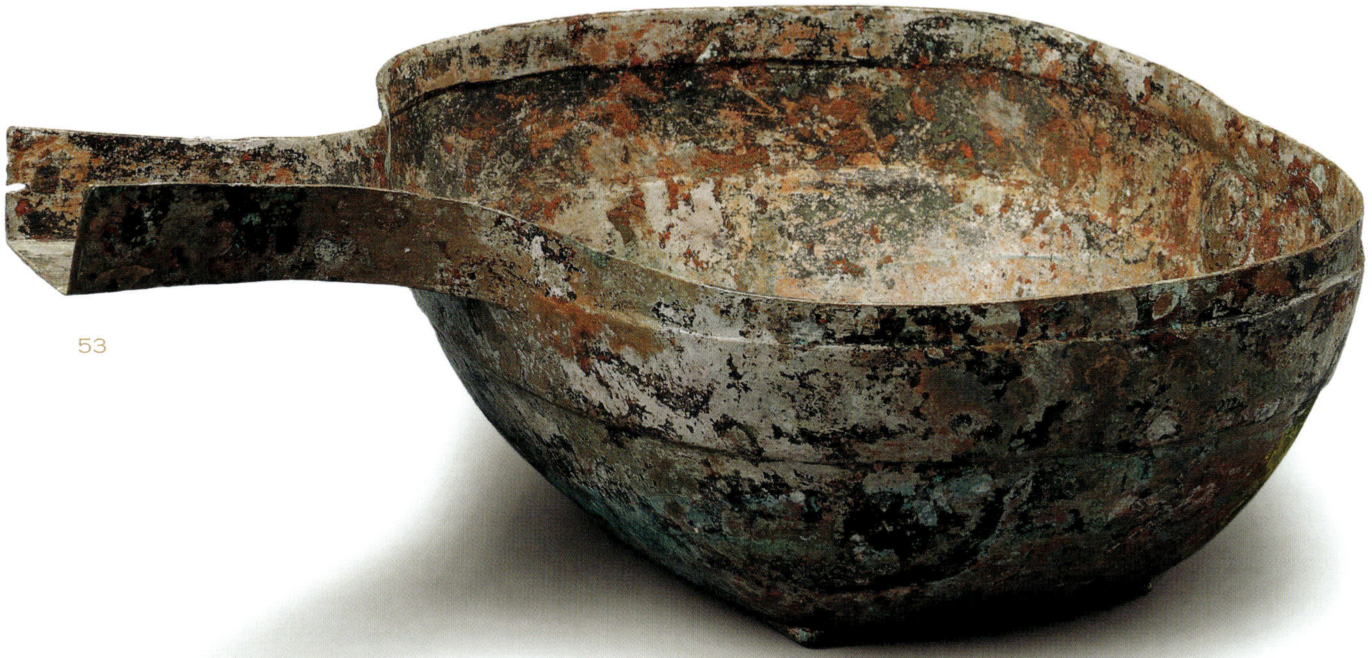

53

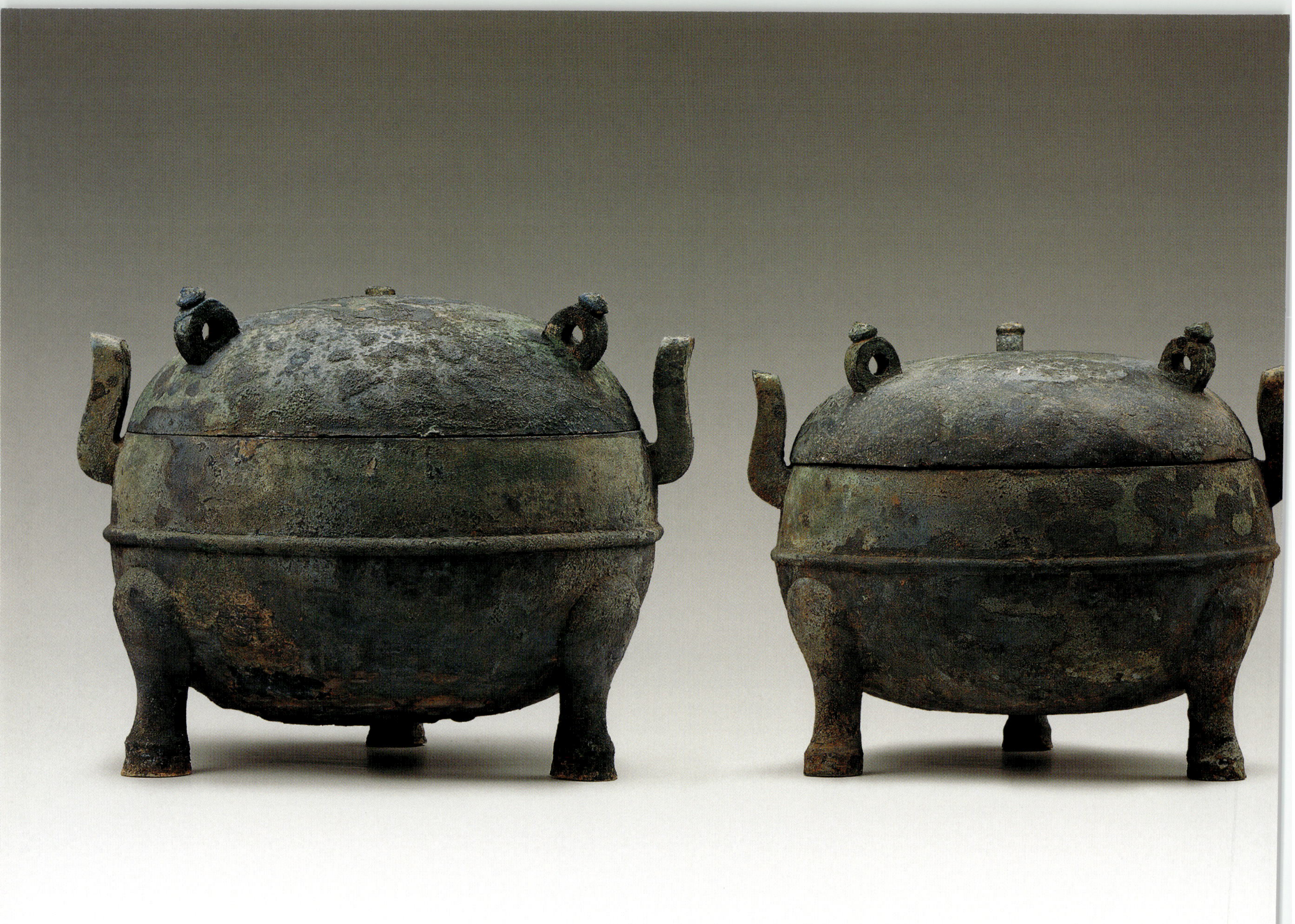

54

54

A set of seven bronze tripods

Second century BC, Western Han dynasty
Height (from left to right): 2 cm, 24 cm, 21 cm, 21.5 cm, 20 cm, 16.2 cm, 16 cm;
Diameter of belly: 31 cm, 27.4 cm, 23.6 cm, 20.3 cm, 19.8 cm, 19 cm, 17 cm
Excavated at the sacrificial tomb at Yangguishan in 2005
Xuzhou Museum, Jiangsu Province

The sacrificial pit at Yangguishan has yielded fourteen bronze tripods in total, seven of which are possibly from a set of decreasing size. All of the seven bronze *ding* were inscribed with their weight and capacity, but their forms are not exactly the same. Ritual bronze vessels unearthed from ancient tombs were often covered with exquisite decorations of geometric forms or zoomorphic motifs representing dragons, animals and birds, executed in incised lines or in high relief, but this set of *ding* is plain in design and has no particular decoration.

The *ding*, originally made for cooking and storing food, was used as an important ritual object from as early as the second millennium BC.[1] Possession of a *ding* was often associated with power and dominance over the land. The most famous examples were the set of nine *ding* said to have been cast in the legendary Xia dynasty (*c*.2070–1600 BC) when the king divided his territory into nine provinces. During the Zhou dynasty (1046–256 BC) the ritual use of a *ding* became fixed and the *ding* was established as a more important ritual bronze vessel than others. The Zhou conquerors justified their defeat of the Shang and reinforced their ruler's political power as following the 'Mandate of Heaven'. It was recorded in *Gongyangzhuan*

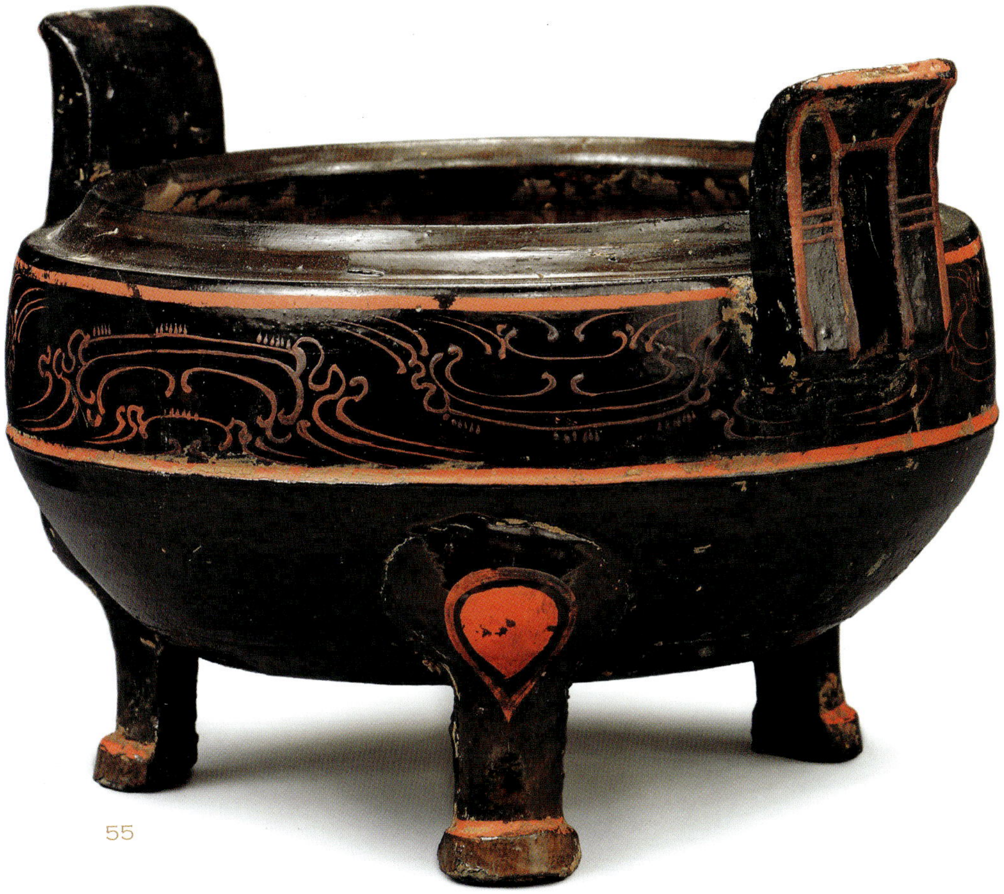

55

55

Lacquer-covered earthenware *ding*

Second century BC, Western Han dynasty
Height: 15.5 cm; Diameter: 20 cm
Excavated at tomb M5 at Bojishan in 1998
Xuzhou Museum, Jiangsu Province

This earthenware tripod is clearly a copy of an earlier bronze vessel. It has a spherical body with three legs and two rectangular handles. The original lid is missing or has perhaps completely decayed. The body is painted with black lacquer and decorated in red with a band of clouds just below the handles. Painted earthenware was common in early Western Han tombs. However, pieces decorated with lacquer are rather rare. Lacquer was a luxury material during this period and this laquer-covered earthenware tripod was probably made to imitate lacquerware for someone of lower social status. Tomb M5, a catacomb tomb, suffered serious looting. Although it is located near the tomb of the rebellious prince Liu Yi (M3) and is roughly contemporaneous, the nature of the relationship between the two tomb owners, if any, is unknown. JCSL

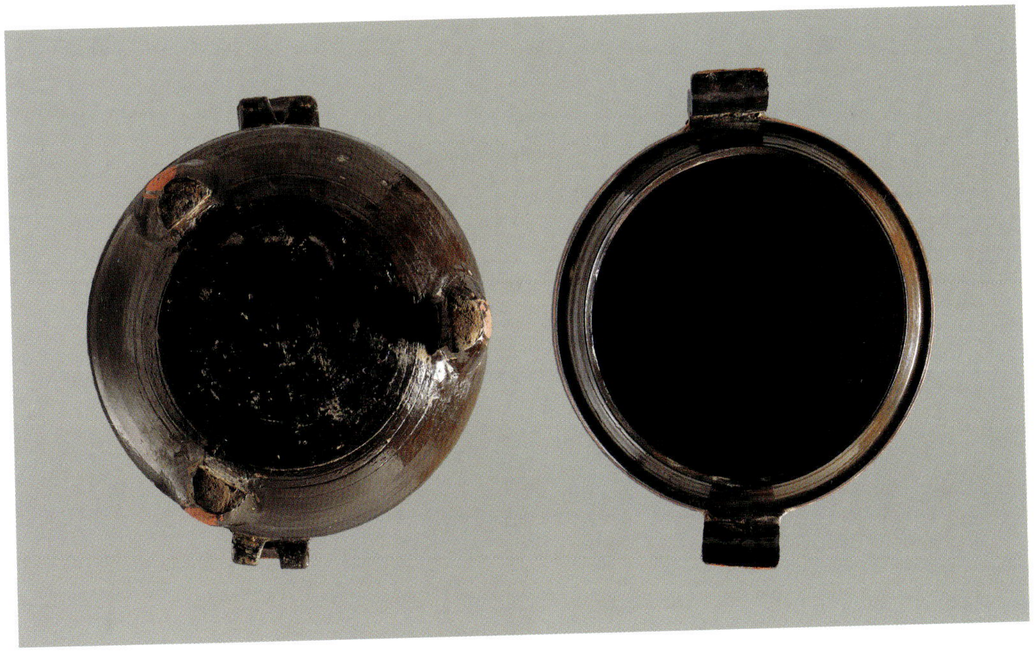

56

Celadon glaze jar

Second century BC, Western Han dynasty
Height: 24 cm; Width: 33 cm
Excavated at the Han tomb at Kuishan in 1972
Xuzhou Museum, Jiangsu Province

Ceramic vessels have been found much more frequently in association with Qin and Han dynasty tombs than in the burial sites of earlier periods. Vessels in Han dynasty tombs include domestic wares such as this celadon glaze jar. It has a bulging body, a close-fitting lid and two handles. The upper part of the jar is divided into three registers and the

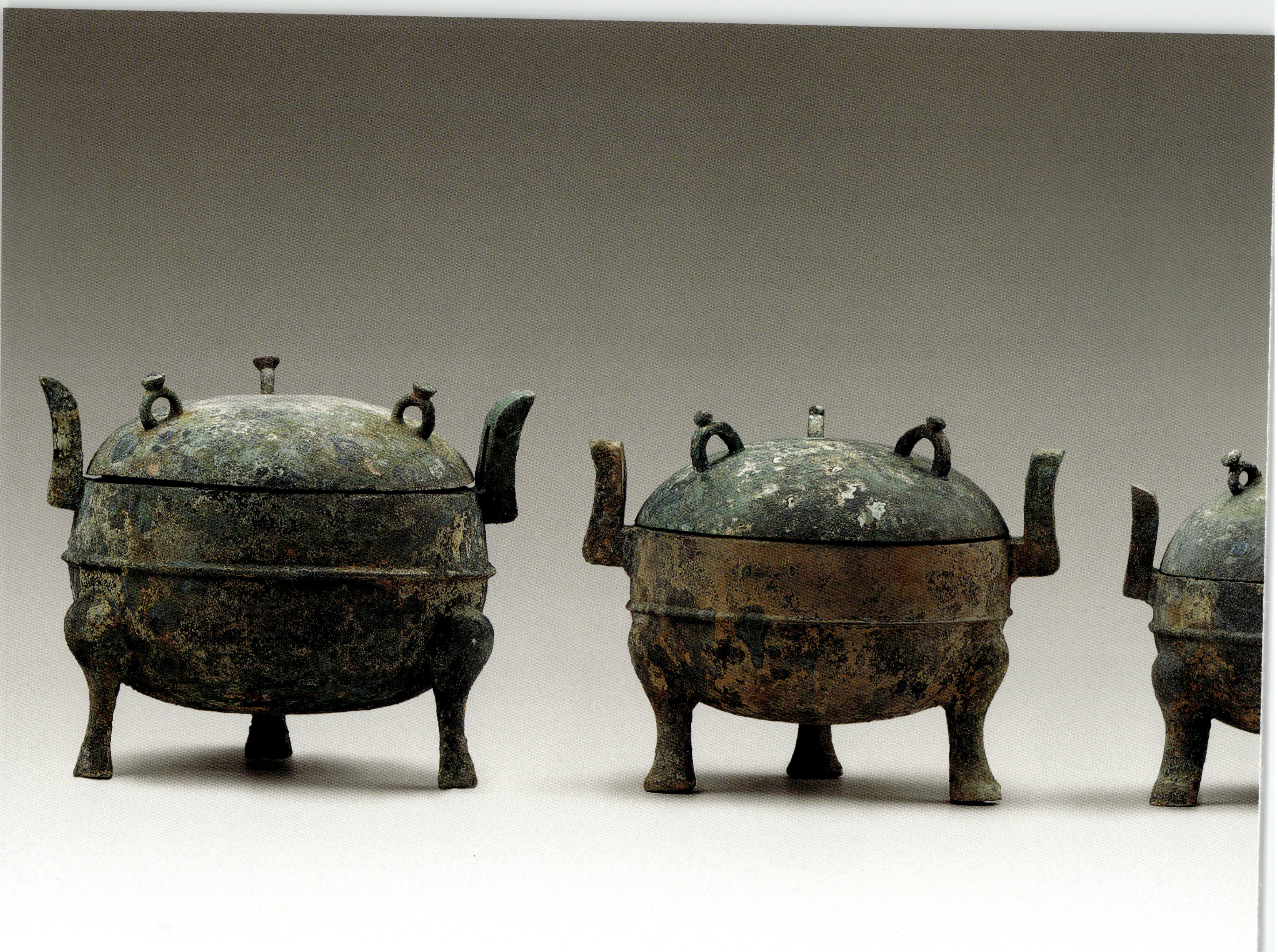

('Commentary by Gongyang') that the ruler, as 'Son of Heaven', can possess nine *ding*, kings of vassal states seven *ding*, noblemen five *ding* and senior officials three *ding*.[2]

The ruling class of the Han followed many traditions handed down from the Zhou dynasty and paid a great deal of attention to the burial of their dead. There continued to be a large repertoire of spectacular bronze objects placed in the tombs. But some of them were no longer made for strictly religious purposes, rather for secular use or as indicators of social status. JX

1 The first *ding* vessel was found in phase four at the site at Erlitou, Khotan (Hetain).

2 It was slightly different in the *Yili*, another ancient text on rituals; the ruler (including vassal kings) can use nine *ding*, noblemen seven *ding*, senior officials five *ding* and *shi* (a social stratum between senior officials and commoners) three or one *ding*.

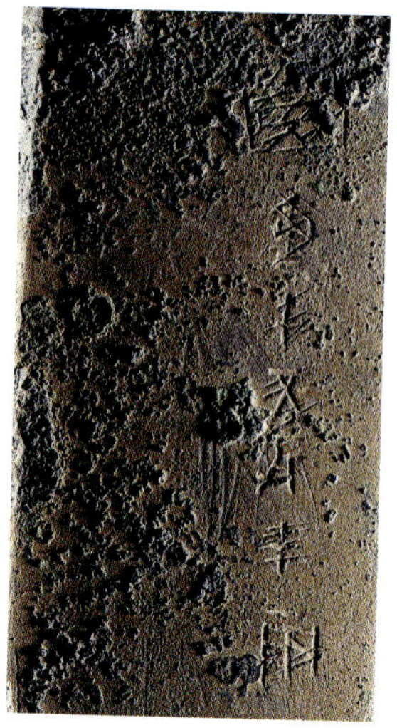

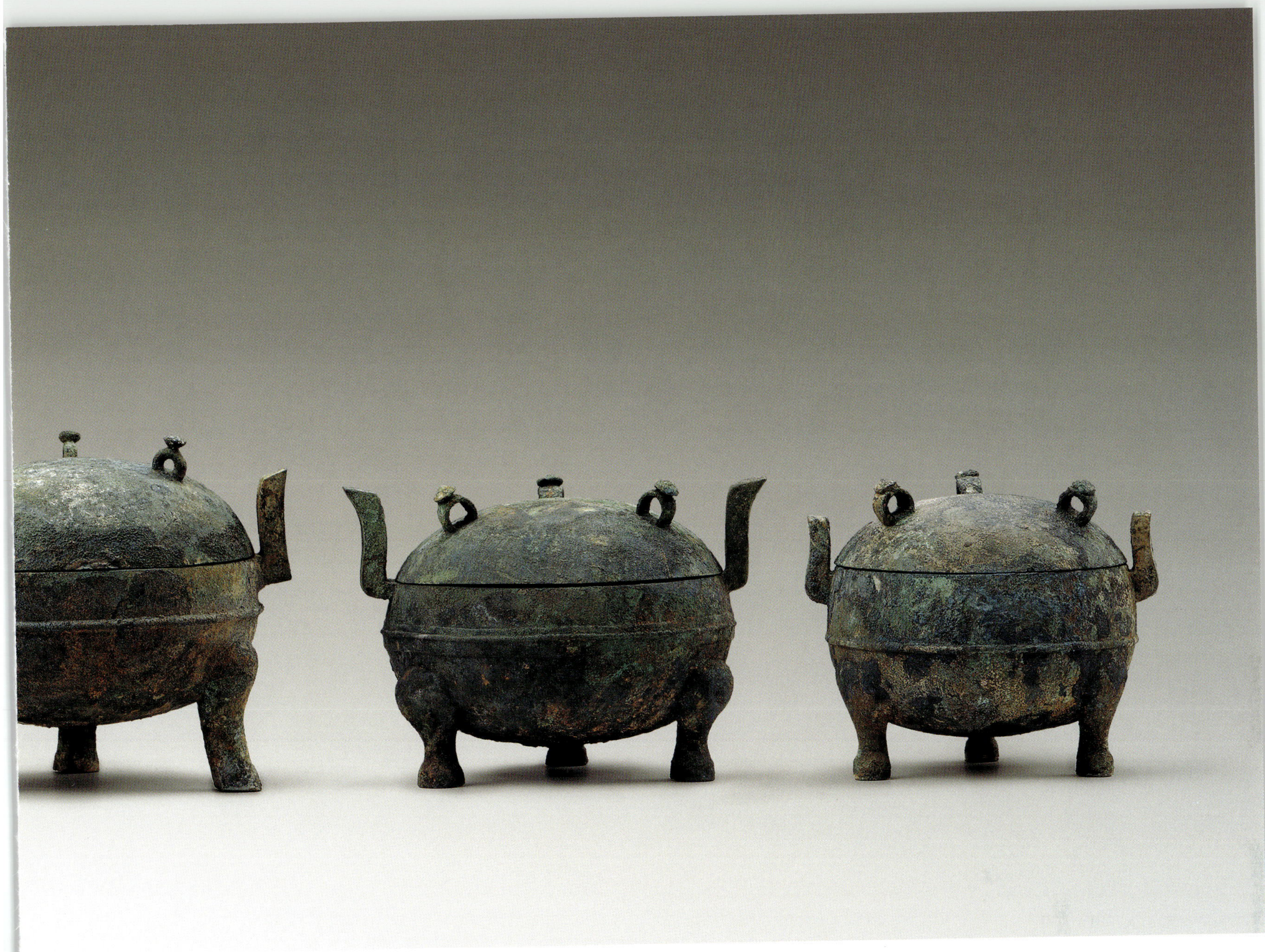

lower two parts are decorated with a repetitive wave pattern. The pattern is probably made by scraping with a comb-like tool before firing. Many ceramic vessels discovered in Han tombs imitate the shapes of earlier bronze vessels. The ear-like protrusions on the handles of this vessel have precedents in bronze vessels, which were decorated with stylized animal heads with deer-like antlers. However, the handles of this vessel no longer have any representational characteristics, and the outward-facing surfaces are adorned with C-shaped curls rather than the animal faces seen in bronze vessels. LKC

57

Jade eared cup

Second century BC, Western Han dynasty
Height: 3.8 cm; Diameter: 11.1–14.3 cm
Excavated at Shizishan in 1994–5
Xuzhou Museum, Jiangsu Province

This jade eared cup, semi-translucent pale green with brown areas, is carved from a single piece of jade. It was found in one of the intact chambers at Shizishan, together with a lidded jade beaker and two narrow-stemmed tubular jade cups. These four jade utensils were placed in a single line, suggesting they were the King of Chu's treasured drinking vessels. The eared cup and lidded beaker are two common forms, often reproduced as lacquer vessels.

Eared cups and a basin with a ladle were used as offerings to the tomb owner. Inscriptions on lacquer eared cups such as 'May you enjoy the food!' and 'May you enjoy the wine!' from Lady Dai's tomb at Mawangdui (fig. 41) reveal that these cups were for food and wine in the afterlife.[1]

The use of durable materials such as jade or stone for offering vessels may have been seen as pragmatic, as they

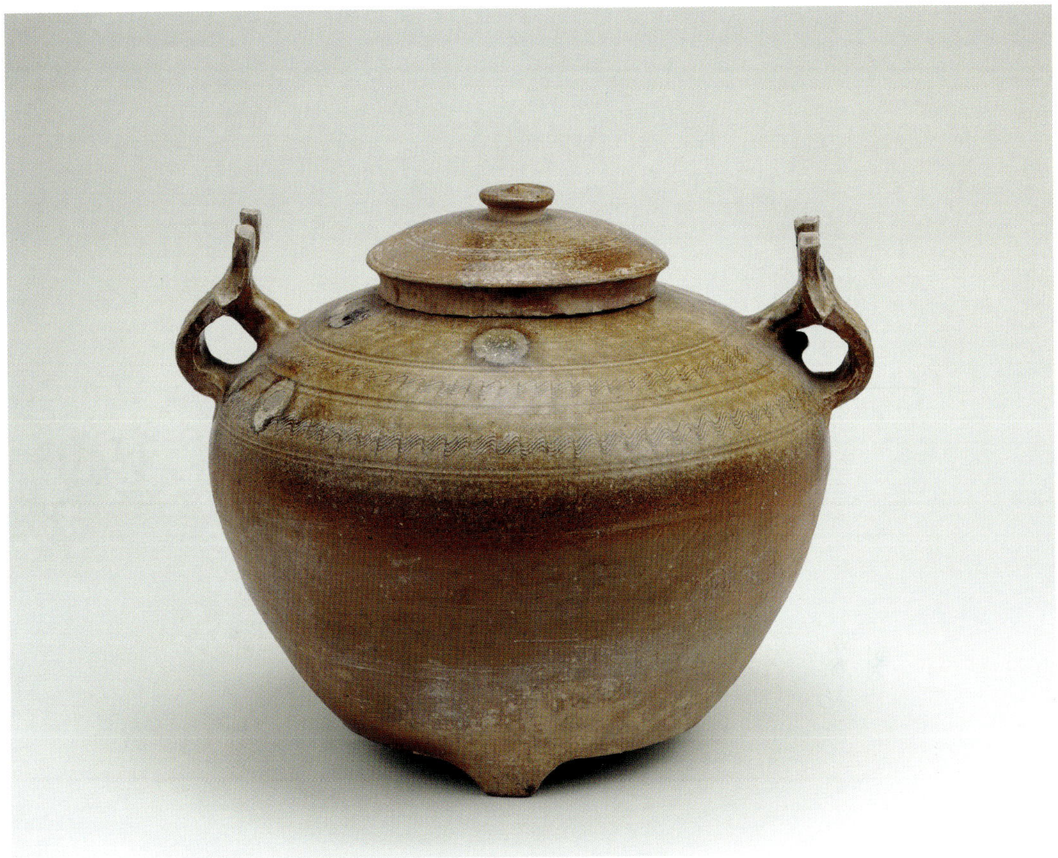

56

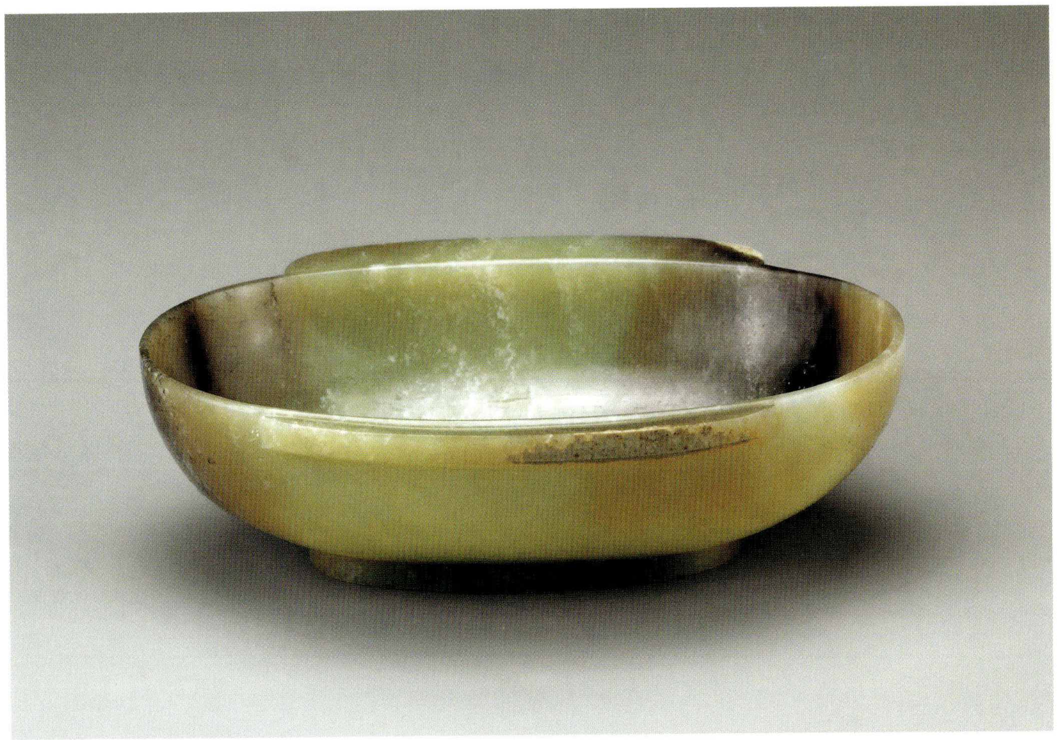

57

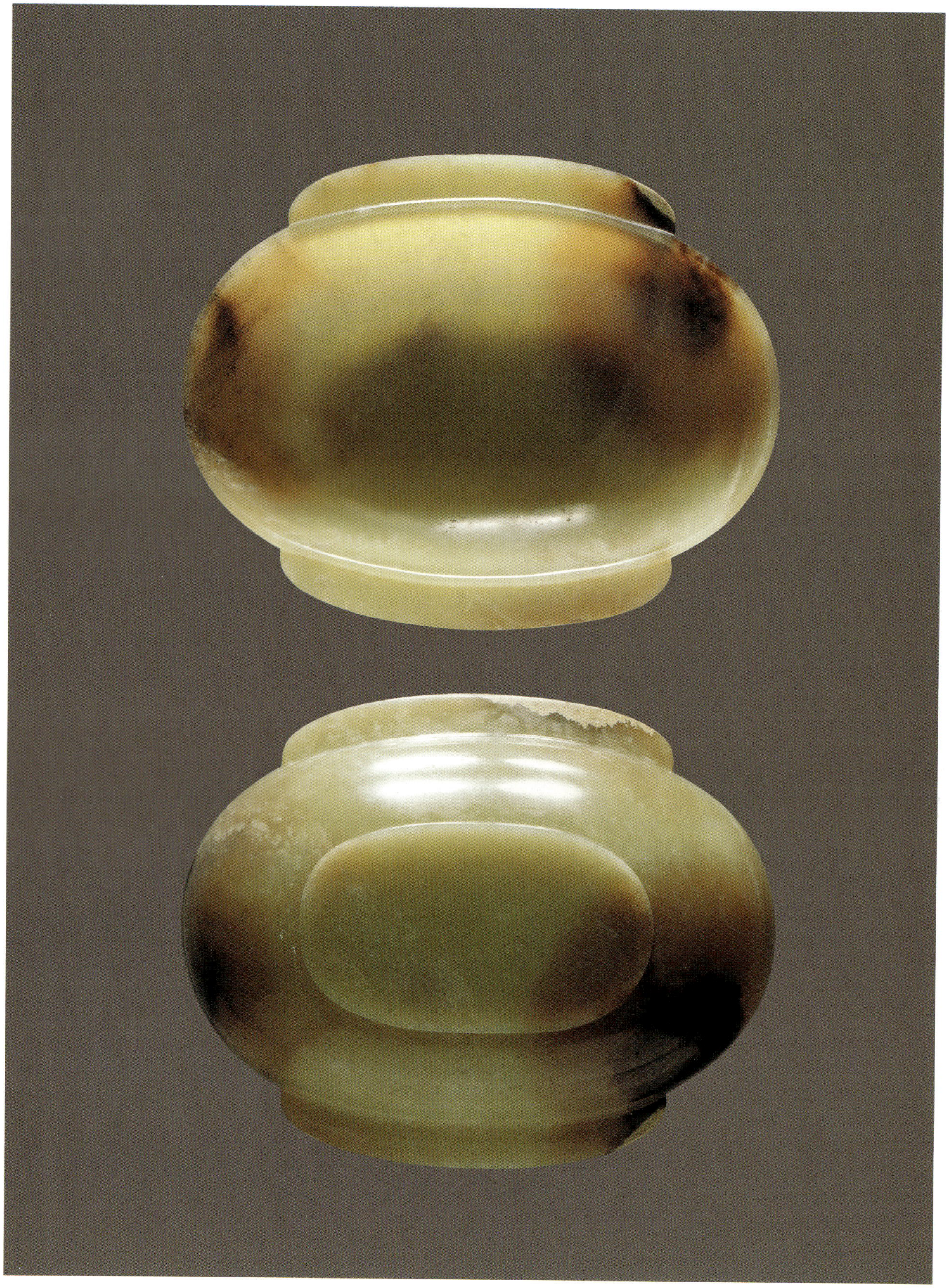

were likely to last for centuries. However, a comparison of the materials from differently ranking tombs reveals a hierarchical system. The most powerful members of the Liu family from Xuzhou used jade eared cups. Liu Sheng, king of the Zhongshan kingdom, used glass in place of jade. In the tomb of a high-ranking non-Liu family aristocrat at Mawangdui in the south, lacquer was the main material, while in the tombs of lower-ranking officials a small quantity of earthenware vessels or images carved on stones was supplied. A similar jade eared cup, also Han, is found in the collection of the National Palace Museum, Taipei.[2]
JCSL

1 Beijing 1973, p. 83.
2 It is 8.8 cm in length; Beijing 2010, vol. 2, pl. 133.

58

Jade cup (*zhi*)

Second century BC, Western Han dynasty
Height: 11.8 cm; Diameter: 6.7 cm
Excavated at Shizishan in 1994–5
Xuzhou Museum, Jiangsu Province

This jade cup was carved from a semi-translucent yellowish-green jade. It has a cylindrical body, three animal-mask feet and a five-petal flower lid. The majority of such drinking vessels were made of earthenware or lacquer; few were made of bronze or jade. Some examples have a ringed handle, such as the one from the tomb of the King of Nanyue (cat. 181). To date, two similar examples have been found in the tomb at Chaohu, An'hui Province.

This drinking vessel is referred to as a *zhi* in both the *Shiji* and the *Hanshu*. Both texts refer to an event when Liu Bang, founder of the Han dynasty, raised a jade cup, or *yu zhi*, and drank a toast to the long life of his father, referred to as the Grand Emperor after Liu Bang's

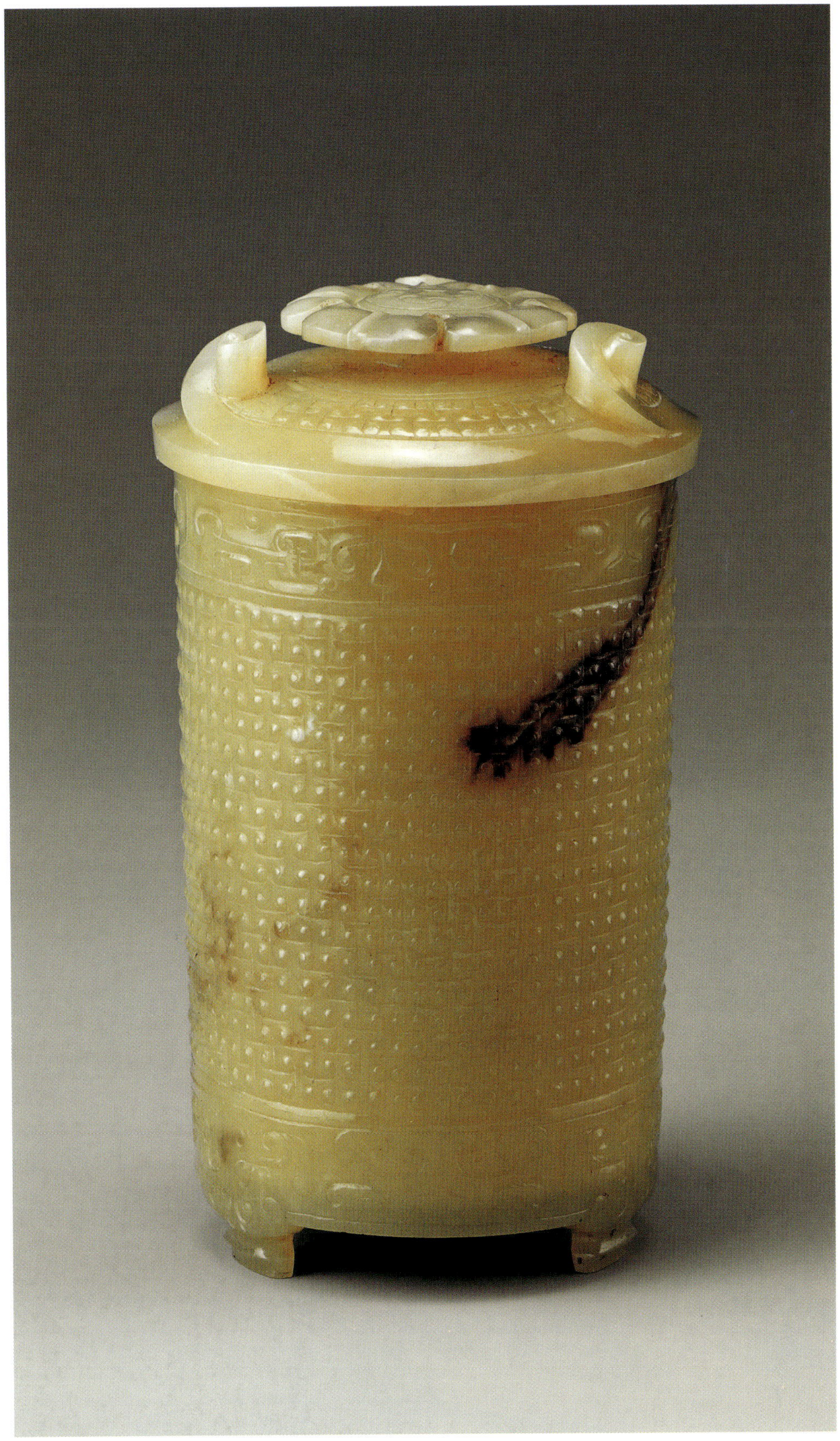

58

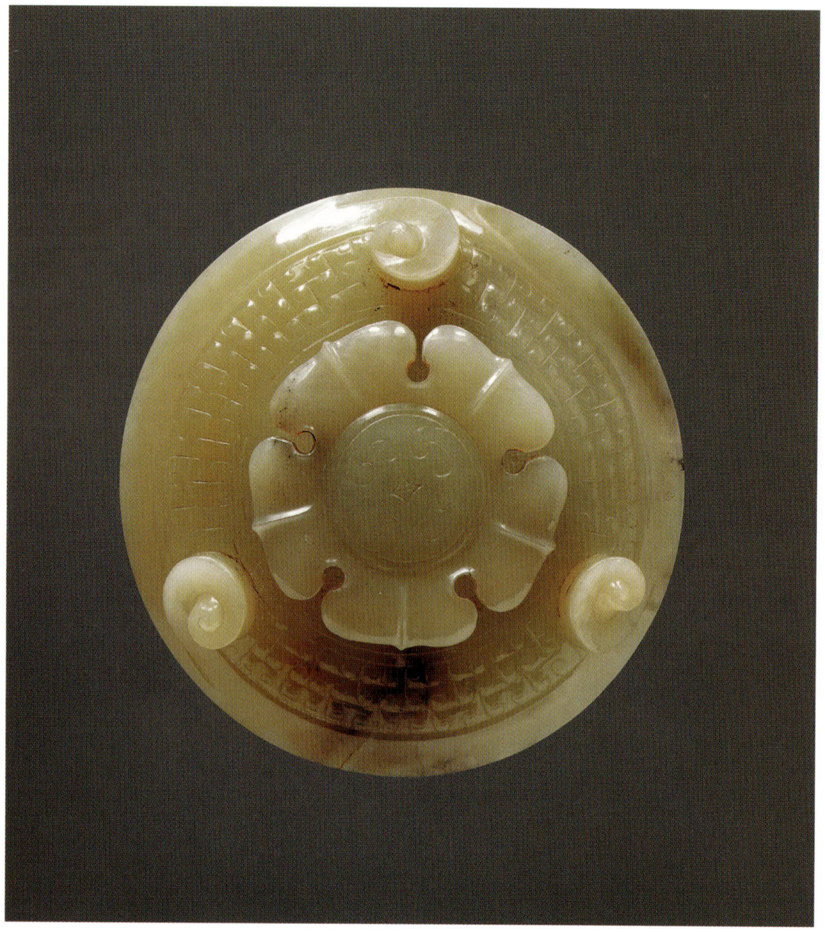

59

Two glass cups

Second century BC, Western Han dynasty
Height: 8.2 cm, 9.4 cm; Diameter 8.3 cm, 8.5 cm
Excavated at Beidongshan in 1986
Xuzhou Museum, Jiangsu Province

Archaeologists unearthed sixteen broken glass cups, one glass animal and fragments of three pieces of blue glass at Beidongshan in 1986. Only these two cups have been completely restored. The light green cylindrical cups are made in traditional Chinese shapes normally found in lacquer or ivory, or sometimes jade. The cups have no decoration, but the traces of three bands from the rim to the end show that they may have been mounted with gold, similar to the design of the lacquer cup excavated from the King of Nanyue's tomb.[1] The different heights and thicknesses of these cups indicate they were probably made from more than one mould.

accession.[1] That cup is believed to be similar in design to this one. Jade itself represents durability and longevity and may have been regarded as possessing special powers – that of conferring long life or immortality – when used for drinking and eating. A similar vessel, with a different pattern and lid, is in the collection of the Palace Museum in Beijing.[2] JCSL

1 *Shiji*, p. 386; Hanshu, p. 66.
2 It is 12.3 cm in height; Beijing 2010, vol. 2, pl. 129

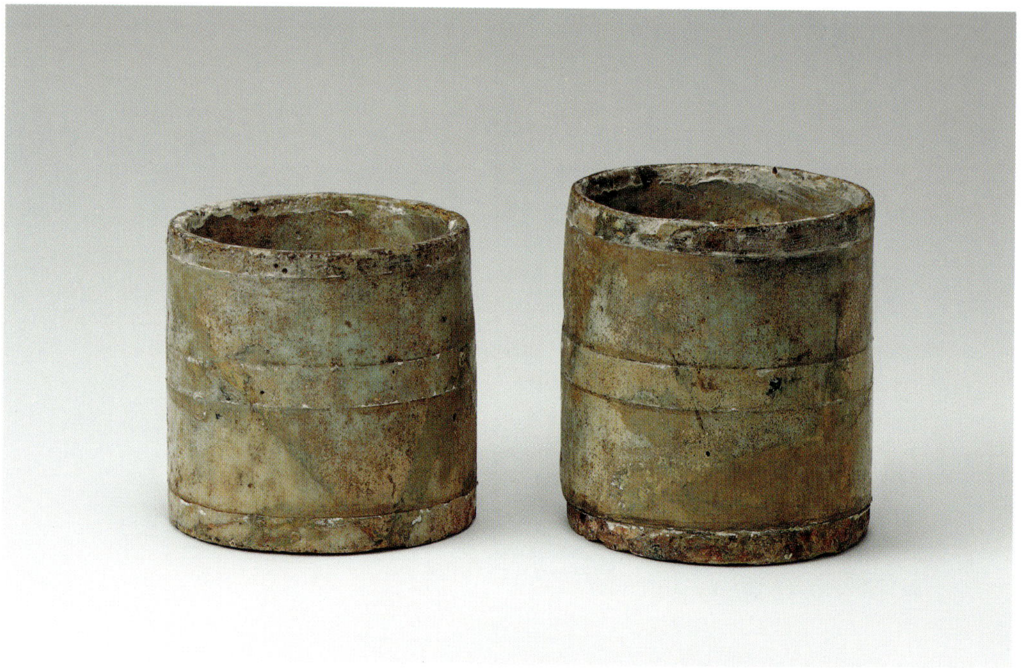

59

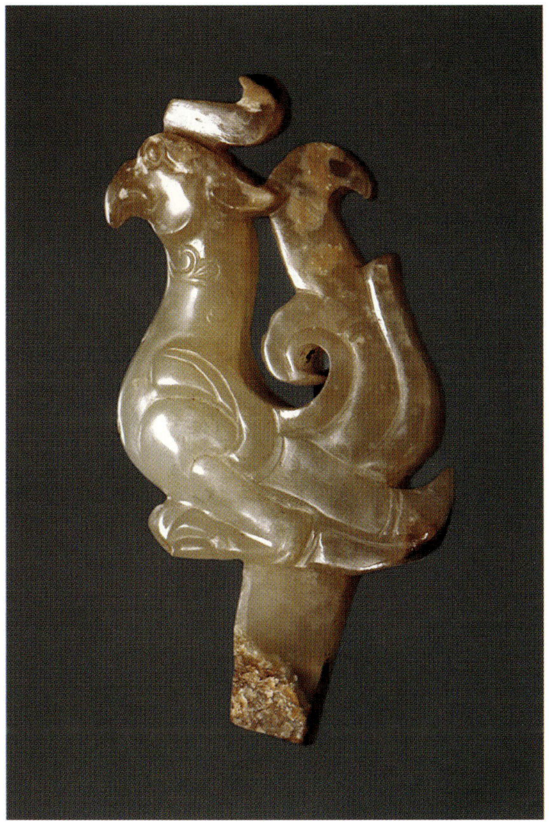

60

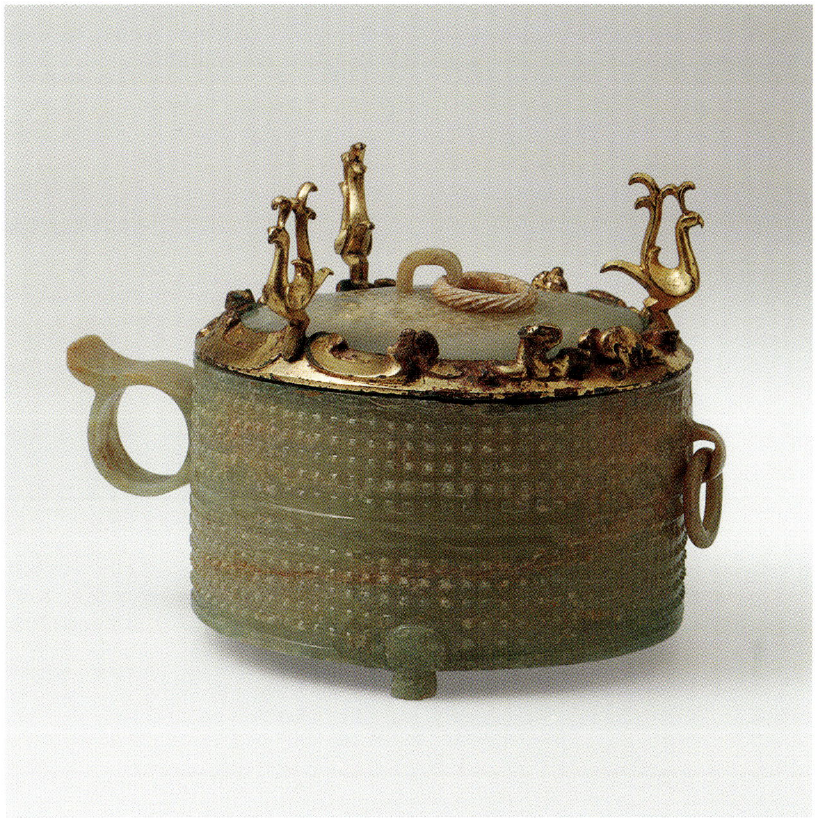

Fig. 54

The glass cups from Beidongshan are considered to have been produced before 128 BC and are the earliest examples of Chinese domestic glass vessels. The glass-eared cups and plates discovered in the tomb of the King of Zhongshan in Hebei were made slightly later, about 113 BC.[2]

Distinguishable from the soda-lime-silica glasses of Western Asia and Mesopotamia, Chinese glass objects during the Han dynasty had a high lead and barium content, which was exclusive to China.[3] Barium was used as a flux to lower the melting point or stabilize the glass and make it less soluble in water. It could also have been added to make the glass opaque to give it a jade-like appearance. Many early Chinese glass objects found in burial contexts were made in the forms of a *bi* disc (a burial suit plaque), sword accessories and vessels, and they are commonly in colours of opaque green, light green and milky white. No doubt they were deliberately made as cheaper alternatives in imitation of jade for lower-ranking aristocrats and officials. JX

1 A lacquer cup mounted with gold bands was found in the western chamber; Beijing 1991, pl. 135.
2 Beijing, 1980.
3 An 1984. 4, pp. 413–48 has a detailed discussion of early Chinese glassware.

54 A *lian* with bronze-bird decoration of similar design in the Arthur M. Sackler Collection, New York. Western Han period.

60

Jade finial in the form of a phoenix

Second century BC, Western Han dynasty
Length: 4.4 cm; Width: 2.4 cm
Excavated at Shizishan in 1994–5
Xuzhou Museum, Jiangsu Province

A piece of light green jade with brown areas is carved as a seated phoenix with a long tail curled back to touch its head. Traces of copper were found in the hole of the tag, which suggests it was a finial. The design of this jade bird is very similar to bronze birds affixed to the lid of a wine container, or *lian*, in the Arthur M. Sackler Collection (fig. 54). This jade phoenix likely had a similar function. JCSL

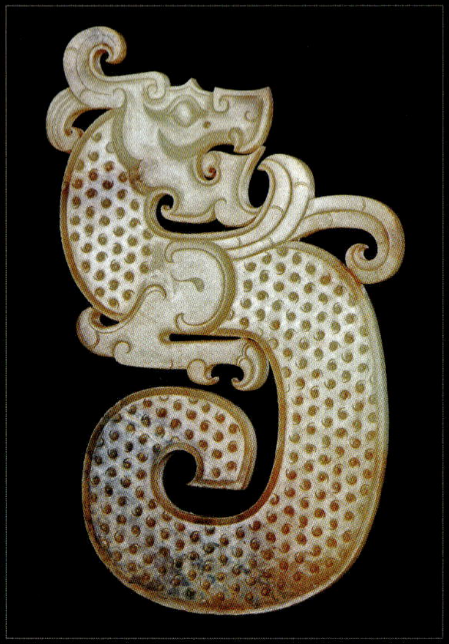
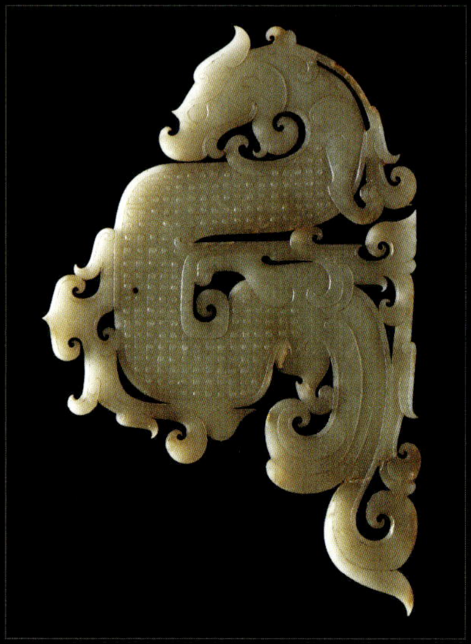
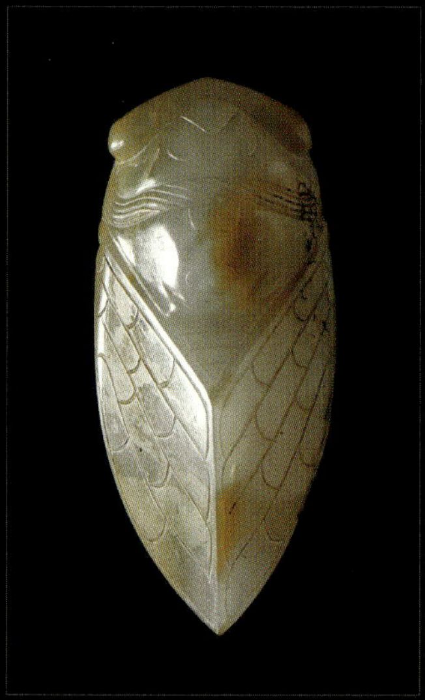
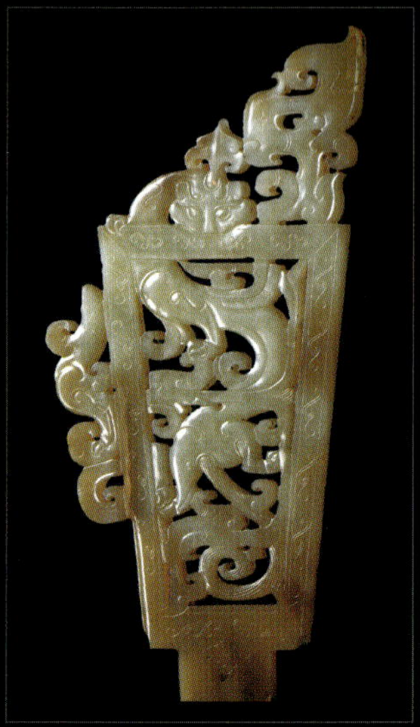

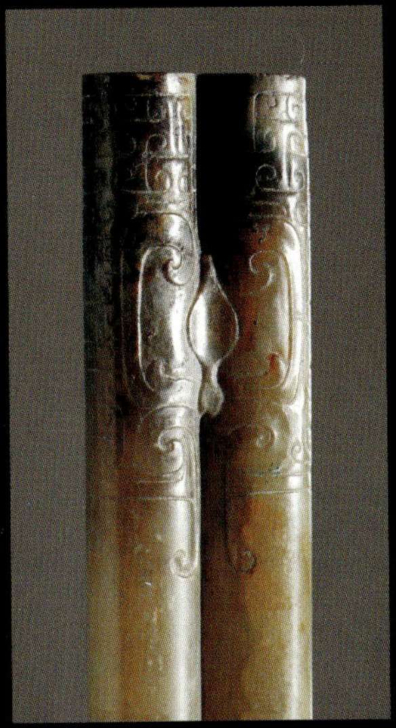
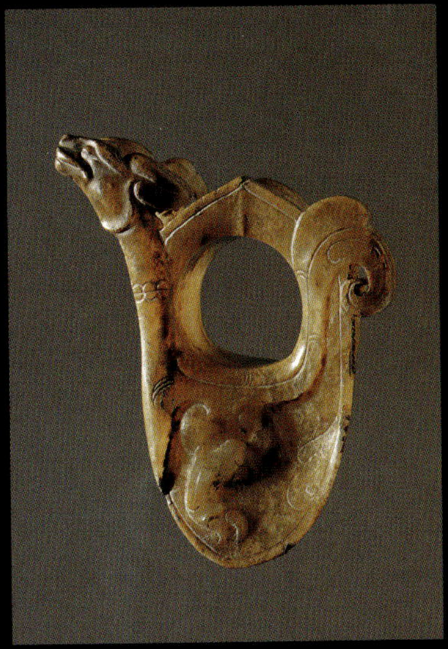
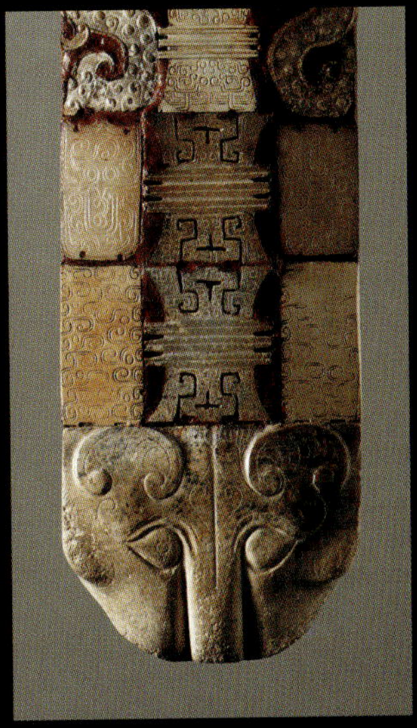
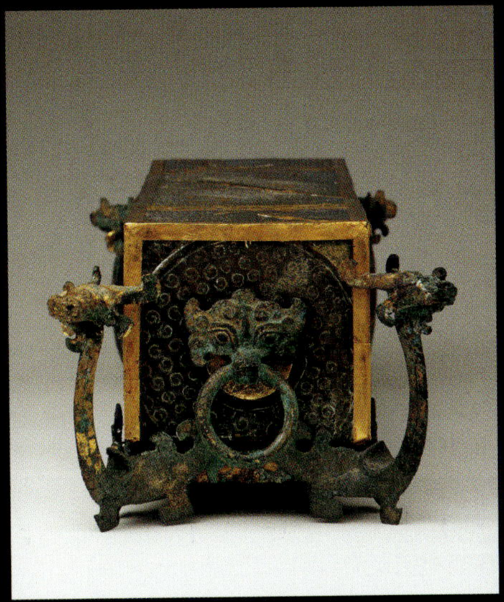

LUXURY BURIAL OBJECTS

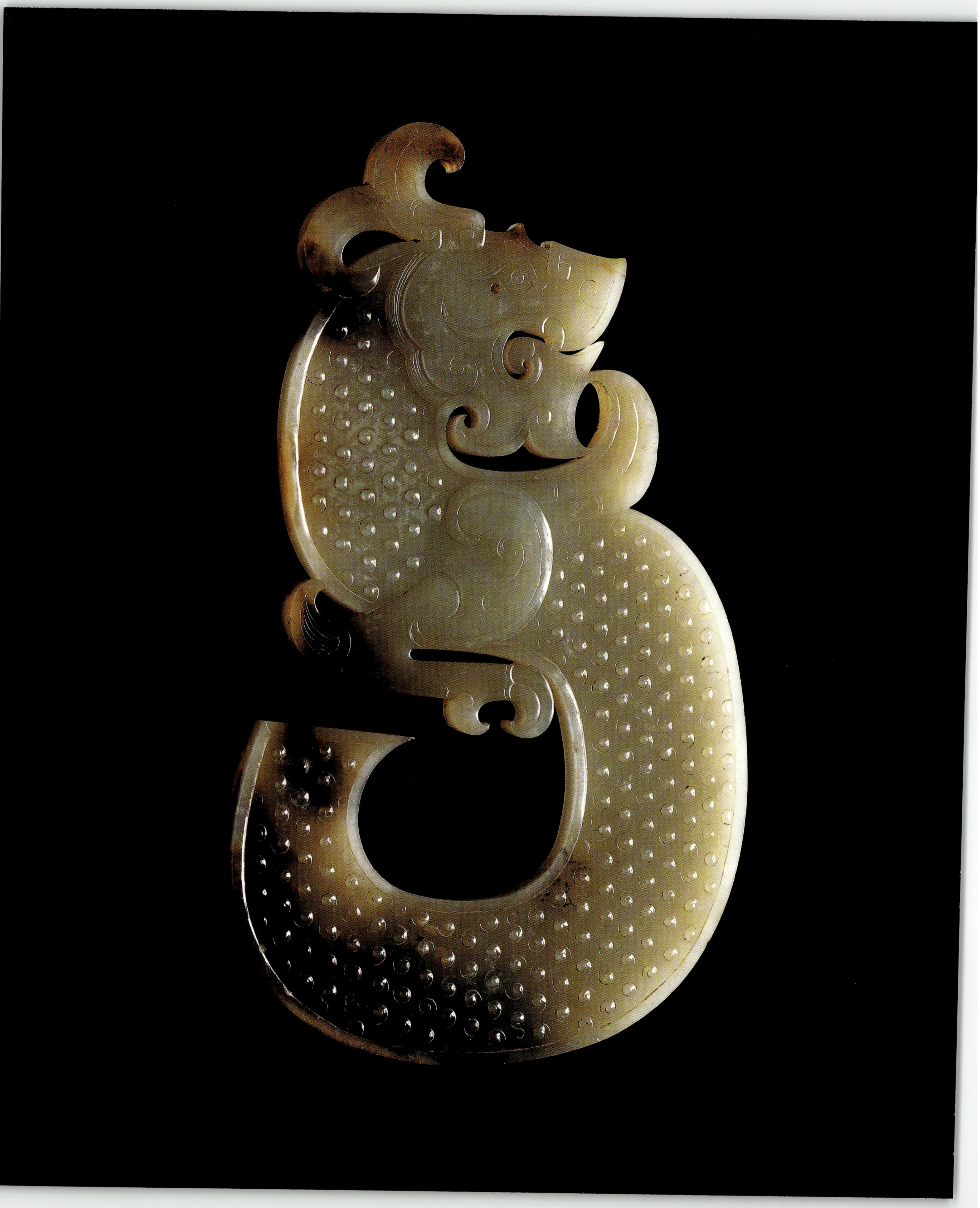

61

Jade pendant in the form of a dragon

Second century BC, Western Han dynasty
Length: 17.5 cm; Width: 10.2 cm
Excavated at Shizishan in 1994–5
Xuzhou Museum, Jiangsu Province
NOT EXHIBITED

Made from semi-translucent jade, this S-shaped dragon pendant is clearly influenced by similar designs from the early Warring States period (476–221 BC). It has exaggerated horns and a beard below the jaw. A perforation below the eye suggests it was used as a pendant. A sharp claw emerges from the upper part of the body and a curved fin emerges from its chest. The curled tail ends in an abrupt manner. The whole body of the dragon is decorated with raised spirals. A similar piece, probably from the Warring States period, was found inside the tomb of the King of Nanyue (cat. 168). JCSL

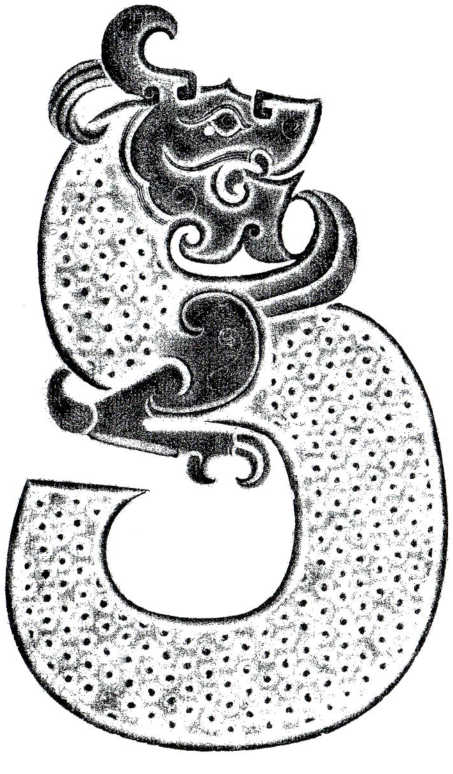

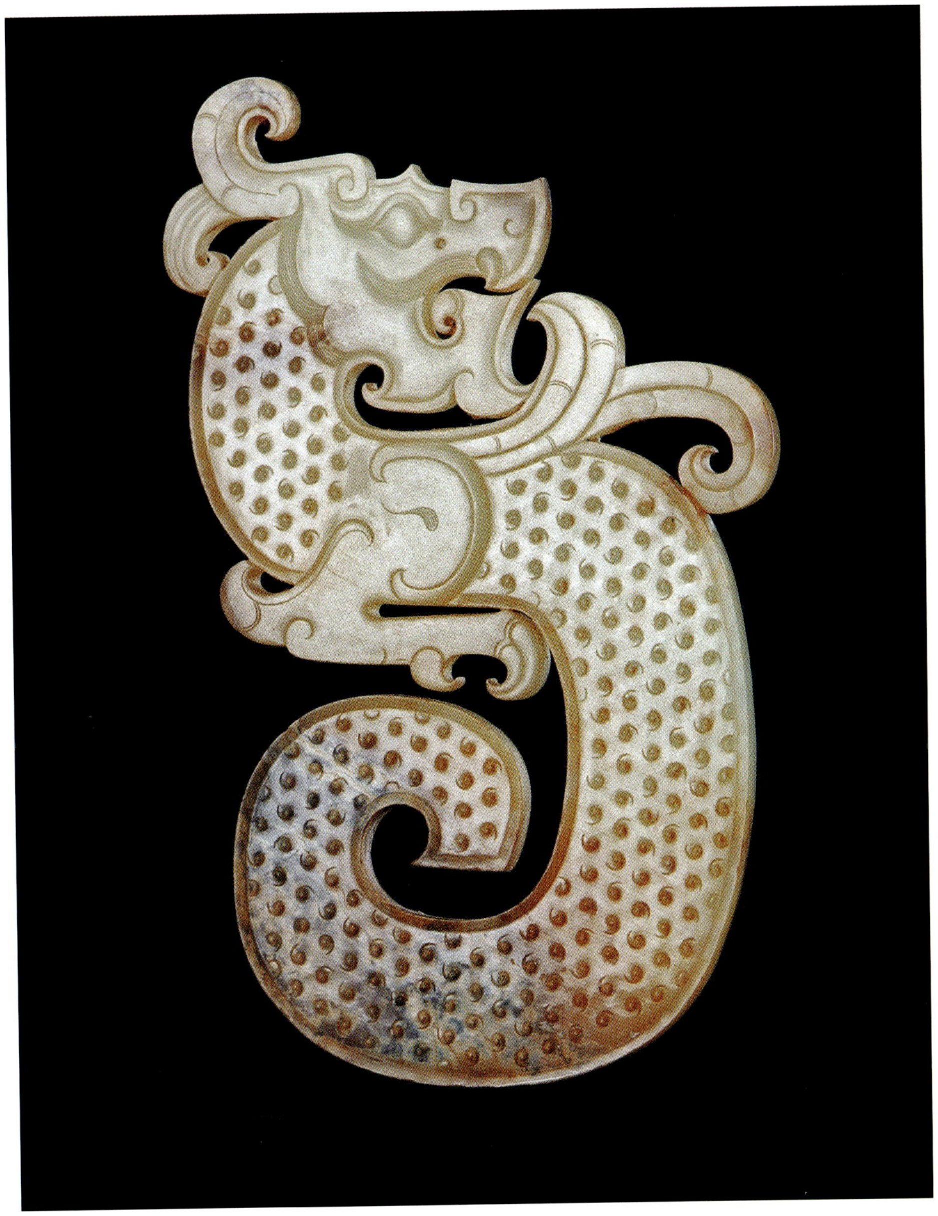

62

62

Jade pendant in the form of a dragon

Second century BC, Western Han dynasty
Length: 17.5 cm; Width: 10 cm
Excavated at Shizishan in 1994–5
Xuzhou Museum, Jiangsu Province

This jade ornament was excavated at Shizishan. The pale and semi-opaque quality suggests that the material came from Khotan (modern Xinjiang). The pendant is designed in the shape of a dragon and its body is arranged in an S-shape. The artisan vividly delineated the dragon's facial features in profile, with a large eye and a prominent snout; moreover, its leg and claw were also carefully treated with fine incised lines. In contrast, the dragon's body is simplified and abstract with a pattern of spiral curls in neat array. The simplicity

FACING PAGE: 61

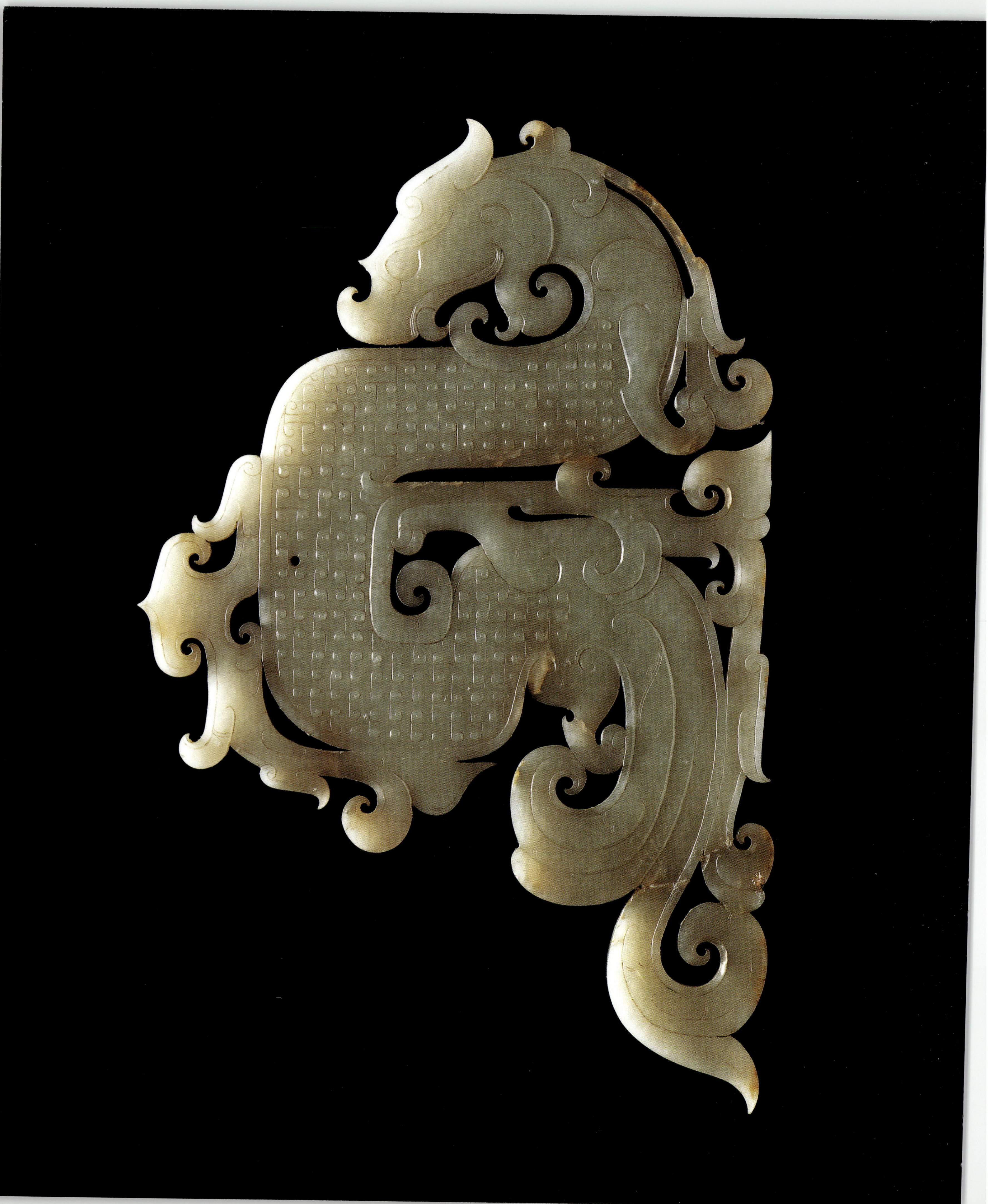

and smooth outline of the dragon's body serve as a foil to the vivid depiction of its facial features and limbs, lending it strength, vigour and an illusion of movement.

Carving jade in the form of dragons has a long history in China. Arranging the dragon in an S-shape developed from the late Spring and Autumn period (eighth–fifth centuries BC) and was popular in the Warring States period (fifth–third centuries BC). This Western Han jade is strongly reminiscent of the style of the earlier period. LKC

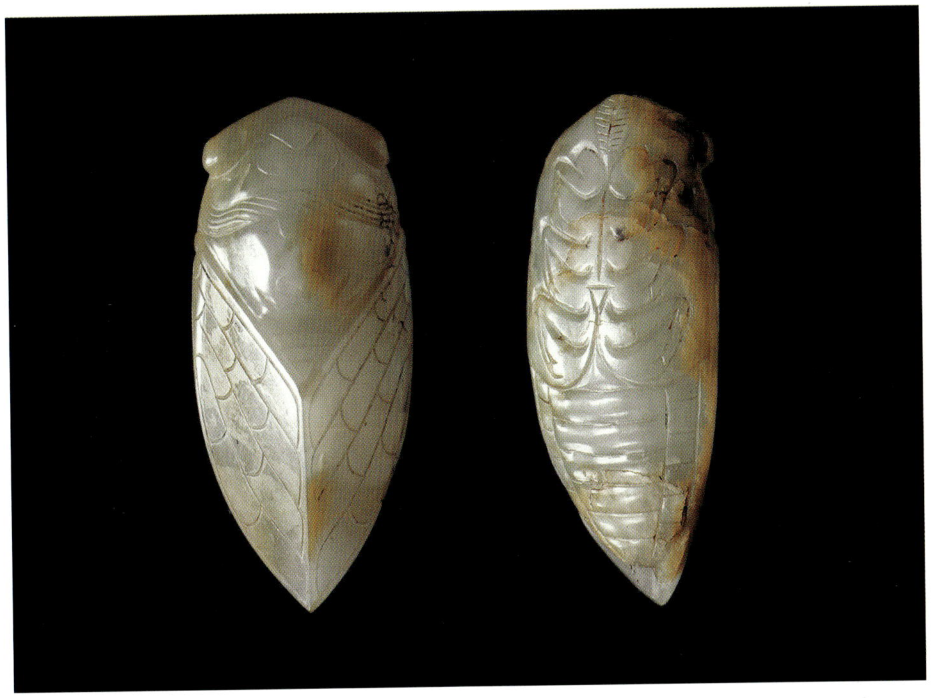

64

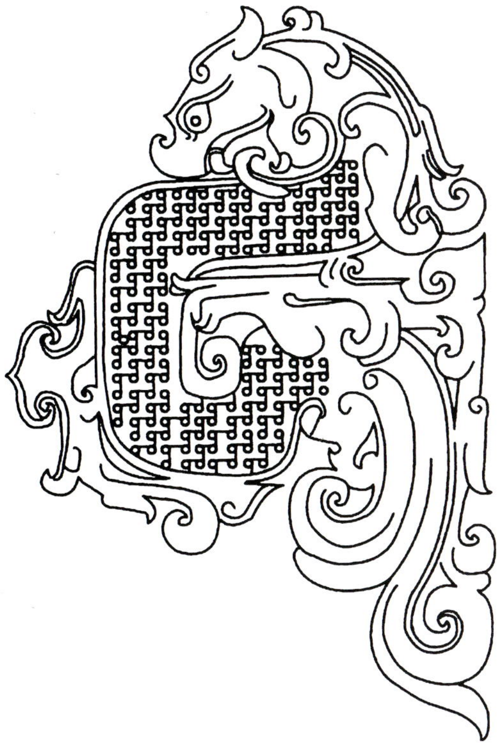

63

Jade pendant in the form of a dragon

Second century BC, Western Han dynasty
Length: 18 cm; Width: 11.9 cm
Excavated at Shizishan in 1994–5
Xuzhou Museum, Jiangsu Province

This jade pendant was excavated at Shizishan, and the material also came from Khotan. The creature has a dragon's head and body arranged in an S-shape and a phoenix tail ending in a flourish of feathers. The perpendicular lines of the dragon's body contrast with the smooth curves of its tail, producing a visual effect that combines both vigour and elegance. The combination of a dragon's body with a phoenix tail is rare in the Western Han. The piece shows fine craftsmanship as the artisan has delineated clouds around the body to convey the impression of flight.

The drilled hole in the middle of the dragon's body was used as the point of attachment for a string. LKC

64

Jade cicada

Second century BC, Western Han dynasty
Length: 4.5 cm; Width: 2.1 cm
Excavated at Shizishan in 1994–5
Xuzhou Museum, Jiangsu Province

This jade cicada is carved from white jade from Khotan with realistic details including prominent eyes, a raised tail and lifelike wings. A perforation was drilled from the head through to the tail, suggesting it was used as a pendant. Other cicada-shaped jades were used as mouth amulets (cat. 91).

Jade cicadas can be traced back as early as the Neolithic period and were commonly seen in Shang tombs. This insect was even more prevalent during the Han period. The life cycle of the cicada is a metaphor for rebirth, making it a popular subject for burial objects. However, cicadas with carving as detailed as this one are very rare from the Han dynasty. JCSL

FACING PAGE: 63

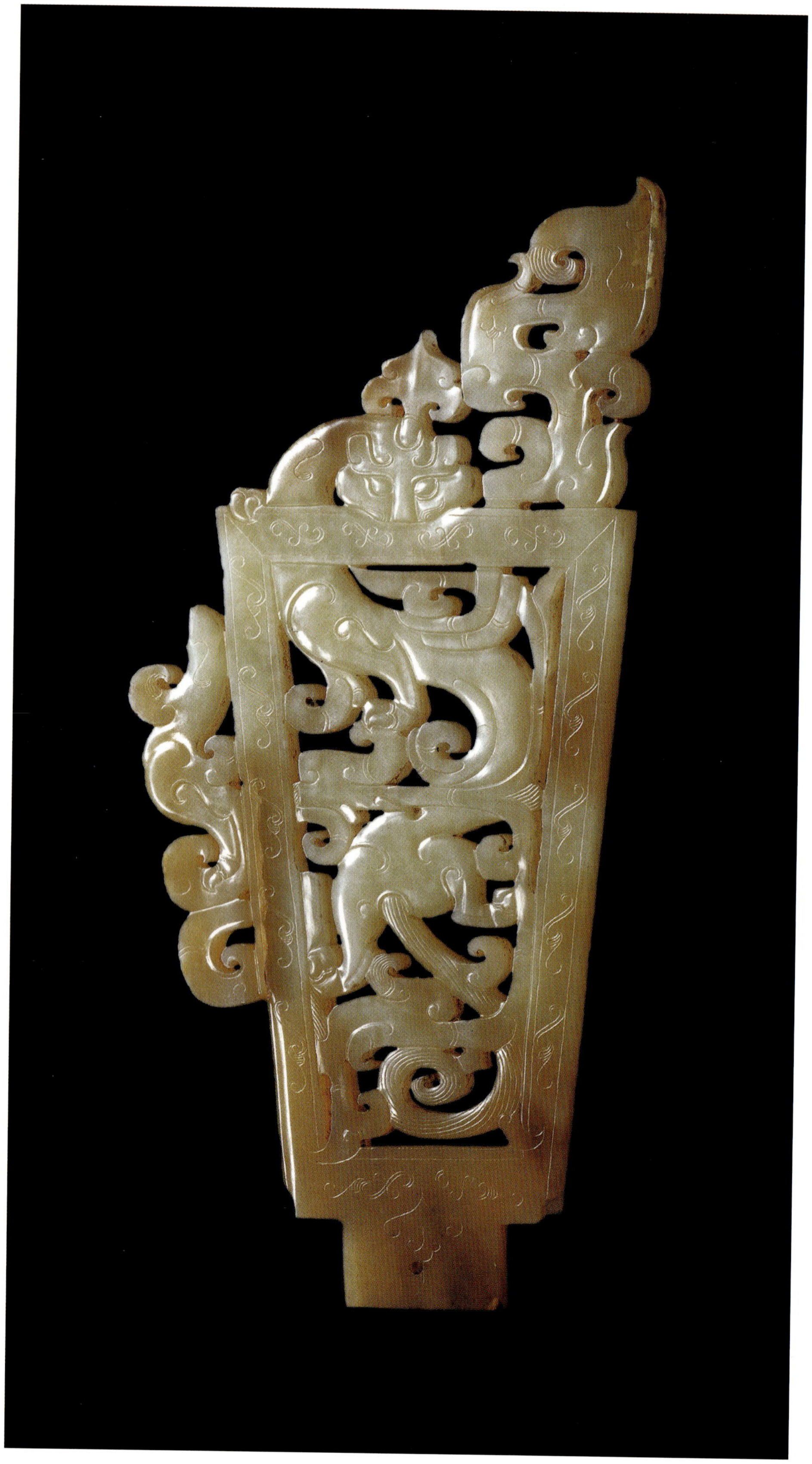

65

65

Jade ornament

Second century BC, Western Han dynasty
Length: 21.5 cm; Width: 4.2–7.2 cm
Excavated at Shizishan in 1994–5
Xuzhou Museum, Jiangsu Province

This unusual jade ornament has a hole on the tag, which suggests it was an attachment or finial for a larger object. It is a trapezoid shape carved in openwork style with an exaggerated design. A feline dragon is climbing upwards with its long curling tail extending outside the trapezoid. Its original function is still being debated. One scholar, Lu Zhaoyin, suggests it was attached to a pole that was used for ritual dancing after sacrificial ceremonies, whereas another scholar, Sun Ji, suggests it was a sword pommel similar to the tomb image found in Xuzhou (fig. 55). JCSL

1 Beijing 2005, p. 43, fig. 4–3.

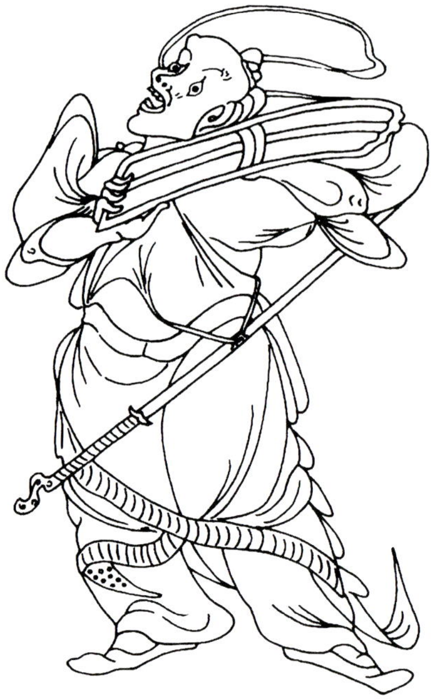

55 Another example of an unusual jade sword pommel in the form of a warrior on the painted tombstone from Bo county, Anhui Province, Eastern Han period (25–220 AD)[1].

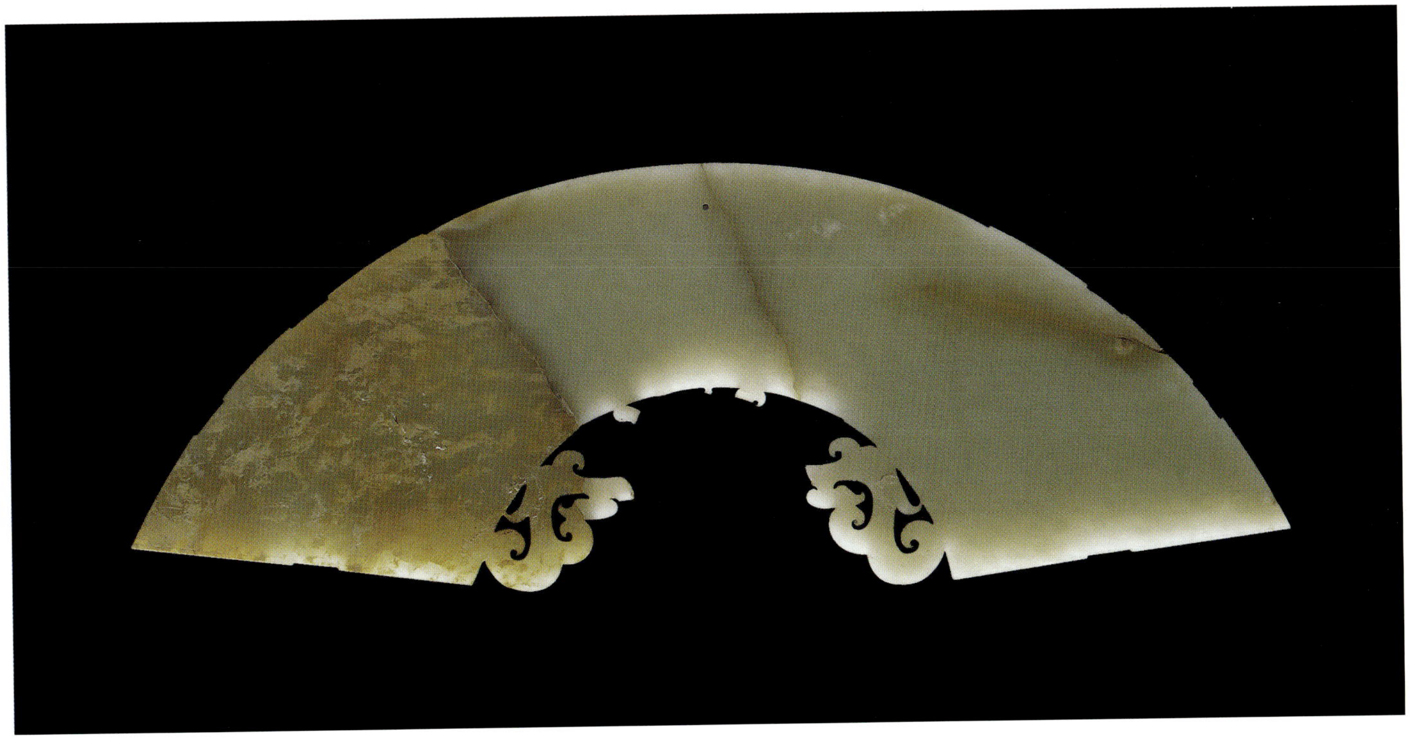

66

66

Jade arc pendant

Second century BC, Western Han dynasty
Length: 34.3 cm; Width: 11 cm
Excavated at Shizishan in 1994–5
Xuzhou Museum, Jiangsu Province
NOT EXHIBITED

This is the largest *huang* arc pendant that has been found to date. At the time of excavation, it was found broken into three pieces in a tomb passage.
The pendant was carved from a superior-quality piece of Khotan jade. It has grooved edges, but otherwise a plain surface. At the base of the arc openwork carvings, very likely of dragons or phoenixes, survived the damage.
A perforation in the middle of this pendant was intended for its suspension.

The inclusion in the tomb of an undecorated jade pendant is unusual, particularly in comparison with other fine and complex pieces found in the same tomb. It is possible that it was buried in the tomb unfinished due to the sudden death of the King of Chu. JCSL

67

Jade arc pendant with dragon and phoenix patterns

Second century BC, Western Han dynasty
Length: 21.1 cm; Width: 4.2 cm
Excavated at Shizishan in 1994–5
Xuzhou Museum, Jiangsu Province
NOT EXHIBITED

This jade arc pendant is the finest one to be found in Shizishan. It was found in the tomb passage, possibly dropped by a tomb looter. It was carved from a piece of white jade from Khotan. Both sides have the same pattern, a symmetrical design dominated by an animal face in the middle and dragons mixed with phoenixes on both sides. It was carved in low relief with grooved edges and decorated with a total of twenty dragons, four phoenixes and two animal faces. JCSL

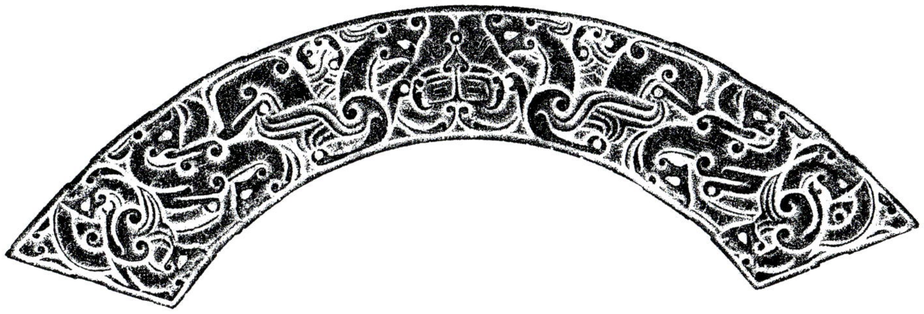

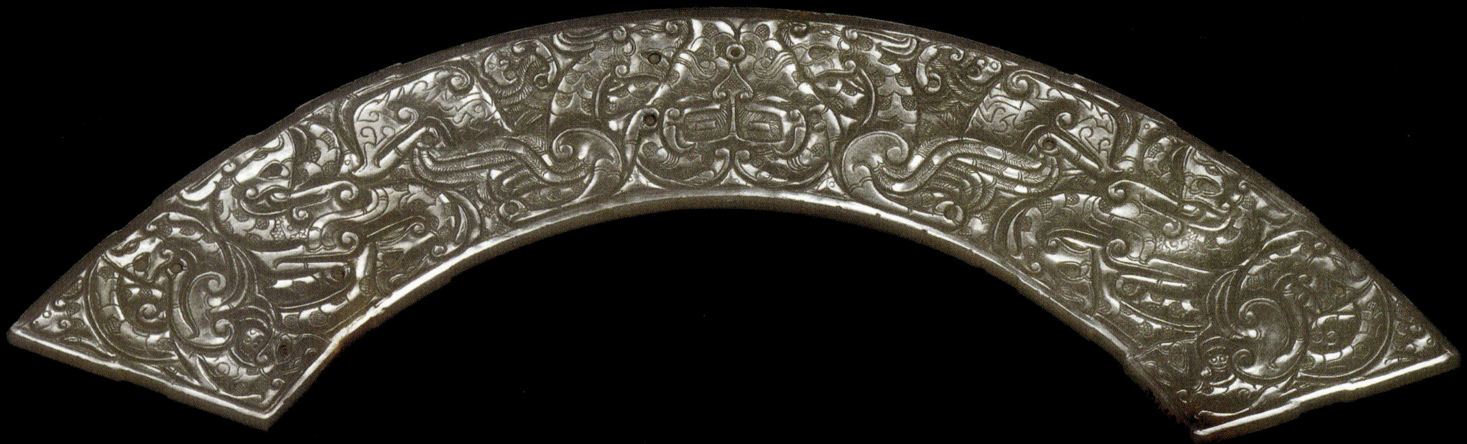

67

68

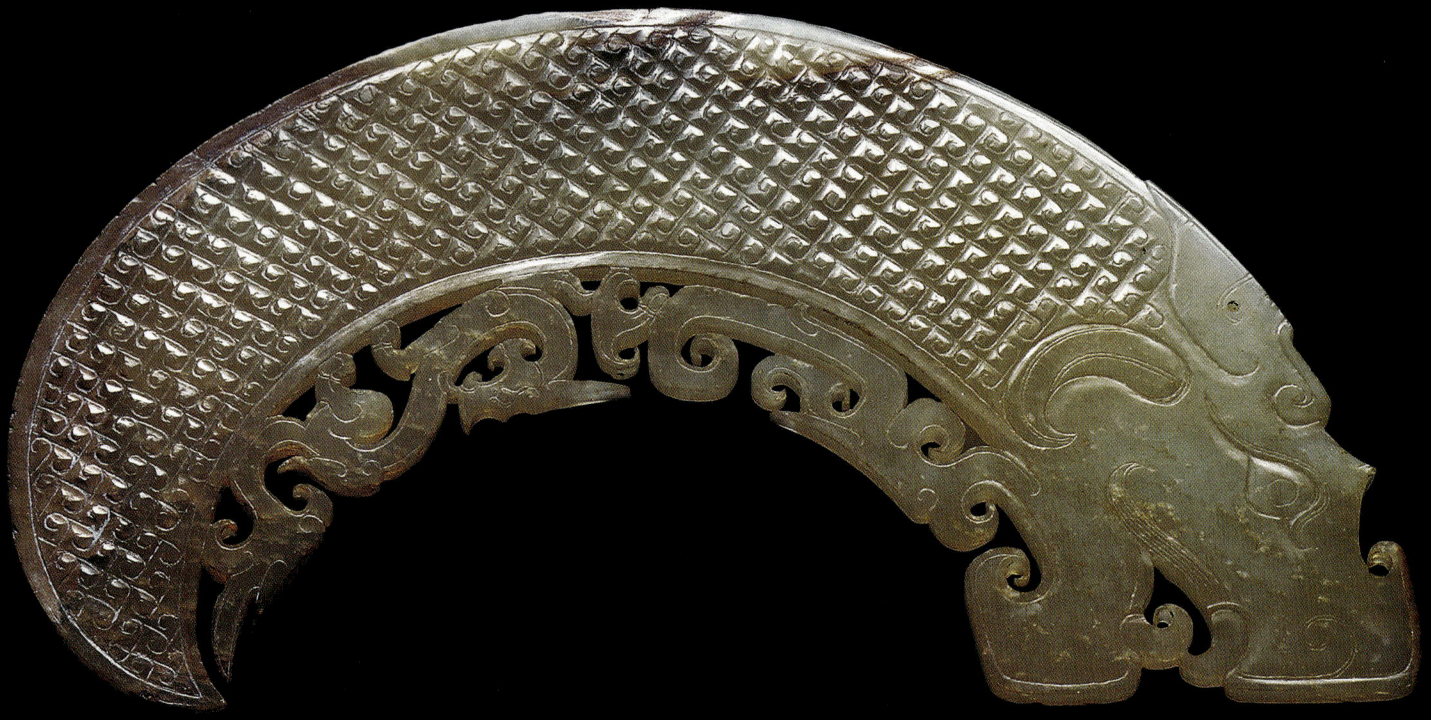

68

Jade pendant

Second century BC, Western Han dynasty
Length: 14.3 cm; Width: 4.5 cm
Excavated at Shizishan in 1994–5
Xuzhou Museum, Jiangsu Province

This light green jade pendant was carved from a piece of Khotan jade in the shape of an arched dragon, ending in a pointed tip. The additional figure under the arc was carved in openwork style, and represents a smaller dragon looking in the opposite direction. The main surface of the pendant is decorated with a fine interlinked scroll pattern. This design was very rare during the Han period. A small hole near the head of the dragon suggests it was used as a pendant. Having been buried in the tomb for more than two thousand years, there is some calcification around the tip of the pendant. JCSL

69

Arc-shaped pendants

Second century BC, Western Han dynasty
Length: 19.7 cm, 25.7 cm, 23.7 cm;
Width: 4.8 cm, 5.2 cm, 7.3 cm
Excavated at Shizishan in 1994–5
Xuzhou Museum, Jiangsu Province

The use of arc-shaped pendants originated in the Neolithic period and became popular in the Shang dynasty (seventeenth–eleventh century BC). During the Western Zhou (eleventh–eighth century BC) they became part of a set of jade ornaments worn by aristocrats. During this period, most of the arc-shaped pendants had a hole at each end of the arc for strings to be tied so that they could be worn around the neck. They were usually worn horizontally with the arc facing upward, but a few examples show that they could also be

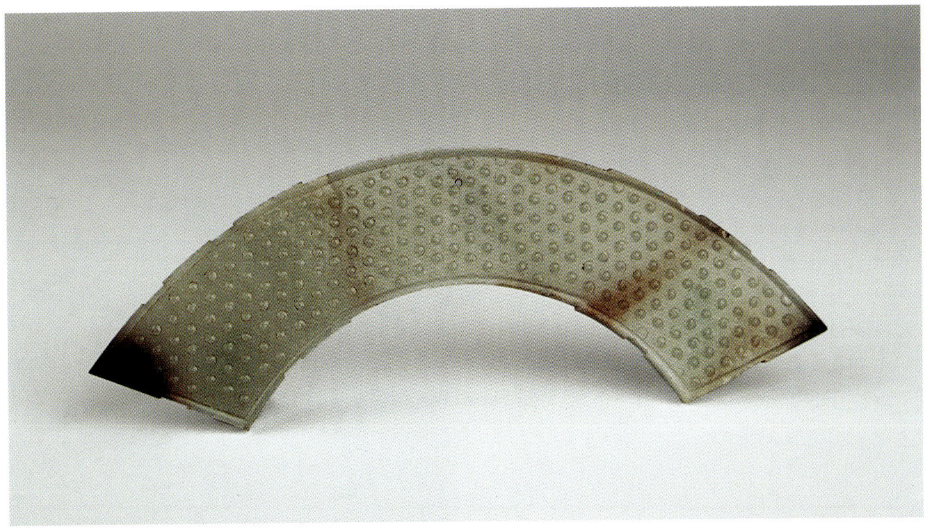

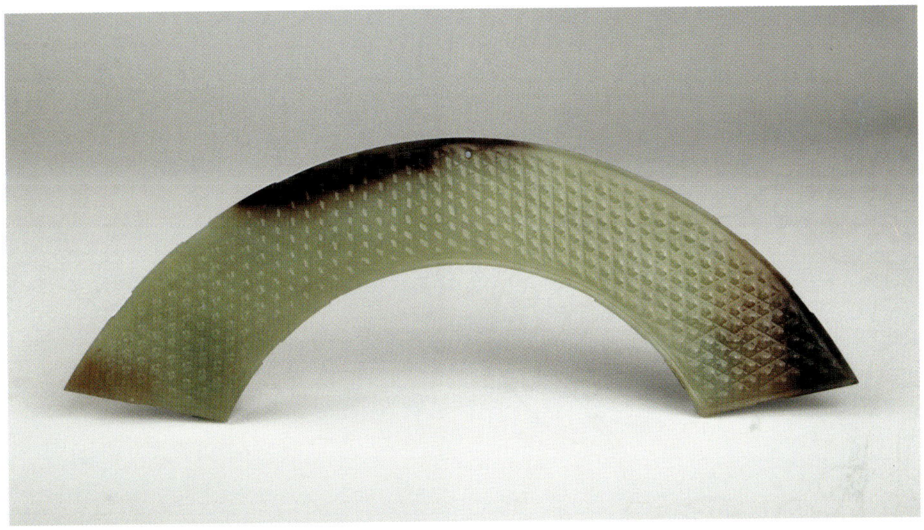

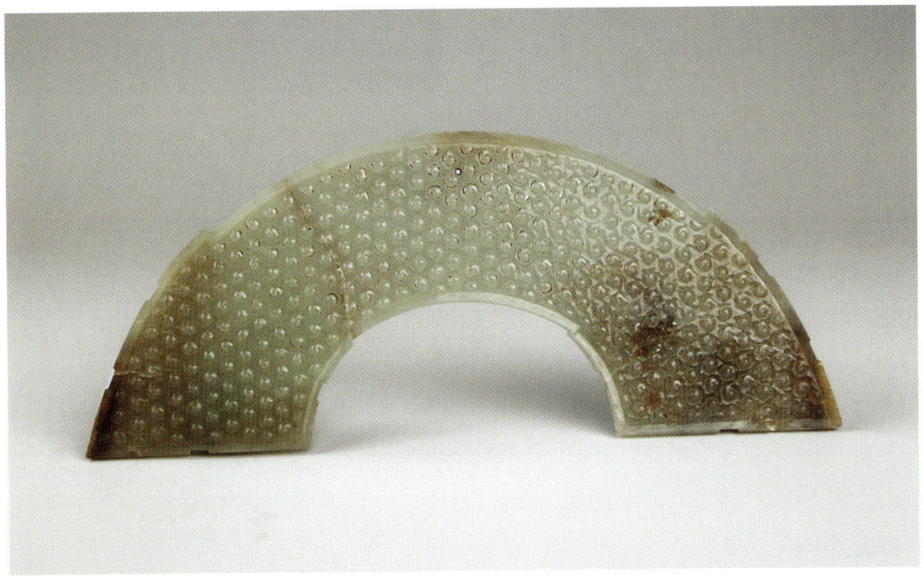

69

worn vertically. After the Spring and Autumn period (eighth–fifth century BC) the style of wearing arc-shaped pendants changed: pendants were tied through the hole at the upper centre and worn with the arc facing downwards. In some cases, the holes at either side of the arc were maintained and used to suspend further jade ornaments.

The three arc-shaped pendants in this exhibition all have the hole at the upper centre. The outer border of the pendants has a stepped edge rather than being completely smooth. Judging from the pale colour of the material, the jade most likely originated from Khotan.

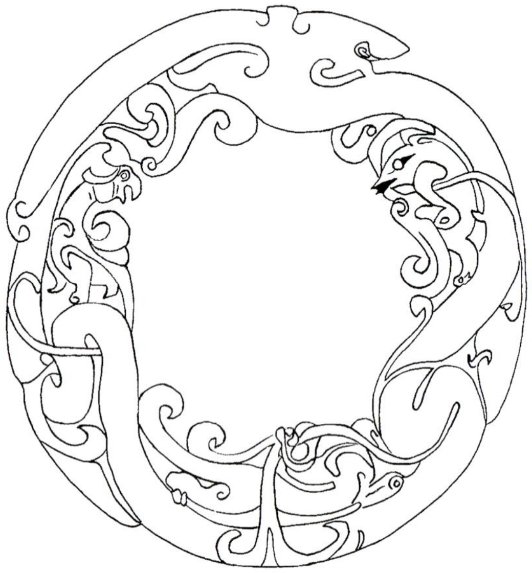

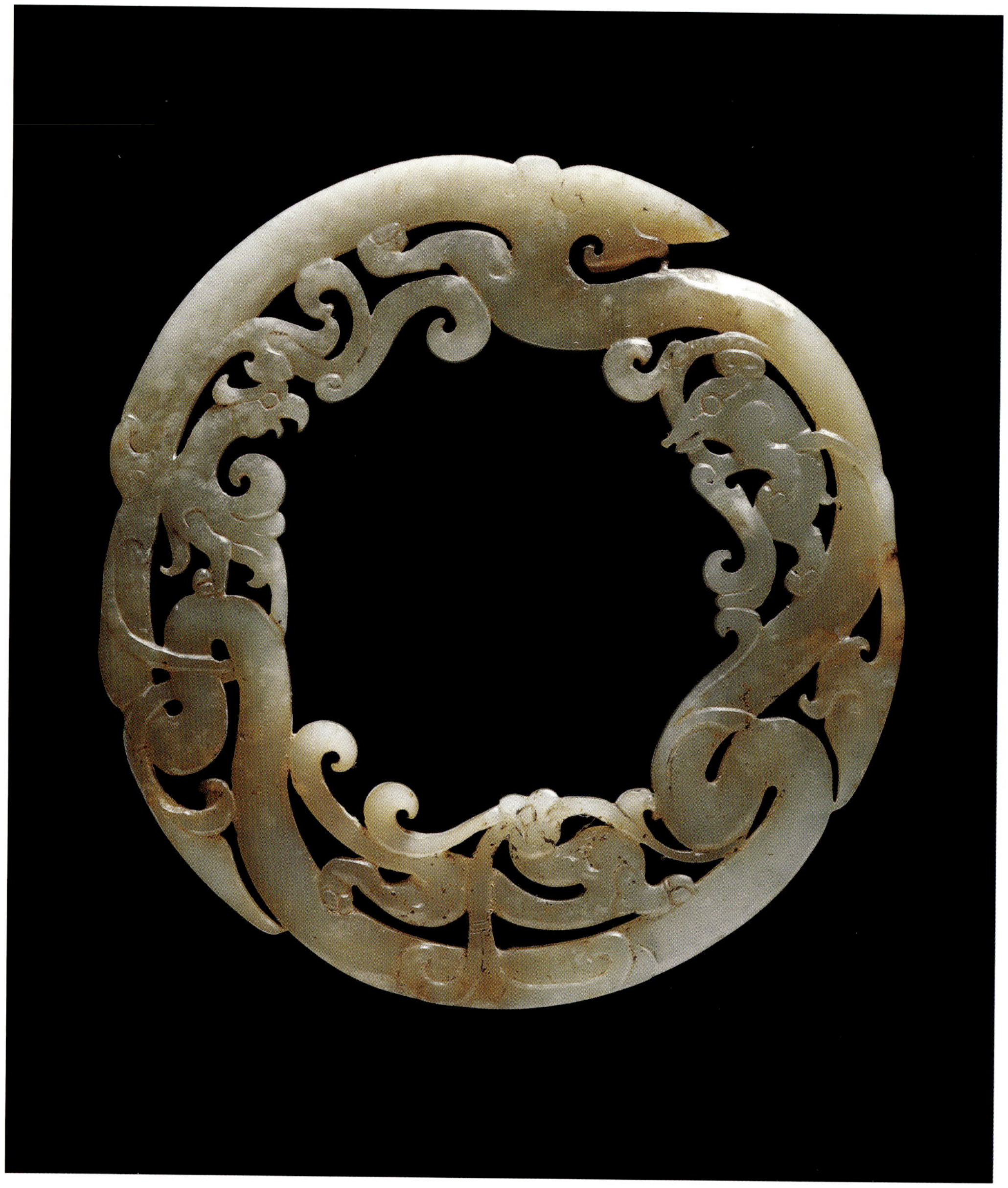

70

70

Jade openwork ring

First century BC, Western Han dynasty

Diameter: 7.9 cm

Excavated at tomb M2 at Dongdongshan in 1982

Xuzhou Museum, Jiangsu Province

This jade ring is a light yellowish-green jade, carved in an openwork style with a phoenix (on the left of the image), a bear (on the right) and a dragon (at the bottom). The ring belonged to the Queen of Chu and was excavated from the M2 tomb at Dongdongshan. The exaggerated designs emerging from the bodies of these three animals are similar in design to the dragon and phoenix on the jade disc from the King of Nanyue's tomb (fig. 3). This style of carving may have been widely used during this period or it may be a design shared by artists in these two kingdoms. A jade ring of this size was usually used as a part of a pendant. JCSL

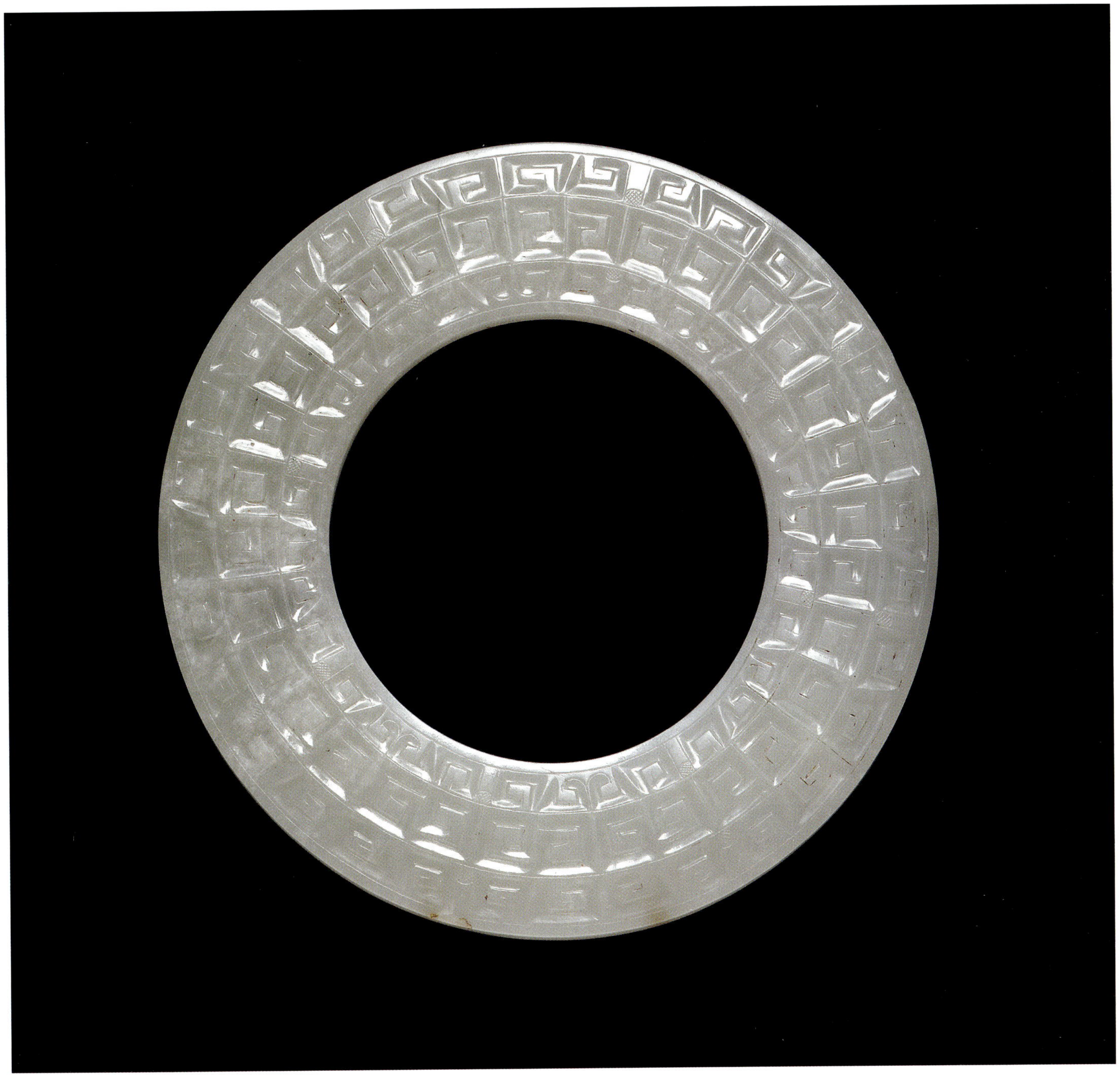

71

71

Jade ring

Second century BC, Western Han dynasty
Diameter: 12.8 cm
Excavated at Shizishan in 1994–5
Xuzhou Museum, Jiangsu Province

This jade ring was carved from a shimmering milky white nephrite stone from Khotan. It is decorated with a repeating meander pattern similar to a Greek key design. This design is similar to the Chinese character *hui* (to return) and is a symbol of rebirth. Jade rings like this were usually part of a long pendant. JCSL

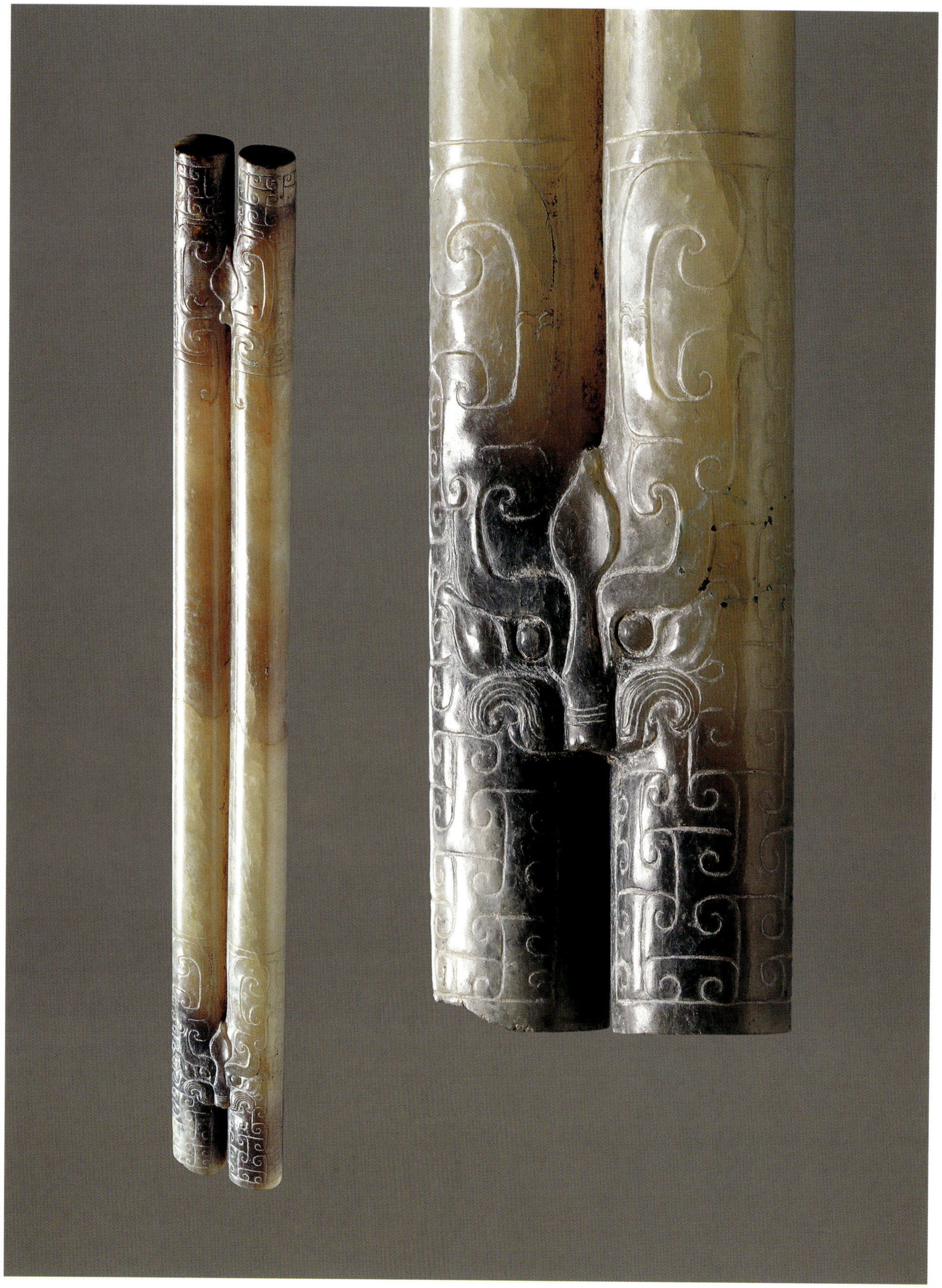

72

72

Jade double-tube

Second century BC, Western Han dynasty
Length: 26.2 cm; Width: 2.9 cm
Excavated at Shizishan in 1994–5
Xuzhou Museum, Jiangsu Province

This double-tube was carved from a piece of light green jade from Khotan. The tubes are hollow inside, although the bottom ends are not drilled through. The joined sections near the top and bottom ends of the tubes are decorated. The bottom end is decorated with a monster face with finely detailed eyes, beard and horns. The top end is decorated with a pattern of interlinked scrolls while the rest of the body is plain. This is the only example of a jade double-tube found to date. Its function is still unknown. JCSL

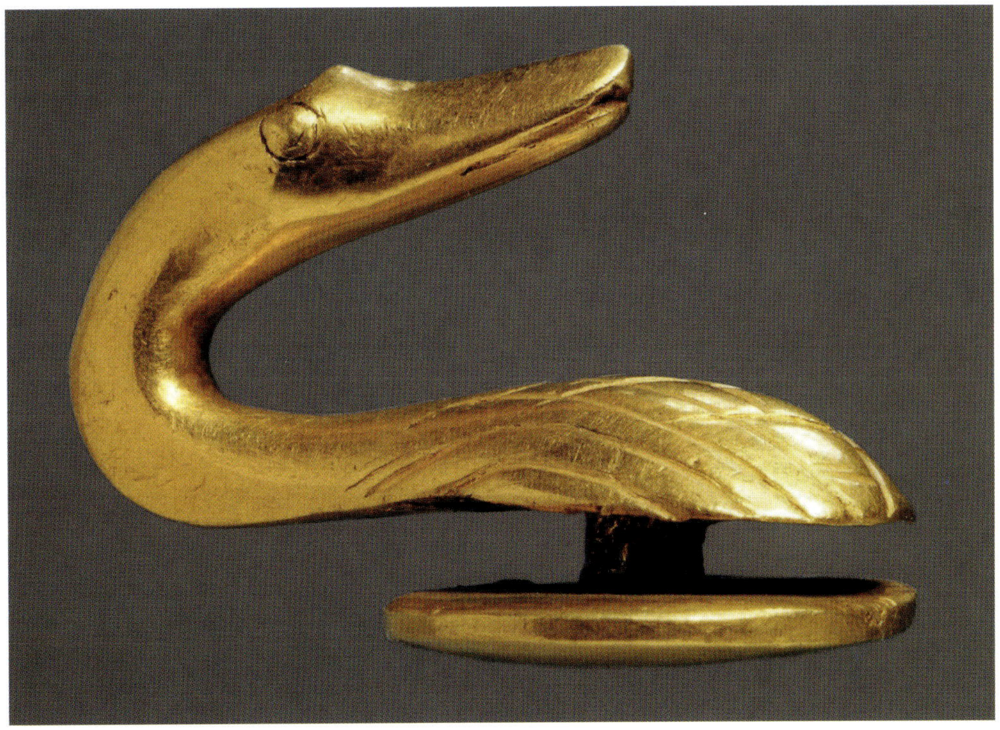

73

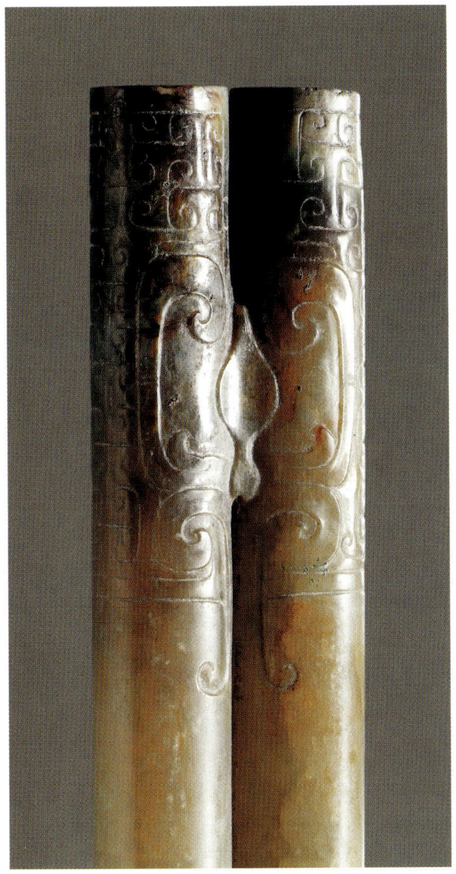

73

Gold belt hook

Second century BC, Western Han dynasty
Length: 3.1 cm
Excavated at Beidongshan in 1986
Xuzhou Museum, Jiangsu Province
NOT EXHIBITED

The use of belt hooks began in the Neolithic period. Metal belt hooks first appeared in the late Western Zhou (eleventh–eighth century BC) and became popular during the Warring States period (fifth–third century BC). In the Han dynasty, the production of belt hooks reached its peak in terms of quantity, technique and craftsmanship. They were used as practical devices and also to mark the users' social status or wealth.

From the first millennium BC, both Chinese people and the pastoral tribes at their northern frontier had widely used belt fasteners with their garments, again both for practical use and to mark status. This exhibition shows two commonly seen types: belt plaque ornaments (cat. 81, 82, 170) and belt hooks (cat. 73, 74, 75, 148, 169). The first two originated among the northern tribes, while the last is believed to be a Chinese innovation.

This belt hook is made of gold, in the shape of a goose's head, and the eyes once had inlay, though this is now lost. Its main body is incised with lines that resemble feathers. LKC

74

Gold belt hook with turquoise inlay

Length: 3.5 cm
Second century BC, Western Han dynasty
Excavated at Shizishan in 1994–5
Xuzhou Museum, Jiangsu Province

The belt hook usually consists of a hook, a main body and a button on the back connected to the main body by a neck. The button was used to fix the hook

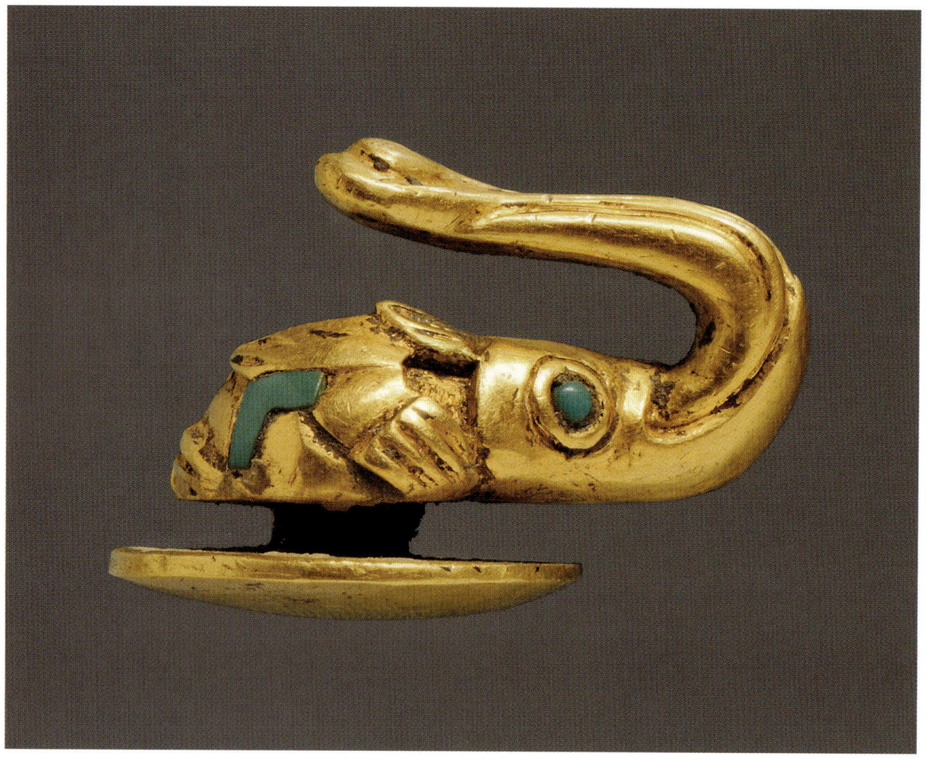

74

onto leather or cloth belts. In the Warring States period (eighth–third century BC) the button tended to be smaller and less conspicuous, whereas in the Han dynasty the button was much larger and some, such as this example, even bigger than the main body.

This belt hook is made of gold and rendered in the shape of a mythical creature, often identified as a *yulong*, a fish-dragon or kraken. Both eyes once had turquoise inlay but only the inlay of one eye survives. LKC

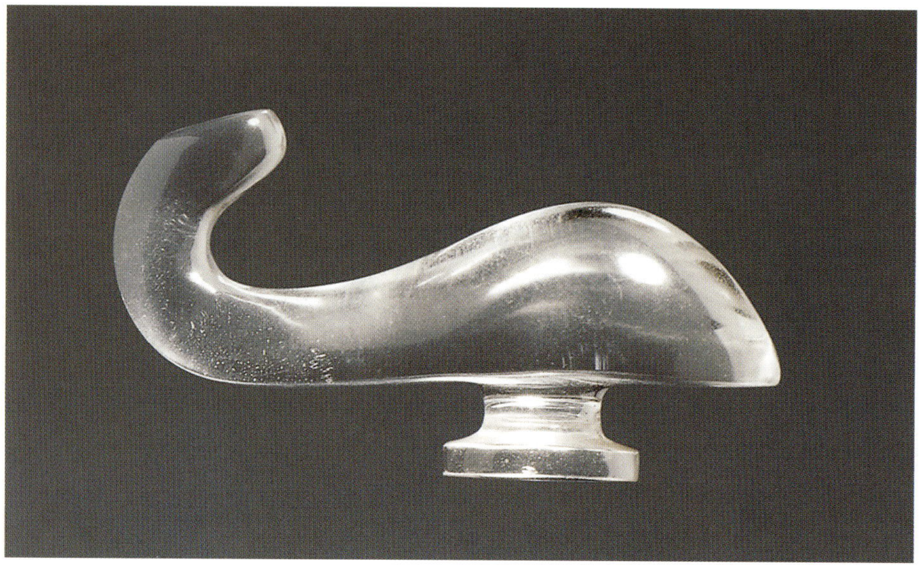

75

75

Crystal belt hook

Second century BC, Western Han dynasty
Length: 5.5 cm
Excavated at Guishan in 1981–2
Xuzhou Museum, Jiangsu Province

Belt hooks were made of a wide variety of materials, including gold, bronze, animal bones and, as in this example, crystal, a rare and precious stone in the Han dynasty. This hook is cut in a simple geometrical shape, which displays to good effect the crystal's purity and brilliance. LKC

76

Gold ornament in the form of a bear's head

Second century BC, Western Han dynasty
Length: 3.5 cm; Width: 2.8 cm
Excavated at the tomb of the King of Chu at Shizishan in 1994–5
Xuzhou Museum, Jiangsu Province

Gold sheet has been found in ancient Chinese tombs as early as the Shang dynasty (*c.*1600–1050 BC), but gold objects were still not common in burial collections during the Han period. Instead, gilt technology was widely used, as shown by a vast amount of archaeological evidence. These two examples of gold animal-design ornaments from the King of Chu's tomb at Shizishan were apparently influenced by foreign cultures from the steppe people of the Ordos region and Inner or Central Asia. The art and iconography of these neighbouring nomads has come to be called simply 'animal style'.

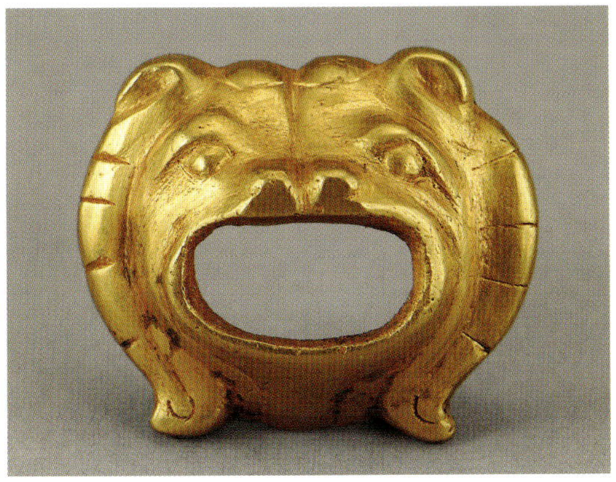

76

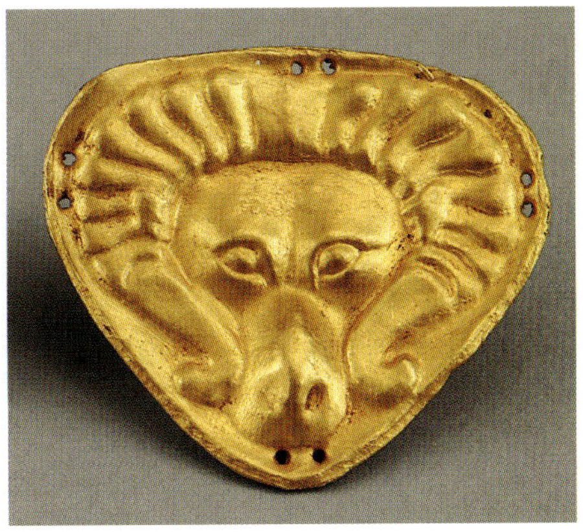

77

The ornament was made from a gold sheet hammered into shape probably over a raised design of a bear's head in metal or other hard material. The mouth was cut out leaving a hole, which, in addition to its aesthetic purpose, may have functioned as a buckle or have been attached to an object for decoration.[1] JX

1 The only similar find is the animal-head ornament from the King of Liang's tomb at Yongcheng, Henan. It has a similar hollow-cut mouth and was made of gold inlaid with turquoise and other brightly coloured stones; Zhengzhou 1996.

77

Gold ornament decorated with a ram's head

Second century BC, Western Han dynasty
Length: 4 cm; Width: 3.4 cm
Unearthed at the tomb of the King of Chu at Shizishan in 1994–5
Xuzhou Museum, Jiangsu Province

The ornament decorated with a ram's head was made from a sheet of hammered gold. It has small holes pierced around the edge of the plaque, which served to attach it to another object. Unfortunately, due to the disturbance of the tomb, the original positions for this ornament and that shown in cat. 76 can no longer be determined. JX

78

Two gilt bronze handles

Second century BC, Western Han dynasty
Length: 11.5 cm; Width: 7.6 cm
Excavated at Shizishan in 1994–5
Xuzhou Museum, Jiangsu Province

These two gilt bronze animal mask handles come from the tomb at Shizishan. The published material does not give their exact location in the tomb, but eight similar masks made of bronze were found in the first side chamber to the west.[1] Two of these are associated with remains of wood, maybe that of a box in which objects were stored. The golden masks may also have served as ornamental handles for such a wooden object.[2]

The major features of this pair of masks are similar to those of the bronze example from Beidongshan (cat. 79). Facial features can be clearly discerned, although the mercury-amalgam gilding has come off in places, giving them a smoother appearance. One of the outward curling ears is damaged. The animal's 'skin' consists largely of scales, while the eyebrows, ears and forehead are rendered to appear like fur. SP

1 *Wenwu* 1998, 8, fig. 7.
2 Beijing 2005, p. 205. This assessment needs to be verified once findings at the Shizishan site are comprehensively published.

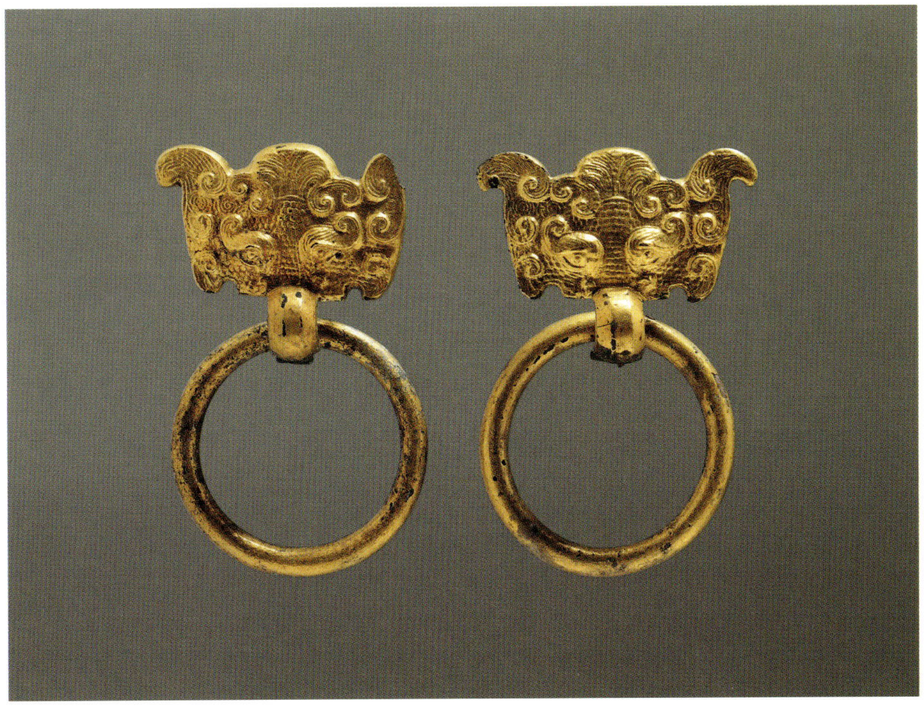

78

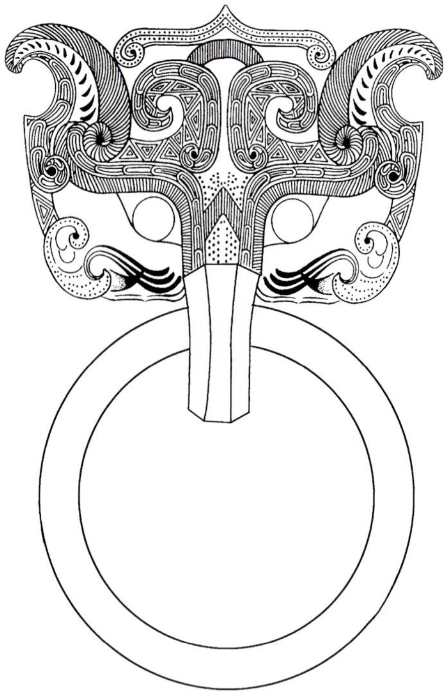

79

Bronze handle

Second century BC, Western Han dynasty
Length: 27 cm, Width: 16.4 cm
Excavated at Beidongshan in 1986
Xuzhou Museum, Jiangsu Province
NOT EXHIBITED

This bronze handle in the form of a mask is one of thirteen such objects from this tomb, five of which are typologically similar, while eight others are generally similar but much smaller. All were excavated from the vicinity of the place where once a wooden double door sealed off the tomb chamber. These ornamental handles were probably attached to this wooden door, which has now disintegrated.[1] In this way they fulfil the classical function of such pieces, usually referred to as *pushou*; the *Shuowen jiezi* explains that a *pushou* is an object holding a ring and is attached to a door,[2] that is, a door handle or ornament.

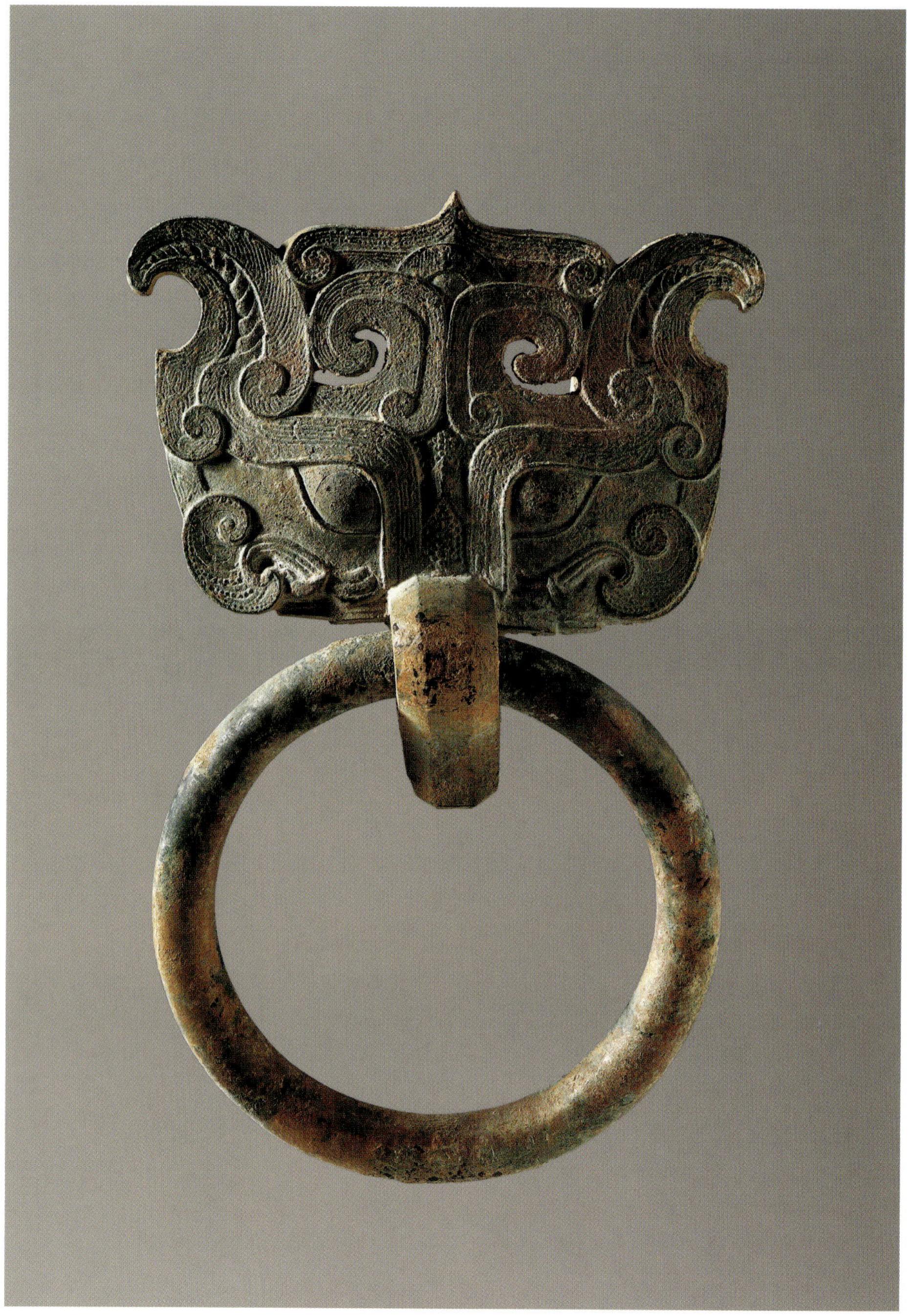

79

Crisply cast and rich in detail, the animal mask has an imposing appearance amplified by its size. Each facial feature is rendered differently, alternating between scale-like dots, fur-like lines, triangular spirals and plain spaces. Parts of the ear appear like a twisted rope. These design features are interspersed with plain spaces and openwork. SP

1 *Wenwu* 1988, pp. 14–15; Beijing 2003, p. 105; Beijing 2005, p. 208.
2 *Shuowen jiezi*, pp. 713–14.

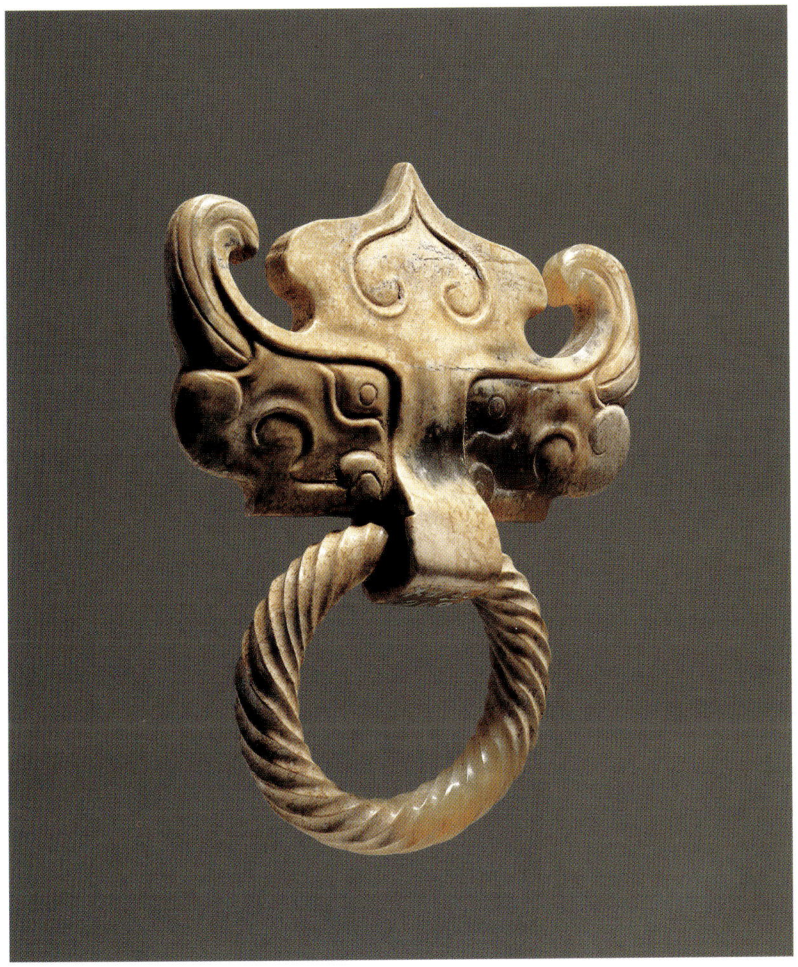

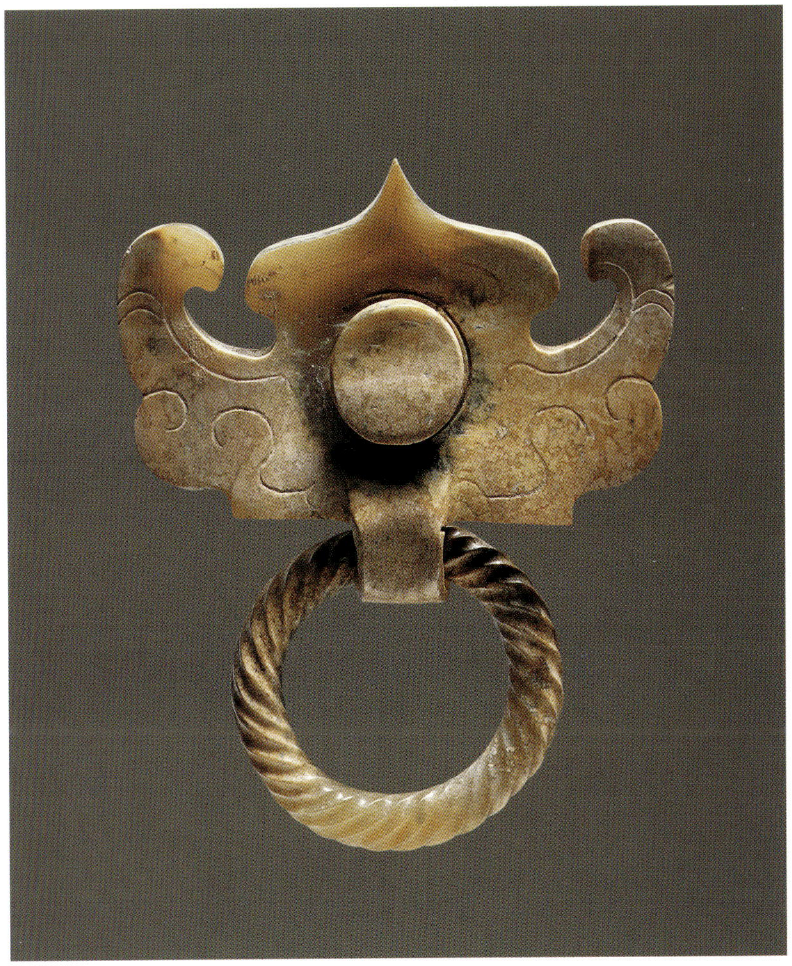

80

80

Jade animal mask

Second century BC, Western Han dynasty
Length: 6.8 cm; Width: 5.4 cm
Excavated at Huoshan in 1996
Xuzhou Museum, Jiangsu Province

Unlike the bronze versions, this animal mask holds a ring that looks like twisted rope. The front is rendered in less detail than those in bronze with only the major features, such as the eyes, cheeks, ears and forehead, clearly depicted. Here there is no rendering of the skin in scales or other decoration. The back is decorated with shallow incised lines tracing the major features.

This example, like the one in gilt bronze (cat. 78), illustrates that these full-front animal masks had a much broader set of functions than their usual use as door handles. The jade mask probably served as a garment hook.[1] Excavation reports of the Huoshan tomb, from which it was unearthed, are so far unpublished, limiting our understanding of the context in which it was found. The round knob on the back of the mask, however, helps to confirm its function as a garment hook as the knob is identical to those found on other garment hooks from the period. The jade mask would have been attached by inserting the knob into a slit in a belt or garment. Similar animal masks of the Han period are used as mounts for ring handles on bronze (cat. 78, 79), lacquer or ceramic vessels. On bronze vessels, such as the *hu* in cat. 120, the rings served as a point of attachment for a chain that was attached to the lid and ended in a handle with which the container could be carried. Animal masks were also used as ornaments (cat. 172). SP

1 Beijing 2005, pp. 206–7.

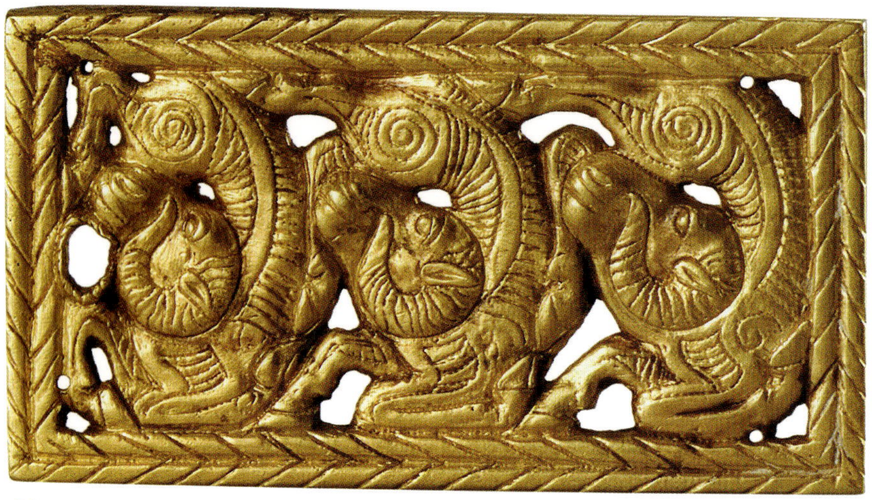

81

81

Gold belt plaque

Second century BC, Western Han dynasty
Length: 8.15 cm; Width: 4.4 cm
Excavated at Tongshan in 1995
Xuzhou Museum, Jiangsu Province

Gold belt plaques of rectangular shape with animal motifs originated among the nomadic tribes of central Asia, although they were later produced in China as items for trade along the northern frontier. These rectangular plaques were usually crafted in openwork and used in pairs on the belt. Some archaeologists speculate that the oval hole on one side of the plaque served as the point of attachment for a cord or ribbon used to fasten the belt around the waist.

This plaque has three rams with large heads in profile with pairs of huge curved horns arrayed in parallel and in the same position. The design of the rams, whose bodies are coiled over their heads with forelegs folded beneath their bodies, is highly stylized. The horns and bodies are adorned with incised lines. The repeating V-shaped pattern of the frame resembles a twisted rope, and can also be seen in the plaque from King of Nanyue's tomb (cat. 170). LKC

82

Gold belt plaque

Second century BC, Western Han dynasty
Length: 13.3 cm; Width: 6 cm
Excavated at the tomb of the King of Chu at Shizishan in 1994–5
Xuzhou Museum, Jiangsu Province

This is one of a pair of belt plaques excavated from the west wing of the antechamber of the tomb. An inscription is carved on the edge of each plaque to state its weight. On the back, two vertical loops are attached to each plaque, used to fix them onto a belt. When they were discovered, the two pieces were tied at the ends of a belt made of three rows of shells tied together with silk.

The plaques are cast in relief and designed as mirror images of each other. The two horse-like animals in each plaque face towards each other, and in each image a wolf and a bear bite into the upper back and the tail of the horse. All three animals are depicted with large round eyes, heightening the drama of the scene. The horse-like animals are delineated with vigorous bodies as if they are forcefully struggling away from their attackers. Fine incised lines represent the animals' hair, making this piece particularly exquisite. Any remaining space is filled in with a decorative pattern of birds' heads, a common Han dynasty convention.

The animal theme of the design and the rectangular shape suggest the influence of nomadic tribes beyond the Han's northern borders of China. However, the method of fastening suggests that this pair was likely to have been made locally rather than imported. Several virtually identical plaques have been excavated from Xi'an, the location of the Western Han capital, and from Kazakhstan, where northern pastoral tribes were active.[1] LKC

1 So and Bunker 1995, p. 144.

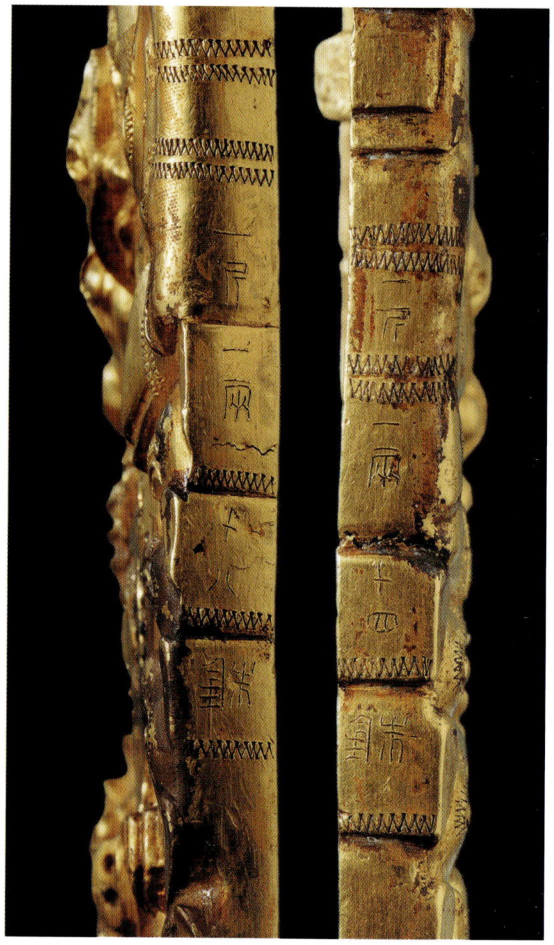

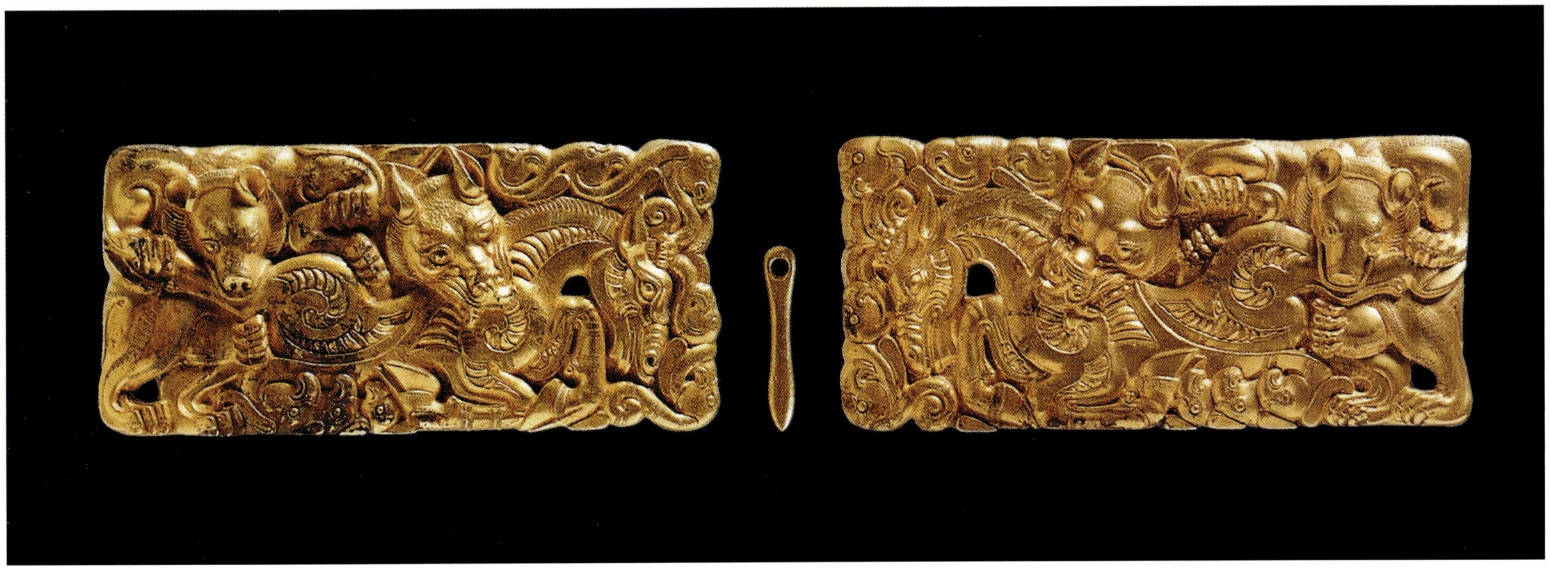

82

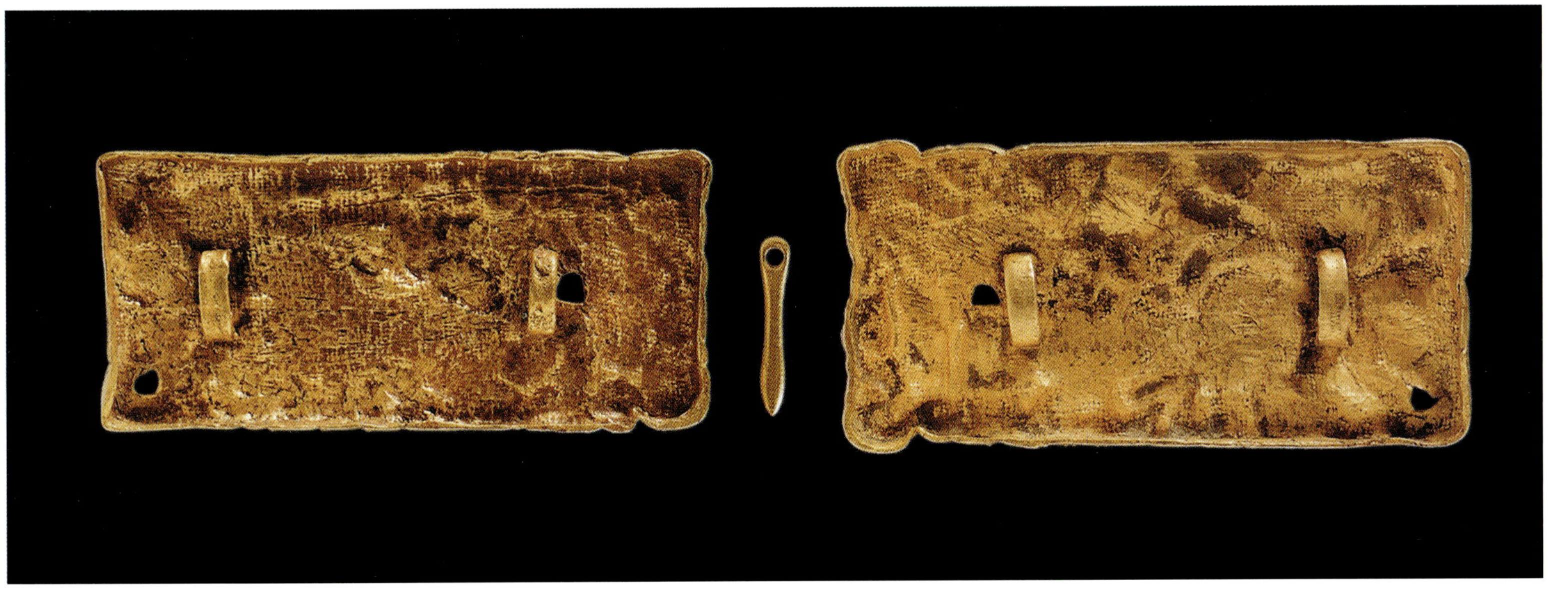

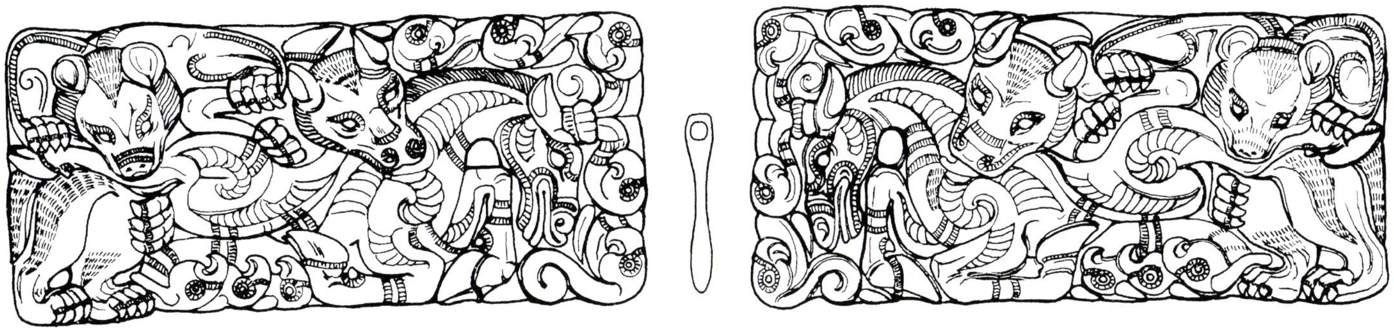

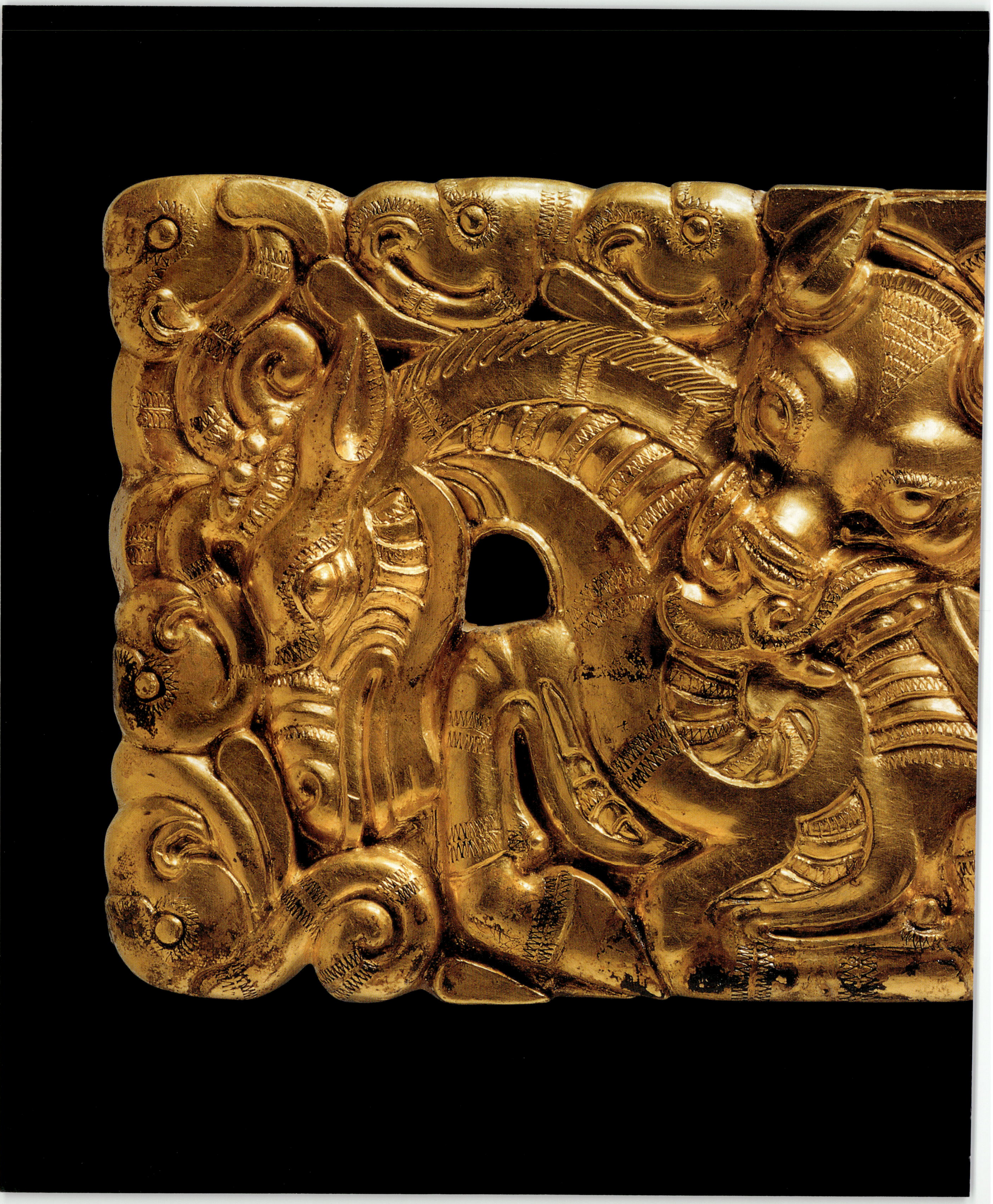

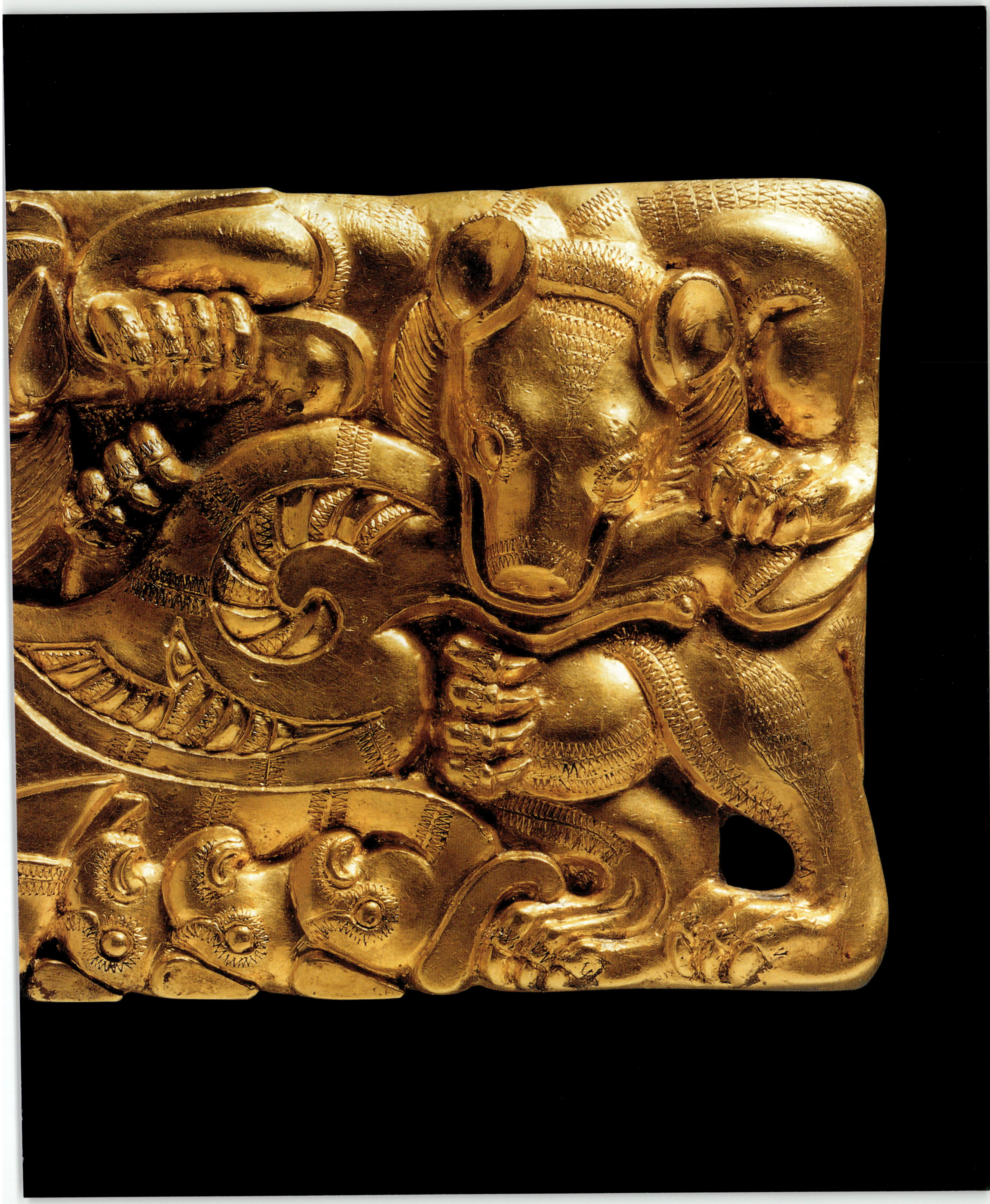

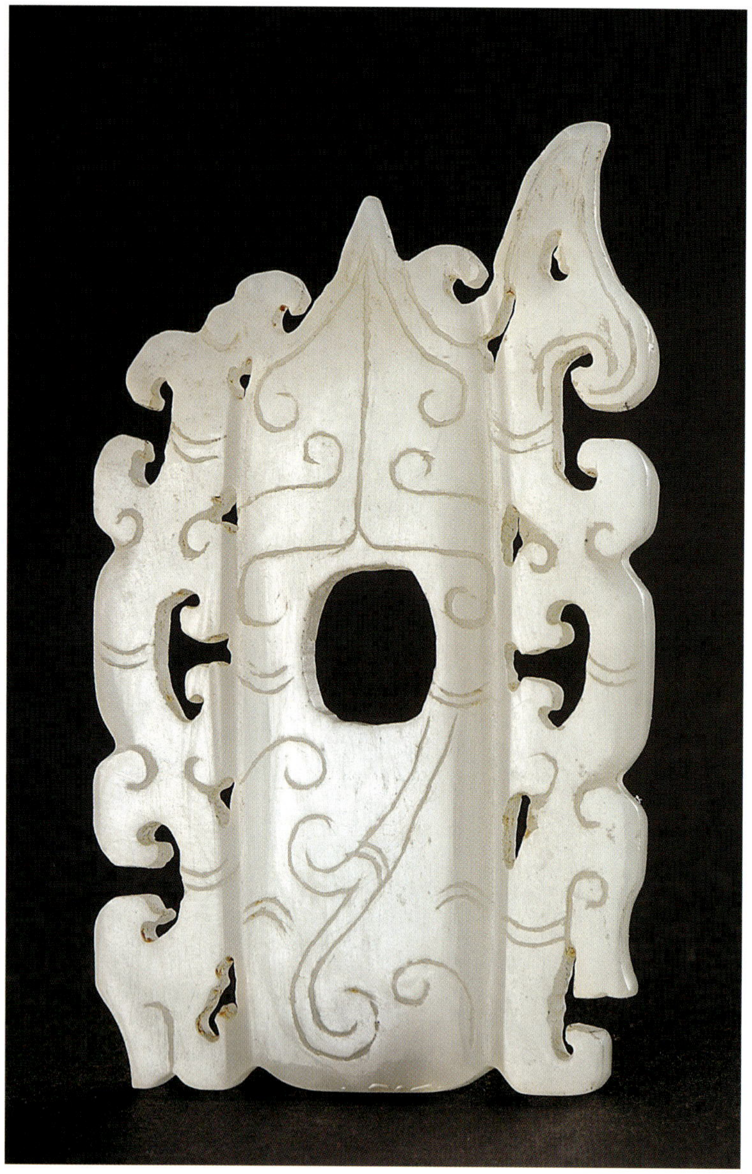

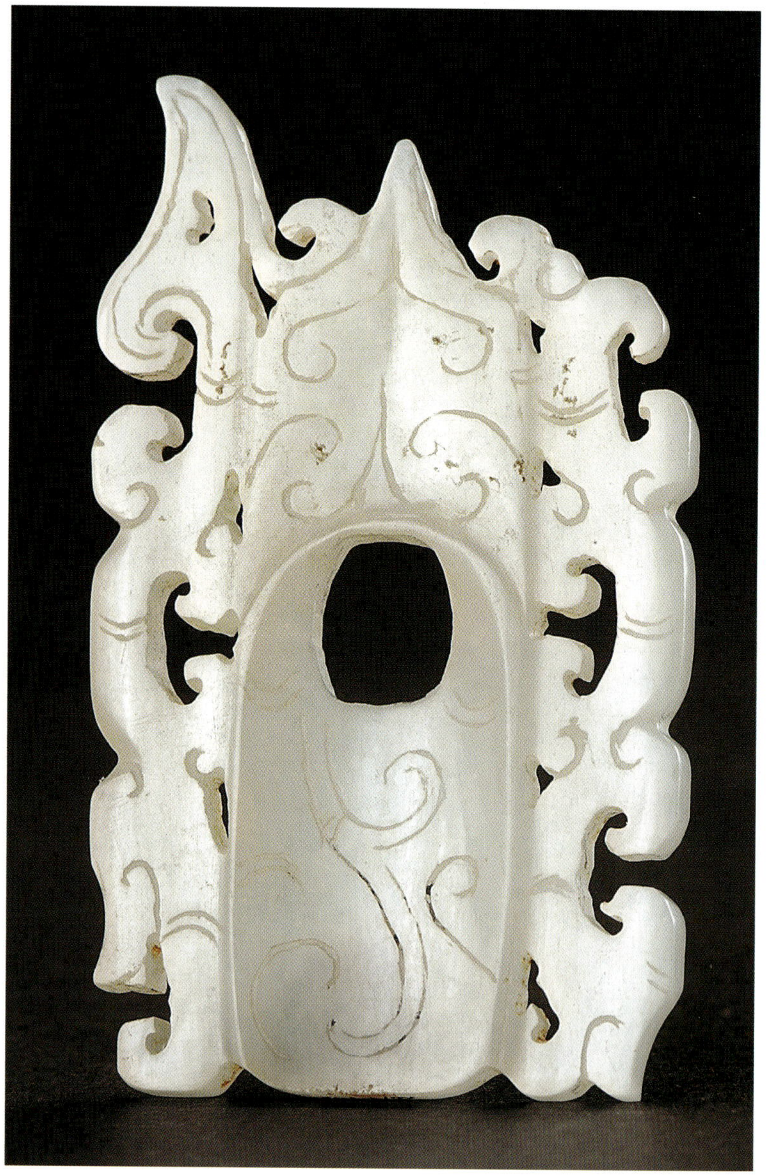

83

83

Jade shield-shaped pendant

First century BC, Western Han dynasty
Length: 7 cm; Width: 4.3 cm
Excavated at tomb M2 at Dongdongshan in 1982
Xuzhou Museum, Jiangsu Province

This unusual type of pendant consists of a shield-shaped element with a hole, usually flanked or surrounded by cloud scrolls, dragons or a dragon with a phoenix in openwork. Its design may have developed from the archer's ring and was used as the central element of a pendant. Pendants like this are usually carved on both sides, with a convex front and concave reverse.

Judging from the pale white colour of the jade, the material may have come from Khotan. Both sides of the pendant are incised with C-shaped scrolls, but the lines are rough and uneven, which suggests that it may be unfinished. LKC

84

Jade pendant in the shape of an archer's ring

Second century BC, Western Han
Length: 7.1 cm; Width: 4.3 cm
Excavated at Beidongshan in 1986
Xuzhou Museum, Jiangsu Province

An archer's ring is worn on the thumb to help pull the bowstring when shooting an arrow. Archaeological evidence from Anyang, Henan, reveals that the use of archer's rings appeared as early as the Shang dynasty (seventeenth–eleventh century BC). Archaeologists have unearthed abundant archer's rings made from jade or bones from sites dated to the Eastern Zhou (eighth–third century BC). They are often discovered close to the tomb occupants' hands, which suggests that the deceased wore archer's rings when they were buried. From the Warring States period (about fifth–third century BC), the archer's ring came to serve a decorative rather than a practical purpose and was worn as a pendant.

In the Western Han, aristocrats often had pendants such as this one in the shape of an archer's ring buried with them. The pendant is carved with a dragon on one side and a phoenix on the other, their heads next to each other. Their claws are cut in low relief with flowing outlines and their bodies are decorated with incised lines showing feathers and some spiral patterns.

Pendants adapted from the shape of archer's rings have frequently been discovered in early Western Han tombs from the areas around Xuzhou, including sites at Beidongshan and Shizishan. However, in the Chu region they have only been discovered in tombs of higher-ranking nobility. LKC

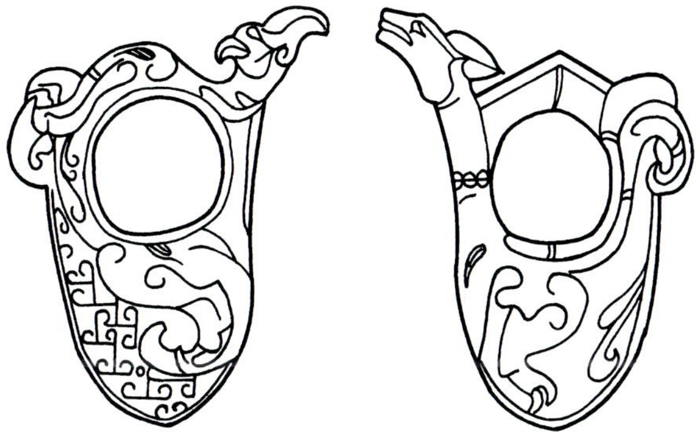

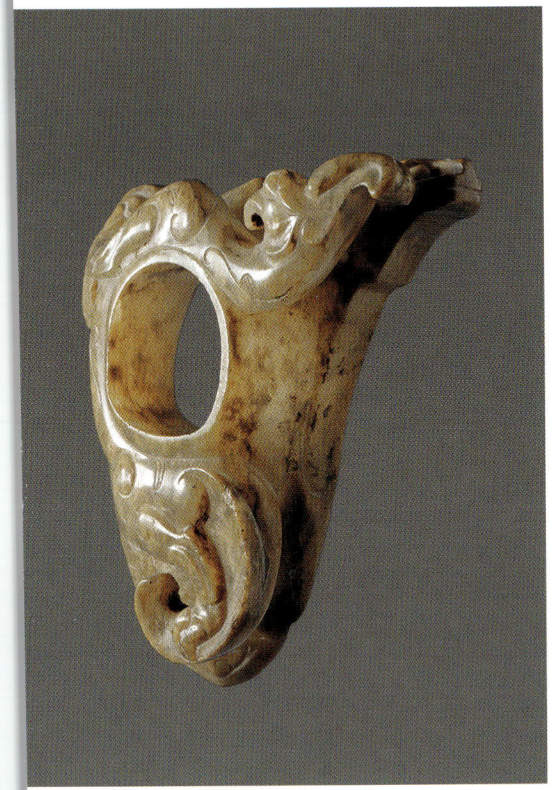

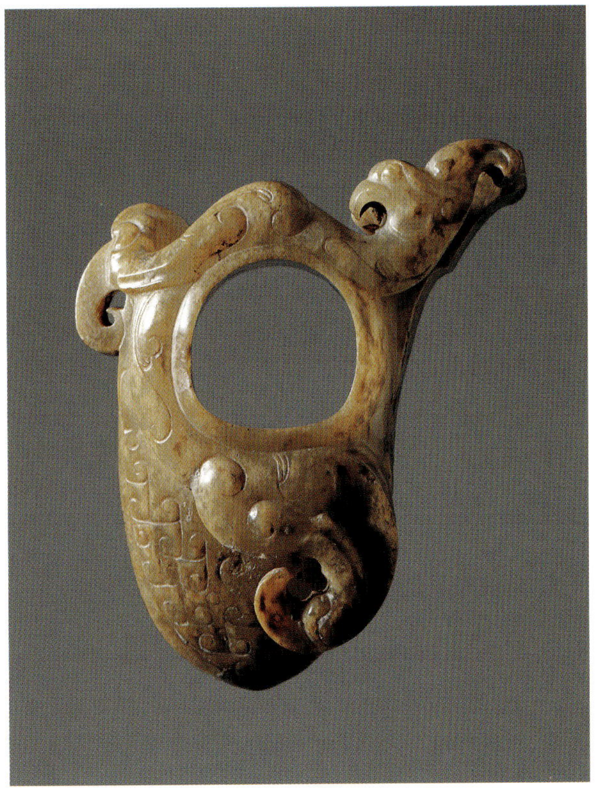

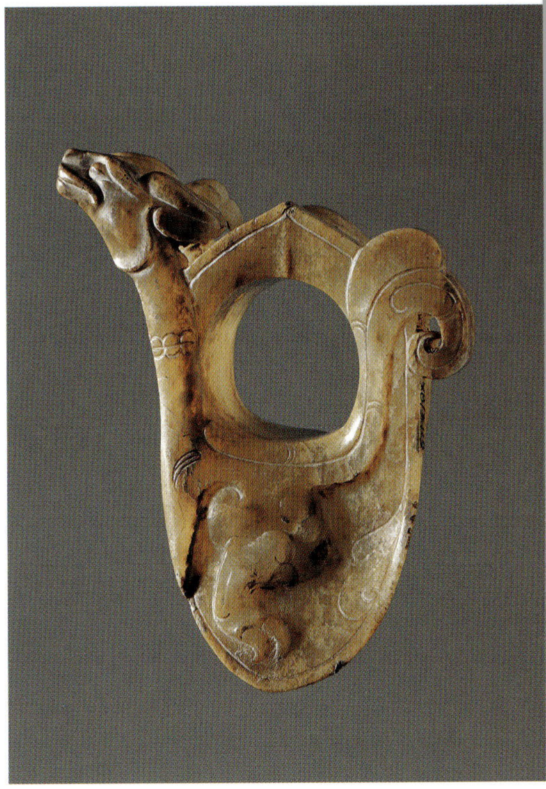

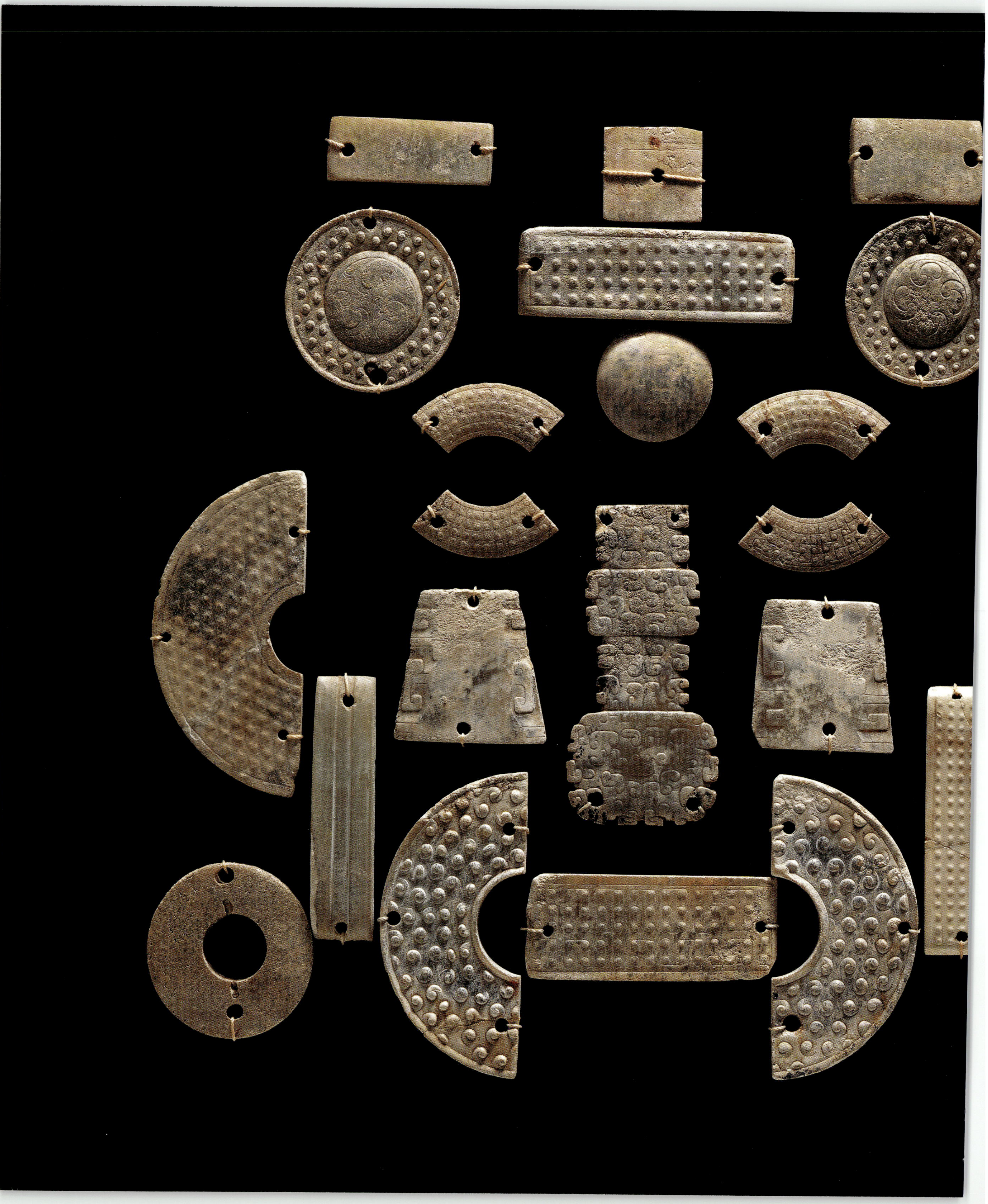

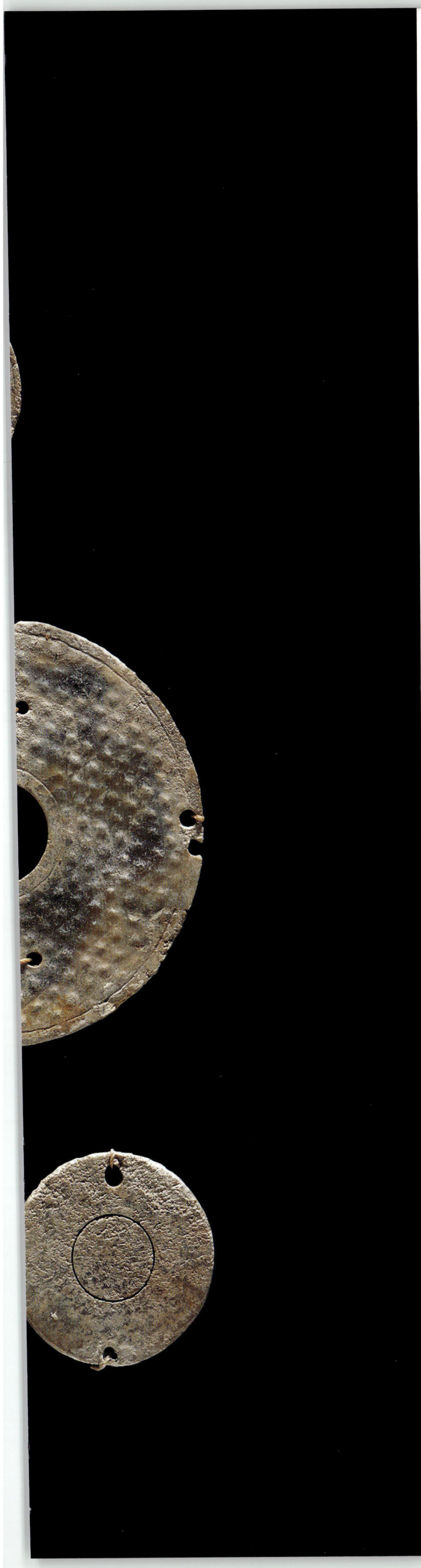

85

Jade veil

Second century BC, Western Han dynasty
Length: 35 cm; Width: 28 cm
Excavated at tomb M3 in Zifangshan in 1984
Xuzhou Museum, Jiangsu Province

This jade veil is composed of twenty-three jade plaques of various shapes: square, rectangular, semi-circular, fan, ring and a nose-like piece. They were used to form human-like facial features. Most of these pieces are decorated and were reworked from sword fittings such as pommels, hilts and scabbard slides. The tomb occupant was identified as an aristocratic official. The tomb itself dates from the very early Western Han (182–140 BC).[1]

Twenty-two of the plaques have between one and four small holes drilled through them so that they could be sewn onto a cloth or silk mask to be placed over the face. Jade veils from Zifangshan retained the appearance of facial features and seem to be based on much earlier types, whereas others from Tuolongshan, Houloushan (fig. 31) and Hanshan, also in Xuzhou, are composed of geometric shapes and share characteristics with jade suits.

The use of jade veils in the Xuzhou area clearly depended on the status of the tomb occupant. Higher-ranking individuals were buried with more delicate and complicated veils or even jade suits. Lower-ranking individuals were buried with veils that were much poorer in quality, simpler in design and made mostly from reworked jade pieces dating from earlier periods. JCSL

1 The date of this tomb was suggested by the archaeological examination of a bronze mirror and *bianliang* coins; *Wenwu ziliao congkan* 1981.4, pp. 59–69.

86

Fish-scale jade plaques

Second century BC, Western Han dynasty
Height: 4.5 cm; Width: 3.3 cm
Excavated at Beidongshan in 1986
Xuzhou Museum, Jiangsu Province

Seventy-three surviving jade plaques were scattered in the main chamber and tomb passages of Beidongshan after incursions by local farmers in 1954 resulted in damage and theft. The majority of those surviving were jade plaques carved to resemble fish scales. This suggests that the tomb occupant was likely buried in a jade suit, which was later destroyed during the looting.

Five to seven holes were drilled in the jade plaques and the edges of the plaques were carefully abraded and polished.

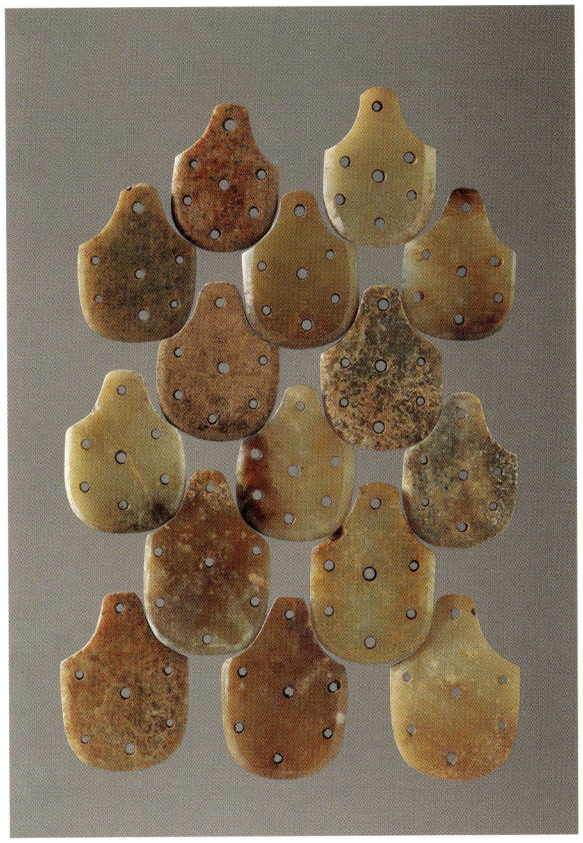

86

LEFT: 85

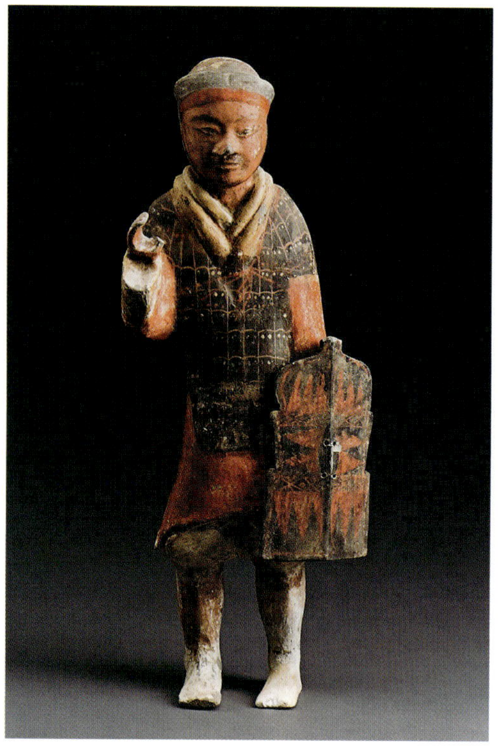

56 Armoured earthenware figure from Yangjiawan tomb, Xi'an, Shaanxi Province. Early Western Han.

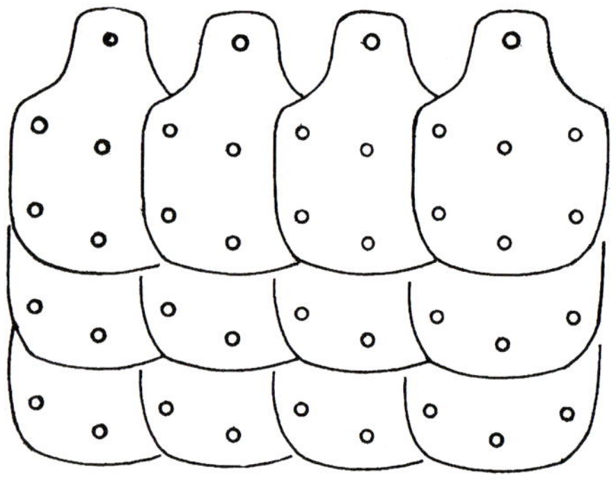

A few had clearly been re-carved from earlier broken discs as they still showed signs of previous decoration. This unusual fish-scale design can be found on armoured earthenware figures from the Yangjiawan tomb (fig. 56) and provides important evidence of the similarities between jade suits and armour.

It is probable that the concept of using jade as a form of armour for the dead arose by analogy with the use of iron (or lacquer) armour to protect the living.[1] More fish-scale jade plaques with even sharper points have been excavated from a late Western Han tomb at Zhangjiabao outside Xi'an.[2] JCSL

1 Lin 2007, p. 189.
2 *Zhongguo wenwubao* 2008.2, 18, pl. 5; Liu 2009, pl. 250.

87

Jade suit

Second century BC, Western Han dynasty
Length: 175 cm; Width: 68 cm
Excavated at Shizishan in 1994–5
Xuzhou Museum, Jiangsu Province

To date, twelve complete jade suits have been excavated in China. Most of the suits or surviving plaques have come from sites concentrated in eastern China, particularly Hebei, Shandong, Jiangsu and

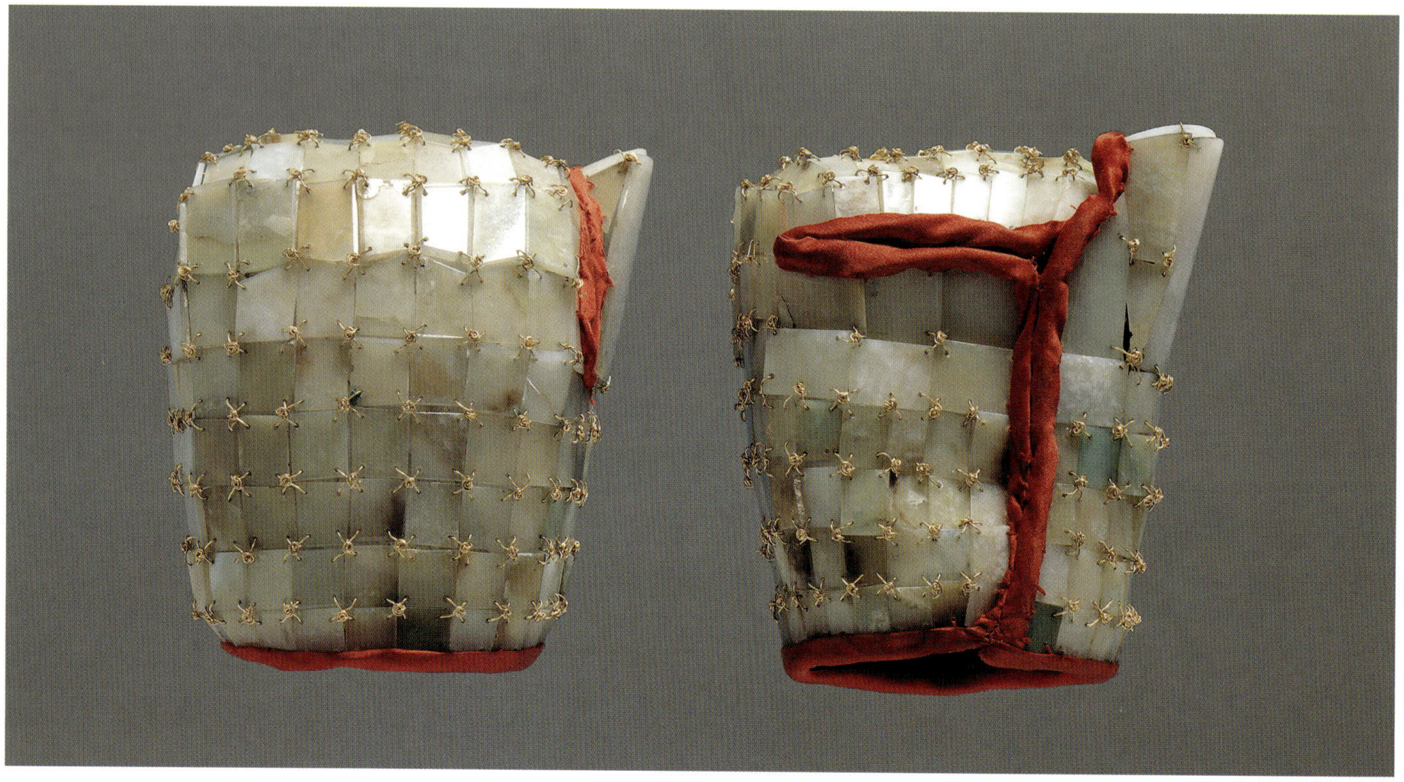

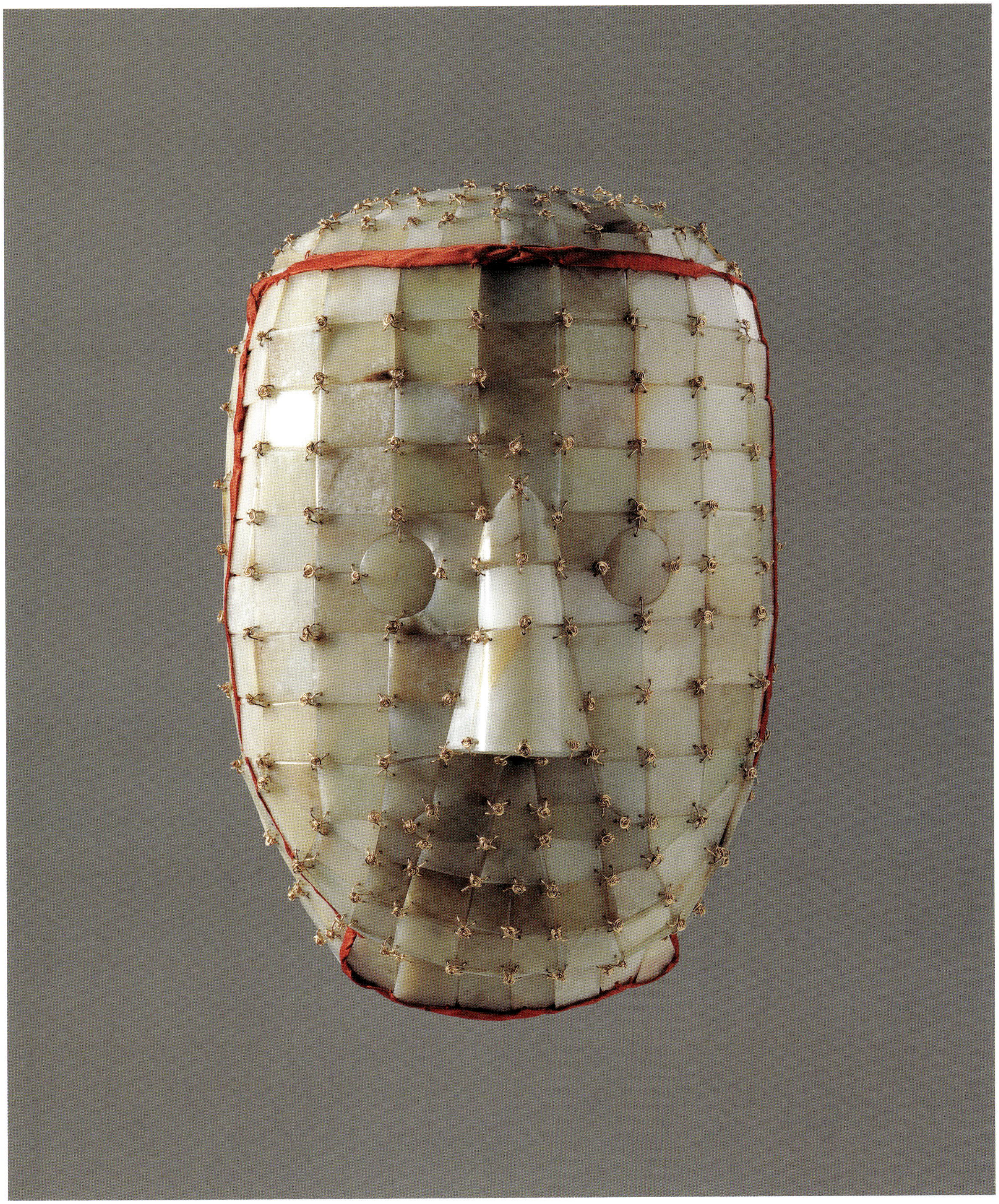

Henan Provinces. These formed parts of the powerful Kingdoms of Zhongshan, Lu, Chu and Liang respectively. Although the exact number of plaques composing a jade suit was dependent on the size of the corpse, it took on average 2,000 pieces to form one. This jade suit from Shizishan is composed of 4,248 jade plaques, sewn with 1,576 grams of gold thread. It is the finest example in terms of material and craftsmanship that has been excavated so far.

The jade suit is bulky in appearance and has a large abdomen. The facial features, eyes and mouth are depicted through the use of differently shaped plaques. The nose is composed of seven narrow plaques. Most of the plaques used in the construction of jade suits were rectangular in shape and on average they were 4.5 cm long, 3.5 cm wide and 0.2–0.35 cm thick. However, a range of differently shaped plaques, including triangular, half-moon, round, rhombic and fan-shaped are used for sections such as the gloves, feet and face covers. The jade plaques used for the helmet, face cover and gloves are smaller and more elaborately carved than those used for other parts of the suit, and on average are 1.5–3 cm long and 1–2 cm wide.

In most cases, a disc was used to form the top section of the helmet, thus leaving an opening at the top, but here the opening is ringed by thirteen small fan-shaped plaques.

The jade material has been identified as originating from Xinjiang, but we do

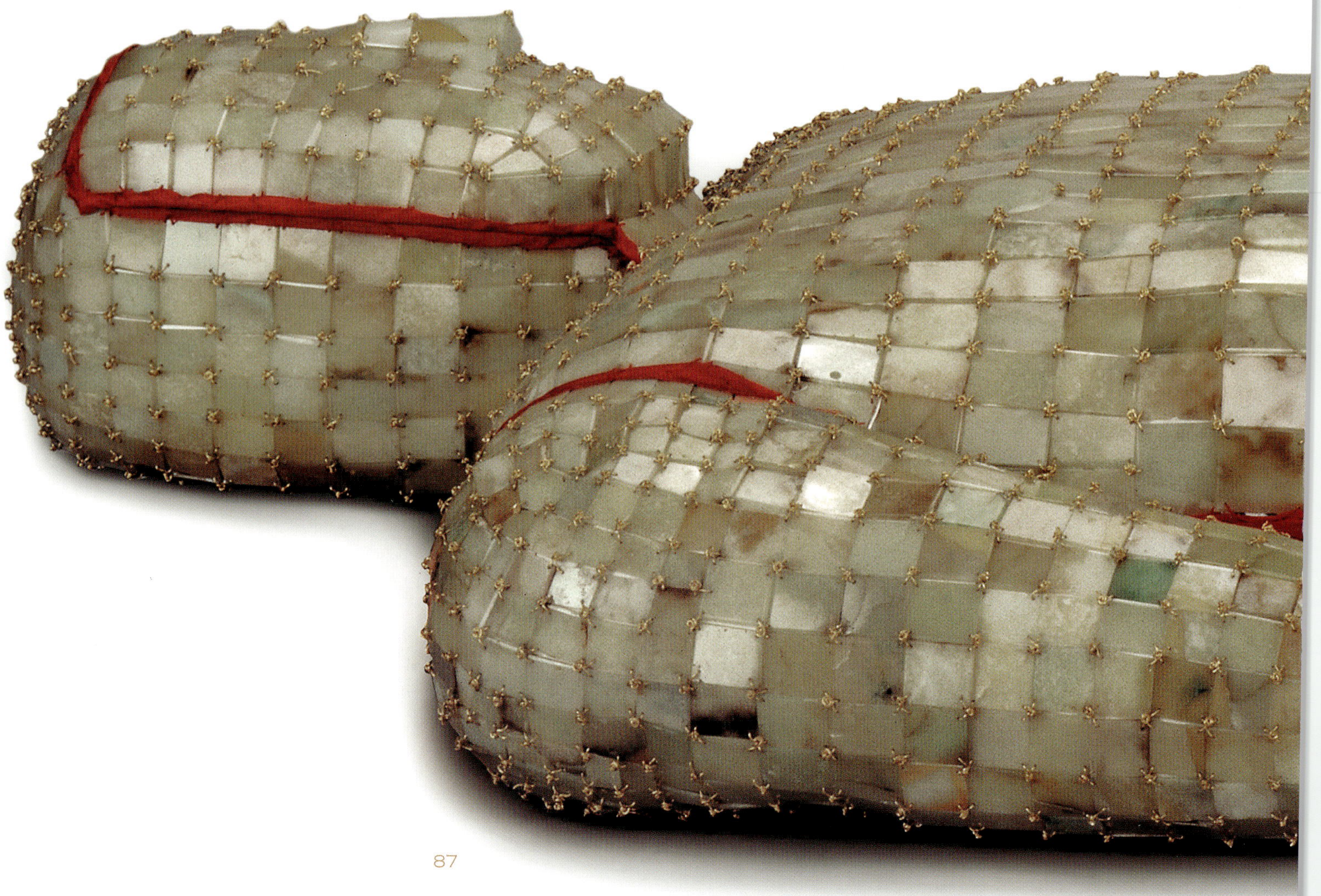

87

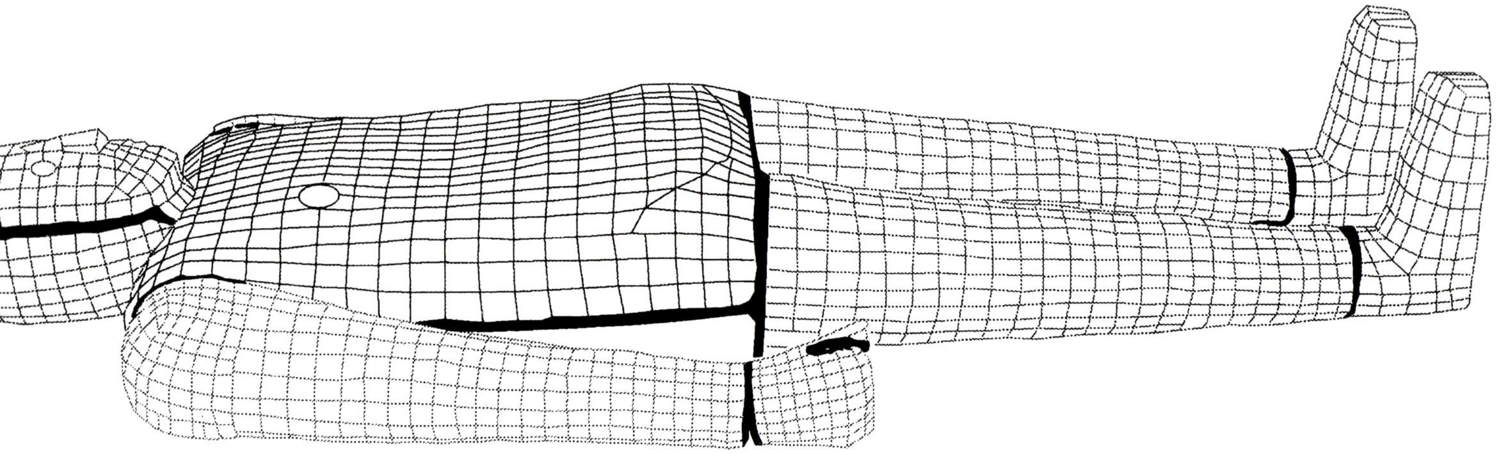

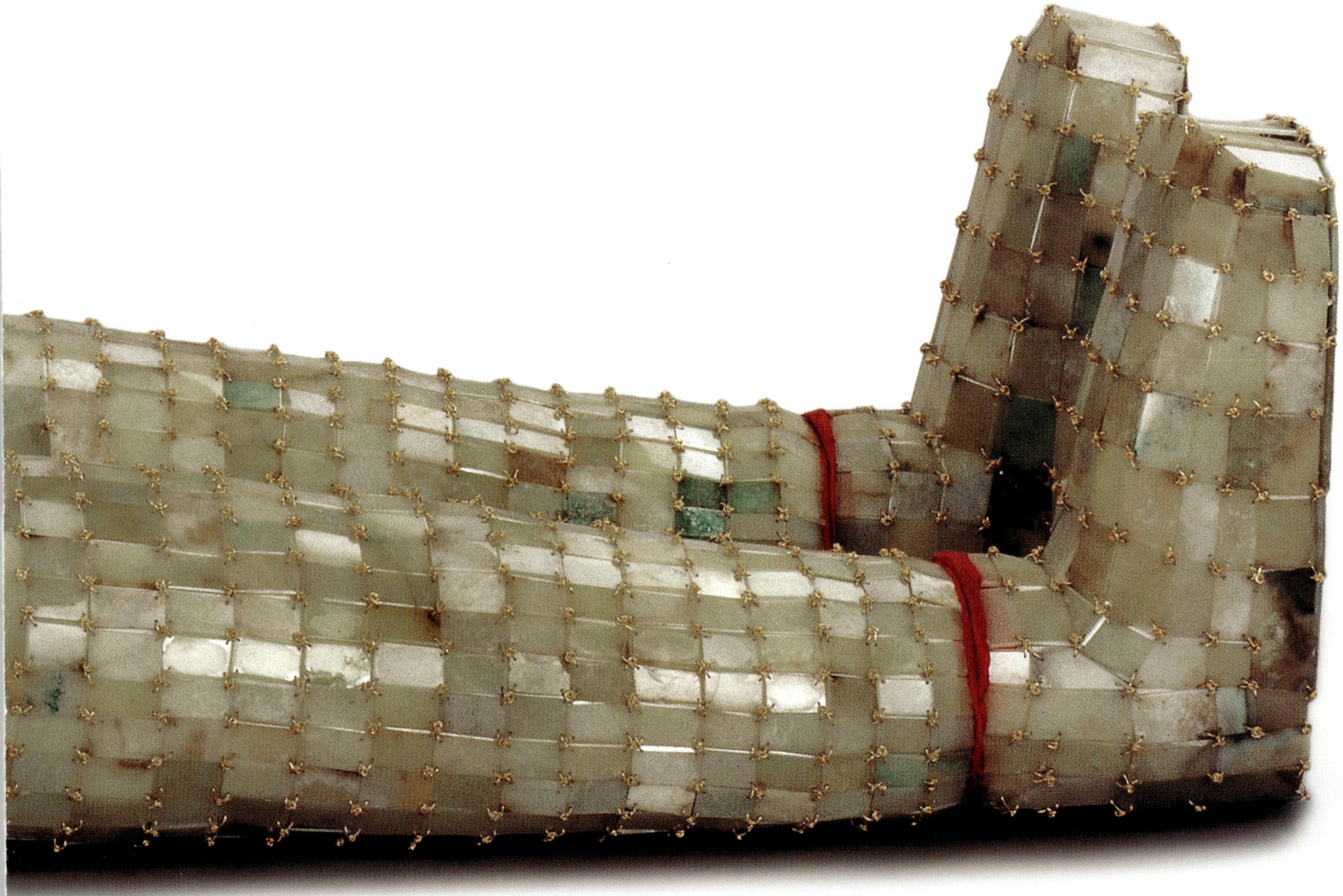

not know how these materials were transported to the eastern part of China. Tomb robbers have looted the original gold thread and some modern jade plaques replace lost originals.

The *banliang* coins found in this tomb, which dates to the early Western Han, reveal that there are two possible owners of this jade suit; Liu Yingke (r. 178–174 BC) and Liu Wu (r. 174–154 BC).

The unfinished giant tomb structure has led archaeologists to believe that the tomb occupant may have been the third generation King of Chu, Liu Wu, who joined the rebellion with six other kingdoms in 154 BC and committed suicide soon after the failure of the rebellion.

However, a large group of terracotta soldiers was found in front of Shizishan, and the jade suit found inside the tomb is particularly delicate. It seems unlikely that the kingdom would have given Liu Wu such a grand burial as this may have risked the possibility that he would pursue his rebellion in the afterlife. General Zhou Yafu, for example, fell out of favour with the Han imperial court and was imprisoned when he purchased 500 sets of armour and shields for his funeral. He was accused of 'underground treason,'[1] the suspicion being that he would commit treason against the spirits of emperors after he died.

Therefore, it seems more likely that the owner of this jade suit is the second King of Chu, Liu Yingke. JCSL

1 *Shiji*, p. 2079.

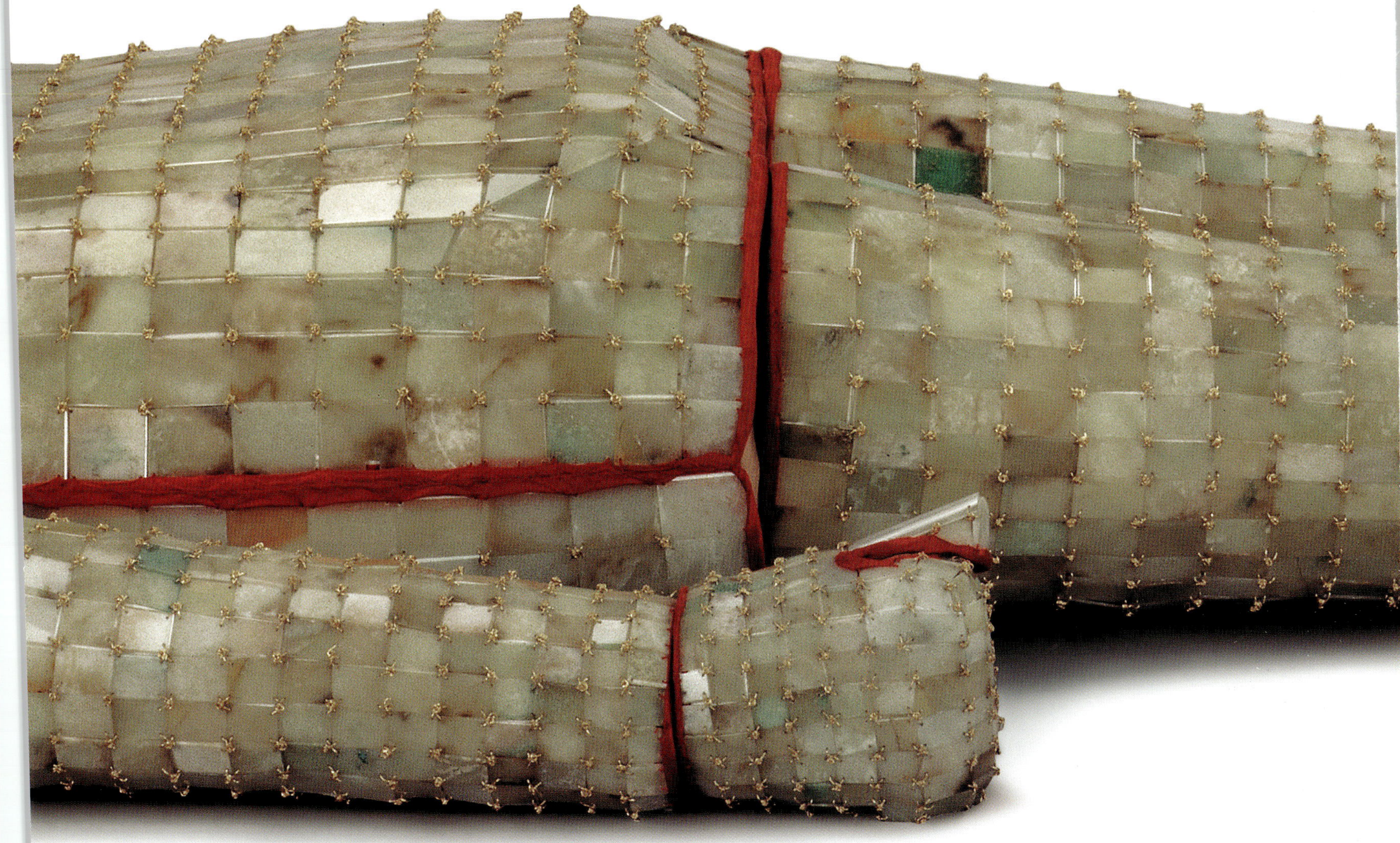

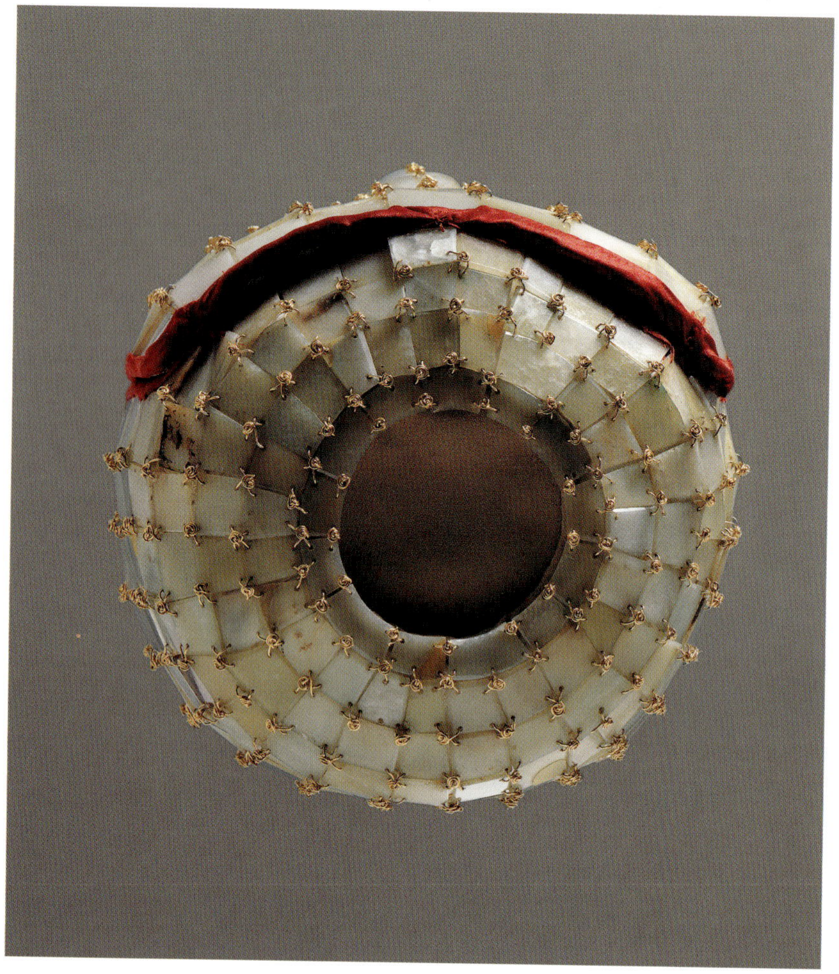

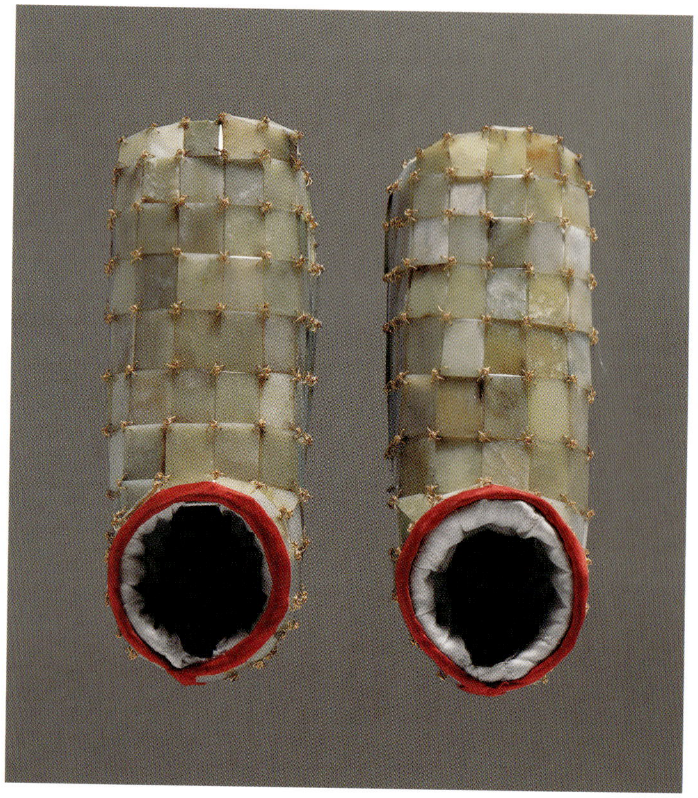

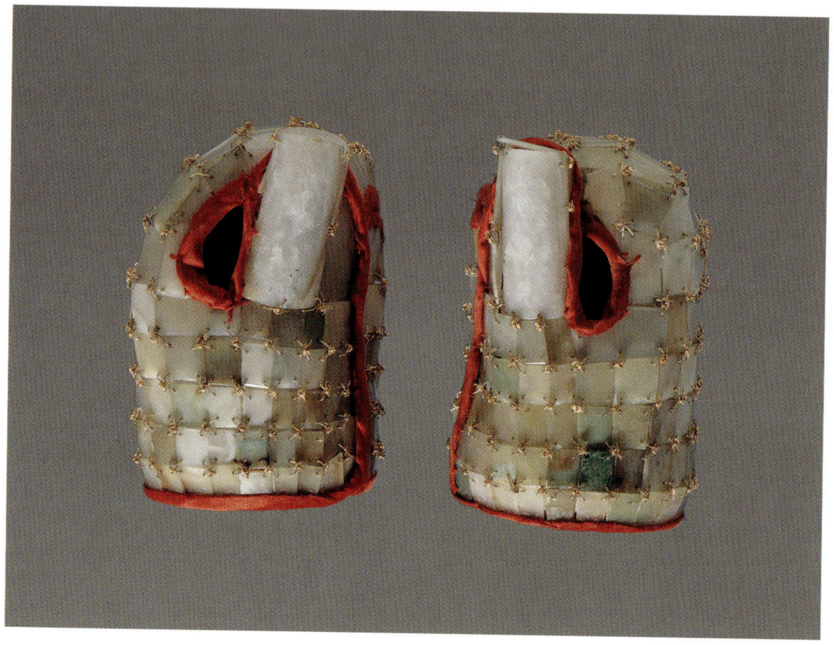

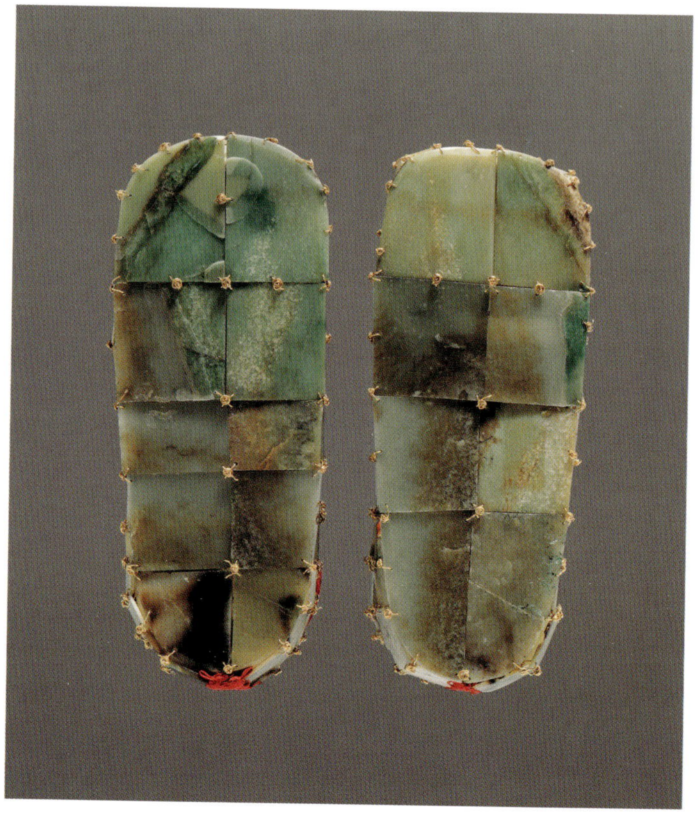

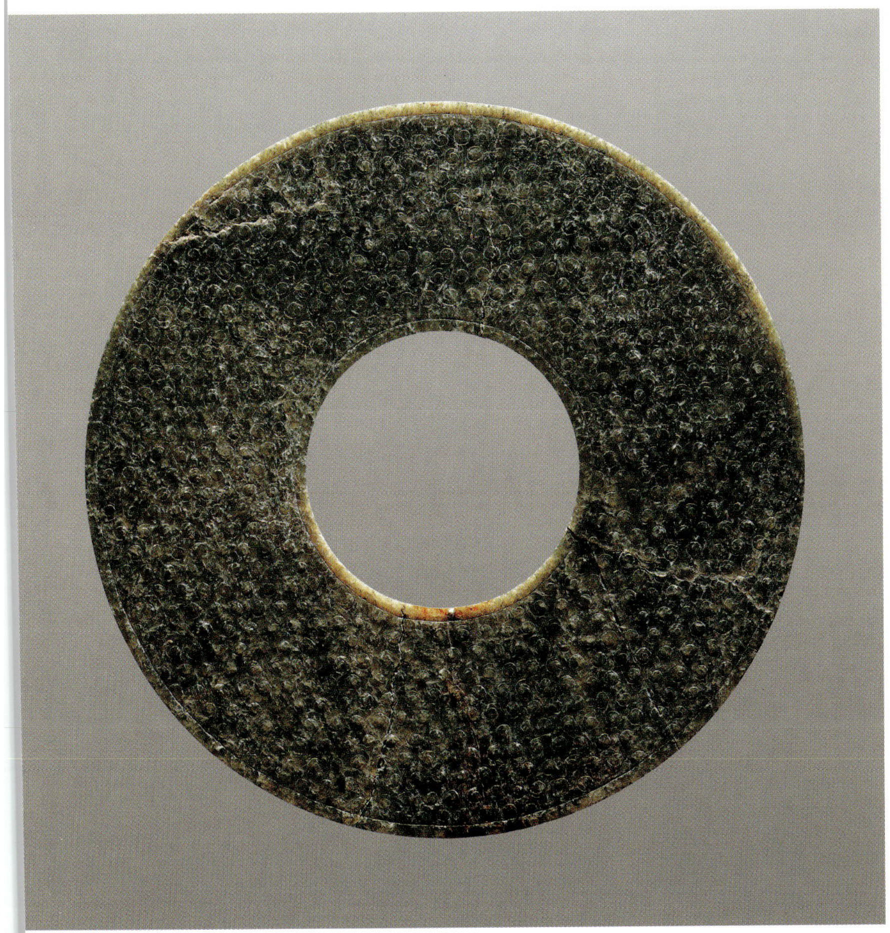

88

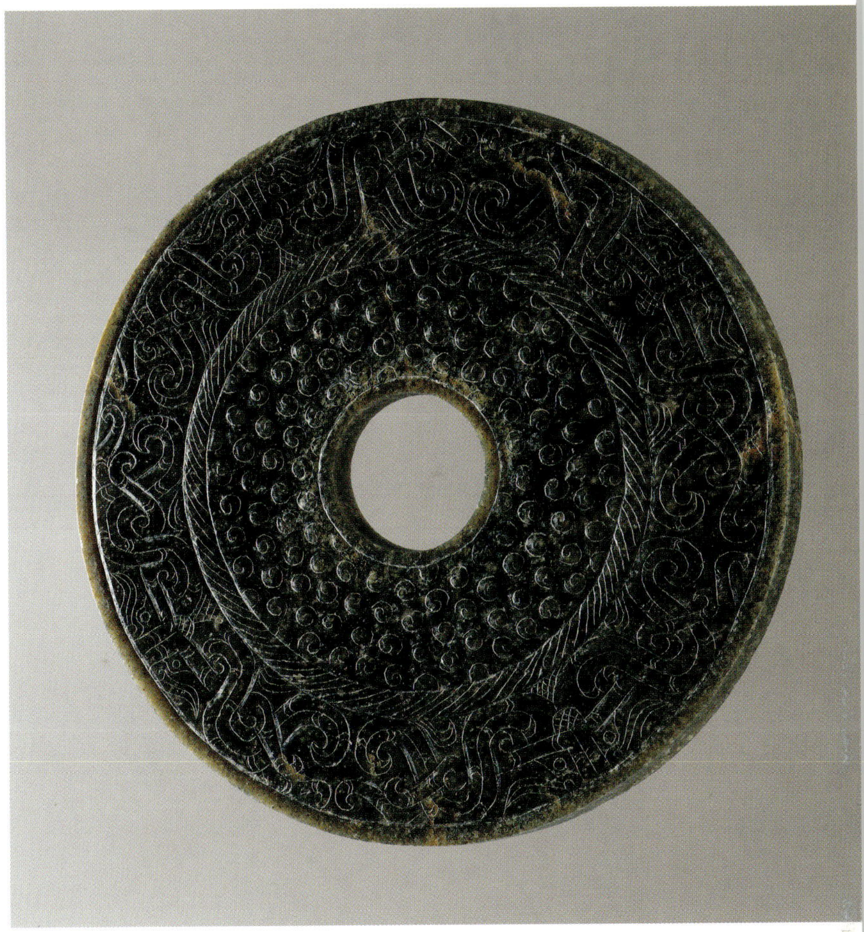

89

88

Jade disc incised with a spiral pattern

Second century BC, Western Han dynasty
Diameter: 25 cm
Excavated at Shizishan in 1994–5
Xuzhou Museum, Jiangsu Province
NOT EXHIBITED

This green jade disc incised with spirals on the surface was found broken into several pieces when excavated. As a result of extensive looting, its original location in the tomb is unknown. However, judging from other intact Han tombs, this type of green jade disc is usually found with aristocratic tomb occupants. JCSL

89

Jade disc with animal-face pattern

Second century BC, Western Han dynasty
Diameter: 22.5 cm
Excavated at Shizishan in 1994–5
Xuzhou Museum, Jiangsu Province

This green jade disc is decorated with four sets of animal heads surrounded by long intertwined scrolls in the outer section and with rows of spirals in relief in the inner section. This type of jade design was very popular from the fourth century BC in the eastern part of China through to the end of the Han dynasty. Such discs were found in large numbers in aristocrats' tombs, on top of and underneath their bodies. Some of the larger discs, such as those from the King of Nanyue's tomb (cat. 156B), have designs that incorporate three distinct sections. JCSL

90

Jade disc with raised spiral pattern

Second century BC, Western Han dynasty
Diameter: 14 cm
Excavated at Shizishan in 1994–5
Xuzhou Museum, Jiangsu Province

Twenty-four jade discs survived the looting at Shizishan, including seventeen of white jade made from stone originating in Khotan. Discs made of green jade are much more common in

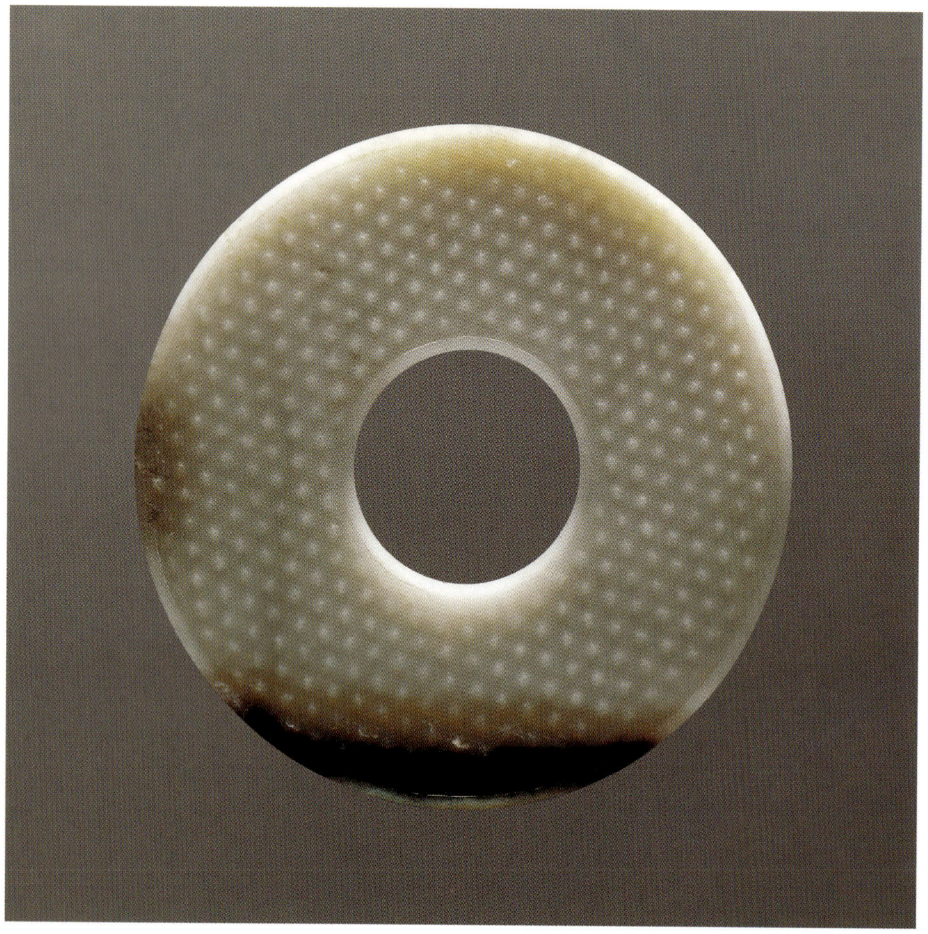

90

Han tombs. They were mainly found with the bodies of aristocrats and may have served a protective function. This particular disc has black areas along its rim and one side is decorated with neat raised spirals while the other is plain. It was probably placed on the body of the deceased rather than being used as a pendant. JCSL

91

Nine jade plugs

Second century BC, Western Han dynasty
Eye coverings: Length: 4.4 cm; Width: 2.3 cm; excavated at Tomb M24 at Wanzhai
Nose plugs: Length: 2.5 cm; excavated at Shizishan in 1994–5
Earplugs: Length: 1.4 cm; excavated at Shizishan in 1994–5
Cicada-shaped mouth amulet: Length: 4.8 cm; Width: 2.5 cm; excavated at Taojiashan
Jade anus plug: Length: 6.1 cm; excavated at Huoshan in 1996
Female genital cover: Length: 5 cm; Width: 2.9 cm; excavated at Hanshan in 1992
Xuzhou Museum, Jiangsu Province

The nine orifice plugs included two eye plates, two earplugs, two nose plugs, a mouth plug, an anal plug and a female genital cover. Archaeological evidence indicates that eye plates were usually almond-shaped and pierced at both ends so that they could be sewn onto a cloth or silk mask that was placed over the face of the deceased. The ear, nose and anal plugs were hexagonal or cylindrical in shape and tapered slightly to a rounded end. A plug was also placed in the mouth of the deceased. In the examples of Liu Sheng and Dou Wan, a crescent-shaped jade was put inside the mouth. The mouth plug later took the form of a jade cicada.

A jade *cong* (in the shape of a square pillar with a cylindrical hole through the centre) from the Liangzhu period was reused as a genital box, which forms part of Liu Sheng's jade suit. Most male genital boxes were composed of small jade plaques joined to form a container. Female genital covers are very rare; the one excavated from Hanshan has a hole in the middle.

The number of jade orifice plugs does not seem related to the status of the tomb occupant. For example, only seven orifice plugs were found in Liu He's tomb (dating to 179–141 BC), and he was buried with a jade suit. The M3 tomb of a low-ranking aristocrat at Zifangshan, Xuzhou dates from the very early Western Han, but contained a jade veil and eight jade plugs.

The term *jiu qiao* (nine orifices) was mentioned as early as the two chapters *shiwen* or ('Ten questions') and *Tianxia zhidao tan* ('Conversations on the loftiest ways under heaven') found on the bamboo-slip texts excavated from the M3 tomb at Mawangdui, dating from the second century BC.[1] In these texts *jiu qiao* were related to *qi* or 'vital essence'.[2] It has been suggested that the purpose of inserting the jade plugs into the orifices of the body was to prevent the 'escape' of vital essence.[3] An alternative view of their function is to prevent evil spirits or ghosts taking up residence in the body and wreaking havoc therein.[4] It is possible that Ge Hong had this in mind when he stated in *Baopuzi* (c.AD 320): 'When gold and jade are inserted into the nine orifices, corpses do not decay.'[5] JCSL

FACING PAGE: 91

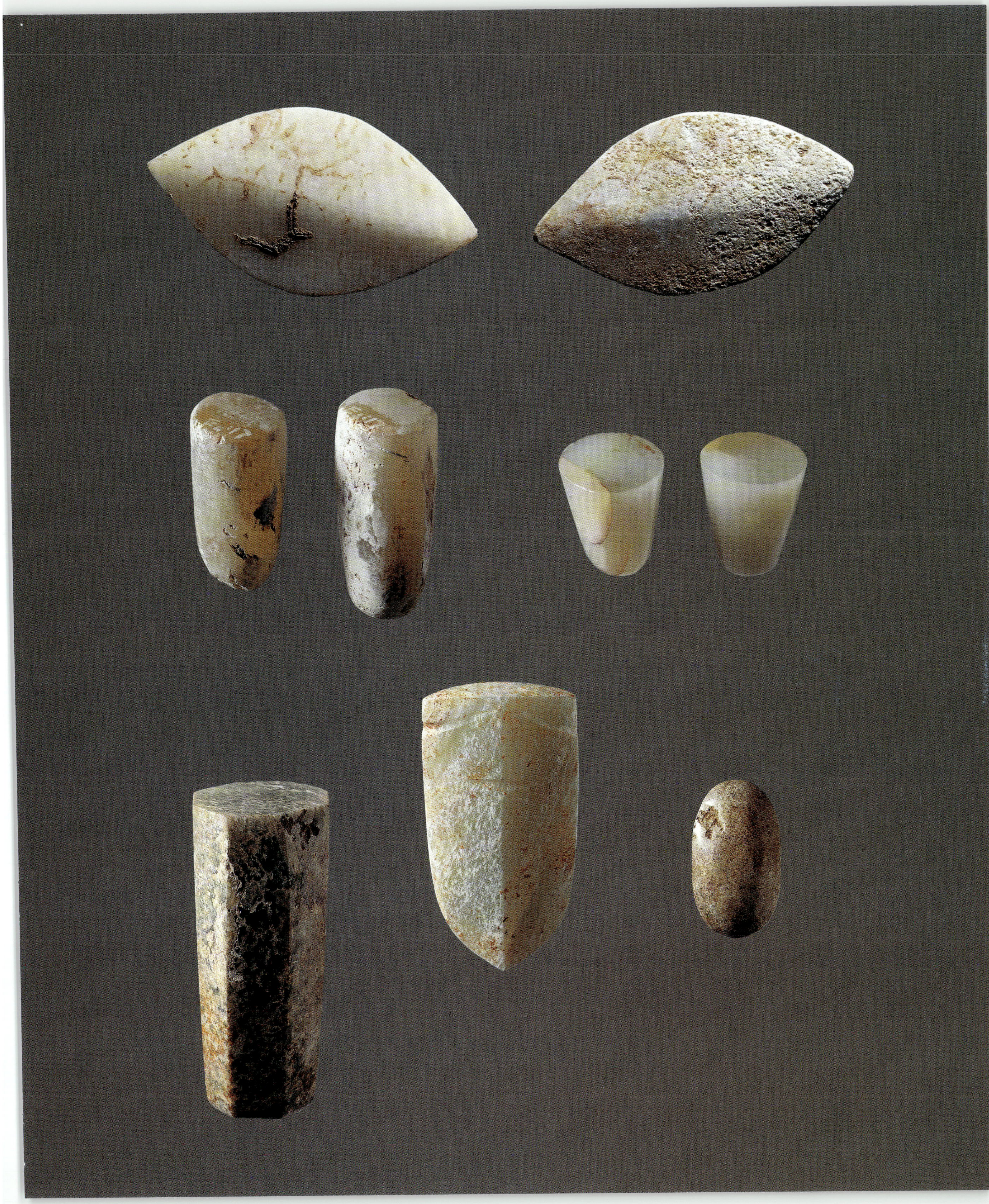

1 The bamboo-slip texts *shiwen* and *Tianxia zhidao tan* from Mawangdui M3 provide theoretical and practical knowledge concerning macrobiotic hygiene in the form of interviews in which noble patrons seek instruction from esoteric masters. The 101 bamboo slips of *shiwen* are approximately 23 cm long and 0.8 cm wide. They contain ten dialogues in which ten macrobiotic specialists respond to questions. The teachings include instructions for executing cultivation techniques, often describing the process in esoteric and metaphoric language. The fifty-six bamboo slips of *Tianxia zhidao tan* are approximately 28 cm long and 0.5 cm wide. The text is primarily concerned with sexual intercourse. See Hebei 1994; Harper 1999, pp. 813–84.

2 The text *shiwen* records that 'He who is skilled at cultivating vapour lets the old vapour disperse at night and the new vapour gather at dawn, thereby penetrating the nine orifices (*jiu qiao) and* filling the six cavities'. Hebei 1994, vol. 1, p. 17; tr Harper 1999.

3 Xia Nai was the first scholar who suggested that the nine orifice plugs were designed to prevent the escape of vital essences; Xia Nai 1983, p. 31. The notion of vital essence, *qi*, was combined with that of *yin* and *yang* (the positive and negative forces) and accounted for all phenomena in the universe. It was widely discussed in Han texts; see Graham 1989, part IV; Harper 1999, pp. 813–84.

4 This was suggested by Yates 1994, p.73.

5 Ge Hong's comment may be the earliest explicit literary statement of this belief, but the evidence from Han archaeology substantiates such concepts and dates to several centuries earlier. It seems possible that he was recording an ancient tradition; *Baopuzi*, p. 45.

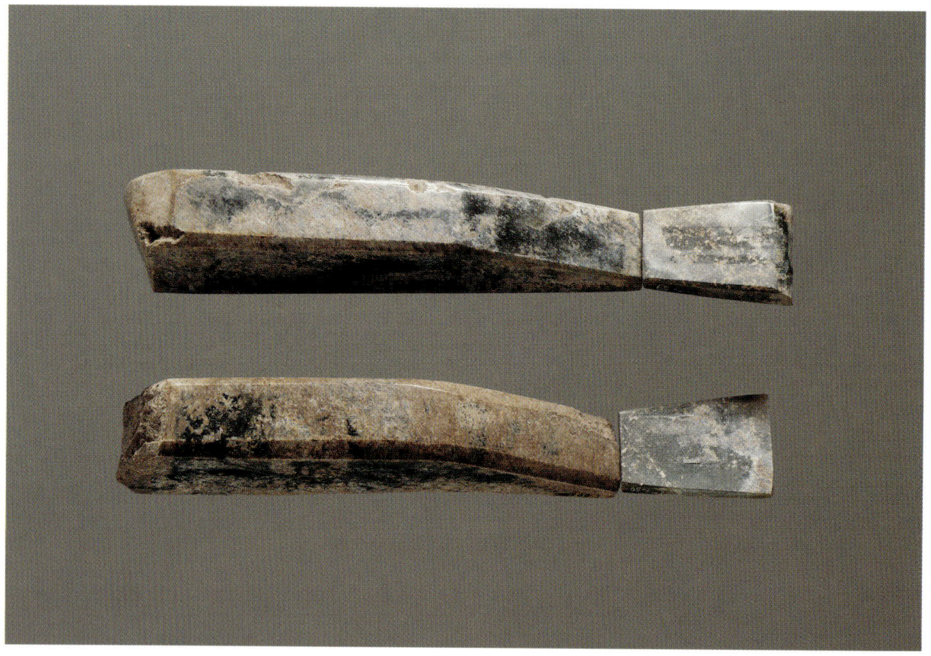

92

92

Jade hand grips from Hanshan

Second century BC, Western Han dynasty
Length: 12 cm; Width: 2.9 cm; Height: 4.4 cm
Excavated at Hanshan in 1992
Xuzhou Museum, Jiangsu Province

Hand grips or *wo* refer to the objects placed in the hands of the deceased. This was a common burial custom dating from the early Western Zhou period (*c.*eleventh century BC) down to the Han. There is no clear division between genders, classes or regions of the objects held in hands. Hand grips made of jade were the most common, although silk ones have also been found in some areas.

Examples from intact tombs dating to the early Western Han period include a pair of jade *huang*, arc-shaped pendants, placed in Liu Sheng's hands at Mancheng, Hebei; a pair of silk aromatic bags placed in the hands of Lady Dai at Mawangdui, Changsha, Hunan; and two *xi* (pointed jade pendants) with different designs found in the right hand of the King of Nanyue at Xianggangshan, Guangzhou (cat. 154).

This pair of jade hand grips from Hanshan, Xuzhou is composed of two sections. The main section is a dark green jade with calcification, carved in the form of a highly stylized pig with a smaller light green trapezoid jade section attached. Both sections have small holes that were connected together, probably with small wooden pegs. In the late Western Han period, jade pigs became the prevalent form for hand grips in most areas and their design became less stylized and more realistic. JCSL

93

Jade pillow

Second century BC, Western Han dynasty
Length: 35 cm; Width: 7.8 cm; Height: 9.5 cm
Excavated at Shizishan in 1994–5
Xuzhou Museum, Jiangsu Province

This pillow belonged to the Inspector of Food Officer of the King of Chu who was buried in the tomb passage at Shizishan. It consists of three sections: two supporting feet, two ornamental ends and a main panel. The main panel was made of wood and inlaid with thirty-five jade plaques in different shapes, either re-cut or reused from earlier pieces. Two ornamental ends were carved with lions' faces with mortises that inserted into the main wood panel. The two supporting feet were carved from a piece of greenish jade with a mortise and tenon arrangement inserted into the main wooden panel to ensure the pillow was secure.

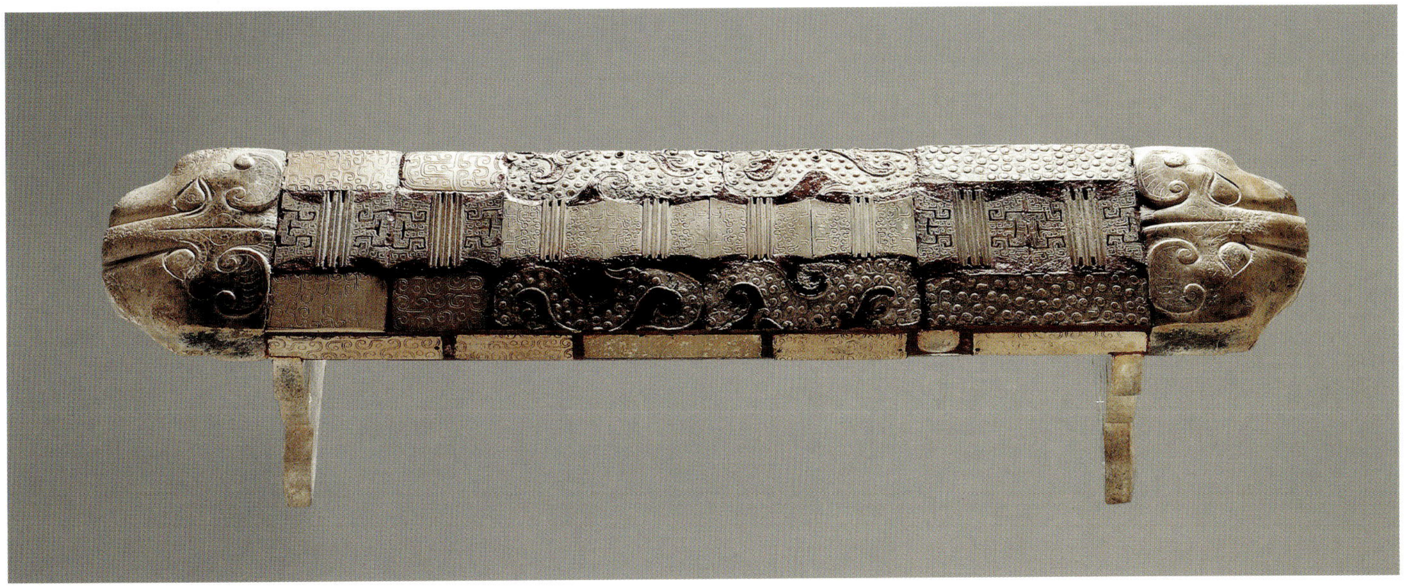

93

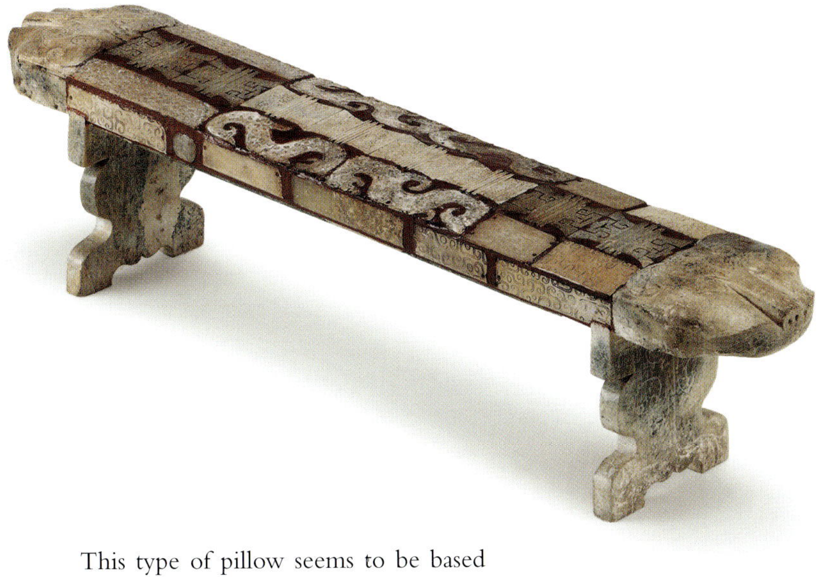

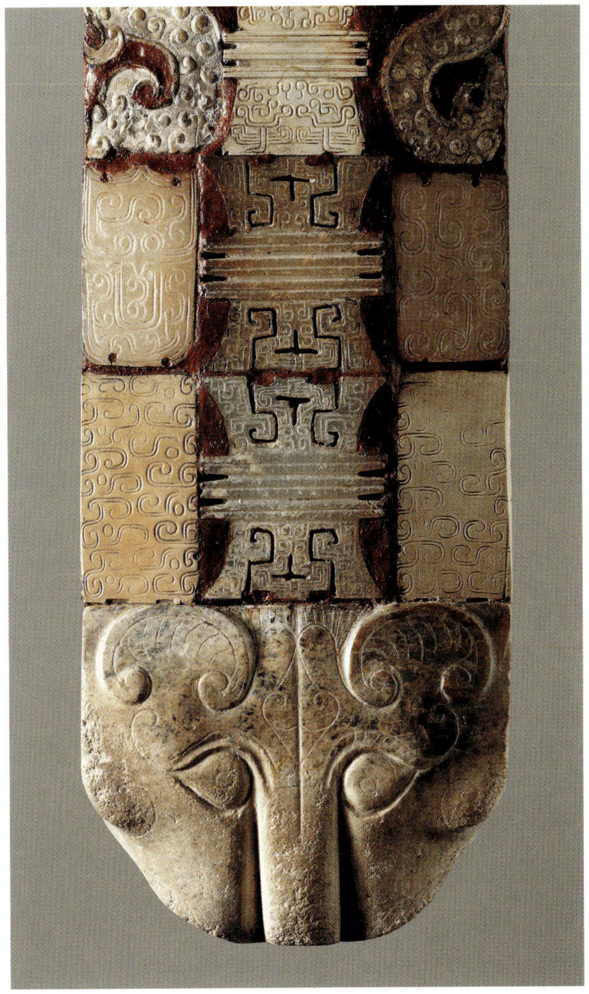

This type of pillow seems to be based on an established form, as a similar one, belonging to the King of Jibei, was found in Shandong Province (fig. 35).[1] Jade pillows usually appear with higher-ranking individuals buried with jade suits or veils. The quality of the jade used in the pillows reflected the owner's social status. JCSL

1 *Kaogu* 1997.3, pp. 1–9; *Gugong wenwu yuekan* (172) 1997.7, pp. 92–121; Tang 1998, vol. III, pl. 448.

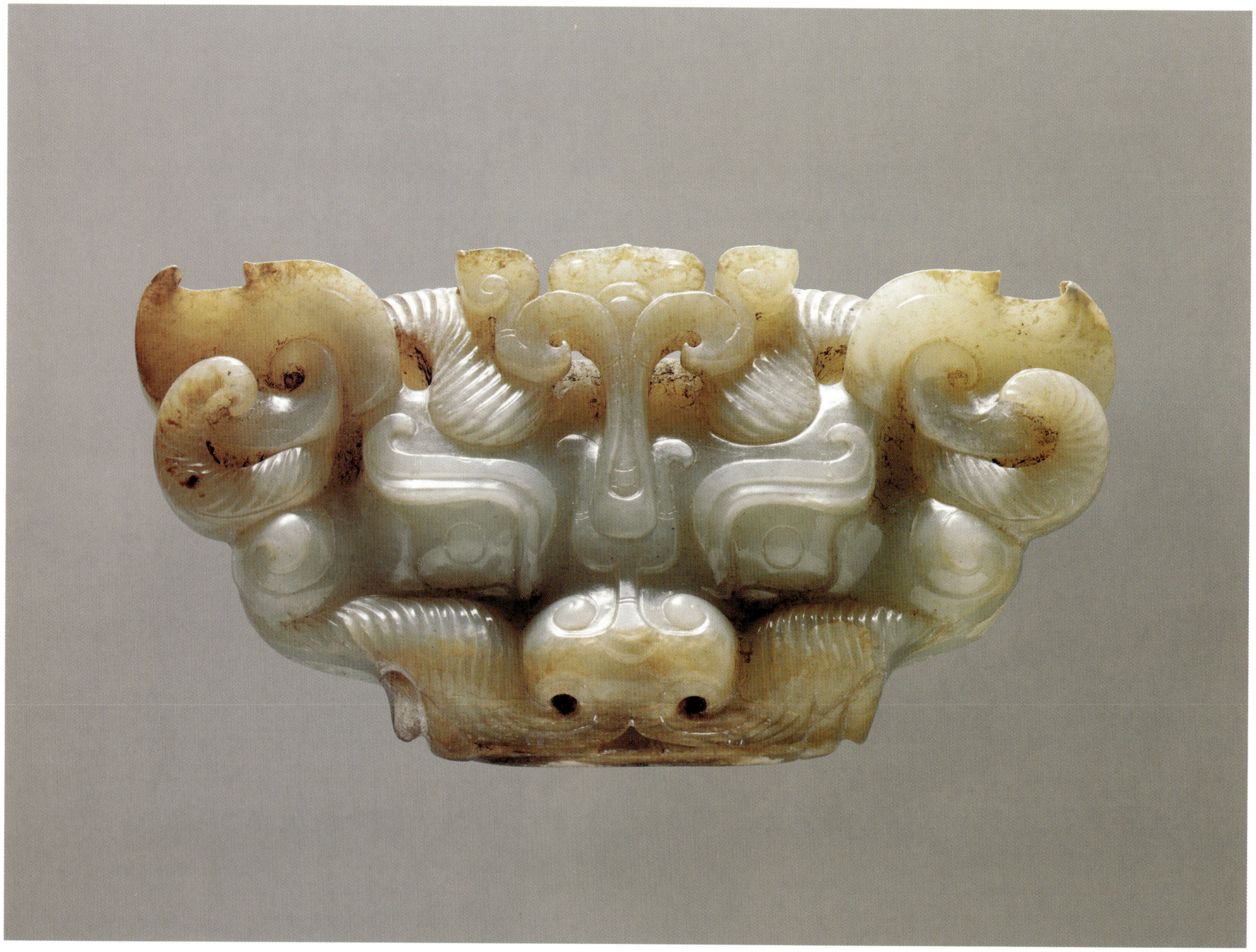

94

94

Jade ornament for a pillow

Second century BC, Western Han dynasty
Width: 5.4–11.5 cm; Height: 5.8 cm
Excavated at Shizishan in 1994–5
Xuzhou Museum, Jiangsu Province

This jade ornament was used as an end piece for a pillow that belonged to the King of Chu. The design is of a lion or monster face with two curly horns issuing from behind the ears, two large eyes with striking pupils, a prominent nose with two large nostrils and powerful jaw muscles. It was carved in high relief and openwork style from a greenish-white jade stone imported from Khotan. This piece is greatly superior to the jade pillow belonging to the king's Inspector of Food Officer (cat. 93), showing more complex carving skills and using a higher-quality jade. JCSL

95

Jade pillow

Second century BC, Western Han dynasty
Length: 28 cm; Width: 9.5 cm; Height: 8.5 cm
Excavated at Huoshan in 1996
Xuzhou Museum, Jiangsu Province
NOT EXHIBITED

This rectangular pillow has four rectangular panels each composed of a large jade plaque at the centre with five much smaller triangular jade plaques at each end. The edges of these smaller plaques are covered with gold foil at the joins. The large plaques on both the front and back panels of the pillow were covered with gold foil to create a rhombus pattern. Both ends of the pillow are square panels composed of two or three jade plaques, with gilt bronze rings. Pillows in the Xuzhou area were usually decorated with gold foil, although the designs varied slightly. This pillow belonged to Liu He, who was buried with a silver-thread jade suit in a catacomb tomb at Huoshan. His name is not recorded in any text, but judging from the jade suit and pillow he must have had a close relationship with the King of Chu. JCSL

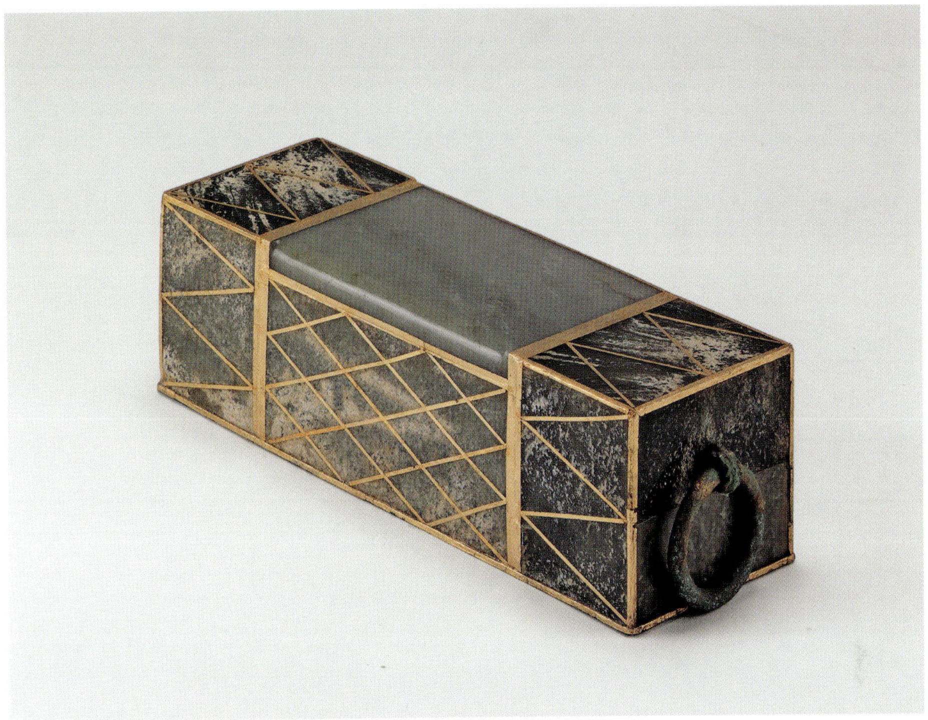

96

Gilt bronze pillow

Second century BC, Western Han dynasty
Length: 37.1 cm; Width: 16 cm; Height: 11.4 cm
Excavated at tomb M1 at Houloushan in 1991
Xuzhou Museum, Jiangsu Province

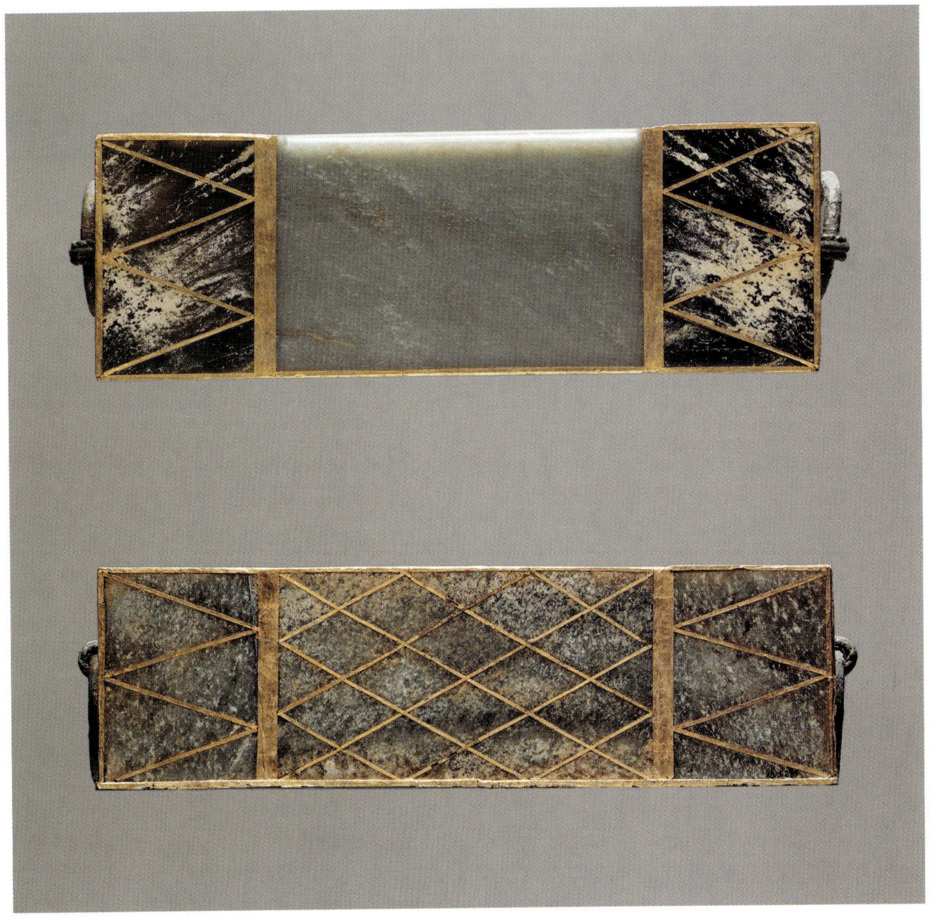

95

This rectangular pillow is composed of two parts: a wooden body inlaid with jade plaques and a gilt bronze frame. The frame has a design of four dragons whose tails and bodies intertwine to form the base of the pillow (D). By the time the piece was excavated, the original wooden body had completely decayed.

The top of the pillow was inlaid with two jade dragon plaques set into undecorated jade to make a uniform surface. The dragons were incised with spirals and were very likely reused from old Warring States pieces (C). The ends of the pillow were decorated with jade discs with ornamental bronze door-knockers at the centre (E). The back of the pillow was inlaid with eight jade plaques including a centrepiece re-carved from a dragon pendant with the original

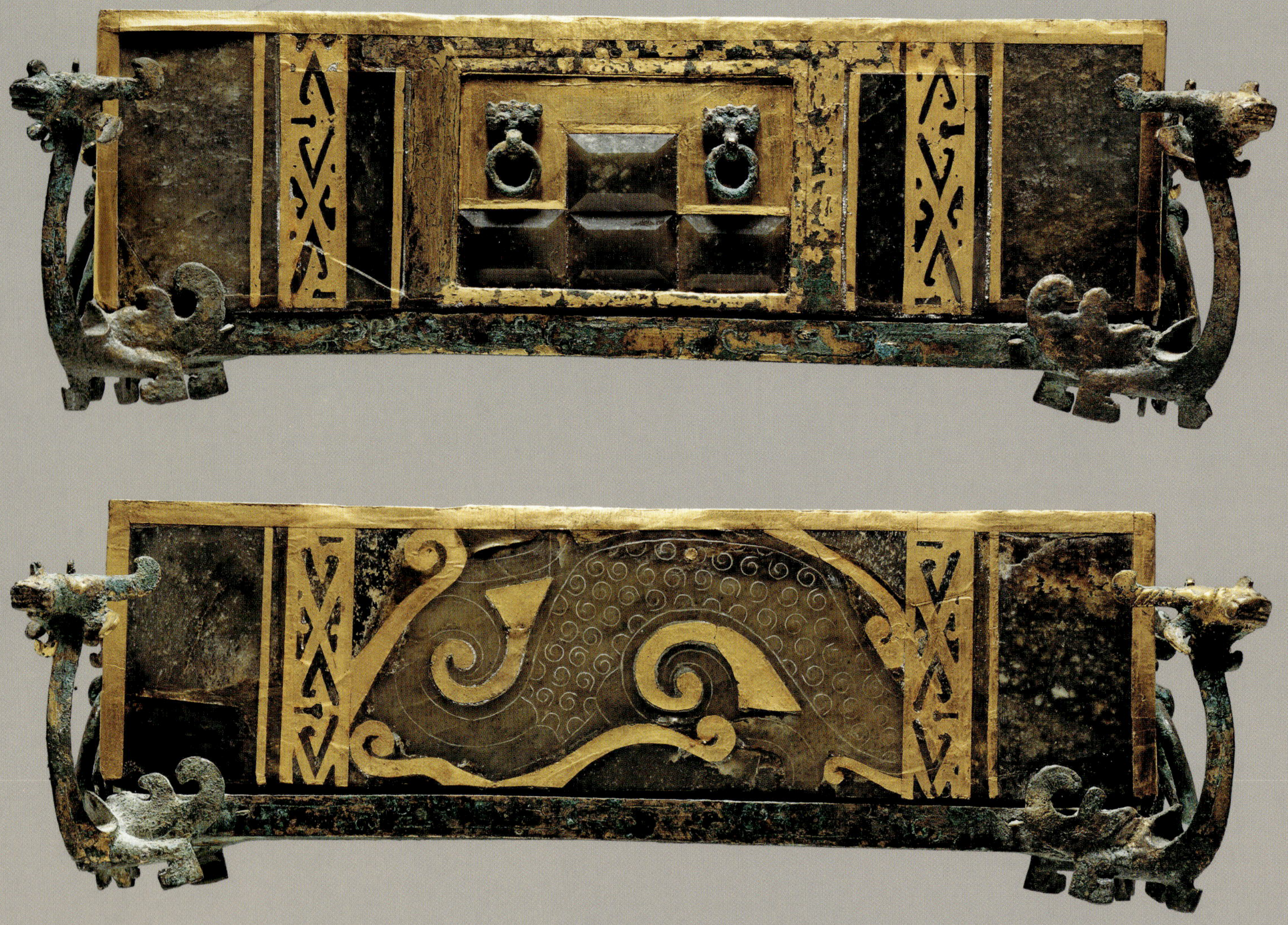

96

drilled hole still visible in the middle at the top (B). The front of the pillow was inlaid with a bronze frame, inserted into which were four jade plaques and two ornamental bronze door-knockers to represent doors (A). It has been suggested by some scholars that it was designed as a gateway for the soul of the deceased. The edges and the main decorated areas were covered with gold foil.

This pillow is probably the most complicated one in terms of design found to date. Together with a jade veil (fig. 31), it was excavated from a vertical catacomb tomb, a satellite grave near the

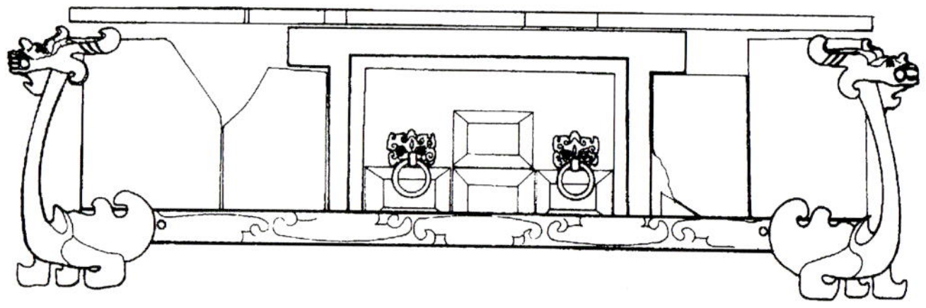

A

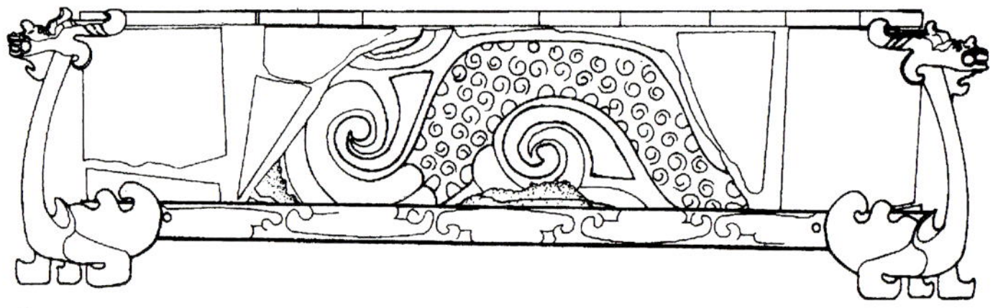

B

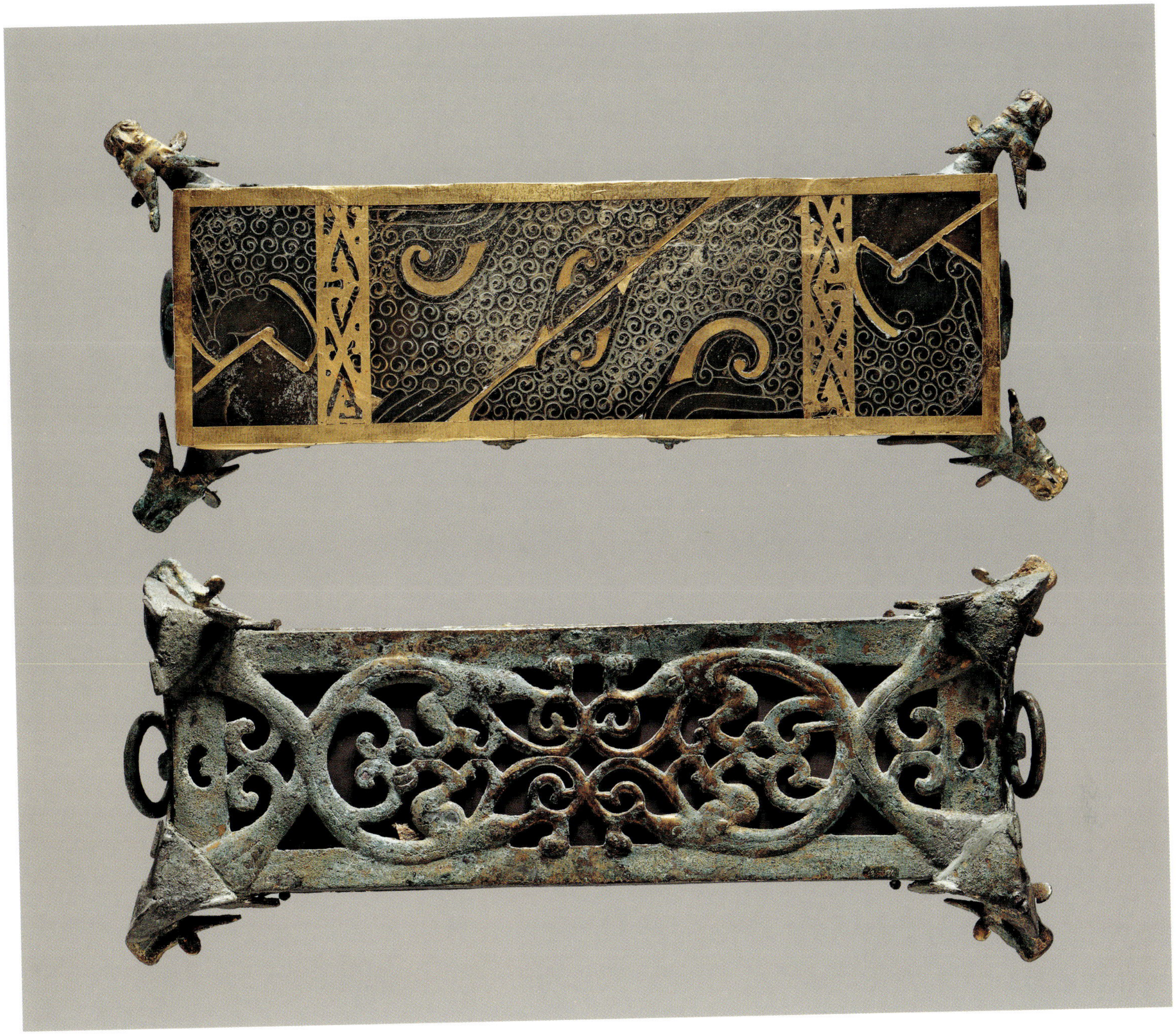

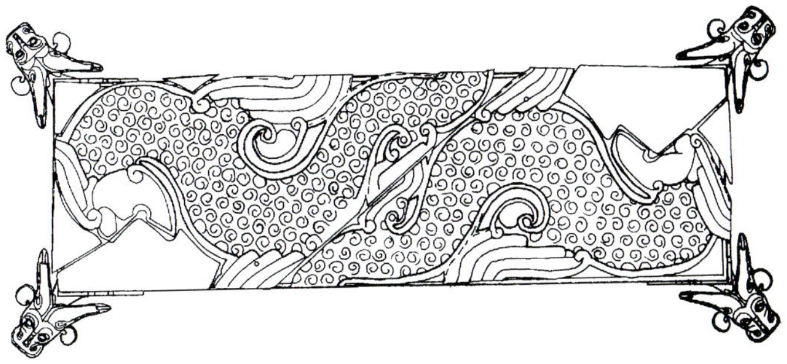
C

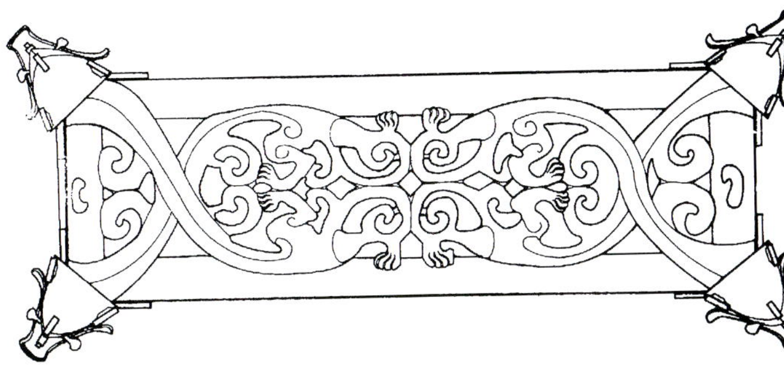
D

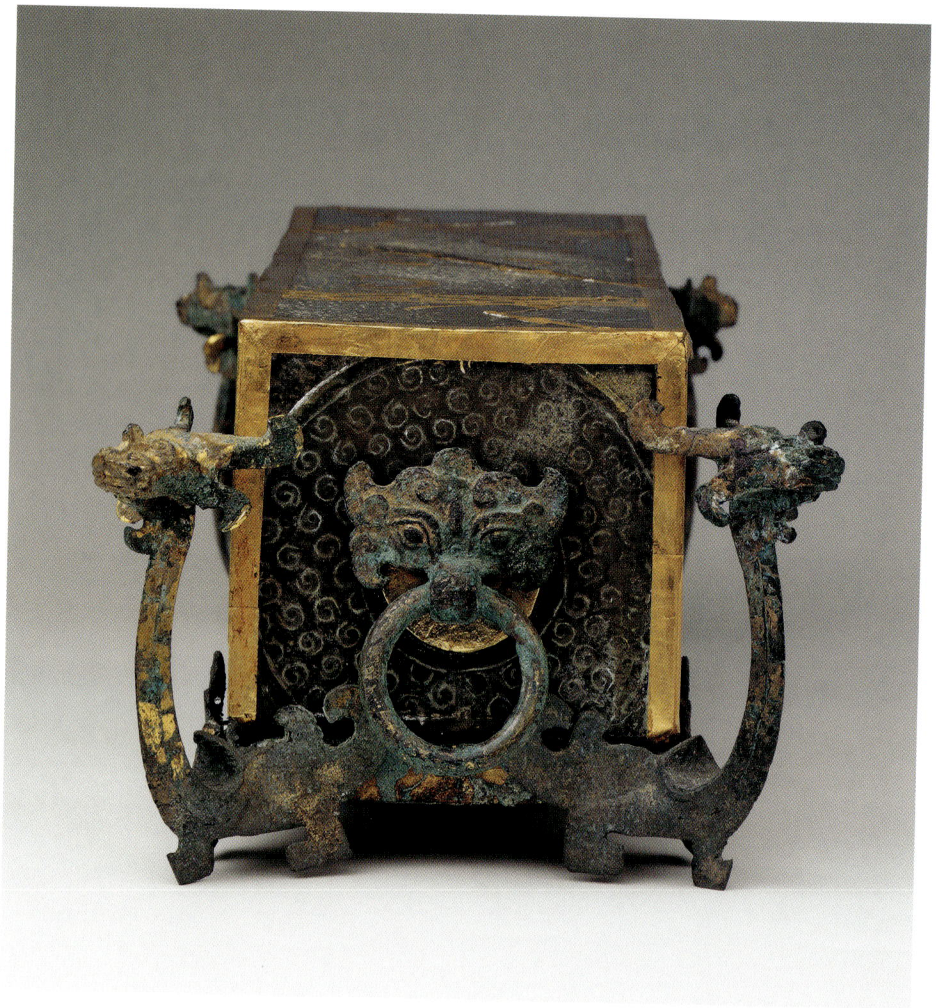

King of Chu's tomb at Beidongshan. The occupant's status is thought to be either that of a relative of the King of Chu or an important vassal of the Chu kingdom.[1] JCSL

1 *Wenwu* 1993.4, pp. 29–49.

97

Jade pillow

Second century BC, Western Han dynasty
Length: 23 cm; Width: 6 cm; Height: 5.6 cm
Excavated at tomb M3 at Zifangshan in 1984
Xuzhou Museum, Jiangsu Province

This jade pillow, together with a jade veil (cat. 85) belonged to a low-ranking noble. The tomb at Zifangshan has been dated to the very early Western Han. Eight jade plugs were also found in the tomb. The design of the pillow is rather simple – a rectangular jade centrepiece with thick gold foil at the edges. JCSL

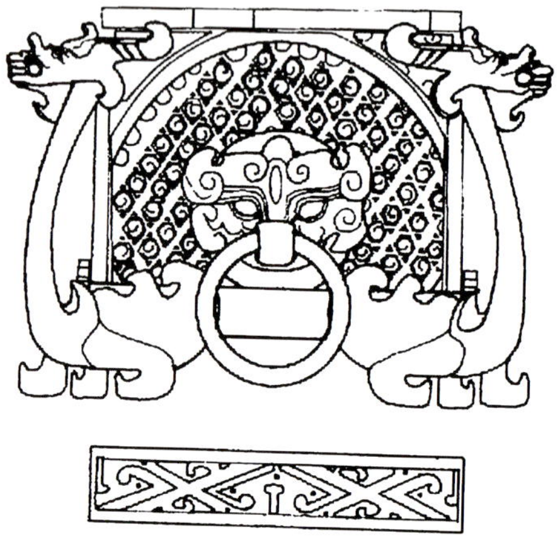

E

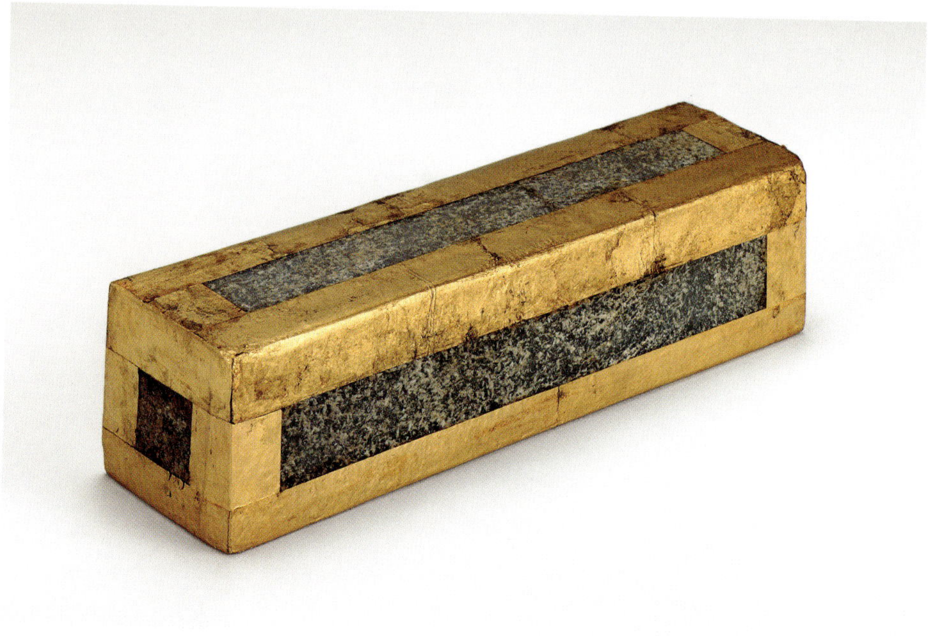

97

98

Jade coffin

Second century BC, Western Han dynasty
Length: 280 cm; Width: 110 cm; Height: 108 cm
Excavated at Shizishan in 1994–5
Xuzhou Museum, Jiangsu Province

This coffin has been reconstructed. During the course of serious looting, a total of 1,781 jade plaques were scattered along the tomb passages, in the fifth eastern chamber and in the fifth western chamber. The plaques were carved into a variety of shapes (triangular, square, rectangular, rhomboid and arching). The majority have inscriptions on the back, which indicate their size and their position on the coffin. These jade plaques were meant to encase a lacquer coffin.

On each side of the coffin are five large rectangular jade plaques that were decorated with a jade disc design. Two large uncovered lacquer spaces on the sides of the coffin may symbolize doors, allowing the spirit of the deceased to get in and out. This is like an outer coffin found in the tomb of Marquis Yi of Zeng (fig. 46).

A total of 2,095 jade plaques were removed to reconstruct this coffin (fig. 57), and it is the largest jade coffin found to date. Originally it would have contained an inner coffin. Gold, jade and turquoise nails were inserted into the coffin, but only a few survived intact.

Lacquer coffins inlaid with jade discs have also been found in the tombs of the kings and queens of the Guangling kingdom at Gaoyou, Jiangsu Province and of the King of Chu at Beidongshan, Xuzhou. The inner coffin of the consort of the first King of Zhongshan at Mancheng, Hebei Province was inlaid with 192 jade tiles on the inside and 26 jade discs on the outside. Imperial family members buried in a jade suit were not necessarily buried in a jade coffin, but those buried in a jade coffin always had a jade suit. This implies that those buried in jade coffins had higher status, regardless of gender. JCSL

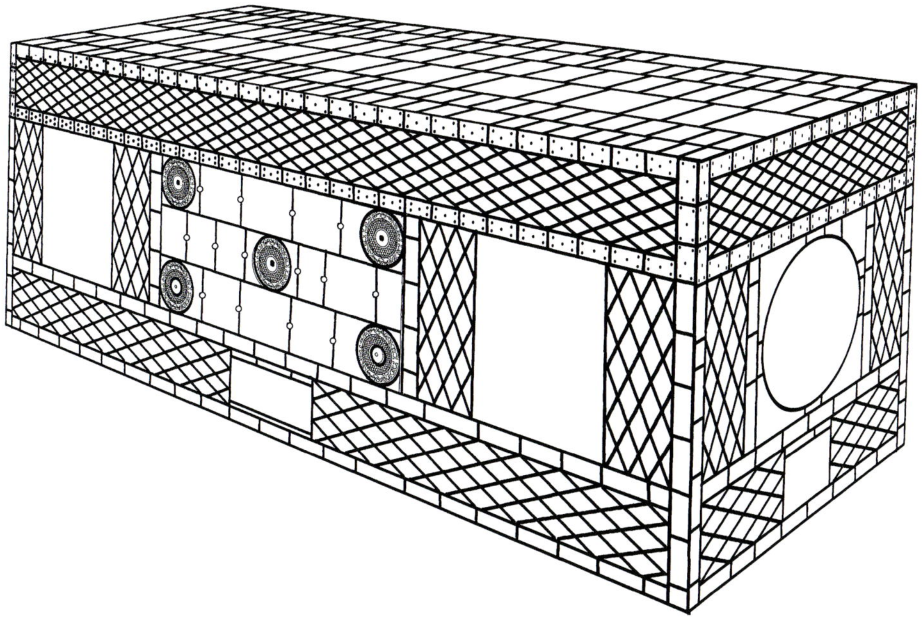

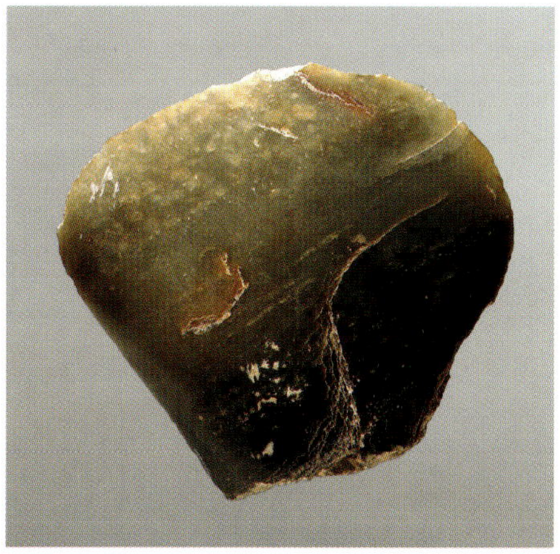

99

99

Jade waste

Second century BC, Western Han dynasty
Length: 13.5 cm; Width: 15 cm
Excavated at Baiyunshan
Xuzhou Museum, Jiangsu Province

Because of its value and rarity, jade carvers always made the best use they could of any available material. Drill waste was not discarded, but used to make small ornaments such as beads. It is very common to see earlier jades rediscovered and reused at a later period. This piece of jade waste was excavated at Baiyunshan from a tomb belonging to an official in charge of jade carving at the imperial workshop.

Jade waste has been found in two other burials. In the tomb of a noblewoman from the Spring and Autumn period (770–476 BC), broken fragments of jade and jade waste were placed in a wooden box and buried with the owner.[1] And in the tomb of the Marquis Yi of Zeng in Sui county, Hubei, dating to 433 BC, jade waste was scattered around the body.[2] JCSL

1 *Wenwu* 2008.1, p. 20.
2 Beijing 1989, pp. 429–30.

FOLLOWING SPREAD: 98

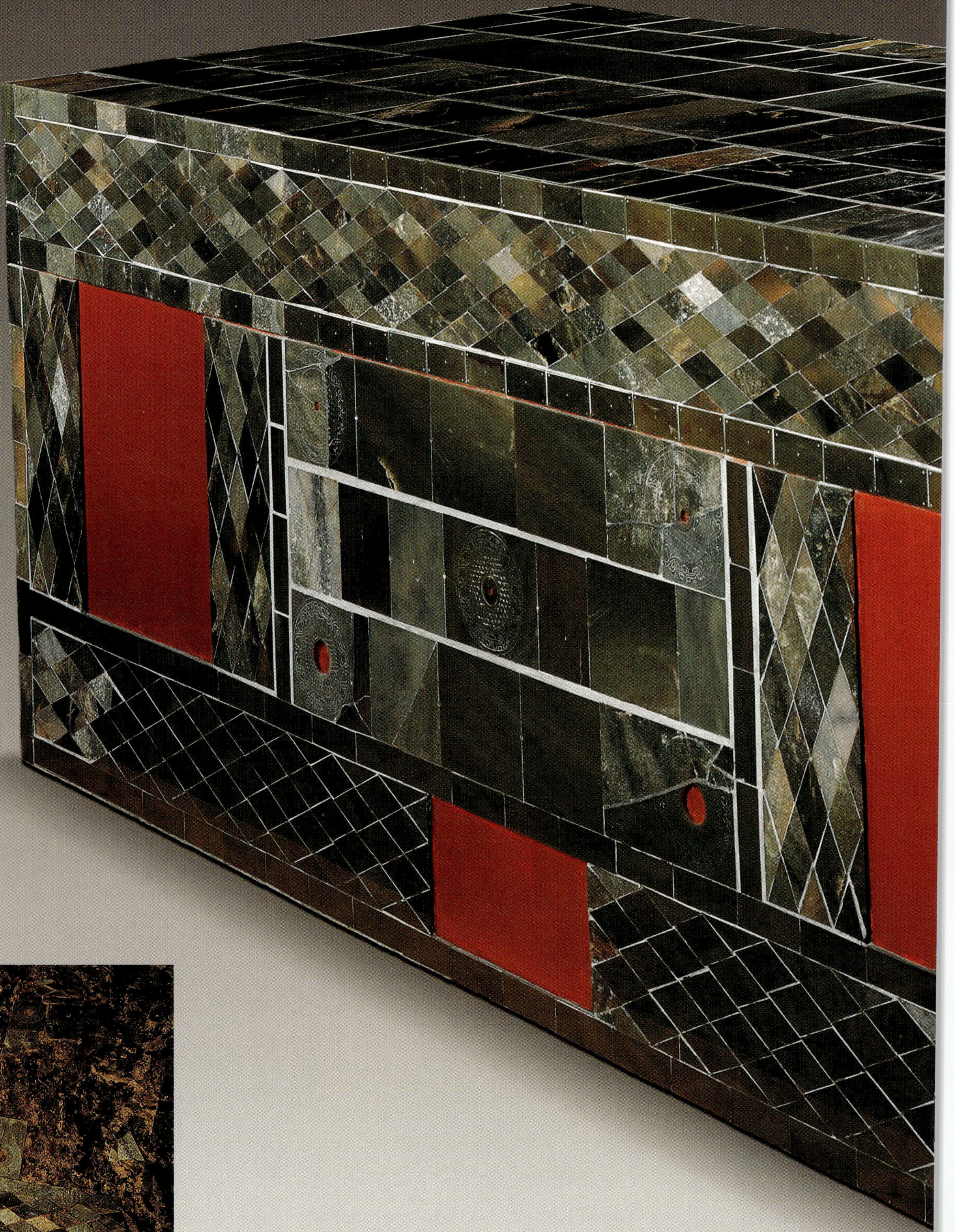

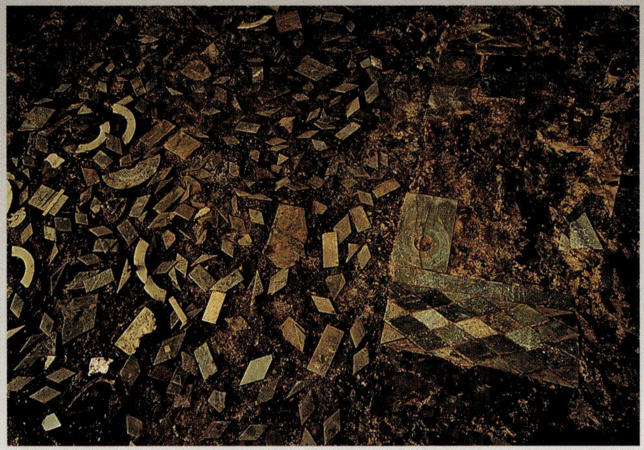

57 The scattered jade plaques of the coffin found during the excavation at Shizishan, Xuzhou. Second century BC.

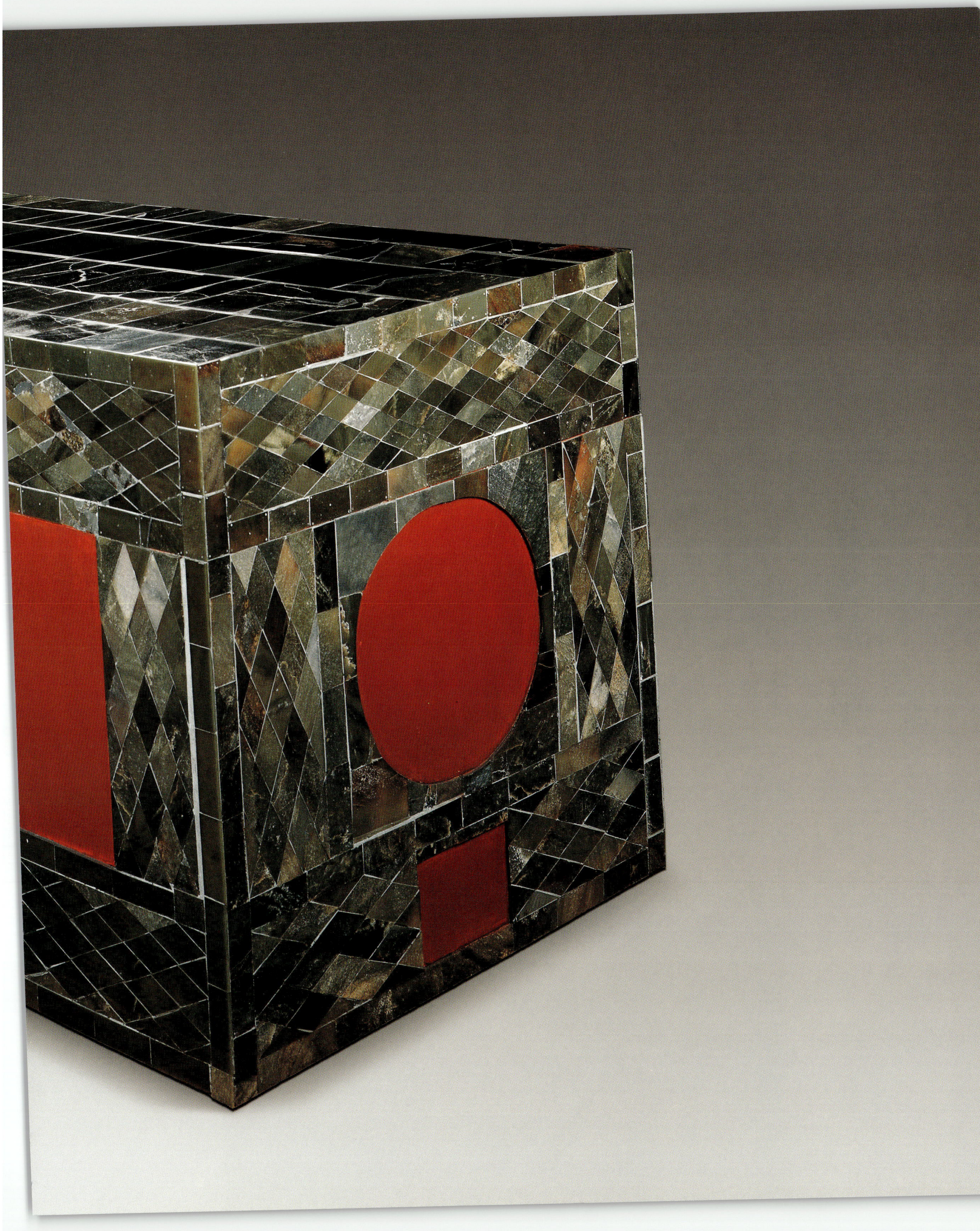

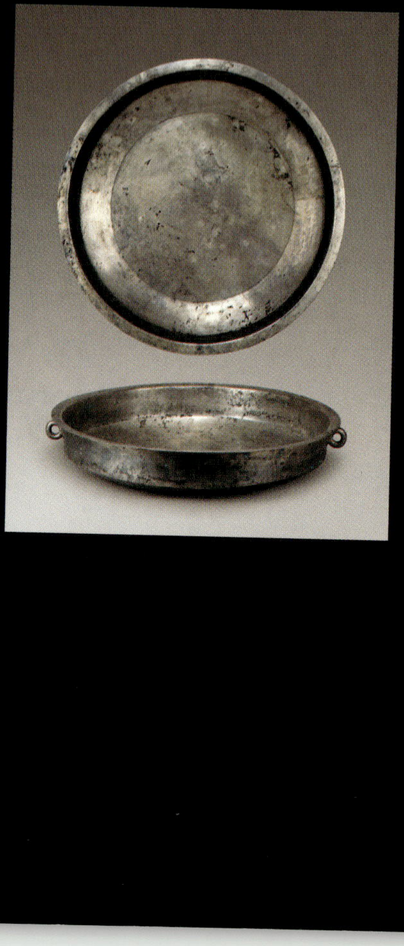
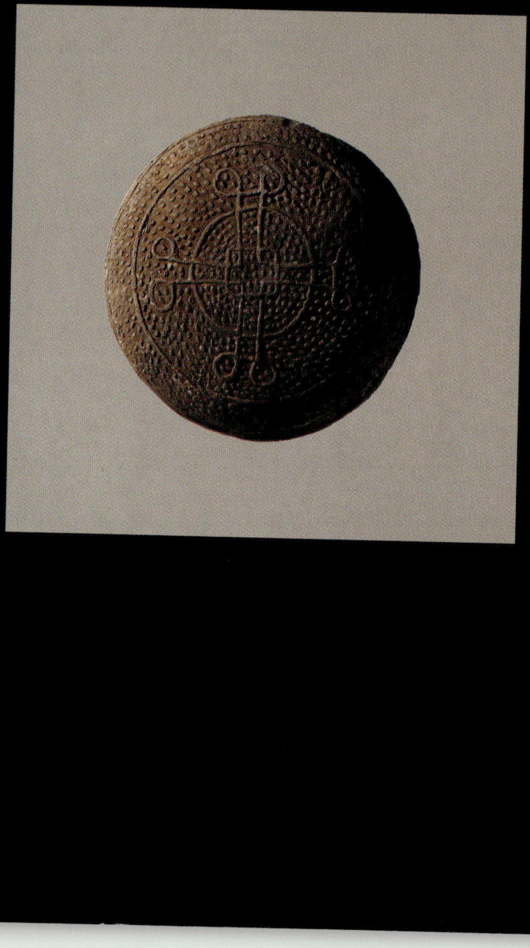
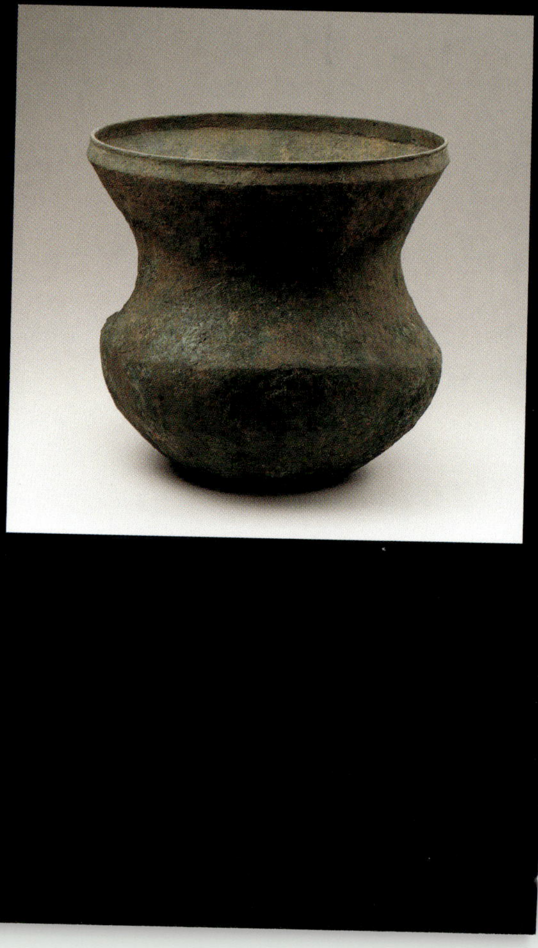

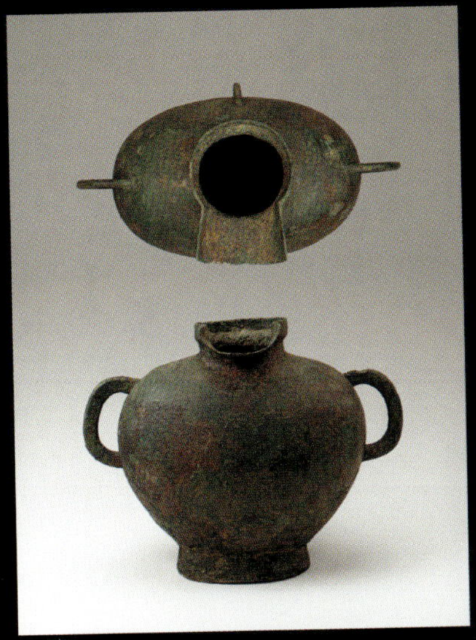
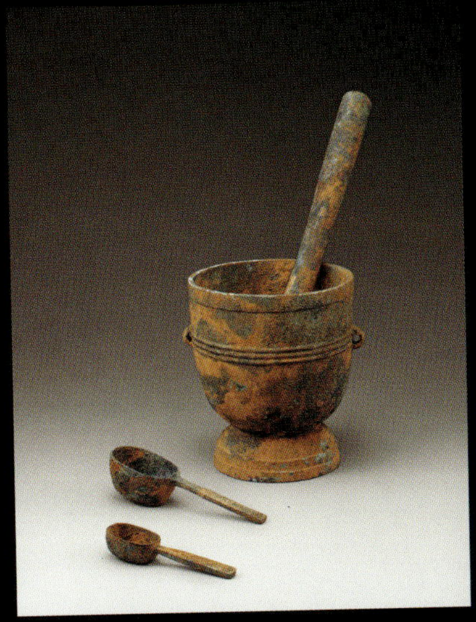
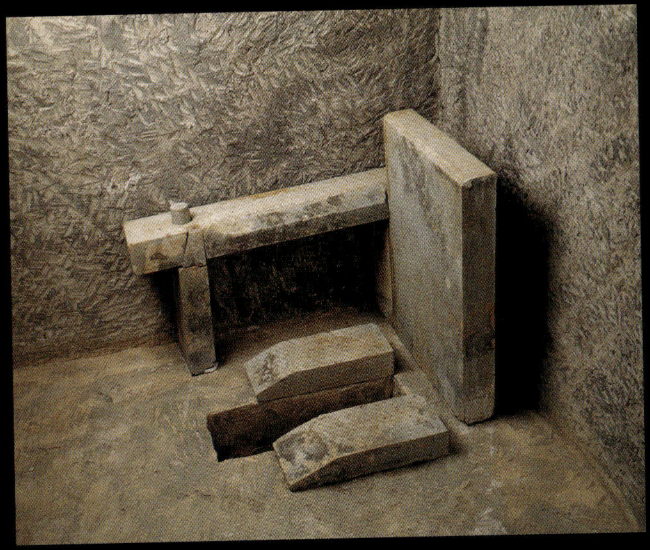

BATH AND TOILET

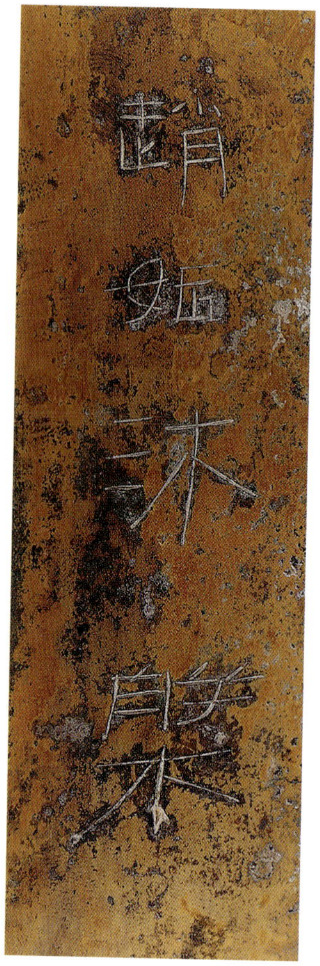

100

Gilt bronze basin (*pan*)

First century BC, Western Han dynasty
Height: 15.6 cm; Diameter: 68.5 cm
Excavated at tomb M2 at Dongdongshan in 1982
Xuzhou Museum, Jiangsu Province

This gilt bronze basin was excavated from the M2 tomb at Dongdongshan and belonged to the Queen of Chu. The basin is shallow with a sloped base, a thin body and little decoration. Four characters, *Zhao Ji Mu Pan* (Concubine Zhao's basin) are incised on the side of the basin. The *Shuowen jiezi* dictionary (compiled in the Eastern Han AD 25–220) includes terms for the cleaning of different parts of the body, for example *mu* for washing hair and *yu* for washing the body.[1] It is possible that the basin belonged to Queen Zhao prior to her elevation to the rank of queen. JCSL

1 *Shuowen jiezi*, pp. 563–4.

101

Silver basin (*jian*)

Second century BC, Western Han dynasty
Height: 11.4 cm; Diameter: 74.7 cm
Excavated at Shizishan in 1994–5
Xuzhou Museum, Jiangsu Province
NOT EXHIBITED

This silver basin, known as a *jian*, was found in the second western chamber together with other washing utensils. Twenty-five characters are incised on the side, recording its capacity, weight and function. The *Shuowen jiezi* dictionary describes a *jian* as a large water basin.[1] Before bronze mirrors were in widespread use, *jian* were used to reflect the image. *Jian* were also used to store ice to cool food. Judging from its location in the tomb this silver basin was clearly used for bathing. However, the inscription incised on it also includes the word *mu* (cat. 100), so it is likely that this silver basin was also used for washing hair. JCSL

1 *Shuowen jiezi*, p. 703.

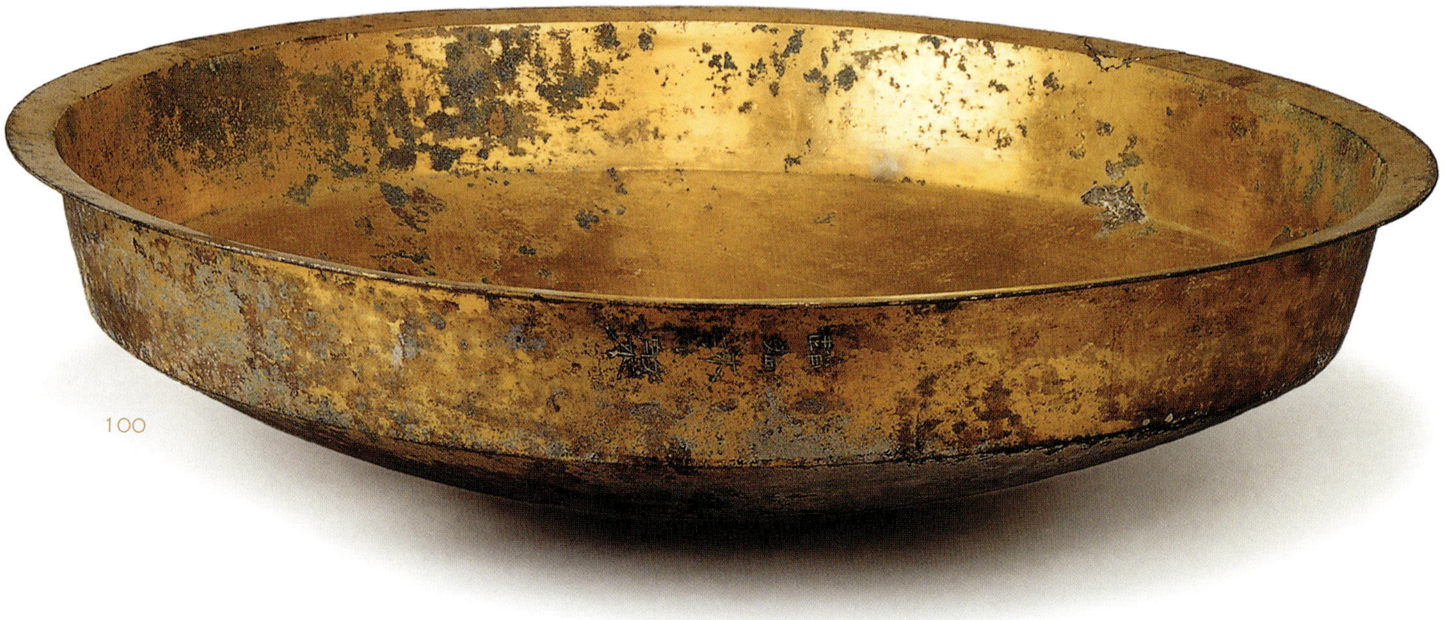

100

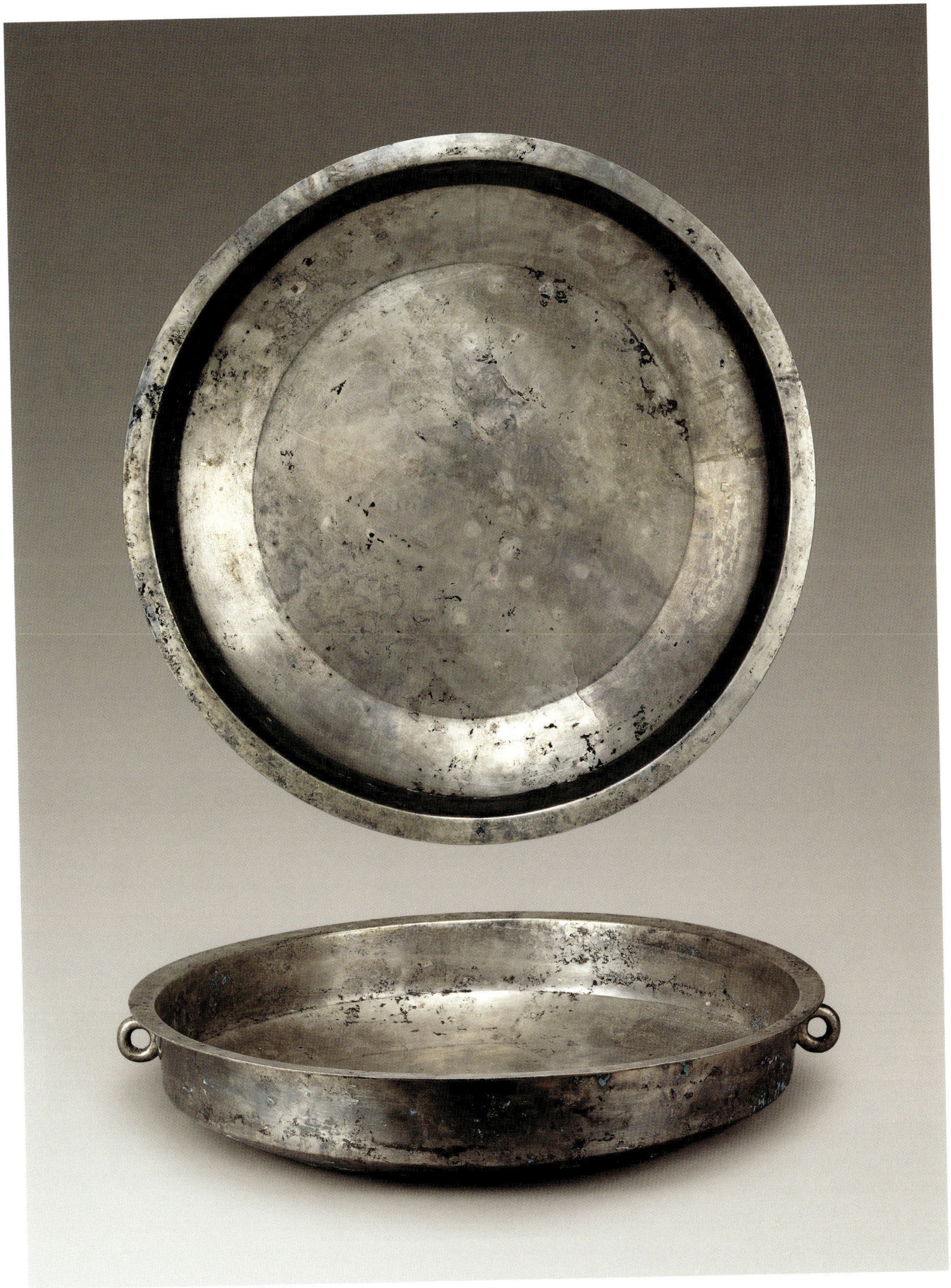

101

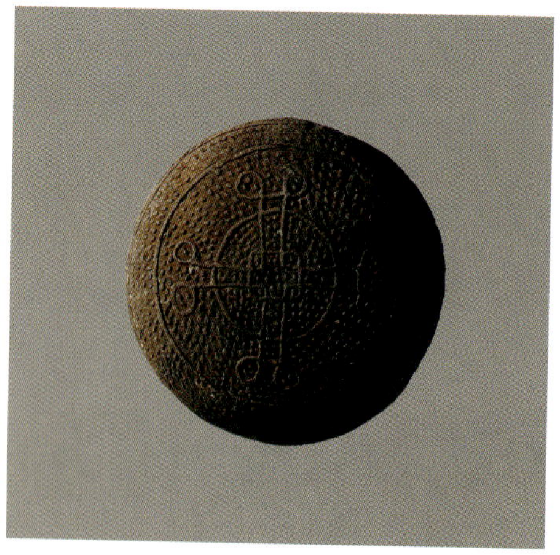

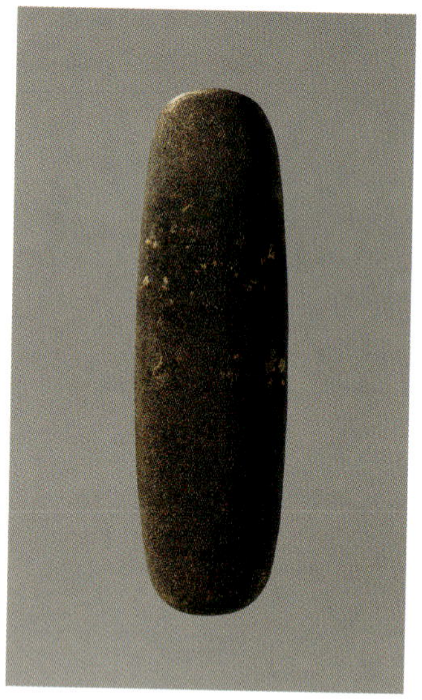

102

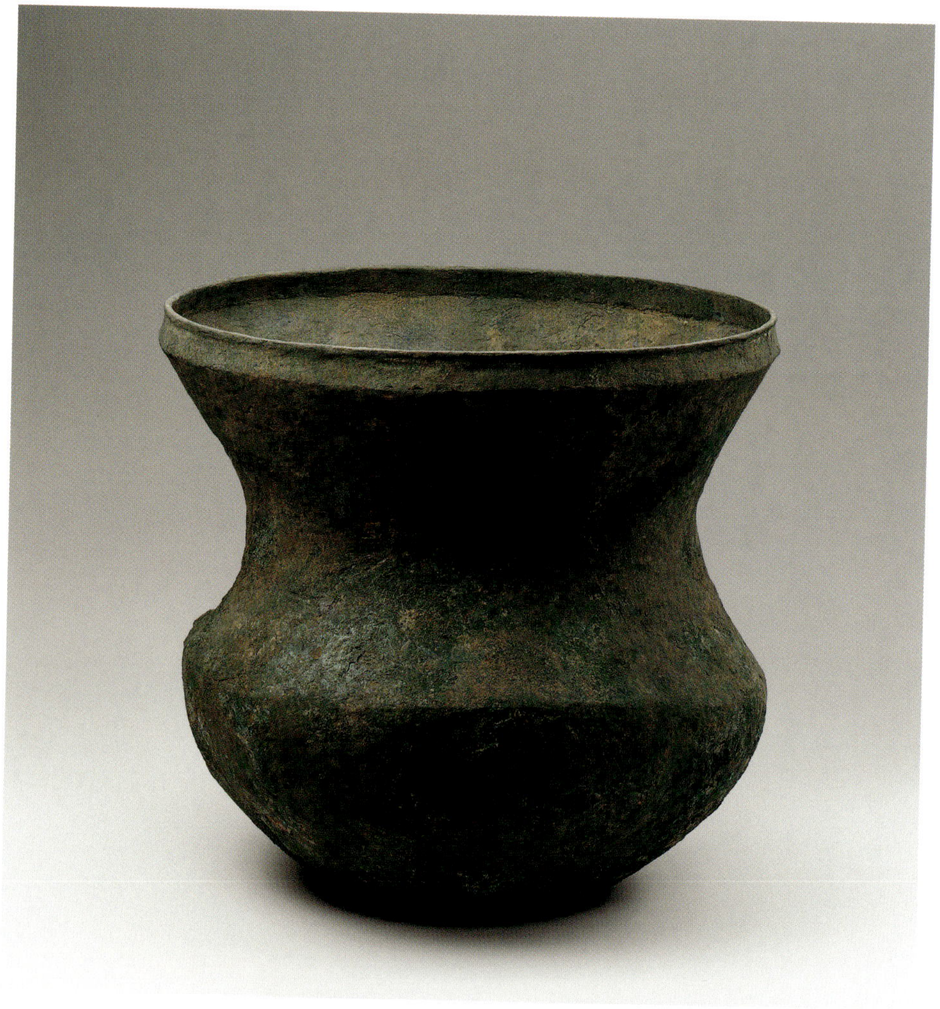

103

102

Two exfoliators

Second century BC, Western Han dynasty
Length: 20 cm; Diameter: 4.5–5 cm
Excavated at Shizishan in 1994–5
Xuzhou Museum, Jiangsu Province

Two pumice-like skin exfoliators of unknown composition were found inside the silver basin in the second western chamber of Shizishan. The round 'stone' has a simple geometric design. One like it was found in the tomb of a king of Guangling at Gaoyou, Jiangsu. The plainer stone has a wide middle section with narrower ends and a plain surface. It is slightly lighter in weight than the round one. A similarly shaped piece made from basalt was found in the tomb of a Zhongshan king at Mancheng, Hebei. These types of exfoliators were probably most popular during the Han period. JCSL

103

Bronze pot

Second century BC, Western Han dynasty
Height: 34 cm; Mouth diameter: 43 cm
Excavated at Yangguishan in 2005
Xuzhou Museum, Jiangsu Province

This peculiar vessel has an hourglass shape with a tall neck ending in a mouth with a diameter wider than that of the shouldered belly, which ends in a round base. This shape is unique to the Chu tombs in Xuzhou and has not been found elsewhere. It is roughly related to what has been called a *mou* cooking vessel,[1] but it lacks the loop handle(s) that are typical for *mou* of this period (cat. 190).

The vessel was found in a pit near the tomb at Yangguishan alongside a bronze flask similar to cat. 104 and a number of bronze vessels, including a large basin and a pestle and mortar (cat. 105), probably used for pounding medicinal herbs for bathing. These vessels from Yangguishan, found together, are thought to have been part of the paraphernalia of washing and bathing. Because this pot was found with these other vessels, it has been suggested that it was used in the same context, perhaps for heating water or keeping it warm.[2] SP

1 Beijing 2005, p. 233.
2 Beijing 2005, p. 233.

104

Bronze water vessel

Second century BC, Western Han dynasty
Width: 42.7 cm; Height: 33.6 cm
Excavated at Shizishan in 1994–5
Xuzhou Museum, Jiangsu Province

This bronze water vessel was found inside a large bronze basin (cat. 108) in the second western chamber at Shizishan. It has a spout, an unadorned simple body with a pair of ringed handles attached just below the vessel's shoulders and another smaller ring on the back.

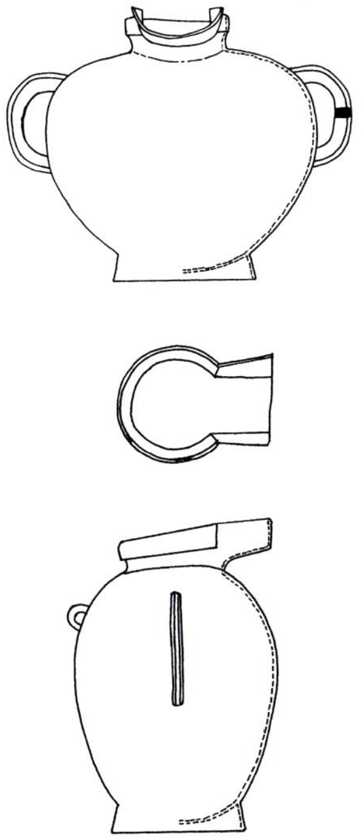

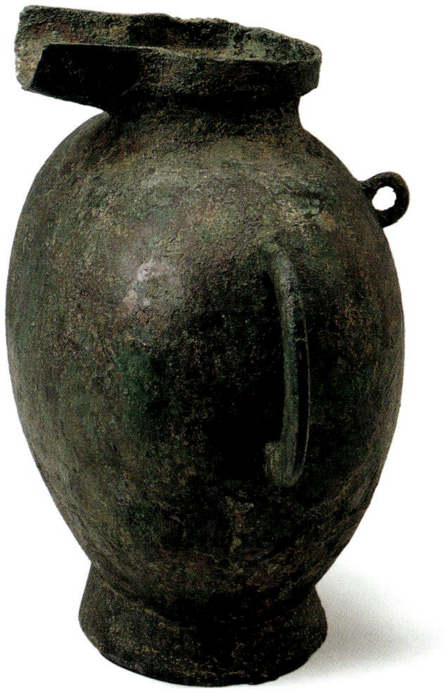

104

Two similar bronze vessels, together with bathing utensils, were also found in a burial pit attached to the subsidiary Yangguishan tomb site in 2005.

The design of this vessel probably originated in Central Asia and may be based on a leather prototype. As four of these bronze vessels have been found in the Xuzhou area, they might have been made locally, copying a steppe design. JCSL

105

Bronze pestle and mortar with measuring spoons

Second century BC, Western Han dynasty
Pestle length: 36.5 cm; Diameter: 3 cm
Mortar height: 18.2 cm; Diameter: 16.3 cm
Measuring spoons length: 12.7 cm, 17 cm
Excavated at a burial pit at Yangguishan in 2005
Xuzhou Museum, Jiangsu Province

This set of pestle, mortar and measuring spoons was found together with a bronze basin and water vessel forming a larger set of bathing utensils. The mortar was

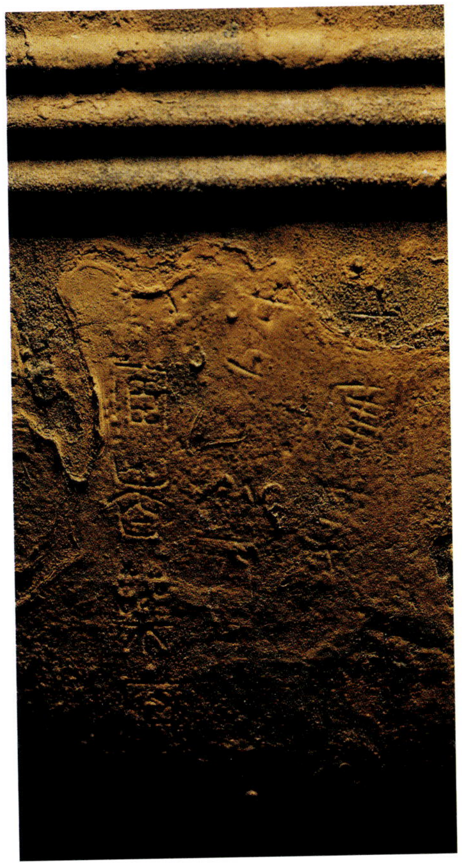

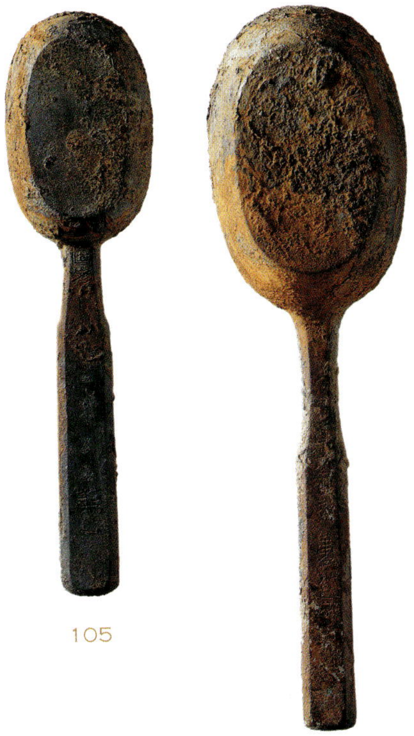

105

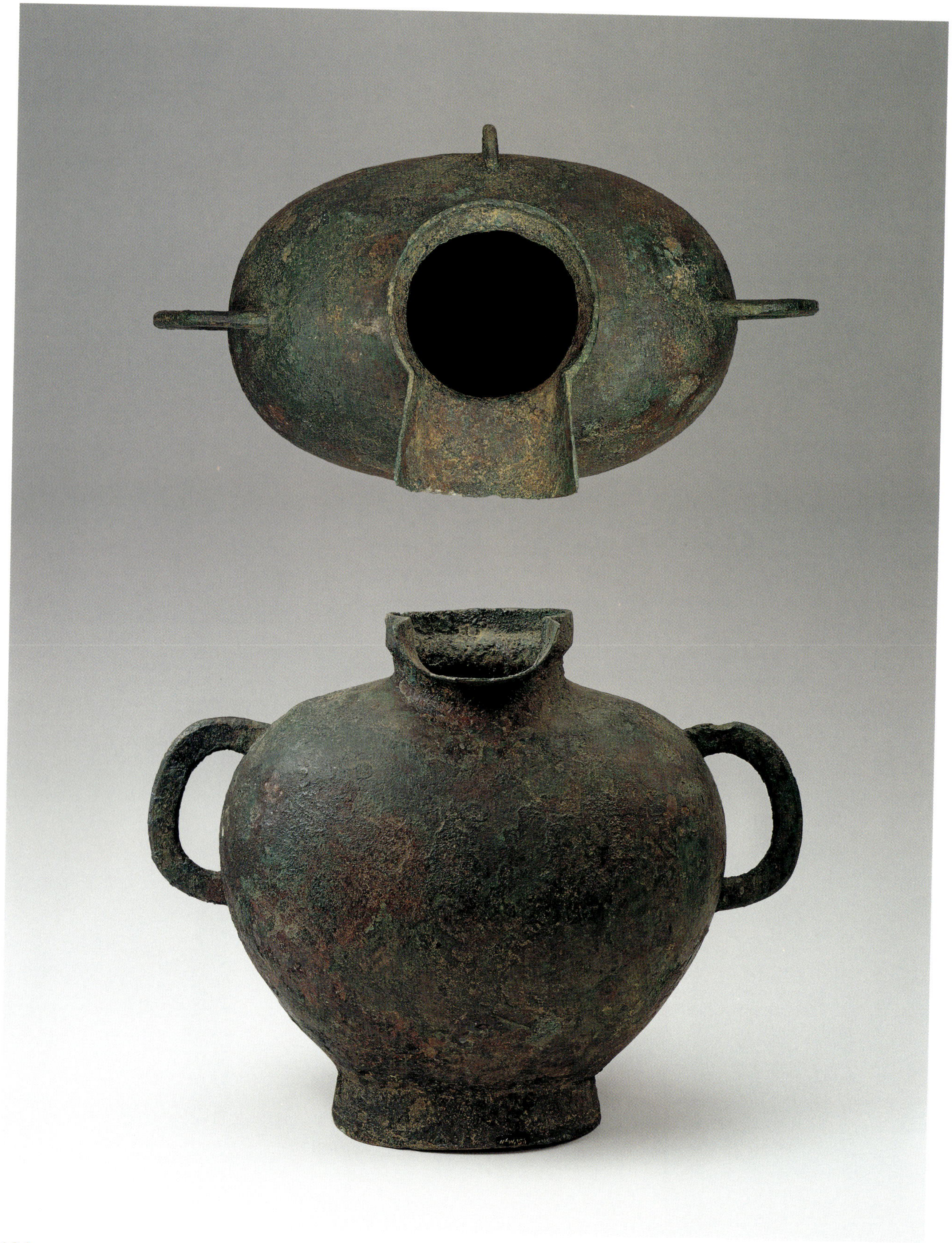

104

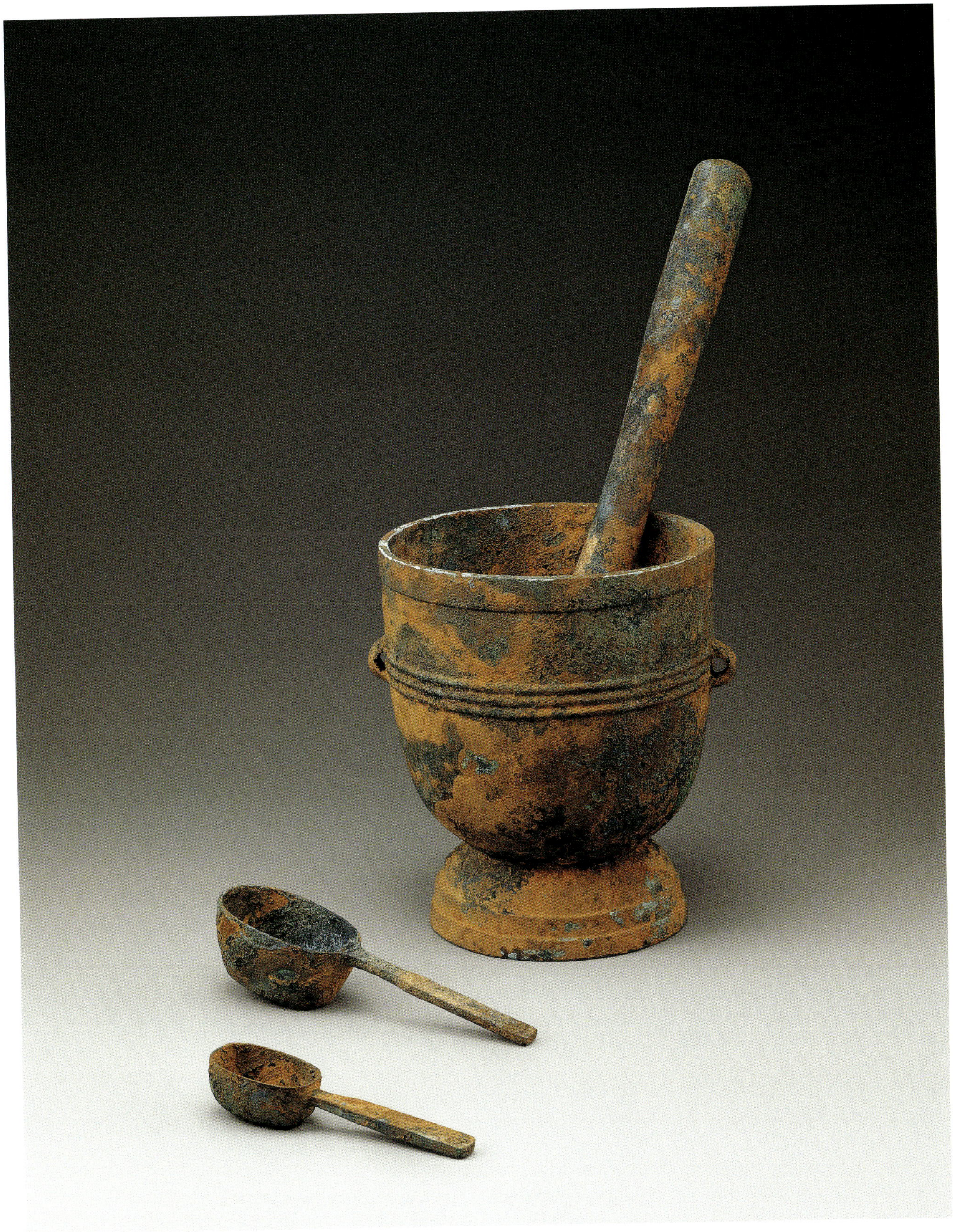

105

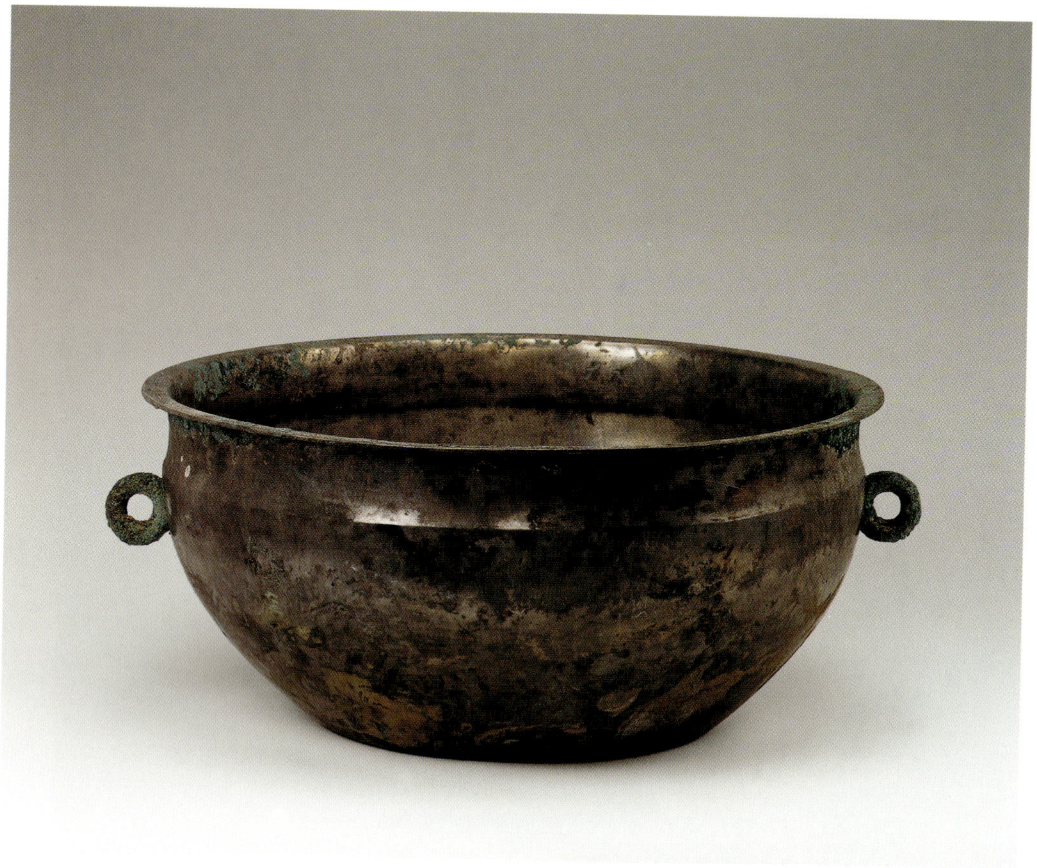

106

cast with two ringed handles, linked by three parallel ridges. Characters incised beneath the string lines indicate this mortar was used to grind herbs. Two differently sized spoons, with their capacities incised underneath the handles, were used to measure the quantity of herbs needed for a bath.

Similar mortars and measuring spoons have been found in other imperial tombs in Xuzhou and Juye, Shandong Province. These utensils were also incised with their capacity. This suggests that bathing with herbs was common among these elites. Bathing was an important ritual during the Han period and government officials were allowed to take one day off every five days to have a proper bath.[1] This explains why most of the tombs belonging to the Chu kings and queens at Xuzhou have bathrooms and the requisite bathing facilities and utensils. JCSL

1 For more discussion see Cai 2003. 2, pp. 71–7; Song 2003.3, pp. 108–13.

106

Silver basin (*juan*)

Second century BC, Western Han dynasty
Height: 19.5 cm; Diameter 45.7 cm
Excavated at Shizishan in 1994–5
Xuzhou Museum, Jiangsu Province

This basin was discovered in a storage chamber containing vessels for food preparation and washing in the tomb at Shizishan. It also contained several exfoliating scrubbing stones, one much decayed lacquered wooden box with traces of cosmetics and one lacquered wooden hamper. The box held the processed stems and leaves of unidentified plants and a bath towel. The plants were probably added to the water used for washing.[1]

The body of the basin bears a twenty-four character inscription detailing the capacity and weight of the object and its purpose, revealing that the King of Chu and his family used it for washing. It was also accompanied by other silver and bronze vessels, including another silver basin, a silver dish and a large bronze basin containing a flask. These silver vessels may also have been used for washing by the king or members of his family. SP

1 Beijing 2005, pp. 228–9.

107

Bronze cauldron (*fu*)

Second century BC, Western Han dynasty
Height: 39.6 cm; Maximum diameter: 59.5 cm
Excavated at Shizishan in 1994–5
Xuzhou Museum, Jiangsu Province

This cauldron was excavated from the second chamber to the west in the tomb at Shizishan and found with a group of storage vessels, including a *hu*.[1] When discovered, the vessel was filled with water and held a ladle-shaped object probably made from wood that disintegrated when the vessel was moved and the water disturbed. The ladle was possibly used to scoop up liquids or food from the cauldron.[2]

Such cauldrons were often used as cooking vessels on a stove or on a tripod over a fire. The chamber also contained fish, bird and animal bones suggesting that this was where food was stored.[3] *Fu* were essential cooking utensils in Han times, either used in conjunction with steamers (cat. 52) or by themselves for cooking stews. They were made of bronze, iron or pottery. The dish *geng* was central to Han cuisine and it underpinned the importance of the *fu* as a cooking vessel. Essentially a stew, *geng* resembles a thick soup with chunks of either meat or vegetables, or both, often mixed with grain. It was frequently served as the opening dish at banquets and it is likely that it was more of a luxury dish than a part of daily fare. Stew was also served as an offering in religious ceremonies.[4] It is also possible that this *fu* was used to boil water for washing,[5] as other bathing and washing vessels and implements were found in this chamber. SP

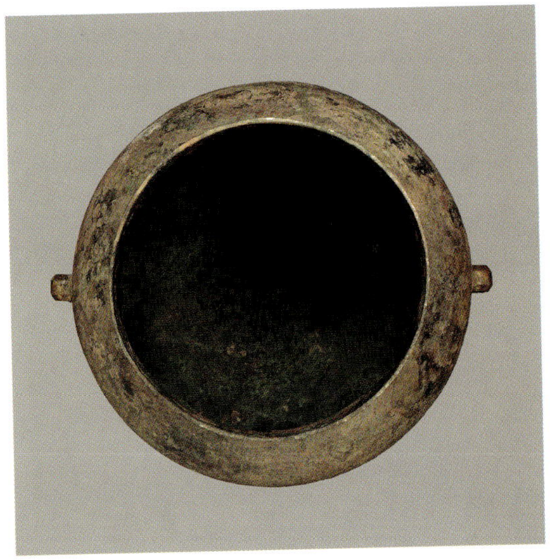

1 *Wenwu* 1998.9, p. 19.
2 Beijing 2005, p. 226.
3 *Wenwu* 1998.9, p. 17.
4 Yü 1977, pp. 57, 69, 74.
5 Beijing 2005, p. 226.

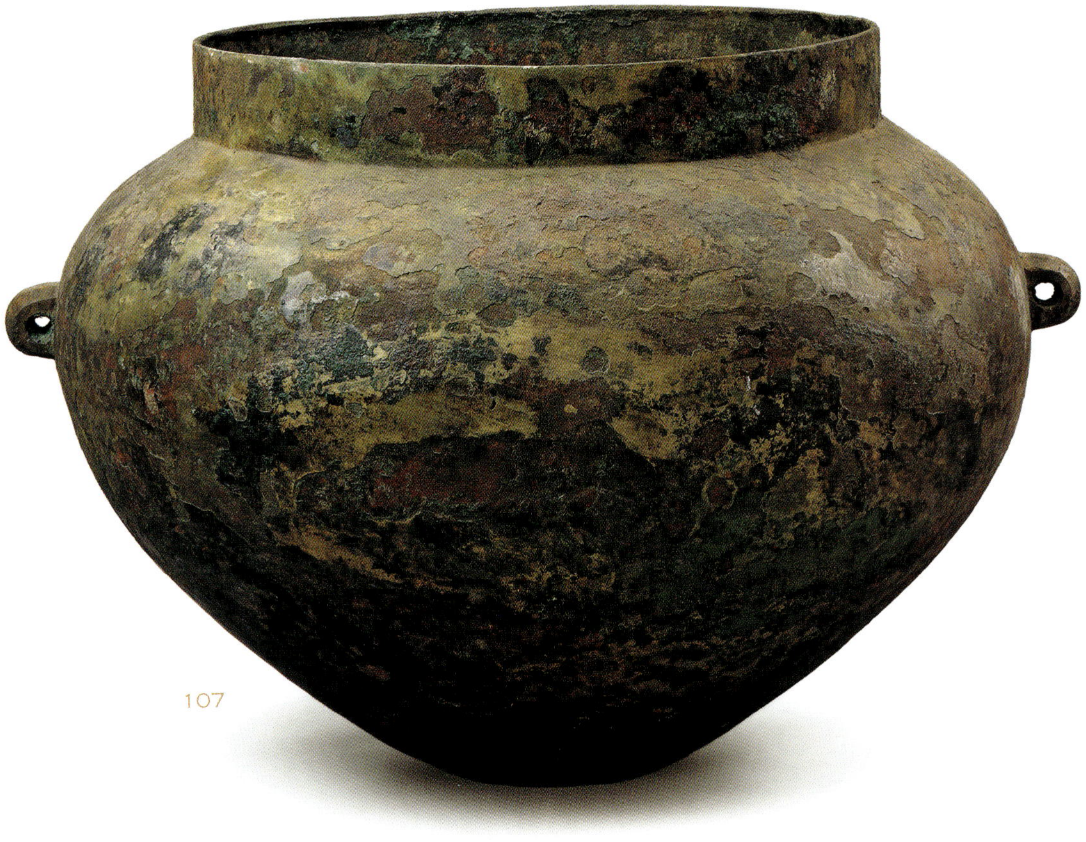

107

108

Bronze basin (*jian*)

Second century BC, Western Han dynasty
Height: 37 cm; Mouth diameter: 88.5 cm
Excavated at Shizishan in 1994–5
Xuzhou Museum, Jiangsu Province

This basin was found in the second chamber to the west of the tomb at Shizishan.[1] It contained a bronze storage vessel (*hu*) and two flat-bodied bronze pouring vessels (cat. 104).[2] These vessels and others with which it was found, such as the silver basins, *jian* (cat. 101) and *juan* (cat. 106), whose inscriptions identify them as vessels used for washing, suggest that this basin was also used in this way.[3] The basin was probably a container for water. SP

1 *Wenwu* 1998.8, p. 9, fig. 9.
2 Beijing 2005, p. 232.
3 Beijing 2005, p. 232 also offers a quote from the *Zhuangzi* as support for the notion that *jian* basins were used for washing.

109

Bronze mirror

Second century BC, Western Han dynasty
Diameter: 18.5 cm
Excavated at Bojishan in 1994
Xuzhou Museum, Jiangsu Province

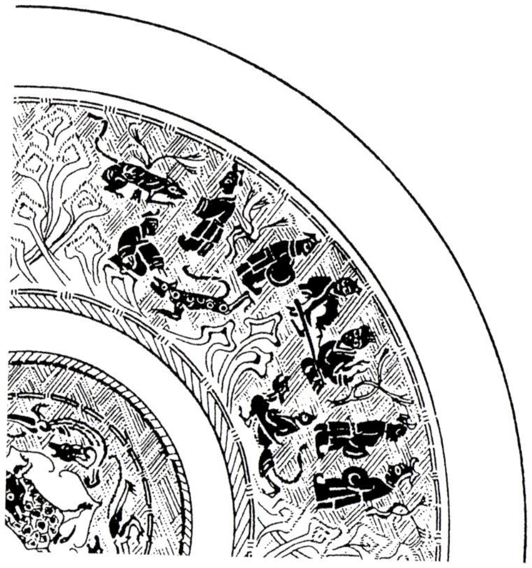

This mirror belonged to the Marquis of Wanqu, Liu Yi, and was found in his tomb beneath his right side. It had been deliberately broken into more than ten pieces during the burial process, according to custom. The mirror is thinly cast, with a suspension loop in the form of a turtle-shaped crouching animal surrounded by four feline dragons in low relief. The outer segment is decorated with four groups of the same image separated by stylized *Boshan* mountains. Each group has images arranged in two layers. The upper layer includes in the centre a man playing a musical instrument known as a *qin* with two onlookers, the seated one clapping. To the left of the trio, a single man tames a tiger; to the right, two standing figures greet one another. Stylized trees separate the three images. The lower layer includes a seated figure taming a leopard and a figure riding a tiger separated by smaller *Boshan* mountains. *Boshan* (Bo Mountain) is a mythical land of immortality.[1]

This is the finest mirror that can be dated to the early Western Han, with a complicated design and complex casting techniques. An identical mirror can be found in the Freer Gallery of Art in

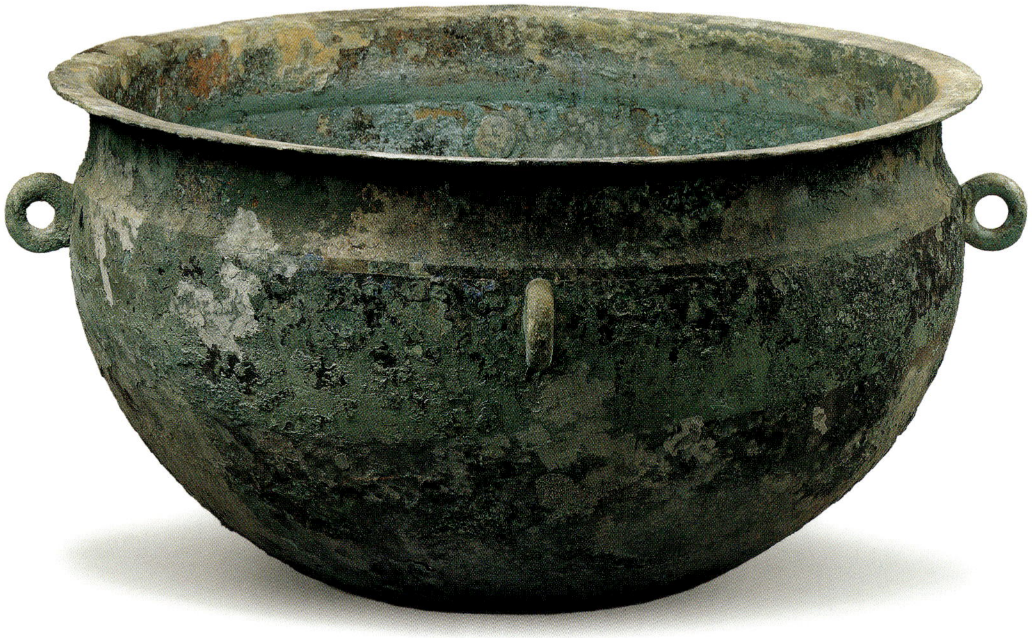

108

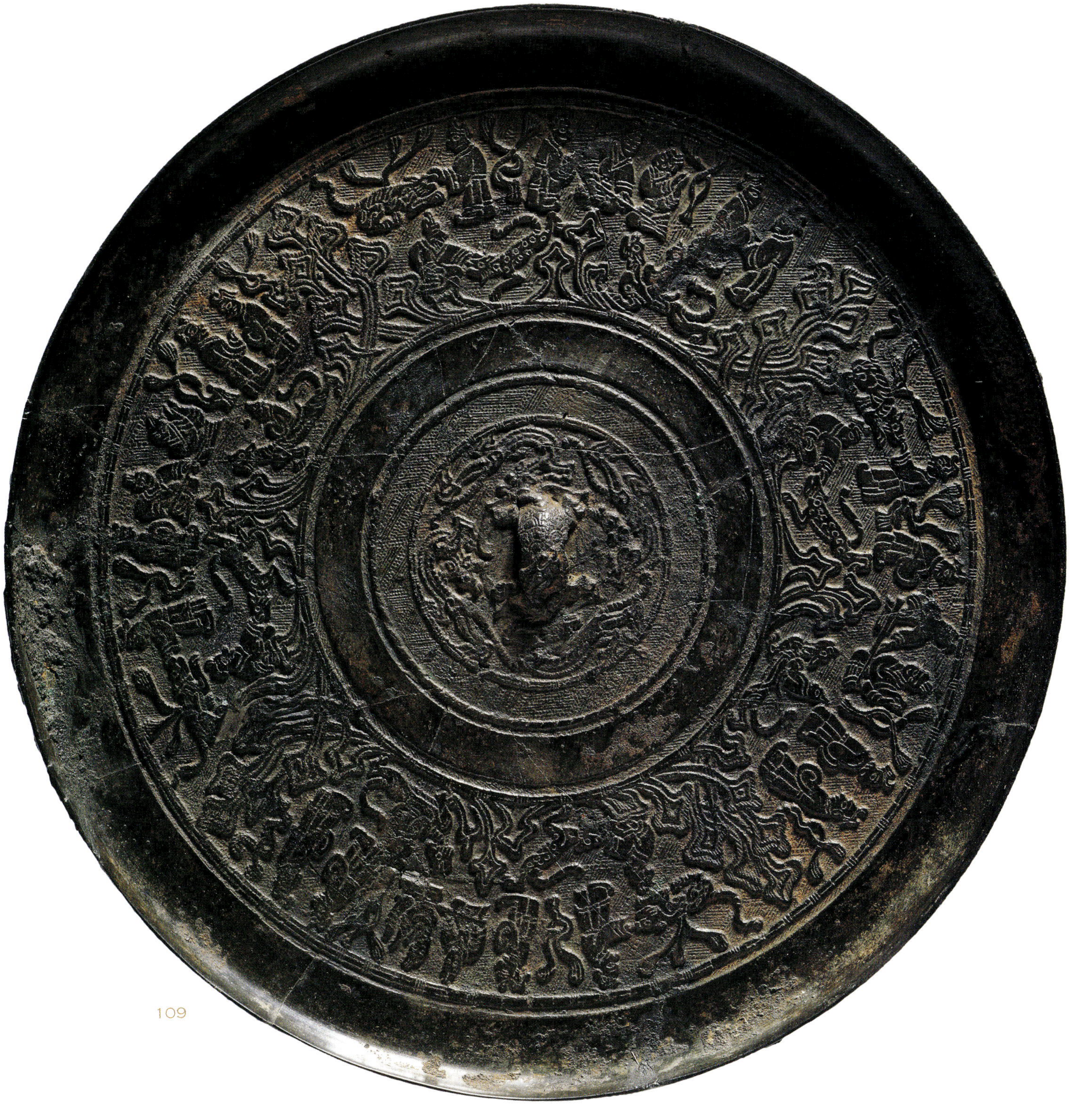

109

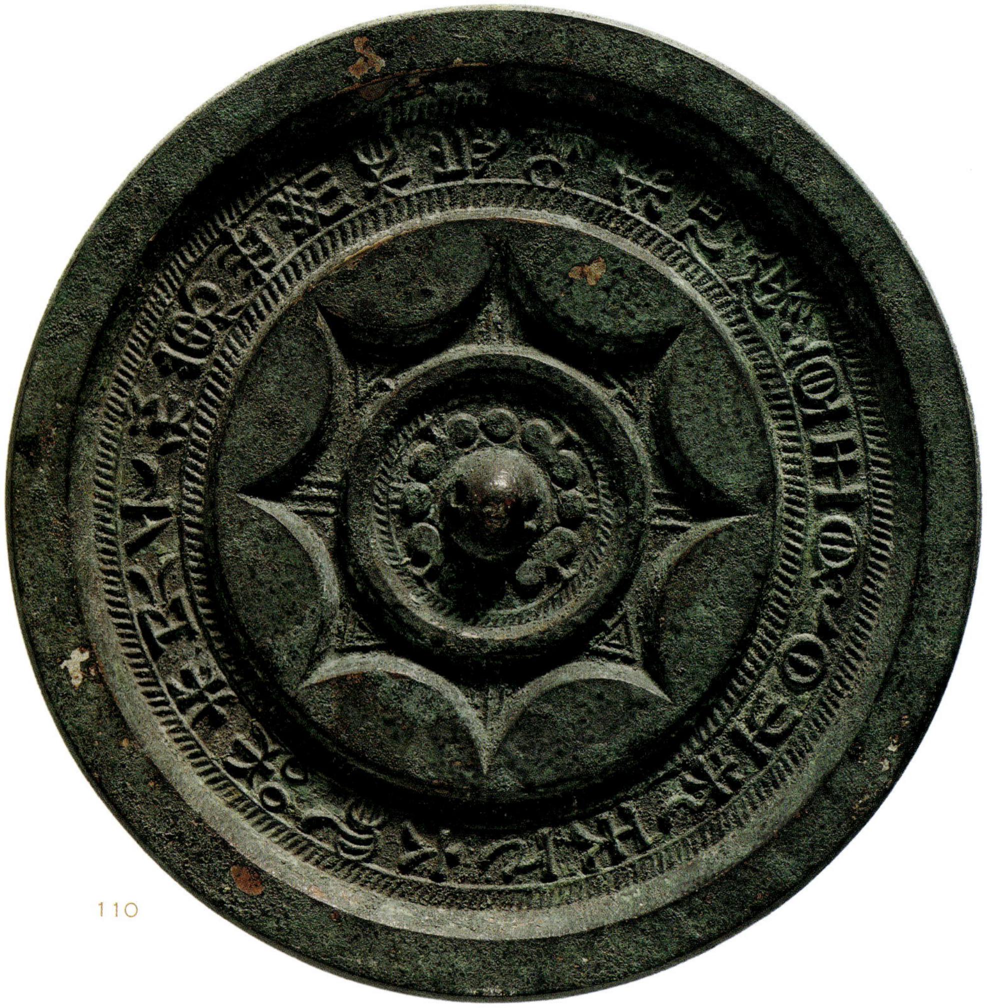

110

Washington DC, suggesting that the two may have been cast from the same mould.[2] JCSL

1 Erickson 1992, pp. 6–28.
2 Umehara 1935, pl. 30:2.

110

Bronze mirror with design of concentric circles and continuous arc

First century BC, Western Han dynasty
Diameter: 17.5 cm
Excavated at the queen's tomb No. 3 at Dongdongshan in 1997
Xuzhou Museum, Jiangsu Province

This bronze mirror features characteristics that appear to emerge in the mid-Western Han period. With a sturdy body, flat rim, concentric circle design and continuous arc motif, its style differs from early Western Han bronze mirrors, which still retain some of the attributes of the Warring States period (fifth–third century BC), such as a thin body and a concave rim.[1]

In between the raised double circles of coiling lines is an inscription, which roughly translates as: 'Seeing the sunshine, the world beneath heaven shines very brightly. Enjoy inexhaustible pleasure. Never forget one another.'[2] Inscriptions on mirrors produced during the Western Han period are often difficult to decipher. Sometimes characters are omitted while meaningless auxiliary characters are added for the purpose of creating a colloquial rhythm. At the time the mirror was produced, however, the inscription was probably sufficient to evoke the intended meaning of the sentence.[3]

As mirrors reflect light they are often associated with the sun or the moon.[4] The inscription on this mirror, which mentions the sunshine, and the sun-like design in the middle reinforce the correlation between the mirror and celestial light. NC

1 Dewar 1994, pp. 102, 124.
2 For the original Chinese inscription, see Beijing 2005, p. 244.
3 Dewar 1994, pp. 124, 126.
4 Nakano 1994, p. 20.

111

Bronze mirror with design of four dragons and three-tiered leaves

Second century BC, Western Han dynasty
Diameter: 18.5 cm
Excavated at tomb No. 1 at Cuipingshan in 2003
Xuzhou Museum, Jiangsu Province

This bronze mirror features a triple-fluted knob and a concave rim, which are characteristics commonly shared among mirrors produced during the second century BC. Apart from designs of raised circular bands, the main decorations on the surface consist of four dragons, which are separated by four flame-like, three-tiered leaf designs. Beneath the four sets of dragon and leaf designs, the surface of the mirror is decorated with geometric patterns made of very fine lines, which testify to the attention to detail that Han craftsmen paid when casting mirrors.

Bronze mirrors are among the most common burial goods excavated at

Western Han tombs in Xuzhou. It has been suggested that the city might have been a centre for the mirror-casting industry in China at the time.[1] Since the early Western Han, it became common for bronze mirrors to be made of alloys different from the ones used for other bronze objects. In addition, special techniques for removing air bubbles during the casting process and finer polishing methods were introduced.[2] NC

1 Beijing 2005, p. 240.
2 Nakano 1994, p. 19.

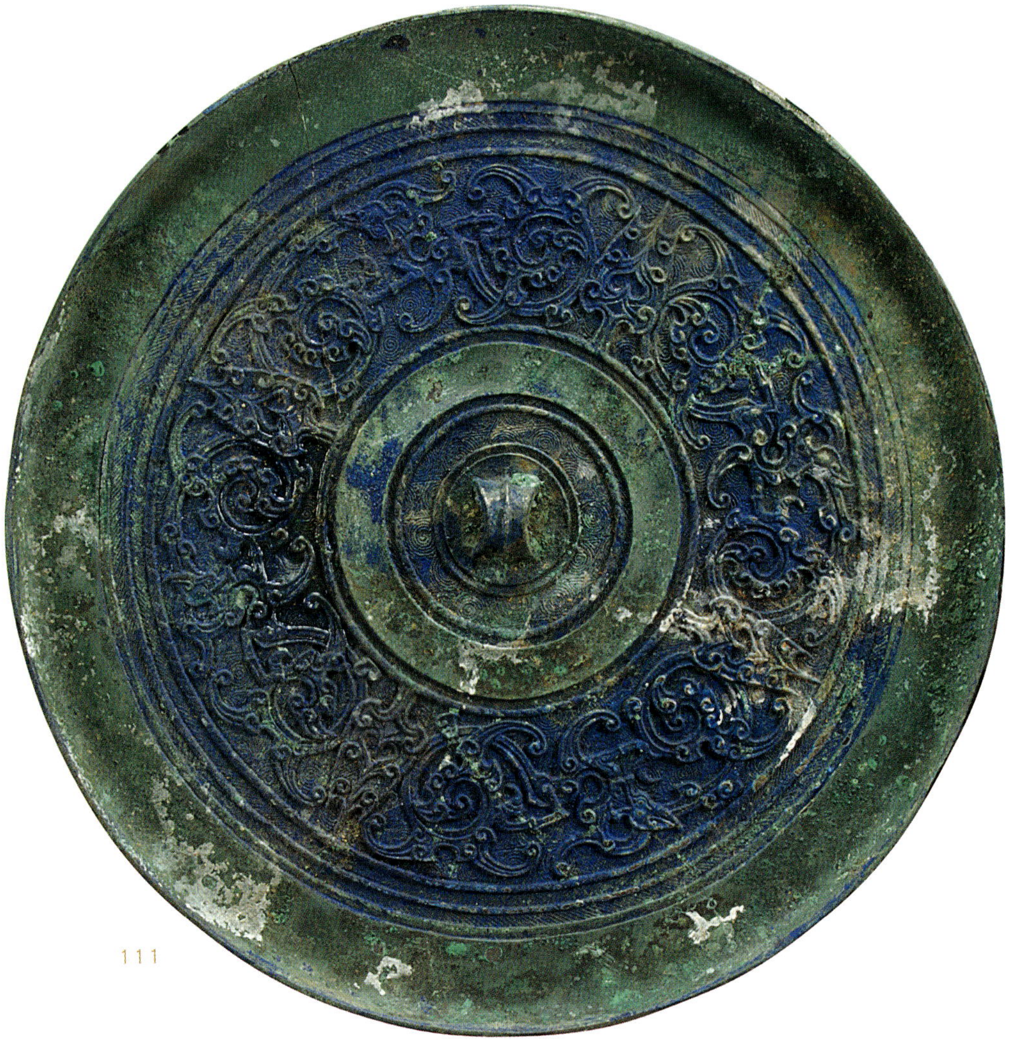

111

112

White metal mirror with TLV design

Third century BC–first century AD,
Western Han dynasty
Diameter: 14.1 cm
Excavated at tomb No. 2 at Yanshan in Xuzhou in 1999
Xuzhou Museum, Jiangsu Province

The TLV design, so named because the patterns resemble the three Roman letters, is commonly seen on the back of bronze mirrors of the Han dynasty. On this mirror, a series of eight roundels and four winged-animal motifs fills the space in between the TLV pattern within the inner circle. On the outer circle, between two raised circular bands is an inscription. A square containing a circular boss occupies the centre of the mirror while cloud patterns adorn the surface of the flat rim.

To ensure the correct spacing of TLV designs, before casting guidelines would be drawn onto the clay mould with tools such as a ruler and a compass-like instrument.[1] On Han mirrors, the TLV design is concave rather than convex.[2] The thick, wide outer rim and the employment of white metal are characteristics of later Western Han period mirrors.

Many believe that the TLV design is derived from the patterns on a *Liubo* game board (fig. 58), which is closely associated with the spiritual world.[3] The inscription on the mirror enhances the link with the realm of immortals, reading: 'Going into a big mountain and seeing an immortal, who eats jade plants, drinks sweet liquid and rides away to the east on a beautiful dragon.' NC

1 Nakano 1994, p. 14.
2 Nakano 1994, p. 15.
3 Cheng 1997; Fu 1986.

113

Bronze mirror with design of concentric circles

First–second century BC, Western Han dynasty
Diameter: 15.3 cm
Museum acquisition
Xuzhou Museum, Jiangsu Province

The bronze mirror has a flat rim and features a design of concentric circles cast in raised lines. There are two inscriptions on the mirror, which also form concentric circles. The inscriptions narrate how the mirror is suitable for a lovely lady to examine her attire and

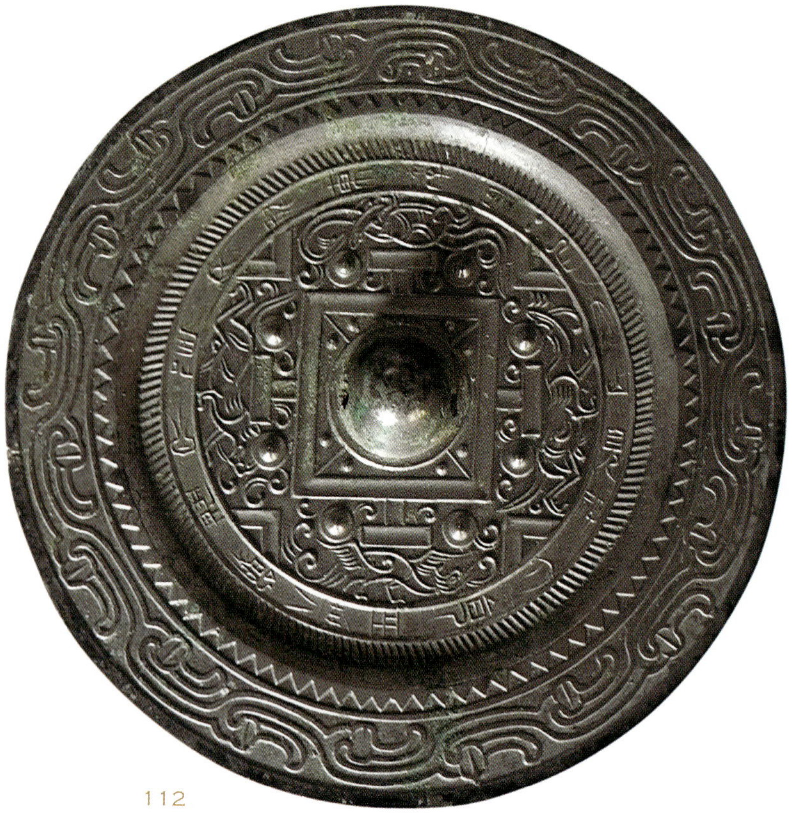

112

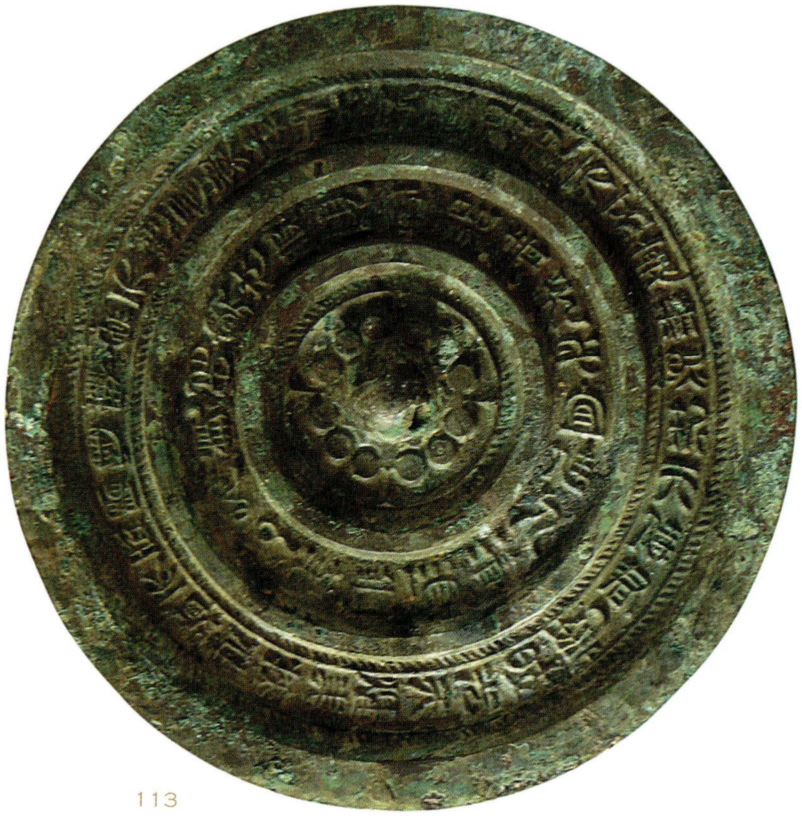

113

appearance and describe the intimate relationship between married couples.

Polished metal mirrors could become clouded due to contact with moisture and oil. A knob was generally affixed onto the reverse side of a mirror so that a cord could be looped through the hole of the knob and tied up, which would help prevent contact with the reflective surface when handling.[1] Mirrors came to symbolize marriage and conjugal fidelity because of the symbolism of the knotted cord, which was associated with the union of a couple.[2] NC

1 Nakano 1994, p. 19.
2 Nakano 1994, pp. 19–20.

114

Stone lavatory

Second century BC, Western Han dynasty
Height: 150 cm; Length: 149 cm; Width: 115 cm
Excavated at the tomb of the King of Chu at Tuolanshan in 1989–90
Xuzhou Museum, Jiangsu Province

Reference to human waste in China goes back as far as the oracle bone inscriptions of the Shang (1200–1045 BC), which include an early form of the graphic denoting human excrement (*shi*).[1] The first mention of a latrine or toilet, *ce*, occurs in the historical chronicle *Zuozhuan* ('Chronicle of Zuo'), which records that, in the year corresponding to 580 BC, the Marquis of Jin died in his lavatory. The verb used here (*xian*) suggests that the unfortunate Marquis fell into a waste hole in the ground. This record also tells that his servant, forewarned of the accident in a dream that same morning, had to carry his master on his back out of the privy only to be buried alive with him later.[2]

Early Chinese texts contain several stories and metaphors identifying the latrine with the lower domains of human morality. According to the opening passage of his biography in Sima Qian's *Shiji*, Li Si, later chancellor to China's First Emperor, was so disgusted at the sight of rats eating the filth in the privy of the clerk's quarters where he served during his youth that he was inspired to become an adept administrator and chief planner.[3] Fragments of a late Western Han calendar excavated sixty miles west of Dunhuang suggest that latrines were also believed to be hiding places of demonic and inauspicious forces. The text contains an incantation to be

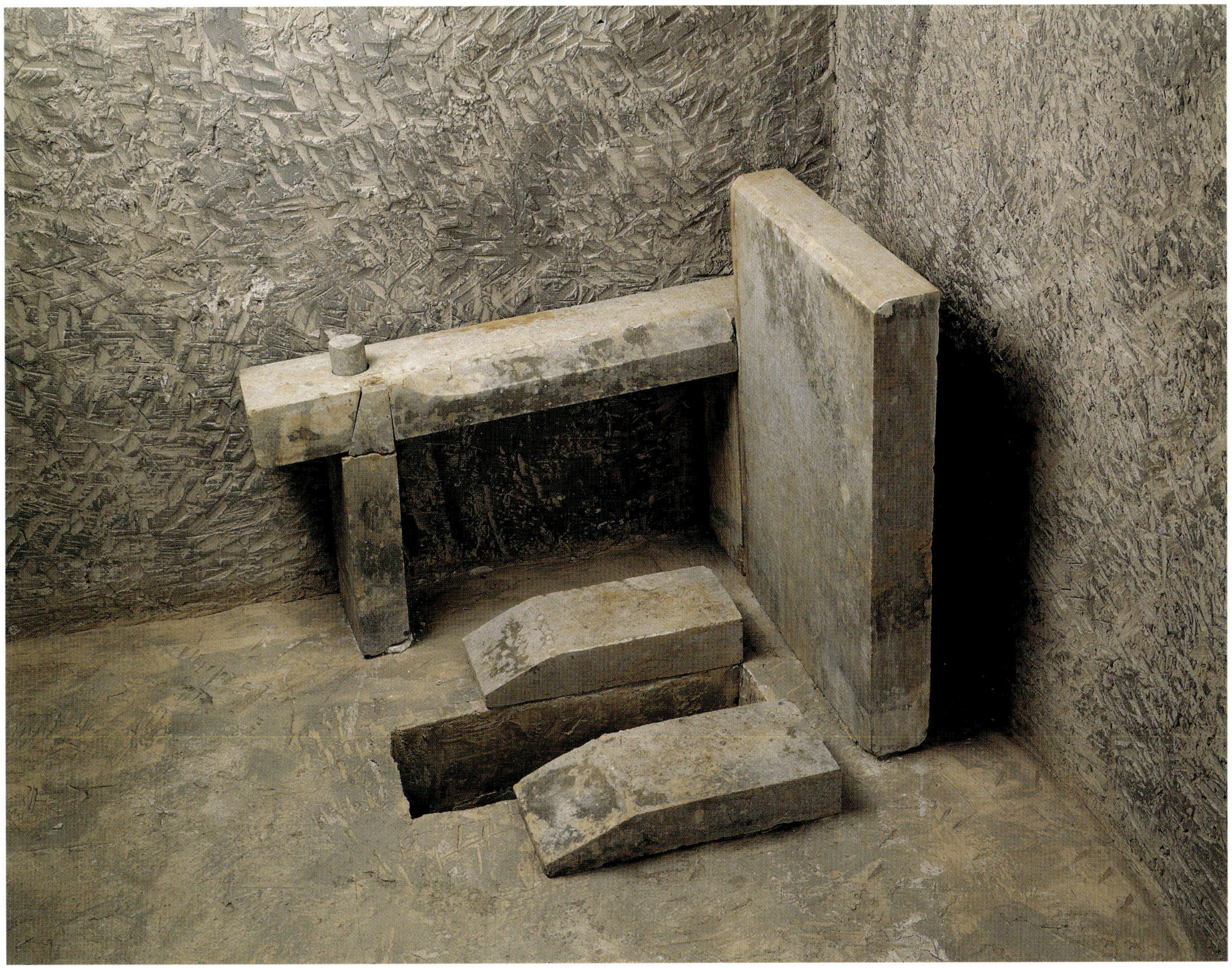

114

pronounced when entering a lavatory, accompanied by the performance of ritual steps known as the Pace of Yu (*yubu*).[4]

The *ce*, generally referred to as a 'privy', was a separate space or room in a residence or other type of building. A treatise associated with the philosopher Mozi (*c.*479–381 BC) allows for the provision of a latrine on a city's defensive walls at intervals of one every seventy metres. It further stipulates that lavatories 'on or below the wall are places for the accumulation of filth', and that 'those entering a latrine should not be carrying anything.'[5]

Replica earthenware lavatories of various designs appear frequently as funerary goods in tombs of the late Western and Eastern Han period.[6] Most of these are latrines constructed above or annexed to a pig-sty or pen. The latter is also reflected in the etymology of an alternative word for the privy, *hun*, which contains an element depicting a pig in an enclosure. Some models suggest that elite Han households had separate closets for ladies and gentlemen. Several tombs of the Chu princes in the Xuzhou area contain separate bathrooms and lavatory compartments that were destined for use by the tomb occupant in the afterlife. RS

1 Wang and Zhang 1961, p. 14.
2 Yang 1995, p. 850.
3 *Shiji* 87.2539.
4 Zhang and Hu 2001, p. 182 (no. 266).
5 Sun 2001, 52.521.
6 Zhang and Fan 1987.

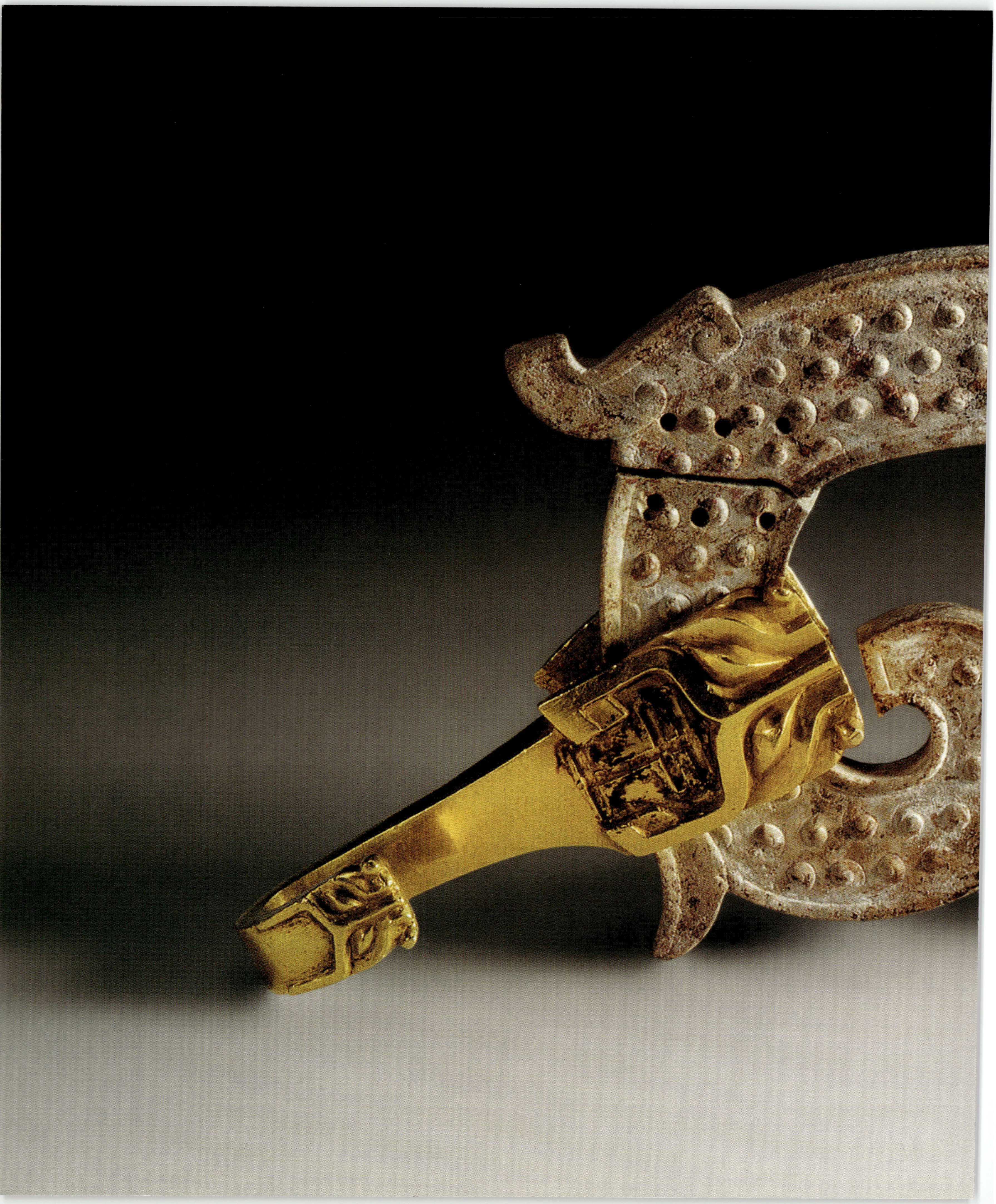

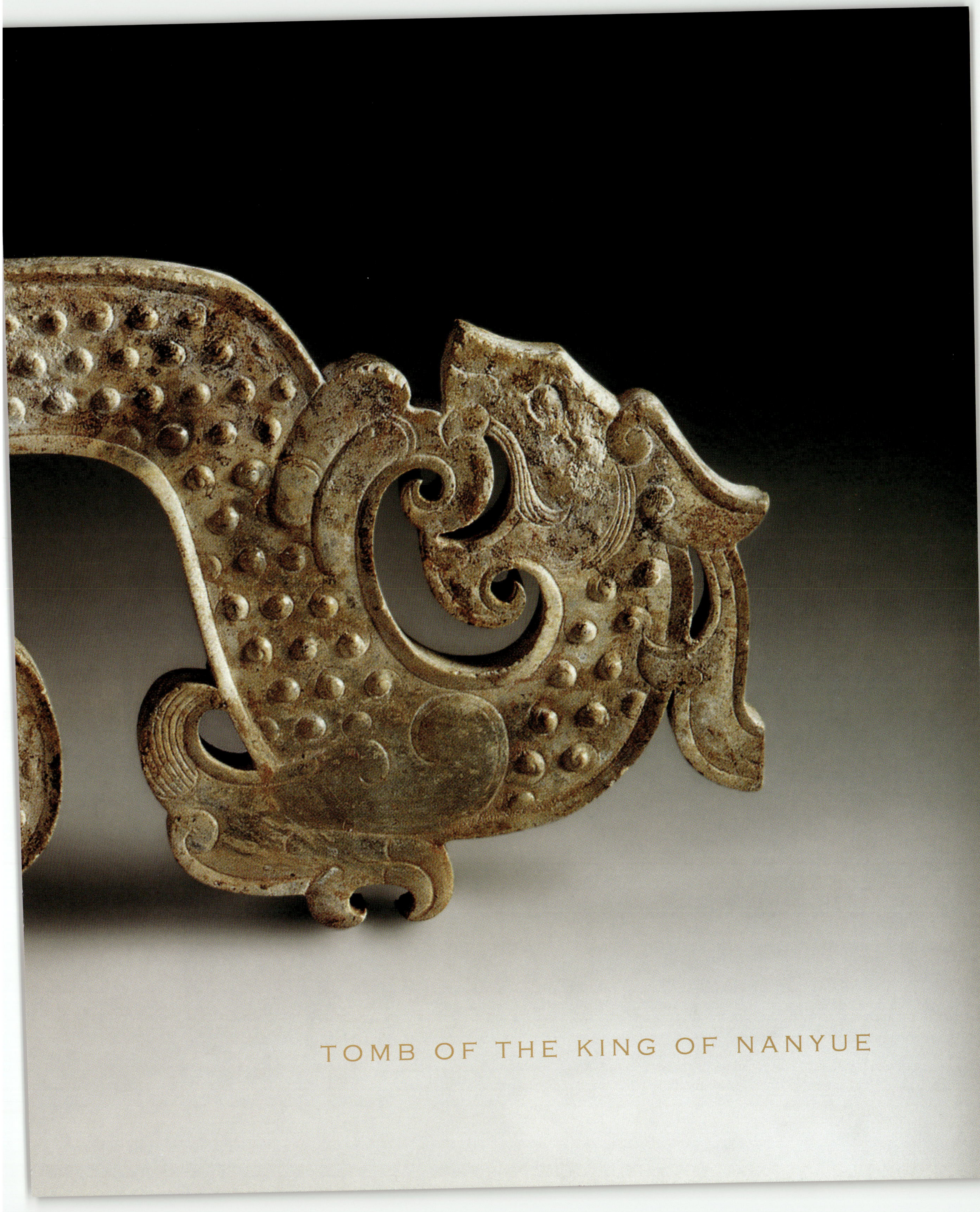

TOMB OF THE KING OF NANYUE

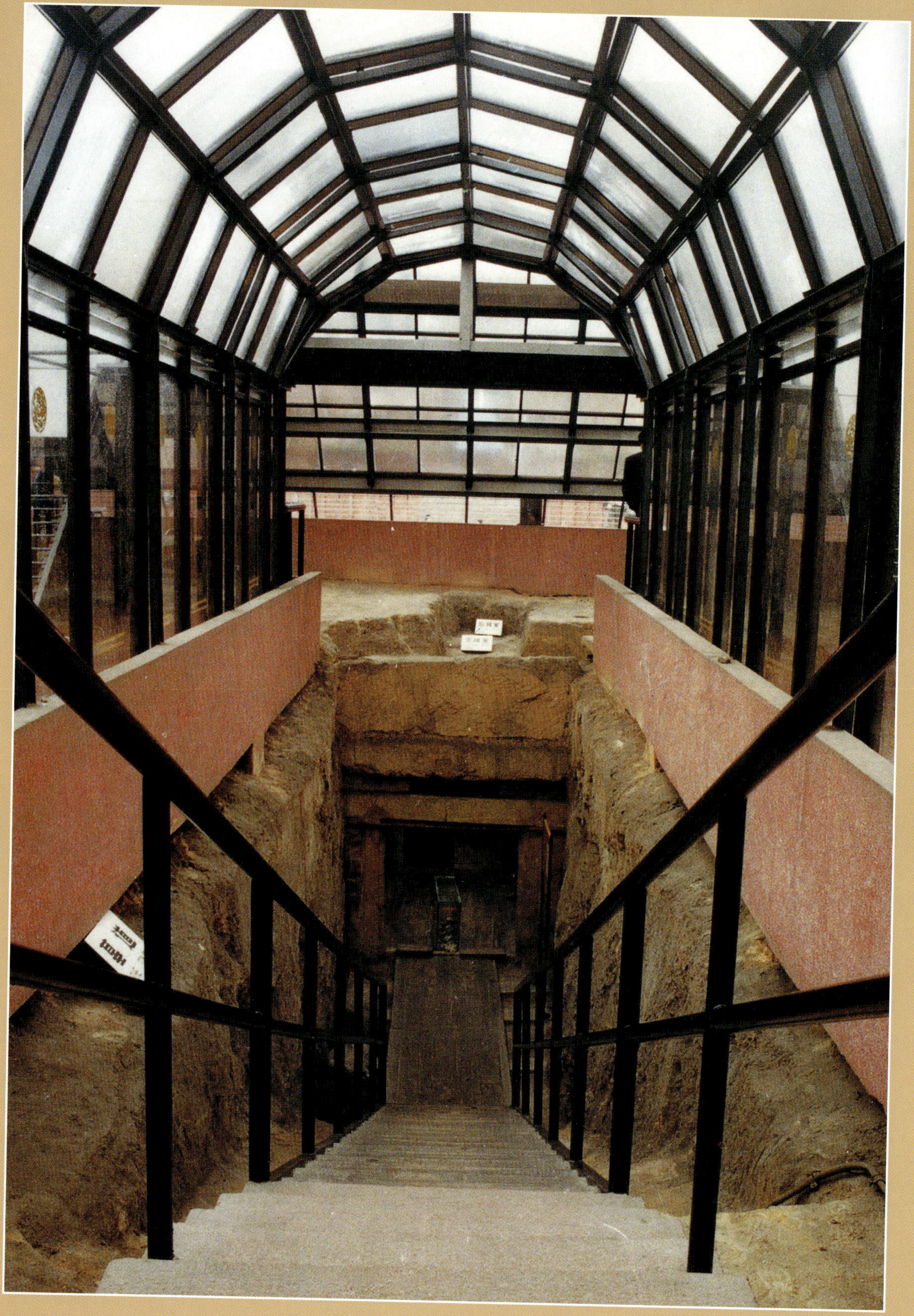

THE TOMB OF THE KING OF NANYUE AT XIANGGANGSHAN

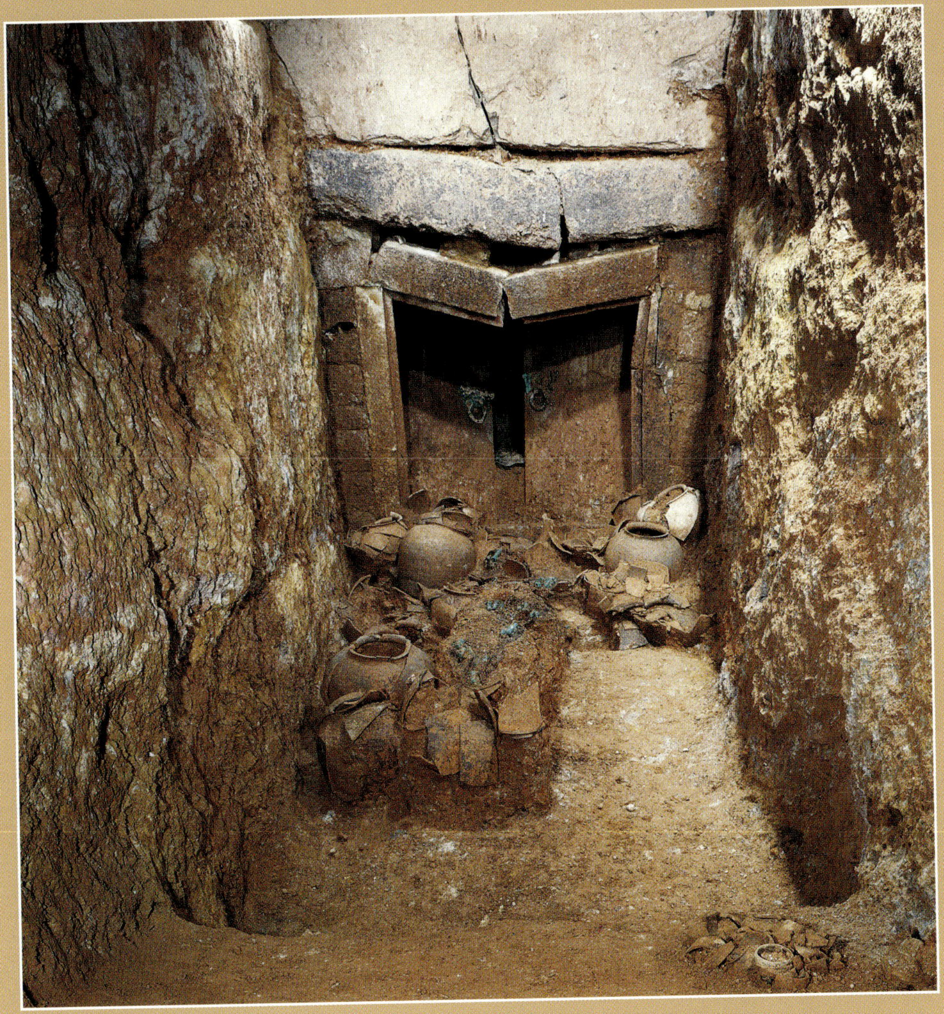

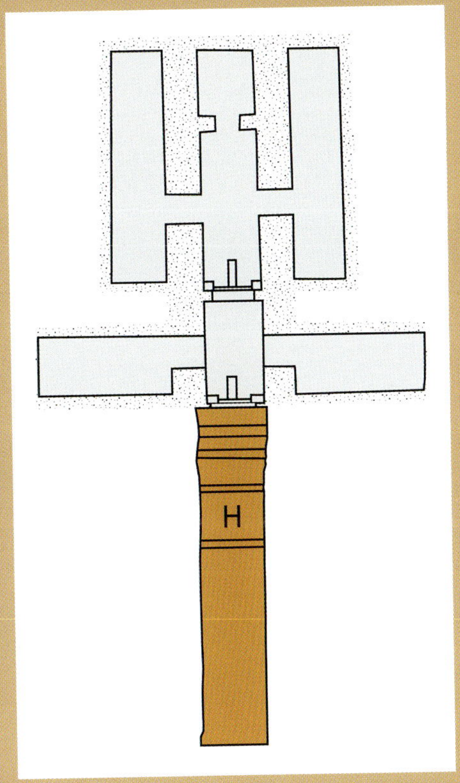

THE TOMB PATHWAY AND THE OUTER COFFIN

On both the eastern and western walls of the tomb pathway, there are no apparent divisional features that separate the pathway from the space containing the outer coffin. However, there is a visible distinction on the ground where the slope turns to a shaft. A set of twelve ceramic utensils, small and unrefined, was found on the eastern side of the pathway. Next to them were a small bronze mirror and a bronze belt buckle. Among the ceramic and bronze objects remained a trace of red colour, which could be the residue of lacquer from the outer coffin. In the opposite direction, on the western side of the tomb pathway, was a pair of gilded bronze ornaments. Judging from these utensils and objects and their positions relative to each other, it was possible to ascertain that a person was buried here.

The shaft in front of the gate of the tomb measures 4.12 by 2–2.3 metres. Inside the shaft was a rectangular wooden outer coffin. Apart from the inner coffin within the outer coffin, burial goods occupied the rest of the space. A wooden model of a chariot may once have been there but has not survived. There was also a wooden crate filled with what may have been ceremonial ornaments. The crate had rotted away. The inner coffin was placed by the south-eastern part inside the outer coffin. Both the inner coffin and the human remains had decayed. Only a pair of gilded bronze ornaments survived.

CATALOGUE NUMBER 115

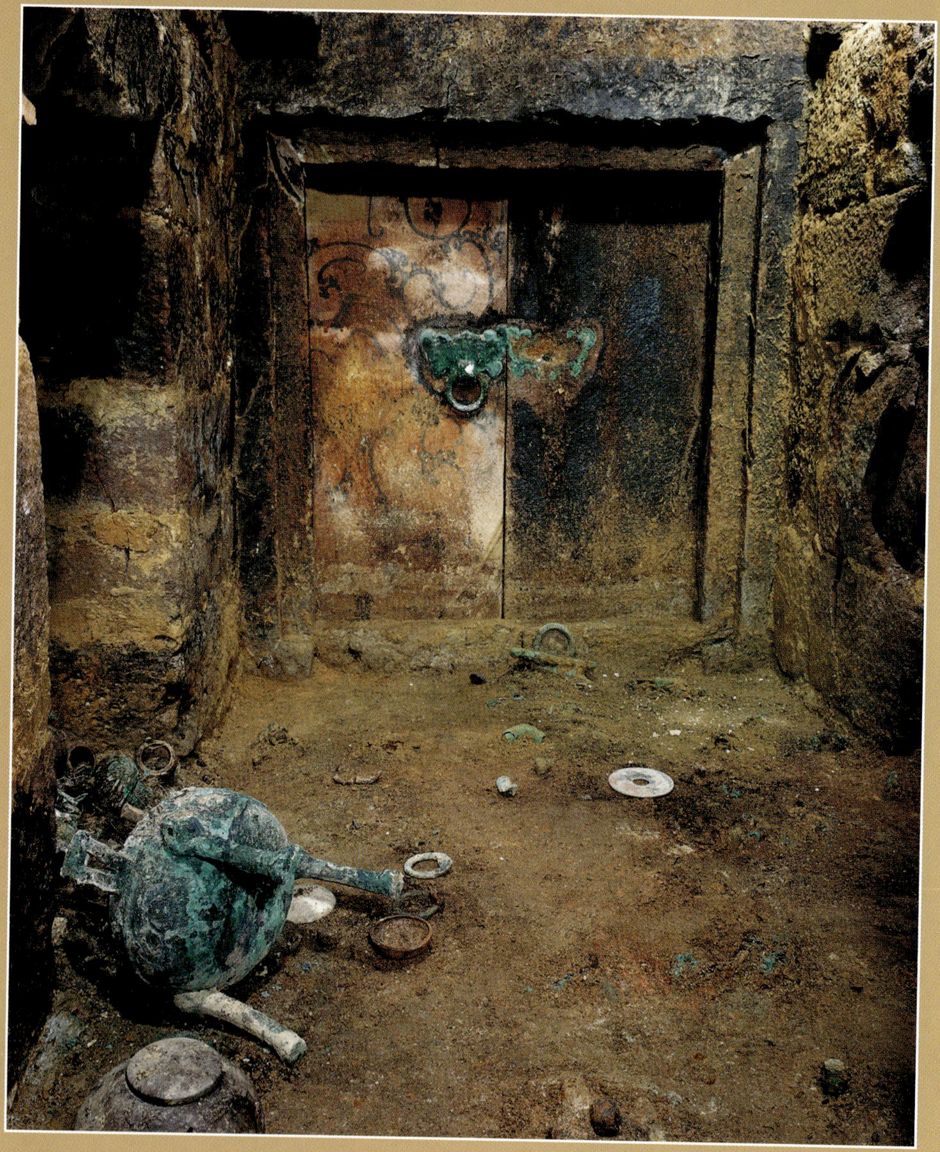

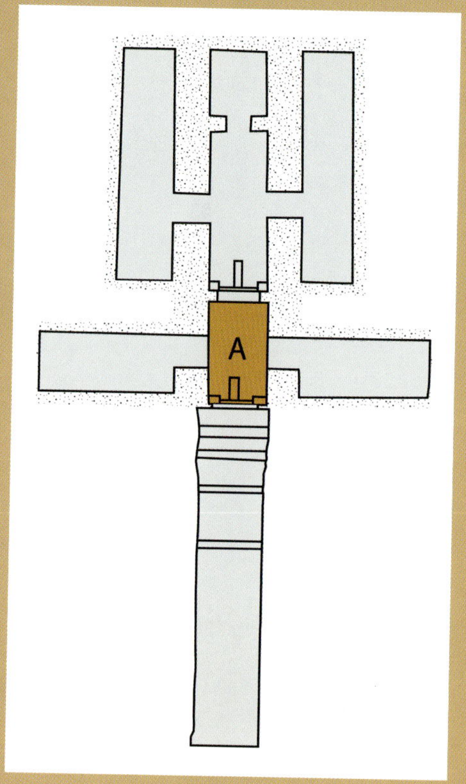

THE FRONT CHAMBER

The front chamber was separated from the tomb pathway by a stone gate, under which a self-locking device was fitted. The room was painted with cloud patterns in red and black. A sacrificial human inside a coffin was found. His seal indicated he was the King's family servant. This room yielded only a few objects including one wooden chariot model, two iron knifes, jade ornaments and mirrors. The most interesting objects from this chamber are two inkstones. Judging from the traces of ink and red color, they were possibly used for the painting of the room. A similar inkstone (cat. 133) from the western chamber is displayed in the exhibition.

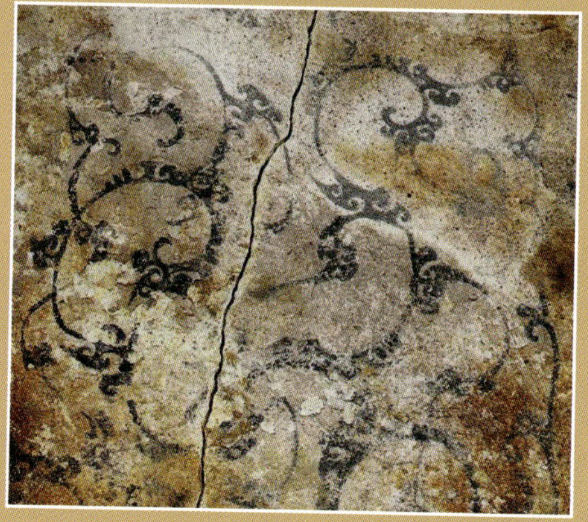

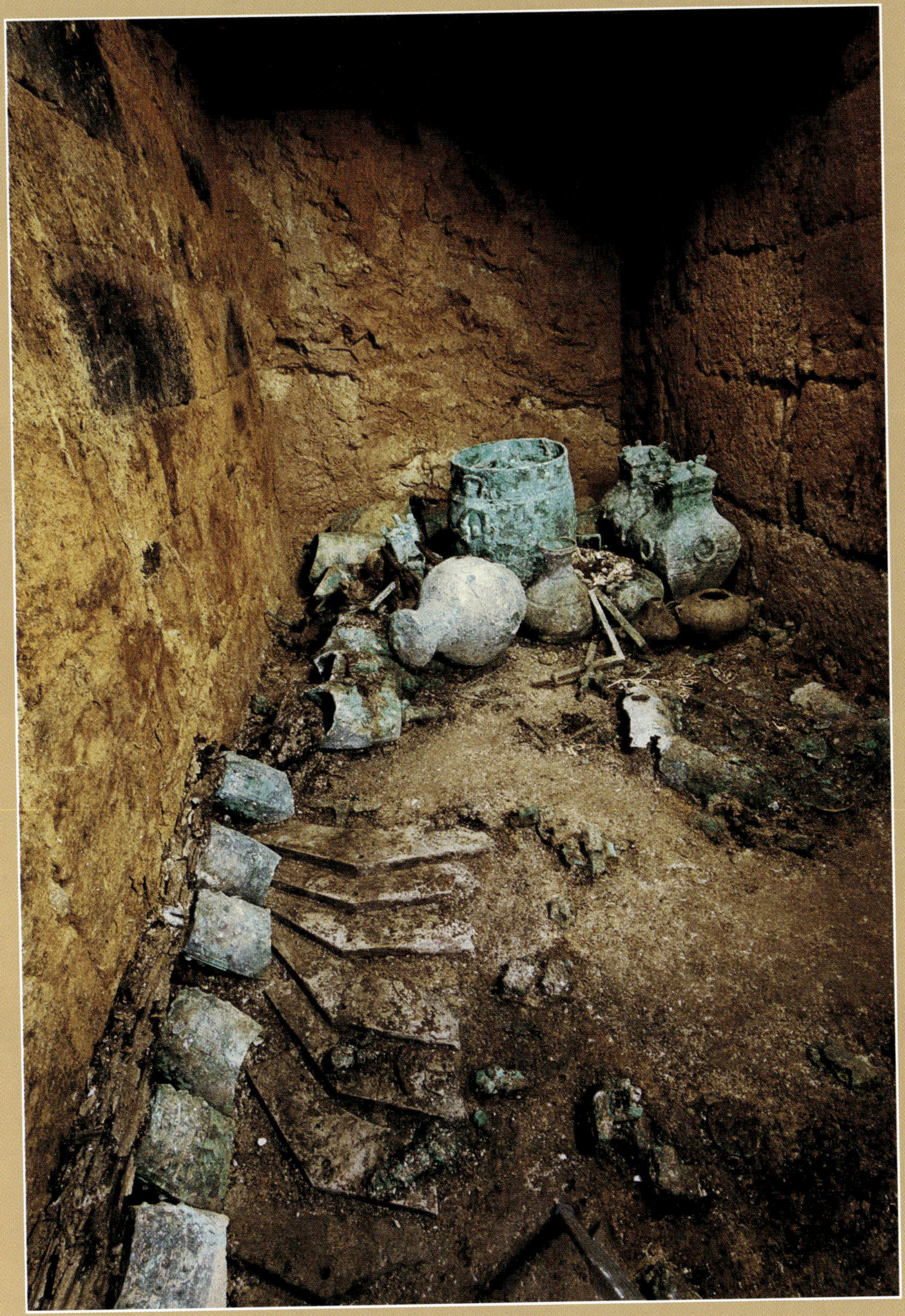

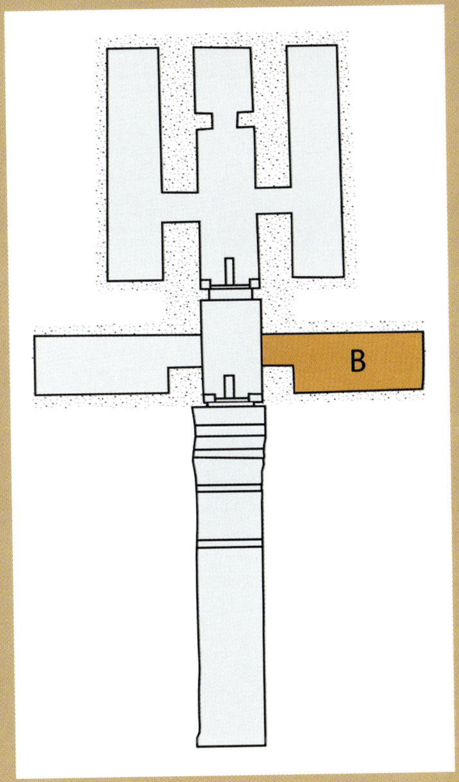

THE EASTERN CHAMBER

The ground was covered with a wooden floor, which has rotted away. Only traces of wood could be seen underneath some of the larger bronze vessels, such as containers (*titong*) and bells.

The eastern chamber was where utensils for banqueting and entertainment were stored and contained many burial goods: sets of instruments made of bronze, stone and lacquered wood and wine vessels were neatly placed inside.

Close to the northern wall was a set of bronze *niuzhong*, all suspended on wooden racks. Not far from the set were two sets of stone chimes, one set of bronze *yongzhong* and *goudiao* (cat. 116), which were all placed on the wooden floor rather than being suspended on wooden racks. In addition, there were other instruments, including *se* and *qing*, which had decayed.

In the south-eastern corner, various types of bronze vessel were stored, some stacked on top of each other, including *titong*, *hu*, *fang* and *pou*. Incense burners (cat. 125), mirrors, belt buckles, a bronze dagger-axe, ceramic vessels, lacquerware and ironwork were also found. Some of the bronze and ceramic vessels contained animal remains, and there were also animal bones scattered on the floor.

CATALOGUE NUMBERS 116–25

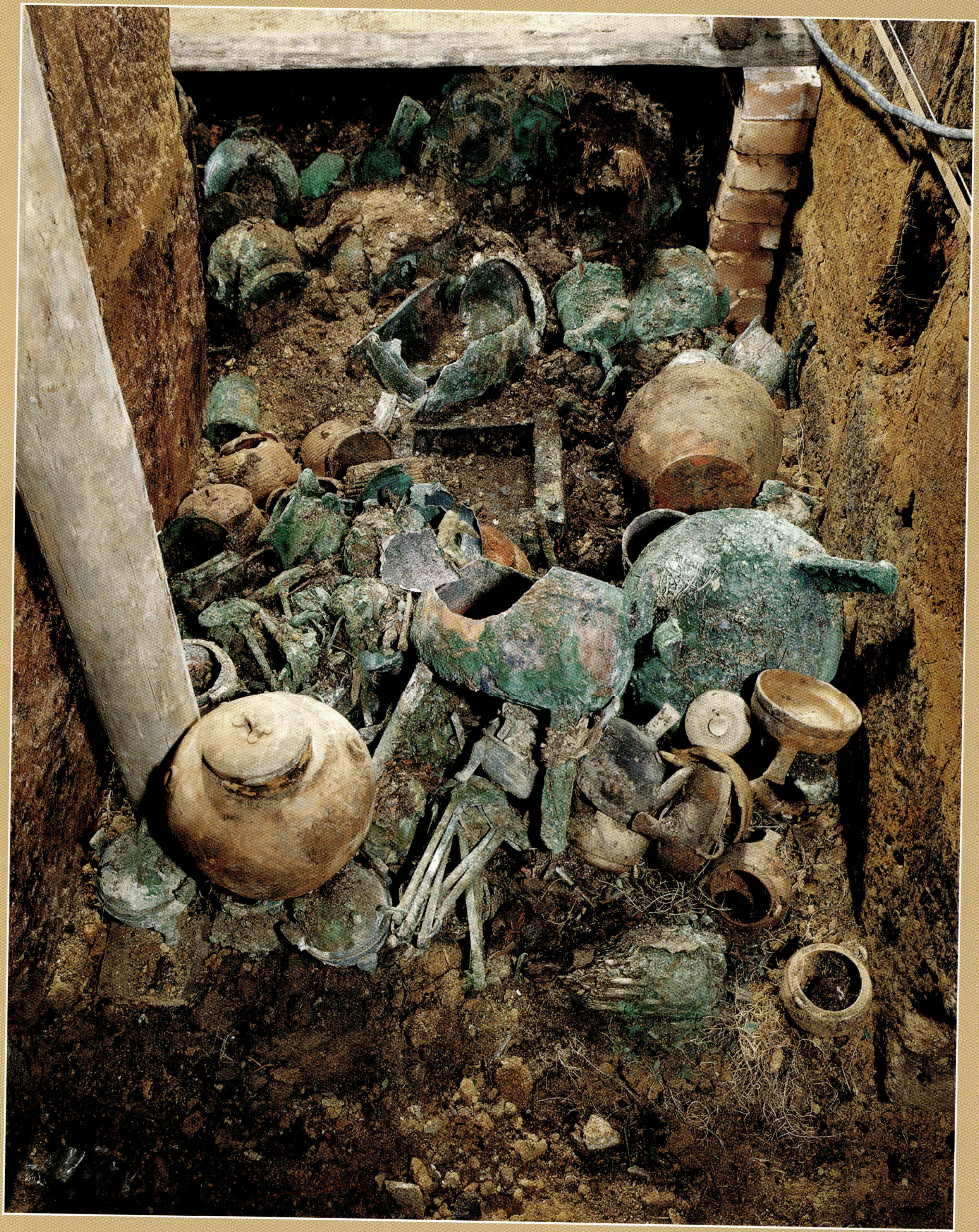

THE WESTERN CHAMBER

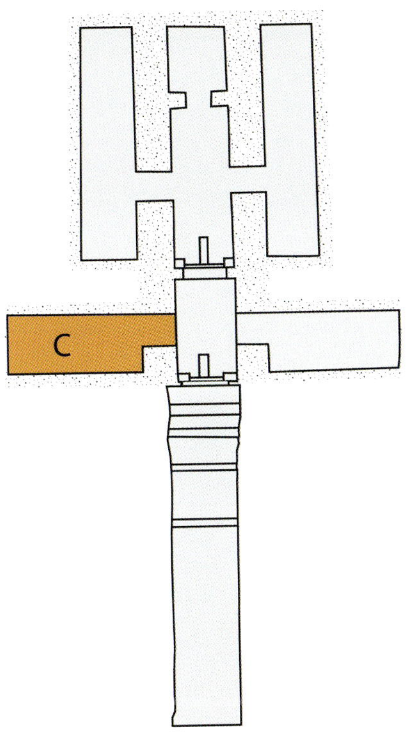

This chamber was formerly covered with wooden floors, which had decayed so only traces of fragments of wood remained. According to the report of the excavation, burial goods were stacked in three layers, possibly on wooden shelves, in this chamber.

On the top layer, three big bronze *ding* were found on a pile of ceramics. A set of nine small bronze vessels and a set of bronze ladles were placed inside a bamboo container. In addition, there were bronze *titong*, ceramic *pou* containing medicine and bronze meat hooks with insect traps. On the south-eastern side of the chamber was a group of ceramic net plummets. In the middle of the chamber, large amounts of lacquerware shards, some discernible lacquered cups with bronze ornaments and lacquer boxes were found. Also in the middle, close to the southern wall, were bronze *juan*, mirrors, arrow shafts and jade and agate seals. Silk textiles, which had been carbonized, were found in the western side of the chamber. On top of the textiles were some wooden boards, which might be the remains of a wooden stack or box that used to hold the textiles.

In the middle layer, close to the passageway leading to the antechamber, decayed lacquerware, gold belt buckles, bronze swords, grinding stones and elephant tusks were unearthed. Lead pellets, bronze vessels and ceramics were found around the elephant tusks. In the south-western corner of the chamber, a lacquered wooden box containing more than seventy iron tools was found. In the middle of the chamber were soapstone pigs, golden bases for lacquer cups, blue glass plaques, incense burners, pegs and bridges of *se* instruments, tiger-shaped *jie* (cat. 143), jade and glass discs, ivory rods, a pestle and mortar (cat. 132) and various minerals. Close to the northern wall was a set of forty-three jade ornaments for swords (cat. 147). They were originally placed inside a lacquer box, which had decayed so that only the lacquer remained.

On the bottom layer, in the passageway connecting to the antechamber, was a pile of ceramics. In the middle of the chamber, two bamboo containers with fittings for horses and chariots were discovered (cat. 127–30). Next to the bamboo container was a bundle of iron arrow shafts. Close to the southern wall were iron armour, large bronze mirrors and silver plates. At the western end of the chamber only textiles were found. In the south-western corner of the chamber a set of chariot fittings and a canopy-supporting pole were discovered (cat. 126). Most of the objects in the chamber contained traces of silk wrappings and bamboo or reed packaging fragments, which indicate that these burial goods were originally stored inside containers that were made of bamboo or reed.

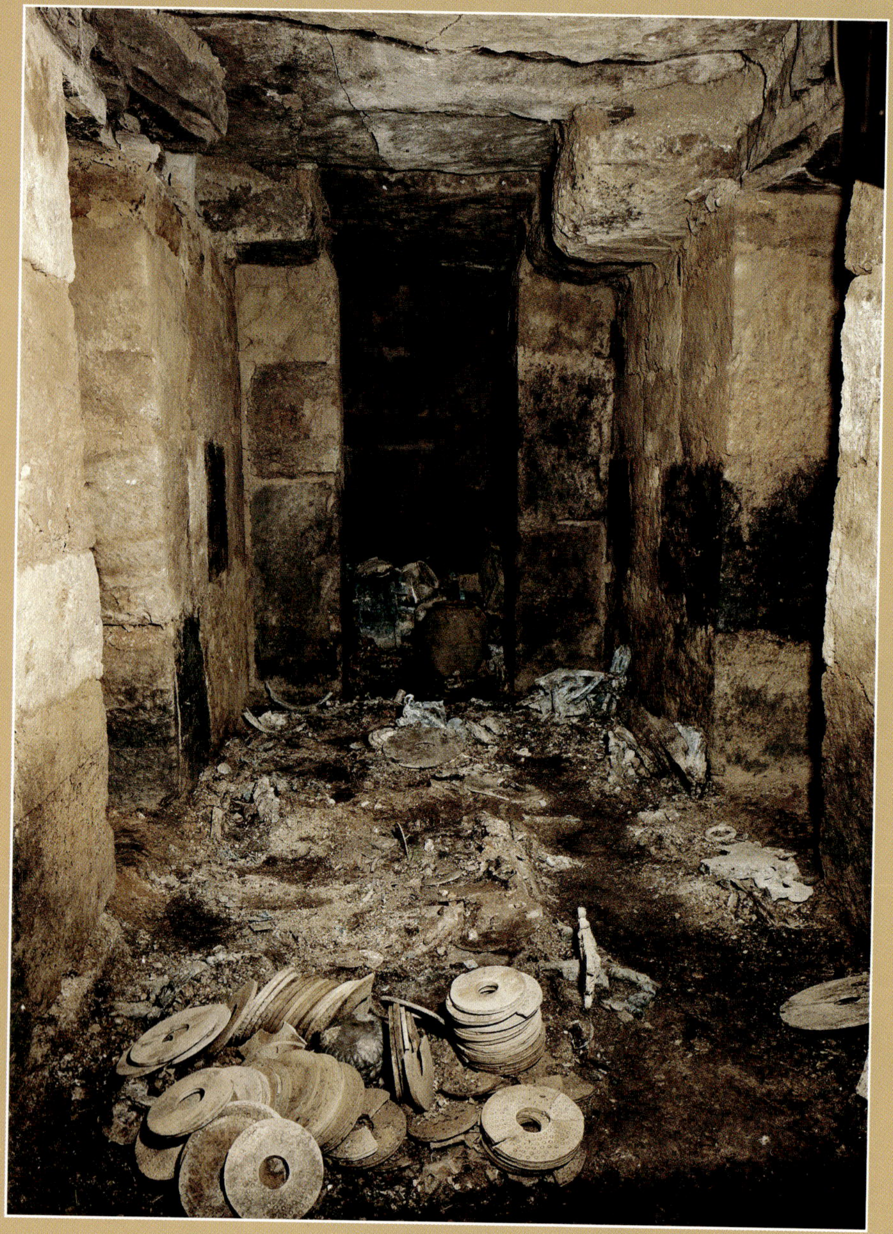

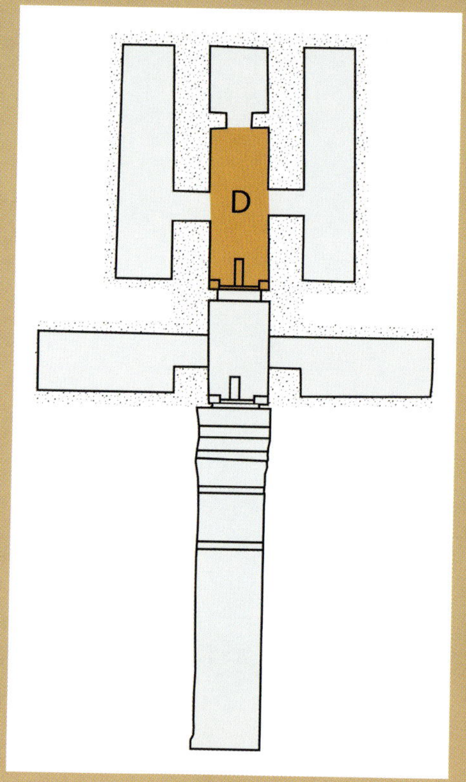

THE KING'S COFFIN CHAMBER

The coffin of the occupant of the tomb was placed in the middle of this chamber. Burial goods were scattered around the coffin. Close to the eastern wall was a large lacquered wooden screen, which blocked the passageway leading to the eastern side chamber. The wooden frame of the screen had rotted away and as a result its original bronze ornaments had fallen onto the ground.

In the northern side of the king's coffin chamber, close to the head of the king, burial goods were discovered. There was an unusual looking jade cup with a bronze base (cat. 164), originally placed inside a lacquerware container, which had rotted away. Only some red and black lacquer was found on top of the jade cup. To the east and the west of the jade cup, large *pen* vessels were placed: on the eastern side a lacquer *pen* with gilt bronze decorations and rotted wooden body; on the western side a deep, large bronze *pen* that was unfortunately smashed by a piece of stone falling from the western wall. In addition, there were two iron spears placed on the doorway leading to the rear storeroom.

To the west of the coffin under the western wall were many weapons, including four iron swords, seven iron spears (cat. 151), a pair of daggers, one bronze dagger-axe and one iron weapon that could not be identified. There were also fifteen pieces of bronze crossbows and many lead pellets and arrowheads. These articles might have been placed on the coffin and fallen to the ground.

Objects were possibly placed in the tomb in the following order: coffins and

CATALOGUE NUMBERS 151–73

burial goods in the western and eastern side chambers first and more than a hundred bronze and iron cooking utensils in the rear chamber. Then the lacquer wooden screen was installed and, finally, the king's coffin was put in position.

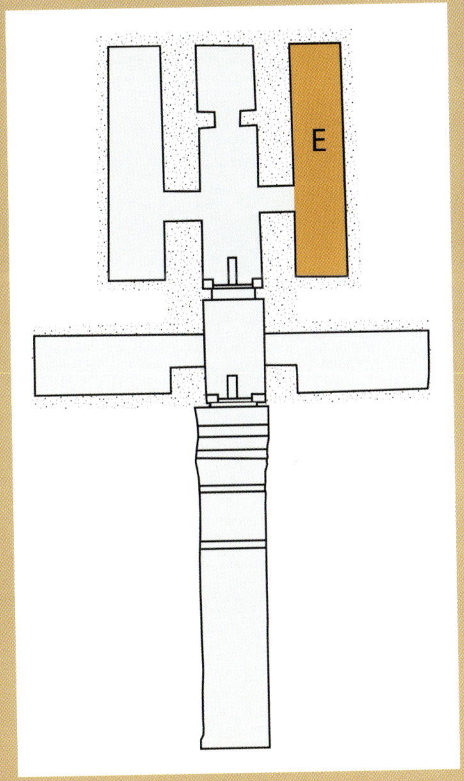

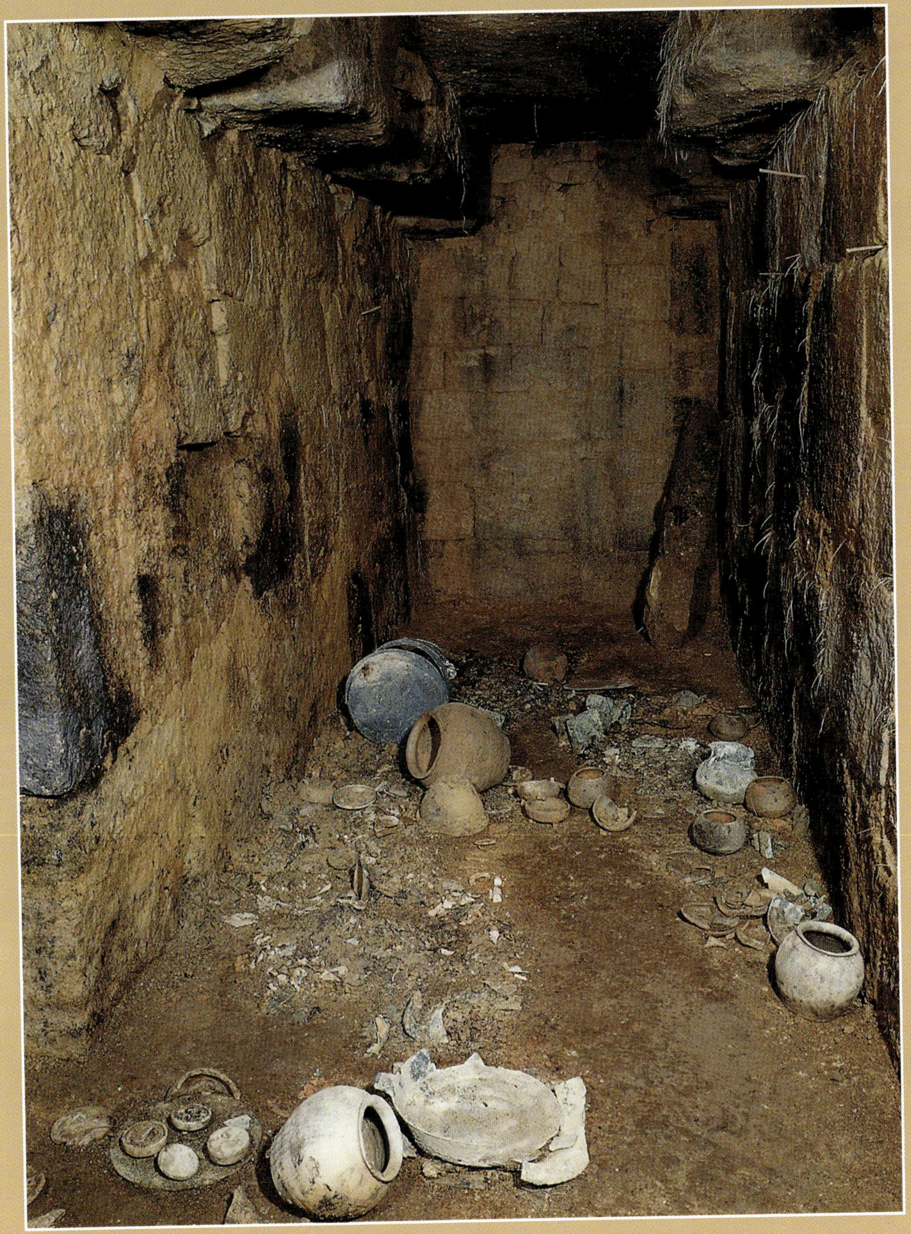

THE EASTERN SIDE CHAMBER

The eastern side chamber was where sacrificial concubines were buried. The burial goods mainly belonged to them, including sets of jade ornaments, seals and bronze and lacquered wooden utensils for daily use. Among the burial goods, four seals had the inscription *furen*, which means lady or wife. On the northern side of the chamber, underneath the western wall were traces of lacquer, which was applied on coffins, sets of jade ornaments and human remains. As a result, the eastern side chamber might be the sacrificial burial site for the four concubines of the king. Due to the fact that the chamber had been flooded several times (traces of lacquer and wood stuck on the ceiling of the chamber show that it was at least once filled with water), the lacquer coffins and the human remains had been severely damaged. According to the excavations, all the sacrificial people were buried inside lacquer coffins.

CATALOGUE NUMBERS 174–80

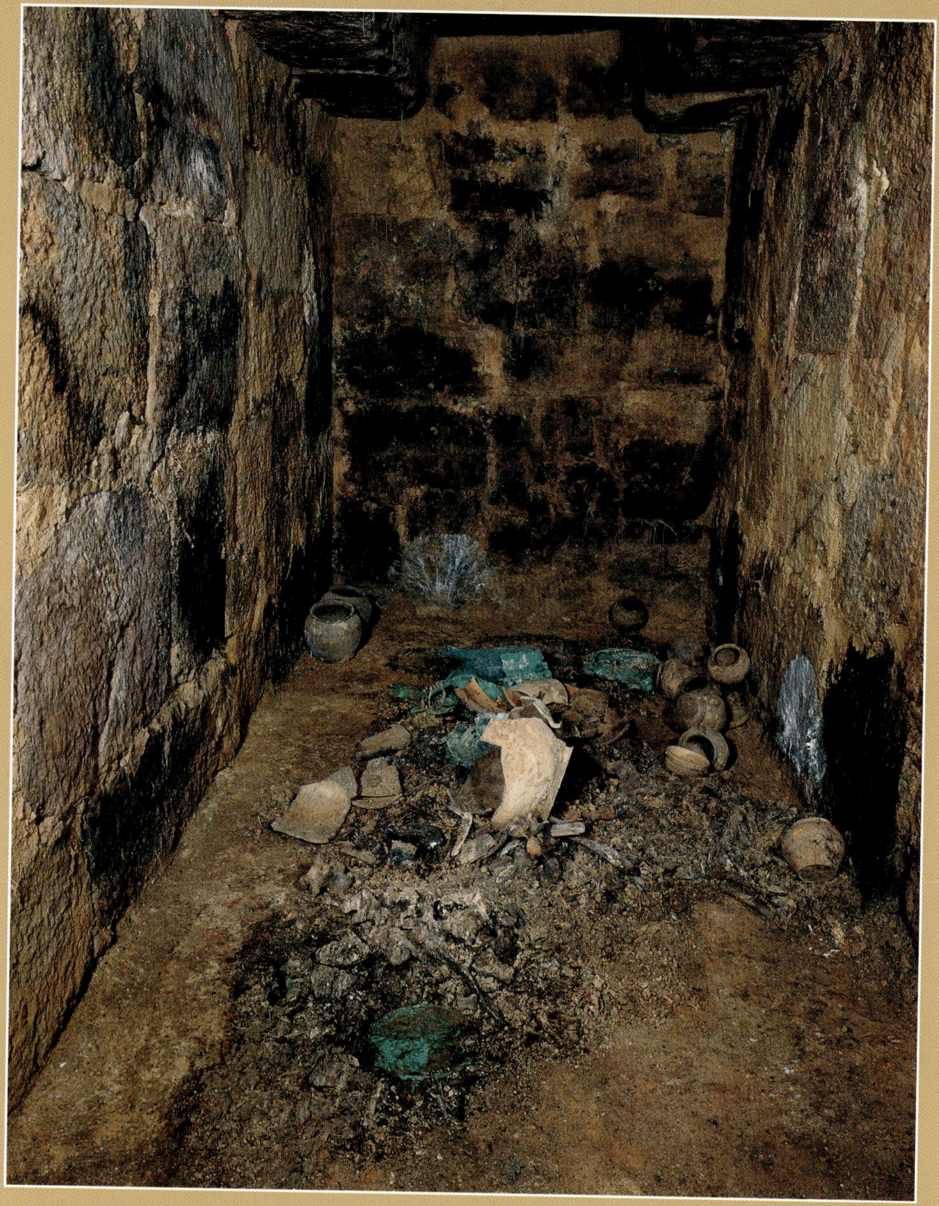

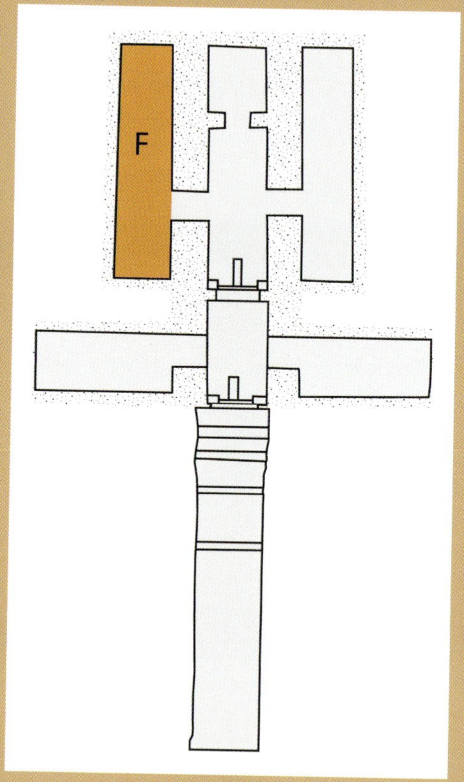

THE WESTERN SIDE CHAMBER

Seven sacrificial people were identified in the western side chamber. Five located in the southern side of the chamber were lying directly on the ground while the other two were found in the northern side of the chamber. Apart from a middle-aged woman, known as R VII who was around forty years old, the rest of the group was relatively young. Judging from the small jade ornaments, belt buckles and bronze mirrors covering their faces, they were most likely female. R VII had the largest number of burial goods and a small jade seal without inscription. She might have been the head of servants.

On the northern side of the western side chamber were piles of bones of oxen, pigs and other animals. These remains were incomplete and seemed to have their heads and tails cut off. They were probably sacrificed for the king. This chamber was meant to function as a kitchen.

CATALOGUE NUMBERS 181–3

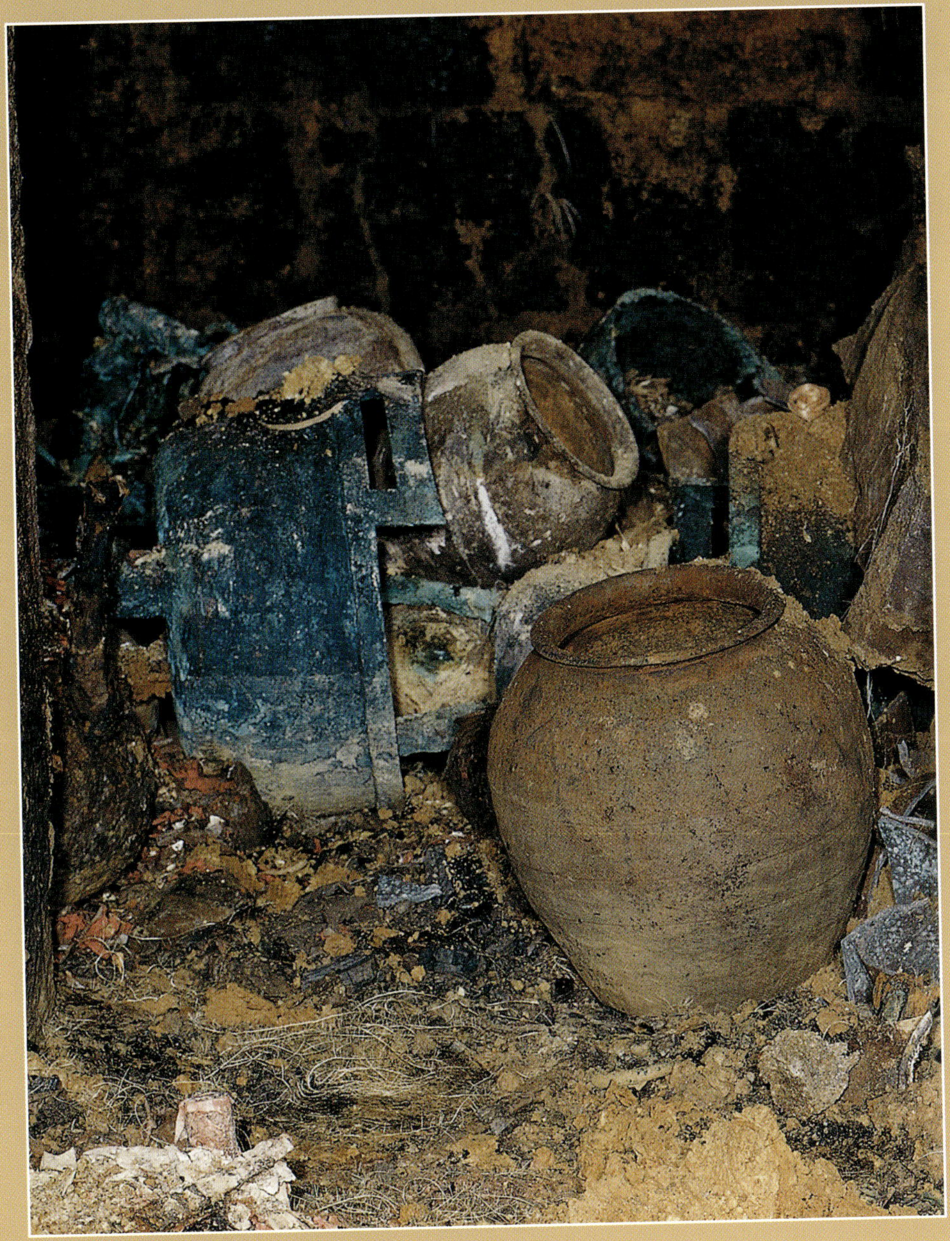

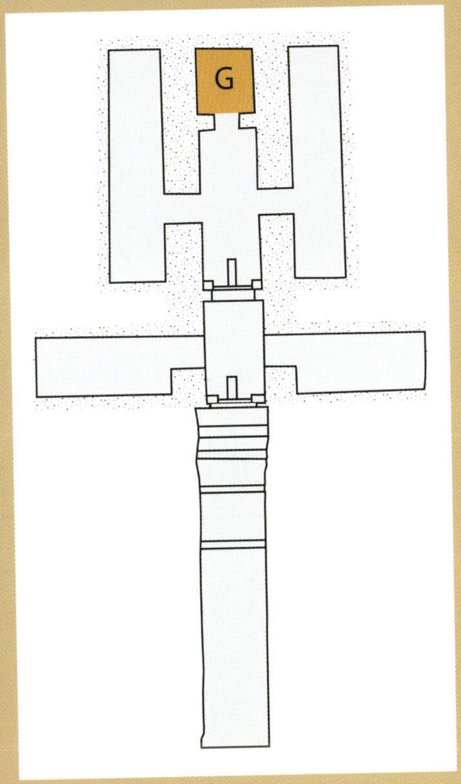

THE REAR STOREROOM

Wooden floors once covered the ground of the rear storeroom. They had rotted away and only traces of ash and decayed pieces of wood could be seen. The room was used to store food, containers, washing devices and cooking utensils, such as *ding* (cat. 184–6), *mou* (cat. 190), cooking stoves (cat. 189), buckets, *jian*, *pen* and ceramic pots and jars. Many objects were stacked on top of each other. Generally speaking, objects of the same genre were placed together and some smaller objects were placed inside larger objects. In between the stacked objects were traces of wooden bars and boards, which indicate that there were originally wooden shelves for holding the objects.

Among the more than one hundred objects stored inside the rear storeroom, most medium-sized and small-sized objects showed traces of wrappers made of silk or reeds. Silk textiles were mainly used to wrap bronze and iron objects. Reed wrappers were used for ceramics and food inside containers. About thirty pieces of bronze and ceramic objects contained poultry, domestic animals and seafood. In addition, there were many clay blocks with the seal impression *taiguan*, which indicates that the burial objects inside the rear storeroom were inspected and sealed up by *taiguan* officials. Furthermore, on the floor at the doorway and in the south-eastern corner of the room, a 3 to 5 millimetre-thick layer of charcoal was found. Because the room had been flooded, charcoal floated around the chamber and some was discovered inside ceramic pots. Charcoal was stored as fuel for cooking.

CATALOGUE NUMBERS 184–93

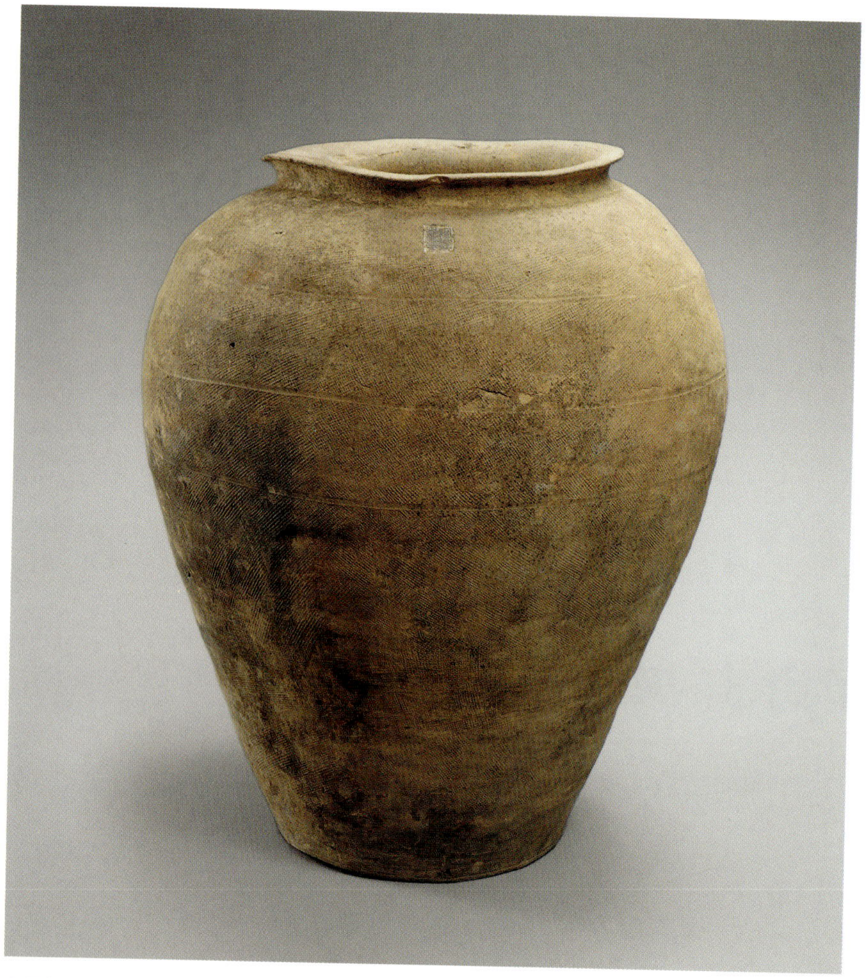

115

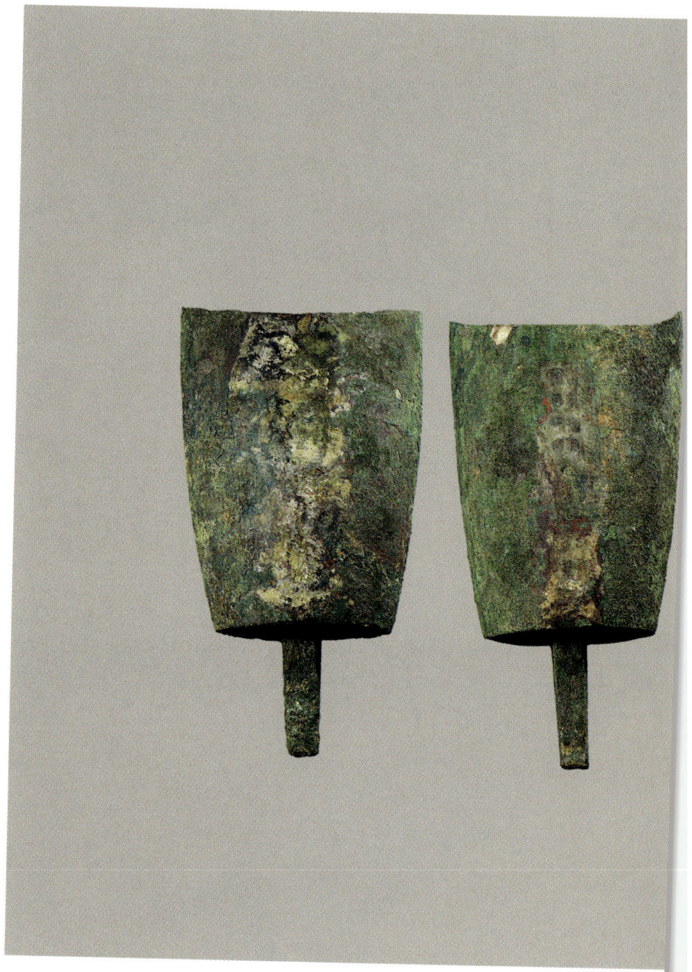

116

115

Changle Palace pottery utensil urn

Second century BC, Western Han dynasty
Height: 53 cm; Diameter: 46.5 cm
Excavated at Xianggangshan in 1983
The Museum of the King of Nanyue, Guangdong Province

This tall pottery urn has a slightly small foot, rising to a rounded shoulder, without a neck but with a contracted mouth and everted rim. It has been made using the clay-strip technique with a trellis and a geometrical pattern, which contains seven designs. Unusually, this urn bears a stamp *Changlegong qi* (utensil from the Eternal Happiness Palace) on its shoulder. Two similar urns are known.

This urn was excavated from the tomb pathway, which is a rectangular pit containing one immolated person, in front of the main tomb door. The tomb has eighteen similarly shaped urns, and seventeen of them are from this tomb pathway. Nothing remains of what was once contained in these urns. However, discoveries in other storage vessels both in this tomb and in other Han tombs in Guangzhou provide evidence that they may have contained foodstuff like fruits, chickens, pigs, shells and fish. It was common to include foodstuff and other material requirements in burials of this kind. KJC

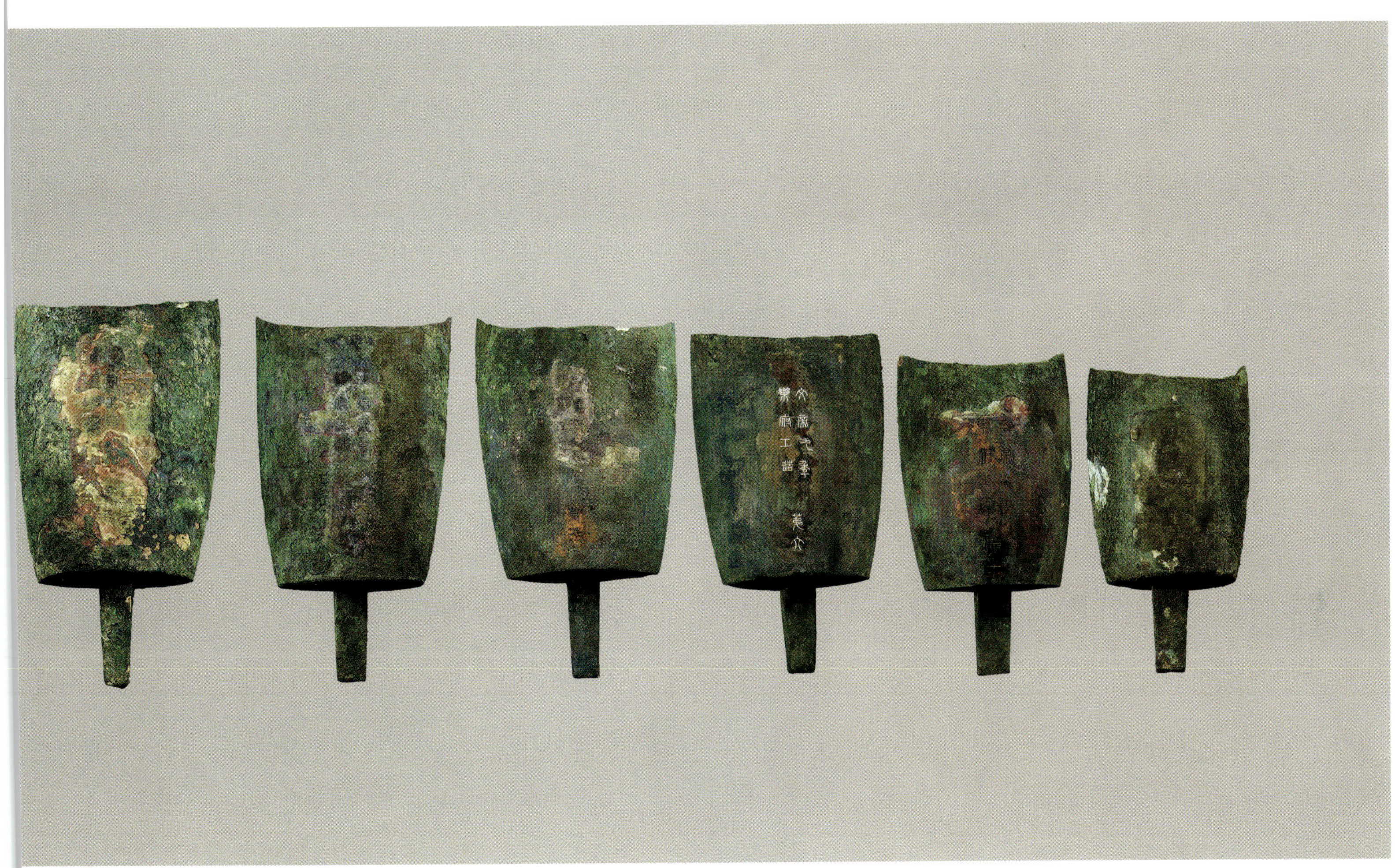

116

Bronze musical instruments (*goudiao*)

Second century BC, Western Han dynasty
Height: 64 cm, 60.7 cm, 55.7 cm, 51.2 cm, 48.2 cm, 43.1 cm, 37.6 cm, 36.8 cm
Excavated at Xianggangshan in 1983
The Museum of the King of Nanyue, Guangdong Province

A set of eight *goudiao* of different sizes and placed one inside the other was stored in the eastern chamber of the tomb. Incised on the surface of each are the characters *wendi jiunian yuefu gongzao* (cast by the musicians of the Music Bureau in the ninth year of Emperor Wen; 129 BC), with a series of numbers from one to eight indicating the comparative sizes of the instruments. Number one is the largest, measuring 64 cm in height and 40 kg in weight, while number eight is the smallest, measuring 36.8 cm in height and 10.75 kg in weight. This set of *goudiao* is probably the least ancient of those that have been excavated so far.

Use of this type of musical instrument seems limited to southeast China, particularly to the Zhejiang and Jiangsu areas, and can be dated from the late Spring and Autumn period to the Warring States period. Occasionally, they have been found in the Shandong area. The name *goudiao* was not recorded in any texts, but was cast on the

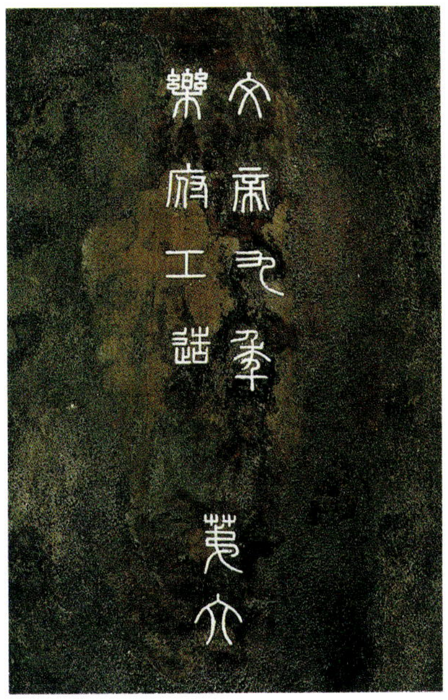

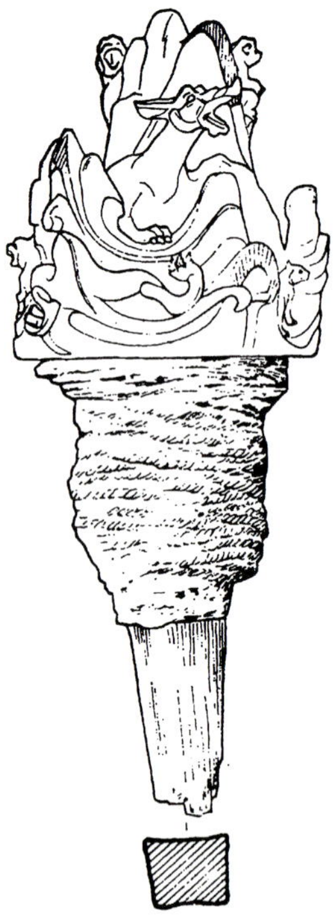

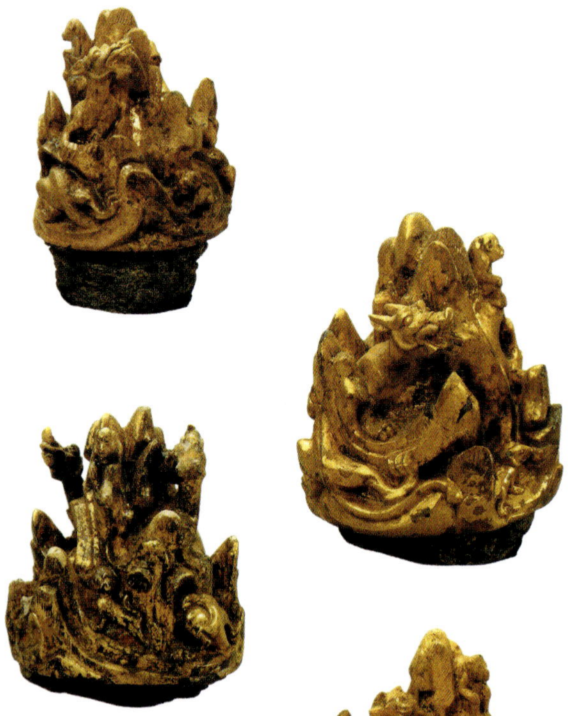

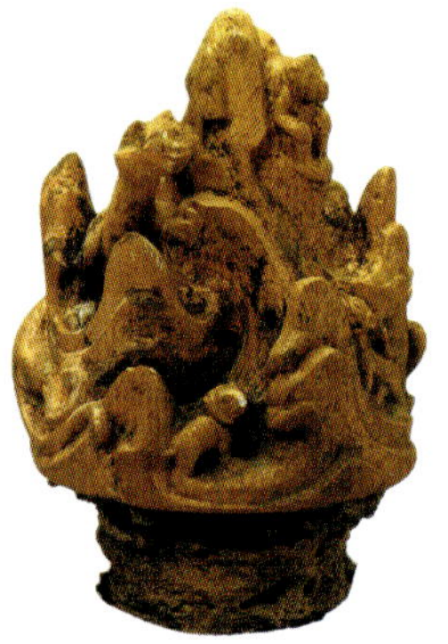

117

instruments themselves. An inscription on one *goudiao* unearthed in Changshu, Jiangsu Province records that it was made for entertainment.[1] JCSL

1 *Kaogu yu wenwu* 1996.6, pp. 38–41.

117

Gilt bronze bridges for stringed instruments (*se*)

Second century BC, Western Han dynasty
Height: 8 cm; Diameter: 5.5 cm
Excavated at Xianggangshan in 1983
The Museum of the King of Nanyue, Guangdong Province

The *se* is a traditional Chinese stringed instrument. In the Han dynasty, the standard number of strings for a *se* was probably twenty-five; one well preserved such example has been excavated from a tomb in Mawangdui and can be dated to the Western Han dynasty (fig. 49). No *se* survives in the tomb of the King of Nanyue, but several bridges have been discovered. The bridges are cast in similar size, but the shapes differ from one another in detail, suggesting that they were crafted individually rather than cast from a single mould. They all have the shapes of layered mountains, with a central peak surrounded by two layers of lower hills. Several mythical and realistic animals, including dragons, monkeys, bears, deer and tigers, are arranged among the mountains. When the bridges were excavated, there were residues of silk on all of them, indicating that the musical instrument was wrapped in silk when it was buried. LKC

118

Bronze wine container (*fang*) on square base

Second century BC, Western Han dynasty
Height: 55.5 cm
Excavated at Xianggangshan in 1983
The Museum of the King of Nanyue, Guangdong Province

This object has a flaring square base that stands on four small protrusions in the corners. The body is pear-shaped and adorned with four ring handles attached to animal masks. Careful inspection reveals that each mask consists of the bodies of two playfully intertwined dragons. Four small abstract ornaments are fitted to the domed lid.

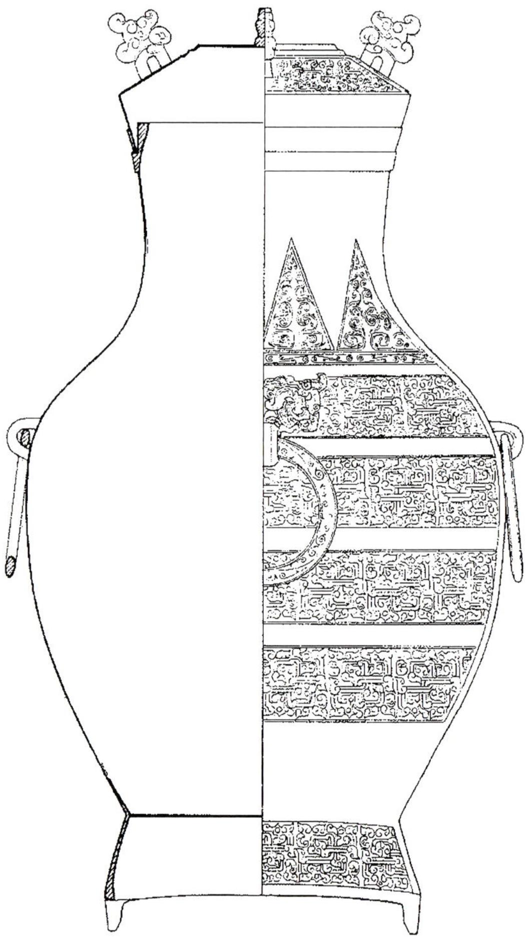

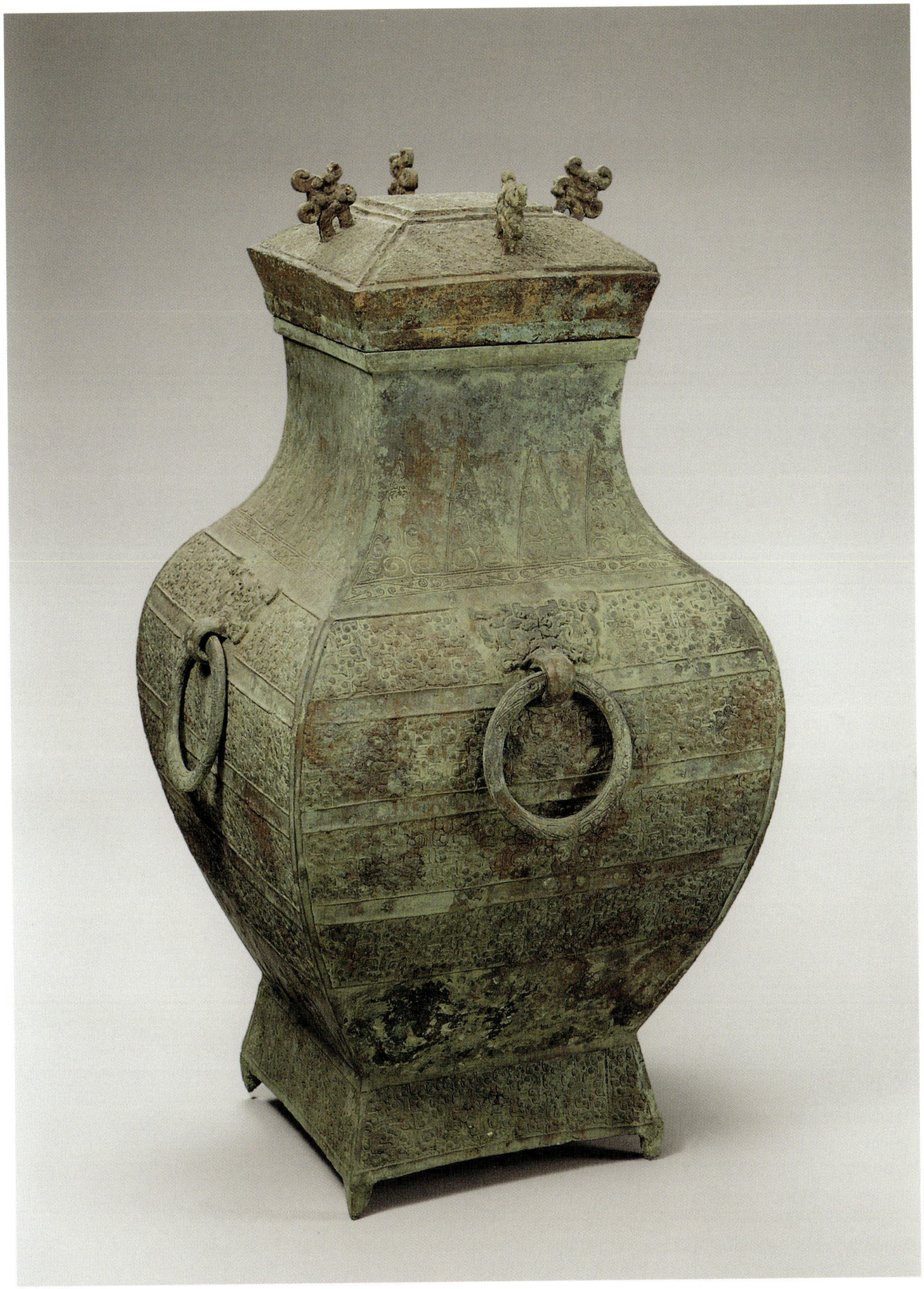

118

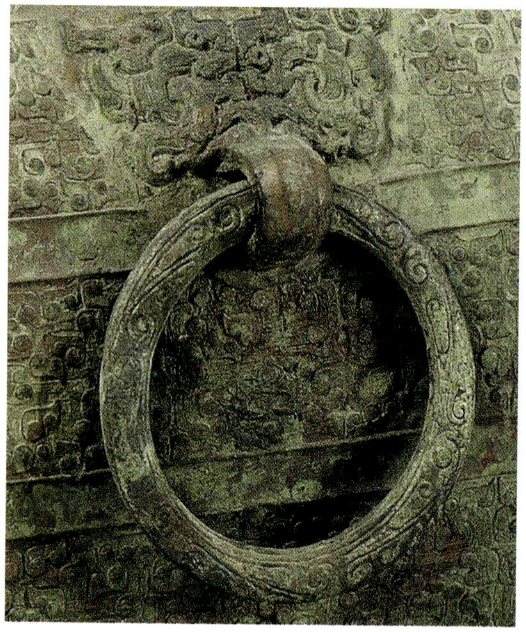

The surface of the vessel displays fine ornament in low relief. Several undecorated bands separate registers of a highly abstracted decoration of irregular geometric shapes and paired volutes. This ornament can be traced back to snake-dragon motifs on bronzes of the sixth and fifth centuries BC.[1] Surface-filling relief decoration as on this object became increasingly uncommon during the Western Han dynasty (cat. 119). When placed in the tomb the jar may very well have been an antique that had already been handed down for generations.

The object was found inside the eastern chamber of the tomb of Zhao Mo, which contained mainly musical instruments. Archaeologists discovered several sets of bronze bells and chime stones as well as remains of wooden string instruments. Inscriptions on some of the bells referring to *yuefu* (the music bureau) indicate that this chamber served ritual functions.[2]

The *fang* was discovered together with a second with comparable features.[3] The latter also displays four ring handles, a low relief covering the body and four abstract protrusions on the lid. Since the actual dimensions of the second jar differ slightly from those of the first, and since the ornamentation is less sophisticated, it may have been cast later to complement the first. During the Han period such jars were often displayed as pairs. LN

1 See the decoration of jars and other vessels from Hunyuan, Shanxi Province, dating to the fifth century BC. Bagley 1995, figs 3, 8, 11.
2 Nickel 1998, p. 60.
3 Beijing 1991, vol. 1, pp. 46–7, vol. 2, pl. 16:1.

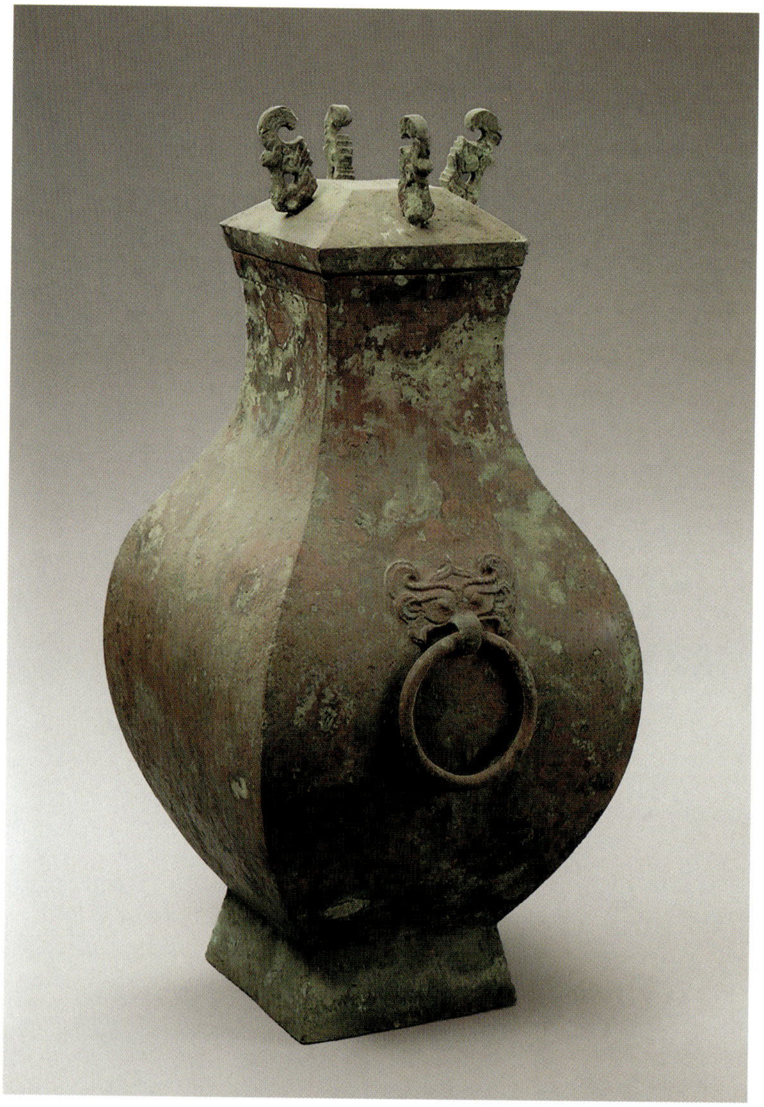

119

119

Gilt bronze *fang* on square base

Second century BC, Western Han dynasty
Height: 44.6 cm
Excavated at Xianggangshan in 1983
The Museum of the King of Nanyue, Guangdong Province
NOT EXHIBITED

The jar has a bulging, pear-shaped body over a high flaring foot, and the mouth is accentuated by a raised band. The domed lid fits tightly into the mouth of the vessel. It displays four ornamental attachments in the shape of stylized birds. On the sides of the body two raised animal masks hold movable ring handles.

Beneath large patches of corrosion, the surface of the vessel is undecorated but bears some traces of gilding. Another Western Han *fang* of quite similar shape and size now in the Metropolitan Museum of Art, New York has a gilt body with silver-leaf geometric decoration.[1] It is possible that when in use at the court of Panyu this *fang* had a similar decoration.

Most vessels from ancient China are categorized in modern terminology as the original names of the Han period are not known. In this case, however, inscriptions on bronzes found in the tomb of Liu Sheng in Mancheng, Hebei indicate that jars on a square base like this were called *fang*, as opposed to comparable jars on a round base that were known as *zhong*.[2] *Fang* and *zhong* were a standard part of tomb equipment across wide parts of Han society. They are found in bronze or as earthenware replicas and it is believed that they served as wine containers. LN

1 Bunker 1988, p. 71, fig. 2.
2 Beijing 1980, pp. 49–51.

120

Gilt bronze vessel (*hu*)

Second century BC, Western Han dynasty
Height: 37 cm; Body diameter: 28.1 cm
Excavated at Xianggangshan in 1983
The Museum of the King of Nanyue, Guangdong Province

Found in the eastern part of the eastern chamber, this storage vessel was deposited with a larger bronze of similar type and others, such as *fang* (cat. 118, 119), a set of bronze *titong* (cat. 122) and ceramic jars. It has been suggested that it formed a pair with the larger example from the same chamber, as is often the case in Han-period burials.[1] However, the western chamber also contained seven similar *hu*, an uneven number, so pairing them up may not have been intended.

The entire surface of the object is covered in mercury-amalgam gilding, which became apparent after it was cleaned. An *in situ* photograph taken during excavation suggests that at its discovery this *hu* was thickly encrusted with patina and there were still traces of a textile in which it had been wrapped.[2] Its broken lid was found inside.

Two lacquered wooden versions of this type and their square counterparts, *fang*, from tomb No. 1 at Mawangdui contained dregs of alcohol, confirming that such vessels were used to store alcohol.[3] *Hu* were also used to store other kinds of food: for example, carbonized remains of jujube were found in bronze *hu* from the western side chamber.[4] A large number of ceramic *hu* in both tombs at Mancheng contained the remains of animals and plants, such as fish and grain, but also the bones of hamsters and other rodents.[5] As nothing remained inside this vessel, it is unclear what it may once have contained. SP

1 Prüch 1998, cat. 9.
2 Beijing 1991, vol. 2, pl. 11:1.
3 Beijing 1973, vol. 1, pp. 79–80.
4 Beijing 1991, vol. 1, pp. 77–8.
5 Beijing 1980, vol. 1, pp. 121, 285.

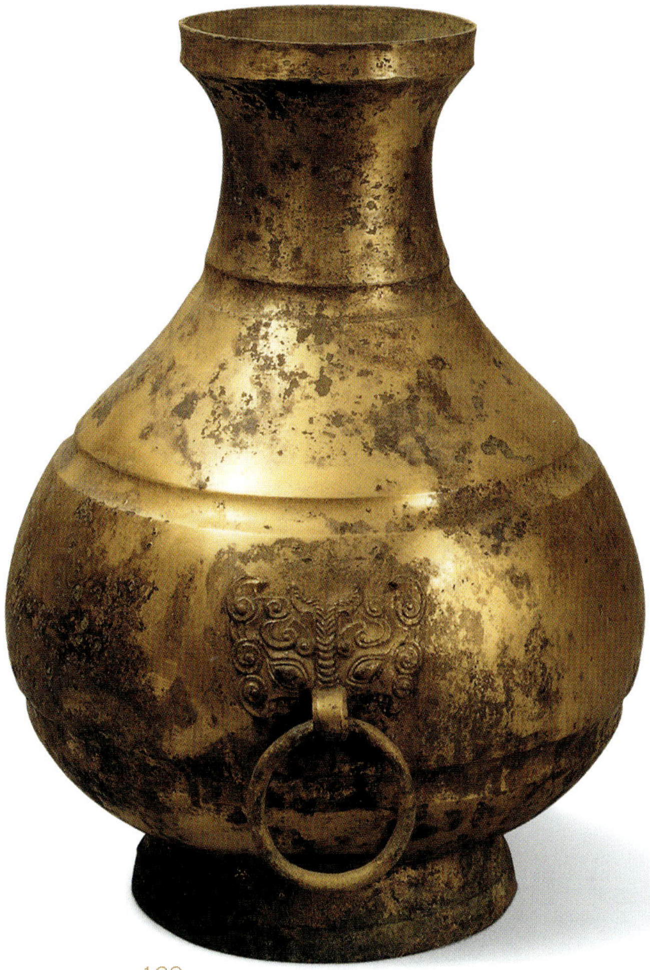

120

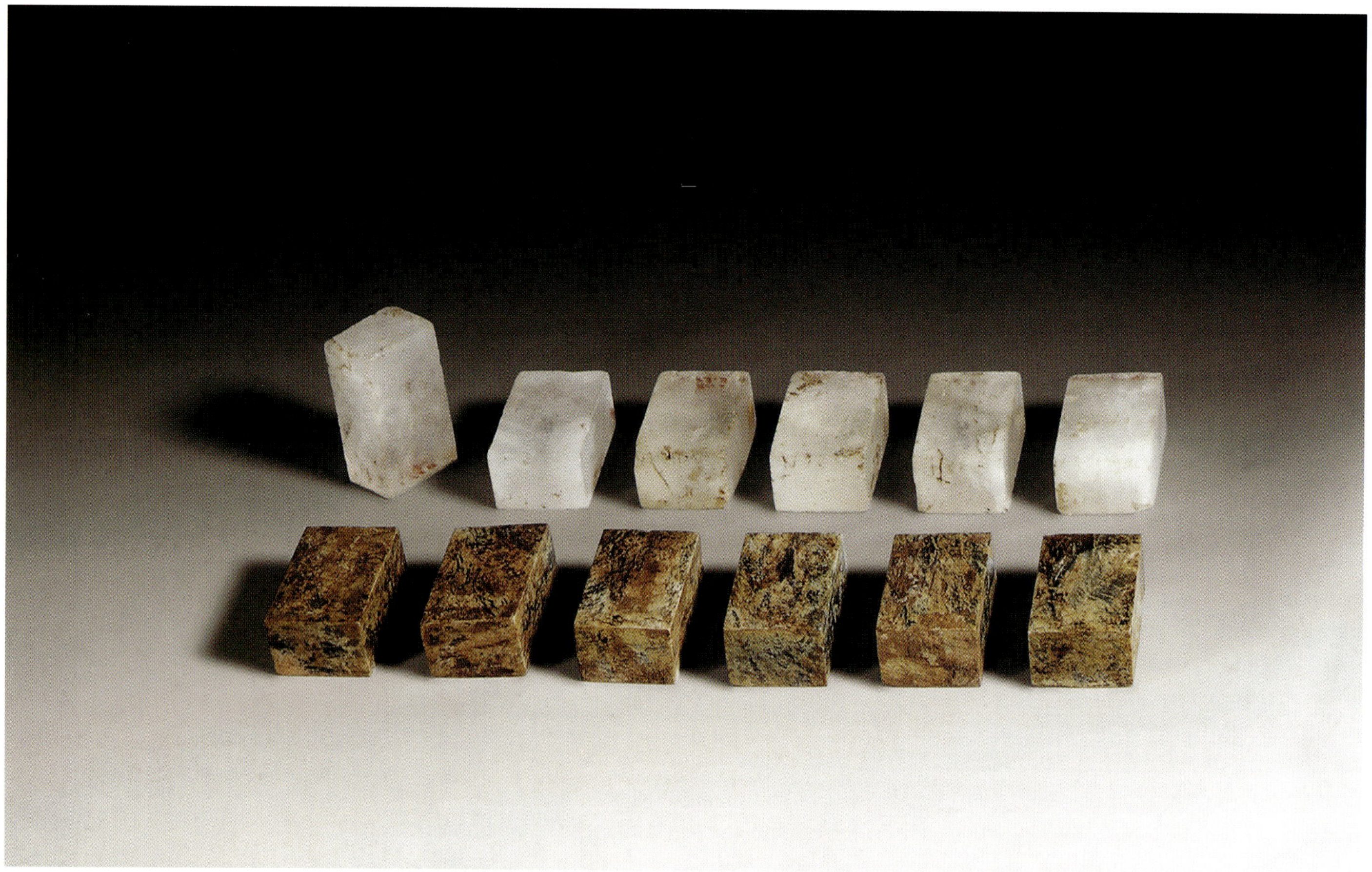

121

121

Counters for *Liubo* board game

Second century BC, Western Han dynasty
Length: 3.3 cm; Width: 2 cm; Height: 1.3 cm
Excavated at Xianggangshan in 1983
The Museum of the King of Nanyue, Guangdong Province

Liubo was a game that involved moving two sets of six rectangular counters, possibly from the outside towards the centre of the game board. Moves were determined by throwing six rods, which functioned as dice (fig. 58). Unfortunately, the precise rules have long been lost.

According to ancient texts, *Liubo* might have originated in China more than three thousand years ago during the Shang dynasty, although the reliability of such claims is questionable.[1] Nevertheless, there seems no doubt that the game had become extremely popular by the Han dynasty. Remains of pieces of the game from Han tombs and images of people playing the game on Han pictorial bricks have been unearthed from all over China.[2] Historical records suggest that both men and women of all levels of society played *Liubo*.[3]

Liubo was a game of chance and therefore came to be associated with the spiritual world and cosmology, which might be one reason why it was deemed an appropriate inclusion among burial goods.[4] Seen as a symbol of good luck, the patterns on the *Liubo* board were often applied as a decorative motif on Han bronze mirrors, known as TLV mirrors (cat. 112).[5]

Two *Liubo* game boards were unearthed from the eastern chamber of the tomb of the King of Nanyue at Xianggangshan. The wooden parts had

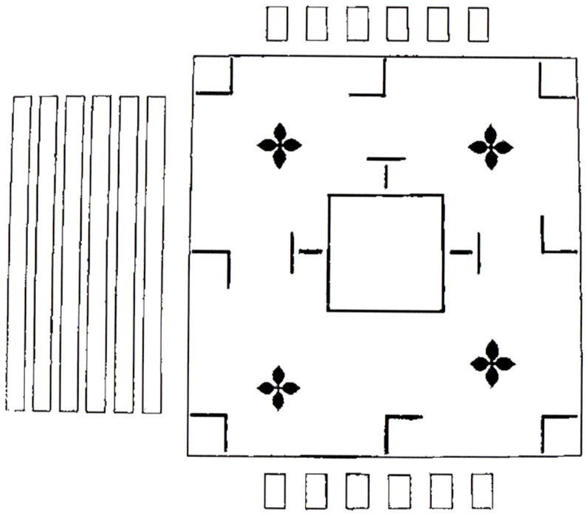

58 Drawing of a *Liubo* board.

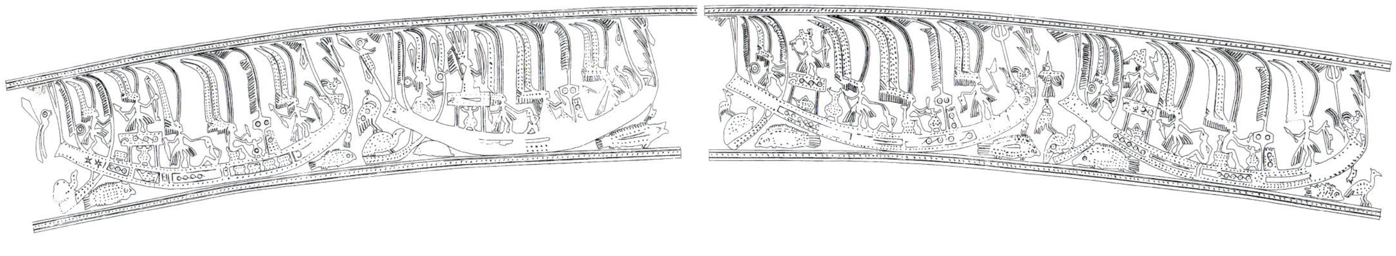

Fig. 59

rotted away and only the gilt bronze frames and gold foil decorations survived. Crystal and jade counters would have been included, but as the boards had been smashed by rocks falling from the ceiling the counters were found scattered throughout the eastern chamber.[6] NC

1 Mackenzie 2004, p. 113.
2 Mackenzie 2004, p. 118; Fu 1986, pp. 21–8.
3 Mackenzie 2004, p. 118; Fu 1986, pp. 36–7.
4 Mackenzie 2004, p. 113.
5 Cheng 1997, pp. 124–6.
6 Beijing 1991, pp. 64–7.

122

Bronze container (*titong*)

Second century BC, Western Han dynasty
Height: 40.7 cm; Mouth diameter: 34–35.5 cm
Excavated at Xianggangshan in 1983
The Museum of the King of Nanyue, Guangdong Province

This container was found in the western end of the eastern chamber together with two larger *titong*, placed one inside the other with this innermost; it in turn contained a bronze *fang*.[1] Among the nine *titong*, seven bronze and two ceramic, found in this tomb this one stands out because of the central band of figures and boats decorating the body (fig. 59).

This scene and the shape of the vessel relate this *titong* not only to others found in Yunnan, Guangxi, Guangdong and northern Vietnam, but also to famous bronze drums found in southern China and northern Vietnam. Boat scenes were a common form of decoration (a contemporaneous bronze drum with similar decoration was found in tomb M1 at Luobowan, Guangxi, within the territory of the King of Nanyue).[2] The closest comparison comes from a bronze drum from the Ngọc Lũ site in the Red River delta in Vietnam.[3] The distribution of bronze *titong* and the similarities they shared have led some scholars to suggest that they may have come from northern Vietnam either as tribute or trade items.[4] SP

1 Beijing 1991, vol. 2, pl. 17:3. For an illustration, see Prüch 1998, cat. 8.
2 Beijing 1988, colour pl. 1.
3 *Kaogu* 1989.9, p. 843.
4 Prüch 1998, cat. 5; *Kaogu* 1989.9, p. 848.

59 Drawings of a bronze container (*titong*) with boat images.

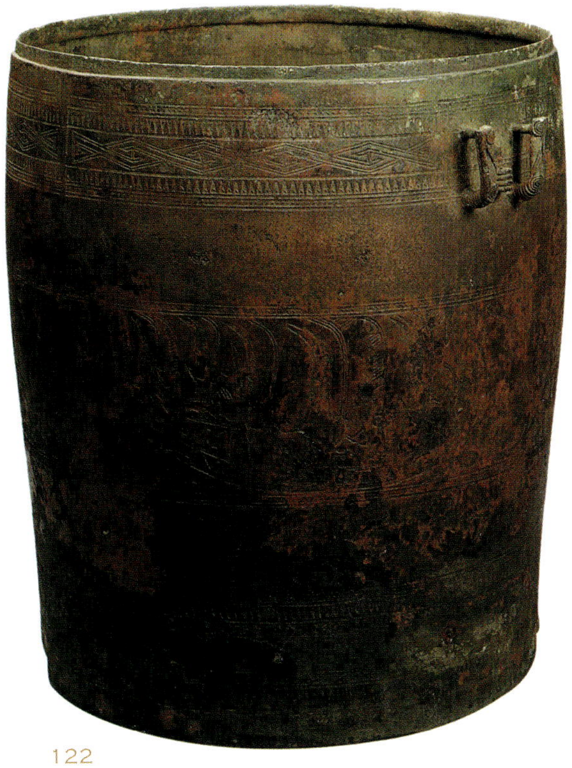

122

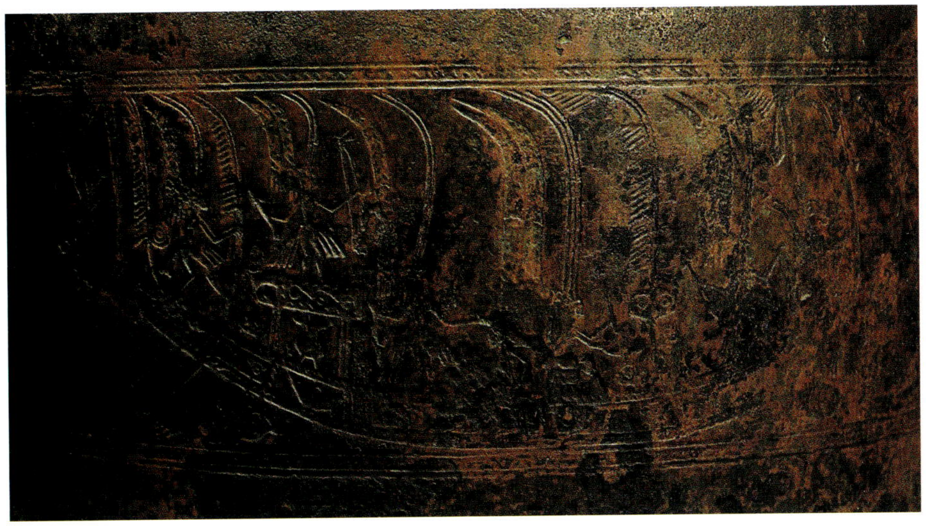

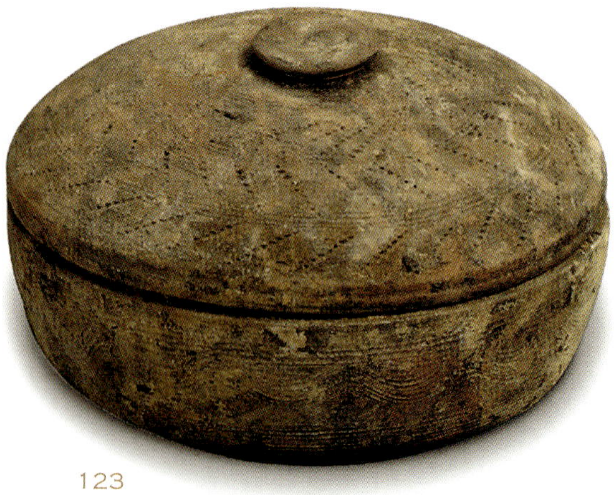

123

123

Earthenware covered box with polychrome decoration

Second century BC, Western Han dynasty
Height: 7.3 cm; Diameter: 10.5 cm
Excavated at Xianggangshan in 1983
The Museum of the King of Nanyue, Guangdong Province

This covered box is decorated with coloured paint. The straight body is decorated with wave patterns and is partly covered with lines of black ink on a geometrical design in red ink. The rounded cover, which fits the body tightly, is also painted. There is a standing knob in the centre of the cover.

Eight boxes like this one were discovered in the tomb of the King of Nanyue. Except for one from the tomb pathway that belonged to the sacrificial attendant and one from the western chamber, the other six were from the eastern chamber, which is believed to have stored mainly objects for banqueting and entertainment, including musical instruments. But no traces of material remains were found inside the box. KJC

124

Earthenware pot in the shape of a gourd

Second century BC, Western Han dynasty
Height: 17 cm; Diameter: 17.2 cm
Excavated at Xianggangshan in 1983
The Museum of the King of Nanyue, Guangdong Province
NOT EXHIBITED

This earthenware pot imitates the shape of a gourd. It has a contracted mouth and a large flat bottom and the upper part is fat and short. The lower part is round and swells outward. A pair of ears with a pattern of three strings is on the shoulder. The lower body is decorated with comb and string patterns and cloud designs in black and red inks.

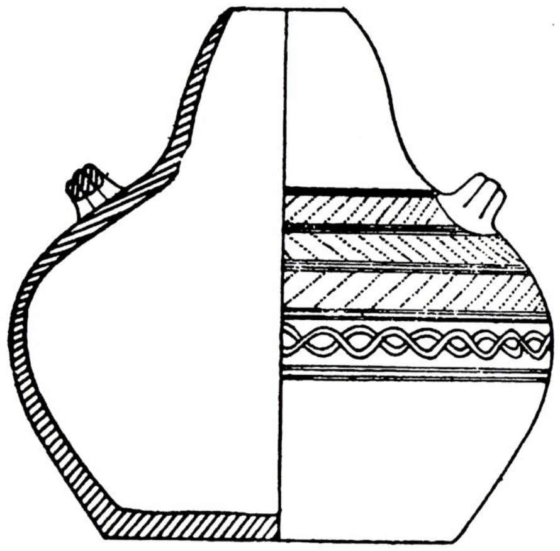

This item is from the eastern chamber, which functioned as an entertainment room. Only three of this special ceramic form have been found, in three different chambers of the tomb. KJC

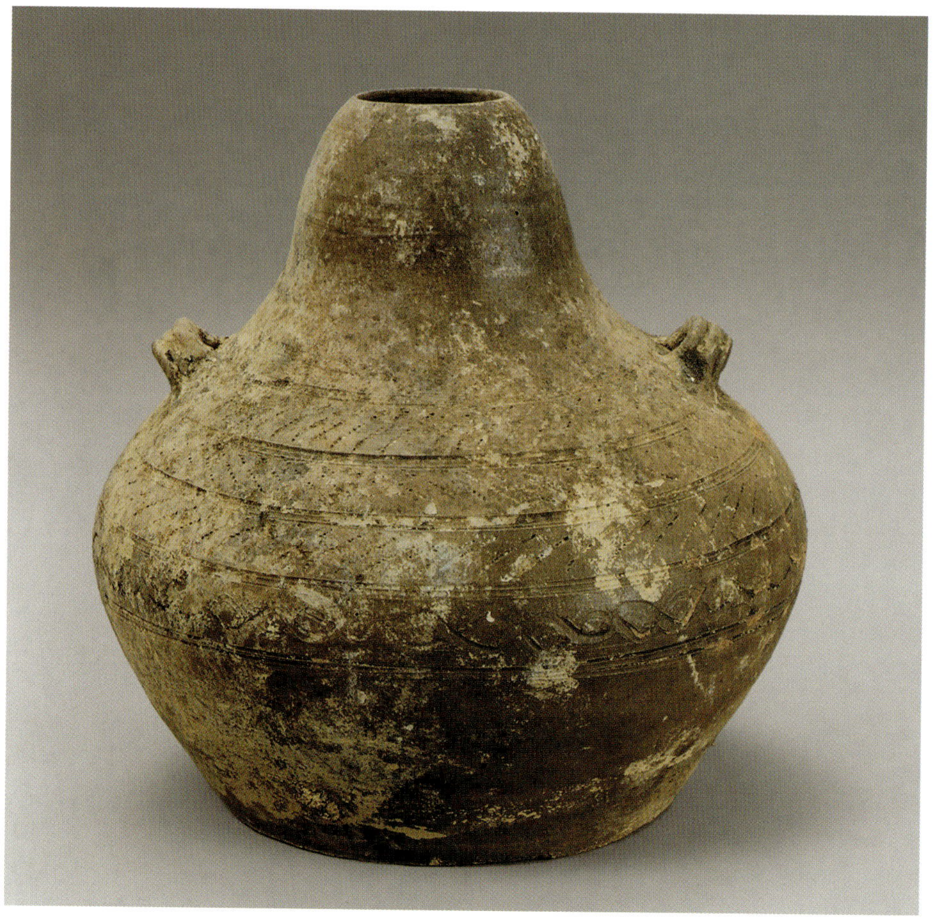

124

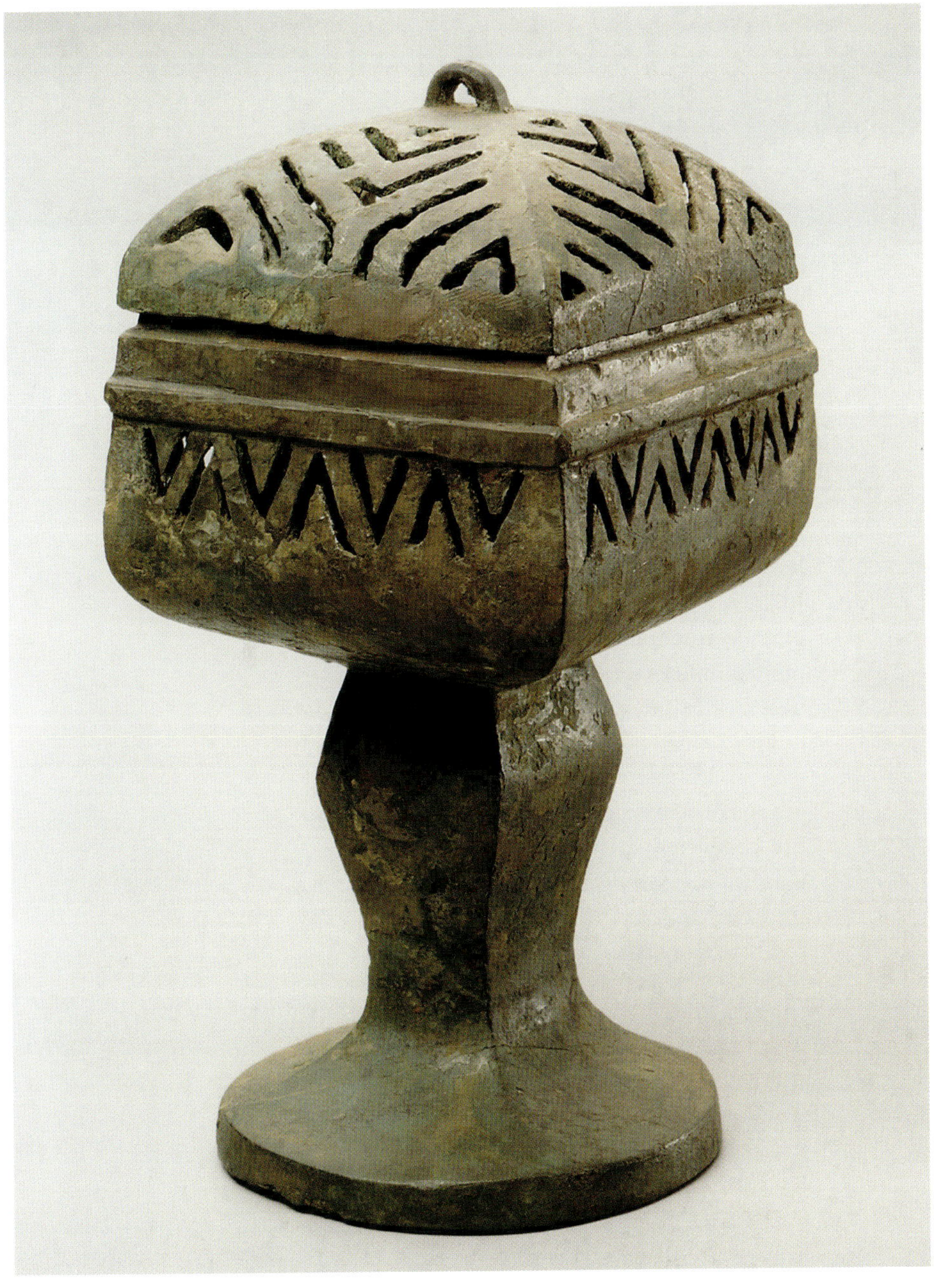

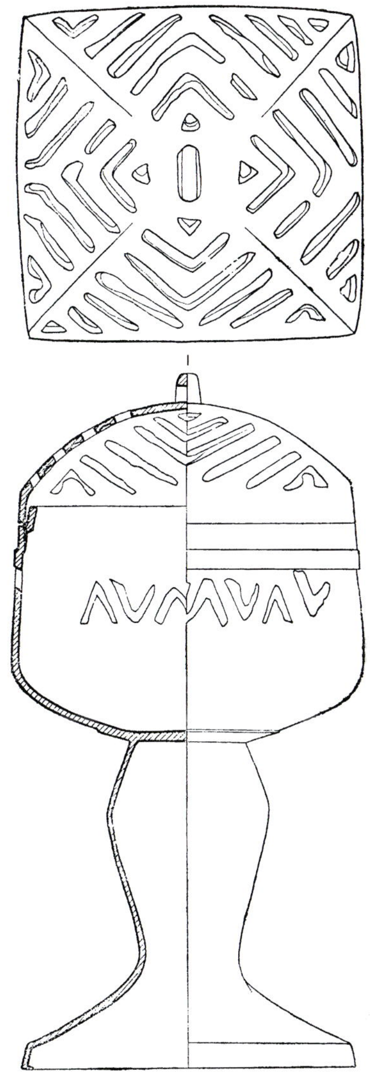

125

125

Bronze incense burner

Second century BC, Western Han dynasty
Height: 17.3 cm
Excavated at Xianggangshan in 1983
The Museum of the King of Nanyue, Guangdong Province

During the Western Han, closer contact with Central Asia facilitated the importation of expensive incense and spices. It became a common practice for the Han people to perfume their rooms, quilts and clothes with incense imported from central Asia. People not only enjoyed the scent but related this practice to the religious pursuit of immortality as the smoke rising through the holes on the lids was thought to resemble the mist and clouds of celestial realms.

Shapes of incense burners vary. This one consisted of three parts: a hollow body, a lid and a stand. It is decorated with simple geometric patterns: the hollowed body is cubic and the perforations on both the body and the lid form a repeating triangular motif.

The incense burner excavated at Dongdongshan (cat. 43) represents another shape that was popular in the Han dynasty. LKC

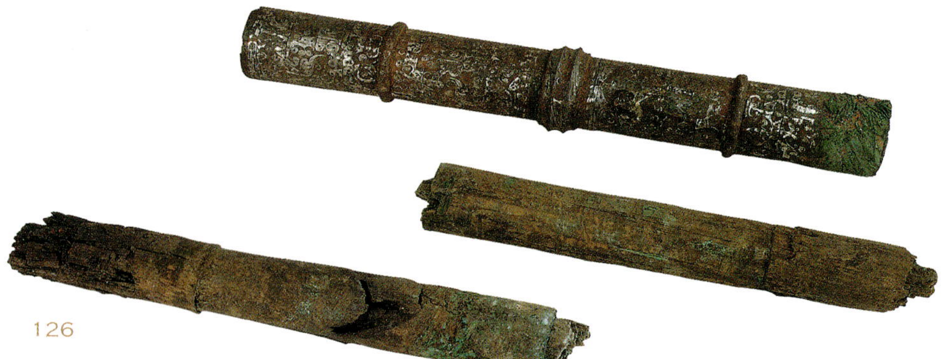

126

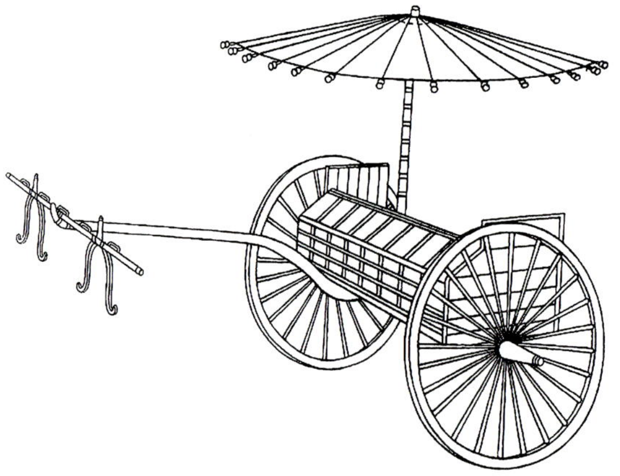

60 Drawing of a canopy placed on a chariot.

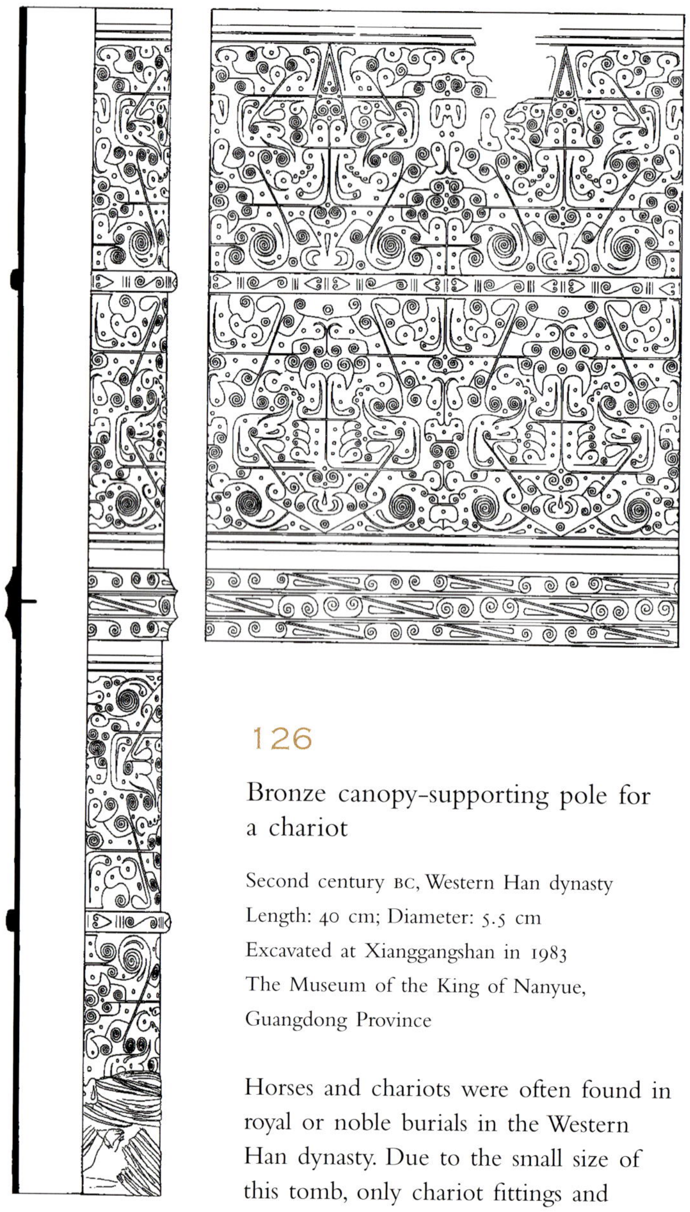

126

Bronze canopy-supporting pole for a chariot

Second century BC, Western Han dynasty
Length: 40 cm; Diameter: 5.5 cm
Excavated at Xianggangshan in 1983
The Museum of the King of Nanyue, Guangdong Province

Horses and chariots were often found in royal or noble burials in the Western Han dynasty. Due to the small size of this tomb, only chariot fittings and ornaments were discovered, mainly from the western chamber, and a model chariot made of lacquer in the tomb pathway. There are fragments of a bamboo basket around some of the fittings, indicating that they were put into a container when buried.

This bronze pole, beautifully decorated with inlaid gold and silver cloud motifs, was originally wrapped in silk, which had completely carbonized. It was part of the shaft supporting the canopy covering on a chariot (fig. 60). A complete section consists of one pole and two wooden cores. Each core has a round projection at one end and a carved hole at the other, which fitted into the other sections. A very similar pole was found in the horse and chariot pit of the First Emperor's tomb.[1] JX

1 Ciarla 2005, p. 148.

127

Gilt bronze *danglu*

Second century BC, Western Han dynasty
Length: 21 cm, Width: 5.4 cm
Excavated at Xianggangshan in 1983
The Museum of the King of Nanyue, Guangdong Province

Four *danglu* have been unearthed at the tomb of the King of

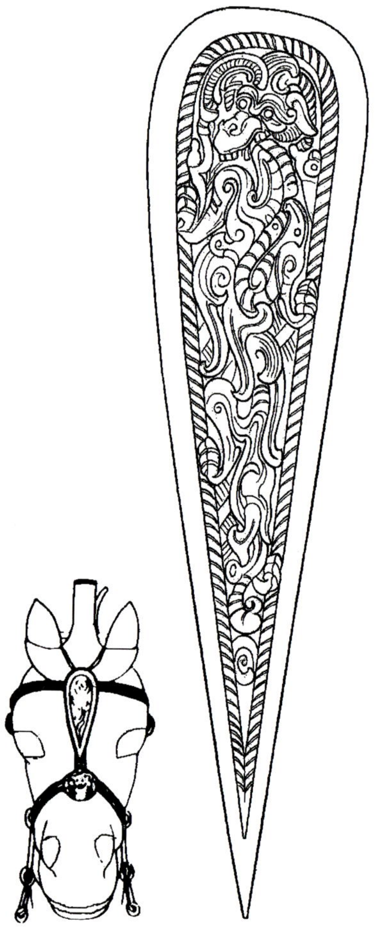

61 Drawing of a *danglu* as part of an ornamental bridle for a horse.

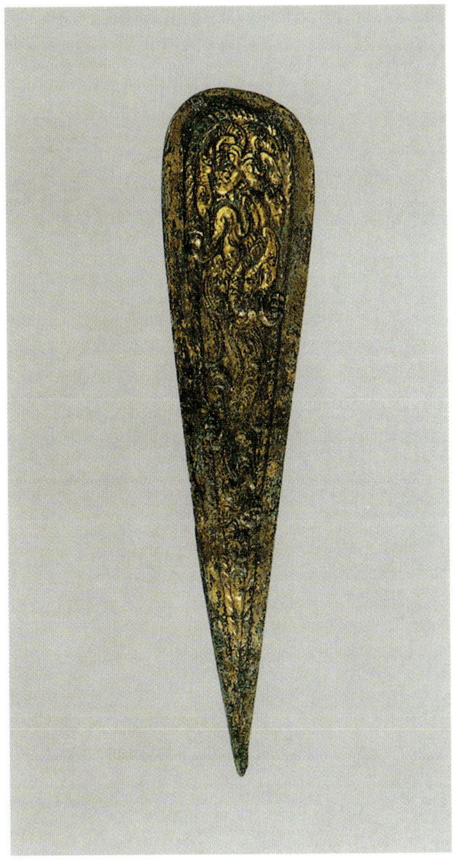

127

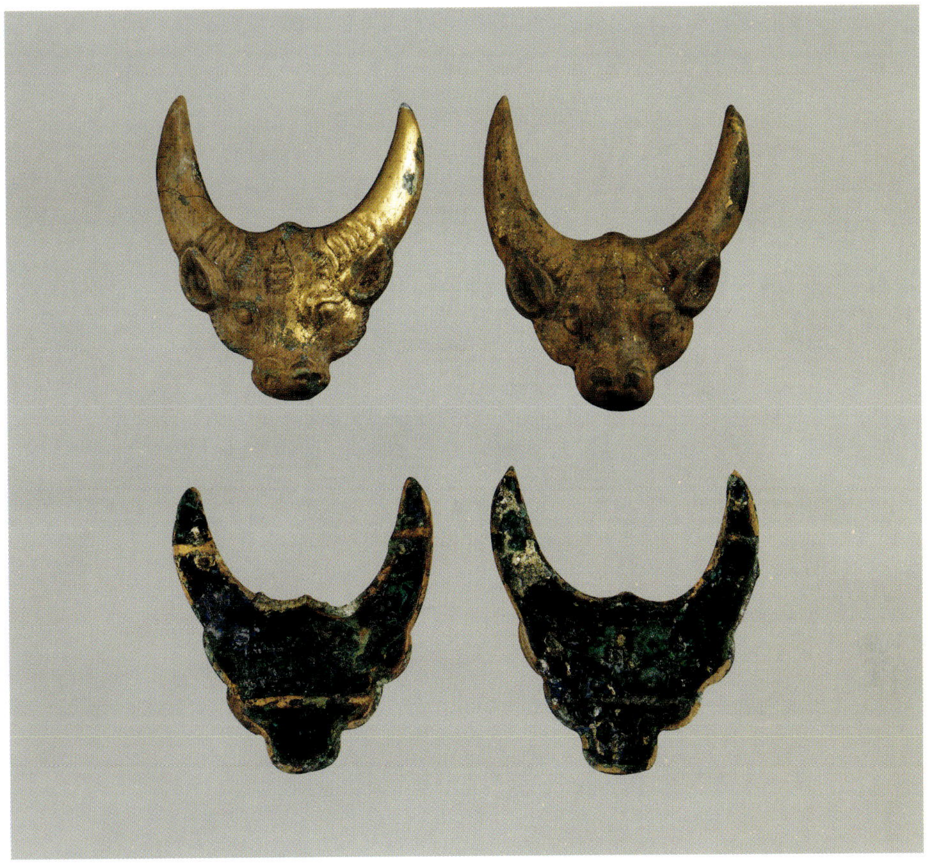

128

Nanyue, of which this is the best preserved. A *danglu* forms part of an ornamental bridle for a horse, placed in the middle of the forehead with the wider side up and the pointed side down (fig. 61). This example has two border sections: the outer layer is smooth and plain without decoration and the inner layer is designed with the pattern of a twisted rope. Inside the border, the main motif is a mythical beast with two large eyes and a long snarling snout. Its long body resembles that of a dragon or a snake. The four claws are depicted on the band of the inner border as if clinging to the rope. On the back are two vertical loops and one horizontal loop, used to fasten the *danglu* onto the bridle. LKC

128

Gilt bronze stud

Second century BC, Western Han dynasty
Length: 4 cm; Width: 3.45 cm
Excavated at Xianggangshan in 1983
The Museum of the King of Nanyue, Guangdong Province

These four studs were found within a bamboo case in the western chamber. Since the items within the case are components of a chariot, they were probably part of a chariot's fittings, although it is not clear which part they were intended to adorn. The studs are cast in the shape of vividly depicted bulls' heads: the artisan skilfully made the curve of the surface accommodate the bull's facial features. A cone, possibly intended to resemble an additional horn, is incised in the middle of the forehead. Judging from the slightly asymmetrical curve of the paired horns of each stud, it is likely that they were cast from the same mould. LKC

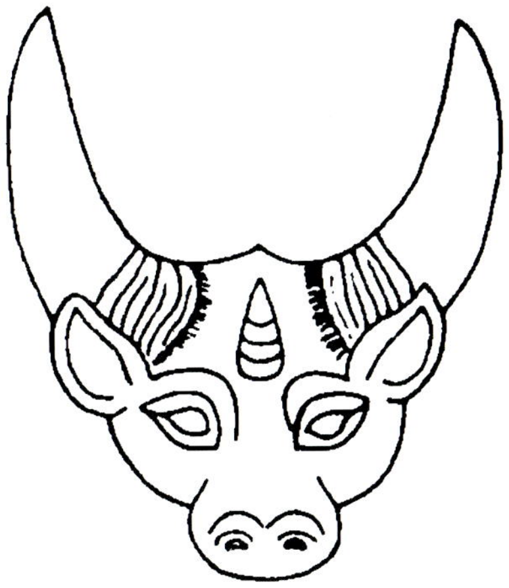

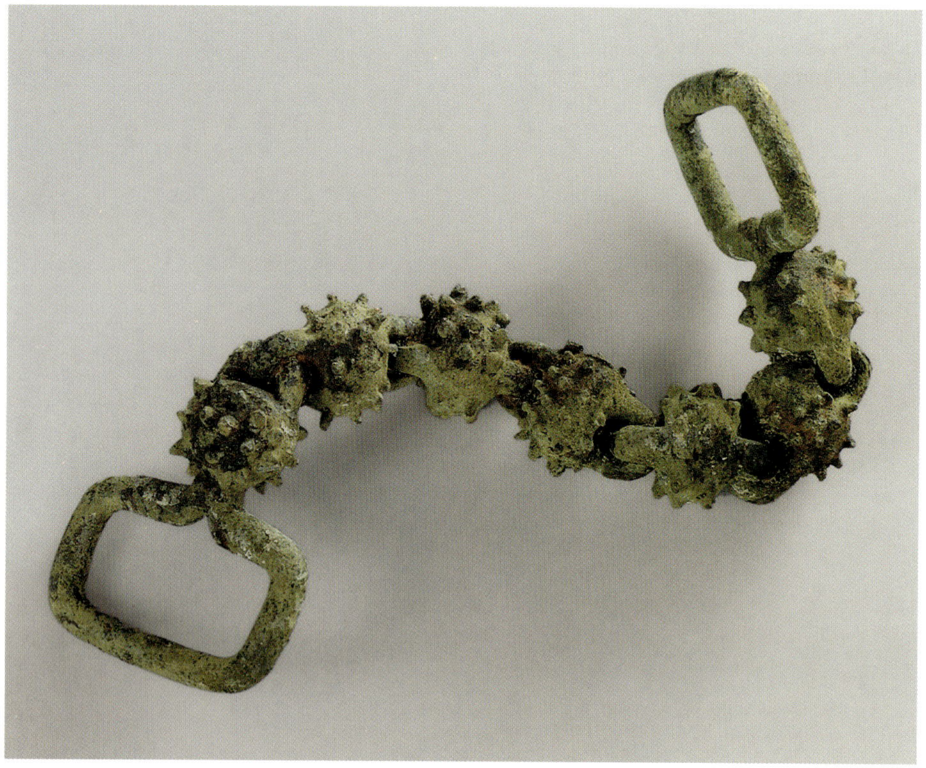

129

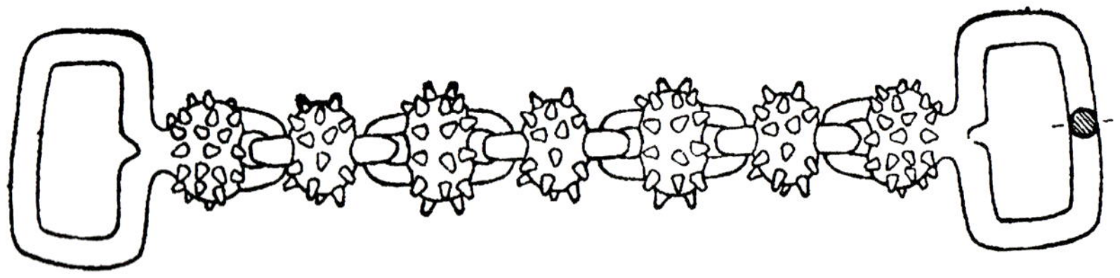

129

Bronze horse bit

Second century BC, Western Han dynasty
Length: 23 cm
Excavated at Xianggangshan in 1983
The Museum of the King of Nanyue,
Guangdong Province

Two woven bamboo boxes found in the western side chamber contained almost exclusively equipment for a chariot. There were more than 1,300 items, mostly fittings of various kinds,[1] including four pairs of horse bits found either in the boxes or in their immediate surroundings. This bit is one of a pair with a similar piece from the second box and together they belonged to a double-harnessed team of horses from the front of a chariot.[2] Their cheek bars were originally made of elephant ivory, as can be gauged from small remains of ivory on one of the rings.[3]

The seven spheres that make up the bit are covered in spikes. These were used to improve the handling of the horse by increasing pressure for control. Such spiked bits are known from as early as the Western Zhou period, about the ninth century BC.[4] Chronologically closer to the tomb from Guangzhou are horse bits from a horse and chariot pit that contained two chariots found to the west of the tomb of the First Emperor of China in Lintong, Xi'an, dated 221–206 BC.[5] The bits actually found in the mouths of earthenware horses consist of a two-part bit plus a peg covered in spikes that probably had the same purpose, to improve the charioteer's control of the horse.[6] SP

1 Beijing 1991, vol. 1, p. 94.
2 Prüch 1998, cat. 40.
3 Beijing 1991, vol. 1, p. 94.
4 Prüch 1998, cat. 40, Dewall 1964, pl. 18.
5 Beijing 1998b, vol. 1, p. 97, fig. 63:1, p. 219, fig. 132:3.
6 Beijing 1998b, vol. 1, p. 220, fig. 133:1.

130

Bronze horse bit

Second century BC, Western Han dynasty
Length: 20.3 cm
Excavated at Xianggangshan in 1983
The Museum of the King of Nanyue,
Guangdong Province

This horse bit was found next to the two woven bamboo boxes in the western side chamber that contained chariot equipment, including another horse bit (cat. 129).[1] They were used as part of the bridle for a pair of horses pulling a chariot (fig. 62). Remains of the silk and hemp in which it was originally wrapped before being placed in the tomb were found on this bit.

The tomb also contained four sets of iron horse bits with S-shaped iron cheek pieces, which may have been used for a four-in-hand carriage. The cheek pieces of the two bronze mouthpieces were probably made of an organic material, such as horn, bone or wood.[2] This type of horse bit appeared first during the Western Zhou period (*c.*1046–771 BC). SP

1 Beijing 1991, vol. 1, p. 76, fig. 52.
2 Prüch 1998, cat. 41.

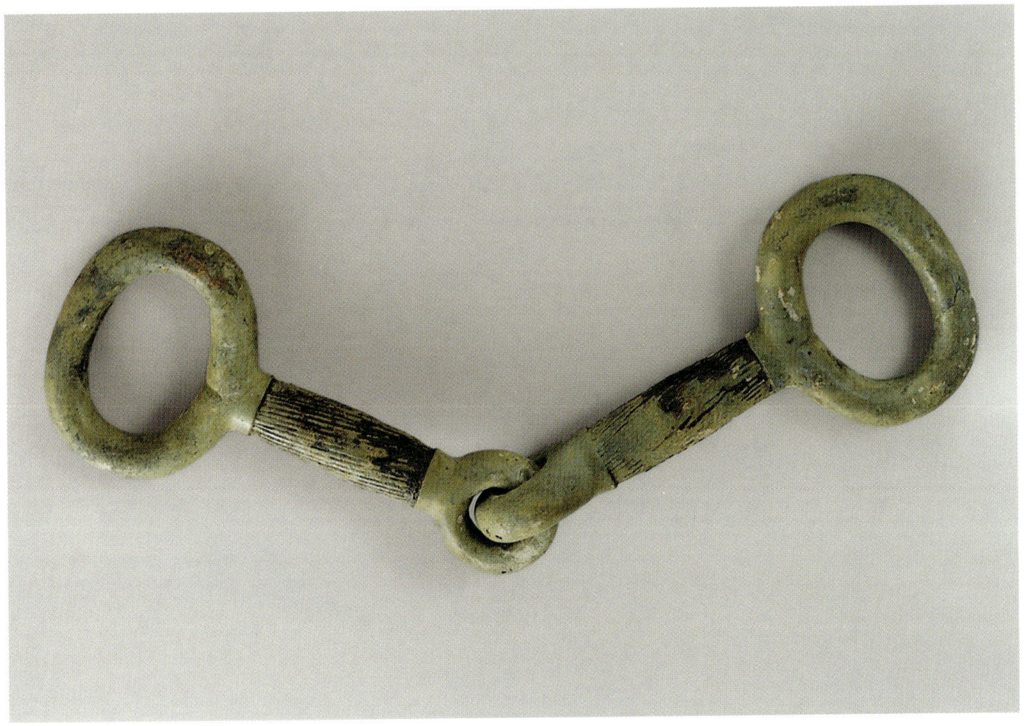

130

the cup is not certain as it has not survived.

According to the archaeological report, this cup support was made of an alloy of about eighty-eight per cent gold and twelve per cent silver. In Nanyue burials gold was often found used to decorate

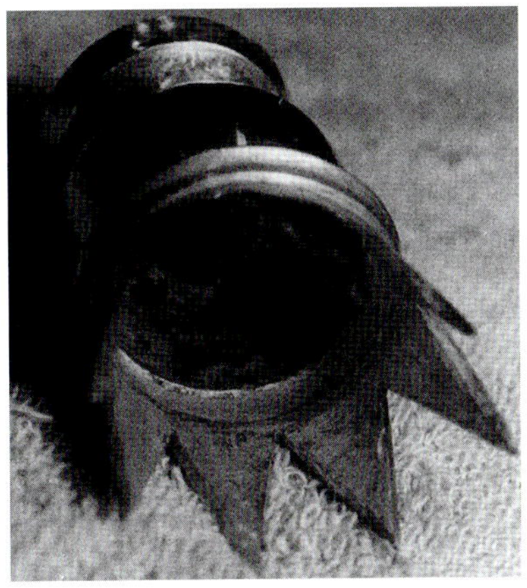

63 Photograph of lacquer traces on the inner surface of the gold support.

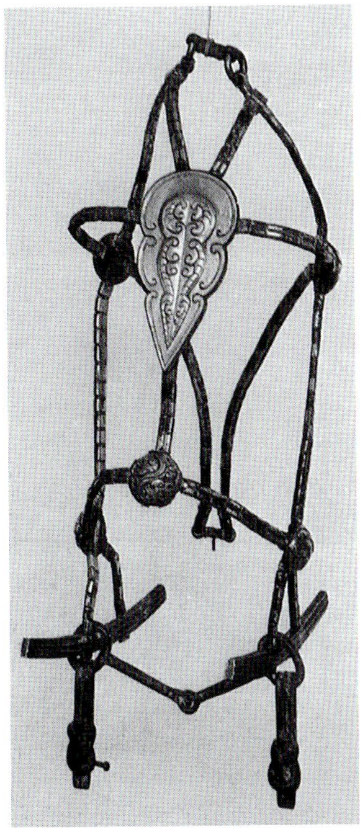

62 A reconstructed ornamental bridle from the Museum of the Terracotta Army, Xi'an, Shaanxi Province.

131

Gold support for a lacquer cup

Second century BC, Western Han dynasty
Height: 6.4 cm
Excavated at Xianggangshan in 1983
The Museum of the King of Nanyue, Guangdong Province

This gold object, discovered in the western chamber, has a hemispheric body with oval-shaped cross-section and a flaring stemmed foot. There are three raised bands at the mouth, on top of which the body extends into eight triangular projections that open slightly outwards. Traces of lacquer were found on the inner surface of the triangular peaks, indicating that it was originally used to hold a lacquer cup, which has disintegrated (fig. 63). This idea has been supported by some similar finds made of wood from another tomb in Guangzhou dating from the early Nanyue period.[1] The original shape of

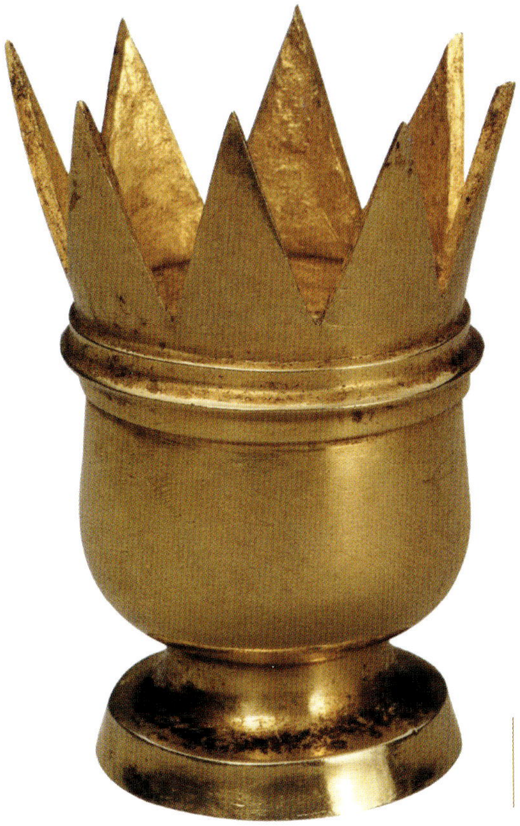

131

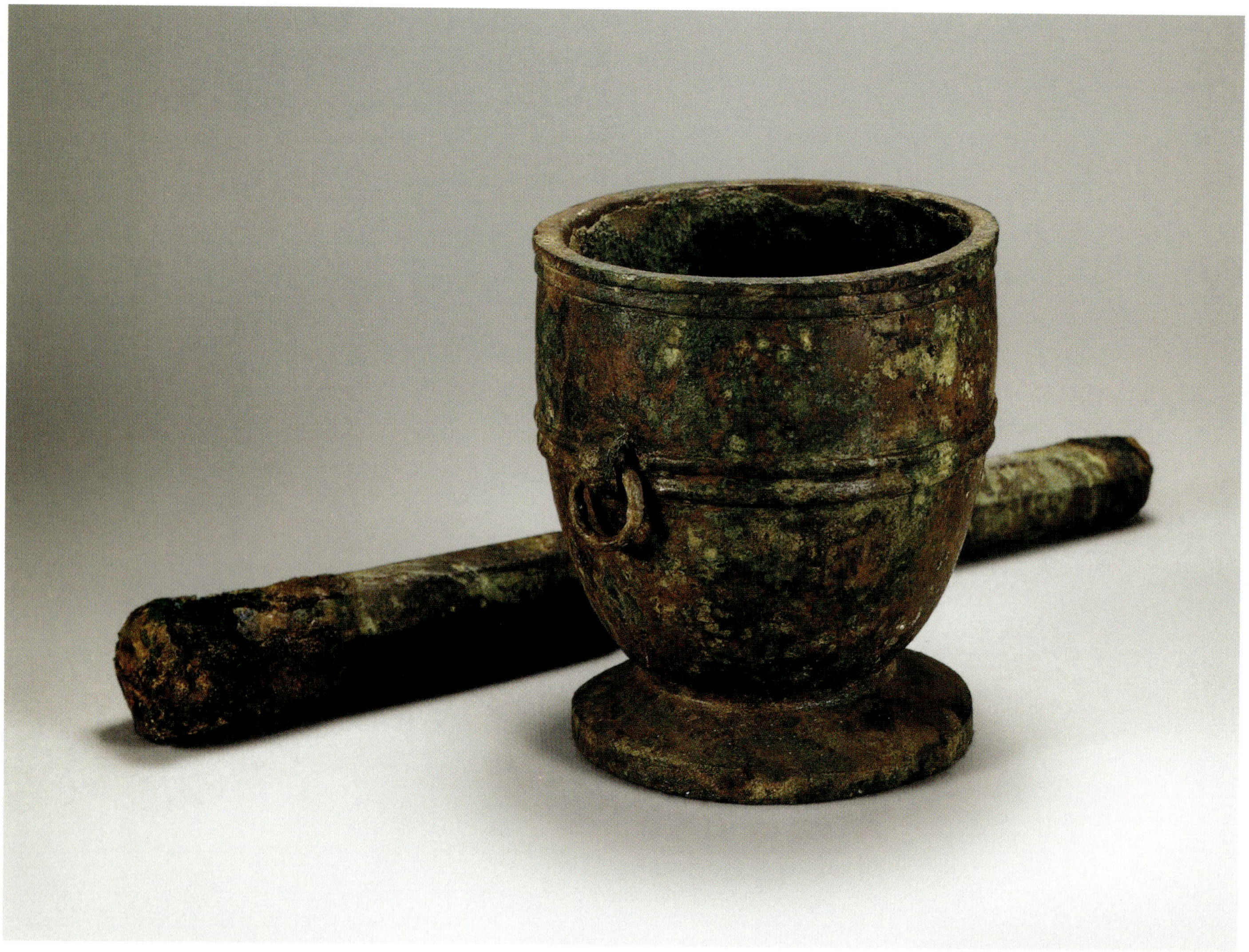

132

lacquer objects. Many finds from the King of Nanyue's tomb, such as a lacquer screen (cat. 173), have gilt decorations. Vessels made of gold seem to be relatively rare. Gilding was very popular during the Han dynasty as it was a less expensive way of achieving the impression of an extravagant use of gold.[2] JX

1 Four similar lacquer cups with wooden bodies were found in the tomb in Meihua village of Dongshan, Guangzhou in 1986, but their details have not been published; Beijing 1991, vol. 1, p. 131.
2 Michaelson 2007, p. 96; Sun 1991, p. 372.

132

Bronze pestle and mortar with minerals

Second century BC, Western Han dynasty
Length of pestle: 35.5 cm; Hight of mortar: 13.5 cm
Excavated at Xianggangshan in 1983
The Museum of the King of Nanyue, Guangdong Province

Two sets of pestles and mortars were found in the western chamber, together with multi-hued minerals intended for medicinal use. One set has a bronze pestle and mortar while the other has an iron pestle and a bronze mortar. The minerals include 193.4 grams of sulphur, 1,130 grams of realgar (red arsenic), 173.5 grams of purple crystal, 219.5 grams of ochre and 287.5 grams of turquoise. Ancient texts often refer to a group of minerals as the *wu shi* or 'Five Stones', although their composition is slightly different from the minerals found here.[1]

The practice of taking mineral substances to prolong life was common amongst the Han elite. According to the *Baopuzi* (*c.*AD 320), the Five Stones were to be liquefied, together with mercury, in

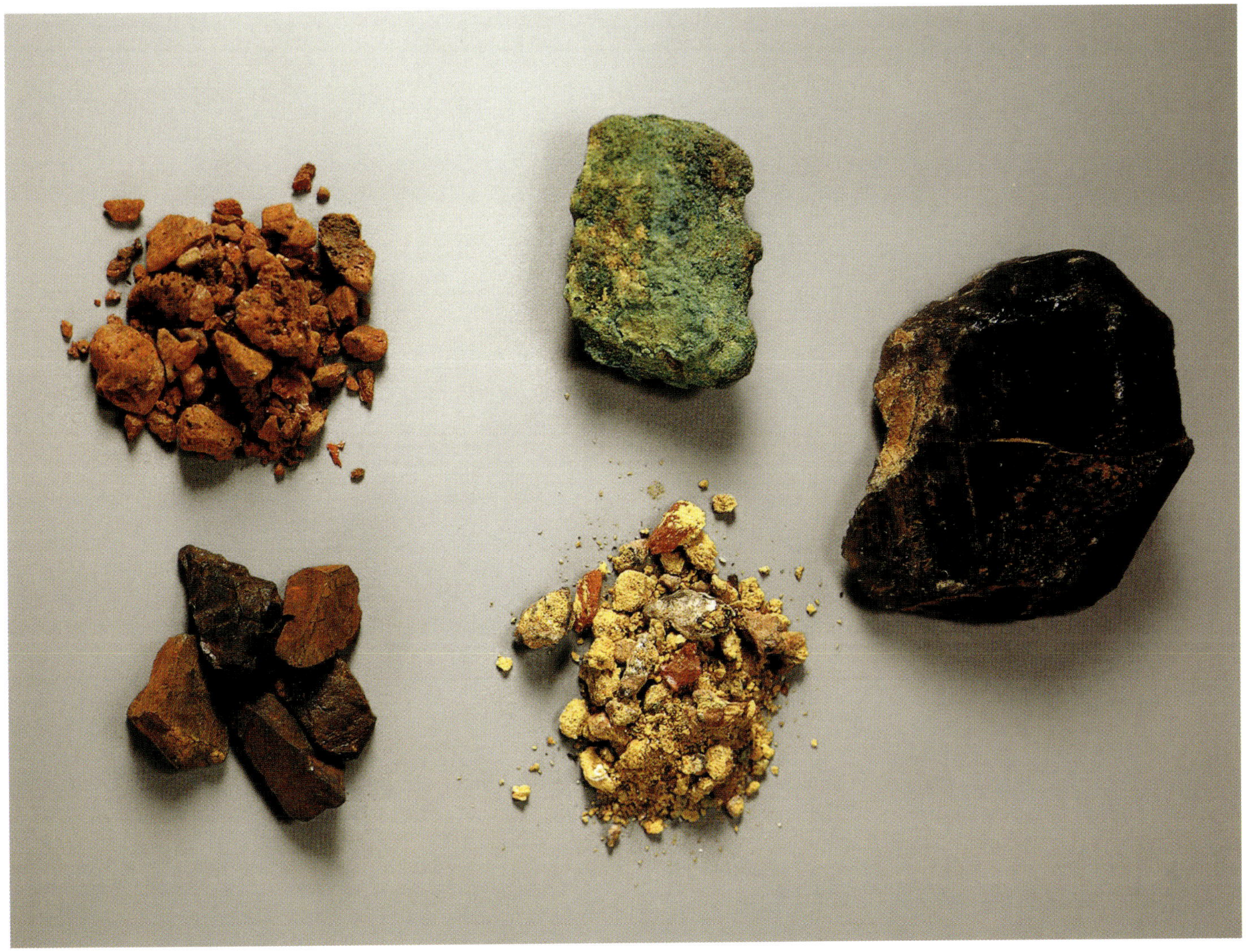

a bronze vessel over heat. Stirred with an iron spoon, the mixture would turn into an elixir of life after simmering for ten days. A single dose of the elixir would rid one of all diseases and taking it regularly would bestow immortality.[2]

These pestles and mortars and minerals were very likely intended for continuing the search for immortality in the afterlife. JCSL

1 Beijing 1991, vol. 1, p. 141
2 *Baopuzi*, ch. 4, p. 14.

133

Inkstone and ink capsules

Second century BC, Western Han dynasty
Inkstone base length: 12.5–13.2 cm;
Thickness: 2.8 cm;
Ink capsules: Diameter: 0.81–1.31 cm
Excavated at Xianggangshan in 1983
The Museum of the King of Nanyue, Guangdong Province

Ink and inkstone, along with paper and brush pen, are the Four Treasures of the Study used in Chinese and other Eastern Asian calligraphic and painting traditions.

This inkstone, found in the western chamber, is composed of two parts: a stone slab and a grinder. The stone slab has a flat square shape with rounded corners. The black cylindrical grinder, made of shale,[1] a rock that consists of various clay minerals and quartz grains, is for grinding the ink capsules on the flat surface of the inkstone. Traces of dyed red textile and straw on both ink slab and grinder indicate that they were carefully wrapped and put into a straw bag before being placed into the tomb.[2] The production of inkstones in China dates back to the Shang dynasty

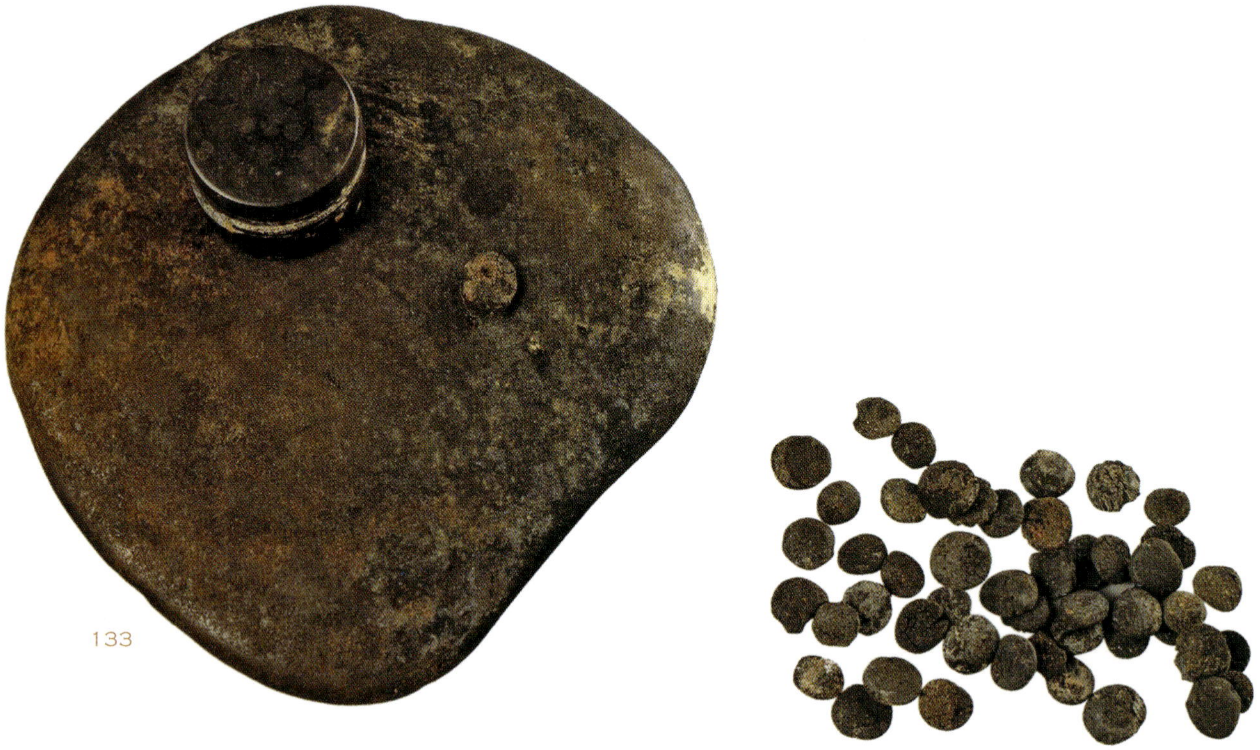

133

(sixteenth–eleventh century BC) and reached its height in the Song dynasty (AD 960–1279) when inkstones became extremely intricate works of art and highly treasured writing implements, as well as ornaments in literati's studies.

4,385 ink capsules were found in a decomposed lacquer box in the western chamber. Given their random shape, it is believed they were formed by drops of liquid ink that were then left to dry and harden. The earliest use of black ink has been found on earthenware and animal bones unearthed at the Shang dynasty site at Anyang.[3] Ink capsules were a primitive form of ink and had to be ground on an inkstone with a grinder. This tradition changed when the Chinese were able to make ink ingots, usually solid and in the shape of sticks or cakes, which could be ground directly on a slab. Sophisticated ink making did not appear until the late Han period. The Eastern Han Chinese character dictionary, the *Shuowen jiezi* ('Explaining Simple and Analysing Compound Characters'), recorded that ink was made from pine soot. However, the composition and production techniques of these ink capsules are yet to be analysed.

Another two sets of inkstones were found in the antechamber. There are residues of red and black ink left on the surface of the slabs. Excavators believe that it was the same ink that was used to decorate the walls in the antechamber. JX

1 A grinder can be also made out of other materials such as pottery or agate.
2 Most of the burial objects in the King of Nanyue's tomb had been wrapped in textiles including silk and linen. Some of the textiles are obviously gifts from the Han Empire. But judging from the large quantity and the historical records on local sericulture, the source of silk could be indigenous. The Kingdom of Nanyue possibly had its own textile workshops.
3 Sun 1991, p. 277.

134

Two silk printing plates

Second century BC, Western Han dynasty
Length: 3.4 cm; Width: 1.8 cm
Length: 5.7 cm; Width: 4.1 cm
Excavated at Xianggangshan in 1983
The Museum of the King of Nanyue, Guangdong Province

Two thin and very fine silk-printing plates made of bronze were found wrapped in silk fabric in the western chamber. They are the earliest tools for silk printing yet discovered. A lot of carbonized silk fabric was found beside the plates. A large quantity of silk was found in the same chamber and some of the images on the silk matched that on these printing plates (fig. 64). JCSL

64 A piece of modern silk printed using the original silk printing plates found in the tomb of the King of Nanyue, Guangzhou, Guangdong Province.

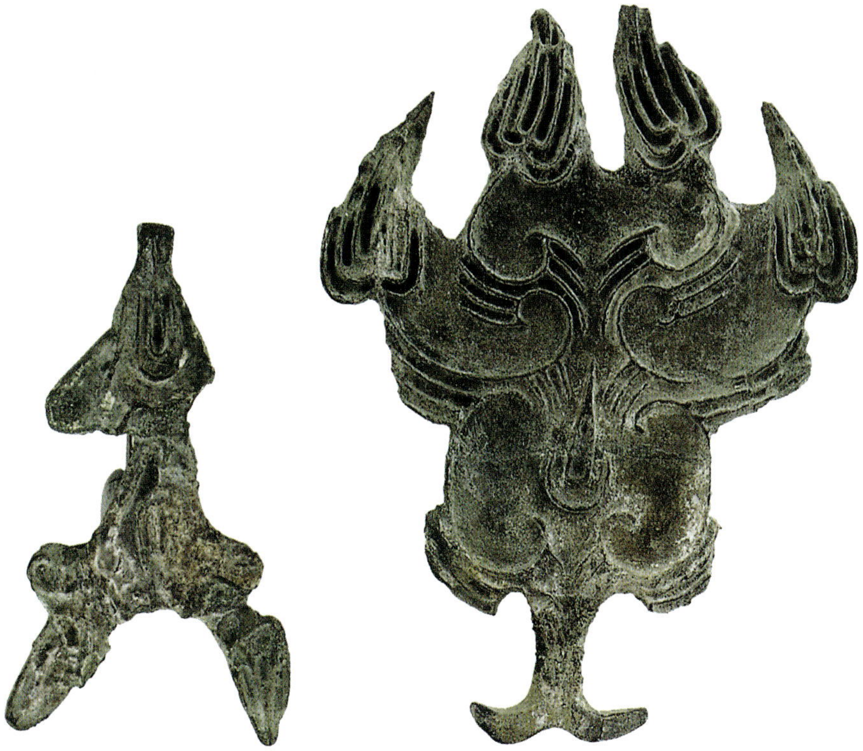

134

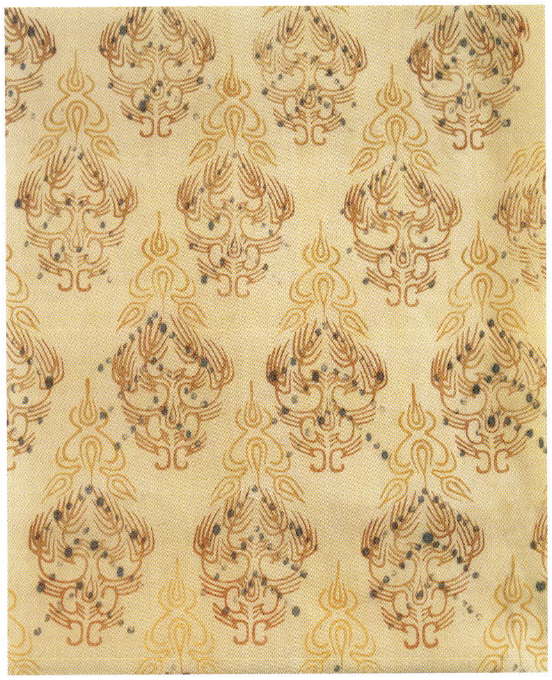

Fig. 64

135

Bronze *ding*

Second century BC, Western Han dynasty
Height 11.4 cm; Mouth diameter 9.2 cm
Excavated at Xianggangshan in 1983
The Museum of the King of Nanyue, Guangdong Province

This is one of fourteen identical *ding* of this type. It was found together with eight others and a group of bronze spoons in the remains of a bamboo basket in the entrance area of the western side chamber. The remaining five *ding* were also found in the entrance area together with a number of larger bronze and smaller earthenware *ding*. Each of the smaller vessels in the basket was individually wrapped in silk and then tied with hemp strings, some of which had not decayed. The spoons were also wrapped in silk. Although no traces of soot attesting to actual use were found

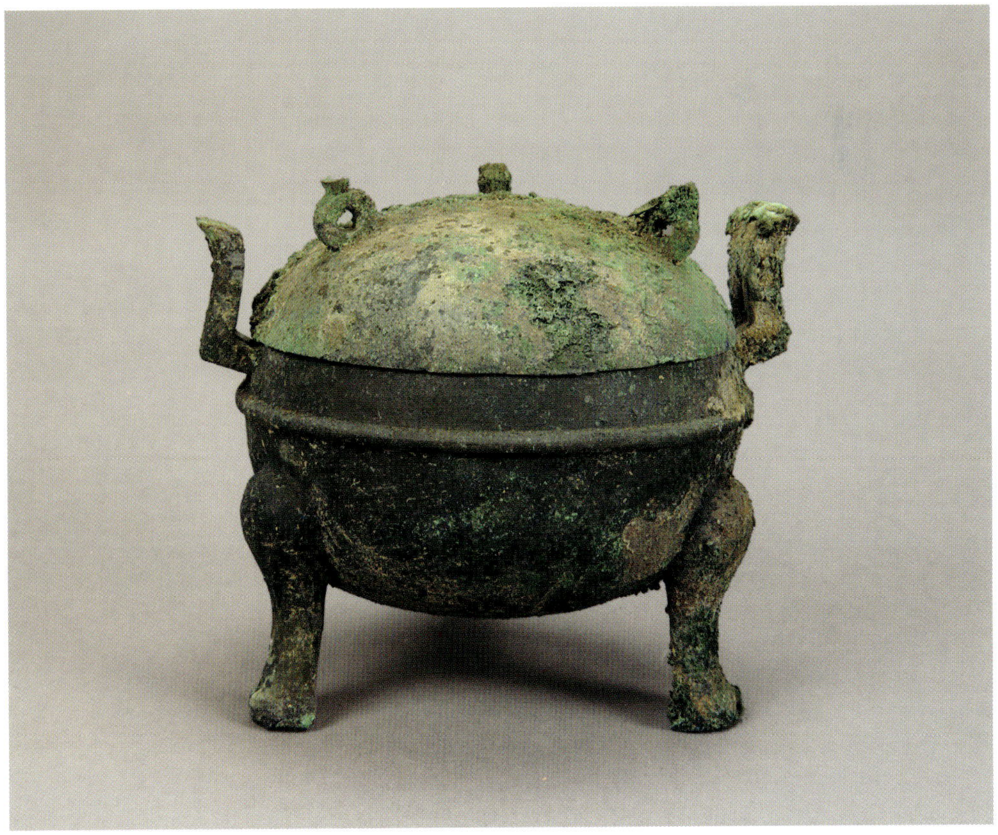

135

on these vessels, a similar example from a Han period tomb in Liuyuangang, a suburb of Guangzhou, bore traces of soot, showing it had been used over fire.[1] The small size of these *ding* has prompted the suggestion that they were used as containers for spices, sauces or other liquids, maybe together with the spoons.[2] Four larger versions of this type of *ding* were found in the rear storeroom (cat. 184).

The shape of this type of *ding* remained very similar from its appearance in the Central Plains area in the middle of the Spring and Autumn period, about sixth century BC, through to the Western Han period.[3] It is often seen in tombs in Nanyue: for example, tomb No. 1,097 in Guangzhou yielded an almost identical but larger example.[4] SP

1 Prüch 1998, cat. 26; Guangzhou and Hong Kong 1983, p. 52.
2 Prüch 1998, cat. 26.
3 *Kaogu yu wenwu* 1981.3, pp. 84–103.
4 Beijing 1981b, vol. 1, p. 136; *Kaogu* 1996.10, pp. 54–65.

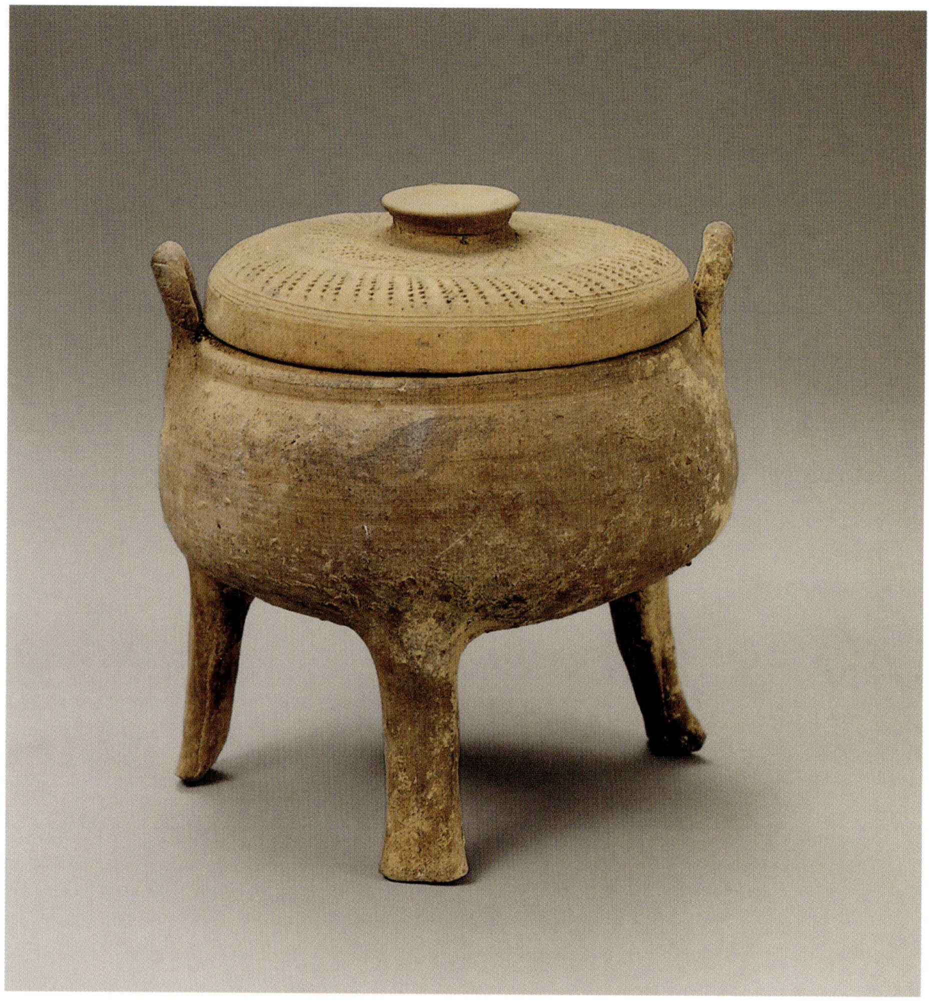

136

136

Earthenware lidded *ding*

Second century BC, Western Han dynasty
Height: 9.9 cm; Diameter: 10 cm
Excavated at Xianggangshan in 1983
The Museum of the King of Nanyue, Guangdong Province

This small earthenware lidded *ding* has a contracted mouth, a flange under the mouth, a drum-shaped body, a round bottom and three long flat legs, which are slightly outwardly extended. There is a pair of loop handles with string decorations on the shoulder and a lid with a knob. The body of the vessel is undecorated but its cover is patterned with bow-string and comb designs. Carbonized material was found inside the vessel, believed to be the remains of food.

There were fourteen earthenware tripods in total in this tomb. Apart from one larger tripod with a deep, round body and animal-feet-shaped legs found in the eastern side chamber, examples were found in four different chambers. This was one of nine found in the western chamber. The western chamber is believed to have been a storage chamber containing many tools, weapons, textiles and other treasures. KJC

137

Bronze *ding*

Probably fourth century BC, Warring States period
Height: 42 cm; Mouth diameter: 31.5 cm
Excavated at Xianggangshan in 1983
The Museum of the King of Nanyue, Guangdong Province

This *ding* was found in the western chamber but its specific location within the chamber is not known. Remains of silk and bamboo show that it was probably wrapped in silk and placed in a basket. The wide mouth, originally covered by a wooden lid, now decayed,

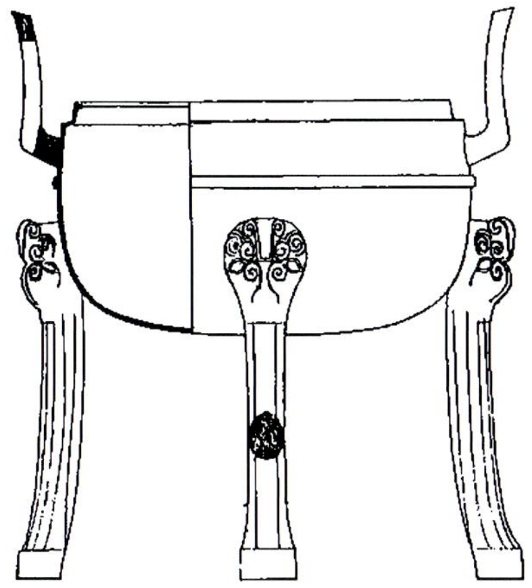

flows into a body with curved sides and a slightly rounded base. Straight, rectangular handles are attached below the mouth. There is a raised ridge around the body between the handles and the legs. The legs are long and round with an animal head in relief, identified as a sheep's head or a ram's head by the excavators.[1] Where the legs meet the body of the vessel there are cloud patterns. This example is unique to the Nanyue area, but is a well-known shape in Hubei, Hunan, Henan and Anhui, where it was found in mid- to late Warring States tombs of the area controlled by the Chu polity.[2] It is possible that this vessel was passed from generation to generation as an heirloom before its final deposition in this tomb.[3] A clue to this vessel's probable date is provided by two very similar examples from tomb Nos 323 and 354, dated to the mid-Warring States period, about the fourth century BC, at Yütaishan, Jiangling Hubei.[4]

Bronze *ding* tripods are among the earliest bronze vessels produced in China and appeared first around 1600 BC in Henan Province, but the shape is based on that of a Neolithic cooking vessel. Produced in large quantities and of considerable typological variety, *ding* were used to cook and serve meat as offerings to the ancestors, the predominant religious practice throughout the Bronze Age. During the second half of the first millennium BC and by the Han period, bronze vessels lost their pre-eminence in religious practices while other materials, such as lacquer, began to be favoured. SP

1 Beijing 1991, vol. 1, p. 78.
2 *Jianghan kaogu* 1983.1, pp. 1–18, 50.
3 Prüch 1998, cat. 25.
4 Beijing 1984, pls 31:1–2.

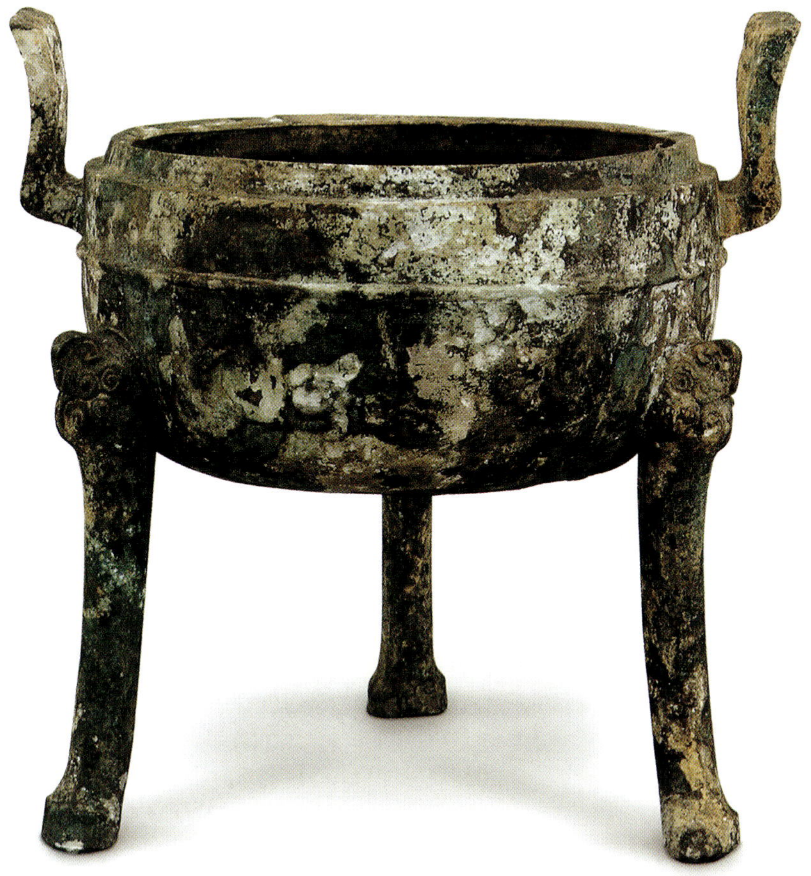

137

138

Earthenware container (*titong*)

Second century BC, Western Han dynasty
Height: 23.5 cm; Mouth diameter: 19 cm
Excavated at Xianggangshan in 1983
The Museum of the King of Nanyue, Guangdong Province

Two empty earthenware *titong* were found in the western chamber.[1] They are based on metal counterparts and were made into the early Eastern Han period, even after metal versions ceased to be produced after the demise of the Nanyue kingdom in the first century BC.[2] Some earthenware *titong* share with those of bronze the same three bands of geometric decoration, but others share their decorative patterns with other types of earthenware vessels.

Titong, both in earthenware and in bronze, had a variety of functions. An example from Yunnan served as a container for cowries, possibly valued as currency. A number of pieces excavated in northern Vietnam served as urns containing the cremated remains of people.[3] Examples from the tomb of the

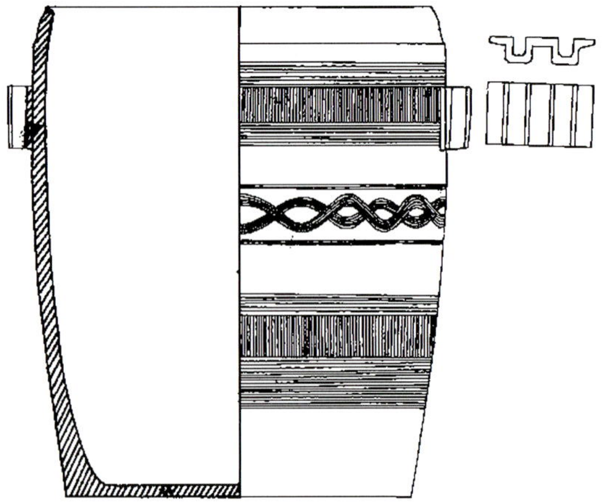

King of Nanyue were probably used as storage vessels as they contained the bones of fish, tortoises, chickens, pigs, oxen and cattle, while others had other earthenware and bronze vessels in them.[4] Earthenware *titong* are also believed to have served as containers for storing or making alcohol.[5] One earthenware *titong* from an early Eastern Han (first century AD) tomb in Guangzhou contained remains of sorghum, which could be used to brew alcohol. An inscription on the inside of the lid details its purpose as a container for alcohol, including the wish that the beverage may grant a long and prosperous life lasting up to 300 years.[6] It is possible that the empty earthenware *titong* from the King of Nanyue's tomb were also used as alcohol containers. SP

1 Like their metal counterparts they may originally have had wooden or, as in this case, earthenware lids. The bronze *titong* from the same chamber was found with a bronze lid and handle; Beijing 1991, vol. 1, p. 78.
2 *Kaogu* 1989.9, pp. 840, 847, 848–9.
3 *Kaogu* 1989.9, pp. 844–5.
4 Beijing 1991, vol. 1, pp. 222–3, 282–4.
5 *Kaogu* 1989.9, p. 845.
6 Beijing 1981b, vol. 1, pp. 322–3; *Kaogu* 1989.9, p. 845; Prüch 1998, cat. 29.

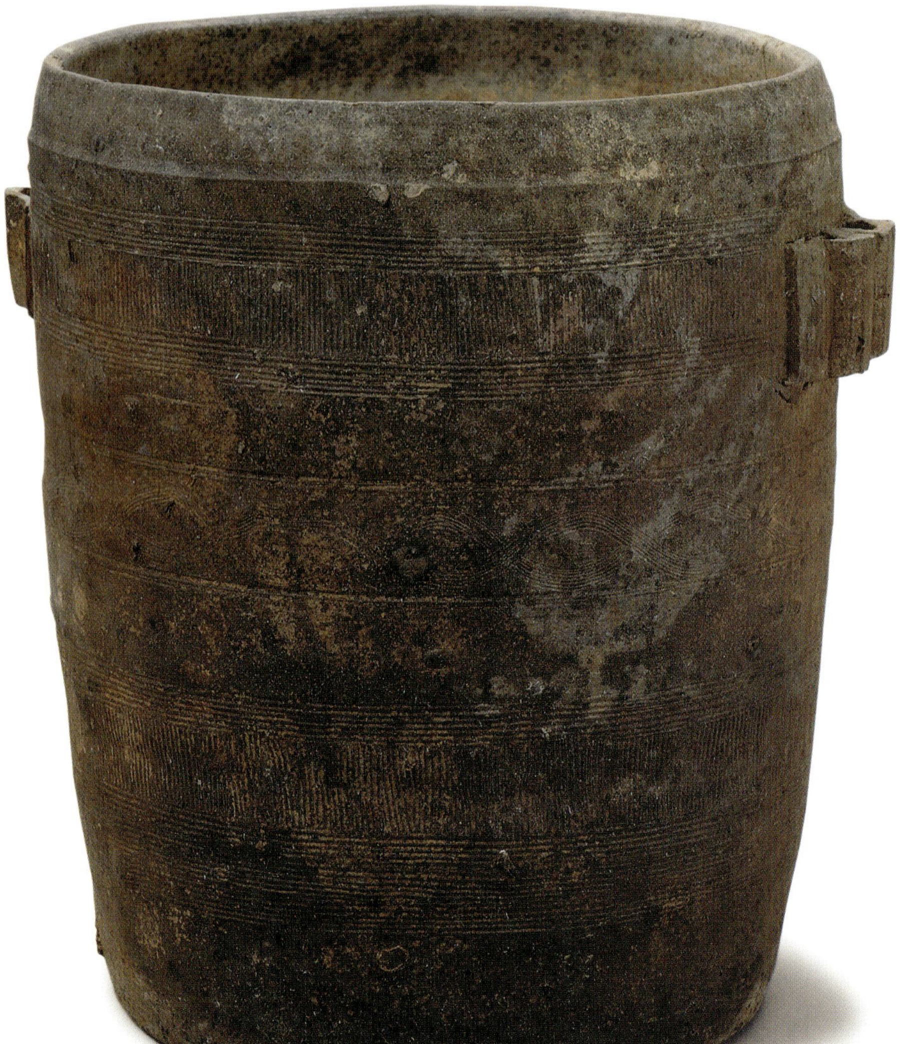

138

139

Gilt bronze ladle

Second century BC, Western Han dynasty
Length: 18 cm; Height: 6 cm; Width: 15.4 cm
Excavated at Xianggangshan in 1983
The Museum of the King of Nanyue, Guangdong Province

The ladle consists of a deep, elongated body on a rectangular base with rounded edges and a long open spout. The vessel was used for pouring liquids into dishes. The ladle was found together with eight similar examples piled up in two stacks in the western chamber of the tomb of Zhao Mo.[1] Both stacks were wrapped in straw mats. Two slightly larger ladles were placed next to them.[2] The gilt surface differentiates the ladles from ordinary dining utensils. Perhaps the three deep gilt bronze basins (cat. 140), a plate, large serving spoons and several other vessels of the same material found in the western chamber belonged to a single set of precious tableware used at the Nanyue court.

Mercury gilding was applied to a wide range of objects in the tomb of Zhao Mo and other Chinese rulers of the

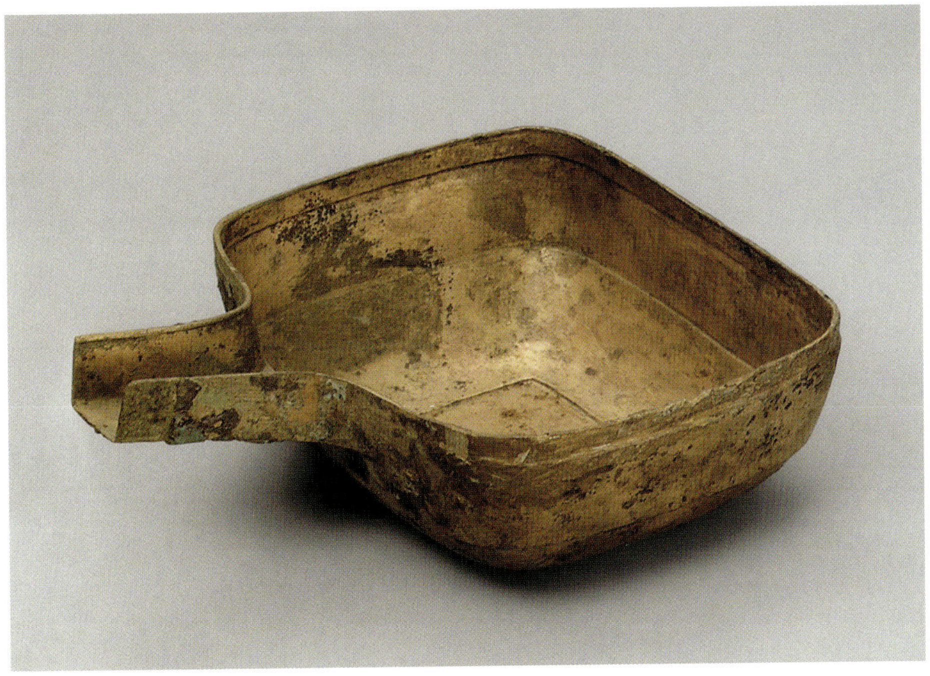

139

second century BC. The appreciation of gold and gilt objects was, however, a rather recent fashion. The technology of mercury or fire gilding had been developed by Chinese craftsmen only in the fourth or third century BC. From China this technology spread throughout Eurasia.[3] LN

1 Nickel 1998, p. 60.
2 Beijing 1991, vol. 1, p. 80.
3 Oddy 1991.

140

Gilt bronze basin (*juan*)

Second century BC, Western Han dynasty
Height: 7.5 cm; Maximum diameter: 20.8 cm
Excavated at Xianggangshan in 1983
The Museum of the King of Nanyue, Guangdong Province

This vessel was found in the entrance area to the western chamber as part of a group of three, stacked together.[1] The chamber contained four more such vessels, one of which contained a gazelle horn.[2] This vessel type is usually referred to as a *juan*, while the names *pen* and *xi* also appear. Typological accounts tend to group these vessels separately,[3] but they may be related functionally despite minor differences in shape. The nine examples from this tomb, including two from the rear storeroom,[4] have round bases, while those of other examples are flat. In terms of Han-period denominations for such vessels there probably was no actual difference as illustrated by almost identical examples from the Mancheng tombs Nos 1 and 2. The inscriptions on two such vessels from tomb No. 1 refer to *pen*, while the inscriptions on two pieces from tomb No. 2 use the term *juan*.[5]

Juan or *pen* were used together with pouring vessels for the washing of hands. They first appeared during the late Warring States period (about third century BC) and became very common during the Western Han period. Fine examples such as this one have the entire surface gilded, which was most likely achieved through fire-gilding, in which an amalgam of gold is applied to the vessel. After heating, the mercury vaporizes leaving a thin layer of gold and creating the impression of a vessel that was made entirely of gold. SP

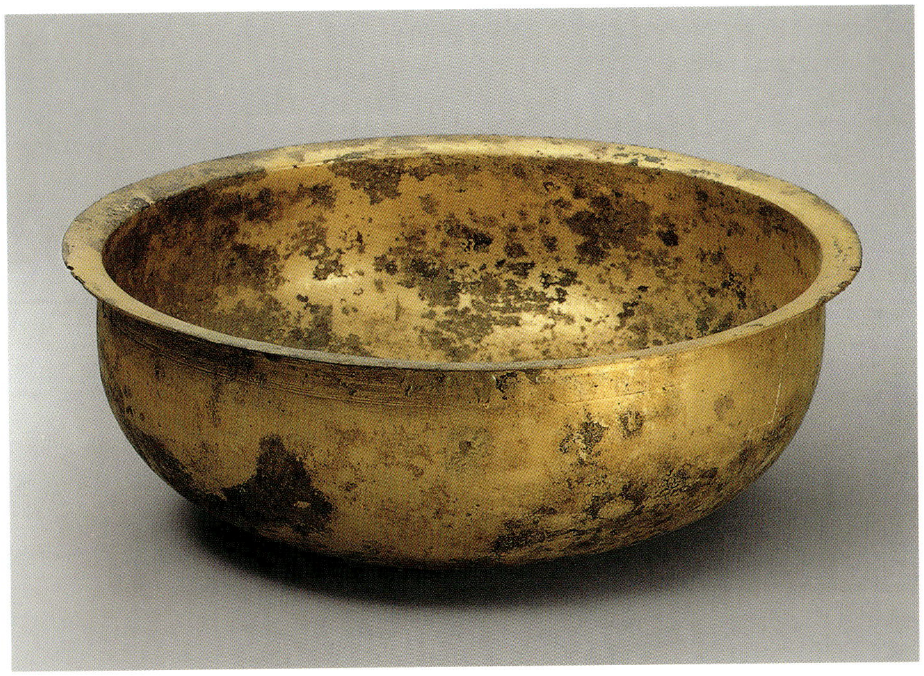

140

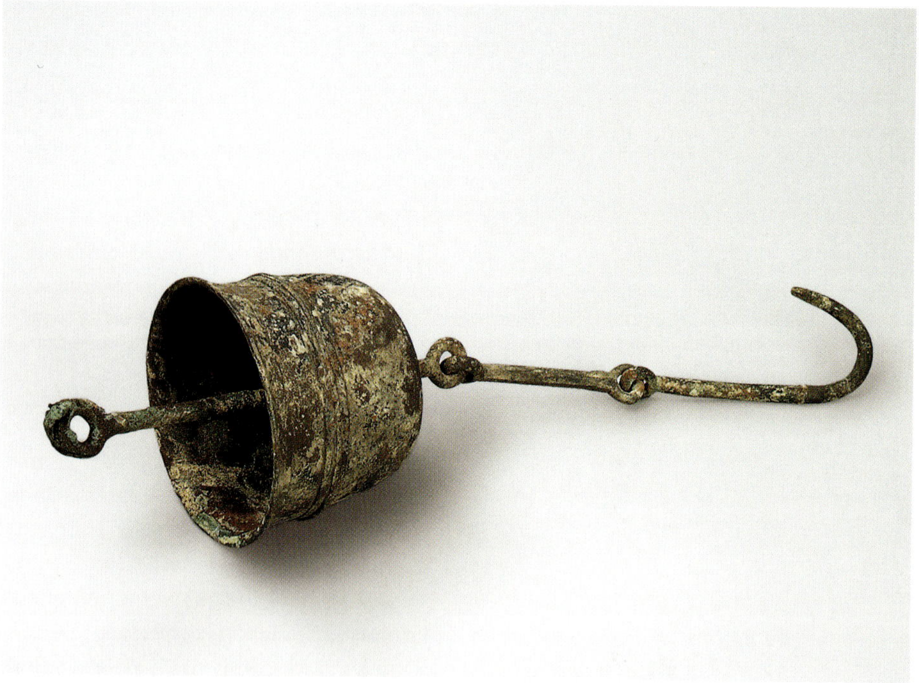

141

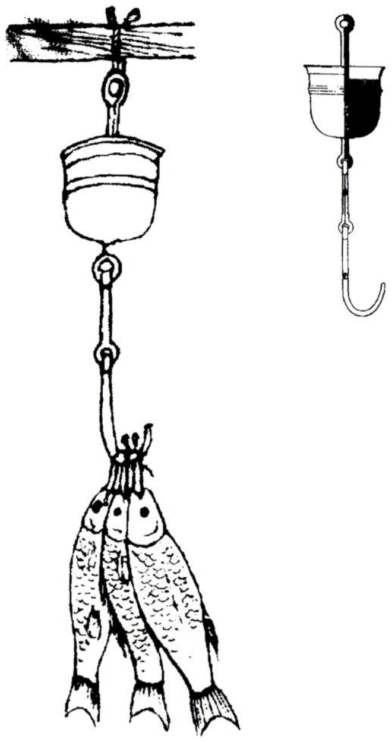

65 Drawing showing how food hook was used.

1 Beijing 1991, vol. 2, pl. 38:1.
2 Beijing 1991, vol. 1, p. 80, vol. 2, pl. 38:3.
3 See, for example, *Kaogu* 1996.10, pp. 57–8.
4 Beijing 1991, vol. 1, pp. 286, 290, fig. 203:1.
5 Beijing 1980, vol. 1, pp. 57–9, 250–2. The *Shuowen jiezi* also makes no distinction between the terms; *Shuowen jiezi*, p. 704.

141

Bronze food hook with an insect trap

Second century BC, Western Han dynasty
Length: 25.5 cm; Mouth diameter: 9.5 cm
Excavated at Xianggangshan in 1983
The Museum of the King of Nanyue, Guangdong Province

This peculiarly shaped item is one of five from the entrance area to the western chamber. Two, including this one, were found next to the mouth of a tripod *ding*, which may have contained them before it was toppled over.[1] For its obvious visual similarities, this item was called a 'bell-shaped object' and 'bell' and illustrated accordingly with the dome upside down in the excavation report.[2] Margarete Prüch's alternative interpretation of it being a food hook with an insect trap, based on similarities to comparable objects found in southern China today, seems more likely.[3] The object was suspended by the loop from the ceiling, or from a rack, and food was hung on the hook. The dome could be filled with water, which would have acted as barrier for insects trying to move their way down the bar towards the food (fig. 65).

Hanging food was a common practice in Han times, as observed by Yü Ying-shih.[4] Racks to which iron or bronze hooks were attached and from which food could be hung, are commonly seen in Han-period kitchen scenes. This way the food was out of the reach of dogs and other animals. The term *roulin* (literally, meat forest) found in texts of the period suggests that storing food in suspension from racks was a common sight. SP

1 The same is possibly true for the other four of these objects that were found in a similar position next to the mouth of a pottery vessel.
2 Beijing 1991, vol. 1, pp. 92, 83, fig. 56:1.
3 Prüch 1998, cat. 28.
4 Yü 1977, pp. 60–1.

142

Bronze ginger grater

Second century BC, Western Han dynasty
Length: 13.3 cm; Height: 5.2 cm
Excavated at Xianggangshan in 1983
The Museum of the King of Nanyue, Guangdong Province

This was found at the northern wall in the entrance area of the western side chamber. Another larger grater, also made of bronze, was found in the back storage chamber inside a *ding* (cat. 186). It has been suggested that it was used to grate ginger or extract plant juices through grating:[1] positioned on its feet, the grater was held by the double loop attached to the rectangular grating section. Fresh

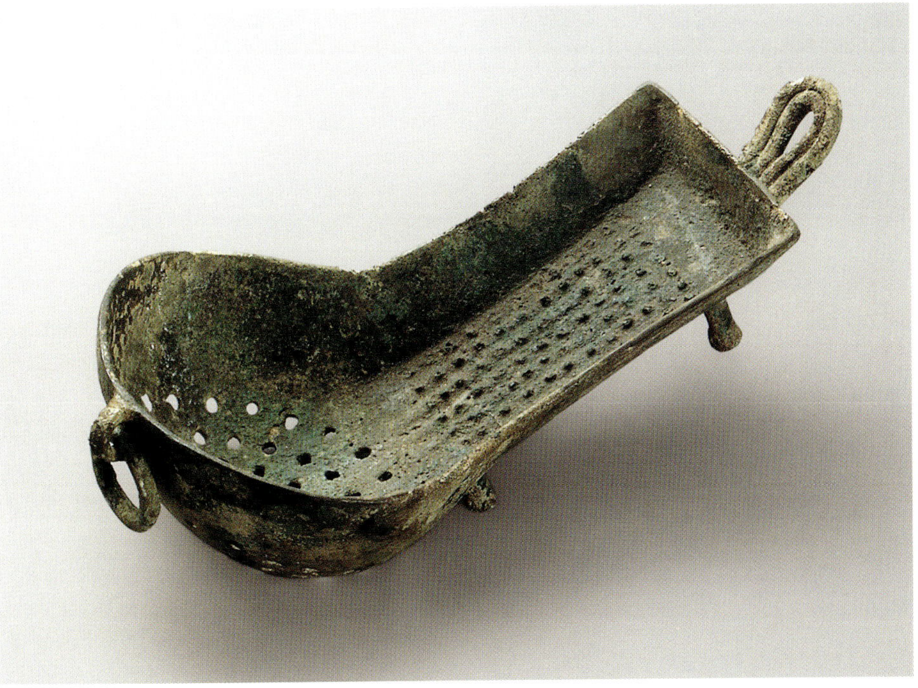

142

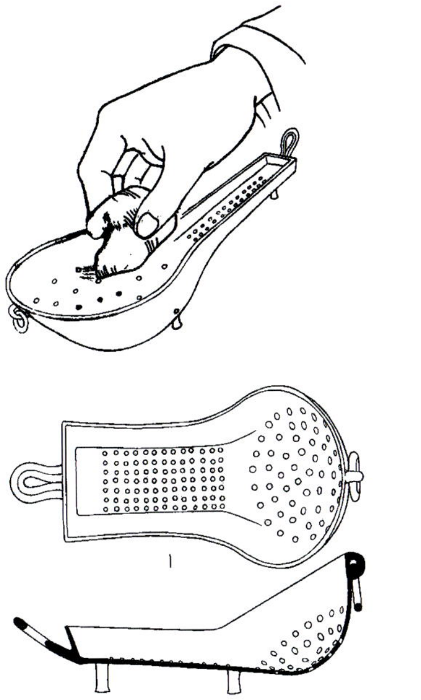

66 Drawing showing how ginger grater was used.

ginger could be grated through the rows of knobs (fig. 66). The juices could be drained by slightly tilting the object and letting them escape through the holes in the bowl, when the juices would be collected in a vessel. When not in use, the object could be hung on a hook with the ring handle that is attached to the bowl. While this function seems plausible as directly gauged from the item itself, this conclusion was drawn by analogy with similar devices still used by peoples in the Lingnan region and Guangdong, Guangxi, Jiangxi and Hunan Provinces, today. These are not made from bronze but mostly from bamboo, but they are mainly used for grating ginger.[2]

Ginger was already known in China in the first millennium BC if not earlier, where it had been cultivated in the southern and central provinces.[3] It has a long and illustrious history in China and was used during the Han period. Finds of ginger were made in tomb No. 1 at Mawangdui and references exist showing that ginger was often used in feasts of the period.[4] SP

1 Beijing 1991, vol. 1, pp. 80, 279; Prüch 1998, cat. 27.
2 Beijing 1991, vol. 1, p. 279.
3 Simoons 1991, pp. 370–2.
4 Yü 1977, pp. 56, 67.

143

Tiger-shaped bronze *jie*

Second century BC, Western Han dynasty
Length: 19 cm; Height: 11.6 cm
Excavated at Xianggangshan in 1983
The Museum of the King of Nanyue, Guangdong Province

This bronze *jie* was moulded flat in the shape of a crouching tiger with wide-open jaws and a curled tail. The body is embellished with sixty fine gold foil strips to represent tiger stripes. Across the middle of the *jie* are five gilt characters, which read 'The king orders the mustering of troops'.

Jie were used to convey orders and messages for military and diplomatic purpose in ancient China. However, *jie* have not often been found in archaeological excavations. To date, a bamboo-shaped *jie* has been found in the Anhui Province and a bronze dragon-shaped *jie* in Hunan. Both pieces are linked to Chu culture. This tiger-shaped *jie* is the only gilt one found so far. Judging from the characteristics of this *jie*, it is possibly from the Chu region. It was wrapped in silk and stored in the western chamber. JCSL

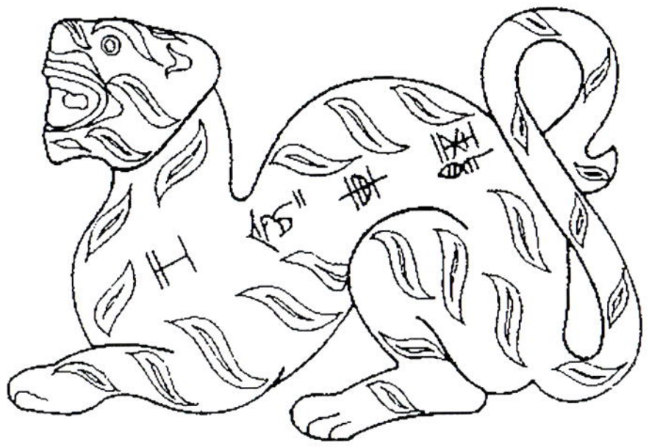

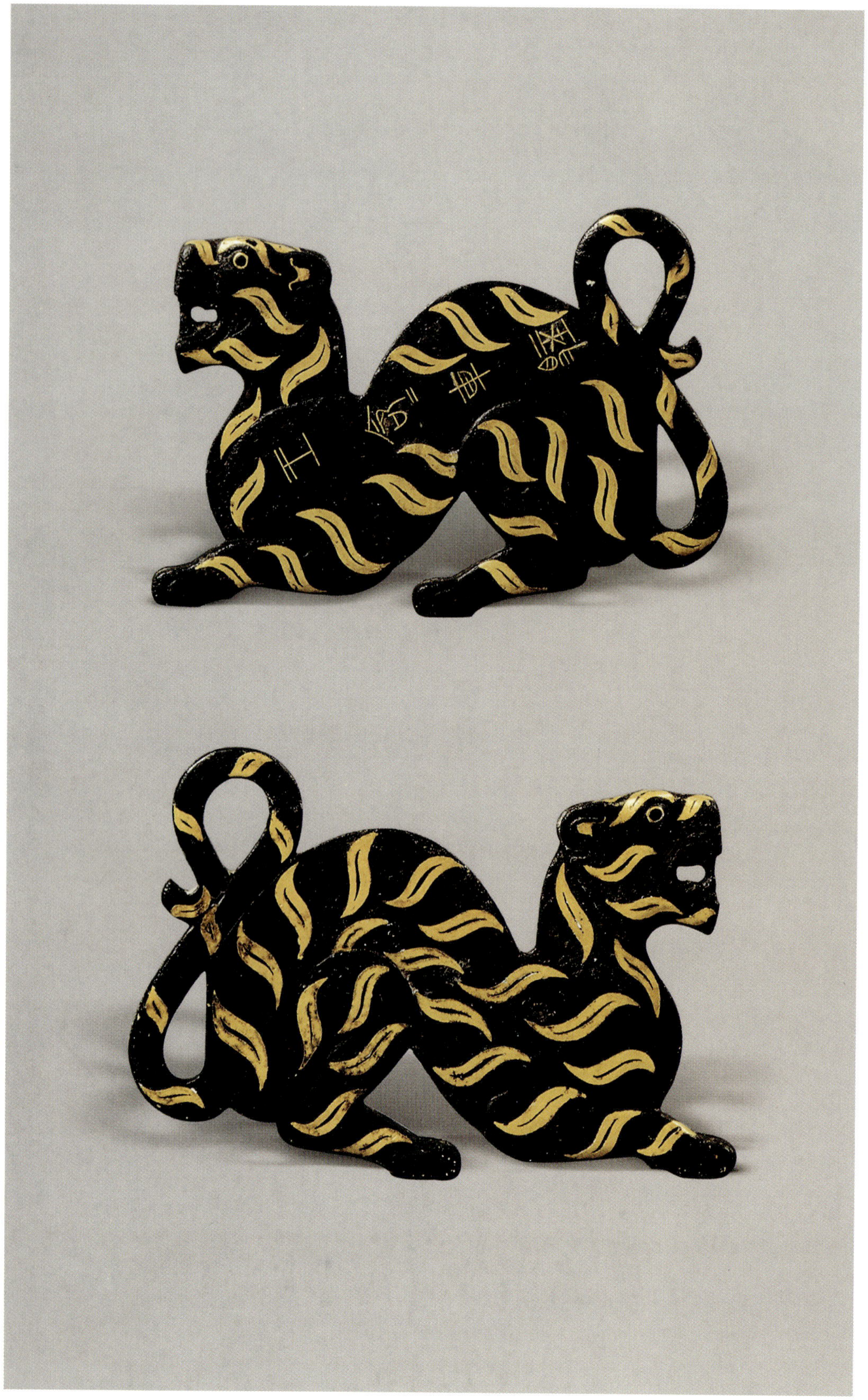

144

Clay seal

Second century BC, Western Han dynasty
Diameter: 1.1 cm
Excavated at Xianggangshan in 1983
The Museum of the King of Nanyue, Guangdong Province

Nine clay seals have been found near or inside objects in the western chamber, which functioned as a storage room. Two of the nine were stamped with *di yin* (Seal of the Emperor) and two with the character *Mo*, the second character in the emperor's name. The shape of this particular clay seal is relatively square with a slightly convex surface. Both the base and edges show traces of a decayed wooden case. Its function was probably the same as that of the seal found at Mawangdui (fig. 67), that is, to prevent tampering with a document or object. These clay seals, along with those found on the body, once again confirm that the tomb owner's name was Zhao Mo, a name that does not appear in surviving texts. JCSL

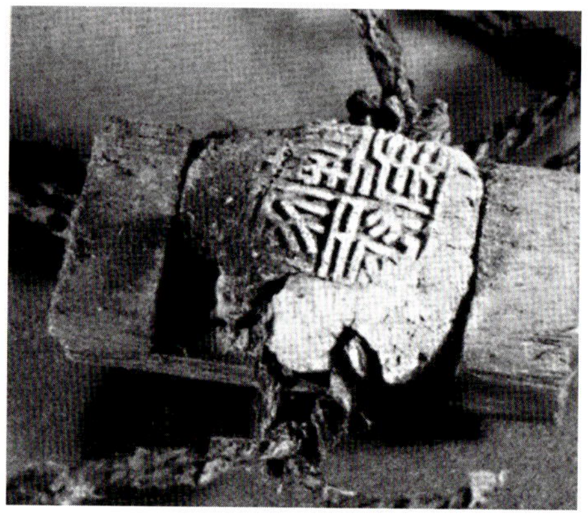

67 Clay seal in a wooden case that was excavated at tomb M1, Mawangdui, Hunan Province. Second century BC.

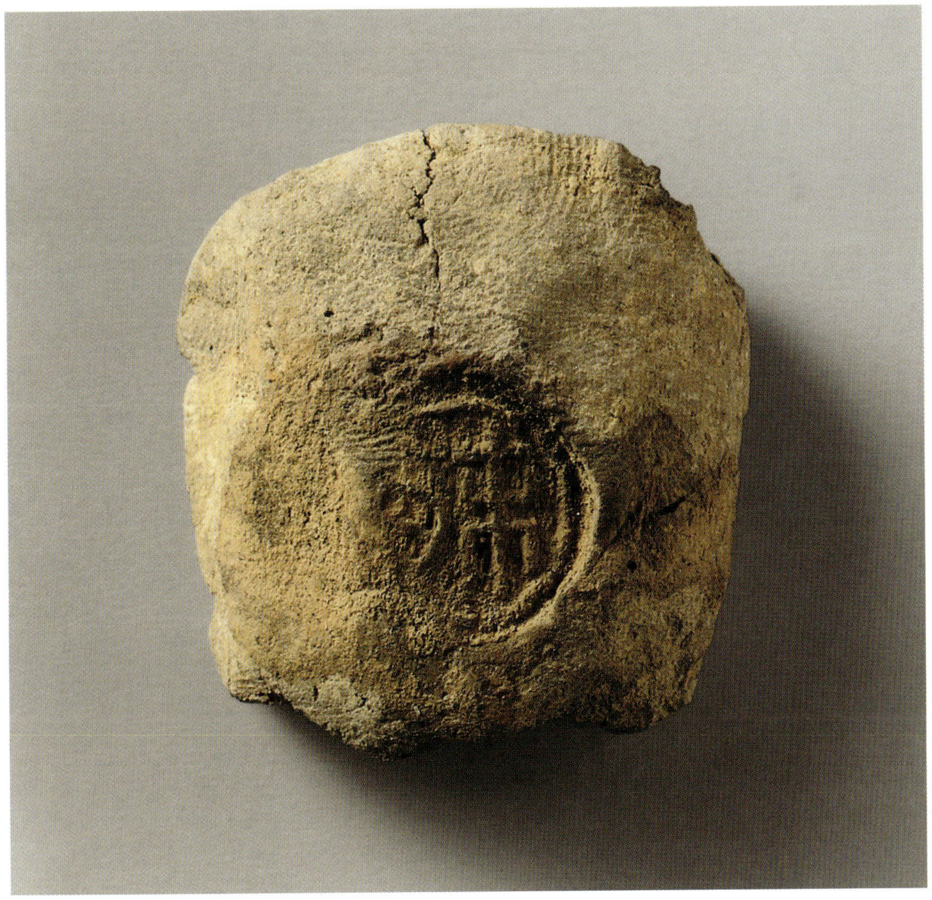

144

145

Glass ornament plaque with bronze frame

Second century BC, Western Han dynasty
Length: 10 cm; Width: 5 cm
Excavated at Xianggangshan in 1983
The Museum of the King of Nanyue, Guangdong Province

Fourteen glass ornament plaques were discovered in pairs in the western chamber. All of the plaques have gilt bronze frames decorated with grain patterns. Separated with thick layers of fine linen fibres and wrapped carefully in textiles, each pair was put face to face in a bamboo vessel when buried. There are also traces of oakum on the back of the plaques. A spectral transmission test has revealed a fairly high transparency.[1] These rectangular plaques were probably made in moulds and refined afterwards. The shape appears to be inspired by bronze ornament plaques with animal patterns, which were popular in the nomadic Xiongnu area in the north. An example of a bronze counterpart is the gilt bronze plaque decorated with a dragon and tortoises discovered in this tomb (cat. 170).

The composition analysis has shown that these plaques are Chinese indigenous lead-barium glass, like the glass cups discovered from Xuzhou. Early examples of lead-barium glass are mainly found in the regions of the Chu state in the Warring States period (fifth–third century BC). The glass discs from this Nanyue tomb are very similar to the pieces found in the former Chu state,[2] indicating an influence from the central region. The ornament plaques and beads, however, are unique to the Nanyue area. Plaques such as this are the earliest examples of Chinese translucent flat glass and its use seemed to decline after the collapse of the Nanyue kingdom as no more such objects have been found since. JX

1 The test done by the Research Institute of Building Materials (China) has revealed that the transmissivity of the test plaque is 70–77% within the spectrum of visible light. See Shi 1991, p. 424.
2 See Shi 1991, pp. 424–6 for a comparative composition analysis of these two plaques.

145

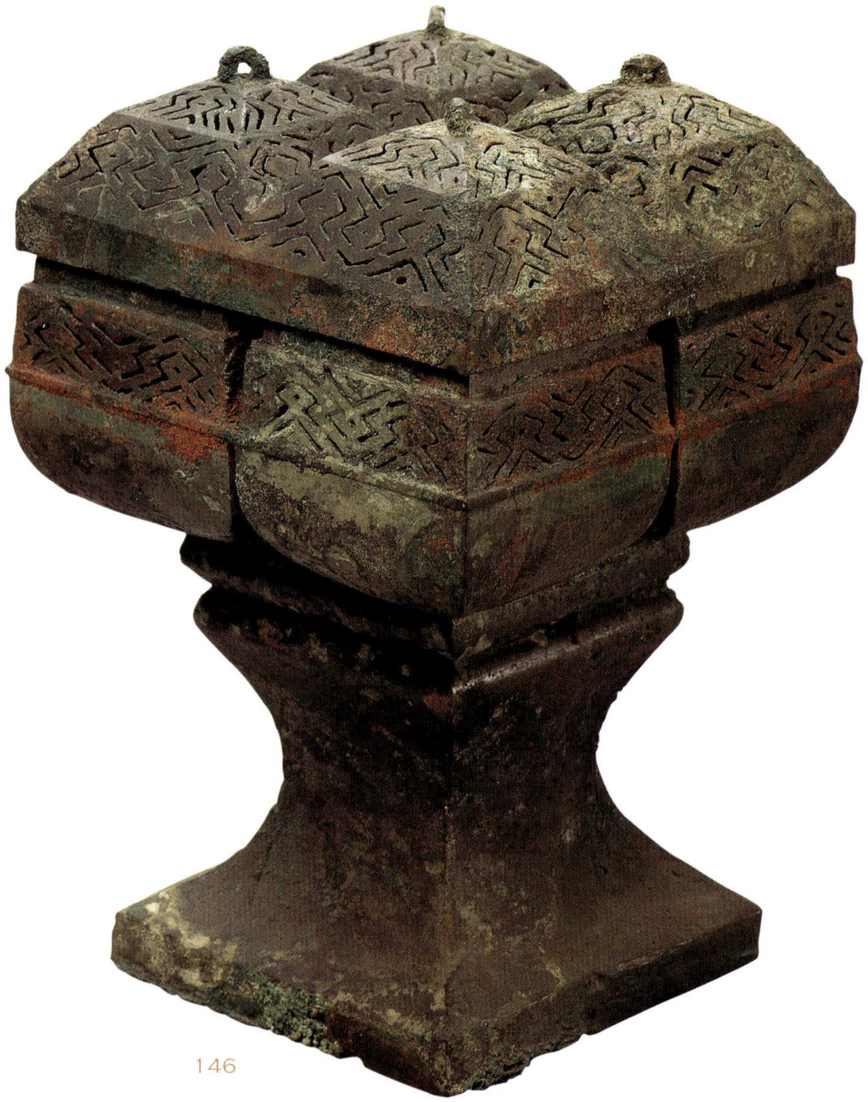

146

146

Bronze incense burner

Second century BC, Western Han dynasty
Height: 16.4 cm
Excavated at Xianggangshan in 1983
The Museum of the King of Nanyue,
Guangdong Province

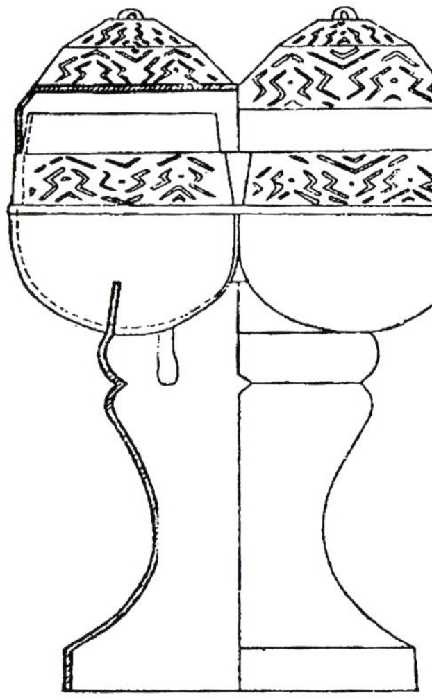

Three similar bronze incense burners were carefully wrapped in several layers of silk and kept in the western chamber. This example has four small containers, arranged side by side but not connected, resting on a bronze support. It may have been used to burn four different types of incense at the same time. Most incense was imported from South East Asia during the Western Han. The use of certain types of incense for their medicinal properties was very common during the Han period, but this particular type of incense burner is only known from the Guangzhou region.[1] JCSL

1 Erickson 1992, pp. 6–28.

147

Jade sword fittings

Second century BC, Western Han dynasty
Pommel diameter: 5.1 cm
Guard length: 4.1 cm; Width: 6.2 cm
Scabbard slides: Length: 7.9 cm; Width: 2 cm
Scabbard chape: Length: 4 cm; Width: 6.8 cm
Excavated at Xianggangshan in 1983
The Museum of the King of Nanyue,
Guangdong Province

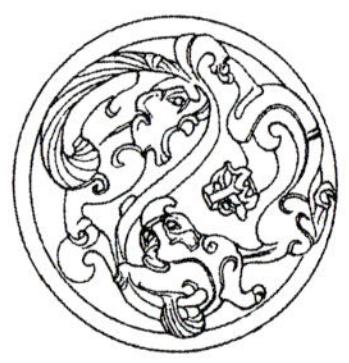

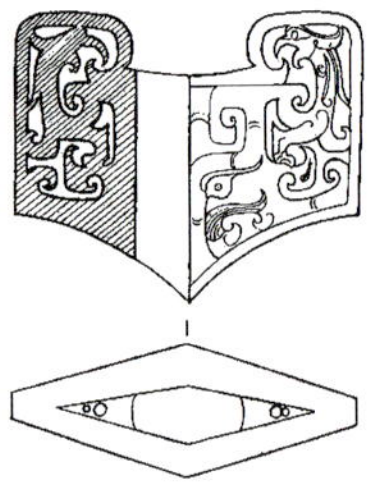

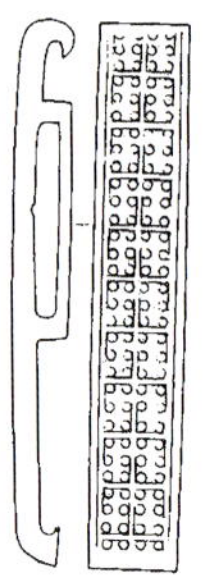

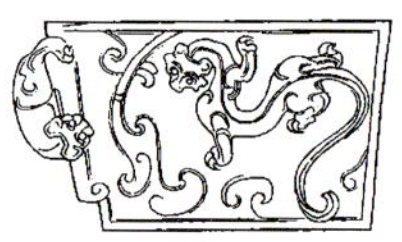

Forty-three jade sword fittings were found in the western chamber, which has been identified as a storage room in the King of Nanyue's tomb. These sword fittings include ten pommels, sixteen guards, nine scabbard slides and eight scabbard chapes. They were carefully wrapped in silk before being stored in a lacquer box. Only a few exhibit signs of use, suggesting that they were collected as pieces of personal interest to the king. Such a large collection of jade sword fittings from a single tomb is rather unusual compared with other excavations. The colours of this group of sword fittings range from pale yellow to light green and dark green. The pieces were covered with cinnabar powder as part of ancient burial practices. Some of the fittings were carved in high relief with feline dragons and some in openwork style. JCSL

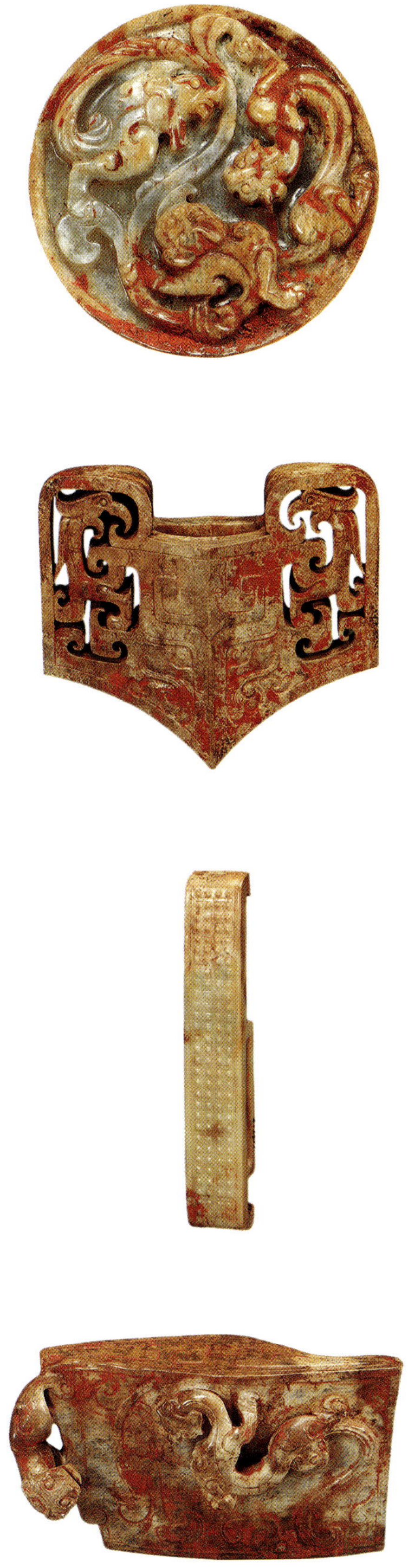

147

148

Gold belt hook shaped in the form of a goose's head

Second century BC, Western Han dynasty
Length: 1.9 cm; Diameter: 2.3 cm
Excavated at Xianggangshan in 1983
The Museum of the King of Nanyue, Guangdong Province

This type of belt hook comprising a hook, a main body and a button was popular in the Han dynasty. Three other examples, from the tombs of the Kings of Chu, are cat.. 73, 74 and 75. However, this belt hook is slightly different from the other three in that the button is much larger than the main body, probably because it was fitted onto a belt of special material that needed one of this size. The goose-head design was popular in the Han (cat. 73). LKC

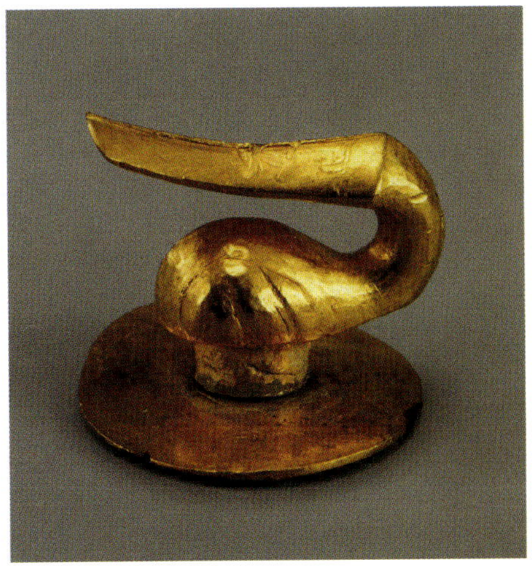

148

149

Jade dancer

Second century BC, Western Han dynasty
Height: 3.5 cm; Width: 3.5 cm; Thickness: 1 cm
Excavated at Xianggangshan in 1983
The Museum of the King of Nanyue, Guangdong Province

This well-carved jade dancer found in the western chamber was the best preserved among a number of jade dancing figures discovered at the same time. The sculpture is made of whitish-green jade, a type of nephrite. The yellowish colour all over the piece is caused by calcification. The figure wears a long robe decorated with carved cloud patterns on the hems and fastened on the right with a belt. The hair is tied up in a unique snail-shell-style bun on the right side of the head. The dancer is kneeling and twisting, with her left arm raised over her head and a sleeve hanging down behind; her right arm is swung back. The mouth is slightly open as if the performer were singing while dancing. There is a small vertical hole from the head through to the bottom, presumably for a hanging string.

Jade objects from the tomb of the King of Nanyue show some local characteristics even though they also preserved rather traditional shapes and designs similar to those found in Han areas. The graceful, flowing sculptural style shown in this piece represents a blending of pre-Qin Chu, Han and local styles.[1] This jade dancer is the only example of a jade figure carved in the round ever found in a Han tomb.[2] In spite of 2,000 years of burial it remains vigorous and lively, not only because of its durable material, but also because of the craftsmanship of its maker. A material analysis of eighteen jade objects from the King of Nanyue's tomb shows that the origin of the nephrite is probably around today's Qujiang area in northern Guzhangdong Province.[3] JX

1 Beijing 1991, vol. 1, pp. 343.
2 Most of the jade dancing figures found in early Han tombs are carved on flat plaques. Examples can be found in many tombs in Shaanxi Province. See Liu 2009, pp. 195–202.
3 Beijing 1991, vol. 1, pp. 372–9.

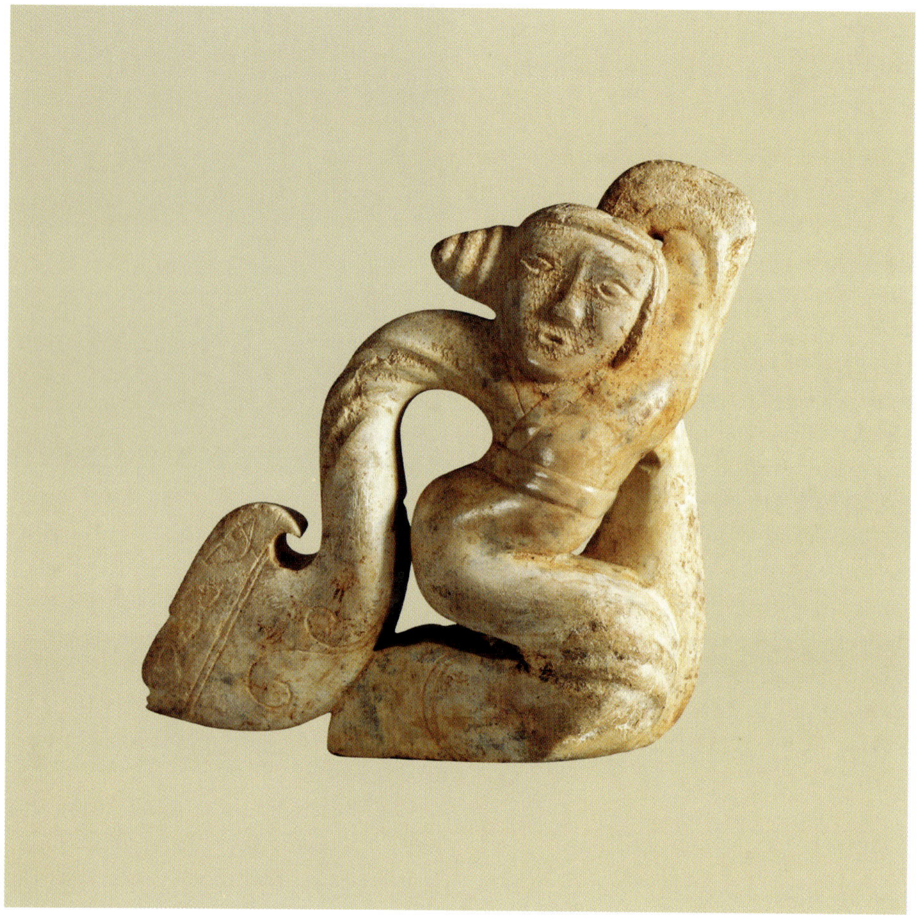

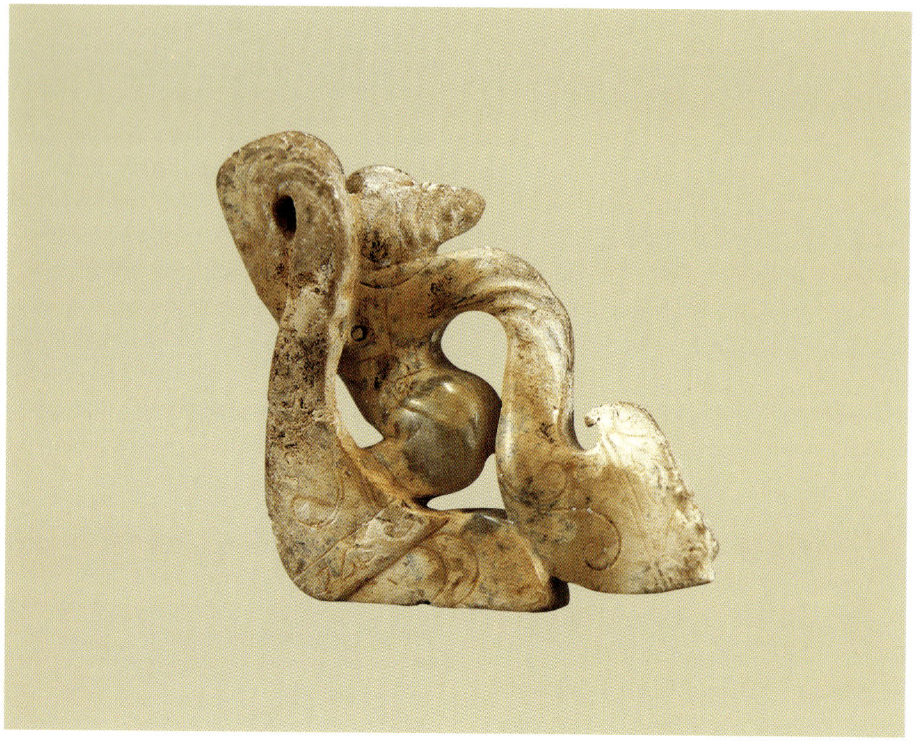

149

150

Earthenware percussion instruments

Second century BC, Western Han dynasty
Diameter: 9.5 cm
Excavated at Xianggangshan in 1983
The Museum of the King of Nanyue,
Guangdong Province

These percussion instruments were discovered in the western chamber. A total of seven such instruments were unearthed from the same room. Like the fish-shaped ones found in the rear storeroom (cat. 193), they were used in dance and music to beat out a rhythm.

Some of the surfaces of the instruments are decorated with small circles, possibly made with a straw or a reed when the clay was still wet, and others are marked with clusters of dots, possibly made by a comb-like object.

When these percussion instruments were discovered, there were fragments of woven reeds and silk remaining on the surface, indicating that they may have been wrapped in silk or put in a reed container when they were buried. LKC

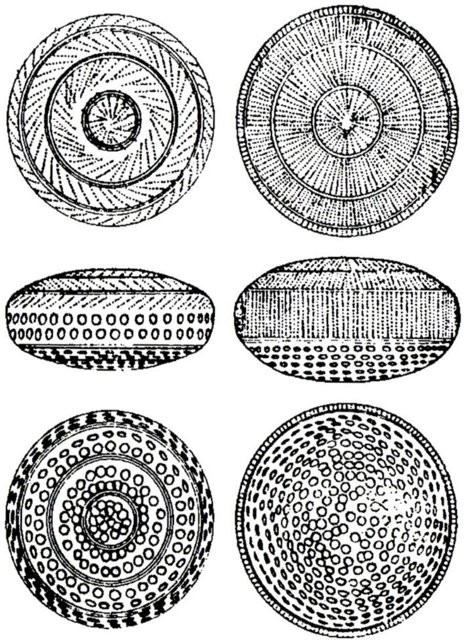

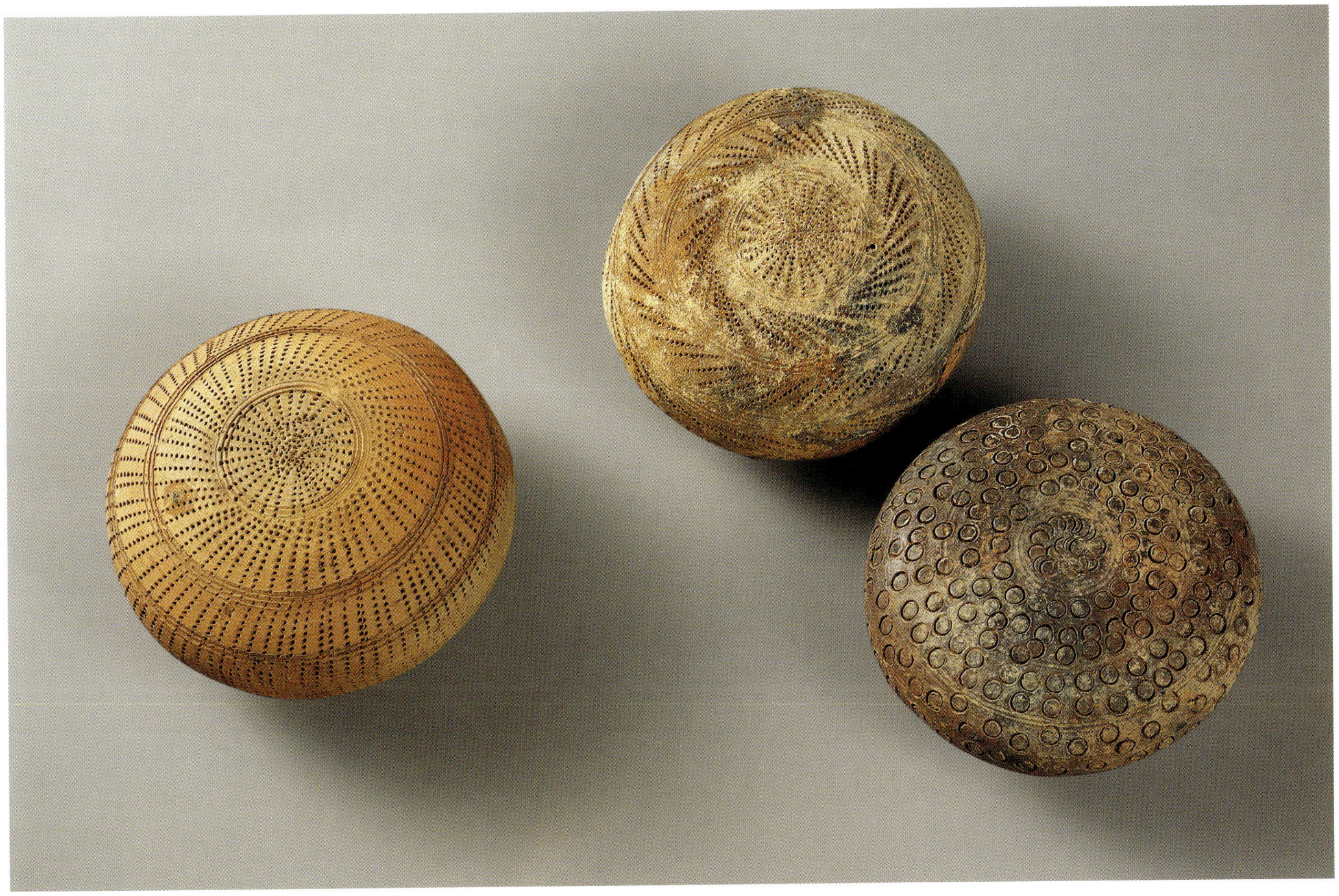

150

151

Iron spearhead

Second century BC, Western Han dynasty
Spear length: 49.2 cm; Ferrule length: 19.5 cm
Excavated at Xianggangshan in 1983
The Museum of the King of Nanyue, Guangdong Province

This iron spear was discovered among a bundle of five spears carefully wrapped in a piece of textile under the west wall of the king's coffin chamber. The ferrule, made of bronze and gilt, has a horizontal band raised in the middle and long triangular peaks in the mouth. There are remains of the original bamboo shaft inside both the spear socket and the ferrule (fig. 68).

In terms of the material and technology, iron appeared relatively late in the Lingnan region, where the Nanyue kingdom was located. The earliest iron objects dated from the late Warring States period (third century BC).[1]

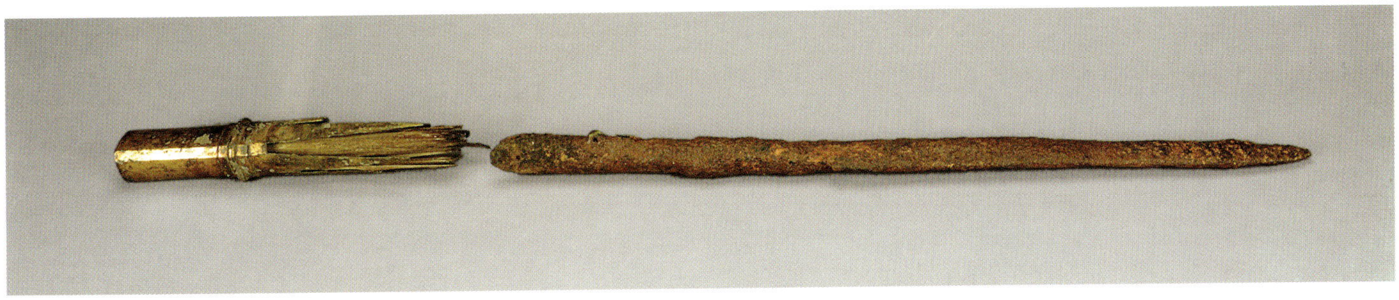

151

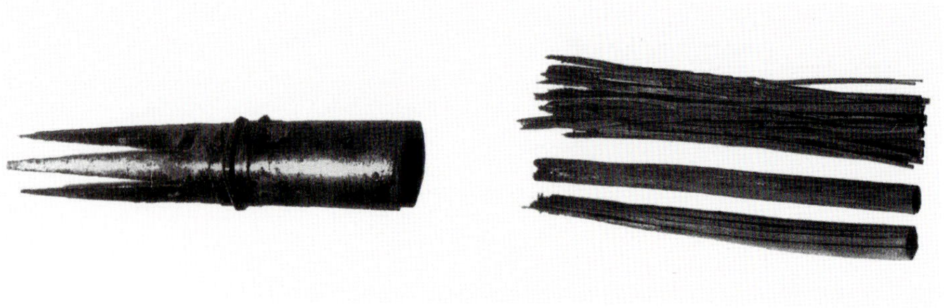

68 Bamboo splicing and spear socket.

Instead of developing its own local style, Nanyue armies mainly used weapons introduced from the former states of Chu and Qin.

Finds from tombs in the Nanyue kingdom show that the Nanyue people were verby skilful at iron casting. Local technology had achieved a high degree of strength but iron making in Nanyue also relied greatly on importation from the central region. Metallographic analysis of iron objects excavated from the tomb of the King of Nanyue has confirmed that most pieces contained materials with a different ratio of carbon content and some of them had obviously been reused.[2] The whole area lacked iron mines in the early Western Han. JX

1 The Warring States site of Baishiping in Shixing, Guangdong Province; *Kaogu* 1963.4: p. 217.
2 Beijing 1991, vol. 1, p. 333.

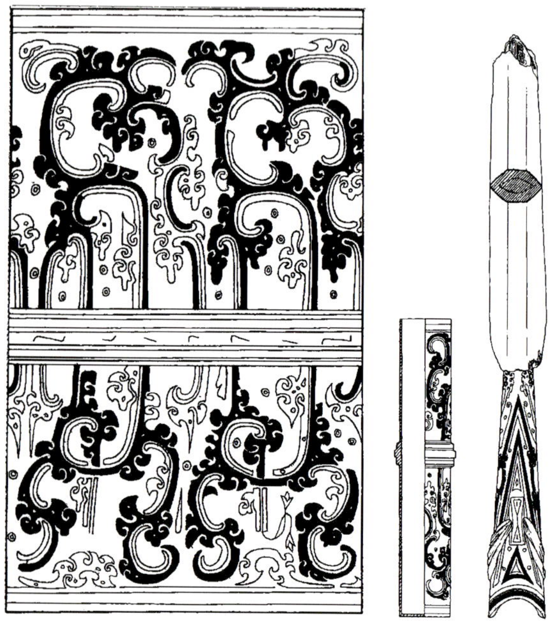

152

Iron spearhead inlaid with gold and silver

Second century BC, Western Han dynasty
Spear length: 27.3 cm; Ferrule length: 14.1 cm
Excavated at Xianggangshan in 1983
The Museum of the King of Nanyue, Guangdong Province

This iron spear and bronze ferrule were found in the same bundle as the spear of cat. 151. The spearhead had eroded so badly that it was stuck to the sheath. The sheath near the point of the blade was broken and the bamboo base inside was partially exposed. The blade was attached to a bronze cylinder decorated with an inlaid gold and silver triangle pattern on the front and back, and a flowing cloud design on both sides. The bronze ferrule was also inlaid with beautiful gold and silver flowing clouds motifs.

According to archaeological evidence, during the second century BC there appears to have been an increasing tendency to replace bronze weapons with those made of iron due to the cheaper material and the development of iron metallurgy. The iron to bronze weapon ratio in the King of Nanyue's tomb is 1 to 4.2. The transition from bronze to iron seems to have happened by the end of the Western Han period, two hundred years earlier than Chinese scholars used to believe.[1] JX

1 Yang 2005, pp. 28–31.

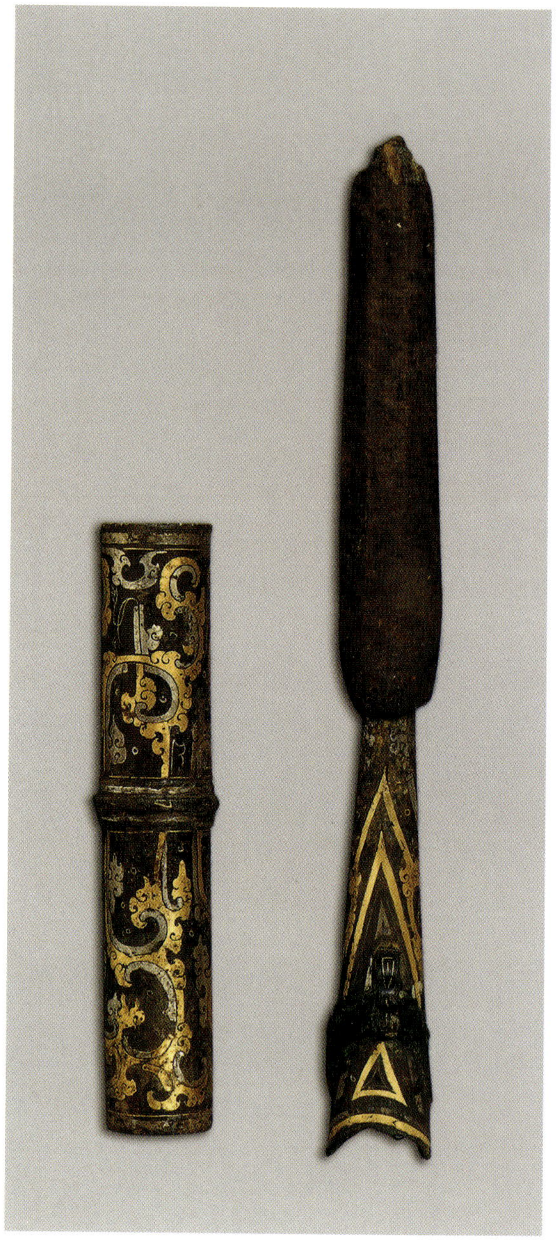

152

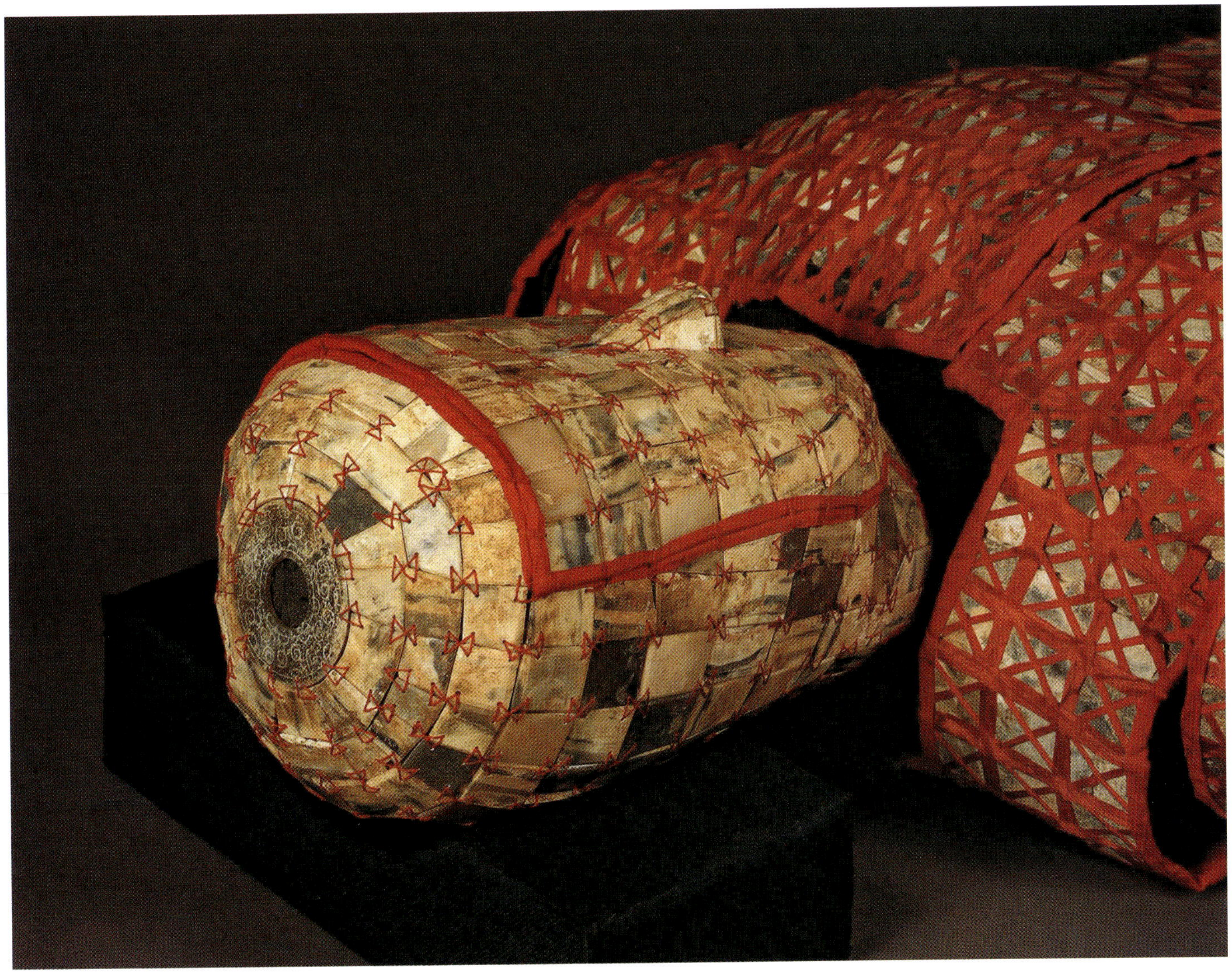

153

153

Jade suit

Second century BC, Western Han dynasty
Length: 173 cm
Excavated at Xianggangshan in 1983
The Museum of the King of Nanyue, Guangdong Province

The King of Nanyue's jade suit was composed of 2,291 jade plaques (fig. 69). It was divided into twelve parts like those from the tombs of the Han imperial family. However, only the plaques for the head, hands and feet were sewn together with silk thread, while the other sections were prepared by pasting plaques onto linen, which was then used to cover the body.

The jade plaques used for the head, hands and feet were carefully cut and polished. Almost all of the jade plaques used for the jacket and trousers were irregular in shape and of different lengths and most of them were reworked from discs and other jade objects. A disc was placed on top of the head. The nose was composed of triangular, trapezoid and semi-circular jade plaques and was the only facial feature. Inside the jade suit, two discs were placed near the head, four discs between the chest and abdomen and another eight between the arms and the body. No genital or other plugs were found on his body.

In order to explain the difference in practice between this and other imperial burials, scholars have advanced the theory that the Han emperor bestowed the plaques for the head, feet and hands as Nanyue was considered a vassal kingdom, and that the King of Nanyue

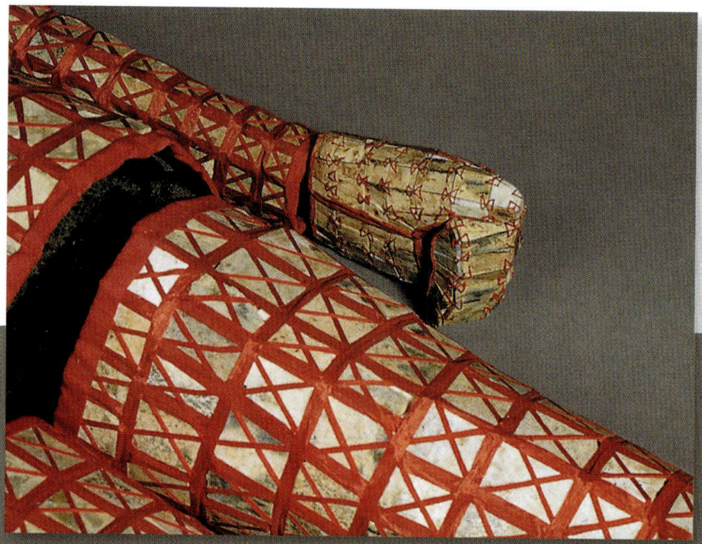

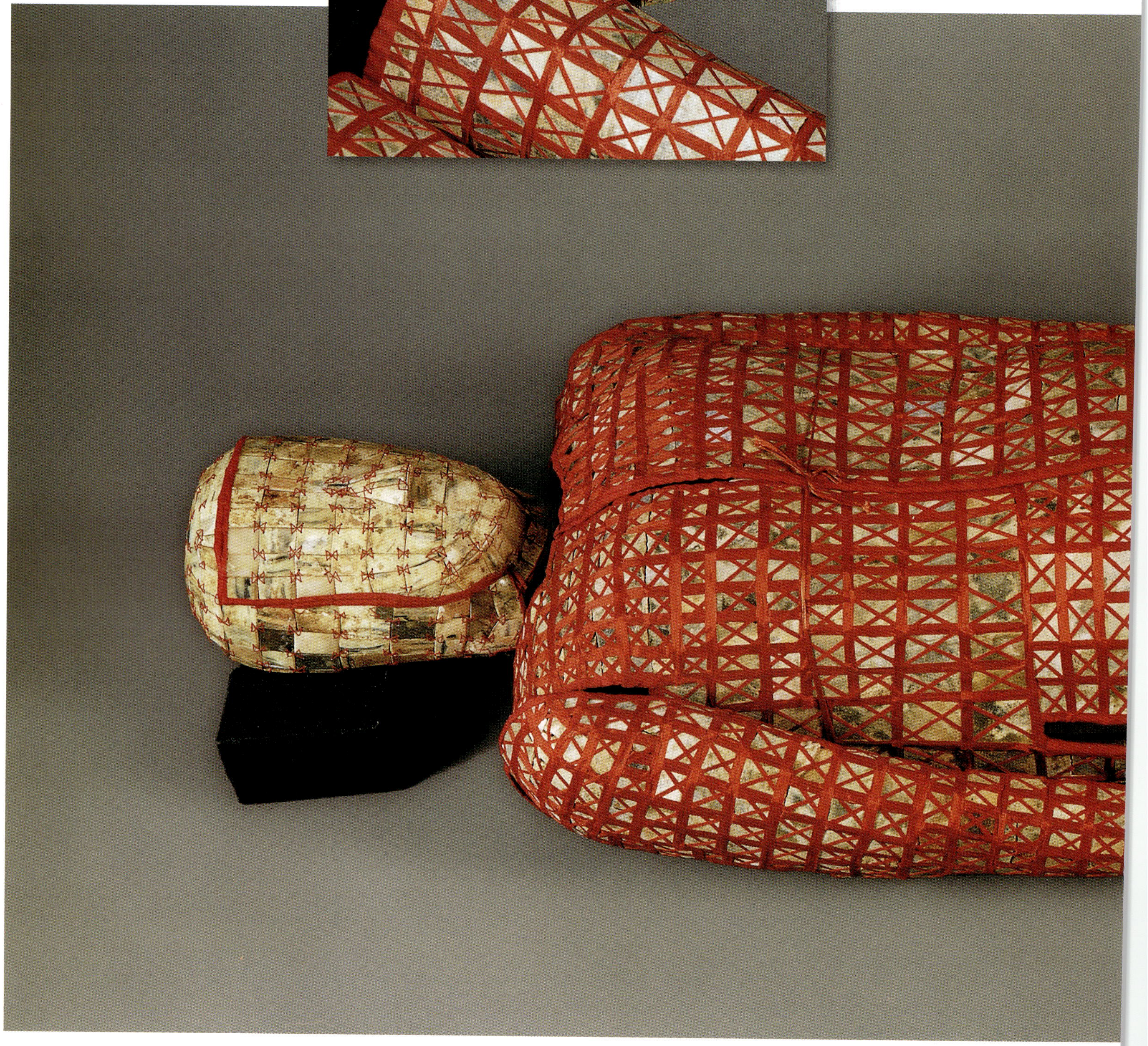

153

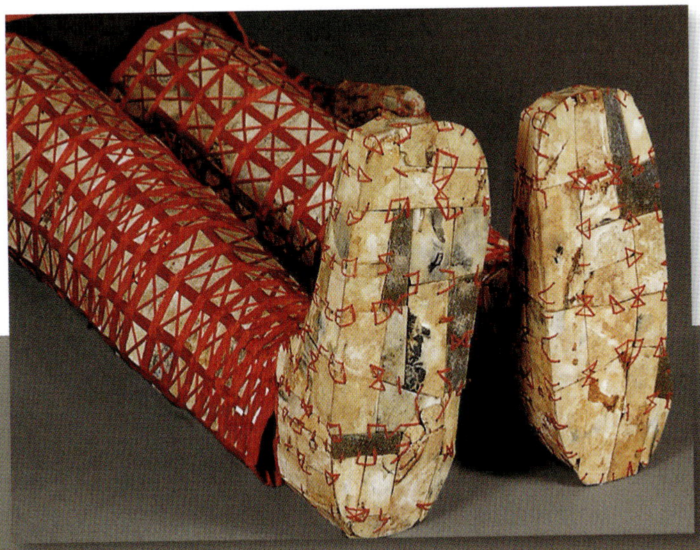

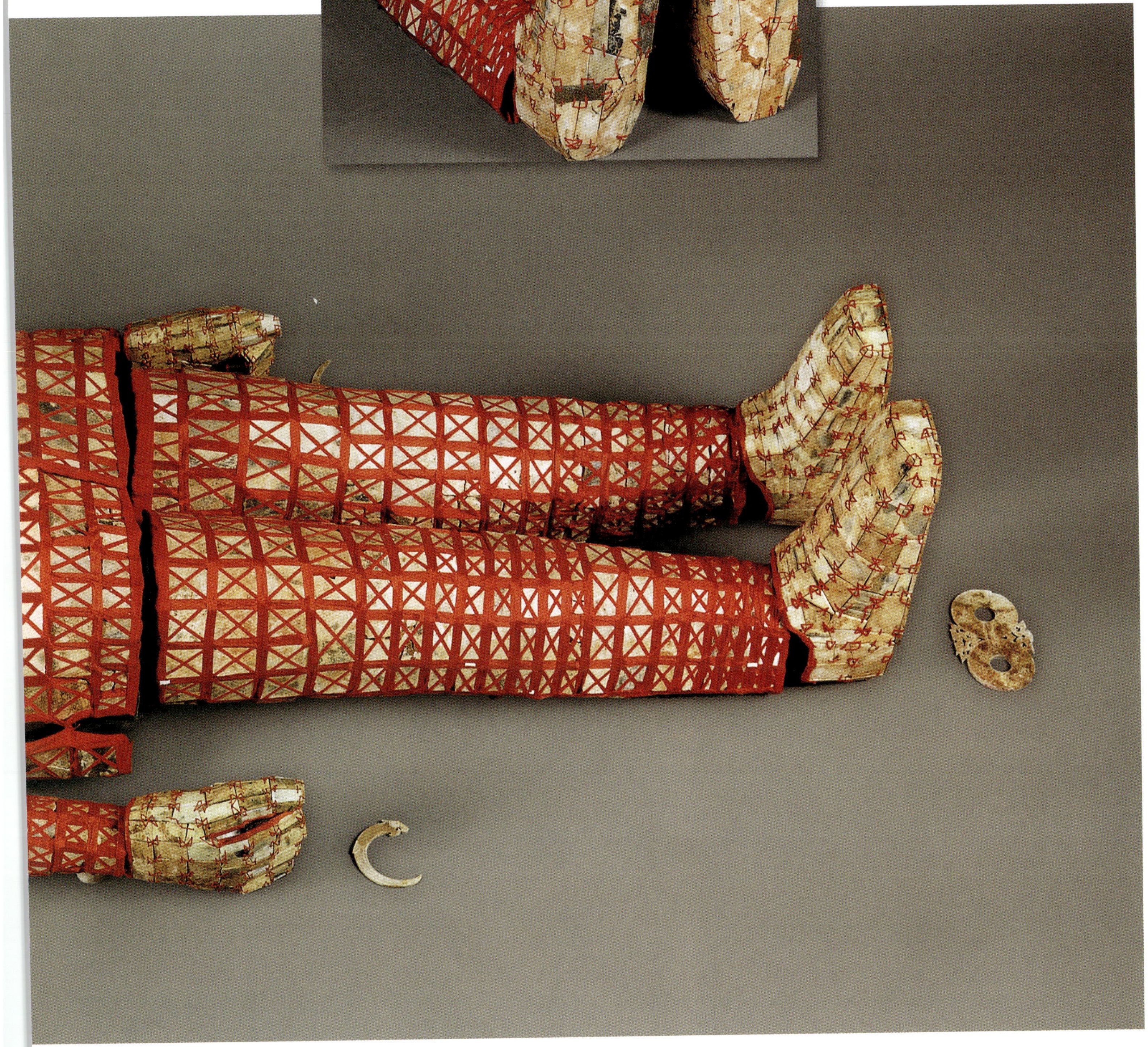

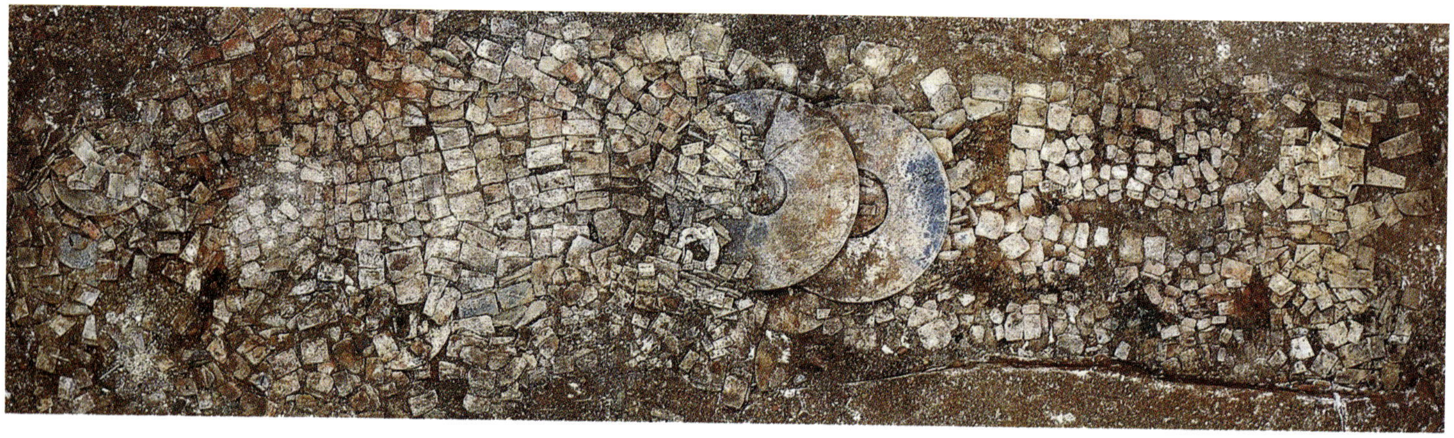

69 The jade suit of the King of Nanyue during the excavation.

commissioned the rest as part of the preparations for his eventual death and burial. JCSL

154

Two jade *xi*

Second century BC, Western Han dynasty
Length: 7.2 cm (left), 9.5 cm (right)
Excavated at Xianggangshan in 1983
The Museum of the King of Nanyue, Guangdong Province

These two curved dragons each ending in a sharp tip are known as *xi*. Both were found in the right hand of the jade suit. The custom of placing objects in both hands of the deceased has a long history in different parts of China. The body of a woman from the Chu tomb M1 at Mashan in Jiangling was wrapped in thirteen layers of cloth and tied with nine brocade ribbons. According to archaeological reports, her face was covered with a piece of silk called a *mingmu* that had small holes in it to represent the facial features. Both her arms and thumbs were bound with cross-knitted cord and her hands gripped silk rolls called *wo*.[1]

The terms *mingmu* and *wo* were referred to in the text *Yili shi sangli*, a record of ancient funerary rituals.[2] The custom of placing objects in the grip of burial figures differs from area to area during the Han period. In most areas, *wo* or hand 'grips' are usually made in the form of jade pigs, which represent fortune. The arched-dragon design was no longer popular during the Han period, so the two pieces found in the

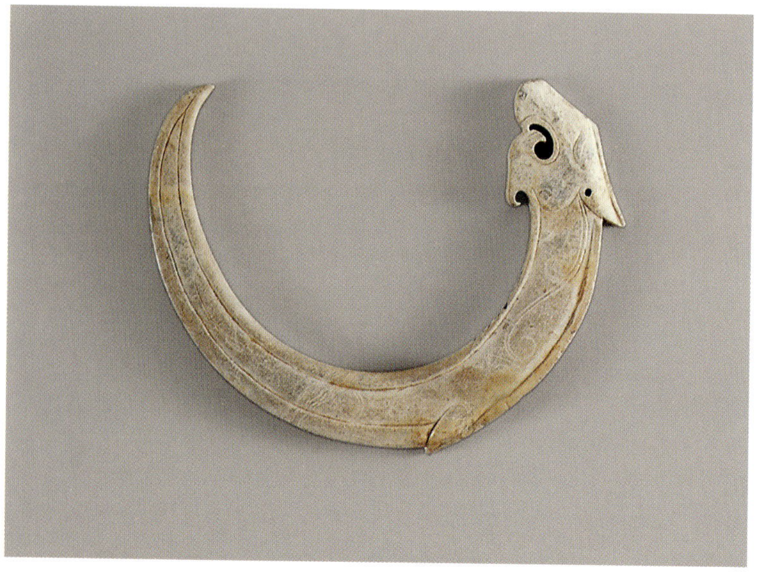

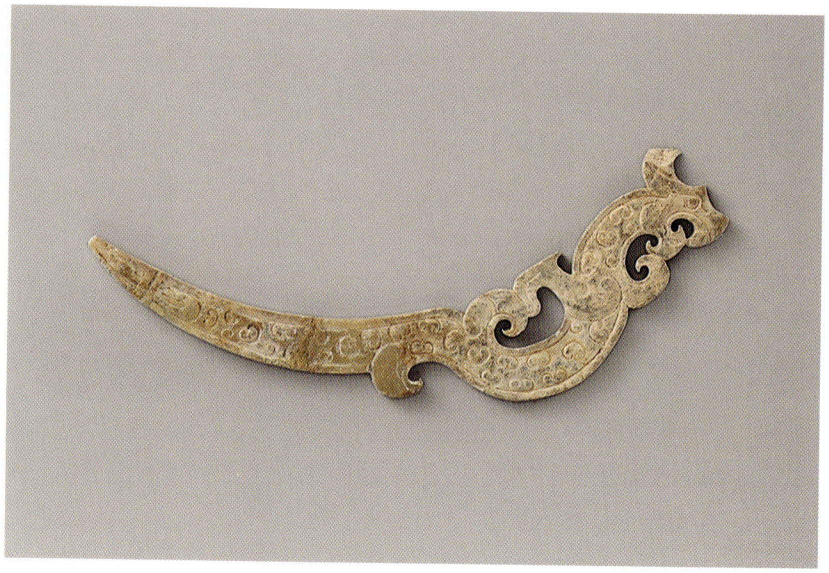

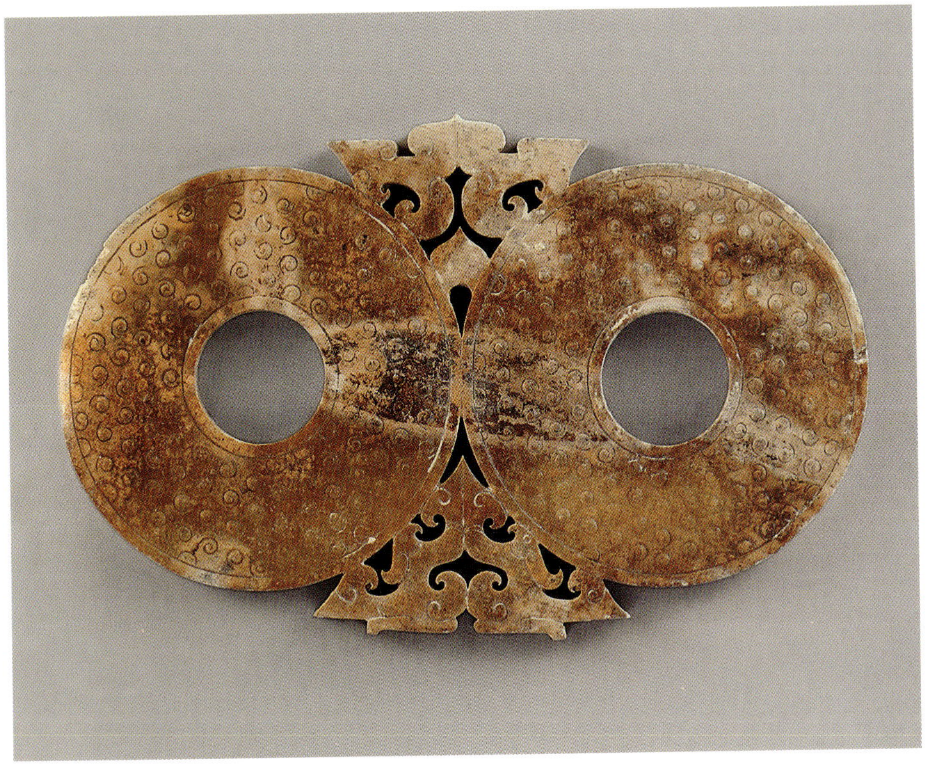

155

King of Nanyue's right hand might have survived from an earlier period. Two objects found gripped in one hand is very unusual in archaeological finds. JCSL

1 Beijing 1985, pp. 97–8.
2 *Yili*, 12.5b.

155

Jade double disc

Second century BC, Western Han dynasty
Length: 12.3 cm; Height: 7.4 cm;
Diameter: 6.2 cm
Excavated at Xianggangshan in 1983
The Museum of the King of Nanyue,
Guangdong Province

This double disc was found near the foot section of the jade suit. It was carved in the shape of two discs linked together by symmetrical openwork triangular appendages. The discs are decorated with raised spirals. The lower appendage shows a pair of rampant birds with spreading wings and the upper one is carved with flying clouds. Judging from the traces of silk on both discs, this double disc might have been tied to the feet of the jade suit. JCSL

156

Two jade discs

Second century BC, Western Han dynasty
Diameter: 28.1 cm (left), 28.5 cm (right)
Excavated at Xianggangshan in 1983
The Museum of the King of Nanyue,
Guangdong Province
156B NOT EXHIBITED

This type of large disc was popular in eastern China from the late Warring States period to the Western Han. They were found in large numbers on top and underneath the bodies of high-ranking individuals. Each disc usually consists of three distinct decorative sections separated by striated bands. In these examples, the inner and outer sections of the disc are decorated with four sets of animal heads surrounded by long intertwined scrolls while the middle section consists of rows of spirals in relief. Jessica Rawson has argued that this animal motif probably evolved from rectangular plaques dating back to the fourth century BC, becoming a standard design during the third–first centuries BC.[1] However, the animal head designs on such discs differ slightly from area to area. In some they were incised

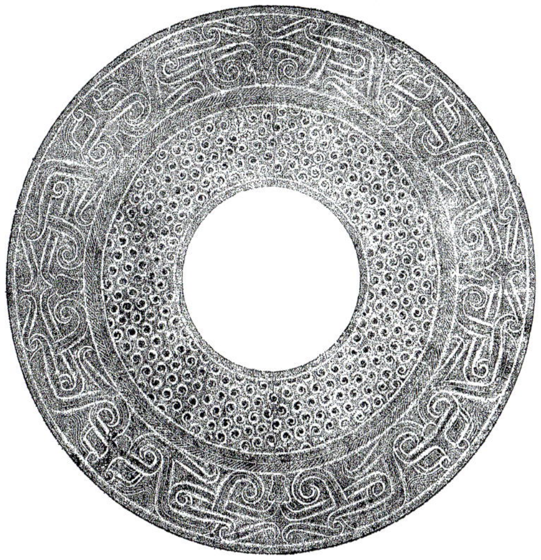

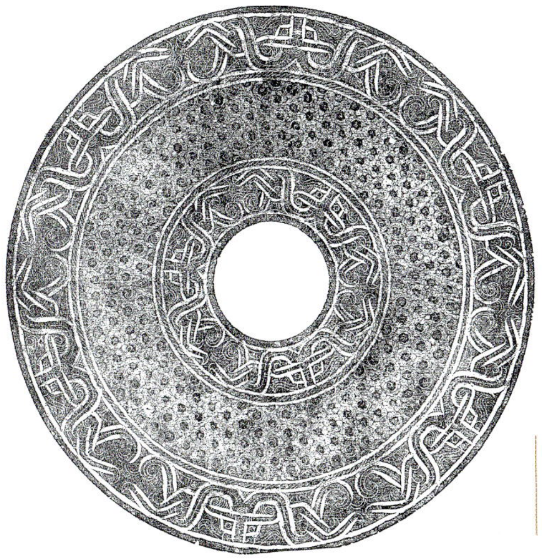

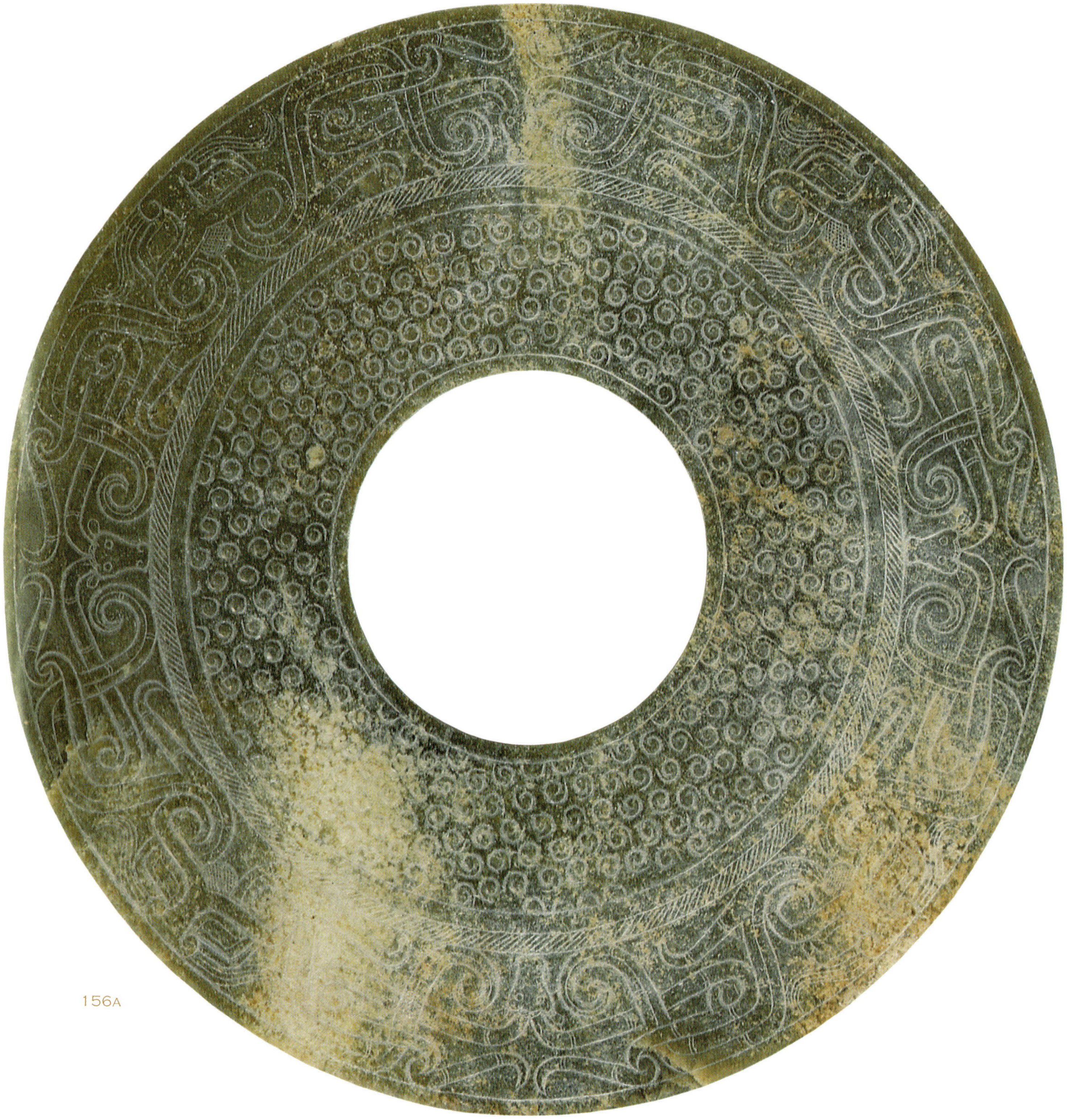

156A

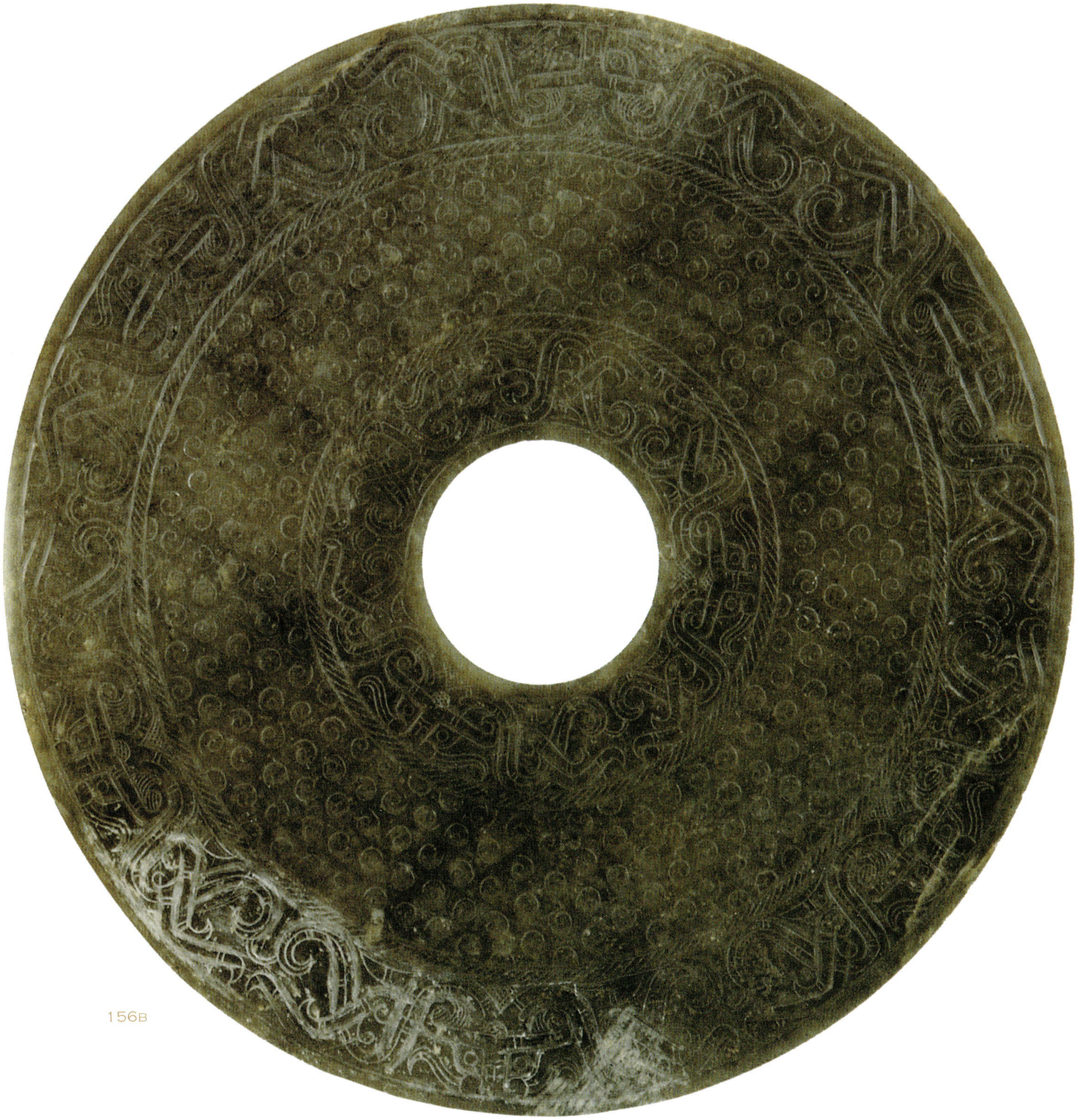

156B

with buffalo heads surrounded by intertwined scrolls.

These discs were arranged in a row and held together by silk threads used to cover the body before enclosure within a jade suit. Decaying silk has discoloured some discs.

Discs played an important role in funeral rites during the Han dynasty. Fourteen jade discs were placed around the King of Nanyue's body, on his chest and under his back, within the jade suit. Five more discs were laid under the suit. Additional jade discs and segments were placed on the top of the outer coffin and in between the inner and outer coffins. All these discs were of finer material than that of the jade suit. Glass and earthenware discs were also used in Han tombs as substitutes for jade. For example, 139 earthenware discs (cat. 157, fig. 70) were found at the foot of the inner coffin in the Nanyue king's tomb. In another example, approximately 200 earthenware discs were found scattered on the top of a coffin in a Western Han tomb at Tongshan, Xuzhou, Jiangsu Province.[2] JCSL

1 Rawson 1998, p. 130.
2 *Wenwu* 1973.4, p. 27.

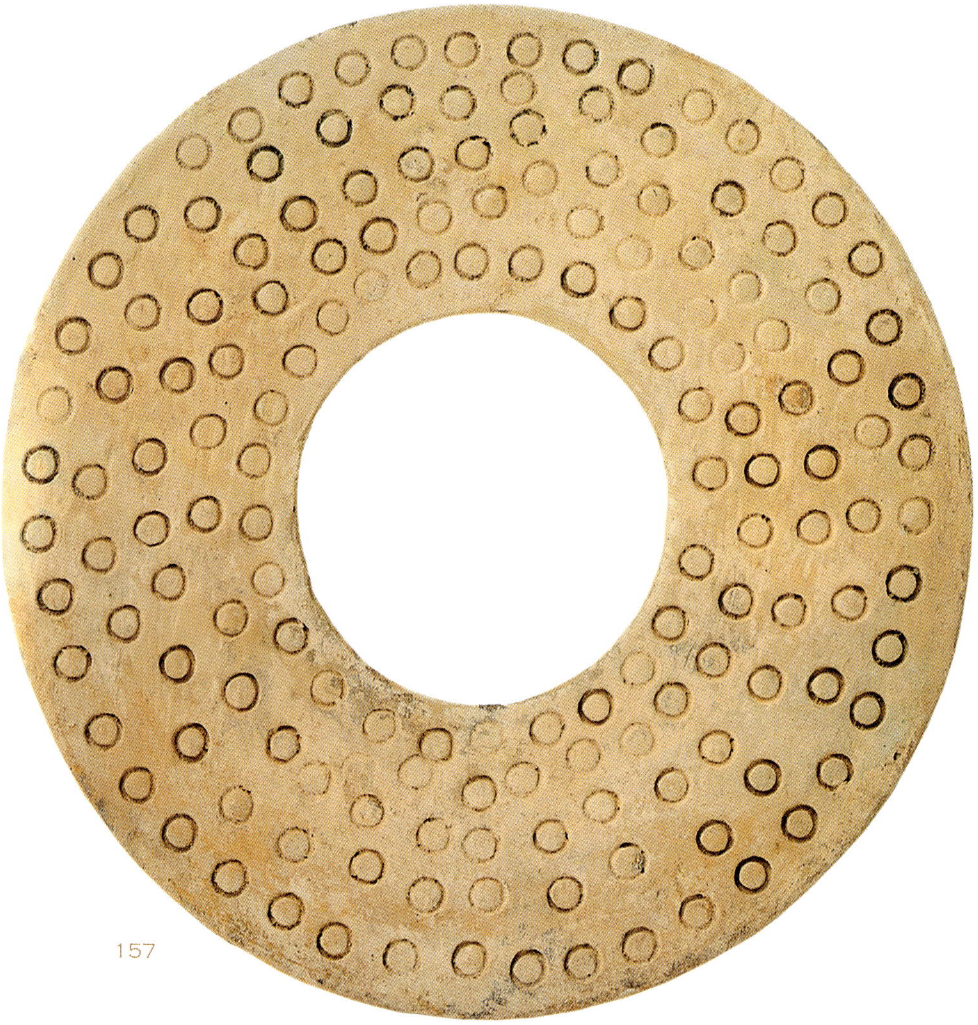

157

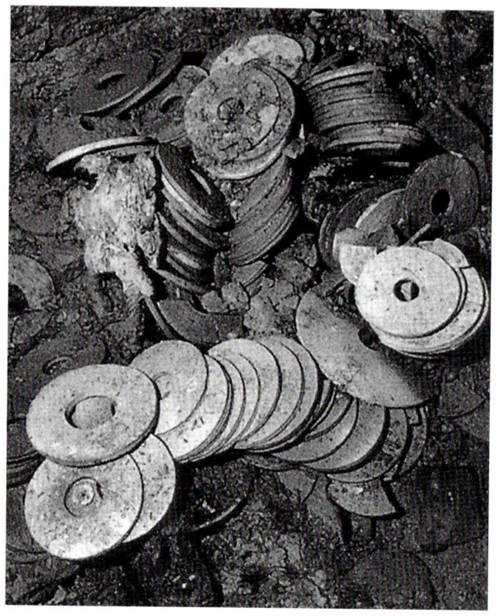

Fig. 70

157

Earthenware disc

Second century BC, Western Han dynasty
Diameter: 15 cm
Excavated at Xianggangshan in 1983
The Museum of the King of Nanyue, Guangdong Province

139 earthenware discs and two jade discs were found at the foot of the king's inner coffin (fig. 70) next to a Persian-style silver box (cat. 167). They were arranged in four piles. Earthenware discs appear to be a substitute for jade for individuals with lower status; the sacrificial servant in the kitchen was buried with earthenware discs. Discs must have had significant meaning in burial rites as they appear in large numbers near the body of the tomb owner. Made of clay, these discs can be mass-produced in a short period. This type of earthenware disc has only simple decorations with three to six sections of circles impressed into the clay with bamboo sticks. JCSL

70 Discs excavated at the tomb of the King of Nanyue. Second century BC.

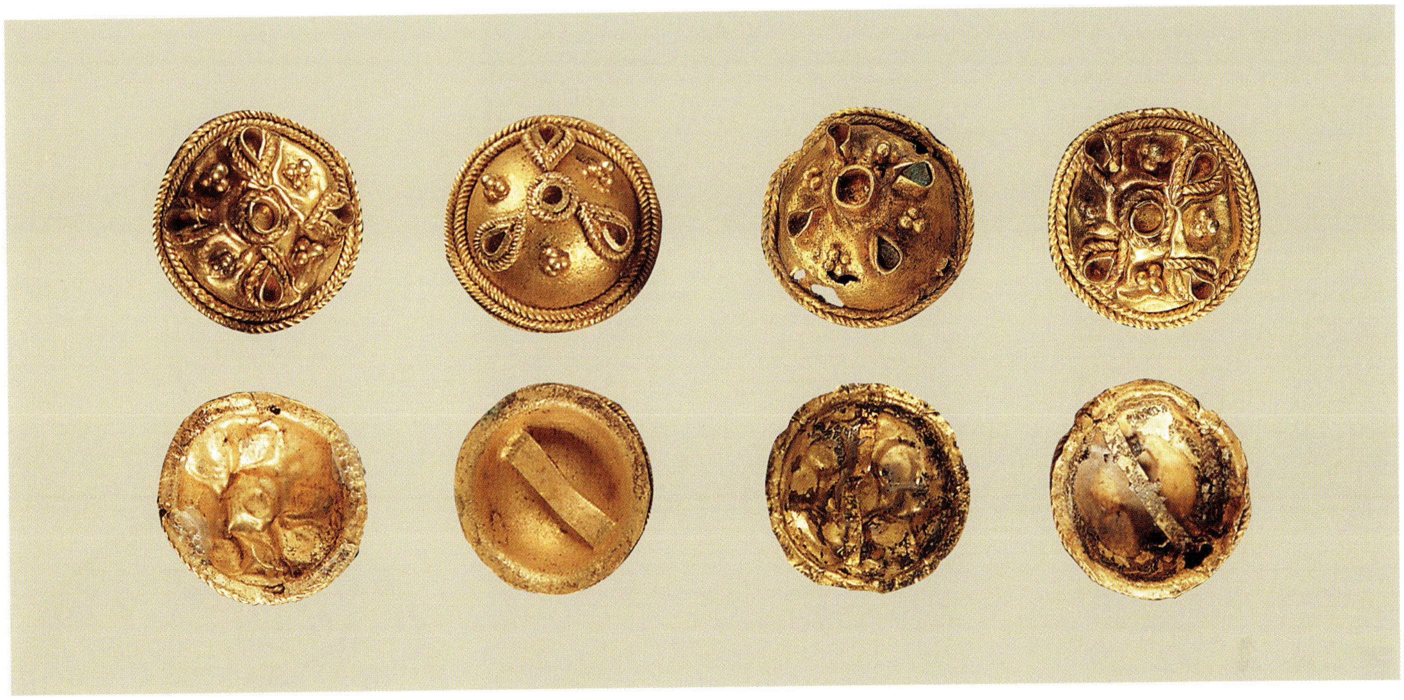

158

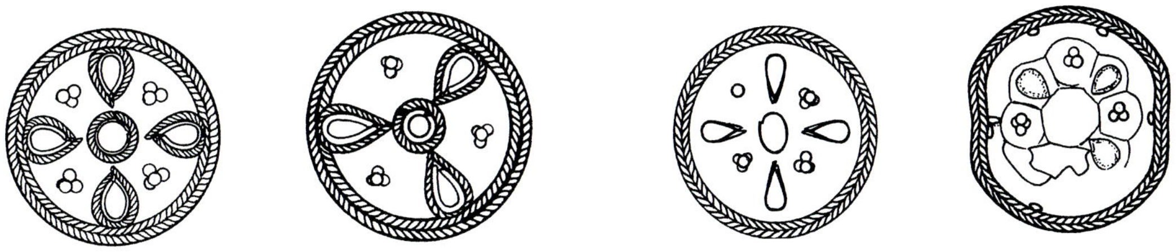

158

Gold ornaments in the shape of buttons with flower designs

Second century BC, Western Han dynasty
Diameter: 1.1 cm; Height: 0.5 cm
Excavated at Xianggangshan in 1983
The Museum of the King of Nanyue, Guangdong Province

These are elaborate examples of the thirty-two gold buttons with flower designs found along with many glass beads, glass shells, gilt bronze buttons and silver buttons, on three belts attached to the lower part of the jade suit that the tomb occupant was wearing in the king's coffin room.

These objects are obviously not originally from Nanyue or Han China. Inlaid turquoise is consistent with the long tradition of using brightly coloured gemstones set in gold in countries like Egypt and Persia. The technique of granulation appeared in Mesopotamia at least by the mid-third millennium BC[1] and then spread to other areas. This exotic design must have found its way to the Nanyue court by way of trade through the flourishing maritime routes of that time. In addition to agriculture and fishing, trade formed one of the most important aspects of the Nanyue economy. Maritime routes to South East Asia through ports like Panyu (present-day Guangzhou, Guangdong) and Hepu (Guangxi) have been recorded in Han texts. They are also reflected in diverse archaeological discoveries, such as the exceptional finds of a silver box and gold buttons in the Nanyue king's tomb. But whether the buttons were imported or locally made under the influence of another culture is still not clear. These beautifully crafted gold buttons are testimony to the superb skills of their maker and material proofs of prosperous trading between ancient China and the outside world. JX

1 Zettler and Horne 1998; Margon 1949, pp. 93–125.

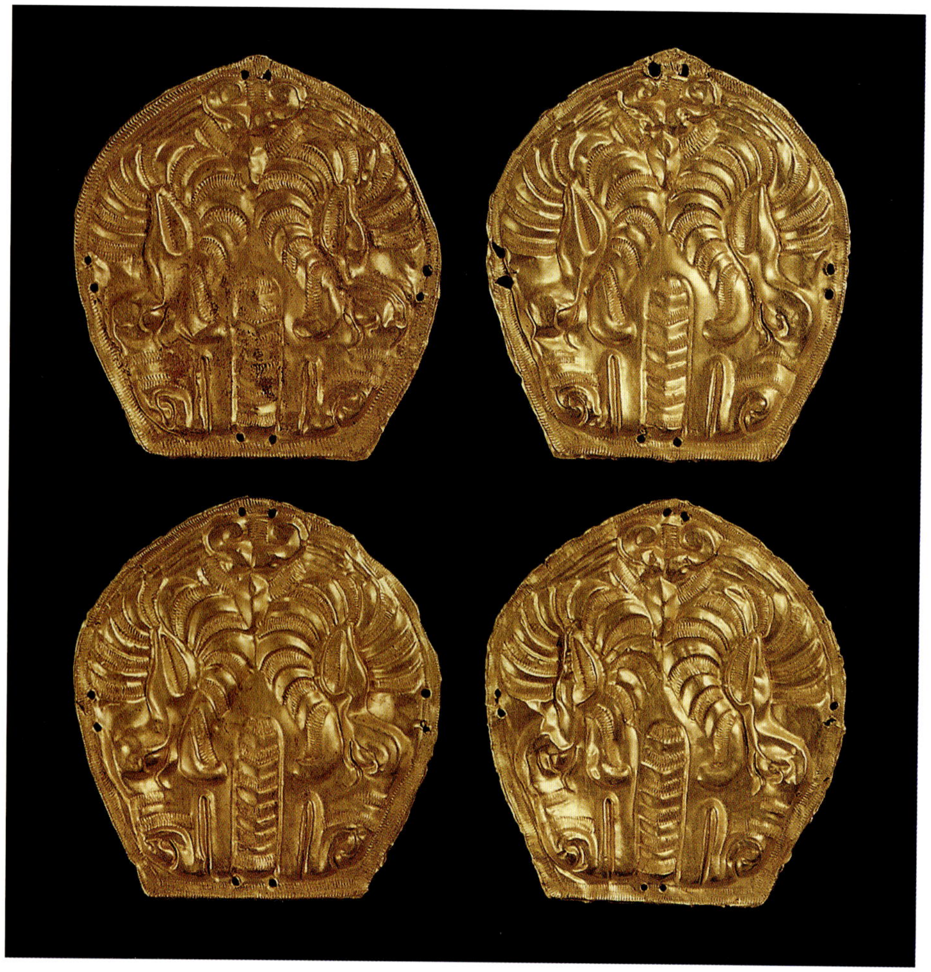

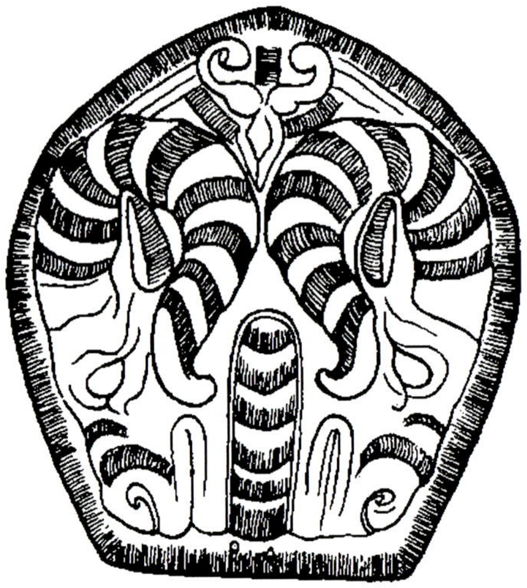

159

159

Gold ornament in the shape of an apricot leaf

Second century BC, Western Han dynasty
Length: 4.6–4.7 cm; Width: 4.3–4.4 cm
Excavated at Xianggangshan in 1983
The Museum of the King of Nanyue, Guangdong Province

Eight gold leaves of the same size and design were found on the face of the decayed king's corpse in the coffin room. They were sewn to the silk face cover on top of the veil of the jade suit, with four in the middle and two on each side. Made from gold sheets, they were hammered into shape and engraved with details of the curving horns of two symmetrical ram heads in profile facing opposite ways and one stylized ram head in the top middle. One pair of small holes in the middle of the rim on each direction is meant for attachment to the silk cover. Another five gold leaves nearly identical in design were unearthed in the early Han tomb at Mancheng, Hebei Province.[1]

Animal motif decoration on gold objects was very much a steppe tradition. When China came into close contact with the nomadic peoples of the steppe from the Warring States period to the Qin and Han dynasties, the Chinese were influenced by their neighbours' interest in gold, along with elements of nomadic lifestyles such as the practice of sophisticated horseback riding. Related objects, including belt hooks, buckles and gilded ornamental plaques reflect the influence of nomadic culture on Chinese habits of dress. However, it is unclear whether these gold leaves were locally made in Nanyue or brought by Qin soldiers who had participated in military campaigns in the North and then came to the conquered southern territory late in the third century.[2] JX

1 Archaeological report of the Han tomb at Mancheng; Beijing 1980, vol. 1, p. 117.
2 See Huang 1996, pp. 55–60 for a discussion on the source of 'animal-style' objects unearthed in Guangdong and Guangxi Provinces.

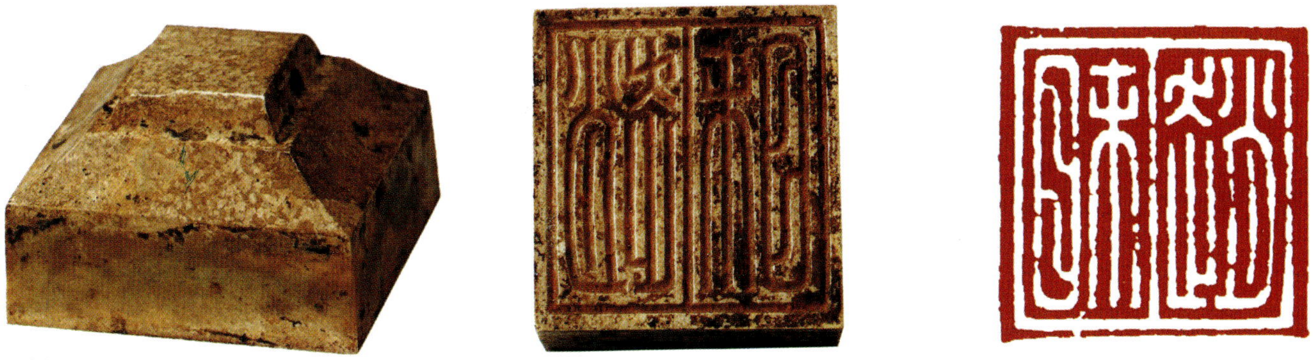

160

160

Jade seal

Second century BC, Western Han dynasty
Length: 2.3 cm; Width: 2.3 cm; Height: 1.6 cm
Excavated at Xianggangshan in 1983
The Museum of the King of Nanyue, Guangdong Province

This jade seal is of pyramid shape and carved with the characters Zhao Mo in negative relief. It was found together with the jade seal carved with *di yin* (Seal of the Emperor; cat. 161) and a plain turquoise seal on the lower abdomen of the owner. A frame separates the two characters. This seal is particularly important because it reveals the tomb owner's name as different from that recorded in the *Shiji*. The historian Sima Qian mistakenly gives the name as Zhao Hu. The character *Mo* also appeared on two clay seals that confirm the owner's identity as Zhao Mo (cat. 144). JCSL

161

Jade seal

Second century BC, Western Han dynasty
Length: 2.3 cm; Width: 2.3 cm; Height: 1.7 cm
Excavated at Xianggangshan in 1983
The Museum of the King of Nanyue, Guangdong Province

This jade seal is square with an ornamental feline dragon knob, edges carved with cloud patterns, and the inscription *di yin* (Seal of the Emperor). The seal has heavy calcification and, as a result, its colour has darkened. Two smaller clay seals found in the western chamber were also incised *di yin* (fig. 71), but the style of the characters is different from that of the jade seal. This is the first time a seal with the inscription 'Seal of the Emperor' has been found in an archaeological excavation. Again it supports texts recording that the King of Nanyue challenged the authority of the Han emperor of his time. JCSL

71 Inscription 'Seal of the Emperor' from the clay seal found in the western chamber.

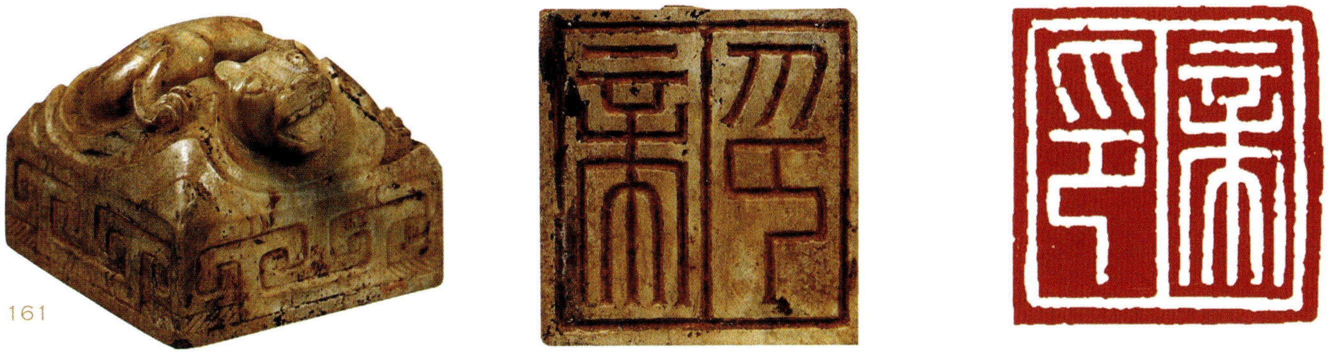

161

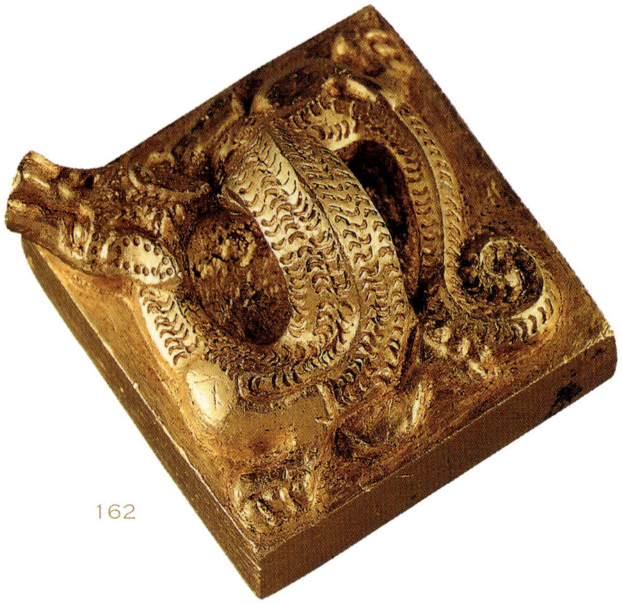

162

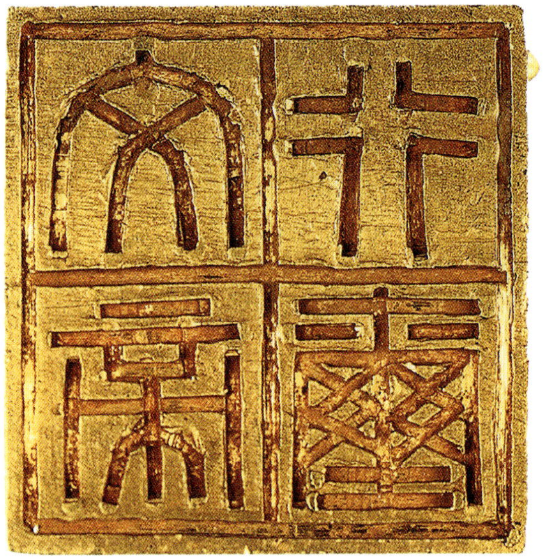

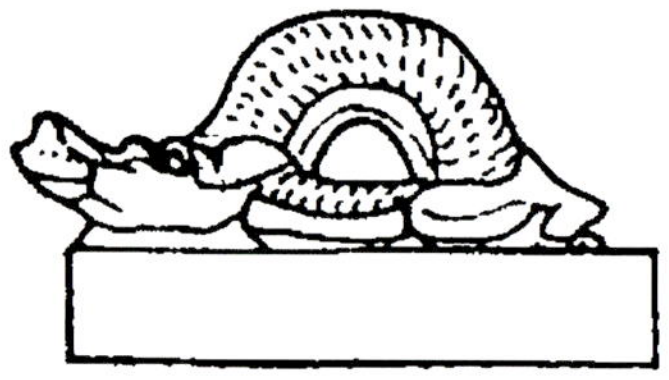

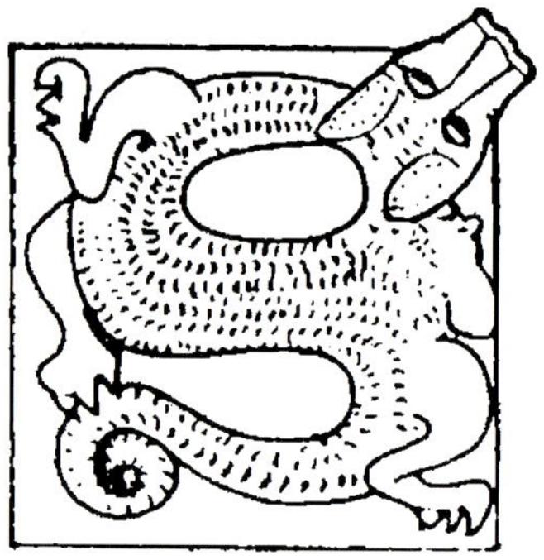

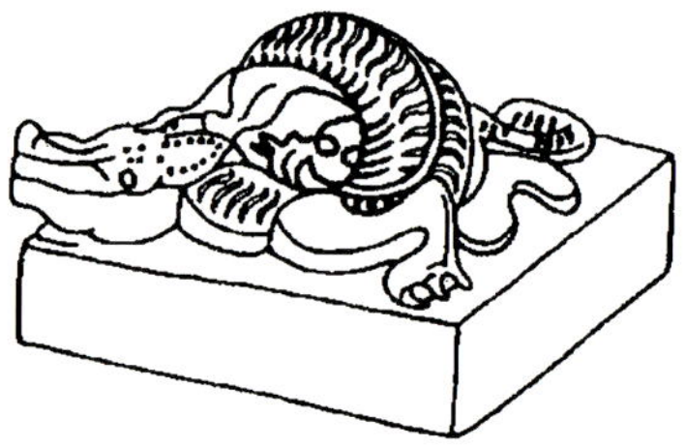

162

Gold seal with ornamental dragon knob

Second century BC, Western Han dynasty
Length: 3.1 cm; Width: 3 cm; Height: 1.8 cm
Excavated at Xianggangshan in 1983
The Museum of the King of Nanyue, Guangdong Province

This gold seal incised *wendi xingxi* (Administrative Seal of Emperor Wen), together with two plain jade seals, was found inside a lacquer box on the chest of the King of Nanyue. The seal is cast with a dragon knob with the dragon's scales and claws incised afterwards. The four characters on the surface were separated by a frame design. Signs of wear and tear on the surface of the seal and the walls of the inkpad suggest that the seal may have been used during his lifetime.

Compared with other seals excavated to date, this seal is unique in many ways. First, most seals belonging to imperial family members, including those from Xuzhou, were cast in gold with turtle knobs. The seals found in Han vassal kingdoms, such as Japan and Dian, or present-day Yunnan Province and part of Vietnam, are cast in gold with snake knobs. This is the only example of a dragon-knob seal excavated so far. Second, the inscription on this seal, *wendi xingxi*, is different from the usual references to 'emperor' in texts from the period as *huangdi xingxi*, and suggests that Nanyue did claim independence. Third, the size of this seal is larger than those belonging to members of the imperial family (usually between 2.7 and 2.8 centimetres). This is the largest gold seal that has been found from the Western Han period. The evidence shows that Zhao Mo, like his grandfather, ignored the authority of the Han emperor and declared himself Emperor of Nanyue kingdom. JCSL

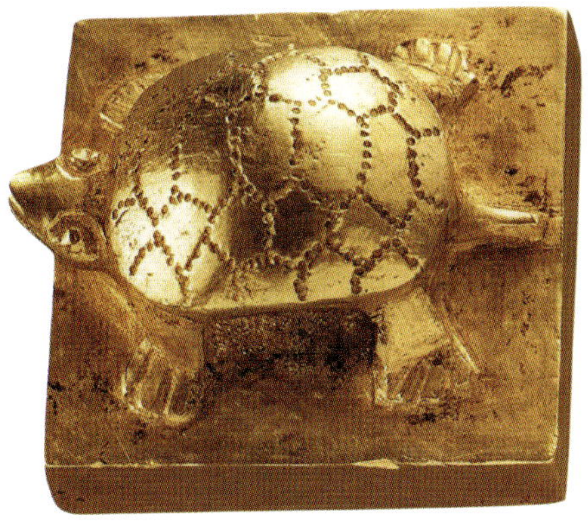

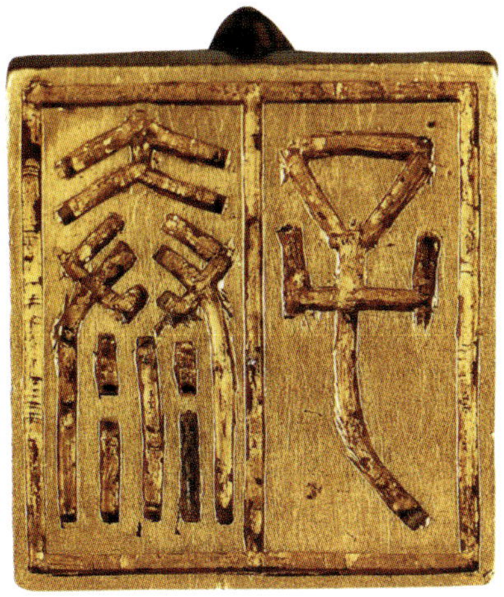

163

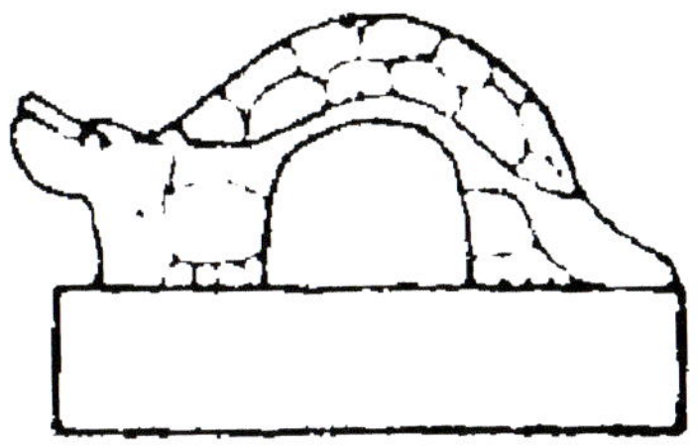

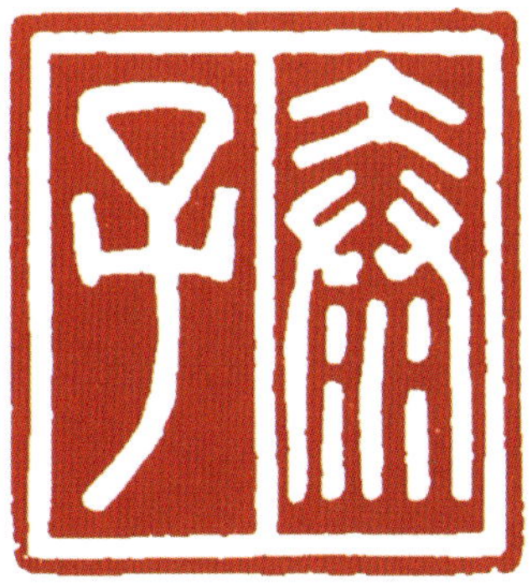

163

Gold seal with ornamental turtle knob

Second century BC, Western Han dynasty
Length: 2.6 cm; Width: 2.4 cm;
Height: 1.5 cm
Excavated at Xianggangshan in 1983
The Museum of the King of Nanyue, Guangdong Province

This gold seal, cast with a standing turtle and incised in negative relief with *taizi* (Crown Prince), together with another jade seal carved with the same title and a plain uncarved seal, was originally found in a small lacquer box placed on the abdomen of the tomb's occupant. The details of the turtle were incised after casting. Under the plastron part of the turtle's shell is a hole through which a silk ribbon was threaded. This seal, together with the jade seal of the Crown Prince, must have been handed down to Zhao Mo from his father. This excavation was the first in which seals inscribed with references to the title of 'Crown Prince' were found. JCSL

164

Jade cup with bronze basin stand

Second century BC, Western Han dynasty
Height: 17 cm
Excavated at Xianggangshan in 1983
The Museum of the King of Nanyue, Guangdong Province

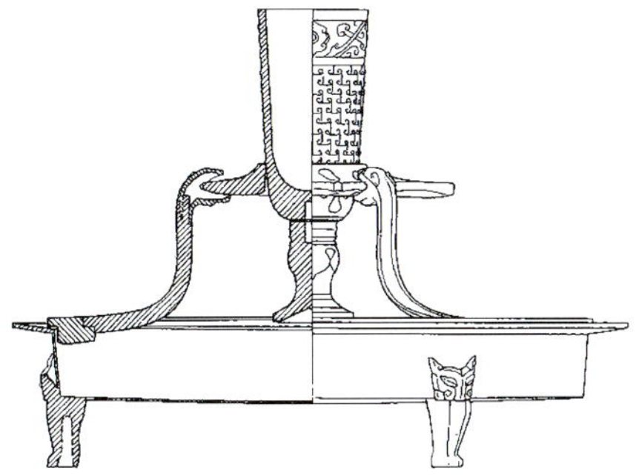

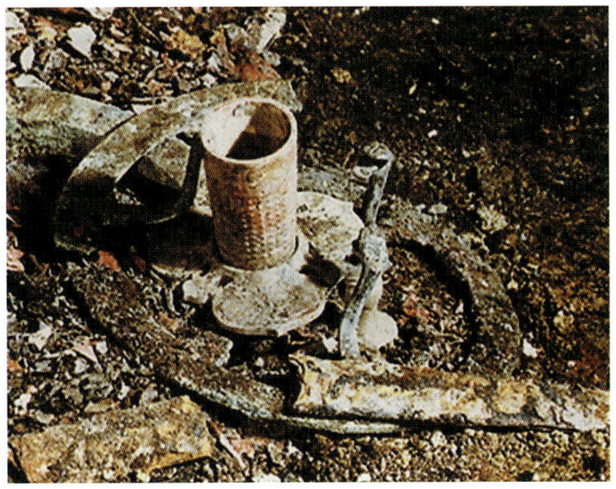

72 Jade cup with a bronze basin stand *in situ* at the tomb of the King of Nanyue.

This light green jade tubular cup is held by a quatrefoil jade disc, which is in turn supported by three gold-headed silver feline dragons soaring upwards from the broad rim of a bronze basin. It was found placed squarely in the middle of the outer coffin. To its left was a lacquer cup with gilt bronze handles and to its right a deep bronze basin (fig. 72). All three were placed in a line in front of the outer coffin, and they were probably related to a sacrificial or burial ceremony. These jade vessels were probably not simply viewed as luxury objects, but may also have had additional functions in ensuring a good afterlife for their owners.

As recorded in the *Shiji*, the Han Emperor Wudi believed that drinking dew and jade powder from a jade cup conferred longevity. He therefore built a

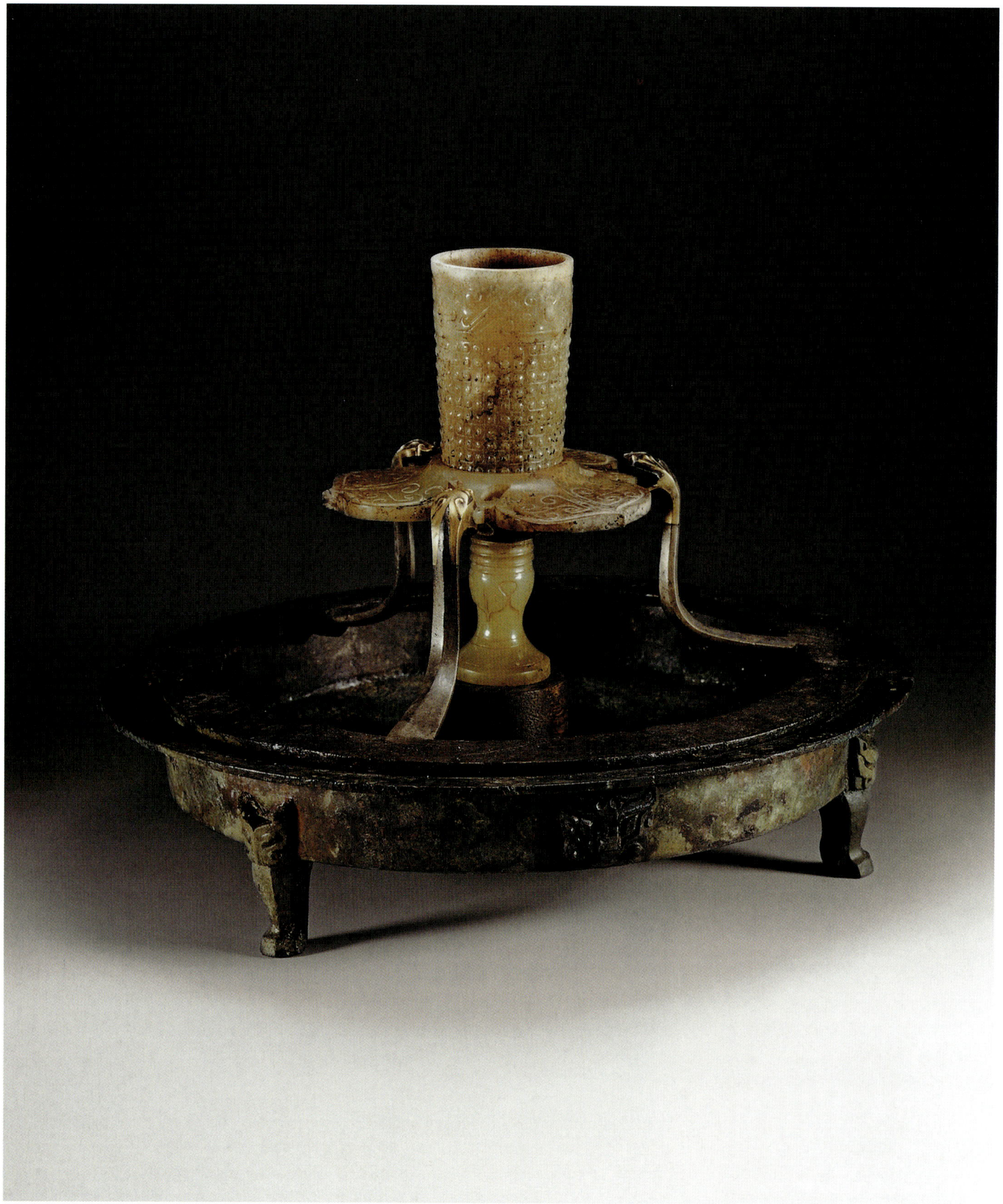

164

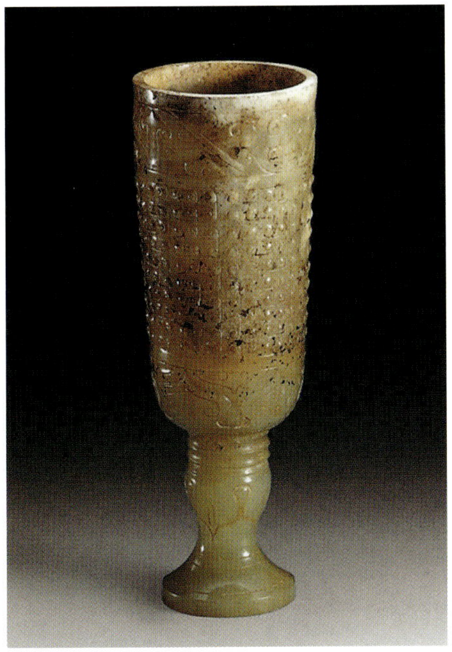

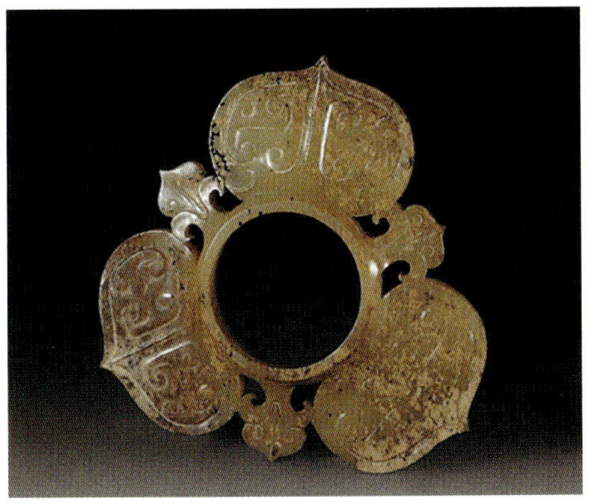

device for collecting dewdrops in the Jian Zhang Palace.[1] This tubular jade cup is likely related to the search for immortality. Two almost identical cups were excavated from the Luobowan M1 tomb, Guixian, Guangxi and from the Epang Palace site at Chezhangcun in Xi'an city, Shaanxi, dating to the Qin dynasty, third century BC. A third cup, likewise with a single ringed handle but of a different pattern, is in the collection of the National Palace Museum, Taipei.[2] This points to a standardized design for this particular type of vessel. However, the scholar Yang Jianfang has suggested that this type of tubular jade cup is likely to have originated in the late Warring States period and been passed on to the later Han dynasty.[3] JCSL

1 *Shiji*, p. 459.
2 *Wenwu* 1978.9, pp. 25–35; Hebei 1991–3, vol. 4, pls 19, 7; Beijing 1993a, pl. 64. The one kept in the National Palace Museum, Taipei is 12.3 cm in height; Beijing 2010, vol. 2, pl. 132.
3 Yang 2008, p. 80.

165

Jade box

Second century BC, Western Han dynasty
H: 7.7 cm; Diameter: 9.8 cm
Excavated at Xianggangshan in 1983
The Museum of the King of Nanyue, Guangdong Province
NOT EXHIBITED

This greenish jade box was discovered in the space between the top of the inner and outer coffins. It is a slightly compressed globular box with grooved rims. The body is shaped like a bowl and decorated with three distinct sections – the upper section in a spiral pattern with additional floral designs, the middle in spirals and the lower in a band. The decoration on the cover is divided into

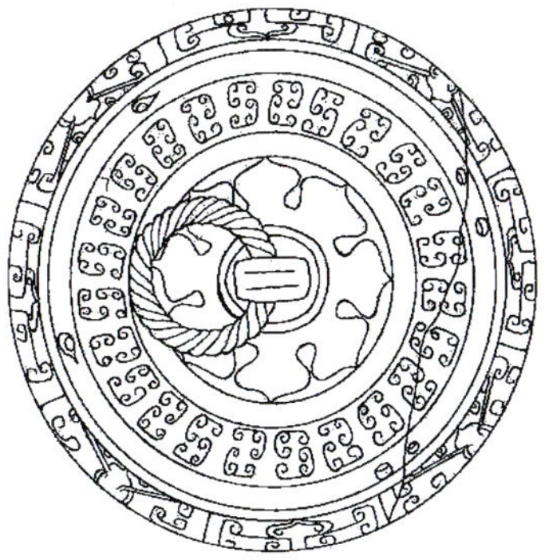

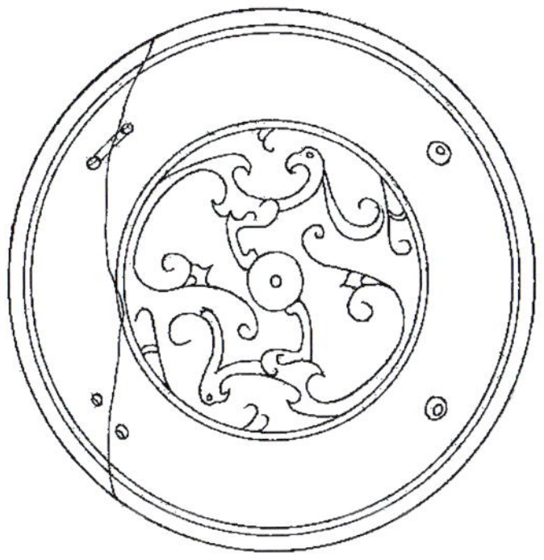

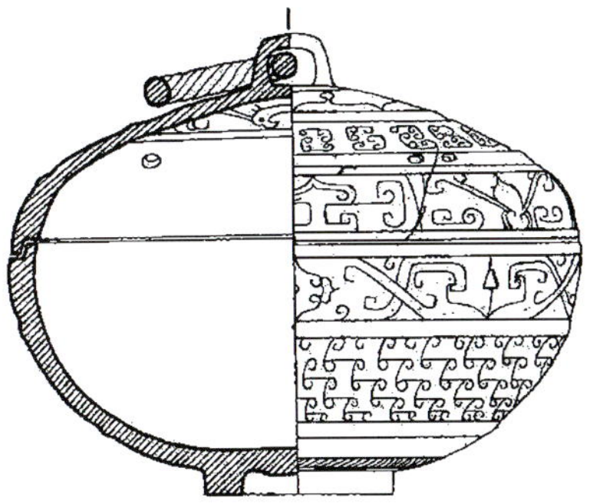

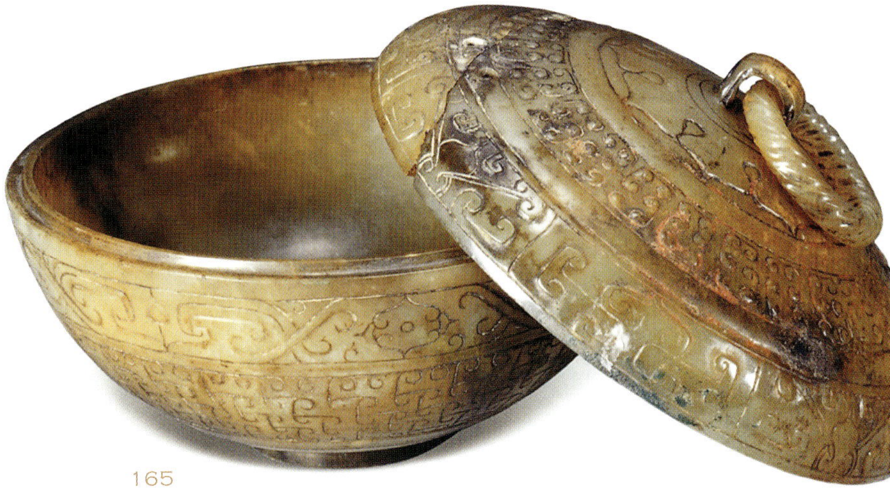

165

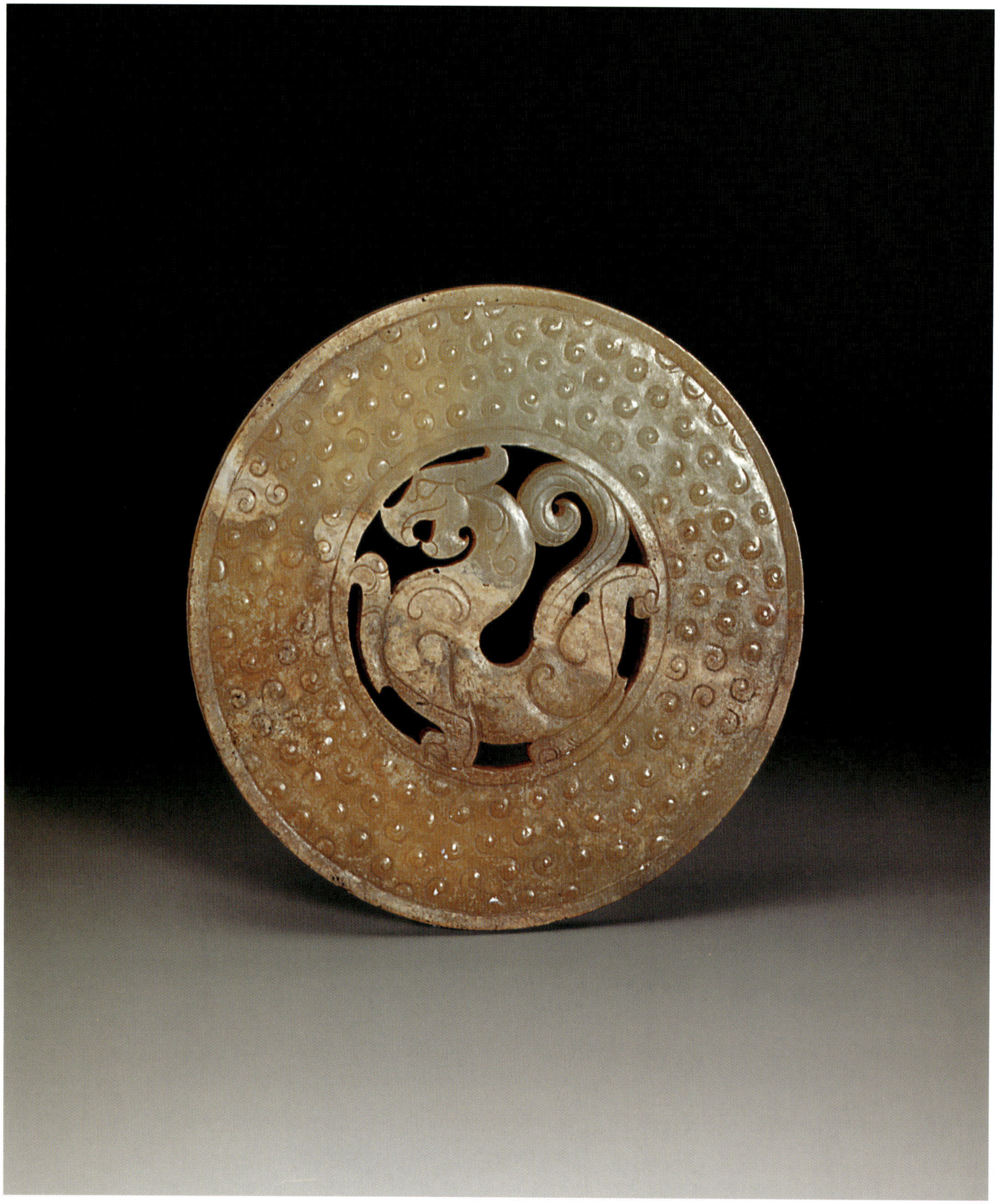

166

three sections. In the centre is a floral medallion made up of eight petals, which is enclosed by the second section, a low-relief band of interlocking spirals. The outer section is decorated with four units of interlocking spirals alternating with formalized floral units. A small ring handle was carved on top of the cover.

Jade boxes of this design are very rare if archaeological finds to date are taken into account. It is rather small, but the surface is covered with delicate patterns. The function of the box is unknown, but four small holes were drilled inside the bowl as part of an ancient intervention to prevent cracks in the cover from spreading, which suggests it was very precious to its owner. JCSL

166

Jade disc with openwork dragon pattern

Second century BC, Western Han dynasty
Diameter: 8.8 cm
Excavated at Xianggangshan in 1983
The Museum of the King of Nanyue, Guangdong Province

This jade disc was originally found on top of the helmet of the jade suit. It is pale green jade with yellowish streaks, carved in an openwork style with a feline dragon at the centre of the disc and an outer ring decorated with raised spirals. The dragon was designed in an S-shape with its tail touching its neck, and wide-open jaws.

A similar design was applied to another jade disc with an openwork phoenix on the outer ring (fig. 3). It was also adopted in a white jade archer's ring that was found in an early Western Han tomb at Xi'an.[1] A white jade disc with brown areas, very similar in design and dating to the Warring States period, is in the collection of the Palace Museum in Beijing.[2] It therefore seems reasonable to suggest that there was a template for this image circulated among artisans. JCSL

1 It is 6 cm long, 4.5 cm wide; Liu 2009, pl. 177.
2 It is 11.1 cm in diameter and 0.4 cm thickness; Beijing 2010, vol. 1, pl. 216.

167

Silver box (partly gilt, with stand of bronze and wood)

Third–second century BC
Height: 12.1 cm
Excavated at Xianggangshan in 1983
The Museum of the King of Nanyue, Guangdong Province

This silver box has a bowl-shaped body and a removable lid. The accentuated rim shows engraved ornamentation and traces of gilding. Tear-shaped lobes worked in high relief form a continuous meander ornament running around the vessel. The stand consists of a gilt bronze outer ring and a wooden core. The core was originally fitted to a conical protrusion below the base of the object. On the lid three irregularly shaped knobs are visible. Most probably they served as bases for three small animal fittings, which may have been lost at an early point in the object's history. Other boxes of comparable shape found in Western Han tombs still retain figures of tigers or little birds on the lids.[1]

The protrusion below the base and the knobs on the lid were soldered onto the surface of the vessel only after the silver box was finished. For this the surface was abraded to allow the solder to adhere. In this process, several characters of inscriptions engraved into the surface were damaged. The alloy composition of the attachments differs from that of the lid of the vessel.[2]

The vessel was found in a prominent place inside the coffin of Zhao Mo, in a compartment below the feet of the ruler. When it was excavated, it still contained remains of some pills that were thought to be medicine.[3]

The vessel shows a series of engraved inscriptions. On the knobs on the lid the numbers 1, 2 and 3 are visible. A short text gives the name of a person, possibly a craftsman, as Gan and the number 141, which may have been an accession number. A longer text on the lid mentions the weight and the capacity of the object and the name of the Provisions Office, *Siguan*, to which the box may

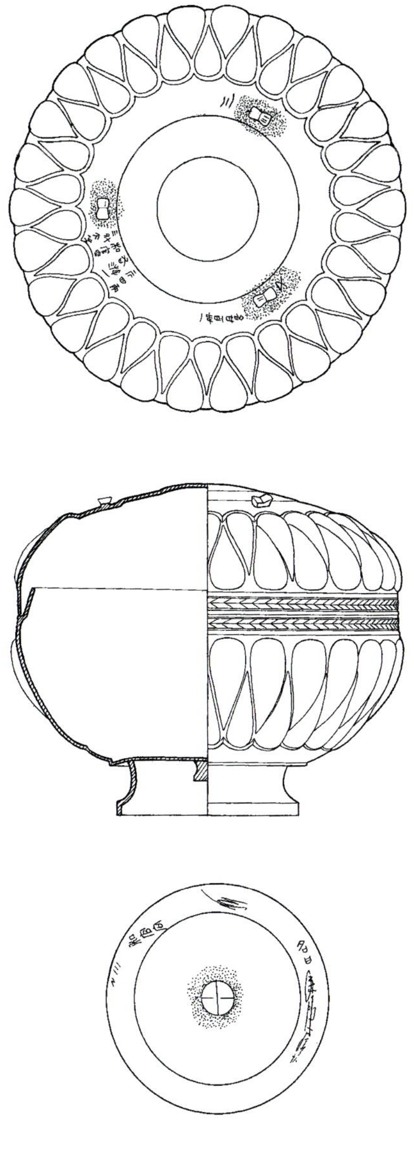

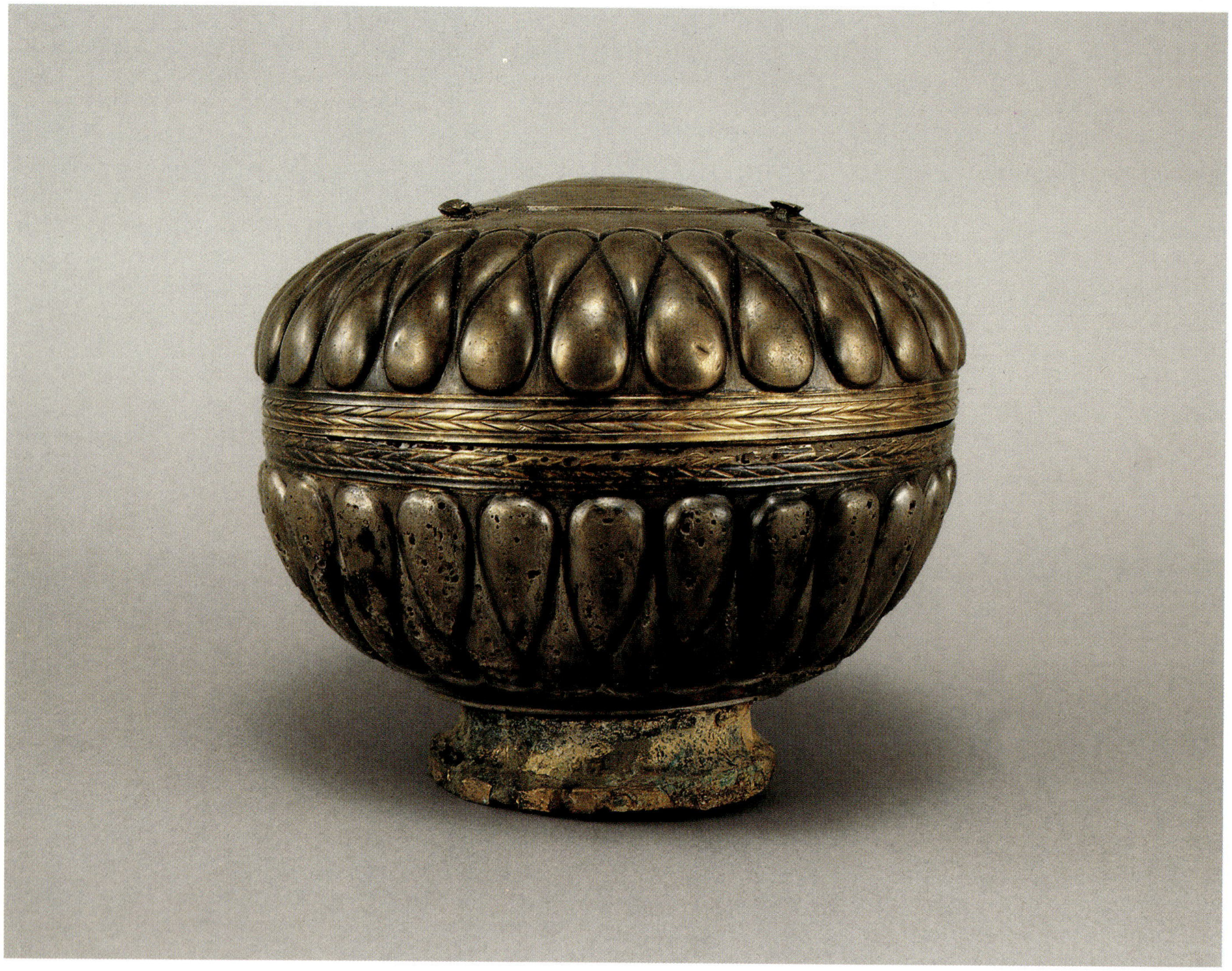

167

have originally belonged. The base of the body shows several characters of an inscription that has been partly erased.[4]

Until the Western Han, Chinese vessels were rarely made out of silver. The lobed decoration has no predecessor in Chinese art. Instead, it can be found on libation bowls made of gold or silver that were used at the Achaemenid court at least from the sixth century BC onwards, and continued to be appreciated by the elites of Parthia and the Asian Hellenistic kingdoms of the third and second centuries BC.[5]

It has been debated whether the box was made in Western Asia or China.[6] When the box was used in China, inscriptions were engraved into its surface and the foot and three finials were added to the object. The craftsmen who converted the box apparently intended to assimilate it to more traditional Chinese shapes such as stemmed bowls (*dou*) that were common during the late Eastern Zhou period.[7] An exotic-looking box with visible references to precious items of Iranian tableware was thus converted into a Chinese luxury object. LN

1 Nickel 2012; Prüch 1998, pp. 262–4; Pirazzoli-t'Serstevens 1990, pp. 531–3; Zhao 2007, pp. 81–8.
2 Prüch 1998, p. 262.
3 Beijing 1991, vol. 1, p. 210.
4 Beijing 1991, vol. 1, pp. 209–10.
5 For *Phialai* and lobed decoration on them see Melikian 1993, figs 6–8; Gunter and Jett 1992, pp. 66–7.
6 For the discussion see Nickel Arts of Asia 2012 (forthcoming).
7 Falkenhausen 2002, p. 227.

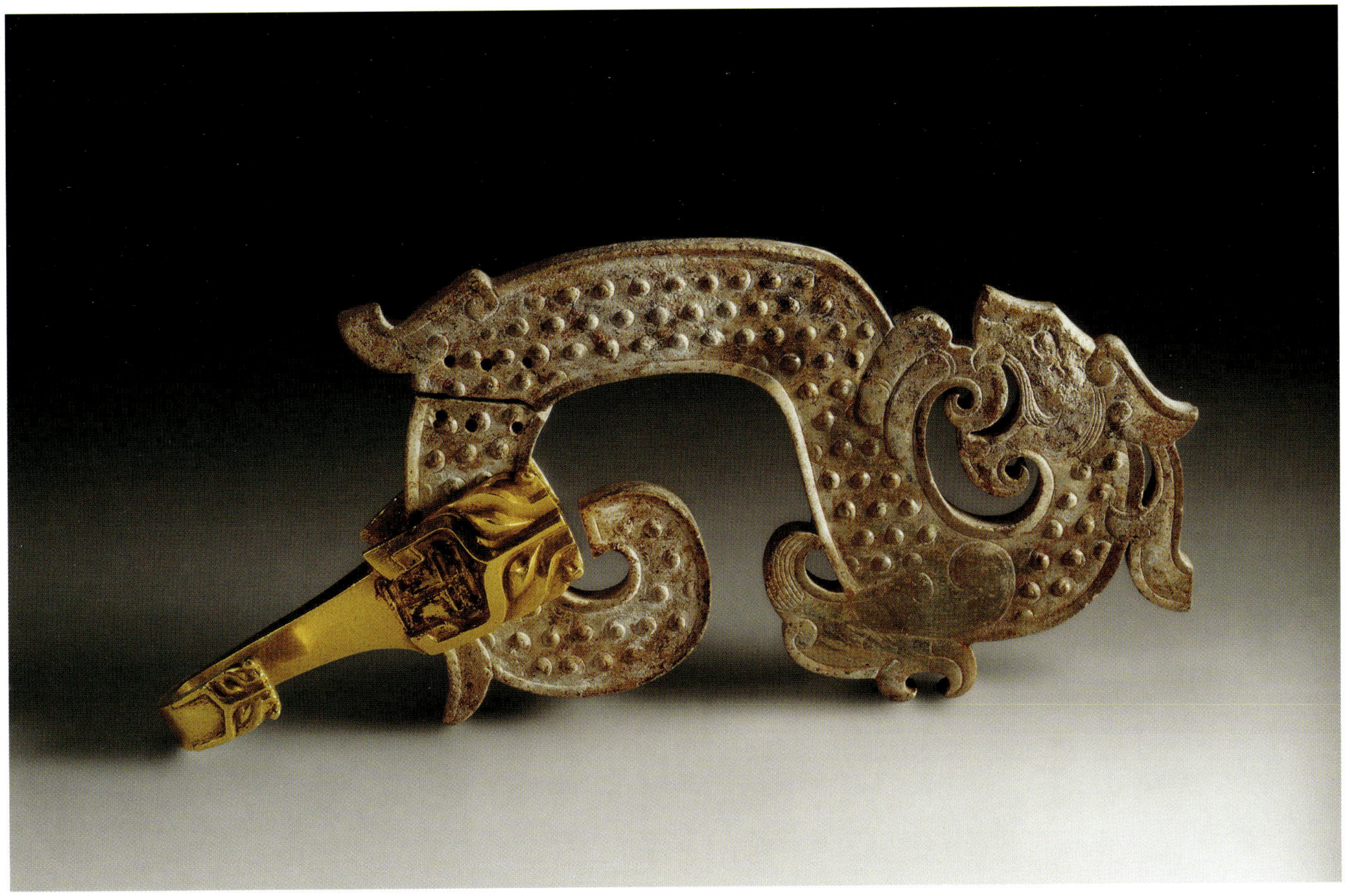

168

168

Jade dragon with gold hook

Second century BC, Western Han dynasty
Length of dragon: 11.5 cm; Length of gold hook: 5.9 cm; Width of gold hook: 2.6 cm
Excavated at Xianggangshan in 1983
The Museum of the King of Nanyue, Guangdong Province

This jade dragon with a gold hook was found on the right shoulder of the King of Nanyue. The dragon is of greenish jade with heavy calcification, and is possibly a piece surviving from the Warring States period. The body of the dragon forms an S-curve, with open jaws biting its own wing and a pointed tail. The hook is moulded in the shape of a tiger head, the mouth of which is biting the tail of the dragon. The Chinese character *wang* (king) was cast on the forehead of this tiger. The tail of the jade dragon was damaged in antiquity and on each side of the broken edges are three holes to join the two halves together with silk.

This combination of two valuable materials, jade and gold, was popular during the Warring States period. Several examples can be found in tombs from this period.[1] JCSL

1 Hebei 1991–3, vol. 3, pls 202, 210, 255, 281, 296.

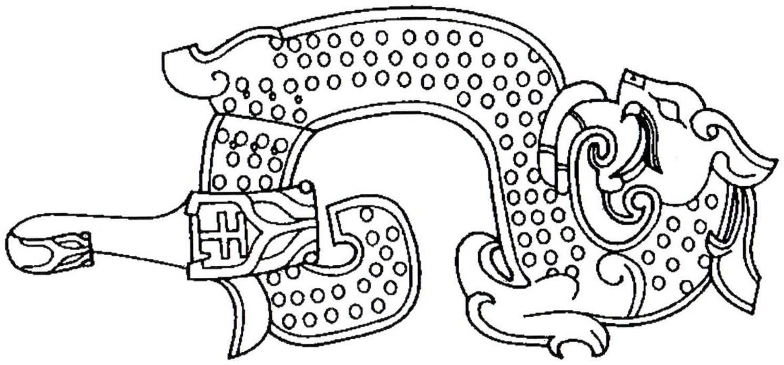

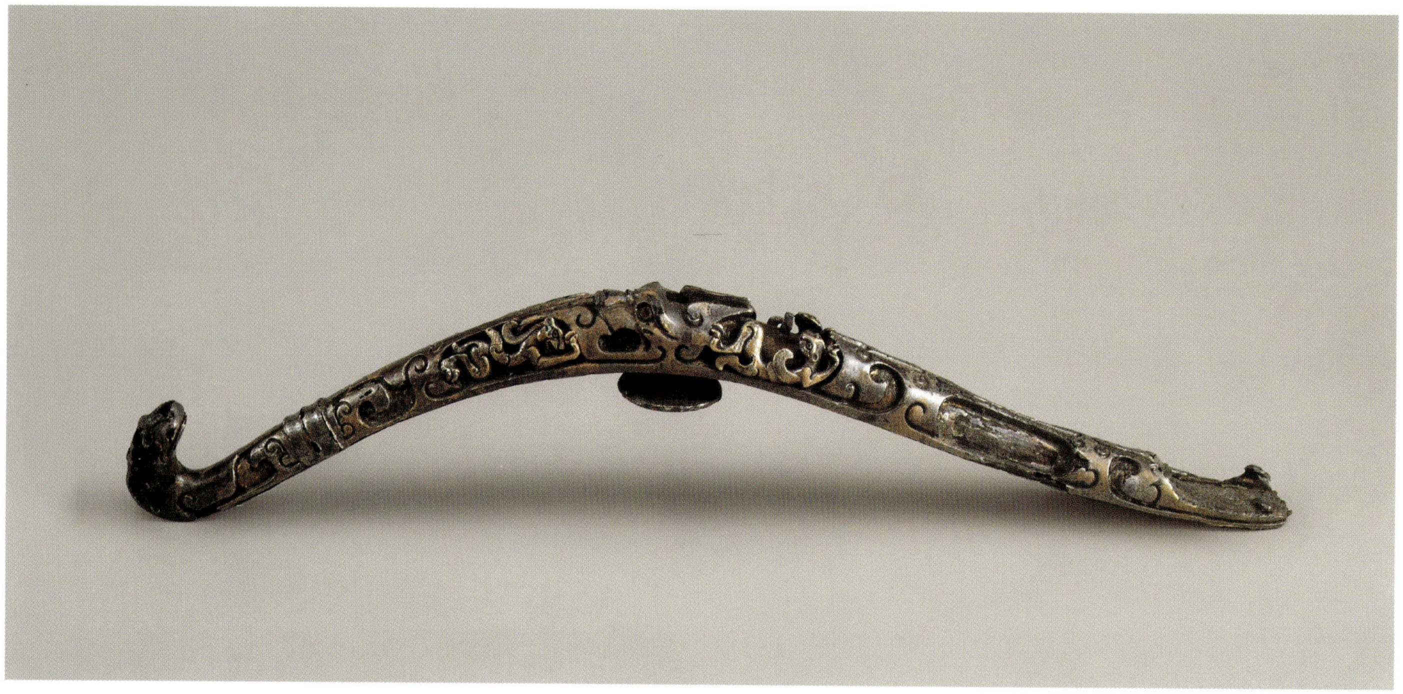

169

169

Gilt silver belt hook inlaid with precious stones

Second century BC, Western Han dynasty
Length: 18.4 cm; Width: 1.3 cm
Excavated at Xianggangshan site in 1983
The Museum of the King of Nanyue, Guangdong Province

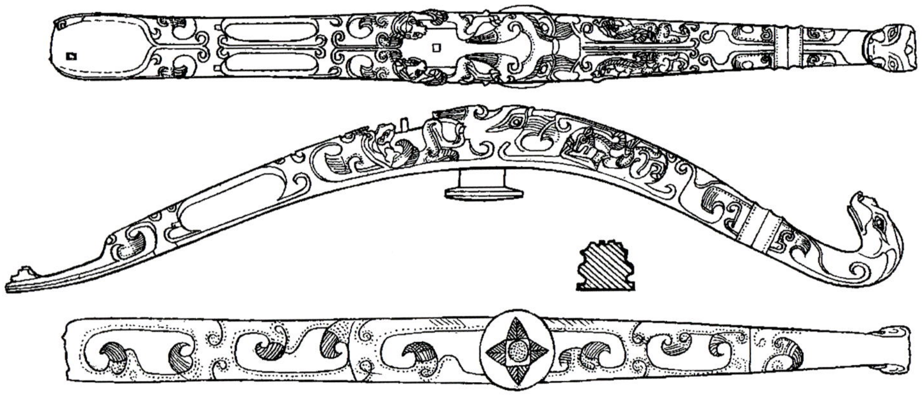

This silver belt hook was discovered in the main chamber of the tomb along with another five hooks (one bronze and the other four jade).

Belt hooks of this shape became popular in the Warring States period, and a large number have been discovered. They differ from the belt plaques displayed in this exhibition (cat. 81, 82, 145, 170) both in their shape and their fastening mechanism, despite the fact that they are all devices used to fasten belts. During the Warring States period, the use of belt plaques was found among both Chinese and steppe people in the north, but the use of belt hooks was predominantly Chinese. The belt plaques serve a more decorative purpose, whereas the belt hooks are more functional, although they too are often fabulously ornamented. While the button and hook are universal features of belt hooks, the styles of the body vary significantly. To use this hook, the button projecting from the back passes through an opening in the belt, while the upward-facing hook secures the other end of the belt. LKC

170

Gilt bronze belt plaque

Second century BC, Western Han dynasty
Length: 8.1 cm; Width: 4.3 cm
Excavated at Xianggangshan in 1983
The Museum of the King of Nanyue, Guangdong Province

This belt plaque is cast in openwork with a twisted rope pattern as its border. This type of rectangular metal plaque

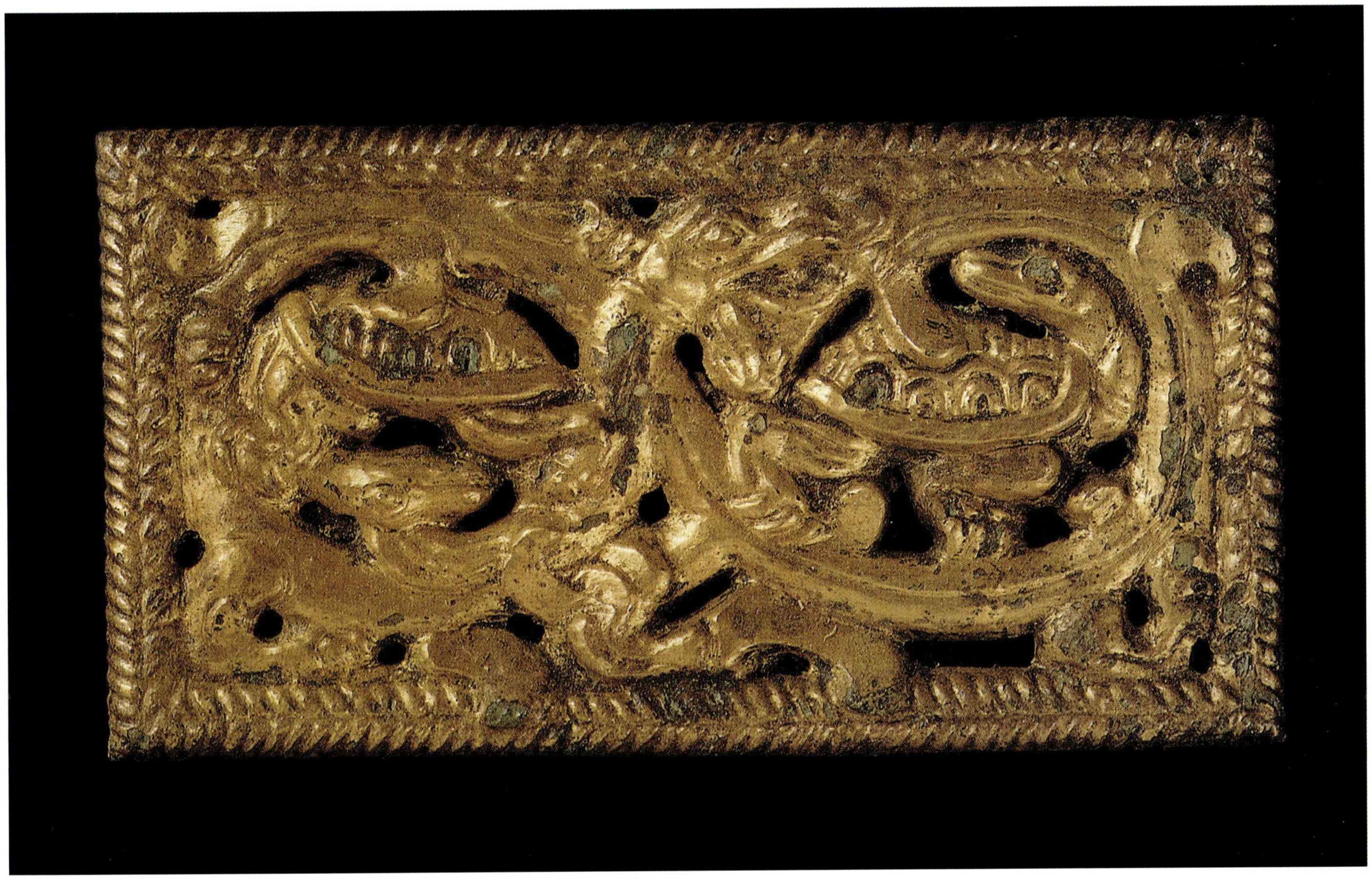

170

originated from the pastoral tribes of northern China, where they often served as belt ornaments. The motifs of these plaques were usually animals, either mythical or naturalistic. The decoration of this plaque depicts two tortoises and a dragon. The dragon's head is placed at the upper centre, facing right, while its body forms a figure of eight, filling the whole space of the plaque. Two tortoises are placed within the loops: the tortoise on the right has its head turning backward, as if it were looking back towards the dragon; the other tortoise looks back from beneath its own body.

The combination of tortoise and dragon was identified as 'black warrior' (*xuanwu*) in the Han dynasty. An earlier example of the combination of tortoise and dragon can be seen in the late fourth century BC in a bronze basin from the tomb of King of Zhongshan. The Kingdom of Zhongshan in the Warring States period was established by a branch of the northern tribe, *di*. As one of the four directional animals, the black warrior symbolizes the north, while the vermilion bird symbolizes the south, the white tiger the west and the green dragon the east. LKC

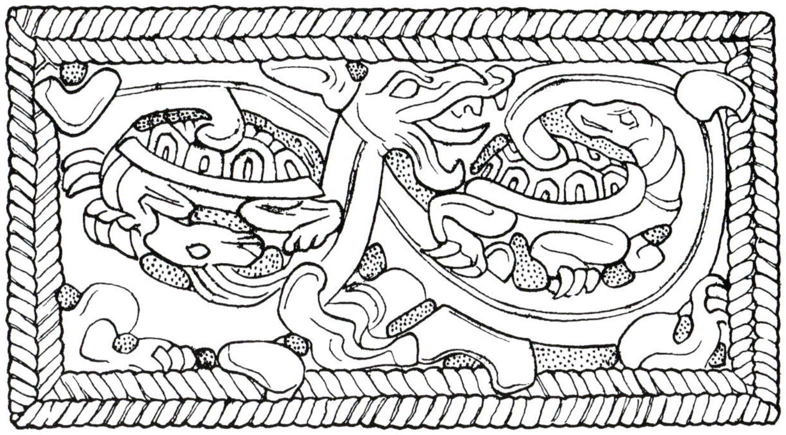

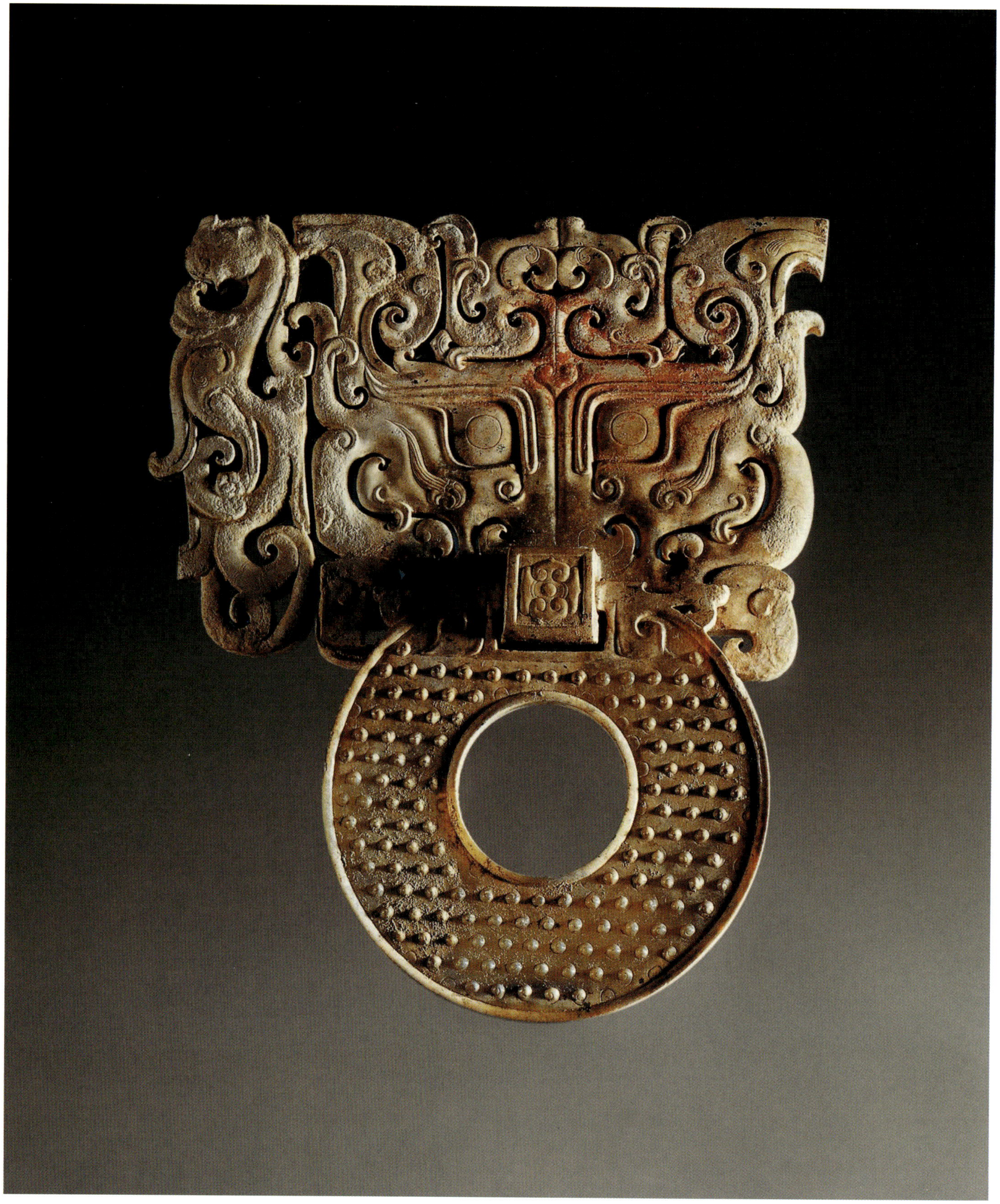

171

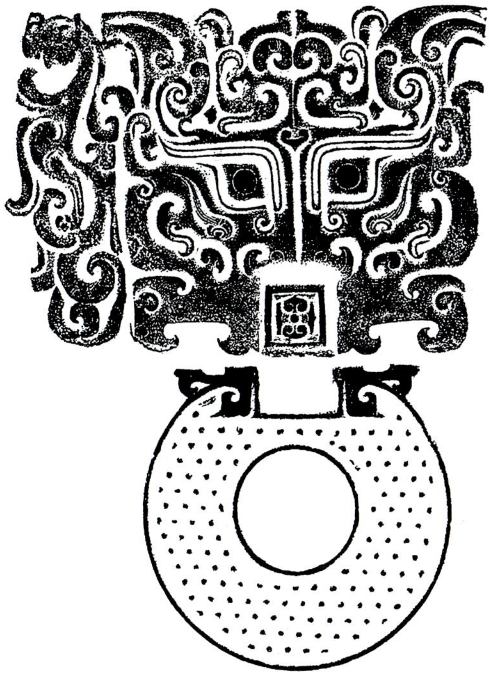

171

Jade ornament with animal mask

Second century BC, Western Han dynasty
Length: 16.7 cm; Width: 13.8 cm
Excavated at Xianggangshan in 1983
The Museum of the King of Nanyue, Guangdong Province

This jade ornament with a mythical animal mask was obviously copied from a bronze door-knocker. It was found on the forehead of the King of Nanyue. It was carved out of one piece of jade in openwork style and consists of a rectangular animal head at the centre with a disc hanging from its nostrils, and an additional feline dragon attached to the left side of the mask. This type of asymmetrical design is very unusual in Chinese art. Most of the surface of this jade piece has suffered serious calcification and only the nose of the mask and a small portion of the disc still retain the original green colour. The back of this jade is without any decoration. JCSL

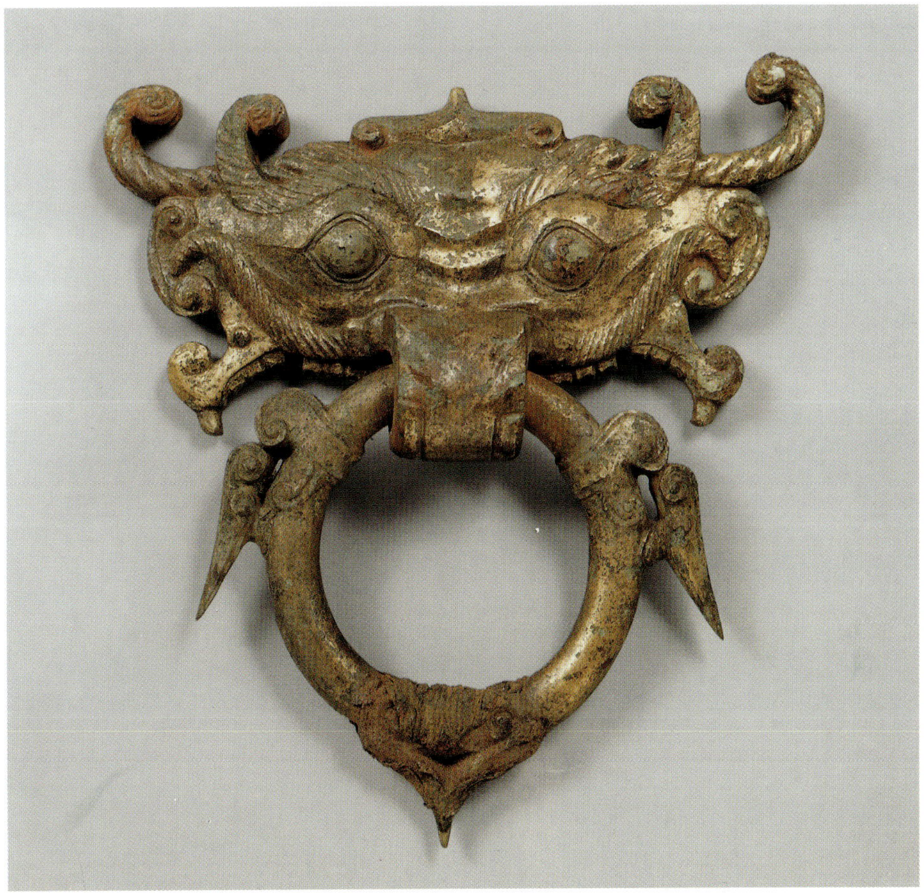

172

172

Gilt bronze ring-shaped coffin ornament

Second century BC, Western Han dynasty
Length: 30 cm; Width: 29.2 cm
Excavated at Xianggangshan in 1983
The Museum of the King of Nanyue, Guangdong Province

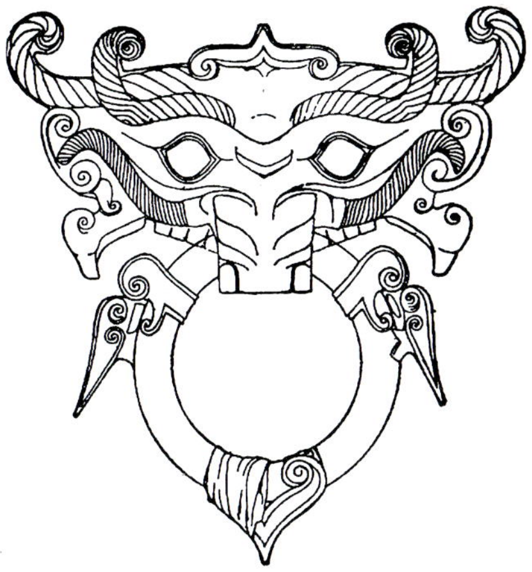

This ring-shaped coffin ornament, along with another five of similar type, was unearthed from the main chamber of the tomb. The six ornaments would have been attached to the exterior of the top, bottom and four vertical walls of the coffin. This type of ornament is commonly found on wooden coffins of the Han dynasty. It is in the shape of a mythical animal, with two large eyes gazing outwards and hair curling out to the sides. The appearance of the eyes was originally highlighted by the use of black pigment, and fragments of silk were found wrapped around the three attachment points on the ring. LKC

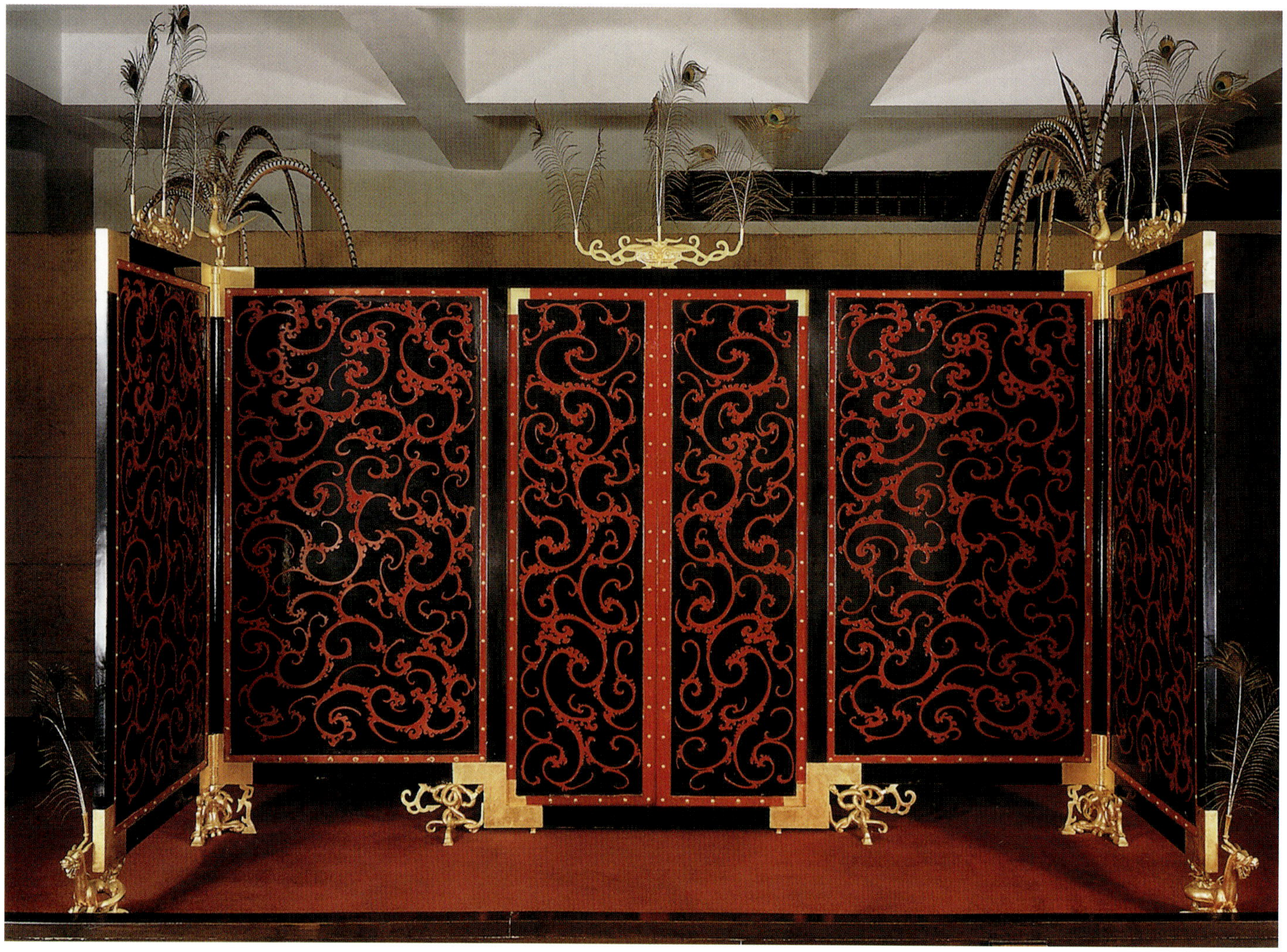

Fig. 73

173

Folding screen fittings and ornaments

Second century BC, Western Han dynasty
Length: 3m; Height: 1.8m
Excavated at Xianggangshan in 1983
The Museum of the King of Nanyue,
Guangdong Province

This lacquer folding screen, found in the east of the main coffin room, is the largest find in terms of size unearthed from this tomb. The wooden frame had rotted away, but 658 gilded nails and twelve main bronze fittings survived, which made it possible to reconstruct the object. The reconstruction (fig. 73) by the museum enabled this early Han folding screen finally to be displayed in its newly found beauty. The model is a meticulous reproduction of the original folding screen buried with the king, based on archaeological evidence. This consisted of the parts and fittings, their locations upon discovery, traces of paint coating and wooden frames and the inscribed numbers on some parts clearly showing the corresponding positions for assembly.

The folding screen consisted of six wooden frames connected by hinges. The middle section was uniquely designed as a pair of doors. The two perpendicular side frames could be folded inwards to save space. The screen is beautifully decorated with pheasant feathers and bronze carvings of snakes and mythical creatures. The wooden frames were originally painted with red and white cloud motifs on a black lacquer background. The colours are almost completely decomposed and difficult to recreate. Lacquer objects from the Kingdom of Nanyue have shown strong

73 Reconstruction of the lacquer folding screen from the tomb of the King of Nanyue.

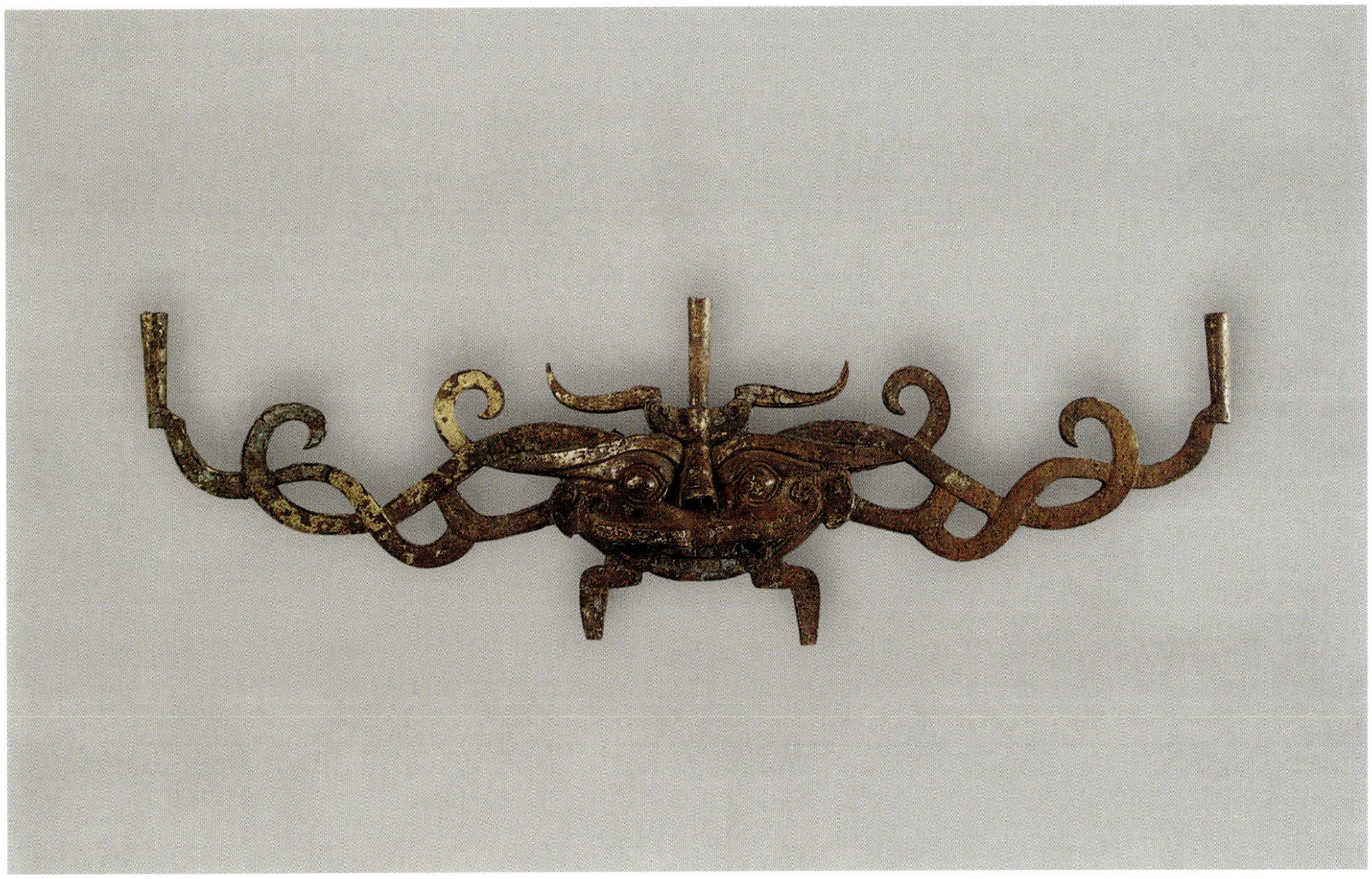

173A

local characteristics, one of which is the use of gilt bronze fittings for large objects such as this screen.[1] The bronze hinges were severely corroded and covered with a thick layer of patina when excavated. Analysis of the composition has shown that the bronze alloy is mainly copper and tin. The techniques of bronze casting seem to be the same as in the Han. When a stone roof collapsed, some fittings in the middle section were destroyed.

A folding screen is a piece of furniture, originating in China, to provide shelter, partition of a space and decoration. The term *pingfeng* (screen; literally screening the wind) was frequently mentioned in Western Han texts such as the *Shiji* and *Hanshu*. However, most screens unearthed of this period or slightly earlier, were made to be burial objects.[2] The Nanyuewang screen is the earliest example of a piece for everyday use with such an exquisite design.

1 Beijing 1991, vol. 1, p. 338.

2 Examples include the screen supports in Tianxingguan tomb No. 1, Jiangling, Hubei Province; the lacquer screen with wooden carving in Wangshan tomb No. 1, Jiangling, Hubei Province; and the lacquer screen from Mawangdui tomb No. 1, Changsha, Hunan Province. See Beijing 1991, vol. 1, p. 451 for a brief discussion of the archaeological finds of burial screens.

A Decorative ornament with a monster's face from top of a screen

Height: 16.7 cm; Width: 56.3 cm

The ornament was inserted in the middle top wooden beam of the screen. It shows a monster's face with clearly defined round eyes, a prominent nose, a big open mouth and a line-shaped moustache. There are two horns. The lines of eyebrows and ears extend to form cloud patterns. The whole piece is

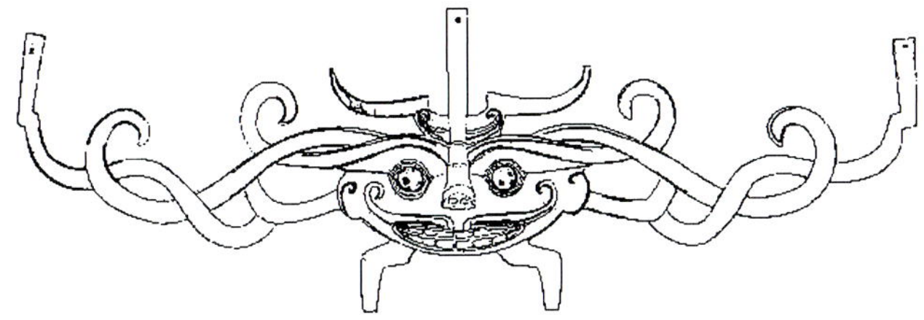

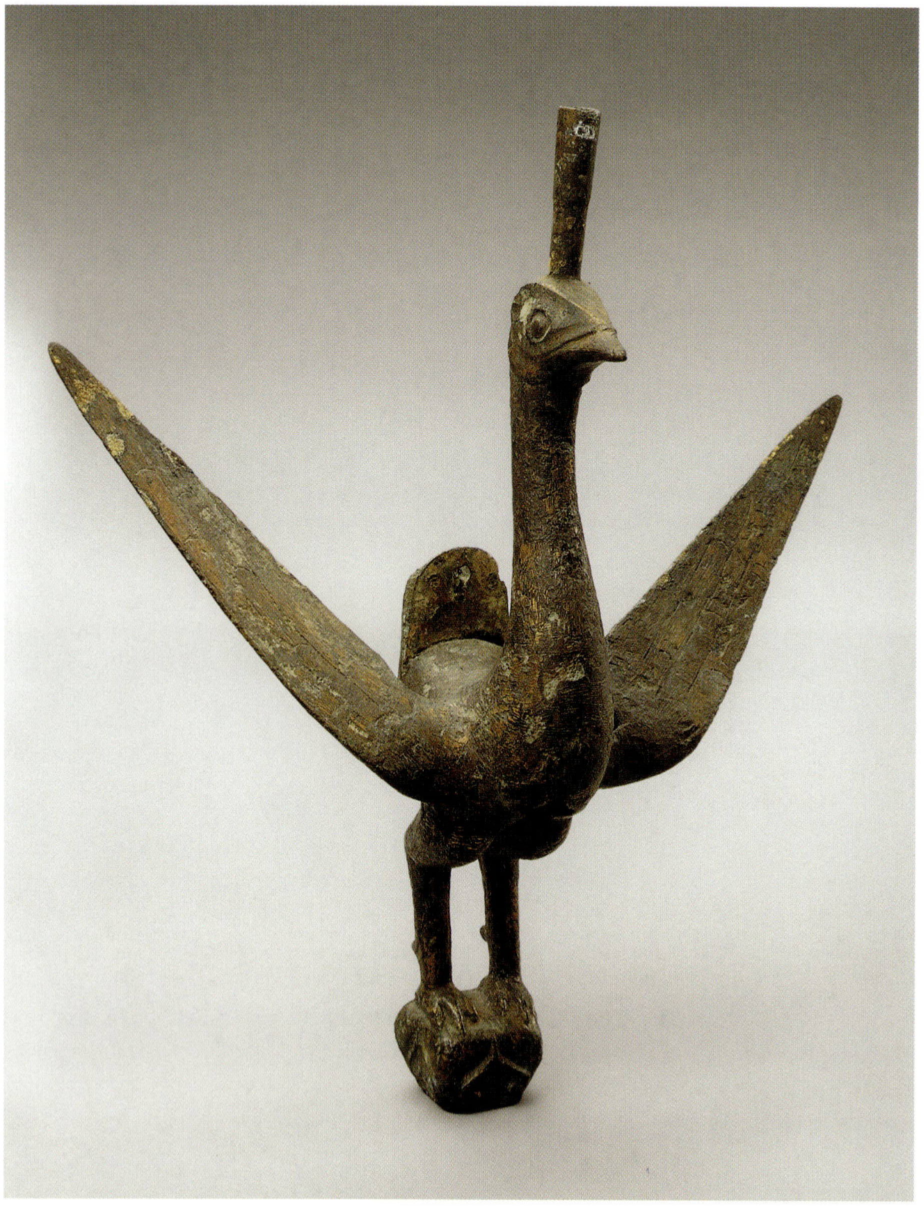

173B

gilt and the horns, eyebrows and clouds are highlighted with black lacquer. Three tube sockets, inscribed with continuous numbers, stand in the middle and both ends of the carving, presumably for holding decorative feathers.

B Decorative ornaments in the form of a bird from top of a screen

Height: 26.4 cm; Width: 24.5 cm

The bird *zhuque* (Vermilion Bird of the South) was a mythological creature of Chinese constellations, and often used in decoration. The bronzes were inserted into the hinges connecting the frames on the left and right. The body and wings were cast with scale-like feather patterns. The bird stands on a square base with flame motifs with a round socket below. There is a tube socket on its head for holding feathers. The tail was originally decorated with feathers as well. Traces of the remains of the feathers were found on top of the gilded bronze ring-holder attachment on the ground 0.8 metres away.

C Bronze screen support with snakes

Height: 23.4 cm; Width: 46.5 cm

NOT EXHIBITED

The gilt bronze support is in two parts: a hinge and a decoration of three interlocked snakes. The hinge consists of a set of three flat rectangular sockets to hold the bottom of the screen frame and the corner of the screen door. The snakes were carved intertwined and tied with flowing strips.

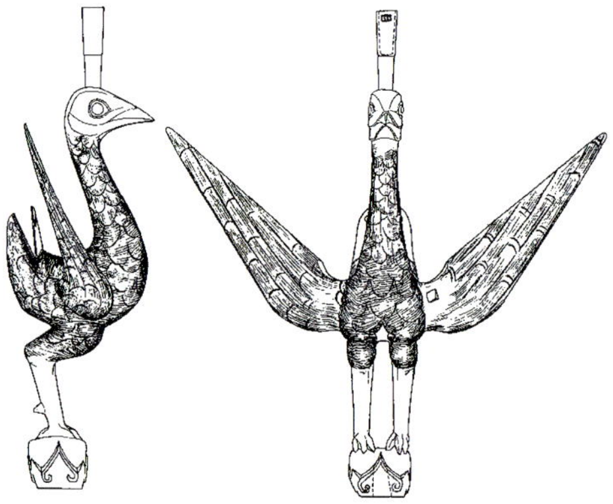

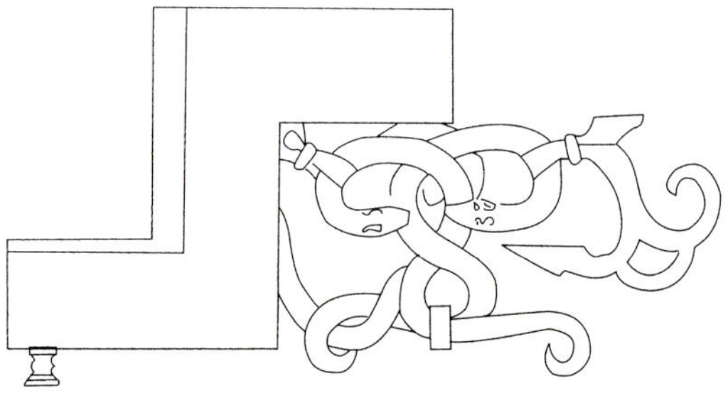

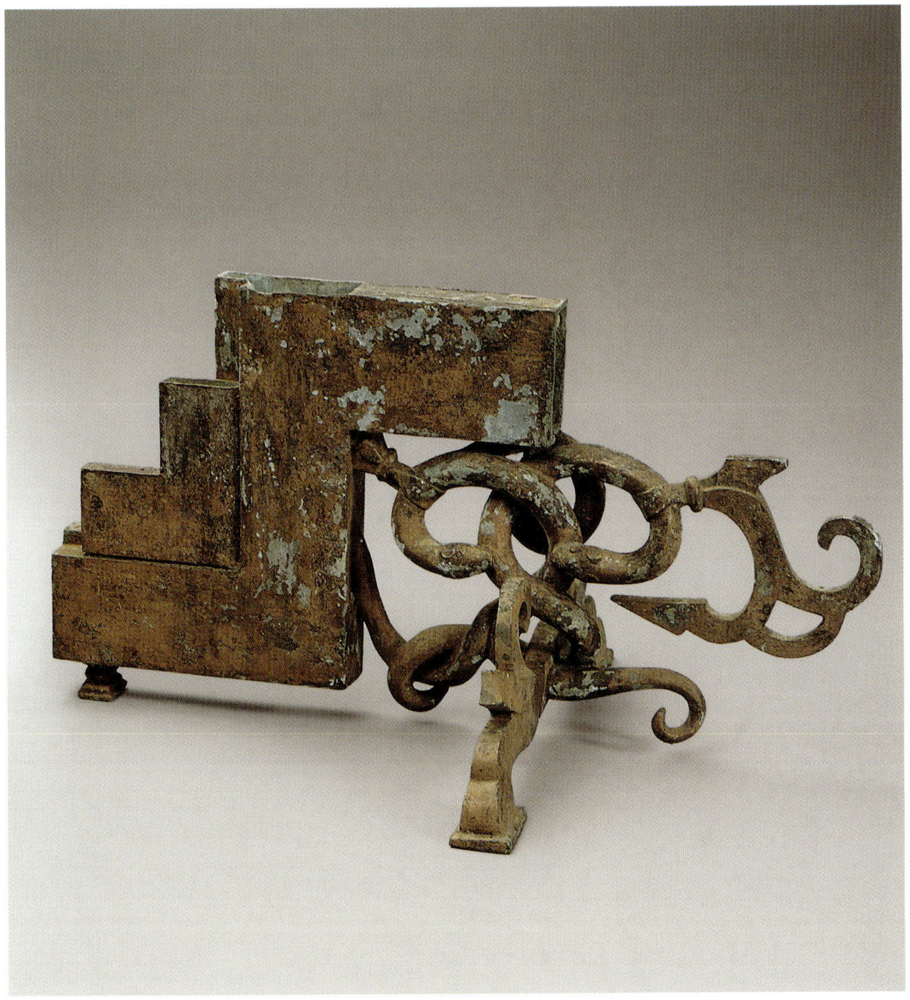

173C

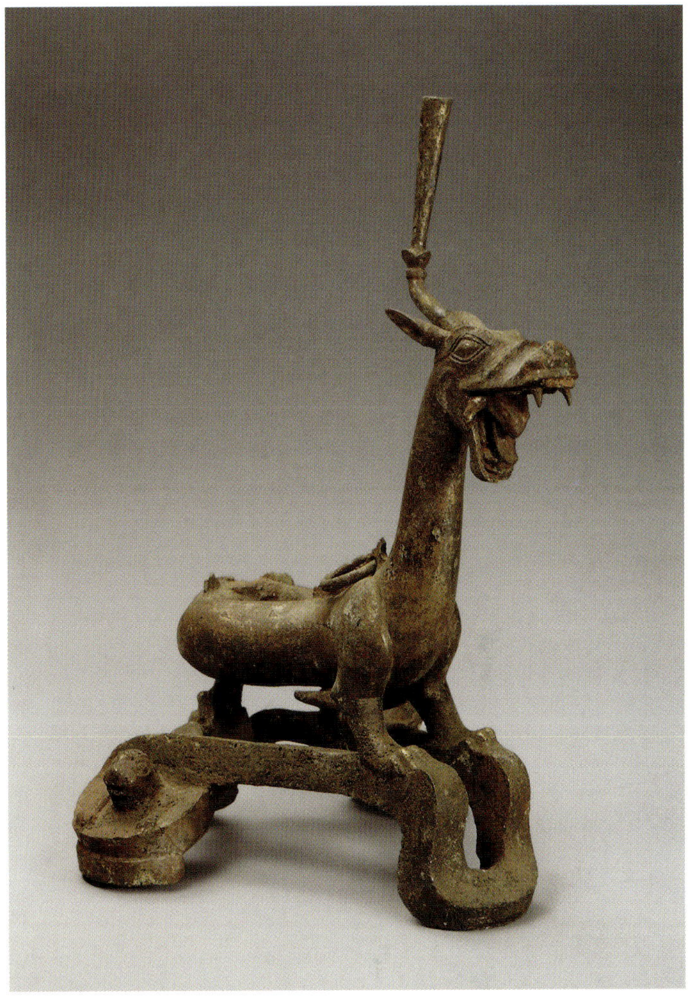

173D

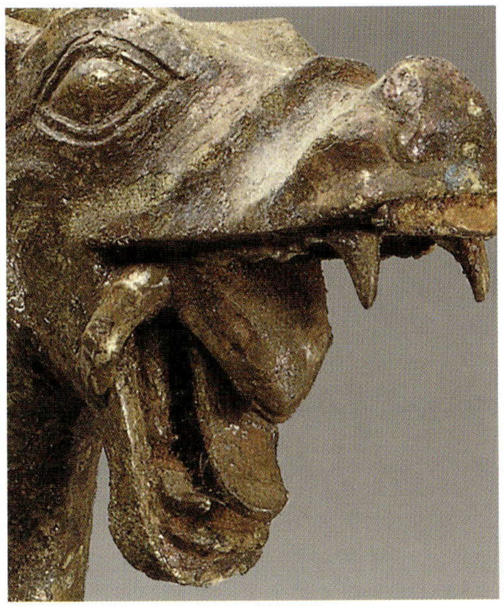

D Bronze screen support with carved dragon and three frogs

Height: 33.5 cm; Width: 27.8 cm

These two identical bronze sculptures are screen supports fitted under the two side frames. The upper section is a dragon with its mouth wide open. A frog is crouching inside and the dragon's tail winds besides its body. A tube socket for decorative feathers is attached to one of the horns. The dragon stands on two snakes merged together. Each snake winds its body to hold a frog striving to escape. Both pieces are inscribed with numbers to indicate positions for assembly.

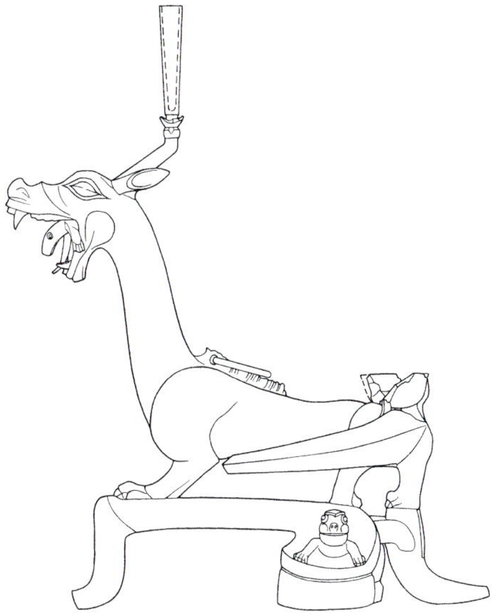

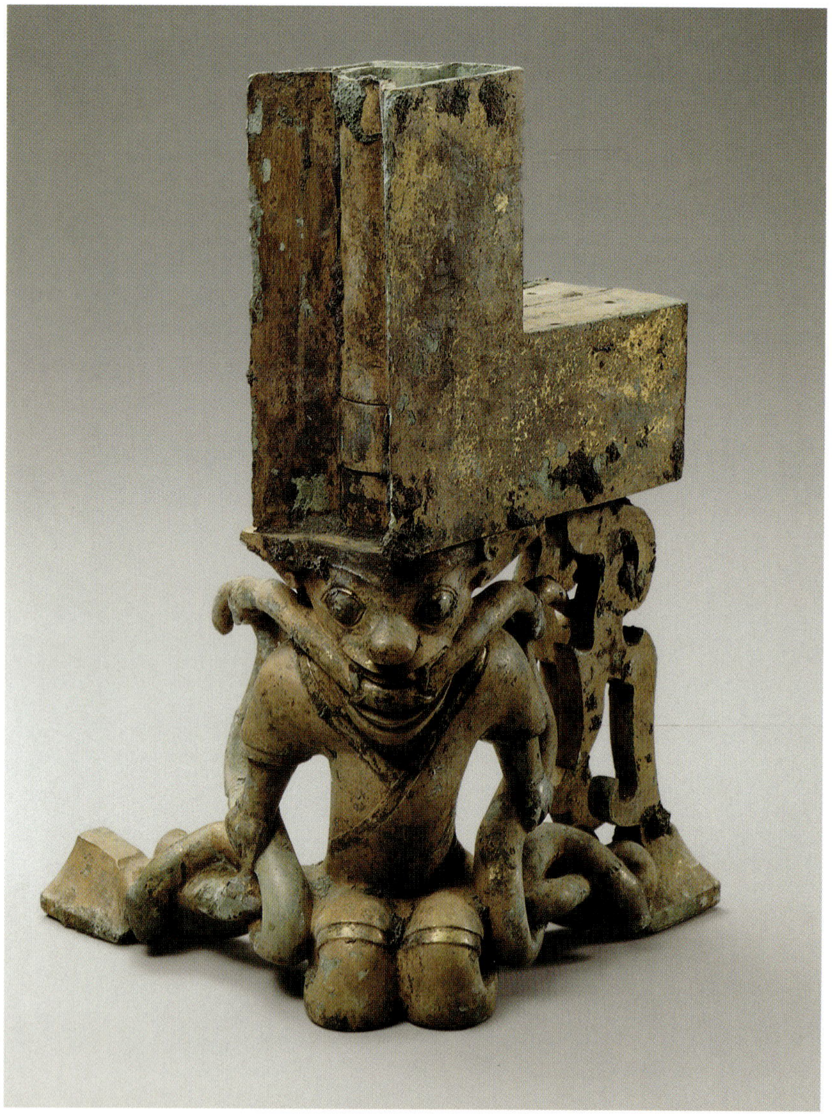

173E

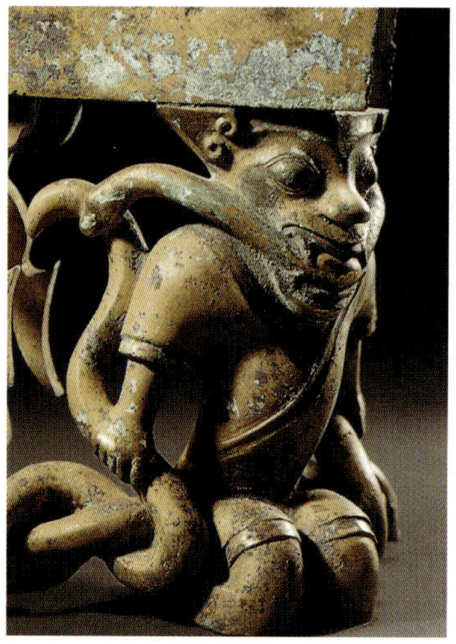

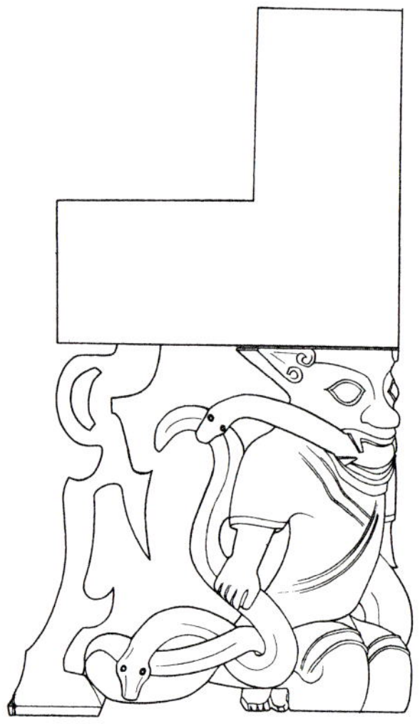

E Bronze screen support with Yue warrior

Height: 31.5 cm; Width: 15.8 cm
NOT EXHIBITED

These two bronze supports were used to hold the bottom corners of the screen. The upper section is a right-angled hinge that fits to the screen and the lower part is a barefoot, kneeling gilt figure of a Yue warrior holding and biting snakes. JX

174

Jade pendant set belonging to the Lady of the Right

Second century BC, Western Han dynasty
First openwork jade ring: Diameter: 7.4 cm
Second openwork jade ring: Diameter: 9 cm
Dancing figure: Height: 4.9 cm
Jade segment with raised spirals: Length: 14.7 cm
Jade segment with dragon heads: Length: 12.4 cm
Two jade tubes: Length: 6 cm (left), 6.5 cm (right)
Excavated at Xianggangshan in 1983
The Museum of the King of Nanyue, Guangdong Province

This is the second set of jade pendants found on the body of the king's first concubine, the Lady of the Right. It is composed of seven pieces of jade: two openwork jade rings decorated with dragons, a dancing figure, a segment with raised spirals, a segment with dragon heads and two jade tubes. Jade pendants were very common burial objects found in tombs of the high-ranking elite from the late Warring States period to the Han. They were a mark of the deceased's status: the higher the status of the tomb occupant, the more delicate the jade pendants. For example, among the eleven sets of pendants excavated from the Nanyue king's tomb, the most elaborate belonged to the king himself. Among those found on the four concubines, the pendant set of the Lady of the Right's coffin is the most elegant. JCSL

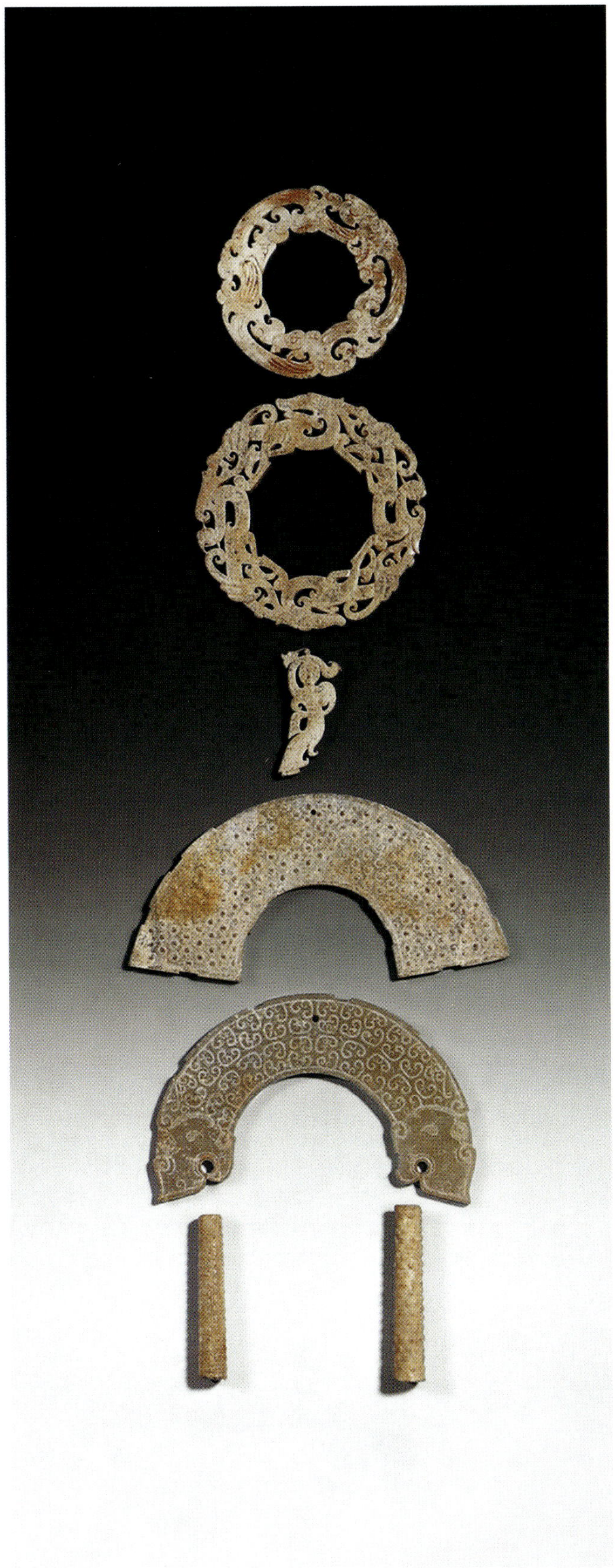

174

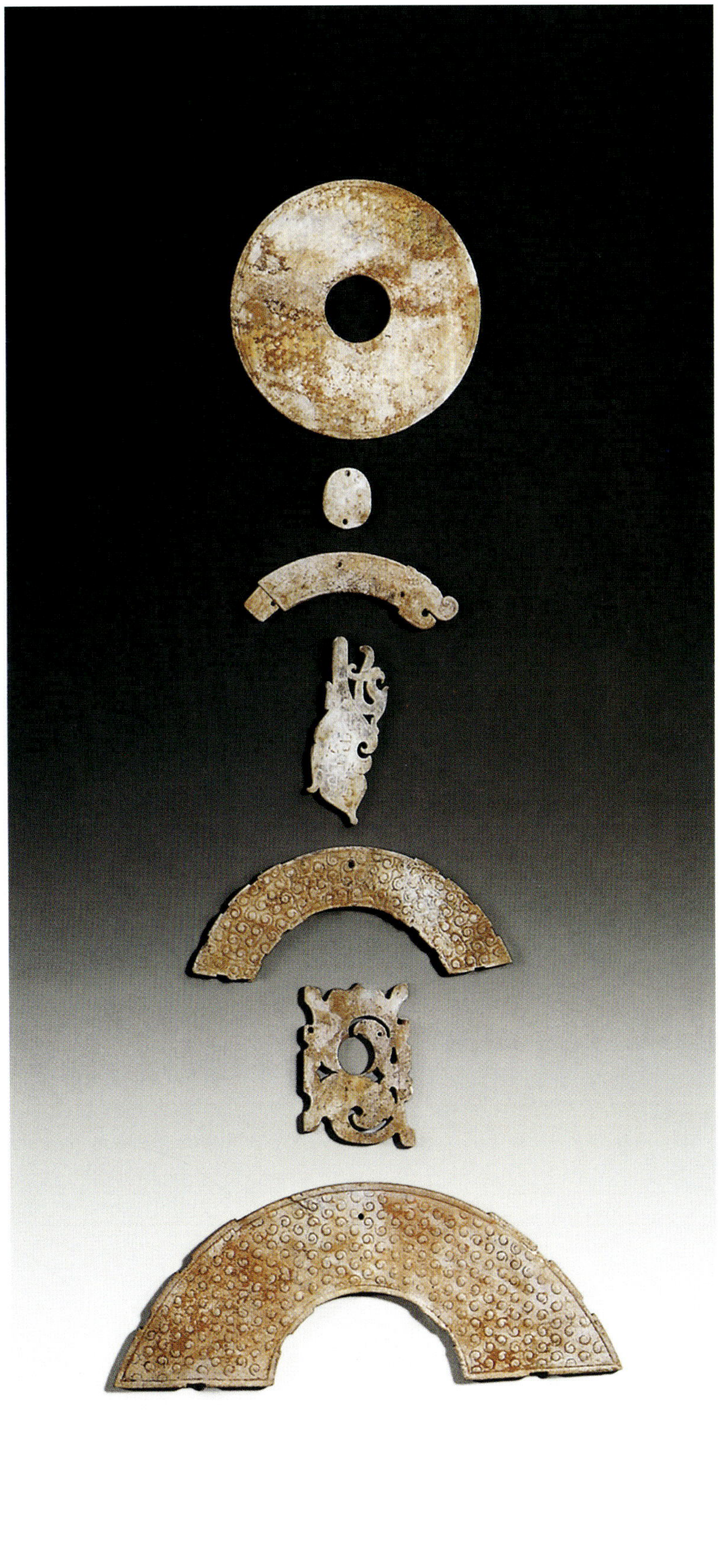

175

175

Jade pendant set belonging to the Lady of the Left

Second century BC, Western Han dynasty
Disc: Diameter: 8.6 cm
Oval pendant: Length: 2.1 cm
First semi-annular segment: Length: 7.5 cm
Floral-shaped pendant: Length: 5.4 cm
Second semi-annular segment: Length: 11 cm
Ornamental archer's ring: Length: 6.3 cm
Third semi-annular segment: Length: 17.6 cm
Excavated at Xianggangshan in 1983
The Museum of the King of Nanyue, Guangdong Province
NOT EXHIBITED

This pendant set was found next to a gilt bronze seal belonging to the king's second concubine, the Lady of the Left. It is composed of seven pieces of jade: a disc, an oval pendant, three semi-annular segments, a floral-shaped pendant and an ornamental archer's ring. Most of these jade pieces were decorated with raised spirals, apart from the floral-shaped pendant and the ornamental archer's ring. The designs on both sides of the floral-shaped pendant are identical, with a phoenix standing on the floral bud. The archer's ring is abstract openwork with a hole in the middle and surrounding bird patterns. JCSL

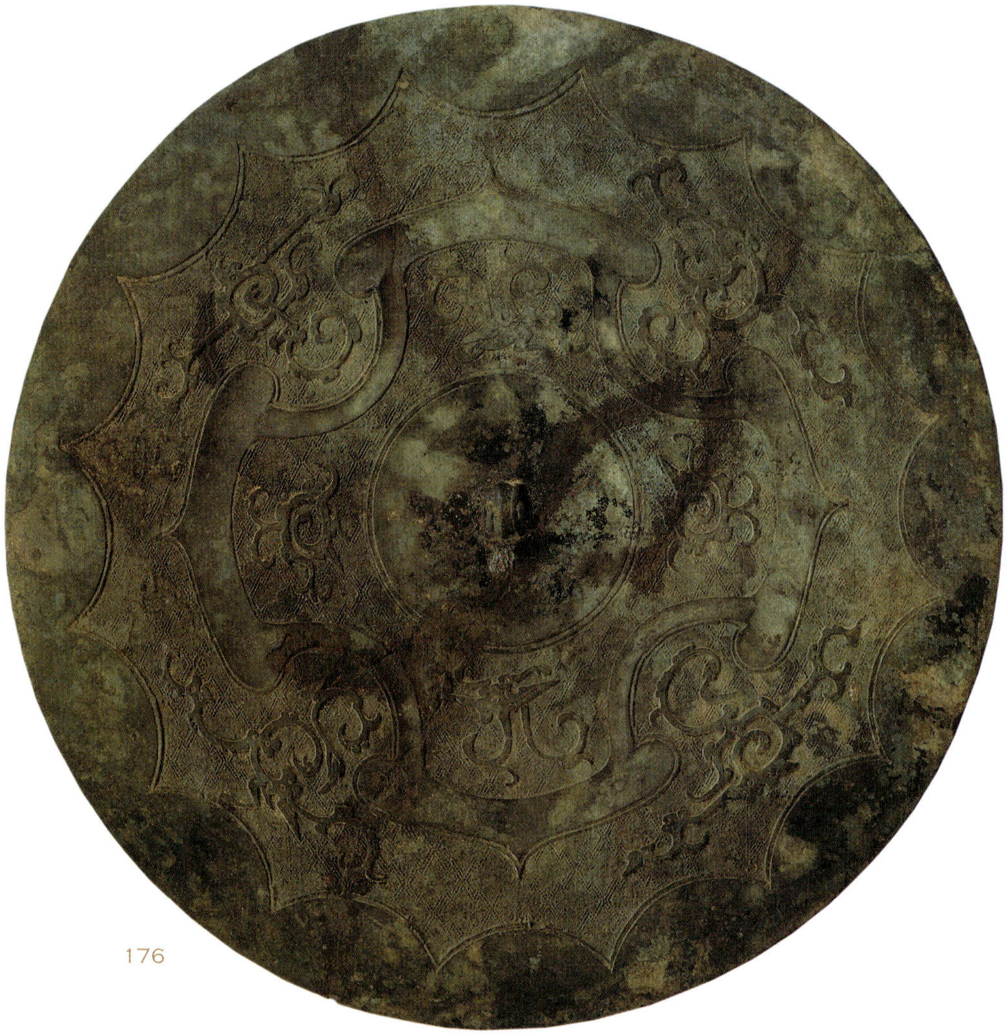

176

176

Bronze mirror

Second century BC, Western Han dynasty
Diameter: 26.6 cm
Excavated at Xianggangshan in 1983
The Museum of the King of Nanyue, Guangdong Province

The outer border of this mirror is composed of a series of sixteen arc-shaped sections, a pattern commonly found in Han dynasty bronze mirrors. Mirrors with fewer than sixteen arcs have also been found, but those with borders composed of more than sixteen arcs are extremely rare.

Both the outer and the inner portions of the design show alternating dragon and phoenix motifs. The dragons and phoenixes in the inner circle are symmetrical, but each dragon and phoenix in the outer circle has a unique form distinct from all the others. These dragons and phoenixes are shown in relief against a background of solid and dotted lines in a diamond-shaped grid pattern. LKC

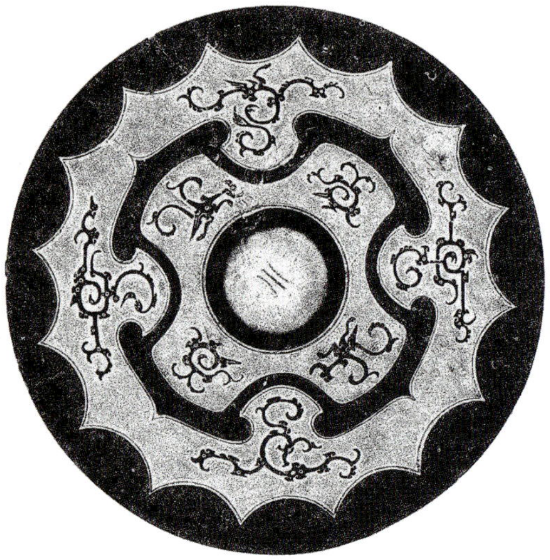

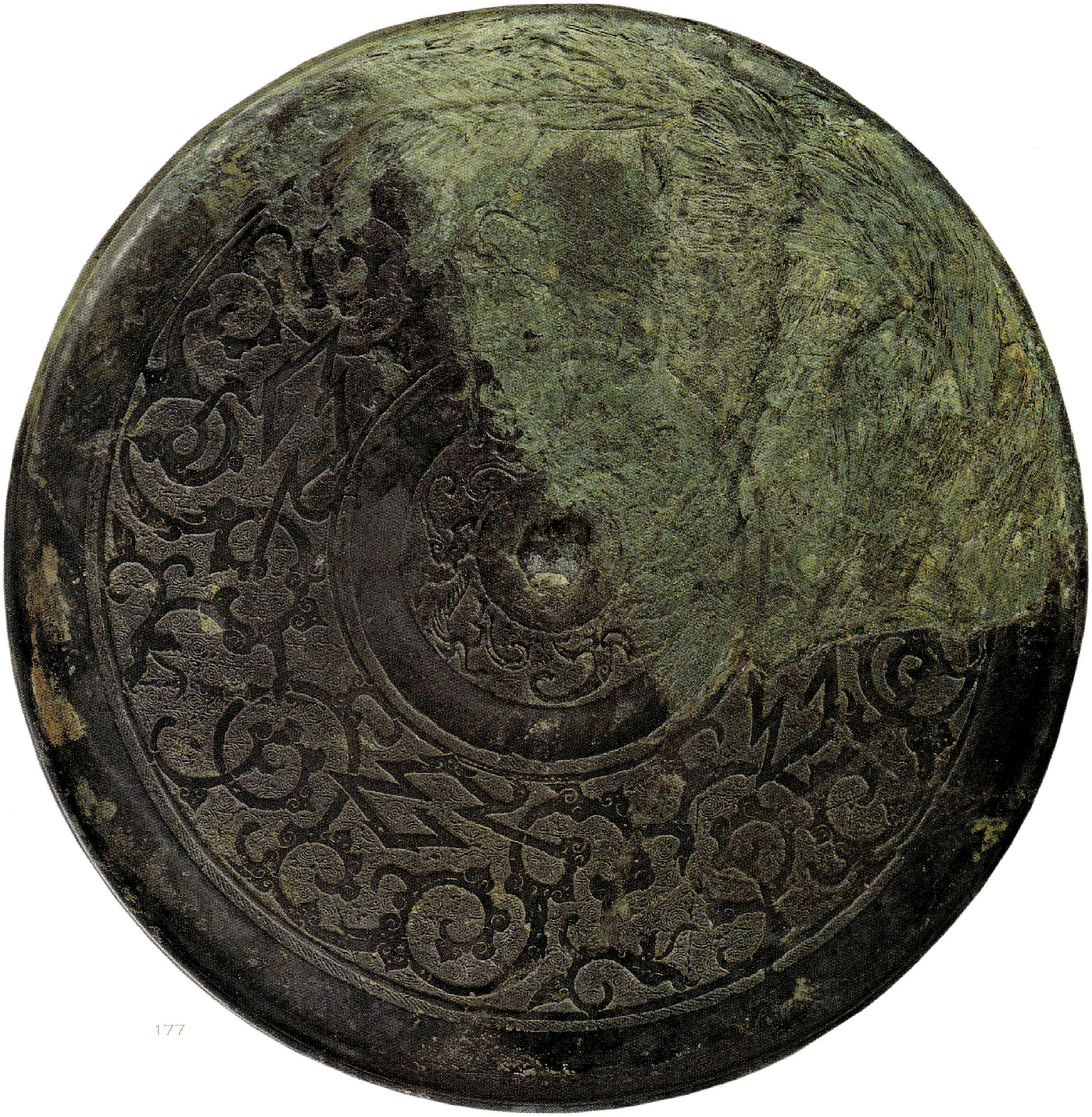

177

177

Bronze mirror

Second century BC, Western Han dynasty
Diameter: 23 cm
Excavated at Xianggangshan in 1983
The Museum of the King of Nanyue, Guangdong Province

Both the inner and outer circles of this bronze mirror show repeating dragon motifs. The dragons in the outer circle are depicted with mouths open and tongues protruding, against a background of fine scrolls representing clouds. The curved forms of the dragons in the outer circle overlap and contrast with the jagged geometric motifs. Jagged motifs similar to these became popular in the Warring States period and were frequently seen on textiles as well as on bronze objects. When this mirror was unearthed, it was surrounded by the remnants of the bag in which it had been placed prior to burial. LKC

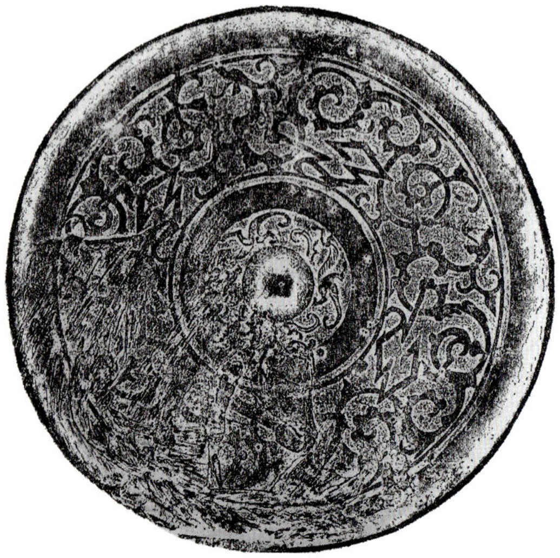

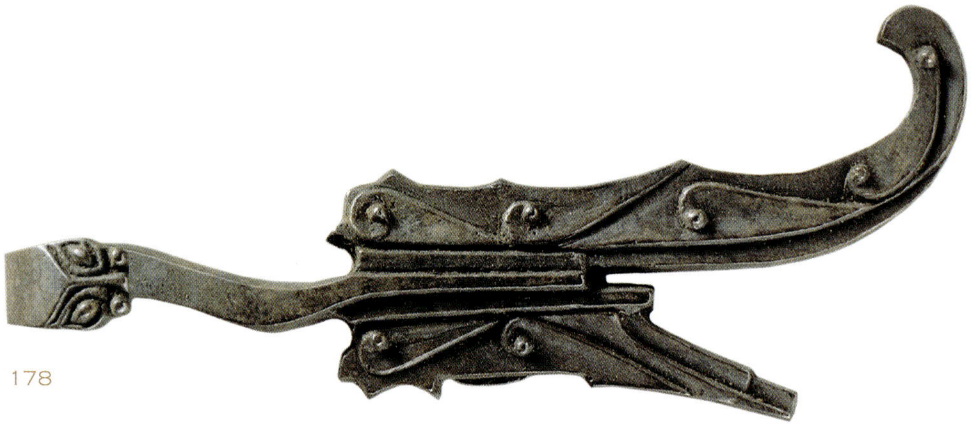

178

178

Silver belt hook with a seven-star pattern

Second century BC, Western Han dynasty
Length: 8.3 cm; Width: 2 cm
Excavated at Xianggangshan in 1983
The Museum of the King of Nanyue, Guangdong Province

This hook is special both in its shape and in its decorative theme. Its overall design is in the shape of a dragon. The hook facing upwards is designed in the shape of a dragon's head with two prominent eyes. The head is attached to a thin neck and a body of irregular shape. Details on the body are simplified, adorned only with several geometrical lines. Even more distinctive, the decorative pattern has seven raised knobs arrayed on the surface, forming the shape of the Big Dipper. The image of the Big Dipper was a popular motif in Han imagery. Many examples can be seen on stone slabs from Han dynasty tombs, including those from the famous Wuliang Shrine. The Han dynasty historian Sima Qian described the central position of the Big Dipper in cosmological terms: 'The Big Dipper is the vehicle of Supreme God. It revolves in the centre [of Heaven], governs the four cardinal points, divides the *yin* and the *yang*, establishes the four seasons, regulates the five elements, moves the quarterly intervals, determines all regulators of time.'[1] This belt hook is the only object in the Nanyue king's tomb bearing an astronomical image. LKC

1 *Shiji*, chapter 27, tr. Fong 1973, p. 13.

179

Earthenware incense burner

Second century BC, Western Han dynasty
Height: 10.3 cm; Diameter: 12.5 cm
Excavated at Xianggangshan in 1983
The Museum of the King of Nanyue, Guangdong Province

This earthenware incense burner was found in the eastern side chamber where the four concubines were interred. It is chalice-shaped with a shallow cup, a short stem and a wide foot. The cover has triangle-shaped apertures to let the fragrant smoke from the incense circulate. The surface is incised with geometric patterns and coloured with added pigments. Horizontal bands of geometric patterns encircle the foot, stem, cup and cover. This type of earthenware incense burner is found only in the Yue area. JCSL

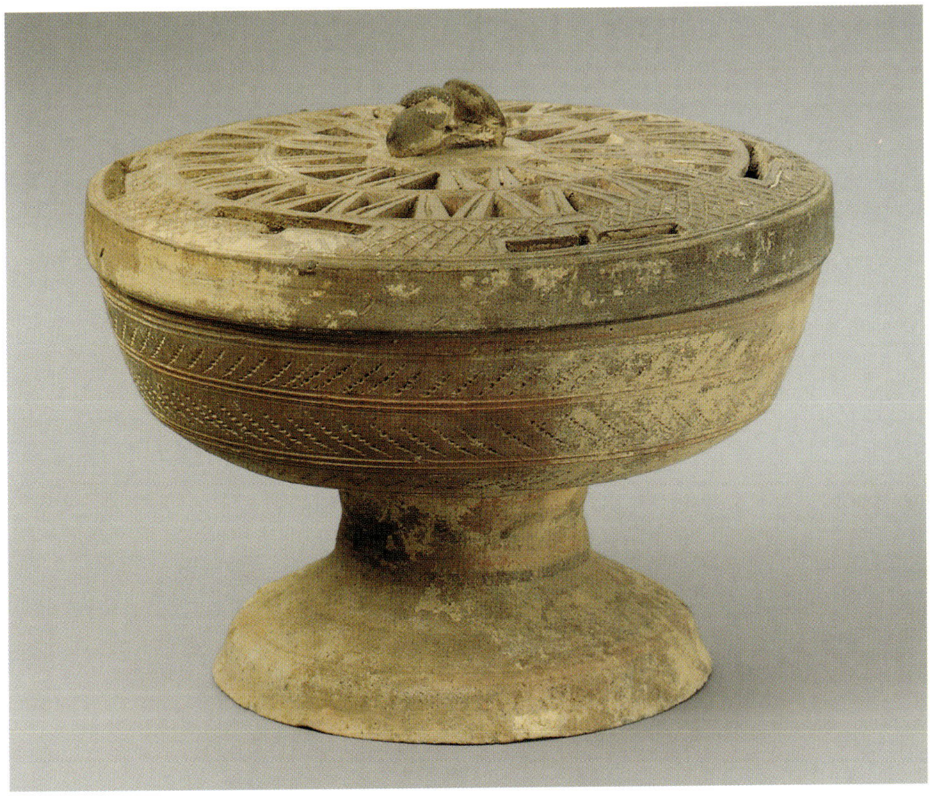

179

from the tomb pathway, seven were from the rear storeroom and the other thirteen pieces were from the eastern side chamber, which is believed to be for the four concubines of the king. KJC

181

Jade beaker with bronze frame

Second century BC, Western Han dynasty
Height: 14 cm; Diameter: 8.6 cm
Excavated at Xianggangshan in 1983
The Museum of the King of Nanyue, Guangdong Province

This jade beaker, composed of nine jade pieces, sits in a gilt bronze frame with a rounded base. It was found in the western side chamber, which was meant to function as a kitchen. It was wrapped in several layers of silk and found next to a sacrificed attendant when excavated.

180

Earthenware lidded *ding*

Second century BC, Western Han dynasty
Height: 8.6 cm; Diameter: 13.5 cm
Excavated at Xianggangshan in 1983
The Museum of the King of Nanyue, Guangdong Province

This lidded tripod has a contracted mouth, a short body and a round bottom. It has three flat legs, split in the shape of an animal foot. Its body is densely decorated with a wave pattern. The tripod has a lid with a knob in the middle and three curved cloud decorations on the edge. The surface of the lid is decorated with comb and string patterns.

A total of twenty-one earthenware lidded tripods, conforming to four sub-types, were found in this tomb. They were from three locations: only one was

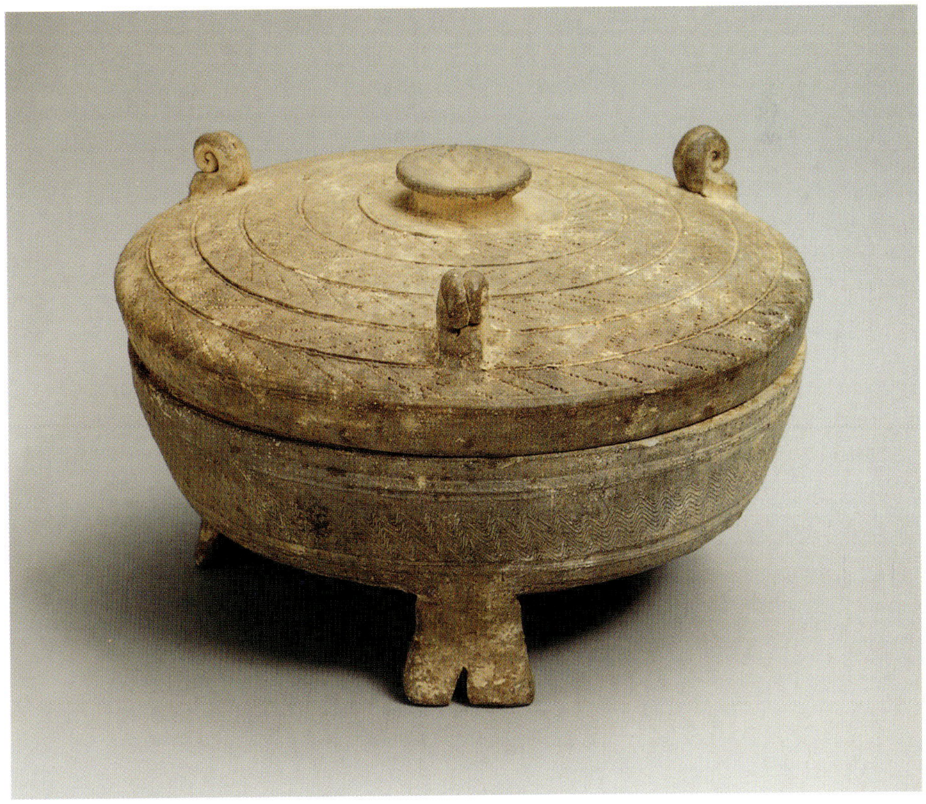

180

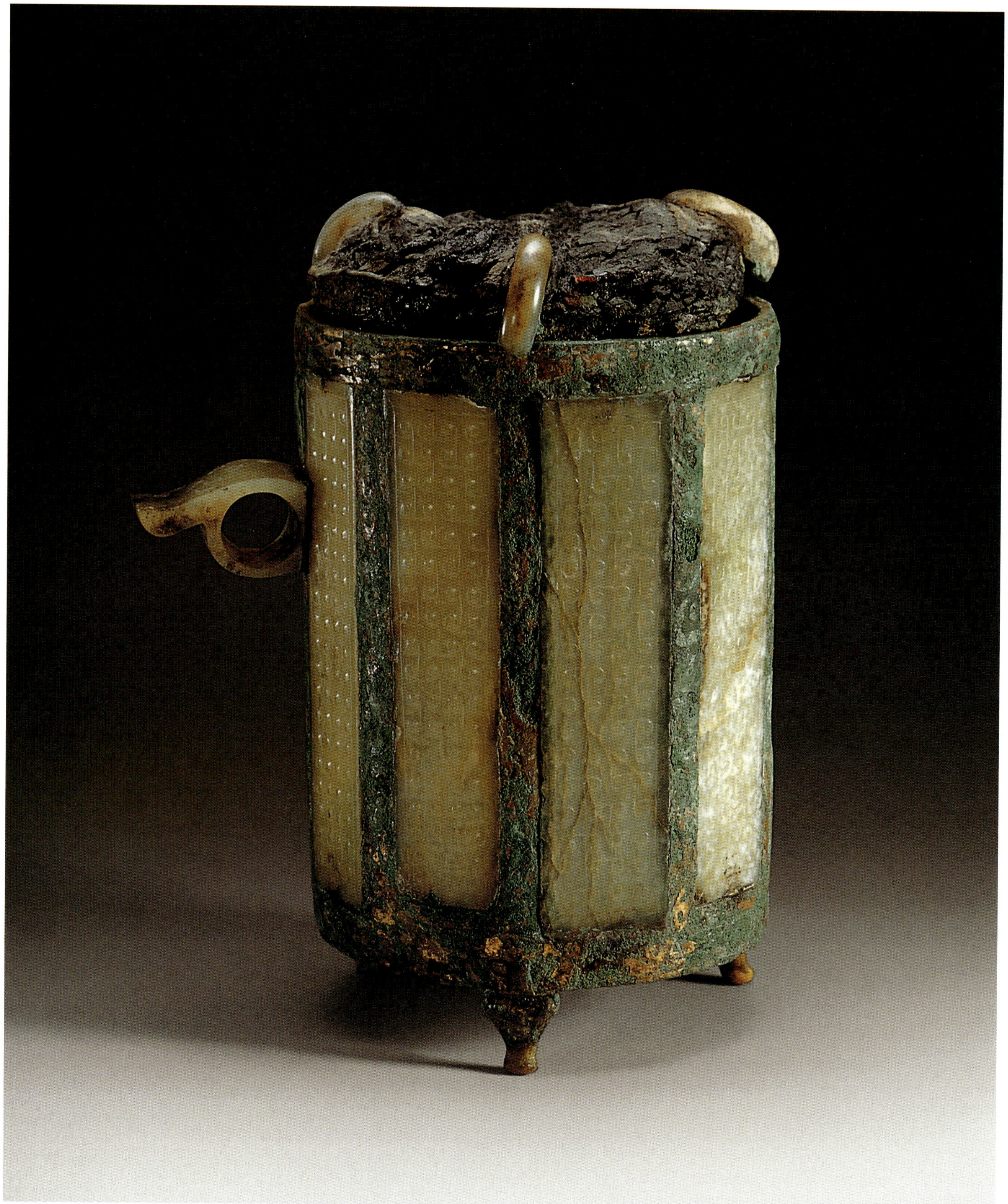

181

The beaker is matched with a delicate jade ring handle and a lacquer wood cover.

The individual found next to the beaker is thought to be the head chef to the King of Nanyue, likely responsible for looking after the king's daily needs. She was identified as the most senior figure among a total of seven sacrificed humans found in the kitchen.

Twelve rectangular jade plaques, ranging from 7 to 10.9 centimetres were excavated from a vertical pit tomb at Zaoyuan, north of Xi'an, and dated to the early Western Han period. The inscriptions incised on the burial bronzes reveal that the tomb occupant was the official in charge of the daily utensils used for the queen.[1] These twelve rectangular jade plaques were very likely inserted into bronze or lacquer frames to form a drinking vessel.

74 Jade beaker with a bronze frame and lid found at the M2 tomb at Mawangdui, Changsha, Hunan Provincial Museum. c.186 BC.

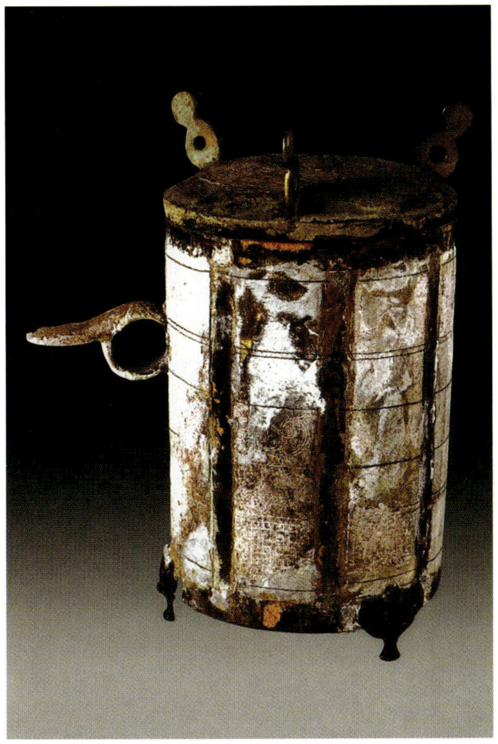

A similar example was found in the M2 tomb at Mawangdui, Changsha, Hunan (fig. 74). It was made up of eight jade plaques, each 11 cm high, 3 cm wide and 0.3 cm in thickness. JCSL

1 Liu 2009, p. 5.

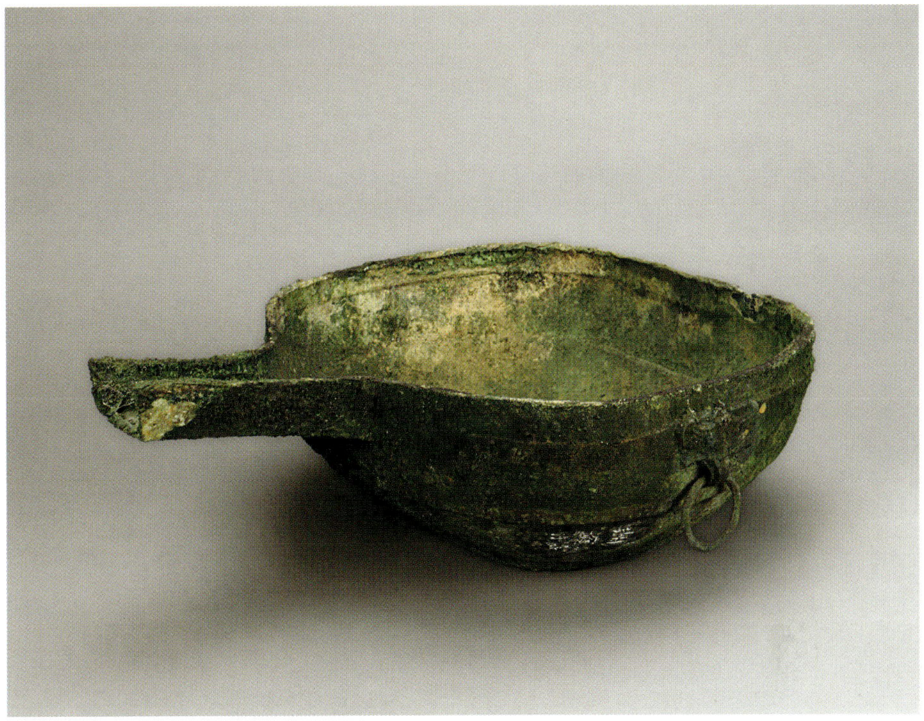

182

182

Bronze ladle with inscription

Second century BC, Western Han dynasty
Length: 33.2 cm
Excavated at Xianggangshan in 1983
The Museum of the King of Nanyue, Guangdong Province

This ladle was found together with a second of the same shape and dimensions. Both have slightly elongated bodies on rectangular bases, accentuated by a raised band running around the bodies. Two ring handles are attached to relief masks on both small sides. The object was to be held in both hands when pouring liquids into cups.

Altogether fifteen ladles were found in the tomb, eleven smaller and simpler ones in the western storage chamber (cat. 139), two in the eastern side chamber, an area assigned to the four concubines of Zhao Mo, and two in the western side chamber. This chamber contained the remains of seven people and rather few and relatively simple grave goods. The excavators suggested that the chamber served as quarters for the servants.[1]

On the lower body of the ladle a short inscription is engraved. It shows the character *Pan*, probably an abbreviation of Panyu, the Nanyue capital,[2] and indicates the capacity of the object: *rong er dou* (capacity [of the vessel is] two *dou*), which equals about four litres. LN

1 Beijing 1991, vol. 1, 254–9.
2 The name of the city was abbreviated in this way in several inscriptions in this tomb; Beijing 1991, vol. 1, pp. 302–3, table 32.

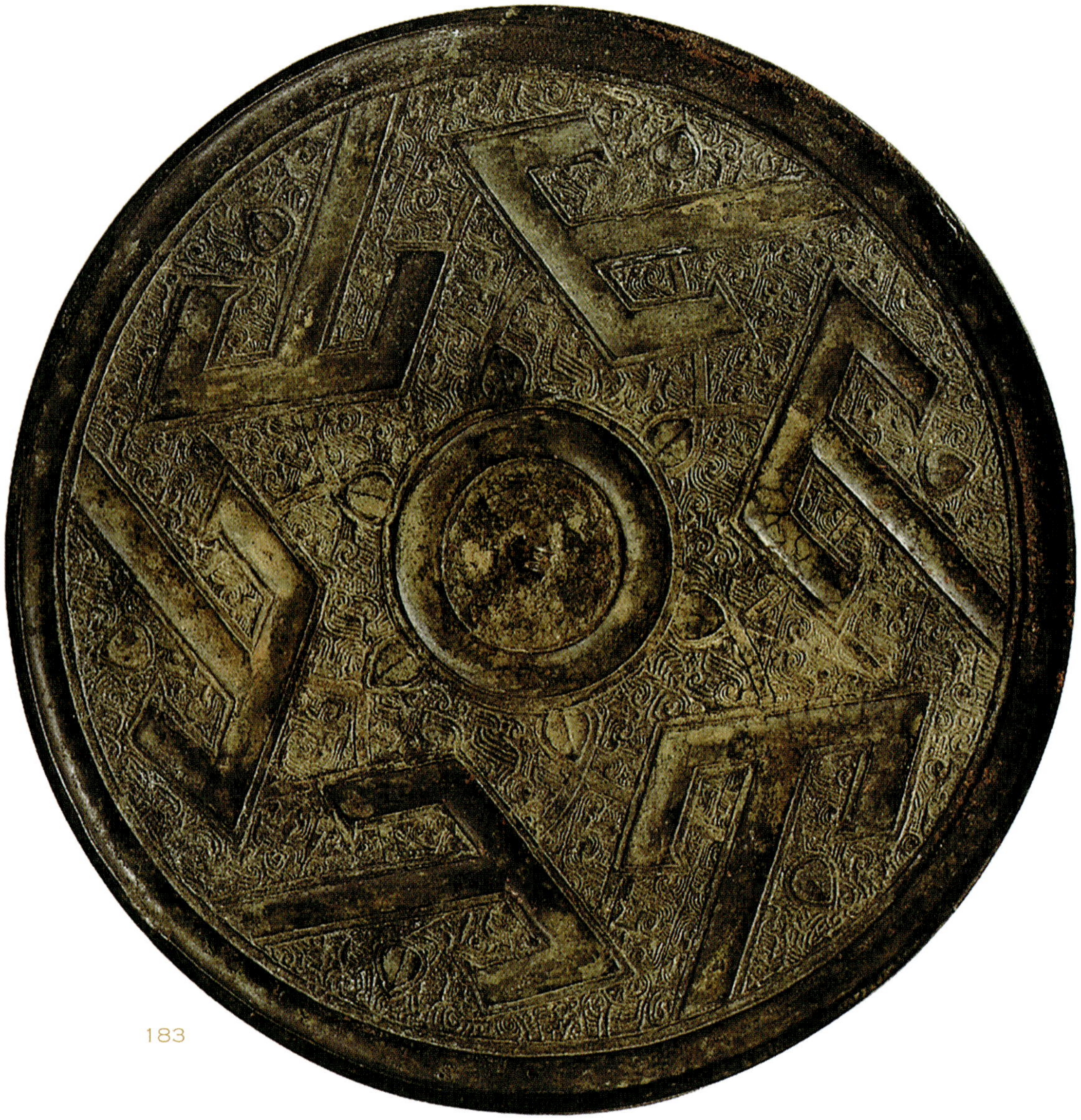

183

183

Bronze mirror with T-shaped pattern

Second century BC, Western Han dynasty
Diameter: 21.1 cm
Excavated at Xianggangshan in 1983
The Museum of the King of Nanyue, Guangdong Province
NOT EXHIBITED

Bronze mirrors with a symmetric arrangement of T-shaped motifs were first produced in large numbers during the fourth and third centuries BC. The earliest mirrors generally had a fourfold repetition of the motif, while mirrors of later date also show fivefold and sixfold repetitions. The finer details in the design of this mirror incorporate both organic and abstract geometric figures, including leaf- or petal-shaped motifs, as well as ripples and scrolls. As is common in mirrors of this type, the raised knob on the back has a hole through which a cord could be threaded, allowing the mirror to be suspended or carried. LKC

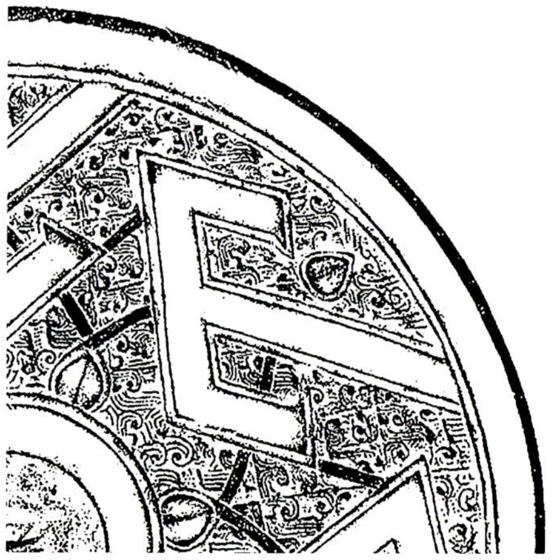

184

Bronze *ding* with inscription

Second century BC, Western Han dynasty
Height: 21 cm
Excavated at Xianggangshan in 1983
The Museum of the King of Nanyue,
Guangdong Province

The tripod has a rounded body with three outward-turned legs and two handles. The lid is removable. Three small handles are attached to it. Apart from a raised band running around the body the vessel is undecorated. Corroded areas of the surface bear impressions of cloth and straw. When placed in the tomb the tripod was wrapped in a protective cover that has later dissolved.

The object was found in the rear chamber of the tomb of Zhao Mo, together with three further bronze

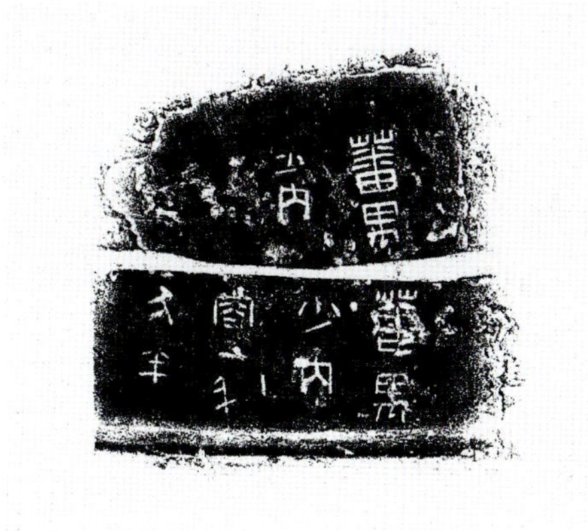

tripods of comparable shape, a range of cooking utensils and other dishes and vessels (cat. 187). In the 'underground palace' of Zhao Mo this chamber apparently represented a kitchen.

When discovered in the tomb, a thick layer of mussel shells was preserved inside the tripod. The other three tripods of the group also contained shells and bones. Some showed soot stains below the belly.[1] Apparently meals were prepared in the vessels before they were placed into the chamber.

The lid and body of the vessel bear short inscriptions. That on the lid reads *Panyu Shaonei*. At the Han Imperial court in Chang'an the *Shaonei* (Privy Treasury) was an office in charge of government funds and accounts.[2] The inscription indicates that the administration of Panyu, the Nanyue capital, was structured after the Han model. The inscription on the body indicates the capacity of the vessel: 'Shaonei office of Panyu (the vessel), contains one and more than a half *dou*' (*Panyu shaonei rong yidou daban*). Since during the Han period one *dou* had the volume of about two litres, the inscription claims that the vessel could hold more than three litres of liquid.[3] The other tripods of this group bore inscriptions of similar character.[4] LN

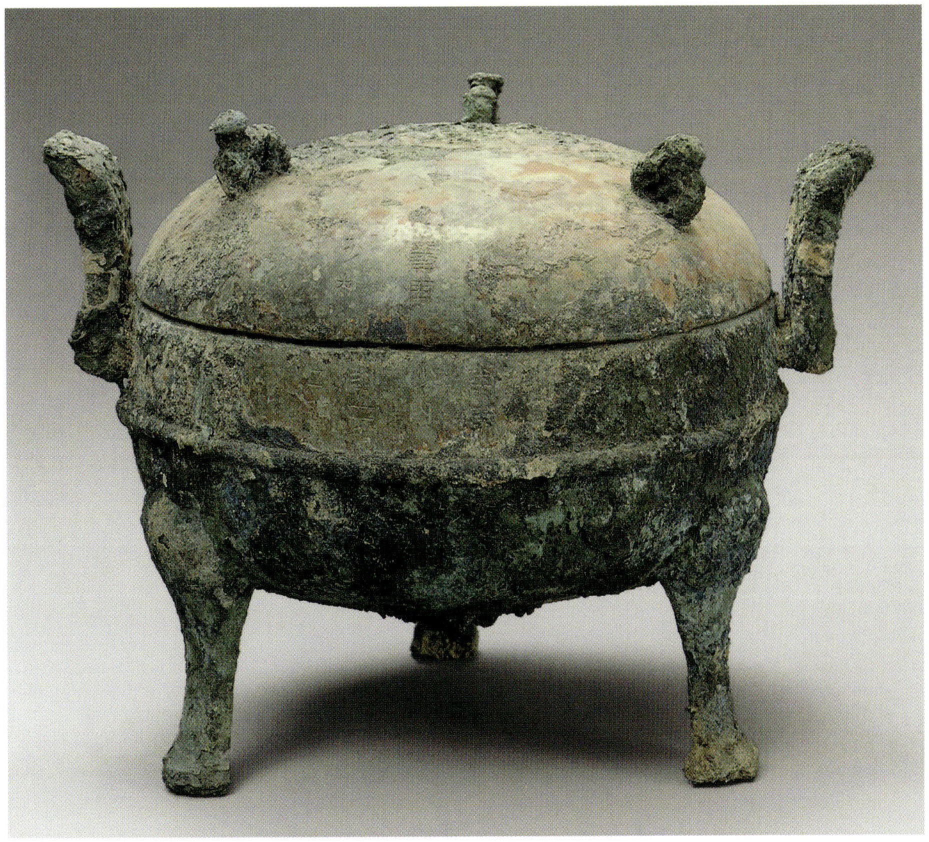

184

1 Beijing 1991, vol. 1, pp. 276–7.
2 Hulsewé 1978, pp. 195–6.
3 For Han measures, see Wilkinson 1999, p. 237, table 17.
4 For the other inscriptions, see Beijing 1991, vol. 1, pp. 276–7; Tsai 1998, p. 316.

185

Bronze *ding*

Second century BC, Western Han dynasty
Height: 54.5 cm; Diameter: 52 cm
Excavated at Xianggangshan in 1983
The Museum of the King of Nanyue,
Guangdong Province

Nine vessels similar to this one were found in the rear storeroom, and while some match its shape exactly, others have a more globular belly, round handles and more splayed legs. Two of these vessels contained the bones of pigs, fish and chickens. One *ding* (G58) contained pig bones and clam shells, but also remains

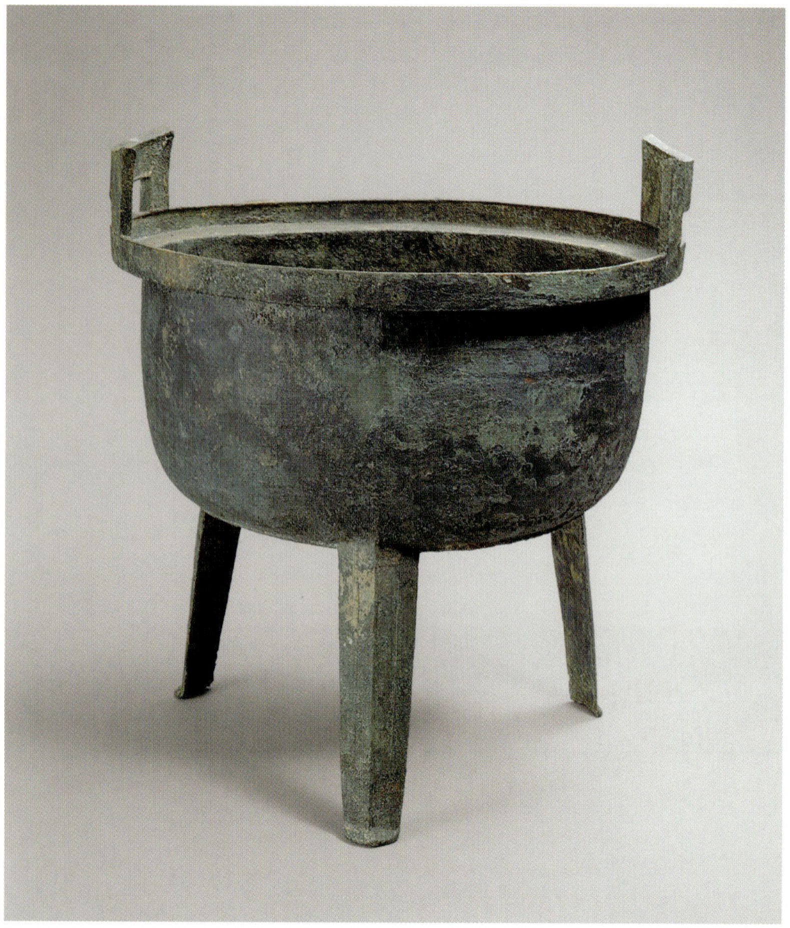

185

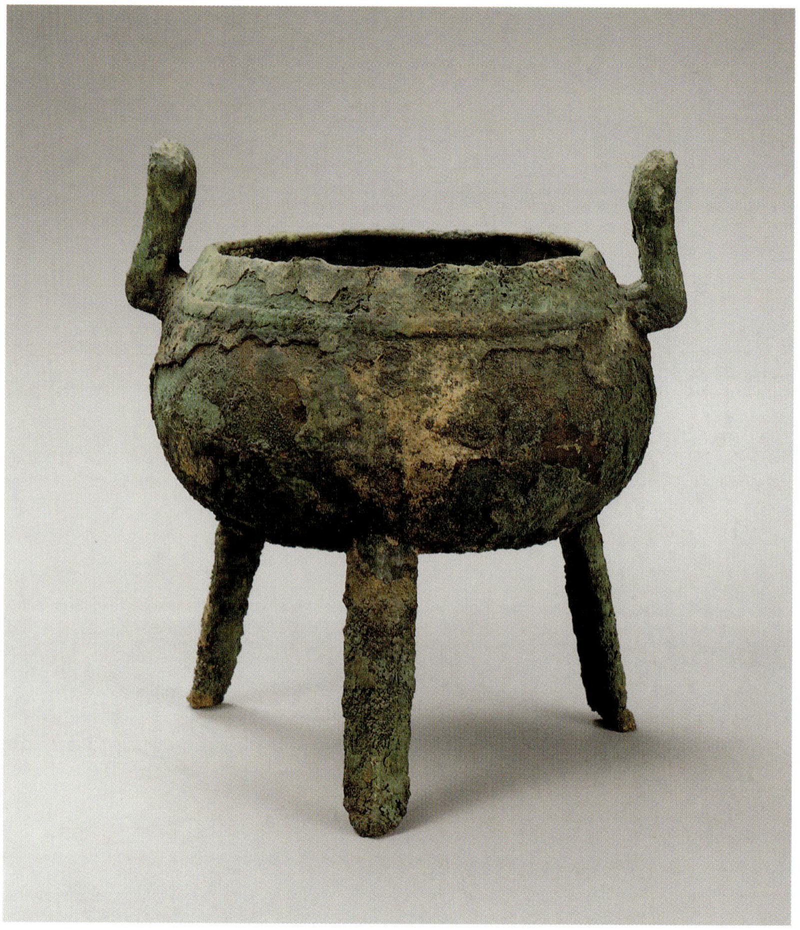

186

of a woven fabric, illustrating that the food may have been wrapped in fabric before being put in the vessel.[1] This *ding* was found lying on its side in the centre of the chamber along with another. It held an earthenware jar of the type *bu* and a clay seal, one of fifteen from this chamber. Seals were used to confirm that the goods conformed to the required quality standards.[2] The seal found in this *ding* and twelve others from this chamber read *taiguan*, referring to the office responsible for providing the king with food, suggesting that the court of Nanyue had such an office.[3] The seals further confirm that the function of this chamber was to store food and supplies.

Originally the *ding* would have had a wooden lid, which has decayed. This *ding* might survive from an earlier period and then have been buried in this tomb, which dates to the second century BC. The earliest was excavated from a burial at Beifushan, Luoding, Guangdong. Several other examples have come from Nanyue tombs.[4] Its distribution is limited to Guangdong and Guangxi, which has earned this vessel the attribution of being of the Yue style. SP

1 Beijing 1991, vol. 1, p. 278.
2 Prüch 1998, cat. 83.
3 Beijing 1991, vol. 1, pp. 309–10.
4 *Kaogu* 1996.10, pp. 55–6.

186

Bronze *ding*

Second century BC, Western Han dynasty
Height: 34.3 cm; Mouth diameter: 22 cm
Excavated at Xianggangshan in 1983
The Museum of the King of Nanyue, Guangdong Province

A total of thirty-six *ding* tripods have come from this tomb; nineteen made of bronze, including this one, two earthenware and one iron from the rear storeroom. Three vessels of this type were found along the chamber's western wall. This example contained a ginger grater, while another vessel contained a spoon. Two of the three vessels, including this piece, had traces of soot on the underside, suggesting that they had been used over fire.[1]

This *ding* has three tall, slender legs supporting a round body with flattened base. It has a wide mouth encircled by a broad ridge below the rim, where two slightly inward slanting, rectangular handles were cast with the body. A lid, probably made of wood, has decayed. This shape has been found in tombs in Hunan, Guangdong and Guangxi, dating from the Warring States period onwards, and in burials of the Nanyue period.[2] As this shape is typical of the very south of China, it was also categorized as being of Yue style. SP

1 Beijing 1991, vol. 1, p. 276.
2 *Kaogu* 1996.10, pp. 54–5.

187

Bronze bottle with garlic bulb-shaped mouth

Second century BC, Western Han dynasty
Height: 36.7 cm
Excavated at Xianggangshan in 1983
The Museum of the King of Nanyue, Guangdong Province

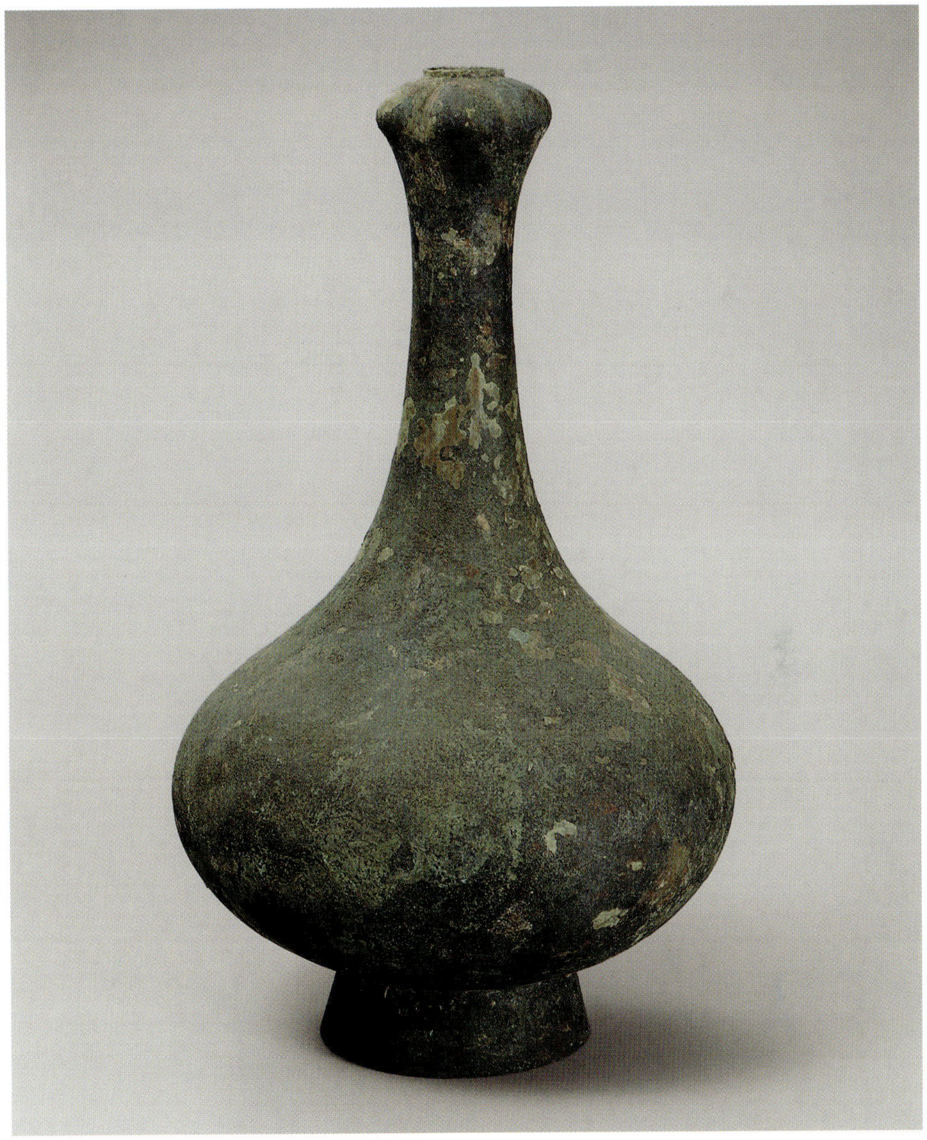

187

The bronze bottle has a high foot ring, a rounded, slightly compressed body, a slender neck and a characteristic mouth in the shape of a garlic bulb. The undecorated surface under the corrosion is smooth.

The bottle was found in the small rear storeroom of Zhao Mo's tomb among piles of bronze and ceramic vessels, iron cooking racks, a bronze lamp, a coal container and a model stove. Some remains of wooden boards found between the vessels suggest that the more than a hundred objects in this chamber were originally put in stacks on wooden shelves along the walls.[1]

Bottles with a garlic bulb-shaped mouth were first used at the end of the fourth century BC in the western Chinese state of Qin.[2] During the third century BC, in the course of the Qin conquest of China, bottles of this distinctive shape spread throughout the country. Almost identically shaped bottles were found in a tomb in Luoyang, Henan Province, dating to the middle of the second century BC,[3] and in a tomb from Shuihudi, Yunmeng county, Hubei Province, that can be dated to the second half of the third century BC.[4] This indicates that the object was produced long before the burial and that the rulers of Nanyue used it before it became a grave good. LN

1 Nickel 1998, p. 63.
2 Tomb no 1 in Yehugou, Gaozhuang, Fengxiang county; *Wenwu* 1980.9, pp. 10–14; Ledderose and Schlombs 1990, pp. 148–9; Tsuda-Hausamman 1998, pp. 336–7.
3 *Wenwu* 1994.7, pp. 34–5; Nickel 2011, pp. 95–6.
4 Beijing 1981b, pp. 43, 46.

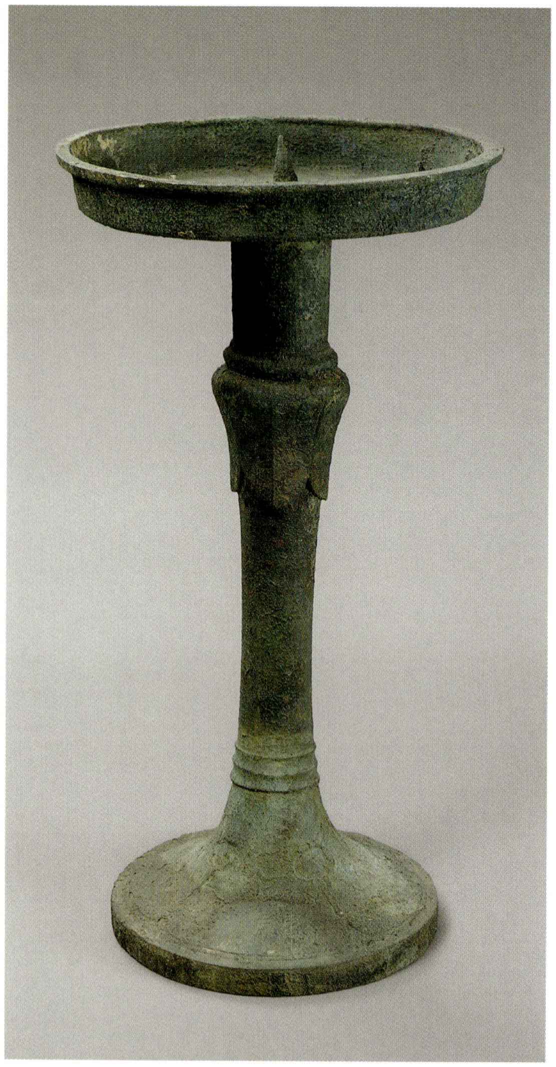

188

188

Bronze lamp (*deng*)

Second century BC, Western Han dynasty
Height: 40.9 cm; Diameter of pan: 23 cm
Excavated at Xianggangshan in 1983
The Museum of the King of Nanyue,
Guangdong Province

This bronze lamp is one of a pair that was found together in the rear storeroom. The inscription on the foot states its weight as '13 *jin* and 11 *liang*'. The second lamp is inscribed as weighing one *liang* more.[1] This type of lamp first appears during the late Warring States period, about the third century BC, then usually with a pan with curved sides.[2] Very popular during the Western Han period, such lamps were found in many burials across eastern China, including Dongdongshan tomb No. 2, Xuzhou, Jiangsu (cat. 41).[3] Many different types of lamps were discovered in the twin tombs at Mancheng, Hebei, including nine of this type.[4] Their inscriptions suggest a use in the palace and it is likely that the examples from the Nanyue tomb once also served in the royal palace at Panyu. This type of lamp declined in use from the mid-Eastern Han period, about 100 AD.[5]

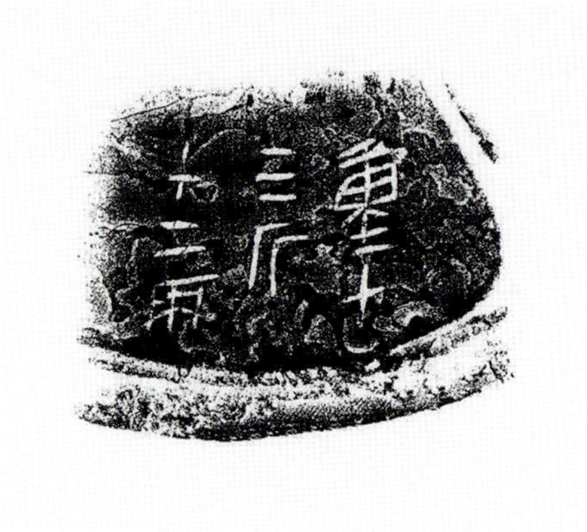

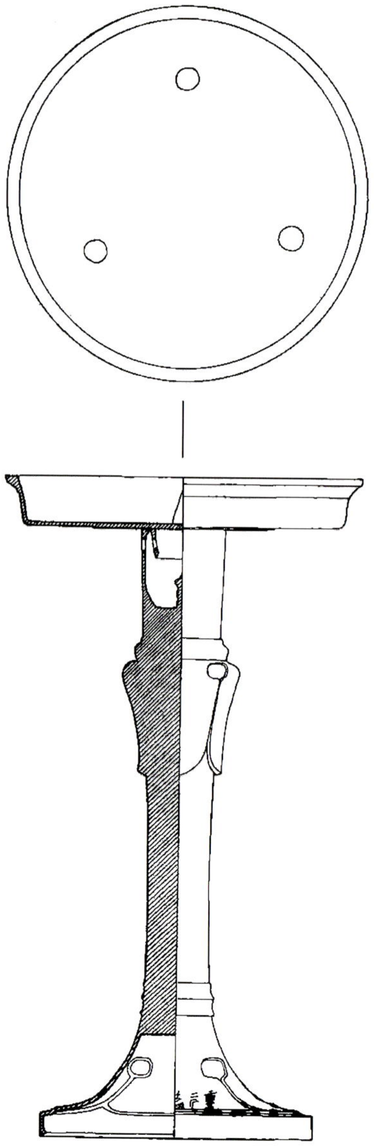

An analysis of the remains of a white substance found in one of the lamps in Mancheng tomb No.1 shows that both vegetable and animal tallow, also in candle form, were used as fuels at that time. While animal and vegetable tallow are a possibility, whether wax was also used is less clear. The earliest textual references are to the Jin dynasty (AD 265–420), but they have not been verified archaeologically.[6] According to some sources, knowledge of the use of insect wax for candles dates as late as the Yuan dynasty (AD 1271–1368).[7] SP

1 Beijing 1991, vol. 1, pp. 288–9. The actual weight of the lamps is 3.475 kg for this object and 3.325 kg for the second lamp; Beijing 1991, vol. 1, p. 349.
2 See the examples from Wangshan tomb No. 2 at Jiangling, Hubei; Beijing 1996, colour pl. 5, pl. 70:5.
3 Three bronze lamps of this type come from this tomb: *Wenwu* 1984, p. 29, fig. 27.
4 See, for example, Beijing 1980, vol. 2, pls 38:1–2.
5 Sun 1991, p. 352.
6 *Wenwu* 1983.7, pp. 85–6.
7 Simoons 1991, p. 334, n. 50.

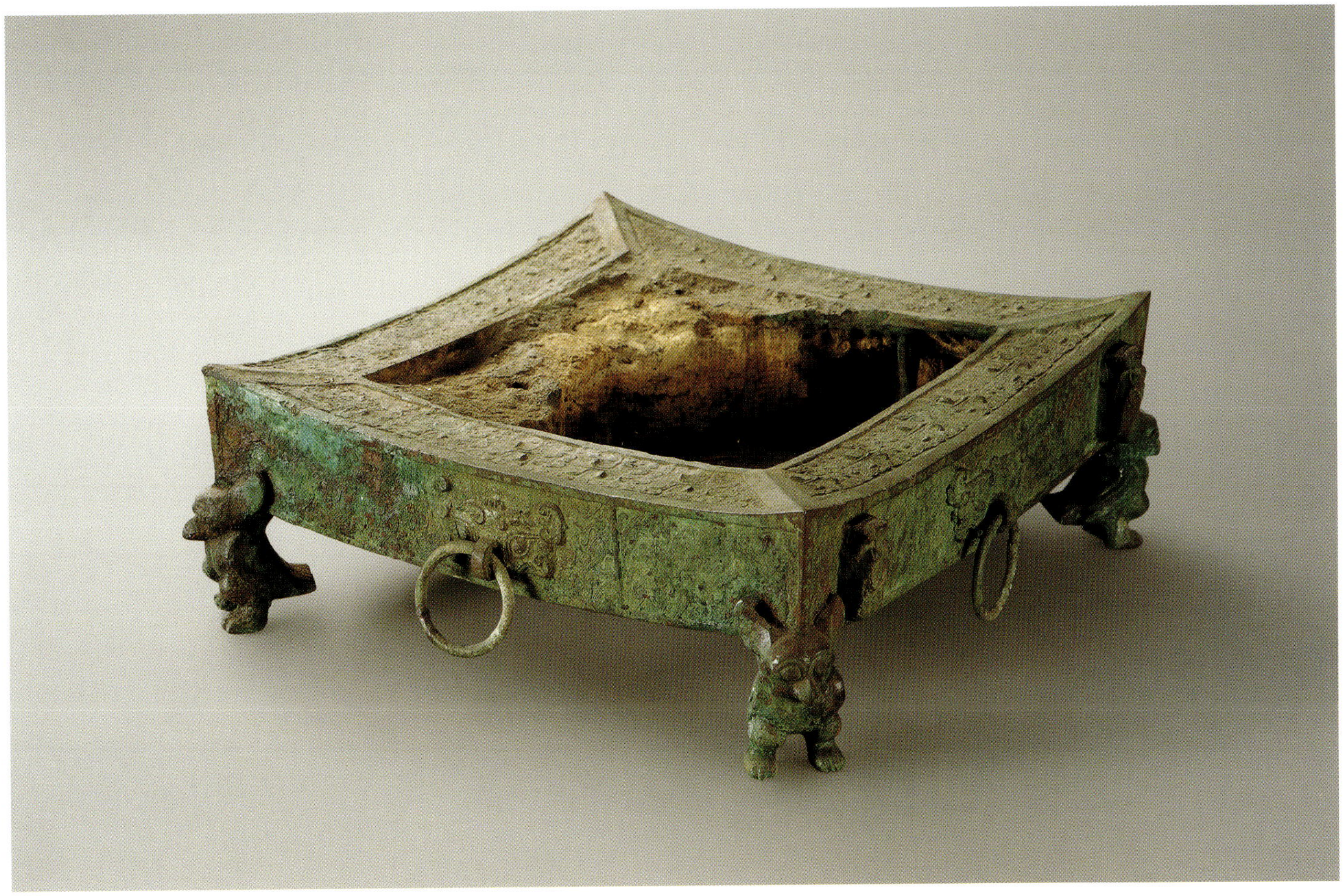

189

189

Small bronze stove

Second century BC, Western Han dynasty
Length: 27.5 cm; Width: 27 cm; Height: 11 cm
Excavated at Xianggangshan in 1983
The Museum of the King of Nanyue, Guangdong Province
NOT EXHIBITED

This very unusual low stove with a wide flat rim was found in the rear storeroom along with other cooking utensils and food for the royal family. Four owl-shaped legs support the stove and its four corners tilt upwards to hold tongs or skewers for roasting meats. Four bronze door-knockers decorate the four sides. Clay material found inside the stove has been preserved as archaeologists are not sure whether or not it constituted part of the stove's original design, helping to maintain the heat of the food.

Eating, drinking and music clearly played an important role in the King of Nanyue's daily life. The Nanyue royal kitchens included several innovative cooking utensils for roasting, baking and frying. This bronze stove is one example. JCSL

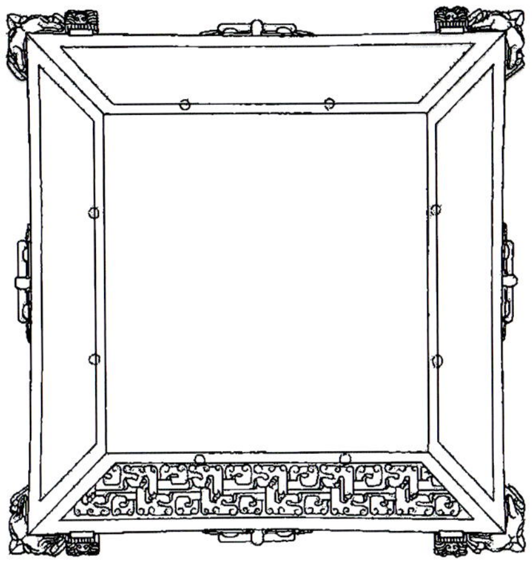

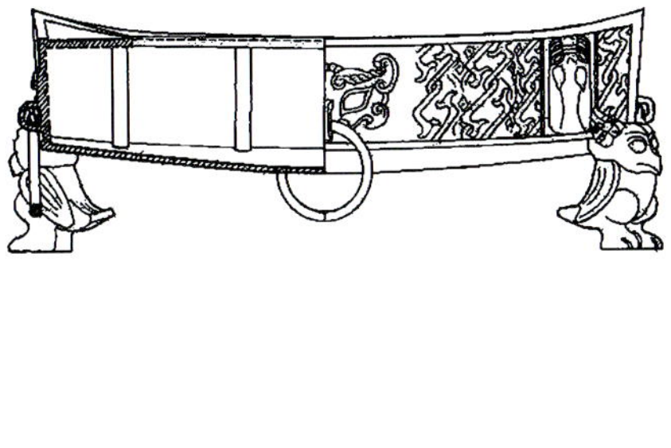

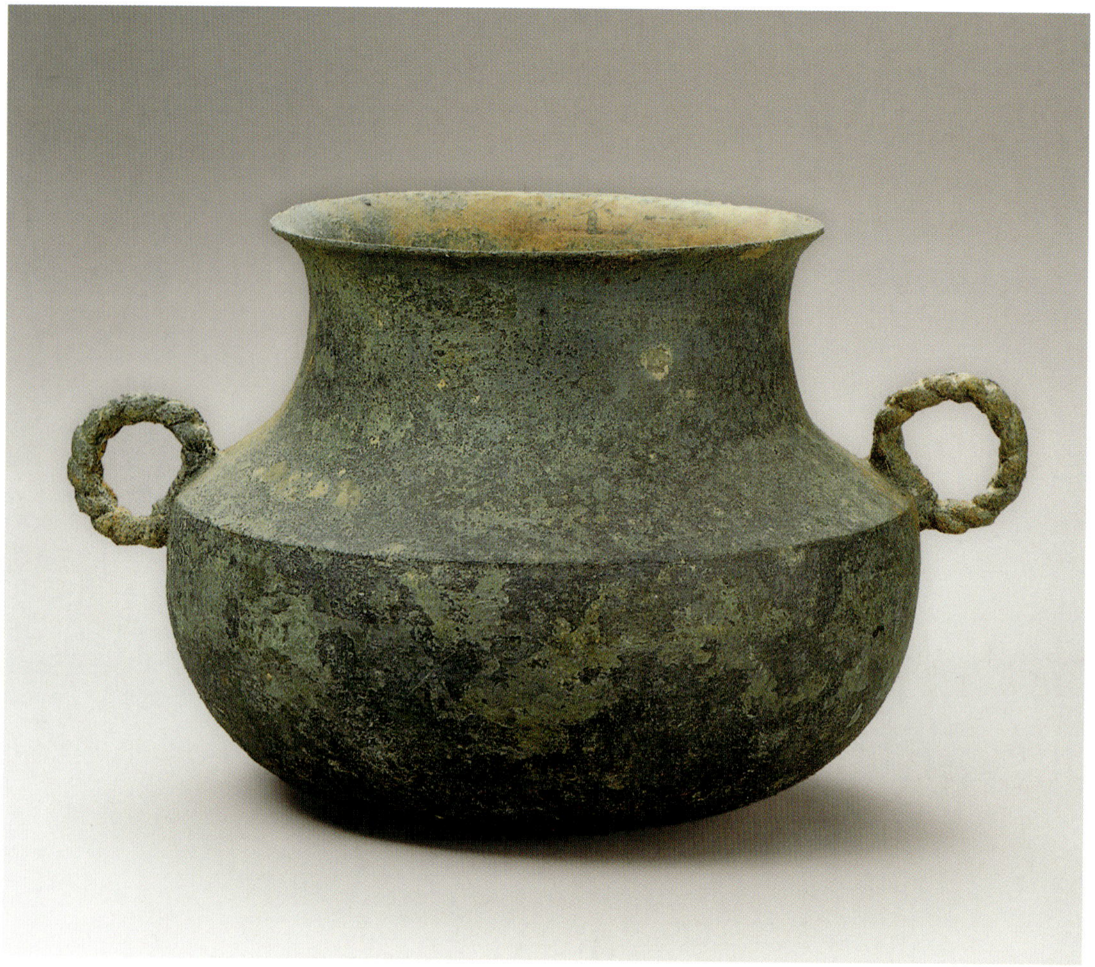

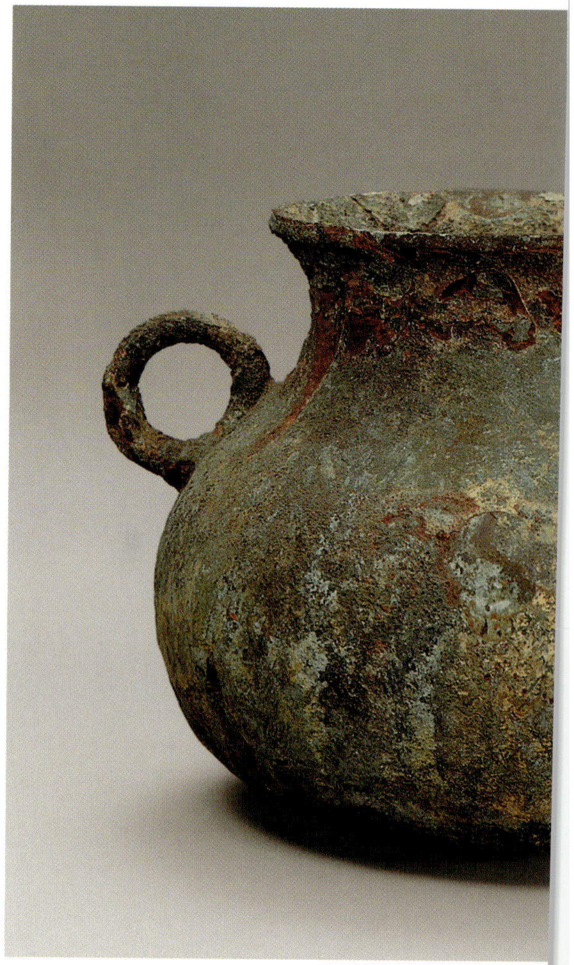

190

190

Bronze cooking vessels (*mou*)

Second century BC, Western Han dynasty
Height: 11.2–22.5 cm; Body diameter: 12.4–30.4 cm
Excavated at Xianggangshan in 1983
The Museum of the King of Nanyue, Guangdong Province

These cooking vessels were found together with around a hundred others and with containers for storing food made of iron, bronze and earthenware in the rear storeroom behind the king's coffin chamber. Remains of wooden beams between the excavated objects indicate that they were once placed on wooden shelves that have since decayed, which may once have served as the furnishings of a kitchen. A large number of cooking vessels of this type, sixteen in total, were found in the tomb. Eleven came from the rear storeroom while four were placed in the western chamber and one in the eastern side chamber.

In some excavation reports, *mou* are often mistakenly called *guan* or *fu*, which are other types of cooking vessel. But an inscription on a heavily damaged vessel of the same type from the late Western Han tomb M201 in Changsha, Hunan, dated to 49 BC, gives not only the weight of the piece, as is often the case in inscriptions on vessels during the Han period, but also refers to the vessel as a *mou*.[1] From this discovery we know the Han period term for this type. *Mou* were mostly made of bronze, although some iron and ceramic examples exist.[2]

From textual sources it is known that *mou* were used as cooking vessels,[3] but the archaeology and the vessels themselves provide even better evidence. In many cases, their bases and sides show remains of soot. Two *mou* from the rear storeroom had the remains of iron tripods attached to the base through corrosion. This suggests that food was cooked in *mou* resting on tripods over fire. Nine iron tripods in varying sizes matching the bases of the *mou* and other cooking vessels, such as cooking pots (*fu*), and steamers (*yan*), were found and

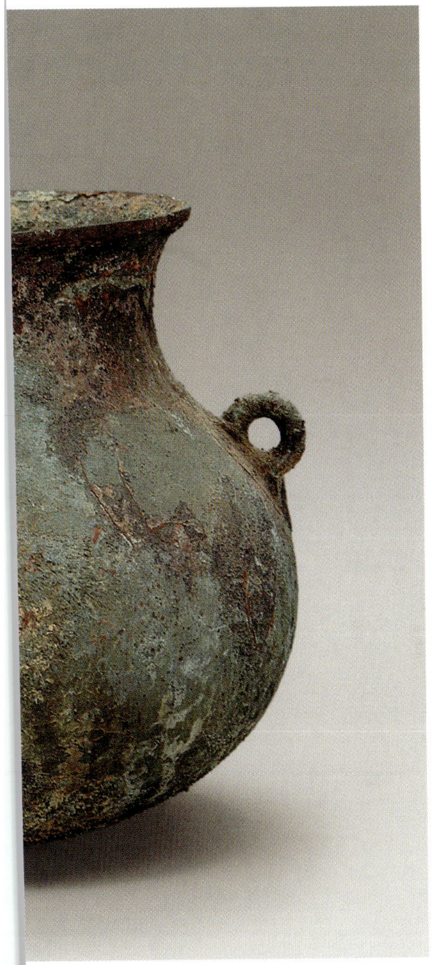

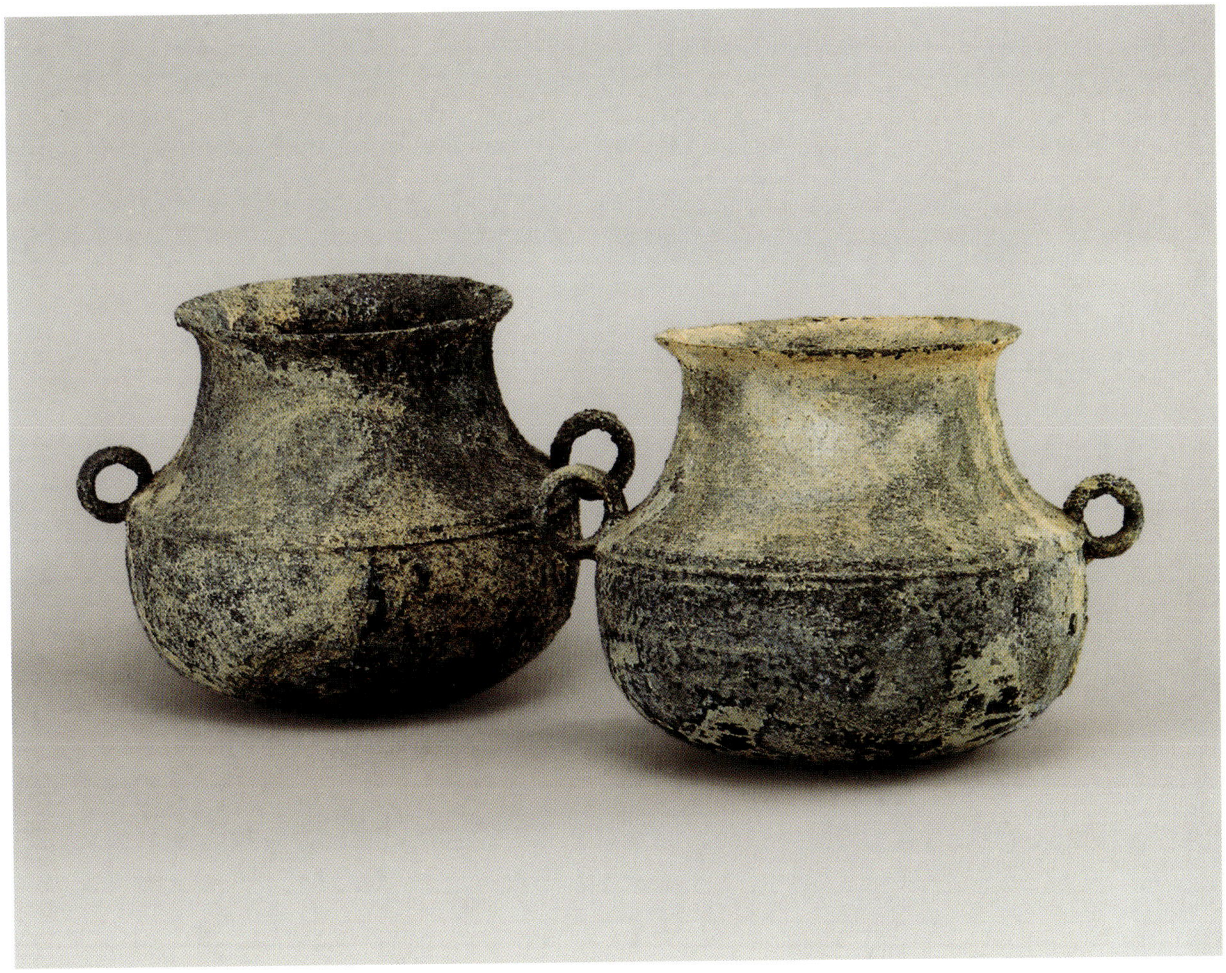

it is plausible that some were used together.[4] Animal remains including those of chickens, fish, tortoises, pigs, shellfish and also eggshells were found in a number of vessels.

Mostly found in burials and hoards, *mou* are widely distributed across China and many were found in Sichuan, Hubei, Shaanxi and Guangdong, but finds have also been made in Inner Mongolia, Henan, Hunan, Jiangxi, Yunnan, Guizhou and Guangxi.[5] The earliest examples with a single ring handle come from the early fourth century BC tombs in Sichuan.[6] *Mou* became especially numerous during the late Warring States, Qin and Western Han periods, which is explained by their transmission from Sichuan through the conquest of much of eastern China by the Qin, but they were probably also traded and exchanged.[7] An explanation less driven by military expansion would be to link the distribution of *mou* to similarities in food preparation that may have had currency across larger parts of southern China.

The latest *mou* were found in burials of the Eastern Han to Three Kingdoms periods (second–third centuries) mainly in Sichuan and Hubei. It has been suggested that the origins of the *mou* can be traced to the late second millennium BC vessels of a similar shape but without handles from Shi'erqiao near Chengdu,[8] but there is no evidence beyond similarities in shape and geographical proximity that plausibly bridges the intervening centuries until the appearance of *mou* in the early Warring States period. SP

1 Beijing 1957, p. 110, pl. 62.
2 See, for example, Beijing 1981a, pl. 27:2–4, 31:2, 39:1–2.
3 *Kaogu yu wenwu* 1994.1, p. 66.
4 Beijing 1991, vol. 2, pl. 181:2.
5 *Kaogu yu wenwu* 1994.1, pp. 71–2.
6 See, for example, the tomb at Xindu, Chengdu; *Wenwu* 1981.6, p. 8, figs 15:1–3; and another one from the western districts of Chengdu; *Kaogu* 1983.7, p. 598, fig. 2:3.
7 *Kaogu yu wenwu* 1994.1, pp. 72–3.
8 *Kaogu yu wenwu* 1994.1, p. 72; *Wenwu* 1987.12, p. 17, fig. 39.

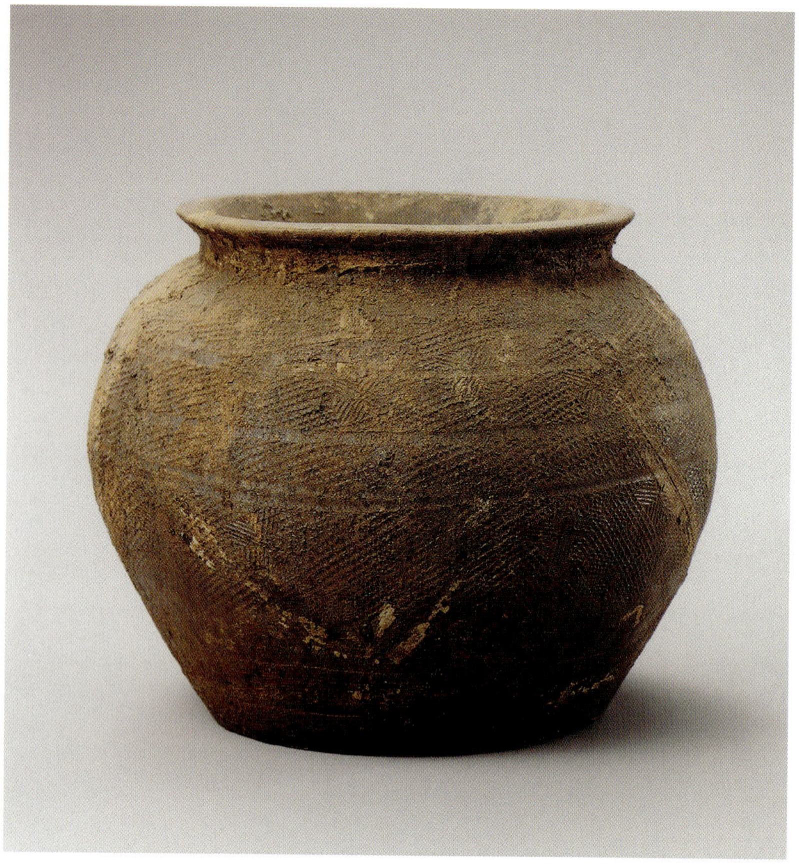

191

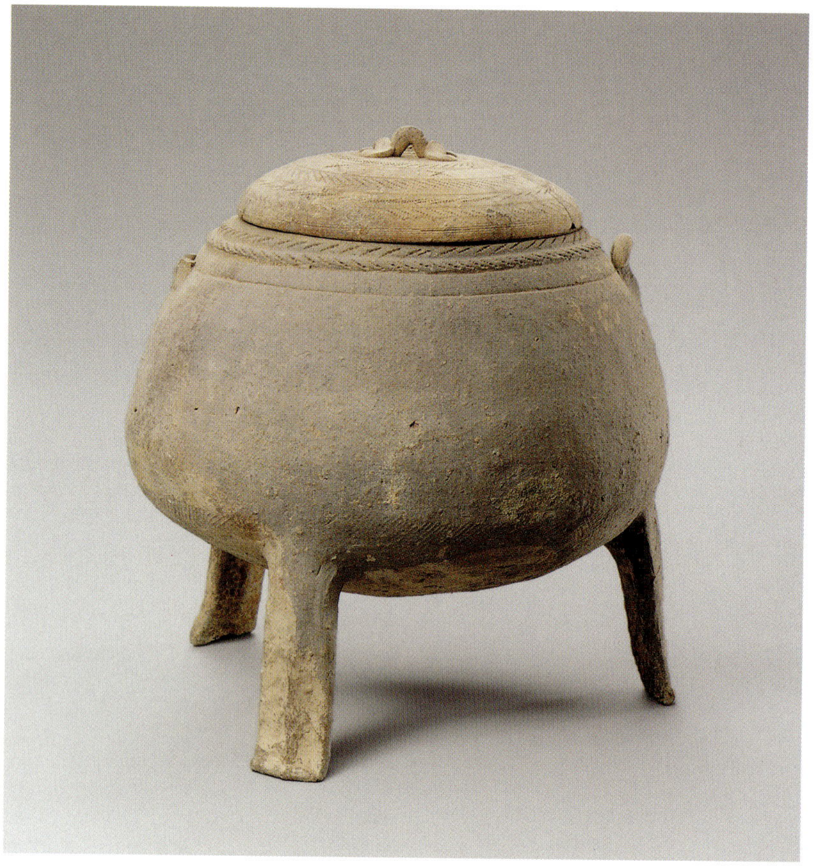

192

191

Earthenware jar

Second century BC, Western Han dynasty
Height: 14.8 cm; Diameter 13.4 cm
Excavated at Xianggangshan in 1983
The Museum of the King of Nanyue, Guangdong Province

This is a small jar with pressed decoration on the body. It has a large mouth with an everted rim, a round body and finishes in a large, flat foot. Its body surface is covered with trellises and geometrical patterns of various designs.

There were more than eighty small jars found in this tomb. Briefly, they can be classified into two sub-types according to their form: the first a strong, tall form; and the second in a fat, short style. The quantity of each sub-type is equal in number. They were discovered in most chambers, except in the antechamber and the king's coffin chamber. However, their distribution varies across different rooms: for example, thirty-six small jars found in the rear storeroom all belong to sub-type two. KJC

192

Earthenware *ding*

Second century BC, Western Han dynasty
Height: 25 cm; Diameter: 23 cm
Excavated at Xianggangshan in 1983
The Museum of the King of Nanyue, Guangdong Province

This earthenware tripod vessel has a contracted mouth, a drum-shaped body and a round bottom with three flat legs. There are several lines of bow-string pattern, together with a comb design, along the mouth. Its body bears the remains of a lattice design. There is a pair of semi-circular handles attached on the shoulder. This tripod has a cover with a semi-circular knob, and the whole cover is decorated with six circles in a comb pattern.

This *ding* was found in the rear storeroom for food and cooking utilities that had more than 130 bronze, iron and ceramic objects. Among them are nineteen bronze, one iron and two earthenware tripod *ding*. This room and the western side chamber, which contains twenty-two items, have the largest number of *ding* of the whole tomb. KJC

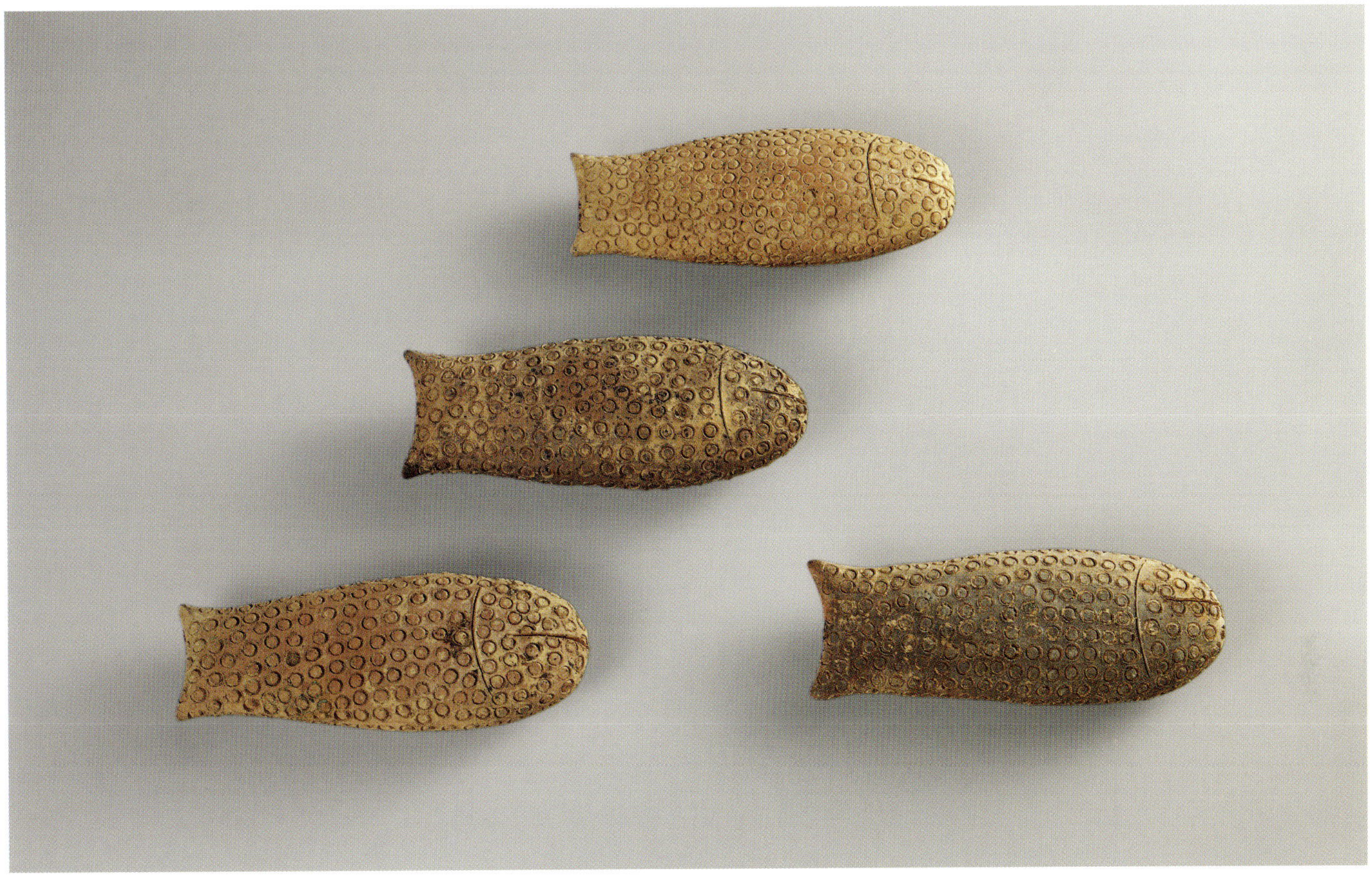

193

193

Earthenware percussion instruments in the shape of fish

Second century BC, Western Han dynasty
Length: 12.3 cm
Excavated at Xianggangshan in 1983
The Museum of the King of Nanyue, Guangdong Province

Fish-shaped percussion instruments, nine in total, were excavated from the rear storeroom. The surfaces of the fish are marked with small round patterns that resemble scales. Two incised lines at the head of each fish represent the gill lids and mouths and there are traces of red, brown and black pigments on the surface.

The fish were constructed from two separate halves; these were joined together and loose sand introduced into the interior cavity before firing, allowing them to be used as percussion instruments. These instruments may have been used for beating a rhythm while dancing or performing, although it is not certain whether they were played by the dancers themselves or by separate instrumentalists.

Other percussion instruments of a different shape were found in the same tomb (cat. 150). LKC

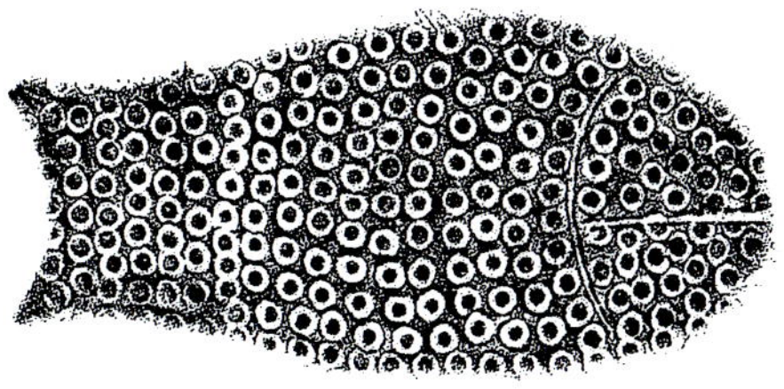

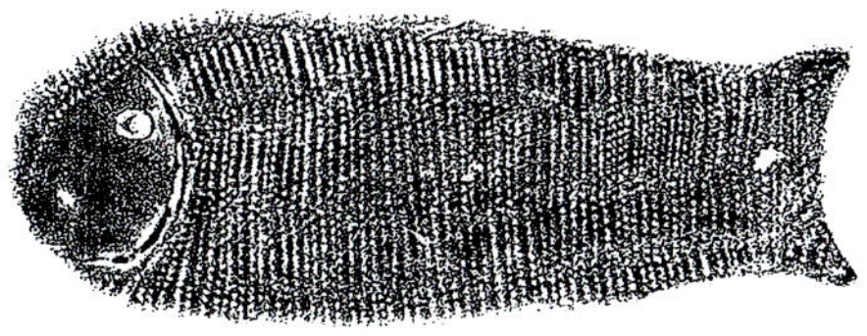

APPENDIX: SITES OF HAN TOMBS IN XUZHOU

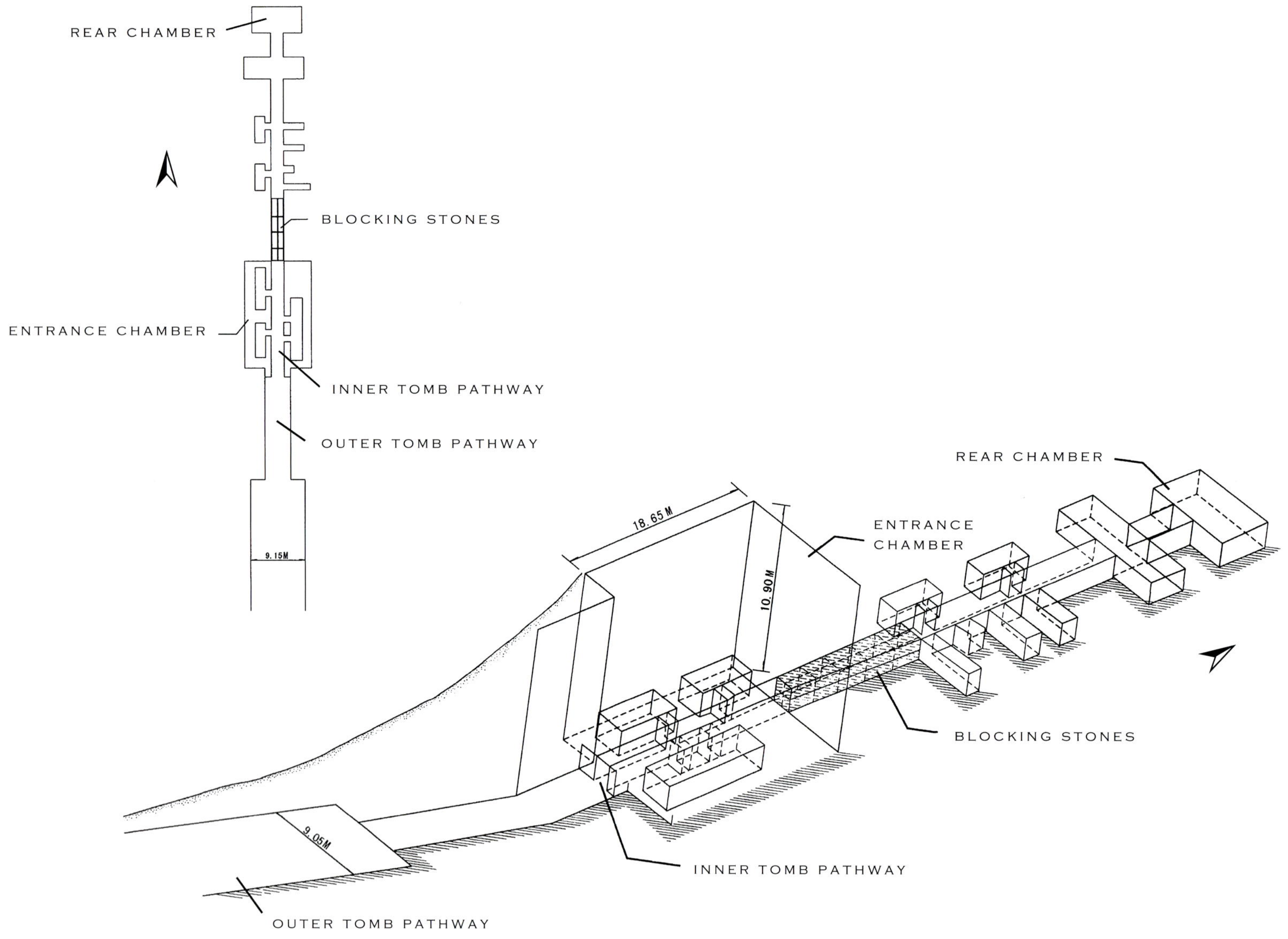

Perspective drawing of the King of Chu's tomb at Shizishan

THE KING OF CHU'S TOMB AT SHIZISHAN

The King of Chu's burial site at Shizishan is the largest of the royal funeral complexes around Xuzhou and has yielded the most spectacular funerary objects. The site covers three hills (Shizishan, Yangguishan[1] and Xiuqiushan[2]) in the eastern suburbs of Xuzhou and contains terracotta armies, sacrificial pits, the king's tomb at Shizishan and his queen's tomb at Yangguishan. The site is named after the hill on which the main tomb is located. The discovery of large quantities of bricks, tiles, eaves and water pipes indicate that there was once above-ground architecture of considerable scale.

The terracotta armies were first discovered in 1984 at the western foot of Shizishan. This was the third terracotta army group unearthed in China, following the finds at the First Emperor of Qin's mausoleum and the Western Han Tomb at Yangjiawan, both located in Shaanxi Province. So far, over 2,000 figurines have been found in the four pits at Shizishan. In contrast to the naturalistic style of the Qin figurines, the Han terracotta warriors and horses are more stylized and are smaller in form.

Seven years after the discovery of the terracotta armies, a massive tomb was found 400 metres east of the pits. The tomb was excavated from December 1994 to February 1995 by a team of local archaeologists and specialists from the Nanjing Museum. Located on the south-facing hillside, it comprises an outer tomb pathway, a vaulted pathway, six side chambers (E1–E6) on the eastern side of the pathway and five side chambers (W1–W5) on the western side, as well as a rear chamber.

The tomb has several unusual features: unpolished walls, scattered building materials across the corridors and chambers, and a rather random way of placing funerary objects. These features indicate that it was an unfinished project and that the king was buried in a hurry. Three sacrificial human remains were found inside the tomb, which is rare in Han tombs since the practice of human sacrifice had been largely abandoned by this period. Unlike the layout of other Han royal tombs, the coffin was placed in one of the side chambers rather than in the rear chamber, which normally resembles the bedroom of the king.

Although the tomb was unfinished and extensively robbed at some time during the Wang Mang interregnum (AD 8–23), it contained more than 2,000 remarkable objects, including a jade suit and a jade coffin, each representing the finest example of its kind. It also yielded a wide range of other jade objects of high craftsmanship, 200 seals and over 100,000 coins, as well as bronze vessels, weapons and other miscellaneous objects.

Judging from the tomb structure, the funerary objects and the fact that the tomb was unfinished, the owner could be the second King of Chu, Liu Ying (referred to as Liu Yingke in some historical records) or the third King of Chu, Liu Wu. In this case, the tomb would have been sealed between 175 and 154 BC. Some scholars argue that Liu Wu was buried in an unfinished tomb because he committed suicide after the failure of his rebellion. However, there is no convincing explanation as to why a rebelling king would be buried with the highest honours, which included wearing a jade suit with gold threads and having terracotta armies guarding the tomb. The identification of the tomb owner remains unsolved.[3]

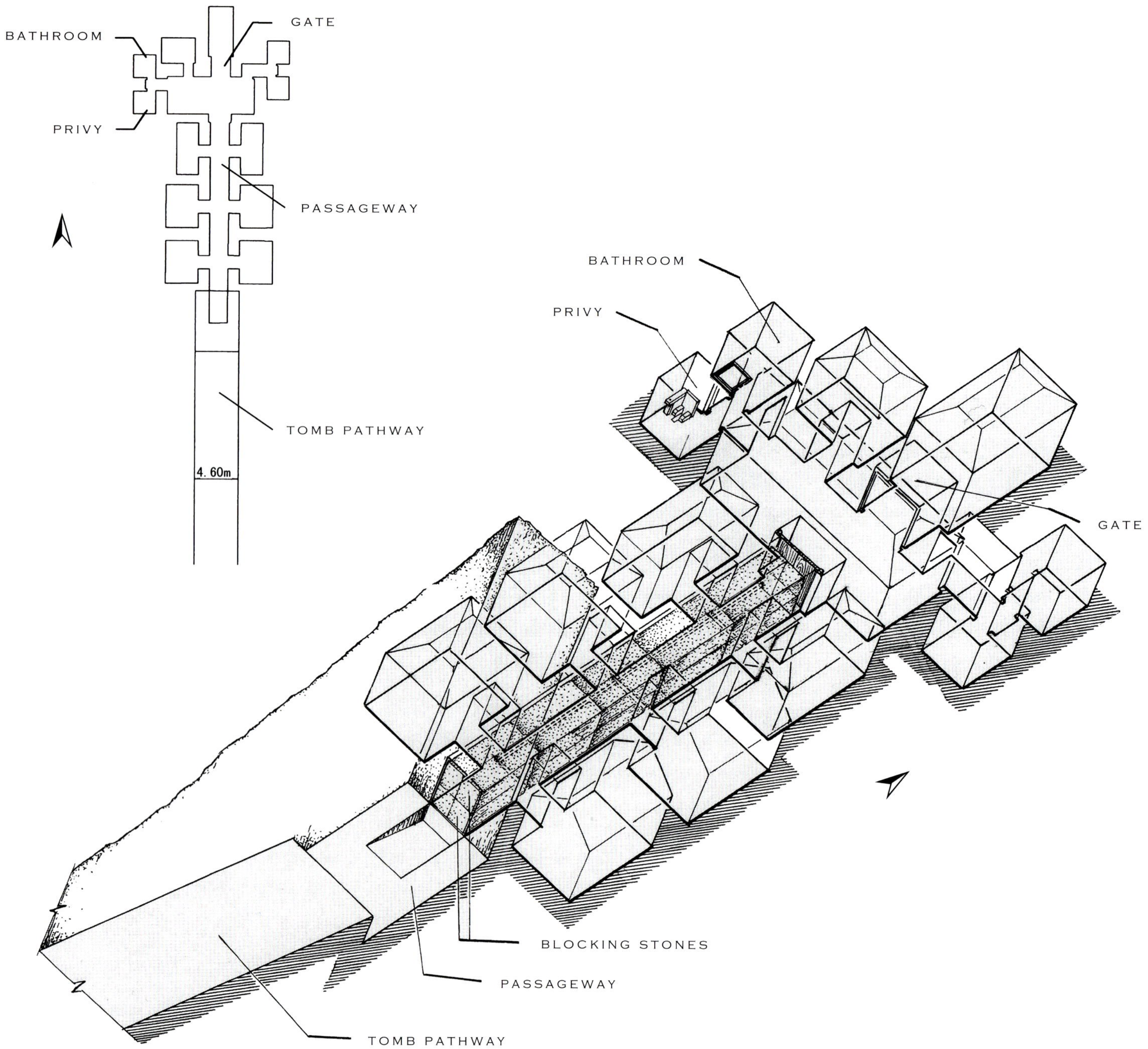

Perspective drawing of the King of Chu's tomb at Tuolanshan

THE KING OF CHU AND HIS QUEEN'S TOMBS AT TUOLANSHAN

The two tombs found on the southern flank of Tuolanshan hill are horizontal tombs cut into the rock and have a wide and long sloping pathway leading to the tomb gate. Similar structures can be seen at the King of Chu's tomb at Beidongshan. Distinctive features of the tombs include a great number of chambers resembling the rooms of a real palace, polished and painted interior surfaces and flat or gabled roofs of different shapes.[4]

Tomb No. 1 faces south and consists of an outer tomb pathway, an inner passage and thirteen chambers designed for specific functions. The tomb covers over 200 square metres. The privy, shown in this exhibition (cat. 114), is made of stone slabs and is most carefully designed, as if intended for use.

Tomb No. 2, also south facing but slightly smaller, has six chambers, an antechamber, a main burial chamber, a side chamber, a privy and a bathroom.

Both tombs were extensively robbed in antiquity. No jade suit was found. Some of the most interesting surviving objects are ceramic figures, which consist of male officials and attendants, as well as female dancers and musicians. These colourful figures are depicted gracefully and fluidly with simple lines. A group of ceramic dancers and musicians, representing some of the most successful attempts at capturing movement during this period, are displayed in this exhibition (cat. 30).

The location, sizes and structures of the tombs, together with their burial objects, help identify tomb No. 1 as a king's tomb and No. 2 as his queen's tomb. During the Han period, couples from royal families and the upper class were usually buried in separate tombs but in the same cemetery.

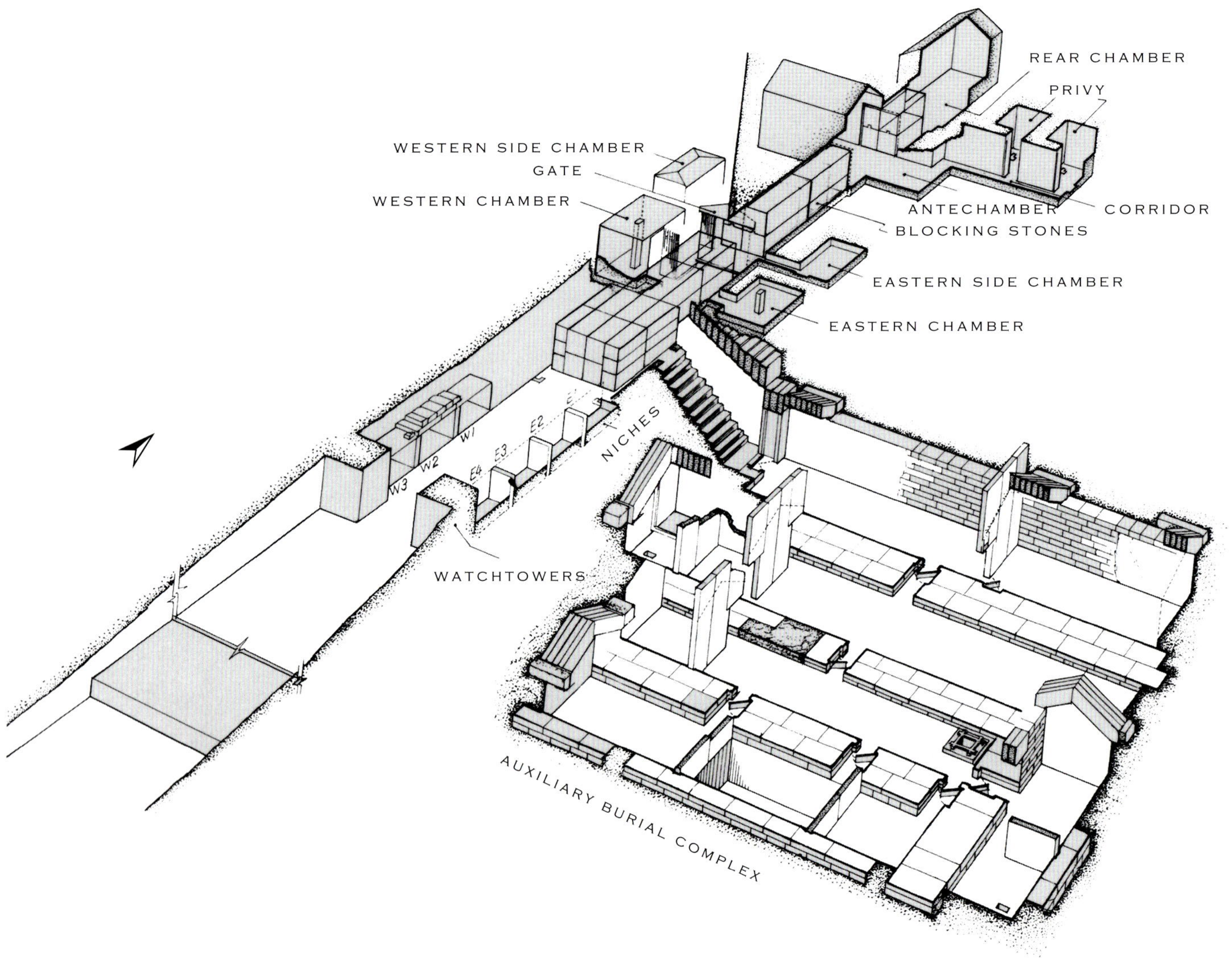

Perspective drawing of the King of Chu's tomb at Beidongshan

THE KING OF CHU'S TOMB AT BEIDONGSHAN

The King of Chu's tomb at Beidongshan was excavated in 1986 in a village ten kilometres north of Xuzhou city in Jiangsu Province. Among the eight Western Han royal tomb sites that have been unearthed so far, this one has the most complex structure and the greatest number of chambers.

The tomb structure follows early Western Han burial practice and is built into the southern flank of the Beidongshan hill. Covering a total area of 350 square metres, it is composed of a long sloping tomb pathway, a main structure and an auxiliary burial complex. There are seven wall niches and nineteen chambers. The tomb is placed in a precise north–south orientation. The tomb pathway is fifty-six metres long and three to four metres wide. Halfway along the pathway are two mounds of earth representing the watchtowers at the entrance of a palace, and beyond them are seven wall niches. The northern end of the pathway is sealed with huge blocking stones, each weighing around 8,000 kilograms.

The main tomb structure, resembling the residential section of a royal palace, consists of two chambers, two side chambers, a corridor, an antechamber, a main burial chamber and two privies. The whole section, including the privies, is painted with cinnabar, which contains a high level of mercury sulphide (HgS) and can be used as a preservative and disinfectant. According to the *Hanjiuyi* ('Ancient Rites of the Han Dynasty'), the First Emperor of the Qin dynasty used this material in his mausoleum, and this practice was then followed by the Han rulers.

The auxiliary structure is built 2.98 metres lower than the main section, comprising a total of eleven functional rooms in four rows: an arsenal and a storeroom in the first row; a separate bathroom and privy and a large entertainment room (46.5 m^2) in the second row; a patio containing a well, a fully equipped kitchen, a firewood store and a privy in the third row; another kitchen, a food preparation room and an ice cellar in the fourth row. The rooms are divided by walls and covered by a sloping roof of stone slabs.

Although the tomb has been plundered several times in the past, archaeologists have excavated a great number of objects. The robbers did not find the seven niches along the pathway. As a result, 224 painted ceramic figures were preserved intact (cat. 9). Another remarkable find of 70,000 or so half-*liang* coins scattered across the tomb testifies to the practice of burying money in large quantities, starting from the early Western Han period. Other important finds include eleven bronze seals, gold belt buckles and two glass cups. Based on the recovered tomb objects and the identifications of other royal tombs in Xuzhou, Beidongshan is believed to be the burial of Liu Dao, the fifth King of Chu in the Western Han period, who acceded to the throne in 150 BC and died in 129 BC.

THE KING OF CHU'S TOMB AT WONIUSHAN

The Han tomb site in Woniushan is located on the northern slope of the Woniu hill in the western suburbs of Xuzhou. The tomb consists of a tomb pathway, corridors, an antechamber, a rear chamber and a side chamber. The tomb pathway is shaped like an elongated trapezoid, which measures eighteen metres in length, two metres at the front end and one metre at the rear end. Apart from the rear end, which leads to the corridor and is level, the rest of the tomb pathway is on a slope that has a roughly fifteen-degree gradient.

The rear section of the pathway leading to the corridor measures two metres in width and 1.8 metres in height. It is divided into two parts by the antechamber. The front part is 2.4 metres long and the rear part is 9.4 metres long. The corridor is carefully chiselled out; the walls are smooth and the corners are sharp. The corridor runs through the eastern side of the antechamber, which is a rectangular room. It is 5.9 metres long from east to west and 3.5 metres wide from north to south. The ridge of the roof, positioned slightly to the south of the chamber, is oriented east to west and is 3.2 metres above ground. No burial goods were found in the antechamber. Judging from its position, the chamber might be for horses and chariots.

The rear chamber is located at the end of the corridor and is 6.5 metres long and 5.6 metres wide. The ridge of the roof runs north to south and is four metres above ground. The walls in this chamber are of different heights. The southern wall is slightly taller than the northern wall and shows natural cracks, which are reinforced by the addition of well-cut stone blocks. The floor is paved with slate. Judging by the number of ceramic roof tiles found in the chamber, there would originally have been a wooden building with a tiled roof within the chamber. Since the wooden building collapsed and the tomb was looted, the ceramic roof tiles are scattered across the chamber and it is impossible to tell what the original architecture might have looked like. In the middle of the rear chamber are human bones, which have also been disturbed.

The side chamber is located to the north of the rear chamber. It has a doorway and is virtually square, measuring 4 metres in length and 3.8 metres in width. Drains ten centimetres wide and four centimetres deep are chiselled out of the ground; they interconnect and lead to the antechamber.

Because the tomb was looted, few objects were unearthed and those that remained were mostly damaged. The objects recovered fall into two categories: architectural materials and burial goods. Architectural materials include flat tiles, curved tiles and eave tiles, which were all found in the rear chamber. The flat tiles are 37 cm long and 30–33 cm wide; the curved 57 cm by 15 cm. The surfaces of the tiles are covered with cord-like and diamond-shaped patterns. The eave tiles are all decorated with patterns of dragons and clouds. Burial goods include a pottery basin, a pigpen and glazed vessels, as well as bronze ornaments and coins. An iron weapon, a jade arc-shaped pendant, a jade seal without inscriptions, a small jade ring and a mortar were also found.

More than a hundred coins with the inscription *daquan wushi* and one coin with the inscription *dabu huangqian* were discovered at the Woniushan Han tomb and date the tomb perhaps to the Wang Mang period (r. AD 9–23). The tomb is a large-scale horizontal cave carved out of rock and was probably made for a king or queen. A jade arc-shaped pendant, which is usually found as part of a set of jade ornaments, was discovered. Judging from the excavations at tomb No. 2 at Dongdongshan, tomb No. 1 at Hanshan and tomb No. 2 at Sushantou, such arc-shaped pendants usually indicate female occupants. In addition, Woniushan has two peaks, the western being the main one. Since the tomb is located beneath the eastern peak, it might belong to the queen of the twelfth Chu king, Liu Yu, who succeeded to the throne in the year 2 BC. In the first year of the Xin dynasty (AD 9–23) his title was reduced from king to duke. The next year, the Chu state came under the rule of Xin.

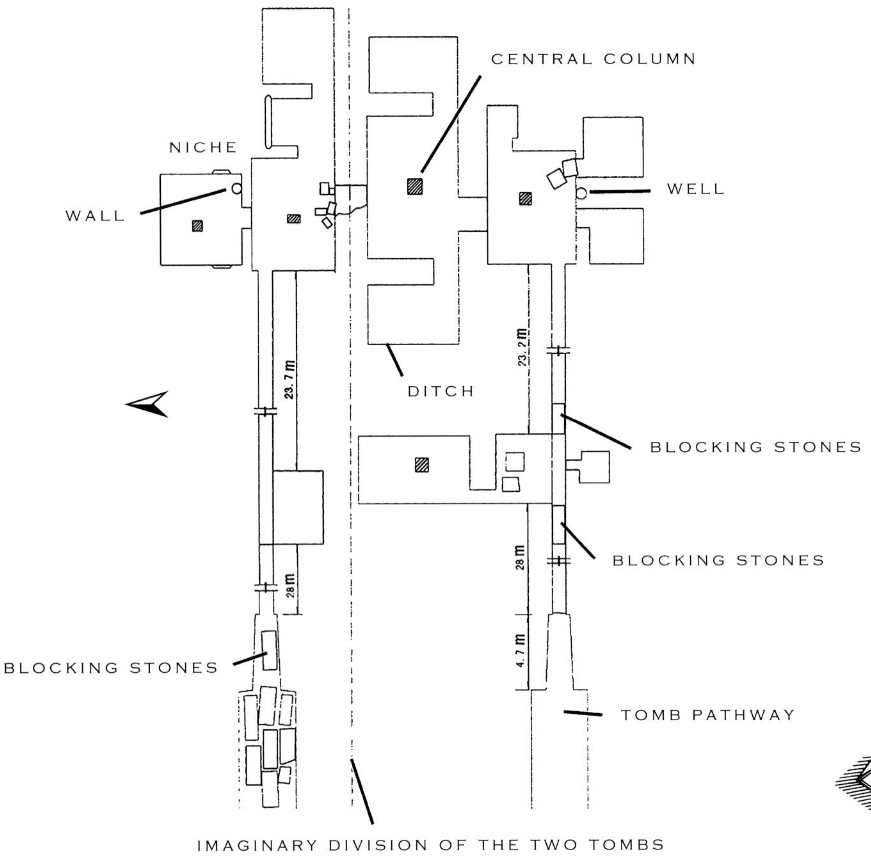

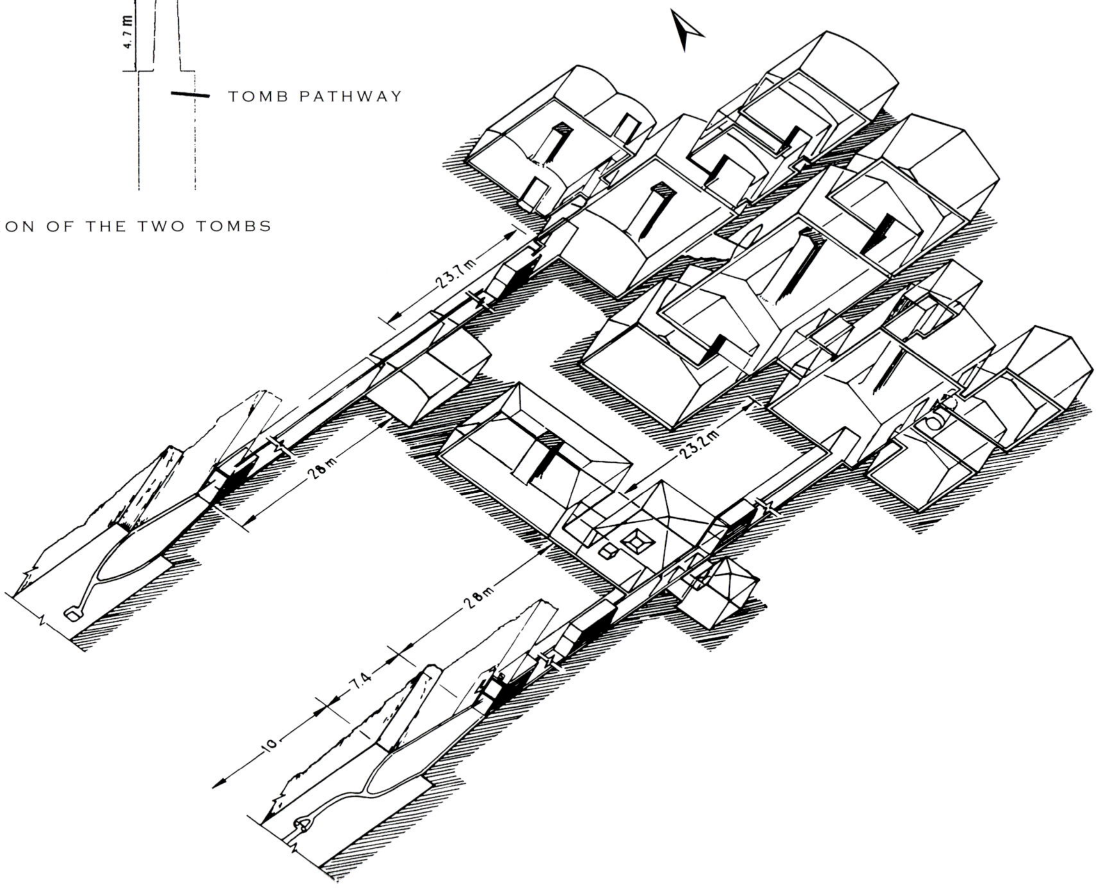

Perspective drawing of the sixth King of Chu and his queen's tombs at Guishan

THE SIXTH KING OF CHU AND HIS QUEEN'S TOMBS AT GUISHAN

Two connected tombs for a King of Chu and his queen were discovered in 1972 on the western hillside of Guishan, part of an ancient battlefield at Jiulishan. Archaeological excavations between 1972 and 1992 revealed one of the largest 'underground palaces' of a Chu king in Xuzhou, covering a total area of 500 square metres.

The tombs were placed in an east–west orientation. Fourteen metres away from each other, they have similar designs, comprising a tomb pathway, an inner passageway and chambers. A drainage ditch was found at the end of the outer passage, which extends to the inside, to drain off rainwater. The eastern end of the passage was sealed with twenty-six blocking stones in two rows. The blocking stones are well polished and marked with their size and location in red at one end. One of them has a painting of an animated tiger looking backwards[5].

The king's tomb in the south has ten chambers and the queen's in the north five. The two tombs are parallel and connected by a corridor as if to allow the royal couple to reunite in the afterlife. Excavation also revealed the traces of timber structures and tile roofs inside most of the chambers.

Like most other royal tombs of the Han period in Xuzhou, this site did not escape the attention of tomb robbers. Fortunately, a silver seal with a turtle knob that had been removed from the tomb (cat. 25) was recovered during a local cultural heritage survey in the 1980s. Its inscription *Liu Zhu* reveals that the tomb belonged to the sixth King of Chu, who reigned 128 to 117 BC. Excavated objects include earthenware figures, iron fittings for chariots and horses, along with bronze weapons. According to the excavators, the most significant finds were the inscriptions on the stone blocks, which provide information for research on the early form of Chinese characters.[6]

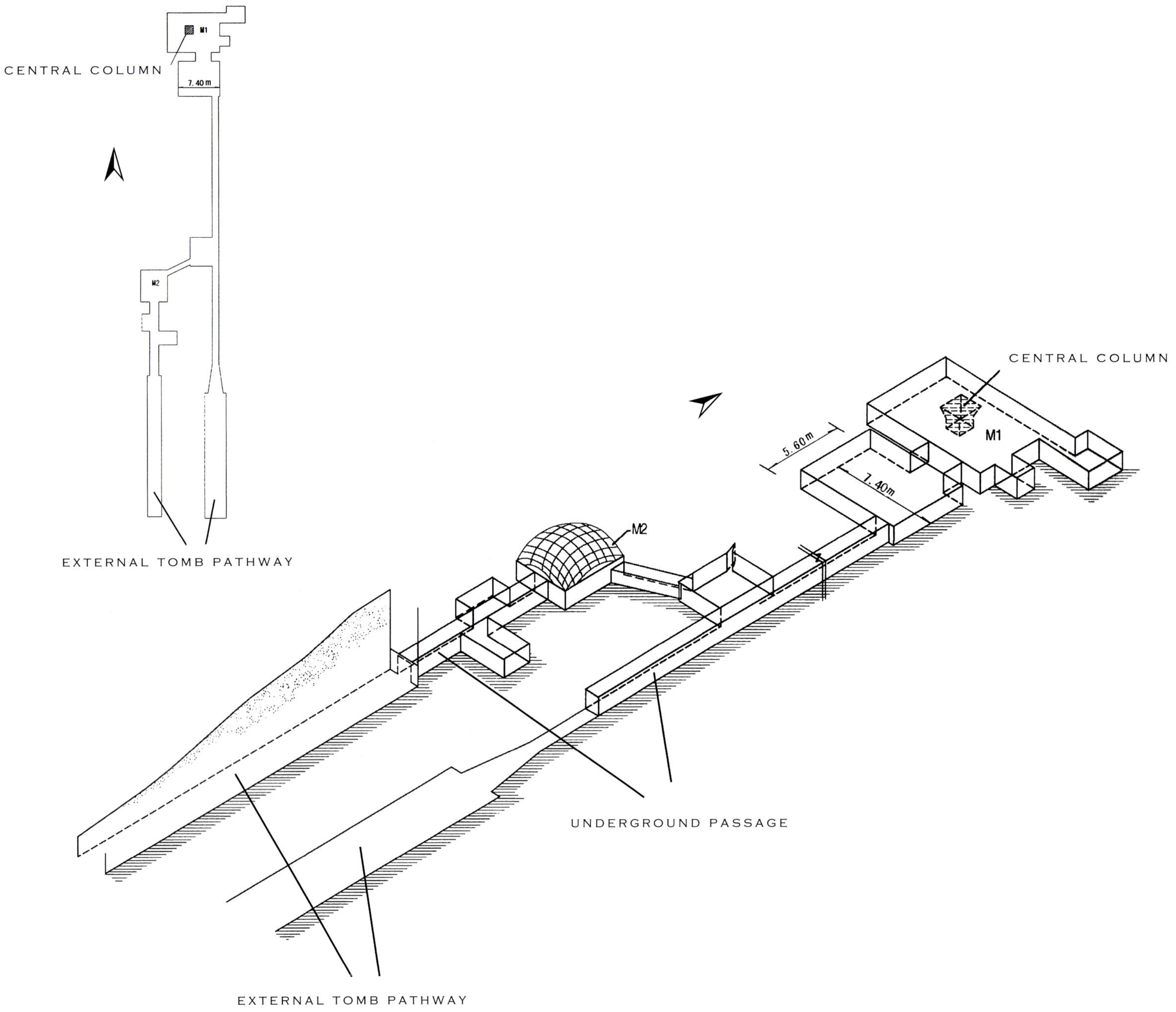

Perspective drawing of the King of Chu and his queen's tombs at Nandongshan

THE KING OF CHU AND HIS QUEEN'S TOMBS AT NANDONGSHAN

Located south of Xuzhou, Nandongshan is a small hill 128.3 metres above sea level. The tombs of a Chu king and his queen were constructed here by cutting into the southern slope of the hill. Graffiti bearing the reign title *Zhida* (AD 1308–11) appears on the western wall of one of the tomb passageways, which suggests that the tombs had probably been looted in the *Zhida* reign of the Yuan dynasty of those dates.

The tombs of the Chu king and queen are connected by a passageway. Both tombs face south and each has a long tomb pathway. Of all Chu kings' tombs of the Western Han period in Xuzhou, this one is located at the highest elevation. Judging from its scale and layout, the tomb site probably belongs to a king and his queen who were active in the mid- to late Western Han period.

Tomb M1 runs along the eastern side of the site. Its scale is larger and should indicate the king's tomb. The tomb consists of an external pathway leading to an underground passageway and the tomb chambers. Its total length reaches over eighty metres. Apart from a small chamber on the western side of the underground passageway, all other chambers, including an antechamber, a main chamber and two side chambers on the eastern side of the main chamber, are located at the end of the passageway. The ceiling of each chamber is slightly domed. Within the main chamber, a stone column, carved out of the hill, stands in the middle. North of the column is a pool and a drainage system.

Tomb M2, located to the west of the king's tomb, almost certainly belonged to his queen. It also consists of an external pathway, short underground passageway and three chambers. Its scale is much smaller than that of the king's tomb. Apart from the side chambers on each side of the underground passageway, there is only one main chamber, which has two unique features. First, the ceiling is in the form of a dome. Second, at the north-eastern corner of the chamber a passageway, 0.8 metres above ground, leads to the side chamber located on the western underground passage of Tomb M1.

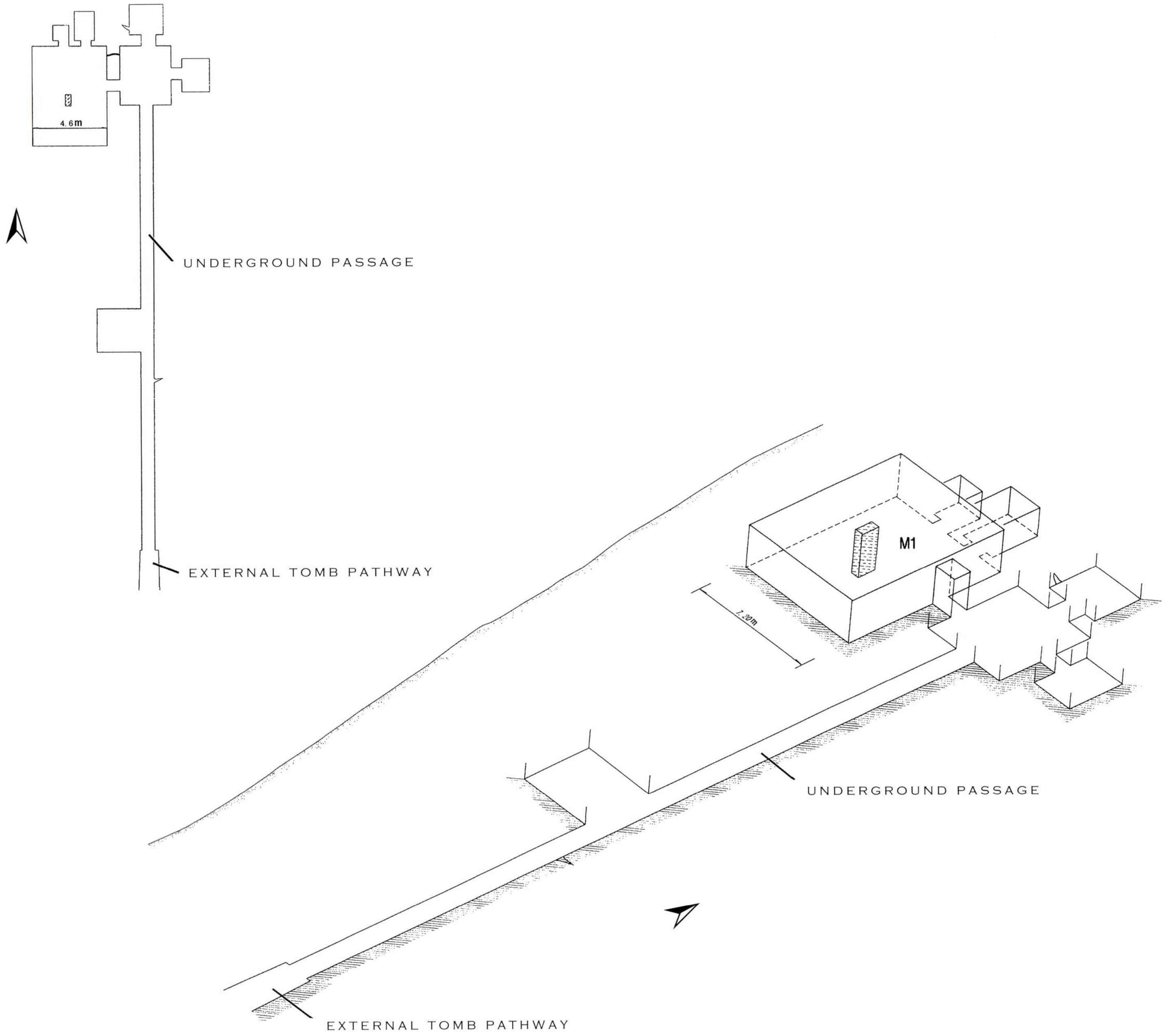

Perspective drawing of the King of Chu's tomb (M1) at Dongdongshan

THE KING OF CHU AND HIS CONSORTS' TOMBS AT DONGDONGSHAN

Two tombs (M1, M2) were discovered under a limestone quarry in 1982 at Dongdongshan. A third tomb (M3) was found and excavated in 1997. The three tombs, from south to north M3, M1 and M2, are roughly parallel and were ten metres apart.

Tomb M1, the largest of the three, was recorded as *Xianren dong* (Cave of Immortals) in the local gazetteer of Pengcheng compiled during the Ming dynasty (AD 1437). The west-facing tomb consists of a 4.2 metre long sloping tomb pathway, a 46 metre long inner passage and seven chambers, covering a total area of 210 square metres. Three Buddhist reliefs, thought to be carved early in the Ming dynasty, were found on the walls of the inner passage, proof that tomb was extensively plundered during the Yuan and Ming periods. The few surviving objects include two bronze vessels, two jade discs, a jade sword ornament and two jade suit plaques. The discovery of a jade suit fragment indicates that this tomb belonged to a King of Chu.

Tomb M2 is located about ten metres north of M1 and has yielded many more finds, consisting of 167 objects. The outer pathway was destroyed during quarrying, but the inner passage and the chamber survived. Interesting finds include bronze objects with the inscription *Mingguanggong* (Mingguang Palace). Historical records state that the Mingguang Palace was built by Emperor Wu around 101 BC and renamed by Wang Mang at the beginning of his reign (AD 9). Combined with the typology of the objects, this allows the tomb to be dated within the mid- to late Western Han period. Since no seal or other attributable objects have been found, the occupant of the tomb is still unidentified.[7]

The unfinished Tomb M3 is 10 metres south of M1 and has no chamber. The burial objects are mainly female accessories such as mirrors, lacquer boxes and bronze brushes. It is thought to be the tomb of another consort of the king.

THE KING OF CHU AND HIS QUEEN'S TOMBS AT CHUWANGSHAN

The Chuwangshan tombs are located within the vicinity of Dapeng town in the Tongshan district of Xuzhou. Several historical records refer to the tombs, as do poems by the Song dynasty scholar Su Shi. According to these texts, the name of the hill on which the tombs are located has been changed many times in history. Chuwangshan has also been known as Tongxiaoshan, Zhetushan and Bawangshan.

The *Houhanshu* states: 'There is a hill twenty *li* west of Pengcheng. On the northern side of the hill is the tomb of the first King of Chu. The *Weishu* ['Book of Wei'] also mentions that: "The tomb of the first King of Chu is in Pengcheng."' In the *Shuijingzhu* ('Commentary on the Waterways Classic') it is recorded that 'The Di River passes by the northern side of Tongxiaoshan. On the northern slope of the hill, there is the tomb of the first King of Chu. It has a dome and a square foundation. The tomb is constructed by layering rocks on top of each other. It measures more than ten *zhang* in height. The width is about a hundred steps. The site contains more than ten burial mounds all made of stone.' *Houhanshu* and *Shuijingzhu* were written only three to four hundred years after the death of the first Chu king, Liu Jiao. As a result, some scholars believe that tomb No. 1 at Chuwangshan could be his burial site.

There are four large mounds on the northern slope of Chuwangshan. Tomb No. 1 is located on the north-western part of the hill and measures fifty metres in height. The mound blends well with the peak of Chuwangshan. Judging from its impressive presence, it should be the king's tomb. South of tomb No. 1 is an escape canal measuring 46 metres long and 3.8–4.2 metres wide. Tomb No. 2 is located north of tomb No. 1. The shape of the mound is similar to the back of a lute. Of all the tombs, it has the greatest bulk and could be the queen's burial place. Tomb No. 3 is located north-east of tombs 1 and 2. Tomb No. 4 is positioned north-east of tomb No. 3. It is the furthest from tomb No. 1 and is separated from the other tombs by a peak. The mounds of tombs 3 and 4 are large, which indicates that the two tombs are quite substantial. They may belong to relatives or close officials of the Chu king.

The four tombs have not yet been excavated. In 1956 the Jiangsu provincial government listed Chuwangshan as a provincial heritage site. In 1996 it became a national heritage site.

THE QUEEN OF CHU AT YANGGUISHAN

Yangguishan, located just north to Shizishan, is a separate hill and is covered with a large mound of tamped earth. Some pottery shards can be seen on the surface. From 2004 to 2005, architectural remains of a tomb were excavated from the eastern side of the hill. Nearby, nearly twenty burial pits were found containing figures of soldiers, ceramic vessels, iron objects, bronze bathing utensils and bronze cooking vessels.

In 2004, the Han tomb at Yangguishan was looted. According to the condition of the ground surface and the state of the tomb interior, it was determined that the tomb is a horizontal cave carved out of the rock. The south-oriented tomb faces the Han tomb at Shizishan and the tomb pathway is made of tamped earth.

The layout of the Han tomb at Yangguishan is quite different from that at Shizishan, resembling instead the plan of the tomb at Tuolanshan: both have a symmetrical layout consisting of a tomb pathway, corridors, an antechamber and a rear chamber. The entire tomb was carefully chiselled out of the rock. The corners are sharp and the surfaces of walls are smooth. Fine clay was applied to the walls, followed by a layer of paint. Apart from the antechamber and the rear chamber, which are painted with brown and red colours, the walls are painted brown. The tomb is installed with various devices to prevent looting. For example, the tomb pathway is filled with smooth boulders and all chambers are fitted with wooden doors with self-locking devices. The tomb also contained a privy and a bathroom.

Shizishan and Yangguishan are very close to each other and belong to the same tomb complex. Since the Shizhishan Han tomb is a Chu king's burial site, it is very likely that the Han tomb at Yangguishan is a queen's tomb.

NOTES

1 Archaeologists have used remote sensing techniques to confirm that there is a consort's tomb at Yangguishan. It has not yet been excavated, but the survey shows that the tomb has also been plundered. There are several sacrificial burials and terracotta warrior and horse pits on the hill. Excavations of these sacrificial pits have unearthed some interesting objects, including bronze tripods shown in this exhibition (cat. 54).

2 See *Dongnan wenhua* 1992, issues 3 and 4. There are two sacrificial tombs at Xiuqiushan, containing pottery, jade objects, bronze mirrors and seals. The most interesting objects include a silver seal with the inscription *Xue Wu Shang*, which is probably the name of the tomb occupant.

3 See The Shizishan Archaeological Excavation Report in *Wenwu* 1998.8. For discussions on the identification of this tomb see Song 2000; Geng 2000; Liang 2001.

4 Liang 2001.

5 *Kaogu* 1997.2, p. 41.

6 *Kaogu* 1997.2, p. 45.

7 Some scholars have suggested that the tomb occupant could be Liu Yanshou, the eighth generation King of Chu from Liu Jiao's clan, based on the evolution of tomb structure in the Western Han dynasty; Liang 2001.

BIBLIOGRAPHY

An, Jiayao 1984
An, Jiayao, 'Zhongguo zaoqi de boli qimin 中國早期的玻璃器皿'. *Kaogu Xuebao*考古學報, 1984.4, pp. 413–48.
Bagley 1995
Bagley, Robert, 'What the Bronzes from Hunyuan Tell Us about the Foundry at Houma'. *Orientations*, January 1995, pp. 46–54.
Baihutong shu zheng
Baihutong shu zheng 白虎通書證. Comp. Ban Gu 班固 (AD 32–92) et al., annotated Wu Zeyu 吳則虞. Beijing, 1994.
Baopuzi
Ge, Hong (葛洪 283–343), *Baopuzi neipian jiaoshi*.抱朴子內篇校釋, Wang Ming王明 (ed.). Beijing, 1980.
Barbieri-Low 2001
Barbieri-Low, Anthony. 'Roman Themes in a Group of Eastern Han Lacquer Vessels'. *Orientations*, May 2001, pp. 52–8.
Beijing 1957
Changsha fajue baogao 長沙發掘報告. Beijing, 1957.
Beijing 1973
Changsha Mawangdui yihao Han mu 長沙馬王堆一號漢墓, 2 vols. Beijing, 1973.
Beijing 1976
A Selection of Archaeological Finds from the People's Republic of China. Beijing, 1976.
Beijing 1980
Mancheng Han mu fajue baogao, 滿城漢墓發掘報告, 2 vols. Beijing, 1980.
Beijing 1981a
Yunmeng Shuihudi Qin Mu 雲夢睡虎地秦墓. Beijing, 1981.
Beijing 1981b
Guangzhou Han mu 廣州漢墓. Beijing, 1981.
Beijing 1984
Jiangling Yutaishan Chu mu 江陵雨台山楚墓. Beijing, 1984.
Beijing 1985
Jiangling Mashan yihao Chu mu 江陵馬山一號楚墓. Beijing, 1985.
Beijing 1986a
E'erduosishi qingtongqi 鄂爾多斯式青銅器. Beijing, 1986.
Beijing 1986b
Xinyang Chu mu 信陽楚墓. Beijing, 1986.
Beijing 1988
Guangxi Guixian Luobowan Han mu 廣西貴縣羅泊灣漢墓. Beijing, 1988.
Beijing 1989
Zenghou Yi mu 曾侯乙墓, 2 vols. Beijing, 1989.
Beijing 1991
Xi *Han Nanyue wang mu* 西漢南越王墓, 2 vols. Beijing, 1991.
Beijing 1992
Treasures, 300 Best Excavated Antiques from China. Beijing, 1992.
Beijing 1993a
Zhongguo wenwu jinghua 中國文物精華. Beijing, 1993.
Beijing 1993b
Mixian Dahuting Han mu 密縣打虎亭漢墓. Beijing, 1993.
Beijing 1995
Cuomu, Zhanguo Zhongshanguo guowangzhimu 嚳墓一戰國中山國國王之墓, 2 vols. Beijing, 1995.
Beijing 1996
Jiangling Wangshan shazhong Chu mu 江陵望山沙冢楚墓. Beijing, 1996.
Beijing 1998a
Zhongguo qingtongqi quanji 中國青銅器全集. *Qin Han* 秦漢. Beijing, 1998.
Beijing 1998b
Qin shihuang ling tongchema fajue baogao 秦始皇陵銅車馬發掘報告. Beijing, 1998.
Beijing 2000
Jingzhou Gaotai Qin Han mu 荊州高台秦漢墓. Beijing, 2000.
Beijing 2001
Mangdangshan xi Han Liangwang mudi 芒碭山西漢梁王墓地. Beijing, 2001.
Beijing 2003
Xuzhou Beidongshan xi Han Chuwang mu 徐州北洞山西漢楚王墓. Beijing, 2003.
Beijing 2005
Da Han Chuwang, Xuzhou xi Han Chuwang lingmu wenwu jicui 大漢楚王: 徐州西漢楚王陵墓文物輯萃. Beijing, 2005.
Beijing 2007
Santai Qijiang yamu 三台郪江崖墓. Beijing, 2007.
Beijing 2010
Chinese Jades in Traditional Collections, 8 vols. Beijing, 2010.

Boardman 2010
Boardman, John, *The Relief Plaques of Eastern Eurasia and China, The 'Ordos' Bronzes'. Peter the Great's Treasure and their Kin*. Oxford, 2010.
Brashier 1997
Brashier, K. E. 'Han Thanatology and the Division of Souls'. *Early China*, 1997 (21), pp. 1–35.
Bunker 1988
Bunker, Emma, 'Charlotte C. and John C. Weber – Benefactors Extraordinary'. *Orientations*, May 1988, pp. 68–72.
Bunker 1993
Bunker, Emma. 'Gold in the Ancient Chinese World: A Cultural Puzzle', *Artibus Asiae*, vol. 53, 1993, 1–2, pp. 27–50.
Bunker 1997
Bunker, Emma, Trudy Kawami, Katheryn Linduff and Wu En. *Ancient Bronzes of the Eastern Eurasian Steppes from the Arthur M. Sackler Collection*. New York, 1997.
Cai 2003
Cai, Wanjin 蔡萬進, Yinwan Hanjian《yuanyan ernian riji》suo fanying de Handai lixiu zhidu 尹灣漢簡'元延二年日記'所反映的漢代曆休制度. *Study of Chinese History*, 2003.2, pp. 71–7.
Cao and Sun 1996
Cao, Zhezhi 曹者祉 and Sun, Binggen 孫秉根. *Zhongguo gudai yong* 中國古代俑. Shanghai, 1996.
Chang 1977
Chang, Kwang-chih (ed.). *Food in Chinese Culture: Anthropological and Historical Perspectives.* New Haven, 1977.
Chang and Guroff 2007
Chang, Claudia and Guroff, Katharine. *Of Gold and Grass: Nomads of Kazakhstan*. Almaty, 2007.
Cheng 1997
Cheng, Zhijuan 程志娟. 'Handai guiju jing yu liu bo 漢代規矩鏡與六博'. *Dongnan wenhua*, 1997.4, pp. 124–6.
Chongqing 2001
Han Yangling 汉阳陵. Chongqing, 2001.
Chuci jin zhu
Chuci jin zhu 楚辭今注. Tang Bingzheng 湯炳正 (ed.). Shanghai, 1997.
Ciarla 2005
Ciarla, Roberto (ed.). *The Eternal Army: The Terracotta Soldiers of the First Emperor.* Vercelli, 2005.
Cook 2006
Cook, Constance A. *Death in Ancient China: The Tale of One Man's Journey.* Leiden, 2006.
di Cosmo 2002
di Cosmo, Nicola. *Ancient China and its Enemies: The Rise of Nomadic Power in East Asian History*. Cambridge, 2002.
Cui 2002
Cui, Dayong 崔大庸. 'Luozhuang Han mu jiuhao peizangkeng chutu beifang caoyuan fengge maju shixi' 洛莊漢墓九號陪葬坑出土北方草原風格馬具試析. *Zhongguo lishi wenwu*, 2002.4, pp. 16–26.
Dewall 1964
Dewall, Magdalene von. *Pferd und Wagen im frühen China*. Bonn, 1964.
Dewar 1994
Dewar, Susan (ed.). *Bronze Mirrors from Ancient China*. Hong Kong, 1994.
Dongnan wenhua
Dongnan wenhua 東南文化. Nanjing, 1985–
Erickson 1992
Erickson, Susan. 'Boshanlu–Mountain Censers of the Western Han Period: A Typological and Iconographic Analysis'. *Archives of Asian Art*, vol. 45, 1992, pp. 6–28.
Falkenhausen 1994
Falkenhausen, Lothar von. 'Sources of Taoism: Reflections on Archaeological Indicators of Religious Change in Eastern Zhou China'. *Taoist Resources*, 1994, vol. 5, pp. 1–12.
Falkenhausen 2002
Falkenhausen, Lothar von. 'The Use and Significance of Ritual Bronzes in the Lingnan Region During the Eastern Zhou Period'. *Journal of East Asian Archaeology*, vol. 3, 2002, pp. 194–236.
Falkenhausen 2006
Falkenhausen, Lothar von. *Chinese Society in the Age of Confucius (1000–250 BC): The Archaeological Evidence*. Los Angeles, 2006.
Fengsu tongyi
Fengsu tongyi 風俗通譯, Ying Shao 應劭 (*c.*AD 140–*c.*206), Wu Shuping 吳樹平 (ed.). Tianjin, 1980.
Fong 1973
Fong, Chow. 'Ma-Wang-Tui: A Treasure-Trove from the Western Han Dynasty'. *Artibus Asiae* 35.1/2 (1973), pp. 5–14.
Francasso 1988
Francasso, Riccardo. 'Holy Mothers of Ancient China: A New Approach to the Hsi-wang-mu Problem'. *T'oung Pao*, vol. 74, 1988, pp. 1–46.
Fu 1986
Fu, Juyou 傅舉有. 'Lun Qin Han shiqi de boju, boxi jian ji bojuwen jin 論秦漢時期的博具、博戲兼及博局紋鏡', *Kaogu xuebao*, 1986. 1, pp. 21–42.
von Gall 1966
von Gall, Hubertus. *Die Paphlagonischen Felsgräber, Eine Studie zur Kleinasiatischen Kunstgeschichte*. Tübingen, 1966.
Geng 2000
Geng, Jianjun 耿建軍. 'Xuzhou shizishan xi Han chuwangmu kaizao shijian kaoxi 徐州獅子山西漢楚王墓開鑿時間考析'. Dongnan wenhua, 2000.3, pp. 73–7.
Graham 1989
Graham, Angus Charles. *Disputers of the Tao: Philosophical Argument in Ancient China*. La Salle, 1989.

Gu 2005
Gu, Fang 古方. *Zhongguo chutu yuqi quanji* 中國出土玉器全集, 15 vols. Beijing, 2005.
Guangzhou and Hong Kong 1983
Sui Gang Han mu chutu wenwu 穗港漢墓出土文物. Guangzhou and Hong Kong, 1983.
Guanzi jiaozhu
Guanzi jiaozhu 管子校注. Li Xiangfeng 黎翔鳳 (ed.). Beijing, 2004.
Gugong wenwu yuekan
Gugong wenwu yuekan 故宮文物月刊. Taipei, 1983–
Gunter and Jett 1992
Gunter, Ann C. and Jett, Paul. *Ancient Iranian Metalwork in the Arthur M. Sackler Gallery and the Freer Gallery of Art*. Washington, 1992.
Guo 2010
Guo, Qinghua. *The* mingqi *Pottery Buildings of Han Dynasty China 206 BC–AD 220*. Brighton, 2010, pp. 86–104.
Hanjiuyi buyi
Hanjiuyi buyi 漢舊儀補遺. Repr. Shanghai, 1930.
Hanshu
Hanshu 漢書. Comp. Ban Gu 班固 (AD 32–92), Ban Zhao 班昭 et al. Beijing, 1962.
Harper 1985
Harper, Donald. 'A Chinese Demonography of the Third Century BC', *Harvard Journal of Asiatic Studies*, 1985 (45), 2, pp. 459–98.
Harper 1999
Harper, Donald. 'Warring States, Qin, and Han Manuscripts Related to Natural Philosophy and The Occult'. *Cambridge History of China*, Michael Loewe and Edward Shaughnessy (eds). Cambridge, 1999, pp. 813–84.
Hawkes 1985
Hawkes, David. *The Songs of the South. An Ancient Chinese Anthology of Poems by Qu Yuan and other Poets*. London, 1985.
Hebei 1991–3
Zhongguo yuqi quanji 中國玉器全集, vol. 6 (Qing), 1991; vol. 1 (Neolithic), 1992; vol. 2 (Shang and W. Zhou), 1993; vol. 5 (Sui, Tang and Ming), 1993; vol. 3 (Spring and Autumn, Warring States period), 1993; vol. 4 (Qin, Han and Six Dynasties), 1993. Shijiazhuang: Hebei Chubanshe, 1991–3.
Hebei 1994
Zhongguo fangnei miji 中國房內祕籍. Hebei: Kexue Chubanshe, 1994.
Henan 2000
Zhongguo meishu fenlei quanji 中國美術分類全集, *Zhongguo huaxiangshi quanji* 中國畫像石全集, 8 vols. Henan, 2000.
Hong Kong 1996
Qilu wenhua-dongfang sixiang de yaolan 齊魯文化—東方思想的搖籃. Hong Kong, 1996.
Houhanshu
Houhanshu 後漢書. Comp. Fan Ye 范曄 (AD 398–446). Beijing, 1965.
Huainan wanbishu
Huainan wanbishu 淮南萬畢術, attributed to Liu An 劉安 (*c*.179–122 BC). See *Congshu jicheng chubian* 叢書集成初編. Hunan, 1939.
Huainanzi honglie jijie
Huainanzi honglie jijie 淮南子鴻烈集解, Liu Wendian 劉文典 (ed.). Taipei, 1992.
Huang 1996
Huang, Zhanyue 黃展岳. 'The "Animal Style" Design Objects Unearthed from Guangdong and Guangxi Provinces 關於兩廣出土北方動物紋牌飾問題.' *Kaogu and Wenwu*, 1996, 2, pp. 55–60.
Hubei 1991
Baoshan Chu jian 包山楚簡. Hubei, 1991.
Hucker 1985
Hucker, Charles O. *A Dictionary of Official Titles in Imperial China*. Stanford, 1985.
Hulsewé 1978
Hulsewé, A. F. P. 'The Ch'in Documents Discovered in Hupei in 1975'. *T'oung Pao*, Second Series, vol. 64, 4/5 (1978), pp. 175–217, 338.
Hulsewé 1979
Hulsewé, A. F. P. *China in Central Asia, the Early Stage, 125 BC–AD 23: An Annotated Translation of Chapters 61 and 96 of the History of the Former Han Dynasty*'. Leiden, 1979.
Jacobson 1984
Jacobson, Esther. 'The Stag with Bird-Headed Antler Tines: A Study in Image Transformation and Meaning'. *Bulletin of the Museum of Far Eastern Antiquities*, vol. 56, 1984, pp. 113–80.
Jacobson 1985
Jacobson, Esther. 'A Reconsideration of the Origins of Chinese Landscape Representation'. *Bulletin of the Museum of Far Eastern Antiquities*, vol. 57, 1985, pp. 133–80.
Jianghan kaogu
Jianghan kaogu 江漢考古. Hubei, 1980–
Jones 1982
Jones, Owen. *The Grammar of Ornament, Illustrated by Examples from Various Styles of Ornament*. London, 1856 (repr. 1982).
Kaogu
Kaogu 考古 (*Kaogu tongxun* 考古通訊, 1955–8). Beijing: Kexue chubanshe, 1959–
Kaogutu
Kaogutu 考古圖. Lü Dalin 呂大臨 (*c*.1092). Repr. Yizhengtang, 1752.
Kaogu xuebao
Kaogu xuebao 考古學報. Beijing: Kexue chubanshe, 1951-
Kaoguxue jikan
Kaoguxue jikan 考古學集刊. Beijing: Zhongguo shehui kexue chubanshe, 1981–
Kaogu yu wenwu
Kaogu yu wenwu 考古與文物. Xi'an: Shaanxi Renmin chubanshe, 1980–

Keightley 1987
Keightley, David N. 'The Quest for Eternity in Ancient China: The Dead, their Gifts, their Names'. *Ancient Mortuary Traditions of China; Papers on Chinese Ceramic Funerary Sculpture*, 1987, pp. 12–24.
Knauer 2006
Knauer, Elfriede. 'The Queen Mother of the West: A Study of the Influence of Western Prototypes on the Iconography of the Taoist Deity'. *Mair*, 2006, pp. 62–115.
Lai 2002
Lai, Guolong. 'The Baoshan Tomb: Religious Transitions in Art, Ritual, and Text during the Warring States Period (480–221 BC)' (PhD dissertation, University of California). Los Angeles, 2002.
Lam 1991
Lam, Peter (ed.). *Jades from the Tomb of the King of Nanyue*. Hong Kong, 1991.
Laufer 1914
Laufer, Berthold. *Chinese Clay Figures: Part 1 – Prolegomena on the History of Defensive Armor*. Chicago, 1914.
Ledderose 2000
Ledderose, Lothar. *Ten Thousand Things – Module and Mass Production in Chinese Art*. Princeton, 2000.
Ledderose and Schlombs 1990
Ledderose, Lothar, and Adele Schlombs (eds). *Jenseits der grossen Mauer – der Erste Kaiser und seine Terracotta-Armee*. Munich, 1990.
Lewis 2006
Lewis, Mark E. *The Construction of Space in Early China*. Albany, 2006, pp. 119–30.
Lewis 2007
Lewis, Mark E. *The Early Chinese Empires, Qin and Han*. Cambridge, MA. and London, 2007.
Li 1990
Li, Yinde 李銀德. 'The Underground Palace of a Chu Prince at Beidongshan'. *Orientations* 1990.10, pp. 57–61.
Li 1998
Li, Jian, et al. (eds). *Eternal China, Splendours from the First Dynasties*. Dayton, 1998.
Li 2005
Li, Yinde 李銀德. Xuzhou xi Han Chuwang lingmu kaogu de faxian yu shouhuo 徐州西漢楚王陵墓考古的發現與收獲. *Kings of Chu in Han Dynasty: A Collection from Xuzhou Kings of Chu Tombs*. Beijing, 2005, pp. 15–21.
Li 2006
Li, Feng. *Landscape and Power in Early China, The Crisis and Fall of the Western Zou 1045–771 BC*. Cambridge, 2006.
Liang 2001
Liang, Yong 梁勇. 'Cong xi Han Chuwang mu de jianzhu jiegou kan Chuwang mu de pailie shunxu 從西漢楚王墓的建築結構看楚王墓的排列順序'. Wenwu 文物, 2001.10, pp. 71–84.
Liji jijie
Liji jijie 禮記集解. Sun Xidan 孫希旦 (ed.). Beijing, 1995.
Lin 2007
Lin, James C. S. 'Armour for the Afterlife'. In Portal 2007, pp. 180–91.
Linduff 1997
Linduff, Katheryn. 'An Archaeological Overview'. In Bunker 1997, pp. 18–98.
Litvinskij and Pičkjan 2002
Litvinskij, Boris and Pičkjan, Igor. *Taxt-i Sangīn, Der Oxus-Temple, Grabungsbefund, Stratigraphie und Architektur*. Mainz, 2002.
Liu 1994
Liu, Lexian 劉樂賢. *Shuihudi Qinjian rishu yanjiu* 睡虎地秦簡日書研究. Taipei, 1994.
Liu 2009
Liu, Yunhui 劉雲輝. *Shaanxi chutu Handai yuqi* 陝西出土漢代玉器. Beijing, 2009.
Loewe 1979
Loewe, Michael. *Ways to Paradise: The Chinese Quest for Immortality*. London, 1979.
Mackenzie 2004
Mackenzie, Colin. 'Liubo: The Five-Hundred-Year Craze'. *Asian Games: The Art of Contest*, Colin MacKenzie and Irving Finkel (eds). New York, 2004, pp. 112–25.
Mair 2006
Mair, Victor (ed.). *Contact and Exchange in the Ancient World*. Honolulu, 2006.
Mao shi zhengyi
Mao shi zhengyi 毛詩正義, Shisanjing zhushu 十三經注疏 (ed.). Collated by Ruan Yuan 阮元 (1764–1849). Rprt. Taizhong: Landeng, n.d.
Margon 1949
Margon, H. 'Working in the Ancient World'. *American Journal of Archaeology*, 1949, vol. LIII, no. 2, pp. 93–125.
Melikian 1993
Melikian-Chirvani, Souren. 'The International Achaemenid Style'. *Bulletin of the Asia Institute* 7, 1993, 111–30.
Michaelson 2007
Michaelson, Carol. 'Qin Gold and Jade'. In Portal 2007, pp. 94–103.
Miho Museum 2002
Miho Museum, *Treasures of Ancient Bactria*. Miho, 2002.
Muscarella 1988
Muscarella, Oscar White. *Bronze and Iron – Ancient Near Eastern Artifacts in the Metropolitan Museum of Art*. New York, 1988.
Nakano 1994
Nakano, Toru. 'Ancient Chinese Bronze Mirrors'. In Dewar 1994, pp. 9–49.
Needham 1974
Needham, Joseph. *Science and Civilisation in China*, vol. 5, part 2, section 33. Cambridge, 1974.
Nickel 1998
Nickel, Lukas. 'Das steinerne Grab des Herrschers von Nan Yue'. In Prüch 1998, pp. 54–69.
Nickel 2011
Nickel, Lukas. *Gräber der Han-Zeit in Luoyang*. Stuttgart, 2011.

Nickel 2012
Nickel, Lukas. 'The Nanyue Silver Box'. *Arts of Asia*. Hong Kong, 2012 (forthcoming)
Nylan and Loewe 2010
Nylan, Michael and Loewe, Michael. *China's Early Empires, A Re-appraisal*. Cambridge, 2010.
Oddy 1991
Oddy, Andrew. 'Gilding: An Outline of the Technological History of the Plating of Gold onto Silver and Copper in the Old World'. *Endeavour*, New Series 15. London, 1991, pp. 29–33.
Özgen and Öztürk 1996
Özgen, Iknur and Öztürk, Jean. *Heritage Recovered: The Lydian Treasure*. Istanbul, 1996.
Pirazzoli-t'Serstevens 1990
Pirazzoli-t'Serstevens, Michèle. 'Ateliers, patronage et collections princières en Chine à l'époque Han'. *Comptes rendus de l'Académie des Inscriptions et Belles-Lettres*, vol. 134, no 2, 1990, pp. 521–36.
Pirazzoli-t'Serstevens 1991
Pirazzoli-t'Serstevens, Michèle. 'The Art of Dining in the Han Period: Food Vessels from Tomb No. 1 at Mawangdui'. *Food and Foodways* 4, 1991, pp. 209–19.
Pirazzoli-t'Serstevens 2010
Pirazzoli-t'Serstevens, Michèle. 'Two Eastern Han Sites: Dahuting and Houshiguo'. *China's Early Empires: A Re-appraisal*, Michael Nylan and Michael Loewe (eds). Cambridge, 2010.
Pitschikjan 1992
Pitschikjan, Igor. *Oxos-Schatz und Oxos-Tempel, Achämenidische Kunst in Mittelasien*. Berlin, 1992.
Portal 2007
Portal, Jane (ed.). *The First Emperor, China's Terracotta Army*. London, 2007.
Prüch 1998
Prüch, Margaret, with Stephan von der Schulenburg (eds). *Schätze für König Zhao Mo – Das Grab von Nan Yue*. Heidelberg, 1998.
Psarras 2003
Psarras, Sophia-Karen. 'Han and Xiongnu: A Reexamination of Cultural and Political Relations'. *Monumenta Serica*, vol 51, no. 1, 2003, pp. 55–236.
Rawson 1984
Rawson, Jessica. *Chinese Ornament: The Lotus and the Dragon*. London, 1984.
Rawson 1995
Rawson, Jessica. *Chinese Jade from the Neolithic to the Qing*. London, 1995.
Rawson 1998
Rawson, Jessica. 'Transformed into Jade: Changes in Material in the Warring States, Qin and Han Periods'. *East Asian Jade: Symbol of Excellence*. The Chinese University of Hong Kong, 1998, vol. 2, pp. 125-136.
Rawson 1999
Rawson, Jessica. 'Eternal Palaces of the Western Han: A New View of the Universe'. *Artibus Asiae*, vol. 59, no. 1/2, 1999, pp. 5–58.
Rawson 2006a
Rawson, Jessica. 'The Chinese Hill Censer, *boshanlu*: a Note on Origins, Influences and Meanings'. *Arts Asiatiques, Volume en homage à Madame Michèle Pirazzoli t'Serstevens*, vol. 61, 2006, pp. 75–86.
Rawson 2006b
Rawson, Jessica. 'Ornament as System: Chinese Bird-and-Flower Design'. *The Burlington Magazine*, vol. 148, June 2006, pp. 380–9.
Rawson 2007
Rawson, Jessica. 'The First Emperor's Tomb: The Afterlife Universe'. In Portal 2007, pp. 114–51.
Reeder 1999
Reeder, Ellen. *Scythian Gold: Treasures from Ancient Ukraine*. New York, 1999.
Ren 1997
Ren Xianghong 任相宏. 'Shuangrushan yihao Hanmu muzhu kaolue 雙乳山一號漢墓墓主考略'. *Kaogu*, 1997.3, pp. 10–15.
Riegl 1992
Riegl, Alois. *Problems of Style, Foundations for a History of Ornament* (trans. Evelyn Kain), Princeton, 1992.
Rudenko 1969
Rudenko, Sergei. *Die Kultur der Hsiung-nu und die Hügelgräber von Noin Ula*. Bonn, 1969.
Rudenko 1972
Rudenko, Sergei. *Frozen Tombs of Siberia: The Pazyryk Burials of Iron-Age Horsemen*. London, 1972.
Sanguozhi
Sanguozhi 三國志. Comp. Chen Shou 陳壽 (AD 233–297). Beijing, 1959.
Schmidt 1970
Schmidt, Erich. *Persepolis III: The Royal Tombs and Other Monuments*. Chicago, 1970.
Seidel 1987
Seidel, Anna. 'Traces of Han Religion in Funerary Texts Found in Tombs'. *Dokyo to shokyo bunka*, in Akizuki Kan'ei (ed.). Tokyo, 1987, pp. 678–714 (also numbered counting from the end, pp. 21–57).
Selby 2001
Selby, Stephen. 'A Crossbow Mechanism with Some Unique Features from Shandong, China'. 2001. Retrieved in September 2010, http://www.atarn.org/chinese/bjng_xbow/bjng_xbow.htm
Shanghai 1998
Silu kaogu zhenpin 絲路考古珍品. Shanghai, 1998.
Shi 1991
Shi, Meiguang. 'Xi Han Nanyue wang mu chutu boli jishu jianyan baogao. 西漢南越王墓出土玻璃技術檢驗報告'. *King of Nanyue Tomb in Western Han Dynasty* 西漢南越王墓. Beijing, 1991, pp. 424–6.
Shiji
Shiji 史記. Comp. Sima Qian 司馬遷 (*c*.145–*c*.86 BC). Beijing, 1959.
Shisanjing zhushu
Shisanjing zhushu 十三經註疏. Beijing, 1980.

Shuowen jiezi
Shuowen jiezi 說文解字. Comp. Xu Shen 許慎 (c.AD 30–124). Beijing, 1963.
Simoons 1991
Simoons, Frederick J. *Food in China: A Cultural and Historical Inquiry.* Boca Raton, 1991.
So and Bunker 1995
So, Jenny and Bunker, Emma (eds). *Traders and Raiders on China's Northern Frontier.* Seattle, 1995.
Song 2000
Song, Zhimin 宋治民. 'Shizishan xihan chuwangling de liangge wenti 獅子山西漢楚王陵的兩個問題'. Kaogu yu wenwu 考古與文物, 2000.1, pp. 22–8.
Song 2003
Song, Jie 宋傑. 'Yuanyan ernian riji suo fanying de Handai junli shenghuo 元延二年日記'所反映的漢代郡吏生活'. *Social Science Front*, 2003.3, pp. 108–13.
Sterckx 2011
Sterckx, Roel. *Food, Sacrifice and Sagehood in Early China.* New York, 2011.
Stierlin 2006
Stierlin, Henri. *Splendours of Ancient Persia.* Vercelli, 2006.
Stockholm 2010
Göransson, Kristian and Rawson, Jessica. *China's Terracotta Army.* Stockholm, 2010.
Sullivan 1962
Sullivan, Michael. *The Birth of Landscape Painting in China.* London, 1962.
Sun 1991
Sun, Ji 孫機. *Han dai wuzhi wenhua ziliao tushuo* 漢代物質文化資料圖說. Beijing, 1991.
Sun 2001
Sun, Yirang 孫詒讓 (ed.). *Mozi jiangu* 墨子間詁. Beijing, 2001.
Taipei 1972
Zhou li jin zhu jin shi 周禮今注今釋. Taipei, 1972.
Tang 1998
Tang, Chung 鄧聰 (ed.). *Dongya yuqi* 東亞玉器. Hong Kong, 1998.
Thompson 1988
Thompson, Stuart. 'Death, Food and Fertility'. *Death Ritual in Late Imperial and Modern China*, James Watson and Evelyn Rawski (eds). Berkeley, 1988.
Thorp 1979
Thorp, Robert L. 'The Mortuary Art and Architecture of Early Imperial China', PhD dissertation. University of Kansas, 1979.
Thote 1991
Thote, Alain. 'The Double Coffin of Leigudun Tomb No. 1: Iconographic Sources and Related Problems'. *New Perspectives on Chu Culture during the Eastern Zhou Period.* Princeton, 1991, pp. 23–46.
Tianjin 1995
Gudai Zhongguo qingtong qi 古代中國青銅器. Tianjin, 1995.
Tsai 1998
Tsai Suey-ling. 'Dreifusskessel *Ding* mit Inschrift'. In Prüch 1998, pp. 316–17.
Tsuda-Hausamman 1998
Tsuda-Hausamman, Nicole. 'Knoblauchkopfflasche *Suantou hu*'. In Prüch 1998, pp. 336–7.
Twitchett and Loewe 1986
Twitchett, Denis and Loewe, Michael. *The Cambridge History of China, Volume 1, the Ch'in and Han Empires, 221 BC–AD 220.* Cambridge, 1986.
Umehara 1935
Umehara, Sueji. *L'étude sur le miroir anterieur à la dynastie des 'Han'.* Kyoto, 1935.
Wang 1995
Wang, Renxiang 王仁湘. 'Kaogu suo jian Zhongguo gudai chushi xingxiang lüeshuo 考古所見中國古代廚師形象略說'. *Di si jie Zhongguo yinshi wenhua xueshu yantaohui lunwen ji* 第四屆中國飲食文化學術研討會論文集. Taipei, 1995, pp. 125–63.
Wang 1998
Wang, Pinzhen 王聘珍(ed.). *Da Dai Liji jiegu* 大戴禮記解詁. Beijing, 1998.
Wang 2007a
Wang, Helen. 'Qin coins'. In Portal 2007, pp. 80–2.
Wang 2007b
Wang, Zijin 王子今. *Zhongguo daomu shi* 中國盜墓史. Jiuzhou Press, 2007.
Wang 2010
Wang, Wangsheng 王望生. 'Xi'an beijiao zaoyuan nanling yihao Xihan mu tongqi shang de mingwen 西安北郊棗園南嶺一號西漢墓銅器上的銘文'. *Wenbo* 2010.1, pp. 9–10.
Wang and Zhang 1961
Wang, Chunyu 王春瑜 and Zhang, Zhangcheng 張占成. 'Woguo gudai nongtian shifei jianshu 我國古代農田施肥簡述'. *Lishi jiaoxue*, 1961.10, p. 14.
Ware 1966
Ware, James R. *Alchemy, Medicine and Religion in the China of AD 320: The Nei P'ien of Ko Hung (pao-p'u-tzu).* Cambridge, 1966.
Watson 1961
Watson, Burton (trans.). *Records of the Grand Historian of China, Translated from the* Shih Chi *of Ssu-ma Chien, Vol. II, The Age of Emperor Wu, 140–c.100 BC.* New York and London, 1961.
Watson 1993
Watson, Burton (trans.). *Records of the Grand Historian: Qin Dynasty.* Hong Kong and New York, 1993.
Wenbo
Wenbo 文博, Xi'an, 1984–
Wenwu
Wenwu 文物 (before 1959, *Wenwu cankao ziliao* 文物參考資料). Beijing: Wenwu chubanshe, 1950–

Wenwu cankao ziliao

Wenwu cankao ziliao 文物參考資料. Beijing: Wenwu chubanshe, 1950–

Wenwu jikan

Wenwu jikan 文物集刊. Beijing: Wenwu chubanshe, 1980–

Wenwu ziliao congkan

Wenwu ziliao congkan 文物資料叢. Beijing: Wenwu chubanshe, 1977–

Wilkinson 1999

Wilkinson, Endymion Porter. *Chinese History: A Manual*. Cambridge, MA and London, 1999.

Wu 1980

Wu, Shuping 吳樹平. *Fengsu tongyi jiaoshi* 風俗通義校釋. Tianjin, 1980.

Wu 1988

Wu Hung. 'From Temple to Tomb'. *Early China* 13, 1988, pp. 78–115.

Wu 1995

Wu, Hung. *Monumentality in Early Chinese Art and Architecture*. Stanford, 1995.

Wu 1997

Wu, Hung. 'The Prince of Jade Revisited'. *Chinese Jades – Colloquies on Art & Archaeology in Asia* No. 18, London, 1997, pp. 147–70.

Wu 2000

Wu, Haigui 吳海貴. 'Xianggang Nanyue Wang muzhu xin kao 象崗南越王墓主新考'. *Kaogu yu wenwu*, 2000.3, pp. 72–7.

Wu 2010a

Wu, Hsiao-yun. *The Zhou Chariot: Politics, Cultural Interaction and Identity*, D. Phil thesis, University of Oxford, 2010.

Wu 2010b

Wu, Hung. *The Art of the Yellow Springs: Understanding Chinese Tombs*. Honolulu, 2010.

Xi'an 2000

Suide Handai huaxiangshi 綏德漢代畫像石. Xi'an, 2000.

Xi'an 2006

Xi'an beijiao Qinmu 西安北郊秦墓. Xi'an, 2006.

Xi'an 2008

Nanyang qilingang huaxiangshi mu 南陽麒麟崗畫像石墓. Xi'an, 2008.

Xia Nai 1983

Xia Nai 夏鼐, *Jade and Silk of Han China* (trans. Chu-tsing Li). The Franklin D. Murphy Lecture III. Kansas, 1983.

Yang 1985

Yang, Hong 楊泓. *Zhongguo gu bingqi luncun* 中國古兵器論叢. Beijing, 1985.

Yang 1995

Yang, Bojun 楊伯峻. *Chunqiu Zuozhuan zhu* 春秋左傳注. Beijing, 1995.

Yang 2004a

Yang, Xiaoneng. *New Perspectives on China's Past: Chinese Archaeology in the Twentieth century*, 2 vols. New Haven and London, 2004.

Yang 2004b

Yang, Yi 楊怡. 'Chushi zhenmushou de shiwei he Han yong de xingqi – jiexi Qin Han linghun guan de zhuanbian 楚式鎮墓獸的式微和漢俑的興起 – 解析秦漢靈魂觀的轉變'. *Kaogu Yu Wenwu* 考古與文物, 2004. 1, pp. 54–60.

Yang 2005

Yang, Hong 楊泓. 'Xuzhou Chu wang lingmu chutu bingqi chulun 徐州楚王陵墓出土兵器初論'. *Da Han Chu Wang* 大漢楚王. Beijing, 2005, pp. 28–31.

Yang 2008

Yang, Jianfang 楊建芳, 'Lun sanjian yubei de niandai, changdi ji qita xiangguan wenti 論三件玉杯的年代, 產地及其他相關問題', *Gugong wenwu yuekan* 2008. 9, pp. 76–83.

Yates 1994

Yates, Robin. 'Body, Space, Time and Bureaucracy: Boundary Creation and Control Mechanisms in Early China'. *Boundaries in China*. London, 1994, pp. 56–80.

Yates 2007

Yates, Robin. 'The rise of Qin and the military conquest of the Warring States'. In Portal 2007, pp. 37–50.

Yili

Yili 儀禮. (Probably fourth or third century BC). Shanghai, 1930.

Yili zhushu

Yili zhushu 儀禮注疏. Annotated by Jia Gongyan 賈公彥 (*fl.* AD 650). Shisanjing zhushu 十三經注疏. Collated by Ruan Yuan 阮元 (1764–1849). Rprt. Taizhong: Landeng, n.d.

Yü 1977

Yü, Ying-shih. 'Han', *Food in Chinese Culture: Anthropological and Historical Perspectives*, Chang, Kwang-chih (ed.), New Haven, 1977, pp. 53–84.

Yü 1987

Yü, Ying-shih. 'O Soul, Come Back! A Study in the Changing Conceptions of the Soul and Afterlife in Pre-Buddhist China'. *Harvard Journal of Asiatic Studies*, vol. 47, no. 2, December 1987, pp. 363–95.

Zettler and Horne 1998

Zettler, Richard L. and Horne, Lee (eds). *Treasures from the Royal Tombs of Ur*. Seattle, 1998.

Zhang and Fan 1987

Zhang, Jianlin 張建林 and Fan, Peisong 範培松. 'Qiantan Handai de ce 淺談漢代的廁'. *Wenbo*, 1987.4, pp. 53–8.

Zhang and Hu 2001

Zhang, Defang 張德芳 and Hu, Pingsheng 胡平生 (eds.). *Dunhuang Xuanquan Han jian shicui* 敦煌懸泉漢簡釋粹. Shanghai, 2001.

Zhao 2007

Zhao, Deyun 趙德云. 'Tubanwen yin, tong he san ti 凸瓣紋銀, 銅盒三題'. *Wenwu*, 2007.7, 81–8.

Zhao and Liu 2009

Zhao, Yun 趙贇 and Liu, Zhaojian 劉照建. 'Jiangshu Pizhou jinian dong Han mu chutu tongren zaoxiang kaobian 江蘇邳州紀年東漢墓出土銅人造像考辨' *Qingtong wenhua yanjiu* 青銅文化研究. 2009, pp 198–201.

Zhengzhou 1996

Yongcheng xi Han liangguo wangling yu qingyuan 永城西漢梁國王陵與寢園. Zhongzhou, 1996.

Zhongguo kaoguxue nianjian
Zhongguo kaoguxue nianjian 中國考古學年鑑. Beijing: Wenwu chubanshe, 1983–
Zhongguo lishi wenwu
Zhongguo lishi wenwu 中國歷史文物. Beijing: National Musuem of Chinese History, 1979–
Zhongguo wenwubao
Zhongguo wenwubao 中國文物報 (*Wenwu bao* 1985–7). Beijing: Zhongguo wenwu baoshe, 1987–

Zhu 1995
Zhu, Fenghan 朱鳳翰. *Gudai Zhongguo qingtongqi* 古代中國青铜器. Tianjin, 1995.
Zhu and Li 2004
Zhu, Zhongxi 祝中熹 and Li, Yongping 李永平. *Qingtong qi* 青銅器. Dunhuang Wenyi Chubanshe, 2004, pp. 211–12.

INDEX

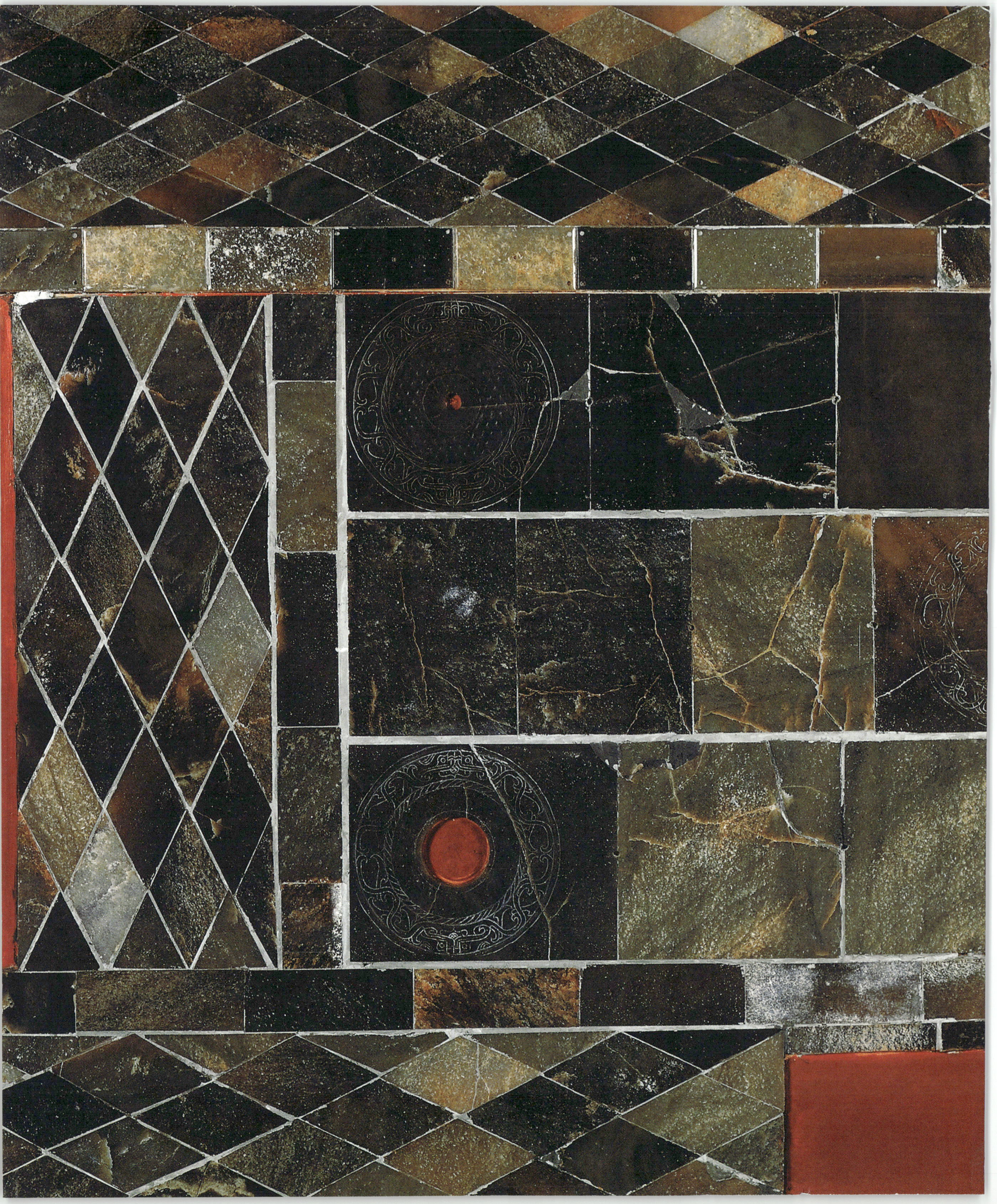